"I WISH TO KEEP A RECORD"

Nineteenth-Century New Brunswick Women Diarists and Their World

Nineteenth-century New Brunswick society was dominated by white, Protestant, anglophone men. Yet, during this time of state formation in Canada, women increasingly helped to define and shape a provincial outlook.

"*I wish to keep a record*" is the first book to focus exclusively on the life-course experiences of nineteenth-century New Brunswick women. Gail G. Campbell offers an interpretive scholarly analysis of 28 women's diaries while enticing readers to listen to the voices of the diarists. Their diaries show women constructing themselves as individuals, assuming their essential place in building families and communities, and shaping their society by directing its outward gaze and envisioning its future. Campbell's lively analysis calls on scholars to distinguish between immigrant and native-born women and to move beyond present-day conceptions of such women's world. This unique study provides a framework for developing an understanding of women's worlds in nineteenth-century North America.

GAIL G. CAMPBELL is a professor emerita of history at the University of New Brunswick.

"I wish to keep a record"

Nineteenth-Century New Brunswick Women Diarists and Their World

GAIL G. CAMPBELL

UNIVERSITY OF TORONTO PRESS
Toronto Buffalo London

© University of Toronto Press 2017
Toronto Buffalo London
www.utppublishing.com
Printed in Canada

ISBN 978-1-4875-0029-0 (cloth)   ISBN 978-1-4875-2018-2 (paper)

♾ Printed on acid-free, 100% post-consumer recycled paper with vegetable-based inks.

___

Library and Archives Canada Cataloguing in Publication

Campbell, Gail Grace, 1945–, author
"I wish to keep a record" : nineteenth-century New
Brunswick women diarists and their world / Gail G. Campbell.

Includes bibliographical references and index.
ISBN 978-1-4875-0029-0 (hardback)   ISBN 978-1-4875-2018-2 (paperback)

1. Diarists – New Brunswick – History – 19th century. 2. Diarists – New Brunswick – Biography. 3. Canadian diaries (English) – New Brunswick – History and criticism. 4. Canadian diaries (English) – Women authors – History and criticism. 5. Diarists – New Brunswick – Social conditions – 19th century. 6. Diarists – New Brunswick – Social life and customs – 19th century. 7. Women authors, Canadian (English) – New Brunswick – Social conditions – 19th century. 8. Women authors, Canadian (English) – New Brunswick – Social life and customs – 19th century. 9. Women – New Brunswick – Social conditions – 19th century. 10. Women immigrants – New Brunswick – Social conditions – 19th century. I. Title.

PS8205.C36 2017   C818'.303099287   C2016-905761-5

___

University of Toronto Press acknowledges the financial assistance to its publishing program of the Canada Council for the Arts and the Ontario Arts Council, an agency of the Government of Ontario.

 Canada Council for the Arts   Conseil des Arts du Canada

*In memory of my mother,
Eva Frances Grace Cox Campbell (1908–2014),
who, by example,
taught her six daughters that there are no ordinary women.*

Contents

Preface ix

Acknowledgments xi

Biographical Information for the Diarists xiii

Map: The Counties of New Brunswick xv

Introduction 3
 1 The Diarists 13
 2 Reading Nineteenth-Century Diaries: A Historian's Perspective 39
 3 The Life Course in Demographic Context: Women's Experience 58
 4 Three Generations: Women of Their Time and Place 77
 5 From Innocent Flirtation to Formal Courtship 95
 6 The World of the Family 115
 7 Households of Independent Women 134
 8 Sociability and Social Networks 153
 9 Schooling and Scholars 171
10 A Sustaining Faith 190
11 Work in the Home 210
12 Beyond the Bounds of Family: Paid Work 227
13 Politics and Social Reform 247
14 A Cosmopolitan Outlook 265
15 In the Midst of Life 284
Conclusion 303

Afterword 311

Appendix 324

   Table 1 New Brunswick Population Statistics to 1911 324
   Table 2 Acadians as a Proportion of the Total Population 1871–1911 325
   Table 3 Rural-Urban Distribution 1851–1921 325
   Table 4a Protestant-Catholic Distribution 1861 325
   Table 4b Protestant-Catholic Distribution 1871 326

Notes 327

Bibliography 391

Index 416

Preface

This book had its origins in an annual event at the University of New Brunswick marking Women's History Month. Since 1993, members of the University and the general public have gathered in October to hear students and faculty read from New Brunswick women's writings (and also, latterly, other women's writings) of the past, grouped around a particular theme, usually of our choosing. But in that first year, Status of Women Canada suggested the theme "Women and Work," and I determined that our examination of this and subsequent themes should be "in their own words." As the organizer of the original gatherings, I went in search of such words, finding them in the diaries and letters of New Brunswick women. At that stage, I confined my search to the Provincial Archives of New Brunswick (PANB) and the University of New Brunswick Archives (UNBA).

Over the years, enthusiastic support for these events came from archivists, colleagues, students, and members of the wider community. Marion Beyea, then Provincial Archivist, provided the venue for several years. Ruth Grattan and Twila Buttimer at the PANB and Mary Flagg and Patricia Belier at the UNBA helped in identifying diarists. While it was they who made the series possible, it was the enthusiasm of my women colleagues in the History Department, our graduate and undergraduate students, and interested Frederictonians who made it all happen, year after year.

Then, encouraged by Gillian Thompson and Beverly Lemire, my only women colleagues in the History Department in 1993, I first set out to prepare a book of readings based on selections made for those annual gatherings. But research projects take on a life of their own. I soon decided to restrict the scope of the project to my own field – nineteenth-century New Brunswick – and to focus on diarists who exemplified the experience of being a New Brunswicker and of regarding New Brunswick as home. In the beginning, I had the diaries of sixteen diarists whose writings, located in Fredericton repositories, had been used at our annual celebrations. A more exhaustive search turned up the diaries of a further twelve diarists who fit my criteria, bringing the total to twenty-eight. Some of the diaries – or excerpts from them – had been published elsewhere but were too important to omit. Because of the existence of numerous local archives, I may not have found all the extant New Brunswick diaries that meet my criteria. But, with the aid of research assistants, I conducted a thorough inventory of diaries held by New Brunswick's major archival repositories.[1] Thus, diarists who are at the core of this book include thirteen whose diaries are held by the PANB, eight whose diaries are held at the UNBA, five whose diaries are held in the New Brunswick Museum Archives, three whose diaries are held in the Mount Allison University Archives, and one whose diary is privately held.[2] I am grateful to the archivists at all four repositories for their help in identifying diaries suitable for inclusion in this study.

Acknowledgments

In the course of research and writing, I have accumulated numerous debts to institutions and people. Chapter 3 is based on work completed with the support of a SSHRC grant. I have been extraordinarily well served by the Provincial Archives of New Brunswick, the Harriet Irving Library Archives of the University of New Brunswick, the Saint John Museum Archives, and the Mount Allison University Archives. Their staff members were always helpful, sometimes identifying diaries within collections that I might otherwise have overlooked. I further wish to thank the research assistants who aided in the transcription of the diaries and undertook background research on their authors: Dorothy Bennett, Gay Fanjoy, Shannon Fougère, Andrew Lockhart, and Shawna Stairs Quinn. I am much indebted to Lisa Griffin, for mapping the diarists and to Stephanie Holyoke for the cover photograph. I am grateful to anonymous readers for critiques that resulted in a better book, to Len Husband for patience as well as encouragement, and to Melissa MacAulay for careful copy editing. And I have been fortunate beyond measure to have the consistent and continuing support of members of the Department of History of the University of New Brunswick, most recently expressed in the provision of a publication subsidy.

Having the opportunity to discuss a work-in-progress with colleagues who have an extensive understanding of the field was invaluable. William Acheson, Margaret Conrad, David Frank, Janet Guildford, Hannah Lane, William Parenteau, and Steven Turner all commented on the text. Their substantive and stylistic suggestions were invariably useful and the encouragement I received from them means a great deal to me. For stimulating conversations about theory and practice in

Canadian history, I have, since our days in graduate school, depended upon Ruth Bleasdale, in whose company I have done some of my best writing, and who read the manuscript "in process." Gillian Thompson, always my severest critic and editor, as well as my strongest advocate, knows these twenty-eight New Brunswick women diarists well, having read and reread chapters with extraordinary patience. I could not have been more fortunate in my assistants, colleagues, department, and friends. To say that I am grateful is an understatement.

Biographical Information for the Diarists

The surname(s) listed here are the surnames used by the diarists themselves and/or by historians and students of nineteenth-century New Brunswick society. The page numbers refer to the pages in this volume where biographical information about them can be found.

	County	Page
Jacobina CAMPBELL (b. 1797)	York	15, 312
Sophia CARMAN (b. 1828)	York	18, 313
Alvaretta ESTABROOKS (b.1869)	Carleton	32, 321
Hannah ESTABROOKS (b. 1871)	Carleton	32, 321
Laura FULLERTON (b. 1870)	Westmorland	34, 321
Violet GOLDSMITH (b. 1880)	Gloucester	36, 322
Isabella GRANT (b. 1807)	Charlotte	16, 312
Marjory GRANT (b. 1800)	Charlotte	16, 312
Sadie HARPER (b. 1875)	Westmorland	35, 322
Mary HILL (b. 1829)	Charlotte	19, 314
Amelia HOLDER (b. 1855)	Kings	30, 319
Bertha JONES (b. 1844)	Kings	23, 316
Catherine LOGGIE (b. 1857)	Northumberland	27, 318
Jessie LOGGIE (b. 1859)	Northumberland	27, 319
Margaret LOGGIE VALENTINE (b. 1853)	Northumberland	27, 319
Ida MacDONALD (b. 1865)	Queens	14, 311
Janet MacDONALD (b. 1795)	Queens	13, 311
Kate MILES (b. 1885)	Sunbury	37, 323
Lucy MORRISON (b. 1823)	York	17, 313
Emma PITT (b. 1857)	Saint John	31, 320
Charlotte REID (b. 1859)	Albert	24, 317
Josephine REID TURNER (b. 1849)	Albert	24, 316
Ann Eliza ROGERS (b. 1837)	Albert	21, 314
Annie TRUEMAN (b. 1851)	Westmorland	26, 317
Laura TRUEMAN WOOD (b. 1856)	Westmorland	26, 318
Annie WALTHAM (b. 1833)	Queens	20, 314
Lillian WILLIAMSON (b. 1861)	Kings	31, 320
Mary WOLHAUPTER (b. 1838)	Carleton	22, 315

Diarists

1. Jacobina Campbell
Near junction of Tay and Nashwaak Rivers - York County

2. Sophia Bliss Carman
Shore Street, Fredericton - York County

3. Alvaretta Estabrooks
Coldstream, Brighton Parish - Carleton County

4. Hannah Estabrooks
Coldstream, Brighton Parish - Carleton County

5. Ida MacDonald
MacDonalds Corner, Washademoak Lake and St. John River - Queen's County

6. Janet Hendry MacDonald
MacDonalds Corner, Washademoak Lake and St. John River - Queen's County

7. Ann Eliza Rogers Gallacher Moore
Hopewell Hill - Albert County

8. Laura Fullerton
Sackville and Point De Bute - Westmorland County

9. Violet Goldsmith
Bathurst - Gloucester County; Fredericton - York County

10. Marjory Grant
Old Ridge, a few kilometres north of St. Stephen - Charlotte County

11. Isabella Grant
Old Ridge, a few kilometres north of St. Stephen - Charlotte County

12. Sarah (Sadie) Harper
Shediac - Westmorland County

13. Mary Whitney Hill
St. Andrews - Charlotte County

14. Amelia Holder
Holderville on the Long Reach, Kingston Peninsula - Kings County

15. Bertha Frost Jones
Greenwich Parish - Kings County

16. Catherine (Kate) Loggie
Burnt Church, Alnwick Parish - Northumberland County

17. Jessie Loggie
Burnt Church, Alnwick Parish - Northumberland County

18. Katherine (Kate) Miles
Maugerville - Sunbury County

19. Lucy Everett Morrison
Morrison's Mills, Lincoln Road, Fredericton - York County

20. Emma Pitt
Portland - Saint John County

21. Charlotte Reid
Harvey Parish - Albert County

22. Annie Trueman
Sackville - Westmorland County

23. Josephine Reid Turner
Harvey Parish - Albert County

24. Margaret Loggie Valentine
Burnt Church, Alnwick Parish - Northumberland County

25. Annie Gilbert Johnston Waltham
Upper Gagetown - Queen's County

26. Lillian Williamson
Greenwich Parish - Kings County

27. Mary Isoline Wolhaupter
Bloomfield, Simonds Parish - Carleton County

28. Laura Trueman Wood
Sackville - Westmorland County

The Counties of New Brunswick

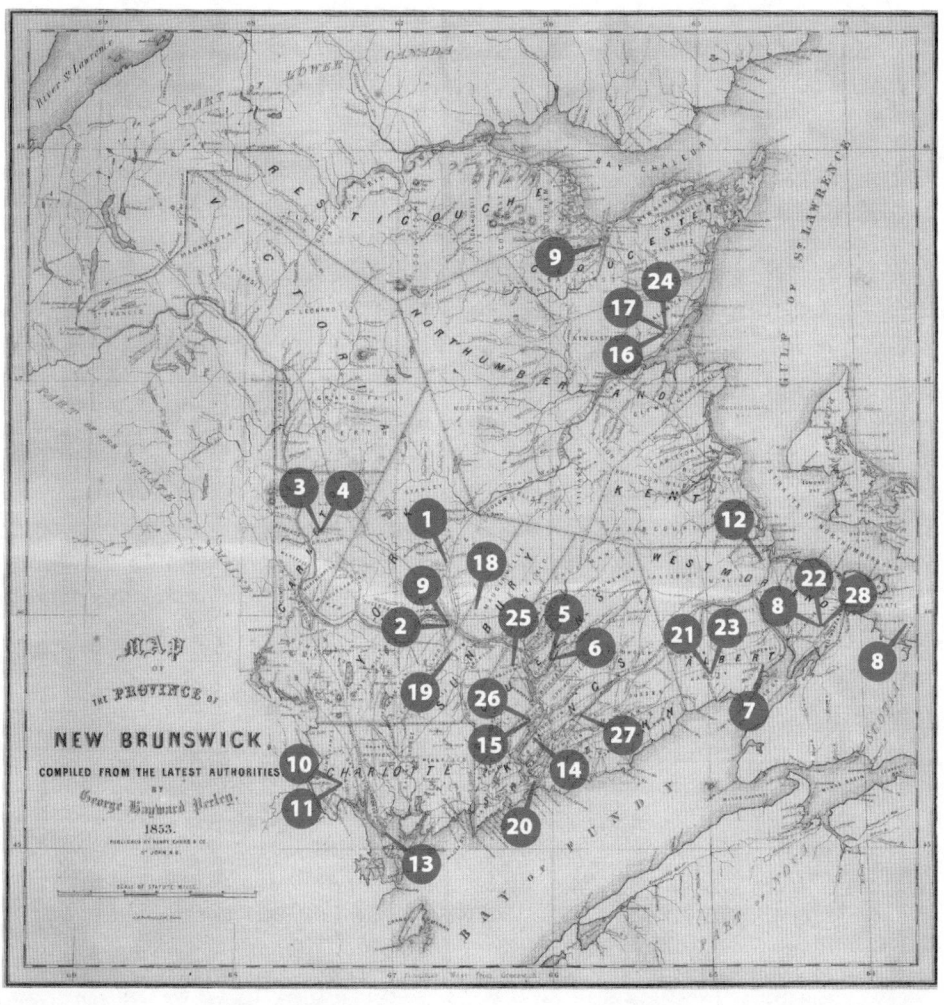

Map of New Brunswick, 1853 (Provincial Archives of New Brunswick).

"I WISH TO KEEP A RECORD"

Nineteenth-Century New Brunswick
Women Diarists and Their World

Introduction

"Aug. 26th, 1880. I wish to keep a record of my daily progress." So begins the diary of twenty-two-year-old Catherine "Kate" Loggie.[1] Opening the small soft-covered black notebook in an archival repository over a century later, the reader is transported back in time to a very unfamiliar world. It is the world of a young schoolteacher in rural New Brunswick. Although Kate Loggie was teaching in a community less than 20 kilometres from her home, the distance was too great to travel on a daily basis. She was, therefore, living independently of her parents, "boarding around," moving from one household to the next, as, following a common practice of the day, her students' parents took turns "boarding the teacher" for a term. Kate Loggie is one of twenty-eight nineteenth-century New Brunswick women whose diaries form the core of this book.

As records of individual lives, diaries offer both the historian and the lay reader a window into that "foreign country" that is the past.[2] Understanding and interpreting such records involves a consciousness of the distance between the writer's world and our own: a historical consciousness.[3] The New Brunswick women diarists who are the subject of this study experienced their world as individuals, and their particular milieu served to shape their particular experience. Our attempts to see their world from their perspective result in partial insights. Yet through the window they have opened we can hear voices, and snatches of conversation that speak of experiences and reflect a world view that are different not only from our own, but also from those of immigrant women whose voices tend to dominate our understanding of Canadian women's experience in past times.[4] One of the purposes of this volume is to suggest that, in analysing nineteenth-century Canadian women's experience, we ought to distinguish more clearly between immigrant and native-born women.

Thematically rather than chronologically structured, this book offers an interpretive analysis while at the same time inviting readers to listen to the voices of the women themselves, through the medium of unfiltered excerpts from their diaries. Twenty of the twenty-eight diarists began keeping diaries as young, single women. Only five were married when their surviving diaries open; two were widows. The group as a whole includes five sets of sisters, two cousins, and a grandmother and her granddaughter. They ranged in age from eleven to seventy-three. Seven of the diarists continued to keep a diary, either consistently or sporadically, for a span of more than ten years. Of these, three married during the period when they were keeping their diaries. The fortunes and futures of our subjects were, in many ways, typical of their society. Four would live to see some of their children leave their community and the province, following a well-trodden path to the United States. One among them had herself made that journey, and might not have returned had her first husband survived. Two others had been among the many New Brunswick young people who spent time as sojourners in the United States. One would settle in Saskatchewan, another in Liverpool, England. Some would travel the globe on New Brunswick's famous sailing ships. They were very much women of their time. That time spans the long nineteenth century, defined as extending to the outbreak of the First World War.

In selecting the diarists, I limited my research to women who came of age during the nineteenth century as I have defined it. In the end, I located twenty-eight women who fit my criteria: my subjects were born between 1795 and 1885, and their diaries were written between 1825 and 1906. A study of women diarists is, by definition, a study of literate women. Furthermore, the diarists are not as representative of New Brunswick's varied cultural landscape as we might wish: I was unable to locate any Acadian, First Nations, or Afro-Canadian diarists, and, as it happens, there are no Roman Catholics among them.[5] At the same time, taken together, the diarists represent the four major Protestant denominations and eleven of the province's fifteen counties, providing material for a valuable analysis of New Brunswick women's wide-ranging experience during the nineteenth century. In cases in which correspondence collections also exist, these have been used to supplement the analysis.

The twenty-eight diarists who are the focus of this analysis were people whom the British of their own period would have labelled "provincials," for they were all born in the Maritime provinces of British North America. All but two were born in New Brunswick.⁶ Such demographic distinctions prove significant in explaining experience. Young women raised in the province, often in farm families whose adult male members spent months in the woods each winter or in seafaring families whose adult male members spent months at sea each year, learned resourcefulness as they watched their mothers manage households and sustain families during those absences. In their turn, such women used the strategies they had learned from their mothers when they themselves faced similar circumstances. That women who had become accustomed to dealing with absent fathers and husbands were well equipped to cope with widowhood is implied by demographic evidence that points to the independence of New Brunswick widows, who were almost as likely as widowers to head their own households. New Brunswick–born women's experience, then, was far different from that of immigrant women facing the challenge of re-establishing themselves and their families in a place they did not consider "home." Our subjects understood their experience not as outsiders or newcomers, but as people who, as one of the diarists put it, "belonged" in New Brunswick.⁷ The experience of "belonging" was more than a mere expression – it was, as one historian has argued, material and sensuous.⁸

From an early period, the majority of nineteenth-century New Brunswick women had been raised in the province and, perhaps for this reason, had, compared to the predominantly immigrant women in some other provinces, a greater stake in their communities. During a century that encompassed both state formation and state building, they helped to define as well as to shape a "provincial outlook," first of a province of Great Britain and then of a province of the new Dominion of Canada.⁹ To recognize that nineteenth-century women had such agency is to recognize both the complexity of their world and the distance between their world view and our own. Shaped by their families and their communities, as well as by the broader society in which they lived, the twenty-eight women who are the subjects of this study reflect the changing attitudes and outlooks of the dominant sector of New Brunswick society that was anglophone, Protestant, and white. Mainly middle-class women, some among them were well-off while others struggled to make ends meet. They lived in towns and cities, on farms and in villages, most in communities dotted along the shores of

New Brunswick's major rivers. They were the daughters of farmers, businessmen, sea captains, lawyers, ministers, artisans, and politicians. Largely evangelical, the group included Methodists, Baptists, Presbyterians, and Anglicans; the preponderance of Methodists and Baptists is not surprising, for members of these two evangelical denominations had a long history of diary keeping.[10] Our diarists' views and values were shaped by a society in which livelihoods were often precarious, and resourcefulness and independence were required of women as well as of men.

Attuned to their environment, the nature of their lives determined by the seasons, our diarists, rural and urban alike, were "students of the weather." In New Brunswick, the changing weather shaped a way of life not only for farmers but for everyone who lived along the banks of the province's major rivers or along the shores of its bays and inlets. All those who depended on the St John River and its tributaries as their main transportation and communication networks watched with regret as the last boat of the season made its way downriver in the autumn and hailed the arrival of the first to make its way upriver each spring. They understood that the lumber economy turned on the accumulation of enough snow to make it possible to haul lumber over rough logging roads, and on the arrival of the spring freshet, to float the logs downriver to market. They also knew that spring flooding helped to renew and maintain the fertility of their intervale farm lands. Daily chores ranging from washing clothes to planting and harvesting fields and gardens depended on the weather. Weather conditioned the state of the roads and the safety of inland waterways and offshore waters for those planning to travel short or long distances by foot, wagon, carriage, sleigh, canoe, fishing boat, steamer, or sailing vessel. For the reader, the weather, briefly recorded at the beginning of a daily entry, situates the diarist within her environment, providing the frame for her day.

Our subjects' voices differ, though in minor ways, from those of other Maritime women, and in this case, regional economic and geographic variations account for differing experiences and differing understandings of their world. Although the majority of nineteenth-century New Brunswickers lived on farms, in contrast to Prince Edward Island, arable land in the province was at a premium. Coastal regions supported a significant fishery, and many of the Acadian communities along the north shore as well as the island communities in the Bay of Fundy were heavily involved in that industry. But the fishery, although important, was not the engine of the economy. The lumbering industry upon which the early New Brunswick economy was built hinged on the rivers that run deep into the interior, providing hinterland communities for the province's major ports. Further, lumbering facilitated the development of a major shipbuilding industry, underwritten by provincial merchants who delivered both lumber and fish to global markets. Saint John, established at the mouth of the river that runs through the heart of the province, grew exponentially, dominating not only its own hinterland region but extending its influence across the Bay of Fundy to the north shore of Nova Scotia. Halifax, with an excellent harbour, but without access to a hinterland, lacked Saint John's advantages. As a result of those advantages, the younger city soon developed a strong secondary manufacturing sector. By Confederation, Saint John had not only surpassed Halifax in population, but was the third largest city in the new Dominion; only Montreal and Quebec were larger. The early choice of the smaller centre of Fredericton as the provincial capital, while initiating a rivalry between the two towns, ensured that no part of the province would be geographically isolated from the seat of political power. Yet despite regional differences, there were also similarities. Looking both southward to New England and eastward to Great Britain, the people of the Maritime provinces, responding to the exigencies of their particular geography and shaped by their particular histories, developed political philosophies, commercial policies, social attitudes, and religious beliefs that reflected a common transatlantic outlook.

Nineteenth-century New Brunswick politicians, who appeared parochial to British-born officials, were surprisingly broad in their vision, and in formulating policy looked well beyond their own borders for the precedents they chose to cite. In comparison to other British North American colonials, New Brunswick leaders demonstrated a considerable degree of political and social enlightenment. New Brunswick was the first province to pass legislation aimed at protecting widowed and deserted women, established a normal school that admitted women in 1848, and was home to the first university in British North America to open its doors to women and the first in the British empire to award a bachelor's degree to a woman. In leading the way on such issues, New Brunswick politicians and educational administrators were undoubtedly influenced by the women in their lives, including at least a few of our diarists.

In conceptualizing this study, I "imagined" a book that would resonate with the widest possible audience: students as well as scholars, the general reader as well as the professional historian. To that end,

I have sought the middle ground, settling on an approach somewhere between those most often found in the existing literature: on the one hand, for example, Kathryn Carter's edited volume *The Small Details of Life* and Margaret Conrad, Toni Laidlaw, and Donna Smyth's *No Place Like Home* are essentially books of documents with scholarly introductions; and, for example, on the other hand, Jean Barman's *Sojourning Sisters*, Françoise Noël's *Family Life and Sociability in Upper and Lower Canada, 1780–1870*, and Marguerite Van Die's *Religion, Family and Community in Victorian Canada: The Colbys of Carrollcroft* are all scholarly analyses which draw extensively on diaries and correspondence collections, but which do not quote from their sources at length.[11]

The structure of the book reflects this approach. Chapter 1 outlines the cast of characters, providing brief biographical sketches of each of the twenty-eight diarists and situating them within their families. This is followed by three more traditionally structured chapters, which provide the necessary context for eleven thematic chapters that analyse different aspects of women's experience by drawing on the diarists' insights into how they understood their world. Each thematic chapter will highlight at least two diarists by including excerpts from their diaries that are long enough to provide the "flavour" of the individual's authorial "style." Unless necessary for clarity, I have not altered idiosyncratic or contemporary spelling or punctuation.[12] Through this somewhat novel approach, I invite scholars to evaluate my interpretation and contribution to the field, students to reflect on the dialogue between the historian and her sources, and all readers to enjoy diaries presented within a historical context.

By intentionally structuring the manuscript to give the diarists a voice, I encourage the reader to interpret their "texts" for herself. Yet, in "sharing the stage" with the diarists, I also acknowledge that interpretation as well as analysis was involved in my "reading" of the diaries. For just as the diarists edited their own lives through their decisions about what to record and what to omit, I have further edited their lives by choosing which portions of their texts to include and which to omit. My intention, throughout the thematic chapters in which I engage the diarists, is to involve readers in the analysis, to raise questions as much as to offer answers, and to move beyond our sometimes narrow conception of nineteenth-century women's worlds. While my "reading" of the diaries is an interpretation, just as the individual authors' writing of them was an interpretation of their world, I trust that the excerpts presented will allow scope for other "readings" and other interpretations.

And I hope that more than a few readers may be moved to visit the archival repositories where these diaries are held and read them in their entirety.

But I aspire to do more than give twenty-eight diarists a voice. In this book, I am using diaries to offer insight into the nature of the experience of girls and women in nineteenth-century New Brunswick. Readers whose primary interest is in the collective experience may regard chapter 2 as their natural starting place. Situating the analysis within a broader scholarly framework, the second chapter is devoted to a consideration of diary writing as genre. In the context of the range of diaries analysed, particular attention is paid to the issue of style vs. substance, to some extent to the contrast between the diaries of adolescents, who were still fashioning a "self," and the diaries of mature women, who had a clear sense of "self," but also to historical vs. literary approaches to the study of diaries. Chapter 3 provides a general backdrop against which the diarists may be viewed. Recognizing that focussing on diaries skews the analysis towards the experience of the middle class, literate women of the dominant culture, in the third chapter, I have drawn on a broad range of routinely generated statistical sources to provide a life-course demographic analysis of New Brunswick society as a whole. A comparative analysis of nineteenth-century New Brunswick women and men at each stage of the life course suggests that the experiences of women and men at this time and place were characterized by converging and diverging patterns of dependence, independence, and interdependence. Those patterns were determined as much by age and marital status as by gender. Intersections of class, ethnicity, and religion proved equally important in determining individual experience. Because not all these distinctions can be captured adequately in an analysis based on diaries, the demographic analysis is intended to provide readers with a broader perspective on New Brunswick society, enabling them to situate the individual diarists within that broader frame. Chapter 4 positions the individual diarists within the context of their own time and place by considering the responses of these three generations of women to New Brunswick's changing economic, political, social, and intellectual circumstances over the course of the century.

The remaining chapters situate the diarists along a continuum that moves outward from family to community to society. Yet the continuum is not a straight line, but rather a series of concentric circles, such as a pebble might create when dropped into a pool of water. In chapter 5, young women are captured at the intersection of family and community as they launch themselves into what might be considered the "marriage market." In chapter 6, the focus is on the nature of family relationships, both within and beyond the confines of individual households. Nineteenth-century New Brunswick women were regularly called upon to exhibit independence both in managing households and in supporting themselves; chapter 7 turns to an analysis of women's strategies in such circumstances. Extending outward from the household into the community, sociability and social networks are dealt with in chapter 8; the evolving world of children as they enter the world of the schoolroom and schoolyard is covered in chapter 9; and the significance of communities of faith in women's lives and the role of women in those communities is examined in chapter 10. Women's work is the topic of the next two chapters, with women's contributions to the family economy through their work in the home, which may or may not have been "paid" work, the focus of chapter 11, and women's work for pay outside the home the focus of chapter 12. Both paid and unpaid work involved women in the local community and larger provincial economy. Women's interest in and impact on New Brunswick society is the subject of chapter 13, in which their interest in politics and their roles as social reformers are considered. New Brunswick women's remarkably broad understanding of the world beyond the province's borders, and the basis for their cosmopolitan outlook, are discussed in chapter 14. The final chapter turns to a topic that no reader of nineteenth-century diaries can ignore: our subjects' experience of and responses to death, in a world in which life often seemed precarious.

Situating women's experience within a framework that takes into account their interactions with their families, their communities, and their society allows scope for the analysis of the complexity of women's lived experience. The three generations of New Brunswick women who came of age during the course of the nineteenth century were grounded not only in their families, but also in their communities and in their society. At the family level, they were embedded in a web of kin that included aunts and uncles as well as parents and often grandparents, cousins as well as brothers and sisters, and nieces and nephews as well as children and grandchildren. The boundaries of women's worlds, like the boundaries of men's worlds, extended well beyond the private sphere of the family. Women, no less than men, defined the parameters of local neighbourhoods, or geographic communities. And women, like men, belonged to other communities as well – communities defined by social interaction as much as by geography.[13] Communities of faith numbered women among their most active members. In some instances, women formed what might be considered communities of interest. In port towns such as Saint John, seamen's wives regularly formed a community of women when their husbands were absent. And young women students at normal schools and universities, forbidden to consort with the young men in their classes, formed close alliances with their female classmates.[14] Over the course of the century, women organized a growing number of gender-exclusive voluntary groups, ranging from missionary societies through temperance societies to local women's councils that had a provincial, national, and even international reach. Nonetheless, like communities of faith, most communities of interest, including partisan political communities, included both men and women.

Just as women usually shared the partisan political ideologies of their fathers, brothers, and husbands, so too they participated in a public discourse that sought to influence public opinion and reform various aspects of their society.[15] They shared and helped to inculcate, disseminate, maintain, and sometimes to change broader societal attitudes, norms, and values. While their ties to Britain remained strong, it was New Brunswickers' North American and Maritime roots that shaped their cultural outlook as well as their economy. To view women as participants in shaping that cultural outlook and in maintaining that economy is not to deny the reality of male power and privilege in the economic and political spheres. Laws and prescriptive literature designed to set societal parameters and to define social norms and values were written by men. The doctrine of separate spheres, a very old concept that identified "woman's proper sphere" as the private world of home and family, was promoted in sermons as well as in advice literature, and it did gain a certain popular currency during the nineteenth century. And, for a significant proportion of men, the workplace became more separated than previously from the home. Yet to focus on the exclusion of women from the formal public worlds of economic and political power obscures women's and men's intersecting, overlapping, and shared lives.[16]

The concept of separate spheres has limited use in understanding the diaries that are the subject of this study. In taking this line, I am in good company. Historians generally agree that, as a framework for analysis, the concept of separate spheres does not capture the reality of nineteenth-century women's lives; at most, it reflects a partial reality for some women.[17] Nevertheless, because literary scholars and others have made use of the concept in their analyses of women's diaries, a review of its continuing relevance and potential for some application in the analysis of diaries is in order.[18] Recognizing that, even with the increasing separation of home and workplace, men, retaining their position as the heads of households, continued to share responsibility in the private sphere of the home, historians have revised our understanding of men's roles as fathers of families, drawing extensively on their diaries and correspondence to discuss their relationships with their wives and children, often with their sons in particular.[19] Yet while men are now "at home" in the private world of the family, women remain uneasily situated in the public sphere. Not only is it impossible to know whether many women attempted either to resist or conform to the standards articulated in the prescriptive literature, even our notion of "the public" and our definition of the concept of a "public sphere" has shifted over time.[20] Historians seeking to situate women in the world outside the household have chosen to avoid this "slippery term" altogether, replacing it with other concepts, such as "civil society," which encompasses all publics except political, or "the social," a mediating category between public and private spheres.[21] Like such scholars, I realize that the public institutions of the legislature, the law courts, and the church were the exclusive preserve of men in so far as men were the elected, appointed, and ordained leaders and that women's influence was normally limited to what they could say or write to the male leadership. But I have chosen an expansive rather than a restrictive framework, which better reflects the experiences and activities of nineteenth-century New Brunswick women as recorded in their diaries.

New Brunswick women shared physical space and regularly interacted with their male counterparts, not only in their homes, but also in their schools and churches, halls and theatres, factories and offices, at fairgrounds and favourite picnic sites, on snow-covered slopes and ice-covered ponds, in the streets and in the shops, on the highways and byways, on the rivers and on the high seas. Acknowledging the complexity of the interactions that occurred in that shared space – their social, spiritual, and informal, as well as formal economic and political aspects – allows us to situate women's varied activities and evolving provincial and national networks as part of an evolving family-to-community-to-society continuum.

Chapter 1

The Diarists

The twenty-eight diarists who recorded their activities and thoughts – beliefs, hopes, fears, concerns, preoccupations, plans, expectations – had a wide range of experience and wrote on a multiplicity of subjects. And their diaries had a multiplicity of purposes. Who were these particular women? They included grandmothers as well as adolescents, single women as well as married and widowed women. This chapter provides brief biographies of the individual diarists to the time when their diaries end, situating them within their families, with diarists who were related to one another introduced as a family. The organization of families is chronological, with the women ordered by their date of birth. In cases where more than one woman is involved, they are ordered by the birth date of the eldest family member. Thus, I begin with Janet MacDonald (b. 1795) together with her granddaughter Ida (b. 1865), and end with Kate Miles (b. 1885).

1. Janet Hendry MacDonald (b. 7 February 1795) (Diaries: 1857–1868)[1]

2. Ida MacDonald (b. 30 November 1865) (Diaries: 1879–1883)[2]

Janet Hendry was born and raised on a farm on the shores of Washademoak Lake in the lower St John River Valley, the eldest of twelve children born to Queens County Loyalists Susan Belyea and George Hendry.[3] In 1818, Janet married Alexander Black MacDonald (b. 1794), and the couple settled on land that was part of her inheritance. There they raised their family of seven: Susan Ann (1819–1867), James Hendry (b. 1821), Donald (b. 1824), George Hendry (1828–1861), Alexander Black (b. 1831), William Lewis (b. 1834), and Malcolm Campbell (b. 1836). In time, Alexander established a sawmill, which supplemented the family's farm income.[4]

In 1857, when the diary opens, the MacDonald household was still large, including four unmarried children, as well as James and his growing family. Susan and George, like James, had married. Readers following the rhythms of life on the MacDonald farm through the pages of Janet's diary not only get a sense of the seasonality of the work, but are also reminded that, even at sixty-two, a farm wife carried a heavy load. Janet MacDonald's strong religious faith surfaces as a recurring theme in her diary. Raised a Presbyterian, at forty-four she converted to the faith of her husband. According to the Baptist record, the conversion of Janet MacDonald, her daughter Susan Ann, and her mother Susan Hendry initiated a "rising tide of interest," which culminated in the organization of the Second Baptist Church of Wickham.[5] During the course of Janet's decade of diary keeping, her son Alexander would become a Baptist minister. Those years brought pain as well as pleasure: George and Susan would die, Donald and Alexander would marry, and William and Malcolm would travel to Boston to further their education.

Meanwhile, a new generation was growing up in her household. When Janet began her diary, her eldest son, James, and his wife, Sally (Sarah) Smith, had four children: Mary Jane (b. 1849), Susie (Susannah, b. 1851), Fred (b. 1853), and Robert (b. 1856). During the period covered by his mother's diary, James and Sally had two more children: Ella (b. 1863) and our second diarist, Ida (b. 1865).[6]

Ida MacDonald began keeping a diary in November 1879, not long before her fourteenth birthday. When her diary opens, Ida, her mother, her five older siblings, and her mother's older sister, Mary Smith, were still living with her paternal grandparents at their farm in Central Cambridge.[7] But Ida's older brothers, Fred and Robert, had taken over their father's work on the farm, for James Hendry MacDonald had died earlier that year. While Janet MacDonald's diary focussed on the day-to-day work of the farm, Ida's diary focuses on school and social life. That the farm routine is largely absent from her diary reflects Ida's own "editing" of her life. Unlike the majority of her contemporaries, Ida attended school regularly, at least until the age of sixteen. Her family placed a high value on education and the local schoolteacher regularly boarded with them. The MacDonalds were an extraordinarily literate family: they were inveterate readers, often reading books or stories aloud to one another in the evenings, a practice only occasionally hinted at in Janet MacDonald's diary.

Like many farm children of her day, Ida lived in the bosom of her family. Yet, as her experience demonstrates, New Brunswick farm life was far from isolated. Members of her close knit extended family – cousins, uncles, and aunts – were in and out of their house frequently. So, too, were friends, for this was a house full of young people. Indeed, Ida MacDonald's diary is dominated by young people. They travelled constantly, back and forth across the lake, and up and down the road that ran like a ribbon connecting the community's farm families.

3. Jacobina Campbell (b. circa 1797) (Diary: 1825–1843)[8]

Descended from Highland Scots who fought for the British in the American Revolution, Jacobina Campbell was the second child of Jacobina Drummond and Dugald Campbell. Although the family owned a substantial farm near the junction of the Tay and Nashwaak Rivers in York County, during much of Jacobina's childhood, they lived in Fredericton. But with the death of her father in 1810, Jacobina's world was turned upside down. Within three years, the family moved to the farm and was soon taken up with the seasonal round of farm activities.

In 1825, when the diary opens, Jacobina was not yet thirty; by the time it closes, she was well into middle age. Her diary, with its terse, economical style, leads the reader into a web of family and neighbourhood relationships characteristic of nineteenth-century New Brunswick life. The careful reader can trace the family's downward mobility, although their situation remained more secure than that of their neighbours. Not only did they own more land, but Jacobina's mother received a pension from the government because her husband had served as soldier and surveyor. By 1825, Jacobina's older brother Sandy (Alexander) had married and he and his wife Caroline had settled on a nearby farm. Her younger brothers, Patrick and Ludlow, moved to their own farms in 1835 following Ludlow's marriage, leaving their mother, Jacobina, and their younger sister Ann on the home farm. Jacobina became the pivot around whom the women's share of the farm work revolved, but she also became central to the intellectual and spiritual life of her community. Between 1814 and 1828, Jacobina kept a commonplace book, in which she recorded sermons and other spiritual texts. As Murray Young has argued, the commonplace book taken together with the diary "reveal two sides of the life of a 'thinking' woman: her inner religious life and its outward manifestations."[9] During the early nineteenth century, the Methodists depended on church members to keep the faith alive in small rural communities, and Jacobina Campbell did just that, arranging the visits of itinerant ministers and organizing the class meetings central to Methodist faith and practice. Jacobina was a community activist, whose influence seems to have been enhanced rather than otherwise as a result of her "independent" state.

4. Marjory Grant (b. 11 April 1800) (Diary: January–February 1827)

5. Isabella Grant (b. 17 January 1807) (Diary: March–May 1827)[10]

Scottish-born William Grant and his wife, Catherine, the parents of diarists Marjory and Isabella Grant, settled at Old Ridge, a few kilometres north of the village of St Stephen in Charlotte County, sometime between 1785 and the birth of their first child in 1788. There they raised their family of ten. Only the four youngest, including our two diarists, were still living in their parents' household in January 1827, when the "Grant diary" opens. Marjory kept the diary between 29 January and 28 February, shortly before her marriage to William Buchanan on 4 March. Her younger sister Isabella took over the diary on 1 March and kept it until 30 May.[11]

The Grant diary offers a glimpse of the life of a pioneer family well into its second generation on a typical New Brunswick farm. William and his sons followed the New Brunswick pattern of farming during the growing season and lumbering in the winter. During the season recorded in the diary, extending from mid-winter to early spring, when the men were busy in the woods, the women regularly came together in each other's homes, sometimes for the purpose of exchanging goods, sometimes for a "quilting," sometimes simply to visit and share a meal. By 1827, six of Catherine and William Grant's ten children had married, establishing a network of extended kin radiating outward from the home farm. Alexander (b. 1788) and his wife, Mary, lived some little distance away, at Oak Hill, in neighbouring St James Parish. Though Jannet (b. 1793), her husband James Buchanan, and their growing family also lived at Oak Hill, she and her children were frequent visitors in her parents' household and her younger siblings were frequent visitors in hers. It seems likely that James (b. 1791) had died, since his wife, Jannet Buchanan Grant, and at least one child, Hesadiah, are mentioned, but he is not. Visits to Jannet are associated with trips to "the shore," where the village of St Stephen and the Marks' store were located. William (b. 1789), his wife Betsy (Elizabeth) Barber, and their family lived near his parents, as did John (b. 1795) and his family. At twenty-two, John's wife, Ann Crockett (occasionally referred to as Nancy Ann), was very close in age to his younger sisters, and was readily absorbed into the family circle. Caty (Catherine, b. 1798) had married Joseph Maxwell, the son of a neighbouring farmer. Of the children still at home, Marjory, at twenty-six, and Isabella, who had just turned twenty, had a good deal of time for sociability during the winter months, whether at home or travelling the countryside together, sometimes combining such trips with necessary errands. While Charles (b. 1803), at twenty-three, joined his older brothers in the woods during the winter, fifteen-year-old Absolam (b. 1811) remained on the farm. Errands fell to him, as did tasks such as chopping the wood to keep the family's various households supplied while the men were in the woods.[12]

The Grants had no pretensions to gentility, yet in many ways their life closely paralleled that of the Campbells. In both cases, family life was characterized by close family relationships, with daughters, daughters-in-law, and sons in and out of each other's homes regularly, with grandchildren spending several days at a time at their grandparents' home, with men spending winters cutting and hauling wood, with trips to the sugar bush when the sap started to run, and with the shift to farm work as soon as the snow had melted. But although the difference in age of the two family matriarchs, Jacobina Campbell the elder and Catherine Grant, was only two or three years, the diarists portray mothers whose role in managing the household economy diverged significantly. Catherine Grant emerges as very much in charge of her household economy, and that economy enters her daughters' diary in a much more concrete way. The rhythms of farm life come through clearly in both diaries, yet, as in Janet MacDonald's case, there is no sense of drudgery, for the farm routine is enlivened by cooperative work and a strong sense of sociability.

6. Lucy Everett Morrison (b. 16 December 1823) (Diaries: 1869–1893)[13]

Lucy Everett was the eldest daughter of Thomas C. Everett and Mary Camber of Saint John. Lucy's sisters, Janie Inches and Belle Stewart, and her widowed mother appear regularly in her diaries; her brothers,

Tom and Will, less frequently. Lucy married John A. Morrison, the son of a Belfast muslin manufacturer, in 1846, on her twenty-third birthday. The couple settled in Saint John where John and his brother owned a dry goods business. By the time that business failed in 1859, they had five surviving sons (their firstborn died in infancy): Tom (b. 1852), Willie (b. 1854), Jack (b. 1856), Frank (b. 1857), and Julius (b. 1859). In 1860, the family moved to Fredericton, where John purchased a sawmill. Stewart (b. 1861) was born there.[14]

"Riverside," their family home, was within walking distance of the mill. As her husband set about re-establishing himself, Lucy took her place in local society as a typical middle-class matron, becoming active in her church (St Paul's Presbyterian), joining the sewing circle, paying visits, and receiving visitors. She also found the time and money to take up a hobby. Hiring a man to help her, Lucy began raising flowers and vegetables on the grounds surrounding their house. What began as a hobby became first a competitive venture, as specimens from her garden took prizes at the annual Fredericton exhibition, and then a paying proposition, as she began to sell her produce. Meanwhile, John's business followed the boom-and-bust cycle typical of the lumber industry. The mill burned three times during the period covered by Lucy's diaries. But the threat of shifting world markets proved even more serious than the threat of fire, and in 1876, the effects of the worldwide Depression brought John Morrison to the brink of bankruptcy. By then, Lucy was embarked upon her own business plan; by the autumn of that year, her second greenhouse was completed. Lucy's diaries record the progress of her business, providing both insight into the running of such a business in the late nineteenth century and a rich source of information on late-nineteenth-century gardening technique and practice. But they offer more, for Lucy Everett Morrison is perhaps the prototype for today's married working woman, maintaining a household and running a business. For Lucy, the work was exhausting, the result almost always rewarding.

7. Sophy (Sophia) Bliss Carman (b. 26 October 1828) (Diaries: 1872–1873; 1883–1886)[15]

Descended from Loyalists, Sophia Bliss was the ninth child and second daughter of George Pidgeon Bliss and Sarah Wetmore. George Bliss, receiver general for the province, died in 1836, when Sophy was just seven. Raised in Fredericton, Sophy married William Carman (b. 1804), a widower with six grown children, in 1859, when she was thirty years old. In 1872, when her first diary opens, Sophy was forty-three and the mother of two young children: ten-year-old Bliss and eight-year-old Murray (Muriel). A third child, a son born in 1866, died in infancy.

Unlike the majority of our diarists, Sophy was a city dweller, with access to all the amenities that even a small urban centre offered. The Fredericton of her day was a "walking city" and Sophy travelled mainly on foot. From her home she could readily walk to the Anglican cathedral, or to visit her mother and younger sister Jean, who lived with her elder brother George. Her sister Emma Roberts also lived within easy walking distance. Like our other diarists, then, Sophy Carman was surrounded by family. Her weekly routines revolved around the rhythms of the cathedral, where she attended services faithfully.

She was well integrated into Fredericton society. William, a barrister, had been appointed clerk of pleas in the Supreme Court as well as clerk in equity, and the Carmans moved in the upper circles of Fredericton society, occasionally dining at Government House. In summer, they enjoyed holidays at Bay Shore near Saint John. Although comfortably well-off, Sophy was far from idle. As well as managing her household and supervising the garden,[16] she played an active role in her children's education, arranging Latin tutoring for Bliss and music lessons for Murray.

By 1883, Sophy's children had reached young adulthood. Bliss, at twenty-two, was attending the University of Edinburgh; Muriel, still at home, was very independent. While Sophy's interests and preoccupations had not changed significantly, first her own chronic eczema and then her husband's failing health severely curtailed her activities. Yet, despite these troubles, which were compounded by financial worries when William was forced to resign his office, family correspondence portrays Sophy as a warm and affectionate parent, with a sharp and lively wit that cut through the pretensions of both church and state officials.

8. Mary Whitney Hill (b. 1829) (Diary: 1878–1879)[17]

Mary Whitney Hill was the second of nine children born to Sarah Upton and George Stillman Hill of St Stephen, Charlotte County. The Uptons and the Hills had been part of a post-Loyalist American migration to Charlotte County. George Hill, a lawyer, married Sarah Upton in 1825. Their first child, Aaron Upton, was born two years later, followed by

Mary Whitney, George Frederick (b. 1832), Hesediah Louisa (b. 1834), Sarah Augusta (b. 1836), Edgar Cutter (b. 1839), Arthur Marcus (b. 1842), Joanna Upton (b. 1844), and Henry Ernest (b. 1848).[18]

We first hear Mary's authorial voice in a letter written when she was eleven years old.[19] By age sixteen, when she left home to attend a private ladies' academy in South Boston, Mary was an accomplished correspondent. Her sophisticated and often satirical comments on school, family, and local affairs suggest that independence of thought was encouraged in her home. At the same time, she sought to maintain home ties through frequent letters, enjoining her family to respond in kind. The Hill correspondence provides unique insight into the nature of family relations in one New Brunswick household.

By the time her father died, in 1858, Mary Hill was living at home and working as a teacher, a profession she continued to pursue.[20] Possibly to ensure his daughters a measure of independence during their mother's lifetime, George bequeathed them each "three shares in the capital stock of the Saint Stephen's Bank."[21] But until Sarah's death in 1874, Mary and her unmarried siblings continued to live in their mother's household.[22] Then, after receiving her share of her parents' legacy – the Hill children would "share and share alike" all remaining real estate, "wherever situated" – Mary moved to the nearby community of St Andrews.

Kept for only a few months in 1878–9, Mary Hill's diary affords us an intriguing glimpse of the life of a middle-aged single woman maintaining her independence by carefully managing her income.[23] In St Andrews, Mary found a community in the Methodist Church, joining the Ladies' Society and teaching Sunday school.[24] She also enjoyed the company of a circle of friends, mainly independent single women like herself.

9. Annie Gilbert Johnston Waltham (b. 1 November 1833) (Diaries: 1869–1877; 1881–1882)[25]

Annie Townsend Gilbert was the seventh of nine children born to Charlotte Amelia Hewlett and Thomas Gilbert, a wealthy farmer and prominent politician, of Upper Gagetown, Queens County.[26] In 1857, Annie married Thomas Millidge Johnston, the son of a Saint John merchant and magistrate. Less than two years later, following the tragic death of her husband and younger sister Hannah in a drowning accident, Annie and her baby daughter, Annie Eliza (b. 1859) joined her widowed mother and two unmarried sisters on the family farm. When her mother died in 1860, Annie assumed the management of the extensive family properties.

By 1869, when she began keeping a diary, Annie Johnston had been managing those properties for almost a decade and headed a household that included her ten-year-old daughter, her sisters Fannie and Lucretia, a cook, and a general servant. Her diary offers clear evidence of her business acumen, detailing regular trips to Saint John to conduct business, shop, and visit. Yet Annie craved the kind of companionship that neither her sisters nor her daughter could provide. In 1871, she thought she had found what she sought in Richard Claude Waltham, a Cambridge graduate, who had come to Gagetown to teach at the local grammar school.

Annie married "Mr Waltham" in 1872. Significantly younger and less experienced than she, Waltham gradually gained control of Annie's property and, with it, the management of her unmarried sisters' financial affairs. Waltham proved a poor businessman. Even before the birth of their child, Adeline (Lena) Miller Waltham (b. 1873), the relationship had seriously deteriorated, exacerbated by Waltham's drinking. Although Waltham was physically abusive, the marriage endured for almost a decade. In 1878, the entire household moved to London, England. Not until October 1881, when the abuse became so serious that she feared for her own, and even more, for the life of her twenty-one-year-old daughter, did Annie decide to end the marriage. During the year that followed, she again emerged as a competent businesswoman, and, still in London, the women resumed a happier, more stable lifestyle, taking in concerts and exchanging visits with a widening circle of friends.[27]

10. Ann Eliza Rogers (b. 12 July 1837) (Diaries: 1852–1876; 1888–1896)[28]

Ann Eliza Rogers was the eldest of five children – our subject (b. 1837), Mary Susan (b. 1840), Maggie (Margaret, b. 1844), James Horace (b. 1847), and John Howe (b. 1851) – born to John Rogers and Eleanor Dodge of Hopewell Hill, Albert County. John Rogers, a prosperous farmer descended from a Nova Scotian Planter family, dabbled in various business enterprises. Eleanor Dodge Rogers had been raised in Maine but had relatives in New Brunswick. In 1852, when her daughter's diaries begin, Eleanor's mother and several siblings were living in Boston.

Spanning the period from her own coming of age through the coming of age of her children, Ann Eliza Rogers's diaries offer insights into individual and community responses to changing times. They also tell a story full of the drama that was the lived experience of an ordinary woman. At age eighteen, Ann Eliza married John McAuley Gallacher (b. 1819) of Glasgow, Scotland, who had come to Hopewell by way of Boston to help set up a chemical works. John was eighteen years her senior, but Ann Eliza was smitten, and remained so throughout their marriage. When the chemical works failed, John, leaving behind his wife and new daughter, Isabelle Plummer (b.1855), returned to the United States to look for work. Over the course of the following decade, the family lived by times in Boston, Hopewell Hill, and Saint John, following job opportunities, but returning home when businesses failed. Ann Eliza gave birth to three more children: Ella Frances (1858–1864), Frank John Howe (b. 1861), and Achsah Georgia (b. 1864). In 1866, John found work in Philadelphia. But within a year, Ann Eliza was back home, tragically widowed as a result of an industrial accident. Three years later, in 1869, she married Lemuel Moore (b. 1842), a neighbour, and settled on a farm near her parents. Lemuel, a farmer and sometime carpenter and storekeeper, became a highly respected member of the community, serving as a school trustee, county assessor, and census enumerator. With him, Ann Eliza had five more children: Ella Kate (b. 1870), Jennie (b. 1872), Archibald (b. 1874), Donald (b. 1877), and Dodge (b. 1880).[29] Over the years, and wherever she was living, Ann Eliza recorded comings and goings, marriages, births, and deaths in Hopewell, revealing hers as a cosmopolitan community, with strong links to the wider world.

11. Mary Isoline Wolhaupter (b. 12 March 1838) (Diary: 1869–1870)[30]

Mary Isoline Wolhaupter of Bloomfield, Simonds Parish, Carleton County, was the second child and eldest daughter of Hanford and Emily Wolhaupter. The son of a New York Loyalist, Hanford Wolhaupter was raised an Anglican but by 1861 had become a Methodist. Mary's mother, Emily Carter, born in the United States, had siblings in both Houlton, Maine, and Woodstock, New Brunswick. The couple settled on a farm in Carleton County, where they raised their six children: Charles (b. 1836), Mary (b. 1838), Samuel (b. 1840), Haddie (b. 1842), Carrie (Caroline, b. 1846), and Benjamin (b. 1848).[31]

The diary opens with thirty-one-year-old Mary preparing to return to her teaching job in a nearby community. Charles, also a teacher, his wife Maggie and daughter Gertrude, were living in the United States; Haddie had just married neighbour George Nye; Samuel and Benjamin were away working in a lumber camp; only Carrie remained at home. Typical nineteenth-century New Brunswick farmers, the Wolhaupter men lumbered in winter and farmed from spring through fall. Also integral to the family economy, the women cared for the domestic needs of their household, sewed and spun for others, and served as agents in procuring homespun cloth for sale.

Well embarked upon a teaching career, Mary Wolhaupter confessed doubts about her choice. Abandoning her position to return home, she exhibited a restless dissatisfaction that spilled over into her family relationships. This conflict resolved itself into an inner struggle, the nature of which was defined by her religious convictions. In the nineteenth-century Methodist world view, obedience to one's parents reflected one's obedience to God, and Mary sought solace and strength in an angst-ridden religiosity. But she also sought economic independence. Casting about for "profitable" work, she considered "going back to Lynn,"[32] tried earning money by sewing, and, finally, began making plans to take on another school. Meanwhile, she demonstrated her acumen and independence by speculating in agricultural products ranging from butter to farm animals, and floating loans to friends and family members.

12. Emma Bertha Frost Jones (b. 23 February 1844) (Diary: 1893–1894)[33]

Emma Bertha Frost was the eldest of the seven daughters of Barbara Smith and Smith Frost, a farmer, of Norton Parish, Kings County.[34] At age thirty-one, Bertha married Zebulon Jones (b. 1832), a farmer in Greenwich Parish, where she had been teaching school.[35] With marriage, Bertha gained a ready-made family, for Zebulon, a widower eleven years her senior, had five young children. The couple had three more children – Ada (b. 1878), Alma (b. 1881), and Hildrick (b. 1887) – by the time Zebulon died in 1891. By then, four of Zebulon's surviving children were young adults. Henrietta Marley, a widow at age thirty, and Julia McKeil (age twenty-eight) were both living in Woodstock. Leander, at twenty-nine, was living in the Dakota Territory. Only twenty-one-year-old Norman was still at home.[36] But by 1893, when the diary begins, Norman, too, was preparing to leave home.

Bertha Jones's diary documents one New Brunswick widow's use of a variety of strategies commonly associated with "respectable" nineteenth-century widows struggling to make ends meet. She used her spinning wheel to good effect, for her own needs and to fill orders for others. Although she taught her daughters to spin, Ada, at fifteen, was still regularly attending school; the children of this former teacher would not be required to cut short their education to contribute to the family income. Even in the absence of Norman, the work of the farm continued, with the help of farm labourers hired temporarily, in season. And, taking advantage of her well-situated, good-sized house, Bertha offered room and board to men who worked in the skate factory. She may have operated something of an inn as well, for she sometimes reported giving travellers a meal and, less often, a bed for the night. Bertha Jones was well served by her community and by her church (Church of England). As was the case in other small nineteenth-century communities, the people of Greenwich were part of an interdependent and interactive economy of barter and exchange, and, as a widow, Bertha had the support of a network of friends and neighbours.

13. Jo (Josephine) Reid Turner (b. 17 March 1849) (Diary: 1884)[37]

14. Lottie (Charlotte) Reid (b. 9 April 1859) (Diaries: 1879; 1881; 1883)[38]

Josephine and Charlotte Reid were daughters of Lucinda Robinson and William Reid, a house joiner and farmer. The Robinsons and Reids had been among the pre-Loyalist families who had settled Harvey Parish, Albert County, and it was there that Lucinda and William raised their eight children: Anna (b. 1845), Mary Eliza (b. 1847), Jo (Josephine, b. 1849), Orpah (b. 1851), James (b. 1853), Merritt (b. 1855), Wat (Watson, b. 1857), and Lottie (Charlotte, b. 1859). By the time Lottie, the youngest, began her first diary, Anna, a seamstress, had married a prominent merchant and politician, Mary, a local farmer, and Orpah, a mariner. Jo, as yet unmarried, was working as a teacher and James, a house joiner like his father, was working away from home.[39] Merritt would soon leave home in search of work as well.

Lottie Reid's first diary, kept during 1879, the year she turned twenty, documented an eventful year for the family. Orpah, her husband, Alden, and their two-year-old daughter came home. And Jo married sea captain James Brewster Turner that August. But there was tragedy as well as celebration. Alden returned to sea, leaving his wife and small daughter behind, but a week later, the family received news that his ship had been lost. Orpah, possibly ill already, never recovered from the shock. She died less than a month later, leaving two-year-old Josie to be raised in the family of her maternal grandparents. Lottie's diaries from 1879, 1881, and 1883, a record of one family's day-to-day life, reveal a rural community which revolved around neighbourhood, church (Baptist in this case), and the farming economy, even as it looked outward to the wider world. By 1881, Lottie, at twenty-two, was the only one of William and Lucinda's children still living at home. Moreover, four of her six surviving siblings had left Harvey, reflecting a pattern of out-migration of young people common to many New Brunswick communities. While her three brothers left Harvey to find work, Jo left to accompany her sea-captain husband on his sailing voyages. On the first such voyage, her youngest brother, Wat, accompanied them.

Josephine Reid Turner wrote her family many letters describing the places she visited, and, in 1884, while she was in Buenos Aires, kept a diary. Although her husband, James, was the son of a farmer, he, like so many other young men from New Brunswick's coastal communities, including two of his three younger brothers, began his working career as a seaman. Unlike the majority, however, James did not return to make his life on the farm, but rose to the rank of captain and made the sea his career. Abandoning her teaching career to marry and go sailing, Jo was a lively observer. Her letters and diary offer an interesting but not uncommon woman's perspective on the sailing life.[40] Jo missed her family when she was away from them and spent most of her time with other seagoing families while on-shore.

Back at home, Lottie, who longed to see her sister, followed the progress of each voyage carefully, just as she kept track of the movements of her three brothers as they followed job opportunities to various destinations in the United States and Western Canada. No less than Jo, James, Merritt, and Wat retained strong family ties, no matter how far away from home they travelled. All three wrote regularly, not only to family members at home, but also to their travelling sister, and those letters – as well as opening a window on the wider world for those left behind – can, for the modern reader, serve to supplement their sisters' diaries, providing further insight into the experience of the women in this close-knit family.[41]

15. Annie Trueman (b. 5 October 1851) (Diaries: 1871–1872; 1885; 1886; 1888)[42]

16. Laura Trueman Wood (b. 14 January 1856) (Diaries: 1868–1873; 1878–1888; 1898–1900)[43]

Annie Rebecca and Laura Sophia Trueman were the daughters of Rebecca Wood and Thompson Trueman of Sackville, New Brunswick. Rebecca and Thompson, a successful farmer, were staunch Methodists and strong supporters of Mount Allison University. Indeed, Thompson Trueman's family had been among the original Yorkshire settlers, all followers of John Wesley, who settled the Sackville region. Annie, Laura, and their younger brother, Albert (b. 1859), were raised in an intellectually stimulating atmosphere. Young professors at Mount Allison sometimes boarded with the Truemans, whose children were raised to be critical thinkers. Annie and Laura attended the female academy affiliated with the college, while their younger brother would attend the university. The sisters kept diaries not only during their time at Mount Allison but also in later periods. An extensive correspondence collection supplements the diaries, offering a complementary perspective on the lives and experiences of the Trueman women.[44]

Annie Trueman's first diary, kept sporadically in 1871–2, stands in interesting contrast to her letters of the same period. Although it is clear in both that Annie was a devout Methodist, the expressive rhetoric of the diary is not reproduced in the letters. Yet her sharp, critical mind is much in evidence in both. Entries in a later diary, dating from the mid-1880s, when she was teaching at Mount Allison Ladies' Academy, were made even less regularly than the entries in her schoolgirl diary and offer the merest glimpses of her life at that time. Unlike her sister, Annie would never be a dedicated diarist, although she was the more regular correspondent.

Laura Trueman Wood's diaries encompass three distinct stages – or passages – in the life course and can thus offer a parallel vision of her world that can be compared to and contrasted with the world portrayed in her letters. The first of the three diaries covers the period 1868–73, when she was attending the Female Academy. Then, in 1874, within months of completing her education, eighteen-year-old Laura Trueman married a cousin, Josiah Wood (b. 1842), a Sackville businessman some years older than she; Josie, as she always called him, had been one of Mount Allison University's first two degree graduates in 1863. Within three years of their marriage, two children – Daisy (Eleanor, b. 1875) and Herbert (b. 1877) – were born. Laura's second diary, which she dubbed a "Journal of Everyday Affairs," was never meant as a daily record, and was kept irregularly between 1878 and 1888. During this period, Laura bore four more children – Annie (1879–1879), Dora (b. 1881), William (b. 1884), and Hester (b. 1887) – and Josie was elected to the Canadian House of Commons. Laura's journal thus depicts her as a wife and mother, surrounded by young children, whose husband was absent in Ottawa much of the time. The sometimes thoughtful, sometimes exuberant entries written during these years presage the reflective, mature opinions of the middle-aged author of her third extant diary, kept very occasionally between 1898 and 1900.

Annie and Laura Trueman's world extended well beyond their home community of Sackville. As teenagers, the girls regularly made extended visits to relatives in other New Brunswick communities. As they came of age, they travelled further afield. Whenever and wherever they travelled, the Trueman daughters and their mother maintained a regular and extensive correspondence with one another. By comparing the diaries and letters written by Annie Trueman and Laura Trueman Wood, we can observe two sides of the same coin. To differentiate between even the warmest of family relationships and the inner life of a reflective individual is to draw a fine but significant distinction. Letters and diaries do not tell the same story but, taken together, they tell a more complete story than either does on its own. And there are, inevitably, important areas of intersection and overlap. The warm, affective relationship between the two daughters and their mother is one such area. In Annie's letters, we see the maturation of her faith and of her understanding of the intellectual underpinning of that faith, while Laura's diaries and letters reflect a parallel inner and shared dialogue of faith and intellect.

17. Maggie (Margaret) Loggie Valentine (b. 1853) (Journal Letter: 1885)[45]

18. Kate (Catherine) Loggie (b. 1857) (Diary: 1880–1881)[46]

19. Jessie Loggie (b. 1859) (Diary: 1887–1888; Journal Letter: 1887–1888)[47]

Maggie, Kate, and Jessie Loggie were the youngest of eleven children born to Alexander Loggie and Catherine Morrison of Burnt Church, Alnwick Parish, Northumberland County. Only eight of the eleven survived infancy: Ellen (b. 1843), Alexander (1845–1875), Donald (b. 1847), John (1849–1876), Mary (b. 1851), Maggie (b. 1853), Kate (b. 1857), and Jessie (b. 1859).[48] By 1880, when Kate began keeping her diary, Ellen, Donald, and Maggie were married and Alexander and John had died. Her father and only surviving brother were prominent businessmen, with interests ranging from fish processing to lumbering.[49] The family was solidly middle class, and we would not expect the unmarried daughters to support themselves by working for wages. Yet, that Alexander and Donald Loggie were the kind of businessmen who can find themselves short of money seems confirmed by a comment in Kate Loggie's diary on 6 April 1881: "They at home want me to go visit Ellen. The only obstacle want of money." Ellen and her family were living in New York, where Kate would, eventually, visit her. But in the summer of 1880, Kate, then twenty-two, was teaching and boarding in Tabusintac, not far from her home in Burnt Church, where she spent most weekends. Her parents, and Mary and Jessie, who were still living at home, figure largely in Kate's diary, as does her brother Donald's family, which included his wife, Mary Jane, and their four small children: Herbert (b. 1873), John (b. 1875), Willber (b. 1878), and Rachel (b. 1880). Kate also mentions writing to and receiving letters and logs from her sister Maggie, sailing the world with her sea-captain husband, William Valentine.

Kate Loggie's diary affords a window on the experience of teaching school in late-nineteenth-century New Brunswick. During this era, even teachers who, like Kate, held a first-class teaching certificate, were hired by the term and then had to make their decision anew: should they continue teaching another term? And, if so, should they agree to continue in their present position or seek a different situation? Although Kate worried about issues of discipline and attendance, and did not look forward to visits from the school inspector, she was popular with administrators as well as with parents, and had her choice of schools. In the end, she decided to continue for another term, her third, at the McRobbie Road School.[50] Kate Loggie, like Mary Wolhaupter, is revealed in her diary to be an intensely serious and devoutly religious young woman. Yet Kate seemed more preoccupied with the nature of duty and true piety than with injunctions to be "good," that constant preoccupation of Mary Wolhaupter. Kate's two sisters, who also recorded their experiences, appear to have been less introspective, but the fact that they were writing their accounts with an audience in mind may explain this difference in tone.

Kate's seagoing sister Maggie was the intrepid sophisticate of the family, as at home in the shops of Liverpool, England, as in her native community of Burnt Church. She met William Valentine, an English sea captain and her future husband, in 1872, when his ship was frozen in at Bay du Vin. During his winter in Northumberland County, Captain Valentine fell in love with Maggie Loggie, and, though he left her behind when he departed in the spring, they married on his next voyage to the port and he took her home to Liverpool.[51] Maggie regularly sailed with William, keeping a "log" of her trips for her family's interest and information. Although Kate refers to such a log as early as 1880, the only surviving example, in the form of a "journal letter," dates from 1885. Entitled "A few remarks on a ten day's trip into the interior of Norway," it is written in an engaging style.[52] In it, Maggie reveals herself as a typical tourist of the day, preoccupied by the search for the picturesque.[53] Through her humourous anecdotes and vivid descriptions, her entire family "participated" in her adventures. And by return mail Maggie was kept abreast of the home news, and responded to it in the next log. It is from this source that we learn that both Kate and Jessie were ill in 1885.

Jessie's illness persisted, with the result that, two years later, in 1887, Alexander and Catherine Loggie decided to send her on a sea voyage with Maggie in the hope that her health would improve, as it did, at least temporarily. Jessie and Maggie travelled by steamship from Rimouski, Quebec, to Liverpool. After visiting and shopping in Liverpool, they joined Maggie's husband on the *Muncaster Castle*, and set sail for Calcutta. In both her travel journal and log of the voyage, twenty-eight-year-old Jessie, like Maggie, emerges as a much more carefree young woman than the serious-minded Kate. Evincing little concern about the state of her soul, she gave herself over to the pleasures of the moment. In so doing, she provides insight into the way women's horizons were broadened by the opportunity to accompany husbands, fathers, and brothers on such travels. Maggie's practice of writing a "log" for her family was continued by Jessie, who, at one stage, pointedly addressed her comments to her mother. Like many other mothers of her day, Catherine Loggie had enjoined her daughters to "'improve their time' through reading." That the three youngest were voracious readers suggests that she had promoted the pastime for pleasure as well.

20. Amelia Holder (b. 25 December 1855) (Diaries: 1867–1879)[54]

21. Emma Alice Pitt (b. 1857) (Diary: 1873)[55]

Susan Amelia Holder was the third child and eldest daughter of Edwin Jacob Holder and Hannah L. Parrett. Born into the most prominent seafaring family in Holderville, on the Long Reach in the Kingston Peninsula in Kings County, Amelia and her siblings – Thomas (b. 1851), Abraham (b. 1853), Aggie (Agnes, b. 1858), Ada (b. 1860), Edwin (b. 1862), Raymond (b. 1864), and Frank (b. 1866) – grew up in an era when New Brunswick's great sailing ships were world renowned. The Holders, like many seafaring families, conformed to the New Brunswick tradition of occupational plurality, involving themselves locally in farming as well as shipbuilding, and internationally in the shipping trade. With her sea-captain husband absent for long periods each year, Hannah, a former school teacher and the daughter of a Methodist minister, became the effective household head, responsible for caring for and provisioning her family.[56]

When, in 1867, Edwin convinced Hannah to go to sea with him, both hoped that a sea voyage would improve her health. Amelia was taken along to help her mother. This was Amelia's first voyage, and, despite her mother's failing health, it was an adventure for the little girl, who had her twelfth birthday at sea. The diary she kept during that voyage was the first of a series of travel journals, the record of six voyages with her father. Those journals enable us to follow Amelia as she moved from precocious child to young adult, a transition that began with the death of her mother, just a few days after their return home in 1868. But Amelia Holder's travel diaries also offer insight into the nature of family life aboard a sailing vessel. Nor was Amelia's experience particularly unusual.[57] Many New Brunswick girls and women sailed with fathers and husbands from the numerous shipbuilding communities that dotted the province's coastline. Having entered the wider world, such women brought the wider world home with them in their own experience and in the stories of their travels passed on to others.[58]

Amelia's diaries do not end with her final voyage, and are supplemented by those of her two younger sisters. Whether at sea or on land, Aggie's journal entries were sporadic. And although Ada, the youngest of the three, did accompany her father and her sister Amelia on one voyage, her occasional diary keeping occurred only when she was at home. Her diary serves as something of a foil to those of her sisters and as a companion to that of their cousin Emma Pitt. Ada's diary, and, indeed, Amelia's and even Aggie's shore diaries, are more introspective than the seagoing diaries, reflecting both adolescent angst and the loneliness of being left behind.[59]

Fifteen-year-old Emma Alice Pitt received a journal in 1873, as "a New Year's Gift" from her eldest brother, Edwin, a twenty-five-year-old sea captain. Their mother, Catherine Susannah Holder (Edwin Holder's sister) had married David Leonard Pitt, a mariner and shipbuilder, in 1844. The couple had six children, two of whom died in infancy. Besides Emma, their surviving children included Edwin Jacob (b. 1848), David Leonard (b. 1850), and Abraham Wilmot (b. 1851). Unlike her cousins, Emma, who grew up in Portland, did not go to sea. The youngest child and only daughter, Emma was an introspective young woman and, in many ways, hers were the typical anxieties of an adolescent girl, caught between childhood and adulthood. Depressed and lonely when she was without company, but readily cheered when company was about, she was very excited when her cousins, Amelia and Aggie Holder, arrived in port on 23 April 1873.

Yet Emma's distress during her year of diary keeping went well beyond adolescent moodiness. Central to her diary is the family drama that unfolded during that fateful year. In the spring of 1873, two of her brothers, Edwin and Abraham, sailed together as captain and mate on the *E. & F. Williams*. In late June, they left Cape Breton with a shipload of coal, but failed to arrive in their home port of Saint John. According to family oral tradition, their father, who refused to believe his sons had been lost at sea, twice consulted a fortune teller. Emma's diary mentions one such consultation and indicates that, as late as mid-August, her father still held out hope for his sons' safe return. By that time, Emma was less optimistic. But not until he dreamed that his sons emerged dripping wet from the St John River, "climbed the hill and lay down in the Holderville cemetery," did her father finally accept that they were "gone forever."[60]

22. Lillie (Lillian) Williamson (b. 1861), (Diary: 1882–1885)[61]

Lillian Williamson was the fourth of five children born to Mary Haviland of Greenwich, Kings County, and Benjamin Williamson, an English immigrant. The couple settled on the Haviland family farm, where their five children – Joe (Joseph, b. 1856), Sam (Samuel, b. 1857), Kate (b. 1859), Lillie (b. 1861), and Fred (Frederick, b. 1863) – were born.[62]

As well as farming, Benjamin Williamson served as a lay preacher, and Lillie's diary reveals her as both a loyal daughter and a committed Methodist, with little patience for some of the practices and teachings of other faiths.

Although Lillie's father ran a successful farm, none of his sons chose to remain on it. By December 1878, when Joe began the diary that his youngest sister would take over four years later, he and Sam were already working away from home, living in Saint John, where they were engaged in the watchmaking trade. By 1882, when Lillie began to keep a diary, Fred, too, had left home and was working as a machinist in Saint John. Joe was working in the United States; before the year was out Fred would be working as a fireman on a tugboat. Only Sam returned home to help his father with the harvest. Thus, it is perhaps not surprising that Benjamin Williamson often thought of selling the farm that had been part of his wife's inheritance.

The Williamson siblings ranged in age from nineteen to twenty-six in 1882 when Lillie's diary opens, and her record charts the ups and downs of their various courtships. This family's young people fell in and out of love, so while some courtships ended in marriage, others did not. Visiting Saint John in the summer of 1882, Lillie was entertained by the Wightmans, with whom her brother Fred boarded. Fred had already begun courting Carrie Wightman and the following year Carrie's brother, another Fred, began courting Lillie. Although the two Freds, who had become fast friends, attempted to start a business, their enterprise proved unsuccessful, and, postponing marriage, Lillie's brother returned to the boats. Fred Wightman had other ambitions, in which Lillie encouraged him, although it further delayed their own marriage, and, as Lillie's diary closed in 1885, their long courtship continued.

23. Alva (Alvaretta) Estabrooks (b. 26 September 1869) (Diaries: 1889–1893)[63]

24. Hannah Estabrooks (b. 2 September 1871) (Diary: 1903–1906)[64]

Alvaretta and Hannah Estabrooks were the daughters of Agnes Carter of Richmond Parish, and Shephard Handy Estabrooks of Coldstream, Brighton Parish, Carleton County. They had two older brothers, George E. (b. 1865) and Arthur Shephard (b. 1867), and a younger sister, Nellie (Ellen J., b. 1879). Shephard, who had taken over the family farm, died in 1883;[65] Agnes, with the help of her children, continued to manage the farm. Three years later, she married the widower George Else.[66] Although Agnes was widowed again in less than a decade, the stability George Else brought to the family economy enabled Agnes's sons to leave the farm.[67] Her eldest, George, married and established his own household in 1888, the year before his sister Alva began her diary.[68] As they came of age, Agnes's daughters also sought independent careers.

Alva Estabrooks was nineteen when she began keeping a diary. In it she recorded the comings and goings of a busy rural household. Relatives, friends, and neighbours visited regularly, and, besides attending sewing circles and prayer meetings, Alva did her own share of visiting. Her brother George was among the frequent visitors at the farm, but, tragically, died in May 1890, as a result of being kicked by a horse.[69] In June, Arthur left the farm to begin clerking in C.A. Harmon's store.[70] Alva helped with the household work, ranging from washing and ironing to hooking mats, quilting and spinning, and making clothes for herself and her two younger sisters. Yet she was rarely too busy for music practice and, with the exception of Sundays, scarcely a day went by when she did not record having "practised" for several hours.

Recognizing Alva's musical talent, Shephard's sister Lucretia and her husband, Amos Hayward, a Baptist minister, helped to fund music lessons and two years at Acadia's female seminary in Wolfville, Nova Scotia, where Alva had the opportunity to develop her skill further. Alva's diary encompasses her time at Acadia, and provides insight into the structure and nature of life at a women's seminary. By 1891, when Reverend Hayward held the pastorate at Florenceville, Alva was dividing her time between the Haywards' home and the family farm.[71] In the spring and summer of 1893, though she had not yet graduated from Acadia, Alva had already embarked on a career as a music teacher in Florenceville and the surrounding district.

We next meet the Estabrooks family through the diary of Alva's younger sister Hannah, a full decade later. Hannah Estabrooks, unlike her sister, was not a disciplined diarist: her attempt to keep a daily record ended after the first two months of 1903. Later entries, while irregular, are longer and more introspective, and, because she used her diary as a confidante, the reader can gain some insight into Hannah's inner life, her disappointed hopes, and her current worries and fears. Hannah's record, though very different, serves as a companion piece to Alva's, providing a glimpse of the family ten years on. Much had changed: their mother was again a widow; Arthur had married Frank

(Frances) Barnes of Queens County and was the father of two small children, Jean and Kenneth;[72] Alva was teaching music and living with their Uncle Amos and Aunt Lucretia; and Nellie was teaching school and being courted by Allan Watters.

In 1903, when her diary begins, Hannah was thirty-one years old, and, by her own account, in indifferent health. Nonetheless, when she went "down home" to the farm, she usually managed to do her share of the labour, whether churning, baking, sewing, or helping with the barn work. In the main, however, Hannah worked as a clerk in a store managed by her brother Arthur in the nearby village of Rockland. On cold winter days, she found the walk back and forth from the farm to Rockland daunting, and, once in the store, the days long and boring. Two years earlier she had been working as a housekeeper in Lewiston, Maine.[73] We cannot know why she decided to return home, but it is clear that Hannah preferred helping with the farm work to the less physically taxing work of clerking in a store. She was happiest at the farm, surrounded by her family.

25. Laura Cynthia Fullerton (b. 1870) (Diary: 1886)[74]

When Laura Fullerton of Mill Village, Cumberland County, Nova Scotia, returned to Mount Allison Ladies' Academy in January 1886, she carried with her a small, brown notebook, for, as she stated in her first entry on 25 January, "I intend to keep a diary this year." The eldest child of Rosamund Lawrence and Burgess Fullerton, a merchant, Laura had two brothers, Walter (b. 1873) and George (b. 1883).[75] Her diary, kept during the 1886 winter term, provides a highly engaging account of life at New Brunswick's premier ladies' academy. Although she was not born in the province, hers was a quintessentially New Brunswick experience. Moreover, although her parents were Presbyterian, Laura had an aunt who taught at the academy. She also had other New Brunswick relatives: an aunt and uncle living in Sackville and another across the marsh at Pointe de Bute. Laura, who was not quite sixteen, could travel to the school by train, since Sackville, as the academy *Catalogue* pointed out, was "situated on the line of the Intercolonial Railway, midway between Halifax and Saint John."[76]

Laura Fullerton's diary provides insight into all aspects of life at Mount Allison during the late nineteenth century. Although academy life is sometimes portrayed by historians as restrictive, with girls closely supervised,[77] what emerges is a nurturing and fairly indulgent environment. Young women attending the academy enjoyed an active social life, establishing close friendships and sometimes flourishing courtships. Yet the Mount Allison of 1886 was no mere finishing school, as some contemporaries feared. Fine arts were certainly taught, and Laura took music lessons and participated in public performances. But equal time was devoted to subjects such as geometry, physiology, and English composition. While Laura disliked composition, she enjoyed and was extraordinarily good at geometry and physiology. She clearly enjoyed her time at school, stimulated by both intellectual and artistic challenges. Yet she missed her family and longed for letters from home. Laura Fullerton's diary spans a single term spent at Mount Allison, but offers a rare portrait of the social as well as the academic life of middle-class schoolgirls of the period.

26. Sadie (Sarah) Harper (b. 7 January 1875) (Diaries: 1890–1892; 1894–1896; 1898)[78]

Sarah Estelle Harper was the fourth of seven children born to Jessie Theal and Duncan Harper of Shediac, New Brunswick. Duncan Harper was a successful businessman, a partner in Harper and Webster's shoe manufactory. Sadie began to keep a diary in 1889, at age fifteen, and continued it off and on to the age of twenty-three. All six of her siblings – May (b. 1869), Winnie (Ethel Winnifred, b. 1871), Nell (Helen I., b. 1873), Blois (DeBloi D., b. 1876), Bea (Beatrice, b. 1878), and Duff (Dufferin W., b. 1883) – figure prominently in her diary.[79]

When the diary opens, Sadie was attending the local grammar school, but her attendance was often irregular. Although the Harpers could afford to hire a servant to help with the household work, retaining them was difficult, and, during periods when the family was without a "girl," the Harper daughters shared the chores. Sometimes this necessitated their absence from school. A mischievous student, Sadie rarely chafed at missing classes. Like our other diarists, Sadie and her siblings were embedded within a network of extended kin, and the Harpers emerge from the pages of her diary as a warm and lively family, whose home served as a magnet for extended family and friends. Their local community seemed equally lively; the little town of Shediac, as portrayed in Sadie's diary, fairly hums with activity. Church-sponsored events played an important role in framing that activity, and the Harpers, though staunch Methodists, also attended Presbyterian, Baptist, Anglican, and, very occasionally, Roman Catholic, events.

In 1893, seeking to develop her artistic talent, eighteen-year-old Sadie enrolled in Mount Allison Ladies' College. In 1894, however, when her father's shoe factory burned down and his health appeared to be failing, Sadie withdrew from Mount Allison. Putting her training to good use, she earned "pocket" money by teaching painting and helped her parents by supplying paintings and plaques to give as gifts. Life in the Harper household went on much as usual; Winnie's marriage to Eddie Talbot of Bermuda in 1895 was a gala affair. That year, Sadie met Frank Allen, a teacher at the local grammar school. Gradually, love between them blossomed.

27. Violet Goldsmith (b. 17 December 1880) (Diaries: 1900–1906)[80]

Violet Goldsmith was the eldest of three children born to Anna Wright and John Goldsmith, a Methodist minister, who had emigrated from the Isle of Man to Prince Edward Island, where he met Anna. After Anna died in childbirth in 1886, John employed a succession of housekeepers to care for Violet, her sister Mabel (b. 1882), and their baby brother, Oliver. Sometime after Oliver's death, at age three, John's sister Margaret, the "Aunt Maggie" of Violet's diary, joined them.[81] In 1900, soon after Violet's graduation from Prince Edward Island's Prince of Wales Ladies' College, John received a posting as "financial secretary of the Chatham District," and the family moved to Bathurst, New Brunswick. As Violet's diary opens, we are plunged into the preparations for that move.

Recording her experiences during her five-year sojourn in the province, Violet Goldsmith's diary provides a series of intriguing snapshots of normal school and university student life in turn-of-the-century Fredericton. Perhaps because she was not a systematic diarist and her summaries are often enlivened by amusing anecdotes, the diary is particularly engaging. Seeking a first-class teaching licence, Violet entered the Provincial Normal School in Fredericton in 1901. There her social life revolved around the Methodist Church, but extended beyond it. She helped organize a Young Women's Christian Association (YWCA) at the normal school and attended concerts and other social events. In 1902, with her first-class licence in hand, she soon secured a teaching post. But despite gaining a superior school licence at the end of that school year,[82] she chose not to continue teaching at that time. Instead, in the fall of 1903, armed with the Gloucester County Scholarship, Violet entered the University of New Brunswick. She was soon immersed in university life, involved not only in the YWCA, but also in the Delta Rho, the women's debating society. Her diary portrays a coeducational institution where men and women lived separate but intersecting lives. Graduating in the first division in 1905, Violet headed, as *The University Monthly* put it, "to the wild and woolly west where she has undertaken the arduous task of imparting her knowledge to the youth of Stockholm, Saskatchewan. No doubt her influence for good will be felt even more there than it was in her short stay at the University of New Brunswick."[83]

28. Kate (Katherine) Miles (b. 9 March 1885) (Diary: 1901)[84]

Katherine Miles was a fifteen-year-old student at Fredericton High School when she began keeping a diary in January 1901. Kate was the third of four children born to Georgianna Harrison and Arnaud Miles, a farmer and surveyor of lumber, of Maugerville, New Brunswick. When Kate's diary opens, her brother Bruce (b. 1882) was studying dentistry in Boston, while her brother Edgar (b. 1883) was an engineering student at the University of New Brunswick. Kate and Edgar boarded in Fredericton during the week but spent the weekends at home. Their brother, George (b. 1893), referred to as "Baby" in Kate's diary, attended the local Maugerville school.[85]

In Kate Miles, we meet a thoroughly modern young woman, the proud owner of a Red Bird bicycle and a passbook for her own savings account. By 1901, grammar schools had been transformed into the more familiar, coeducational "high schools" and, although schooling did not become compulsory in New Brunswick for another five years, the young people who attended them were likely to do so regularly. Yet high schools remained middle-class institutions, for the poorer urban adolescents rarely continued beyond the elementary level and few rural families could afford to board their children in town. Even so, Kate's entries would resonate with any modern adolescent: reflecting a favoured pastime of today's teens that has a long history, Kate regularly reported, as she did on 7 January, "Sade[86] & I downtown at noon and after school."

If Kate Miles's twenty-first-century counterparts would recognize her, so, too, would young New Brunswick women of an earlier generation. In Maugerville, Kate's world revolved around the activities of her nuclear and extended family. Her maternal grandfather lived just down the road and aunts, uncles, and cousins also lived nearby. In Fredericton, her life revolved around school and school activities. When examinations loomed, she curtailed her social life and settled down to study.

Yet, like other diarists, she recorded little about her classes. In contrast, she did report the progress of the "Decorating Committee ... for graduation." In short, Kate Miles's diary provides insight into the life and priorities of a middle-class sixteen-year-old in turn-of-the-century Fredericton.

These, then, are the women whose lives are analysed in this book. The interpretive challenge involved in "listening" to the "voices" of women at different stages in the life course, who expressed themselves in very different ways and kept diaries for a variety of reasons, is the topic of the next chapter.

Chapter 2

Reading Nineteenth-Century Diaries: A Historian's Perspective

Since the appearance, now nearly three decades ago, of Margaret Conrad's path-breaking articles on Maritime women's diaries,[1] many diaries have been published. Aimed at popular as well as at academic audiences, they have been produced by both academic and popular presses, and edited by writers with a wide range of interests. Historians using diaries as primary sources for their research now share the field with popular writers as well as with scholars in other disciplines. More significantly, in the analysis of diaries, literary scholars have taken the lead in shaping the genre. In doing so, some have attracted a popular as well as an academic audience, while others have brought new and intriguing theoretical insights to the interpretation of diary writing as an expressive medium.[2] Crossing disciplinary lines, they have engaged other scholars, including historians, in a broader discussion of this burgeoning field. Historians have a long tradition of borrowing approaches, methodologies, and even interpretations from their colleagues in other disciplines, and the influence of those literary critics who specialize in the analysis of life writing – and particularly the analysis of diaries – has led to a new and fruitful interdisciplinary collaboration. But while both sides are enriched by such collaboration, historians and literary scholars ask fundamentally different questions of their sources and bring very different perspectives to the analysis of the past.

Literary scholars, drawn to the diary as an aspect of life writing, have debated the question of whether or not diaries should also be included within the broader category of autobiographical writing. In decrying "the tendency to obscure the difference between the two forms [that] has accompanied the diary's recent passage into literature," Harriet

Blodgett cogently argues that "the special appeal" of the diary as literature is "its immediacy, the sense of being involved in actual life in process, no matter what the embellishments may be." This sets it apart from "autobiography, life retrospectively, shaped to a coherent whole."[3] Like Blodgett, May Sarton, who was both a diarist and an autobiographer, "insists on the 'huge difference' between the diary form and the autobiography ... because the latter is memory, a past time summoned back, whereas the former concerns 'what I am now at this instant.'"[4] Like Blodgett and Sarton, I have rejected the notion that diaries either can or should be treated as autobiography.

While literary scholars tend to focus on what the diary reveals about the individual life, historians tend to focus on what the diary reveals about the experience of people in past times. Yet diaries are rarely straightforward historical documents and, in reading a diary, the historian, like the general reader, cannot escape the feeling that she is something of a voyeur, gaining illicit entry into a diarist's interior dialogue. Take, for example, the diary of schoolmistress Kate Loggie. Although Kate begins her diary with an apparently straightforward statement, she turns abruptly inward, plunging the reader into the very private world of a young woman coming of age: "Aug. 26th, 1880. I wish to keep a record of my daily progress. Had 12 scholars today. Spent the evening very idly & I fear sinfully. Yielded to the temptation to idle reading. Oh Lord help me to be more watchful & strengthen me against falling into my besetting sins." For Kate, "daily progress" involved a spiritual journey as much as it involved her evolving teaching career. And her "record" involved a continuing interior dialogue as much as it involved the "daily" details of her life. For the historian, no less than for the literary scholar, that interior dialogue is at least as interesting and exciting as the insights she provides into the experience of teaching in nineteenth-century rural New Brunswick, for this record of a young woman's spiritual journey can offer insight into the nature of religious faith and practice during a period when evangelical denominations competed for adherents and religion played a fundamental role in social and intellectual life. But that private dialogue also reminds us that the diary, with its multiple messages, is a challenging and complex historical source.

Bringing a historical consciousness to the analysis of diaries involves both the way we understand the past and the way we understand our distance from it. Above all, it involves a recognition that although we may empathize with people in past times, we cannot bridge the distance between their understanding and our own. Drawing on personal diaries to develop an understanding of people's experience in past times offers a unique opportunity to engage readers in the analysis by sharing passages rich in the kind of "evocative details that can illuminate ordinary lives and common experience."[5] At the same time, invoking a consciousness of the distance between the past and the present poses a unique challenge. Indeed, the dilemma of how to avoid imposing our modern attitudes and assumptions in our interpretation of an individual's private thoughts and public actions is perhaps the most significant challenge facing the historian in analysing diaries.[6]

A further dilemma that is directly related both to the desire to engage a popular audience and to the desire to participate in an interdisciplinary dialogue involves the temptation to privilege literary merit over historical significance, for it is those diaries with literary merit that both draw the reader in and seem to "speak to us without the need of a mediator, an authority who can initiate us into the mysteries of the text."[7] Such diaries have convinced scholars – even those who recognize that "one can read a poem or a novel without coming to know its author, look at a painting and fail to get a sense of its painter" – that "one cannot read a diary and feel unacquainted with its writer."[8] Certainly it is true that, a decade ago, upon opening a small (yet a little larger than octavo), soft-covered, medium-brown cloth notebook housed in the archives at Mount Allison University, I found myself immediately engaged, drawn into another world, another life.[9]

– My Diary – 1886 –

January – Monday – 25th.

> *I intended to keep a Diary this year, but am rather late in commencing however I will record as near as possible the principal events of this year as memories and then proceed with daily records. New Years Day was spent at Grandpa Lawrence's. All the family present but Aunt Janie. To a supper at Mr Tucker's New Years evening, got home about three, pleasant time. Came home on Saturday afternoon. To Parrsboro Tuesday, got my dress and coat, got home about 12 o'clock. To Uncle James' to tea Thursday. Called at Uncle Jessie's & Hubert's Friday afternoon. Over to Mr [Lenwise]'s to tea. Gordon took me. Miss Moore got home that afternoon. Pa and I started for Sackville Saturday at 9 p.m. When we left home it was quite fine but before we got to West Brook it was snowing very fast.*

42   "I wish to keep a record"

Pa decided to put me on board the train at W.B. instead of going to Athol Station as he intended. I got safely to Spring Hill Junction. A little delay was caused by a car being off the track but we arrived in time to meet the train going toward St John. There I met fifteen other girls, all bound for Sackville. Mr Bordon[10] was at the station to meet us and after luncheon we made ourselves as comfortable as possible until our trunks came.
We soon got established in our old way and thus began school life at Mt Allison again. Nothing of note has happened. We have had our Reception, been out tobogganing twice and had a pretty good time generally. Yesterday, that is Sunday, I was to Methodist Church in the morning, heard Mr Wedall preach from Luke 19: 41, 42 verses.[11] To prayer meeting at College in the afternoon. Mr B. led in the service. To church in the evening. Mr Dunn preached from the text "One on either side, Christ in the midst" (St John 19:18). A very nice sermon. Weather clear and cold.

– Monday – 25th

I did not hear the riser this morning, but Mrs Townsend kindly wakened me in time to get almost ready for breakfast by the time the bell rang. Got [on] with today's work as usual. We had our first prayer meeting of this term in Annie Mosher's room. The room was crowded. Net Chase led. Misses Ross and Frazer were in here at recess. Miss Frazer is very nice. I have not been out today. Mr Lunn fix[ed] my radiator and the room is exceedingly warm. Weather clear and cold. Wrote home today.

Tuesday – 26th

Tuesday – To-day had been dull and dissagreeable – snowing and raining alternately. Instead of going out in procession, Mr Bordon gave Miss Bishop permission to take us to the Rink for a short time. There were quite a number of skaters and the ice was very good. We got home shortly after four o'clock. Miss Campbell gave me two plum biscuits, Auntie an apple and a cake so I have fared pretty well today. I was in Miss F.'s room at recess. She had been sick today, but is better now. Ida Trenholm called this afternoon.

Wednesday – 27th

I am more tired tonight than I have been since I came here. I find practicing four hours very tiresome. We had a very nice prayer meeting

tonight. O! What a help they are to one. You can talk of God's love to us
with such mutual feelings. I was in Auntie's room a short time tonight.
She gave me a real nice apple. Weather fine.

Thursday – 28th

Today has been dull and rainy but tonight it cleared up and we were
allowed to attend the service held in the College Chapel. Today has
been set apart for prayer on behalf of the various Colleges & Academies
of the Dominion. We had a very good service. We had a very nice
Physiology Class today. Mrs Archibald[12] had a microscope and we had
the pleasure of looking at different species of butterflies from India. It
was indeed interesting.

Friday – 29th

Another rainy day, but not so dreary looking without. The dullness of
yesterday has been relieved by the beautiful silver thaw. The landscape
is covered with ice. Though this is very beautiful it is also destructive,
especially of fruit trees. I did not go to singing class tonight.

Saturday – 30th

Today has been dull and the beauty of yesterday is slowly passing away,
under the influence of wind and rain. I was down shopping this morning,
but went more for the walk than to purchase. We had Reception tonight but
it was indeed a dry affair. Only a few were over. Mr McC was not over so I
was all about. Miss Campbell brought me a full cup of sugar and I am going to have some candy for a change. I have not done much today. Started
my apron but did not get much done at it. Expected a letter from home
today but got none. O dear! I have my lessons for Monday to learn yet.

Sunday – 31st

I was out to meeting this morning. Mr Pickard preached from Gal 1:4.[13]
I slept with Annie last night & she spent this afternoon with me – we
had quite a luncheon of candy, apples and biscuits. We decided not to
go out to church this evening, so I spent the evening in Annie's room.
Annie is just lovely and I hope that our friendship may be strengthened.
Weather still dull and thawing.

Thus we meet Laura Fullerton, a boarding school veteran at not quite sixteen. Hers is the kind of diary that draws one in, that seems to beg for publication. Laura is a diarist who could be said to "speak to us without the need of a mediator."[14] Her engaging and confiding style allows even the uninitiated reader the vicarious pleasure of entering the private world of an exuberant young woman. Yet, though Laura is a thoughtful and generous adolescent, her diary nonetheless offers readers a self-centred narrative, as she unselfconsciously uses the medium of the diary to construct a self – or to express her self. And even with these caveats in mind, readers seeking to understand her responses to her experiences, her aspirations, and expectations as expressed in her diary, must situate her within the context of her own particular time and place.

The world of other diarists proved far more difficult to penetrate. On another day in another archive, I examined a fragile volume, fifty years older than the first, and, reflecting the more straitened circumstances of its author, compiled from salvaged paper, sewn together to form a book that is somewhat larger in its dimensions than Laura Fullerton's tidy notebook, and much, much thicker.[15] Opening it carefully, I was initially more puzzled than drawn in by this potential gateway to another, much earlier time and another, much earlier life.

August 1825

19	Go to Mr Steward's to hear Mr M. He does not come. Drink tea at McLe[ans].
20	Mr Marshall does not come.
21	Mr Bunnil preaches from X Heb[rews].
22	Wean the last of the calves.
24	Mr James preaches and stays the night.
25	Go to see Mrs Ross. Sally at Capt McLean's.
26	Aunt McLean and Prue stay all night.
27	Boys get out two loads of wheat.
28	Mr Bunnil preaches from XIII Acts at Fraser's in fore & afternoon.
29	Gather white top.[16]
30	Children go to Abernethys for a sheep. John Cary here.
31	Caroline over. Sandy's Birthday.
September 1	Sandy has court here.
4	Nancy Casey here.

5	*Ludlow goes down with his colt. Mama & Patrick go to Duffs.*
6	*Miss Harry and the McLeans here.*
7	*Caroline over.*
8	*Ann & Sally carding for her.*
9	*Mama gets home.*
10	*Funeral. Mr Manyin has meeting in the chapel.*
11	*Mr Bunnil up. Go up with him to Frasers. Cap't & Aunt McLean here.*
12	*Patrick and Archy go to the woods.*
15	*McLean, Mrs Ross, Caroline here.*
16	*Boys begin the garden fence.*
[17]	*... Mr Piccard & Mr Desbrisay get here late.*
18	*He preaches morning in the chapel & afternoon in the house.*

The diarist in this case is twenty-eight-year-old Jacobina Campbell, at home and at work on the family farm on the Tay River, just north of Fredericton, New Brunswick. Although her diary is not accessible to the uninitiated reader – this is no "folk diary," as one scholar of popular culture has characterized such diaries – it is, no less than Laura Fullerton's diary, the record of a life in process.[17] The style is spare, the author recording her own activities within the context of those of her family and, indeed, her community. This diary requires "a mediator, an authority who can initiate us into the mysteries of the text," and through whose good offices we learn that, within the first month of her diary keeping, Jacobina recorded the activities of the various members of her immediate and extended family. These include the families of her older brother Sandy and his wife, Caroline, and of her maternal Aunt McLean, as well as the members of her own household: her widowed mother, her younger brothers Patrick and Ludlow, her younger sister Ann, and Sally, the hired girl. During that month, the family visited or was visited by members of nine neighbouring families, and no less than six itinerant preachers travelled up the Nashwaak to hold meetings in a Methodist community among whose most prominent leaders were the two Jacobina Campbells, mother and daughter. The "authority," to whom I am grateful for working all this out, is historian Murray Young. His first task was to identify the writer of the diary as Jacobina Campbell.[18] Without the intercession of the historian, then, even the author of this diary would have remained a mystery.

These two diaries provide compelling evidence that, as Rachel Cottam has pointed out, "both on an individual level and as a class of writing, the diary is characterized by its hybridity and diversity (it is a mixed bag)" and, further, that whatever its individual nature, "it is continuous with the lived life: it is source material." While, as a historian, I might question Cottam's characterization of a diary as "an art*less* presentation of the self, a text that can be looked through, to catch a glimpse of undistorted life," I can readily agree with her that, "in the creation of a published diary, the annotations and arrangements of the editor create one of many possible 'Lives' from the debris of the lived life: the shape of the subject is determined by the particular story the editor tells."[19]

Examining the physical nature of a diary that is "the debris of the lived life" can, in itself, provide some clues about the diarist and her condition in life. In the first third of the nineteenth century, living miles from a stationery shop and almost certainly without the means to purchase any notebook that might have been available, Jacobina Campbell constructed her own diaries. She salvaged quality paper, rescuing unused portions of envelopes, letters, and even bills, trimming each page carefully to size and wasting no space with her terse, single-line entries. Later diarists, living in more comfortable circumstances, used a variety of more standard forms. By the mid- to late-nineteenth century, bound books manufactured especially for diary writing, and referred to as "diaries," were widely available and often used.[20] These varied in size and shape. Sadie Harper had a penchant for tiny diaries, which she filled to overflowing with her minuscule yet very legible handwriting. Lucy Everett Morrison's diaries of choice, though somewhat larger, could also be considered "pocket diaries." Although they were designed as one-year diaries, Lucy normally used the same volume for three to four years. Some diarists, particularly the younger women among them, had received their diaries as gifts. Emma Alice Pitt's diary was, as noted on the flyleaf, "a New Year's Gift" from her brother Edwin. Adolescents like Emma Pitt and Kate Miles, who had received their diaries as gifts, rarely continued as diarists beyond a single year.[21] But even after the advent of manufactured diaries, women such as Kate Loggie, Mary Hill, and Hannah Estabrooks could find it more convenient to use a general-purpose notebook rather than purchase one designed for the particular purpose.

An original diary, not only by its content, but also by the construction and quality of the prose, by changes in penmanship, by omissions and blank spaces, and, sometimes by its very format, can provide clues about its author. But even in archives, original diaries are not always available for perusal. In some cases, only photocopies, and in others, only transcriptions, have been deposited in the archival repository. The transcribed diary raises significant questions for researchers. Has the diary already been edited and, if so, by whom – the original author, or perhaps a descendant? Occasionally, different versions of the same diary surface in different repositories, as has occurred in the case of the New Brunswick loyalist Sarah Frost, as well as for the seagoing schoolgirl, Amelia Holder.[22] Something is lost, even in the case of the most careful transcription. Thus, for example, internal evidence suggests that, on the day of her marriage, Marjory Grant passed her diary along to her younger sister Isabella, but because the only copy available is a transcription, there is no change in penmanship to alert the reader to this change in ownership.[23]

The two halves of the Grant diary exhibit an amazing congruity, but, on the whole, the contents of nineteenth-century diaries are as varied as the people who wrote them. While diaries are, by their very nature, personal records, those that have survived rarely appear to be intimate documents. Indeed, if the temptation to read nineteenth-century diaries for the vicarious pleasure of learning the most intimate details of the author's life is strong, only the most assiduous readers will persevere, for the extraneous material usually dominates: the births and deaths, the weather, and the routine. In other rarer diaries, the routine, or context, remains in the shadows while the drama is highlighted. And the historian, like all interlopers into diarists' worlds, is drawn into the drama, responding to an echo from the past, such as the *cri de coeur* "God help me for no one else can," which captures the sense of desperation that surfaces regularly in Annie Waltham's diary.[24] Yet, curiously enough, a sense of what life was like in past times often emerges most clearly in entries of diarists who reported, tersely or in some detail, the daily routine of life rather than focussing on the drama.[25] Moreover, even in their omissions, obliqueness, and sometimes formulaic pattern of reporting life's daily routine, as Donna Smyth has observed, "even here, where life-as-text is recorded, more or less unfaithfully, even here are epiphanic moments where a phrase, a word, reveals a world of self."[26] The drama of such lives appears suddenly and sometimes jarringly, as a break in the rhythm, alerting the reader to leaf back, then forward. Sometimes research is necessary to discover what happened, to clarify connections between cause and effect. Tantalizing as such glimpses are, the seemingly mundane details are the greater gift, the building blocks that can be used to reconstruct a life, a family, a community. The intimate detail, piercing the surface but rarely, adds leaven to the whole.

The author's private purpose in keeping a record influenced, and even determined, her diary's nature and contents. If written as a record for oneself, the diary was a record of what the diarist deemed significant or important enough to include at a particular stage in her life. In her "first attempt to keep a diary," nineteen-year-old Lottie Reid often found she had "nothing worth relating," with "everything ... going on as usual," or "no news, everything very quiet." But in the very selection of news or activities "worth relating," Lottie was, in effect, editing her own life.[27] If written to be shared, the diary was usually meant to be shared with the diarist's nearest and dearest. Maggie Valentine and her sister Jessie Loggie kept a "log" of their sea voyage to send to their parents and siblings; Sadie Harper's 1894 diary, written during her term at Mount Allison, was kept with a similar purpose in mind. Lucy Everett Morrison and Ann Eliza Rogers wanted to keep records for their own future reference, although while the former kept a record of her garden, the latter kept a record of vital events – births, deaths, and marriages – both in her family and in her community. Mary Wolhaupter used her diary as a confidante, as did Annie Trueman. Whatever their purpose, and whatever their style – from the spare entries of Jacobina Campbell, scarcely more than a catalogue of a life, through the careful "accounting" of Mary Hill, the rhythmic cadences of farm wife Janet MacDonald, the introspective struggles of Kate Loggie and Mary Wolhaupter, the discursive dialogues of Annie Trueman and Violet Goldsmith, the schoolgirl diaries of Laura Fullerton and Kate Miles, to the lively travelogues of Amelia Holder, Maggie Valentine, and Jessie Loggie – the diaries analysed in this study served many different purposes and are as individual as their authors. Yet they are, at the same time, reflective of the families, communities, and society in which those authors lived.

The diversity of style and substance among the various diaries speaks to the personalities of the women and to the nature of the lives they led, but also to their particular stage in the life course. Above all, the diaries of the young differed from the diaries of the middle-aged. In the analysis of life writing, coming-of-age diaries may usefully be considered as a separate category. In drawing such a distinction, Lynn Bloom defines adolescence as the period that "begins with the onset of puberty and ends when the subject arrives at maturity (itself another variable and debatable term)." Bloom defines maturity as the point at which "some measure of independence and autonomy is reached."[28] But even this tentative distinction is problematic, for autonomy deserves its own definition. Certainly the relatively carefree schoolgirls among the diarists – Amelia Holder, Ida MacDonald, Laura Fullerton, and Kate Miles – can be classified as adolescents by any definition of the term. They had achieved neither independence nor autonomy. Categorizing Kate Loggie, Alva Estabrooks, and Violet Goldsmith, young single women who were just beginning to embark on working careers, proves more difficult. Readers must judge for themselves whether or not the young teachers among the diarists could be considered autonomous agents. The achievement of independence and autonomy in nineteenth-century society has usually been associated with marriage. But one might well question whether marriage afforded Laura Trueman Wood[29] greater autonomy than her elder, unmarried sister, Annie, was able to achieve.

Diaries provide an intriguing window on the lives of single women, offering a basis for comparison with their married counterparts. Mary Wolhaupter, unmarried at thirty-one, discovered that she did not fit in easily at home after having spent time away, both working in Massachusetts and teaching (and boarding) in a nearby community. Mary's determination to "be a good girl," even as she chafed at the strictures inherent in the household hierarchy, highlights the clear tension between the role for women prescribed by societal norms and the single woman's lived experience. Despite her internal struggles, Mary Wolhaupter was clearly an independent actor, in charge of her own life. Hannah Estabrooks slipped more easily back into her family home after her sojourn in the United States. Although she was living in Maine and working as a domestic servant when the 1901 census was taken, by 1903, when her diary opens, Hannah was back at home on the family farm in Carleton County, living with her widowed mother and commuting, usually on foot, to the nearby village where she worked in a store.[30] While Hannah enjoyed family life, she did not enjoy her job, confiding in her diary one Sunday evening, "Tomorrow I must go back to work. Oh how dreary it seems up there, not one pleasant word from one day to another and yet it seems I must stay on."[31] Yet despite her dissatisfaction, Hannah had made her own decision not to return to Maine, and her job at the store undoubtedly provided her a certain measure of autonomy.[32] Jacobina Campbell achieved autonomy in a farm household headed by her widowed mother, following in her mother's footsteps to become a leader in her Methodist community of women. Mary Hill, at age forty-nine, maintained her independence largely through careful management of her modest inheritance, an income she supplemented by teaching music.[33]

Faced with earning their own living, a "precarious independence"[34] was, perhaps, the best even middle-class single women could hope for in a society that still, at the turn of the twentieth century, deemed marriage and motherhood woman's "proper sphere." As single women watched their old school friends marry and begin families, they became increasingly conscious of time slipping by. Some, like Annie Trueman and Mary Hill, attempted to hold time at bay by shaving years off their age when the census enumerator called.[35] On her thirty-first birthday, Mary Wolhaupter noted in her diary that she was "quite an old girl but do not feel as though I was so old as that."[36] Hannah Estabrooks was just thirty when she commented bleakly, "How strange to think that I have lived my life long ago and now … have only to look for the end which may be a long way off with much suffering between. (When I lived it I don't know.) My only hope now is to be able to work if only enough to keep my self going."[37] This kind of age-consciousness reflected the fact that the majority of young single women of the period not only expected to marry but also preferred marriage to spinsterhood. Lillie Williamson, recording her recent engagement in her diary, went on to confide that she had been "feeling as though I was getting to be an old maid." She was twenty-two.[38]

The lives of the married women among the diarists demonstrate that marriage did not necessarily bring security, however. Lucy Morrison's husband's dry goods business failed at a time when the couple had five small sons to support. Annie Waltham's second husband spent much of her inheritance before she finally determined to part company with him, after eight years of marriage, on a night when, she reported, "he kicked me in the chest, pulled my hair, struck me on the head, on the nose, kicked me in the back as I was getting off the side of the bed – and said at different times I'll shoot you, I've a revolver all ready for you, I'll put one ball through your head one through Annie's" (her daughter).[39] Ann Eliza Rogers Gallacher would be left a widow with three small children to support at age thirty; her husband died as a result of an industrial accident in Philadelphia in 1867. Bertha Jones was also left with three dependent children when her husband Zebulon died in 1891. But Bertha was more fortunate than Ann Eliza, for the family owned a working farm, which she continued to manage with the aid of an adult stepson whom she had helped to raise.[40] Sophy Carman's husband, twenty-four years her senior, was forced into retirement at a time when their young adult children remained dependent on their parents.[41]

Only Janet Hendry MacDonald would find both a true partnership and a modest security in her marriage to Alexander Black MacDonald. Even at sixty-one, Janet worked hard, yet the cadence of her diary, bespeaking the daily and seasonal rhythms of farm life, implies a companionable division of labour between men and women. Thus, on a windy and rainy October day in 1857, she reported, "They are sawing, we are quilting. George and B. and Jemima has gone over the lake. Father gathering apples. Malcolm's birthday, he is twenty-one." And even after a busy washing day there was time for contemplation: "N.E. wind, clear and fine. They are digging. G. finished this forenoon, then helped James. D. in the shop to work. This is washing day. I picked a bowl of blackberries this afternoon. The comet looks beautiful; I go and look at it every evening." In that solitary pleasure, at the end of a late September day in 1858, Janet MacDonald unselfconsciously situated herself within a much wider frame, for, like people the world over, she was watching Donati's Comet, the brightest comet of the period.[42]

Clearly, a careful reading of diaries takes us well beyond the individual life, providing a comparative framework for the analysis of women's experience. Moreover, for the historian interested in broader community patterns, the mundane daily entries of the middle-aged prove more intrinsically interesting than the often livelier entries of the young. Diaries that draw one immediately into the narrative were more often written by young women who were, like Laura Fullerton, constructing selves. Yet, diaries like Jacobina Campbell's, which may, at first glance, appear too terse to be of much interest, can offer important insights into the nature of family and community life. In her analysis of the diary of Martha Ballard, a late-eighteenth-century Maine midwife, historian Laurel Thatcher Ulrich explained that while for her it is in "the exhaustive, repetitious dailiness, that the real power of Martha Ballard's book lies," it was this "very dailiness" that put others off.[43] Ulrich argues that the problem with diaries such as Martha Ballard's is that they introduce "more stories than can easily be recovered and absorbed."[44] Kathryn Carter has similarly argued that "what seems like unforthcoming writing may actually contain a wealth of concrete information about the texture of women's lives." Carter uses the account-book diary of Emma Chadwick Stretch to "reconstruct women's role in a 19th century rural economy," in this case, on Prince Edward Island.[45] "To make effective use of such sources," she notes, "scholars need to learn how to navigate the ellipses and compressions found in this form of writing."[46] Ulrich and Carter each serve as mediators, initiating us into the mysteries of the texts they are analysing. And in lamenting the dearth of such diaries among the many women's diaries which have been published, Carter, a literary scholar, is implicitly urging researchers not to privilege literary merit over historical significance.[47]

When all manner of diaries are taken into account, and comparative analysis, juxtaposing one diary with another, is possible, attention to historical context yields further insights, situating women within their communities and exposing both the parameters of community and the niceties of social distinctions. Lucy Morrison and Sophy Carman were contemporaries, both middle-class matrons living in Fredericton during the period from 1872 to 1885, when their diaries overlapped. Yet although Fredericton was a small city, with a population of just 6,218 in 1881, their social circles rarely intersected. To some extent, this reflected the continuing relevance of a phenomenon James Robb, a young Scottish lecturer at King's College, had identified a generation earlier: "There are two sets in Fredericton. 1st, the Government officers, Clergy and professional men – that is my set. 2d, shop and store keepers and businessmen. There I am found by exception only and on rare intervals. It is death without benefit of clergy if you are caught out of your set."[48] John Morrison was a mill owner, while William Carman was a barrister. But there were other significant social divides. In the case of the Presbyterian Morrisons and Anglican Carmans, denomination proved an even more accurate predictor of membership in particular social "sets." Mapped as a pattern of concentric circles, an individual diarist's social interaction can be traced as she moves beyond the safety net of her nuclear and extended family to claim membership in a particular circle of friends. A comparative analysis of a significant number of diarists provides the opportunity to identify the parameters of social networks and to develop a more layered and nuanced understanding of the nature of community on a variety of levels.

Comparative analysis of diaries serves other purposes as well. Ann Eliza Rogers and Jo and Lottie Reid grew up in neighbouring parishes along the Bay of Fundy in Albert County. As their diaries demonstrate, these coastal communities faced seaward, and shipping and shipbuilding were not only fundamental to the local economy, but also shaped a way of life. Many young men spent a season or two at sea, deckhands on New Brunswick's famous sailing ships. Fewer made their careers on the sea, but sea captains were by no means rare in Albert County. A significant number took their wives and families with them on their voyages. In 1879, thirty-year-old Josephine Reid exchanged her teaching career for the seagoing life when she married Captain James Turner, the son of a neighbour and a longtime friend. Her diary account of her travels and her letters home tell a story that would have been as familiar to Ann Eliza Rogers as to Jo's sister Lottie. And, as Lottie's and Ann Eliza's diaries record, young women as well as young men took advantage of regular sailings from Fundy ports to travel to the "Boston States" in search of adventure or opportunity.[49] For some, the move was temporary, while for others it proved permanent. But most went no further than a few days' sail away and they could always find a ship in Boston harbour that would soon be sailing for home. Taken together, the diaries contextualize the individual experience, providing insight into a typical New Brunswick experience, a "toing and froing" that became a way of life for many young people and the basis of a cosmopolitan society in a rural New Brunswick landscape.

While the comparative analysis of diaries offers important insights into the broader society, the diarist remains an individual with her own story to tell. If there ever was a time when historians believed they "owned" diaries as a subject for analysis, that time is long past. The analysis of the diary as a form of life writing has become the purview of the literary critic, and historians have gained immeasurably from the insights offered by literary scholars. Thus, as Cynthia Huff points out, in interpreting the "'we' of the collective narrative" of a woman whose diary may have been meant more as a family chronicle than as a construction of self, researchers "need to be attuned to the ways in which her record portrays ... a woman whose use of the plural person suggests that her definition of self is relational, a woman whose spatial orderings and inclusions put others forward rather than herself."[50] Viewing diary reading as "a personal encounter," Huff cites Patrocinio Schweickart's caution that "the reader is a visitor, and ... must observe the necessary courtesies. She must avoid unwarranted intrusions – she must be careful not to appropriate what belongs to her host, not to impose herself on the other woman."[51] From the historian's perspective, this means maintaining a historical consciousness – a distance consciousness – in reading even the most engaging diary. Laura Fullerton's diary is valuable not only for what it can tell us about one young woman constructing a self as she comes of age, but also for the insights it can provide into the nature of student life at a ladies' academy in the 1880s. There, the curriculum was more academically rigorous, the atmosphere more nurturing, and the supervision less restrictive than we might suppose. Even so, students' lives, values, and expectations were far different from those of young women of either earlier or later generations.

Literary scholars, and particularly those who have brought postmodernist insights to the discussion, have done well to remind us that, just as the diarist constructs herself and her world in the diary, so the reader constructs that same diarist and her world in the reading. Lucy Everett Morrison's granddaughter, passing her grandmother's diaries on to a niece, reported that they were "just about her garden." Reading the diaries, one can understand this characterization:

> *March 12, 1884: Wednesday. Cloudy all day. Men hauling snow out of yards & shovelling out roads. Radcliffe here & bricked up room & climbing rose Marshal Neil & put in fresh soil round it & other climbers & cut leaves off climbers & repotted ferns. D Glasier buried.*
>
> *March 13: Thursday. Sunny day. Beb here for flowers. I sent box of parsley & flowers to Mrs Hatt for Methodist tea meeting. A great deal of watering to do. Put in some cuttings of Pollocks, fuchsias, lautanas & Duetsia. Smoked small green house. Found celery in cellar slightly frosted. Mild today. Men turning manure in cellar. A number of fuchsias in bloom.*
>
> *March 14: Friday. During day Mrs McLellan & Mr Holly in green house, also Miss Coburn & Mrs Wilson. Put in another saucer Feverfew. Houses warm, mild outside. All the ventilators open. Men getting snow out of hot bed yard. Verbenas I got from Beb doing very well, also seedlings.*

Yet the niece saw something more. Penetrating beneath the surface of the gardening record her great grandmother kept for almost a quarter of a century, she used the diaries as the basis on which to build a family genealogy, mining them carefully for information before donating them to the Provincial Archives of New Brunswick.[32]

Certainly there are moments of drama to be found in Lucy Morrison's diaries, times when family concerns took precedence. In mid-March 1884, Lucy's two-year-old grandson became ill. Roy was the Morrisons' only grandchild, the son of their son Jack and his wife, Kate Hodge. Kate's firstborn had died in 1881. The families, including Kate's sister Fanny and Jack's brother Frank, as well as the Morrisons'

Reading Nineteenth-Century Diaries 55

longtime housekeeper, Agnes McNabb, drew together, united in their determination to save this baby.

> *March 15: Saturday. Roy was very sick all day. I was there good part of the day. Sent Mrs Wilsons plants to St John. Mrs Hodge staid all night with Kate.*
>
> *March 16: Sunday. Fanny Hodge came down when her Mother went home. Roy is better. Sunny day. Cut 5 roses of Glorie de Dijon & 1 Le Marque. Roy worse. Fanny went home & her Mother came down.*
>
> *March 17: Monday. Steaming Roy with unslacked lime, poultices of flax seed on his back & chest.*
>
> *March 18: Tuesday. Kate sent for Dr & me, 3 a.m. Roy worse. Dr told Mr Hodge he was dying. Jack got a frame up covered with sheets with Roy inside & kept up steam all day & night. Frank taking turns with Jack. I sat up, also Kate, all night. Left Roy easier, 6 a.m.*
>
> *March 19: Wednesday. Dr says Roy is better. Steamed him off & on during day. Father & Mrs Hodge sat up.*[53]
>
> *March 20: Thursday. Mrs Hodge & Father sat up with Roy. He is better. I went over 7 a.m. Returned & worked in green house & was there after dinner while Kate slept. Mrs Hodge went home after tea. Father & I sat up till 3 a.m.*
>
> *March 21: Friday. Went home from Jacks 3 a.m. Went over there after breakfast for a little. Agnes went after dinner & I worked in green house. Travelling breaking up. Roy better. Paid Agnes to date.*

The crisis over, the diary immediately settles back into a familiar pattern.

> *March 22: Saturday. I was busy in green house most all day, looking over & potting the plants & cuttings. Filled a box with ageratum cuttings. Verbenas I got from Beb looking very well, also seedlings. Scarlet verbenas did not come up. I put in saucer of stock seed.*

The work of the greenhouse did not stop, but for a brief period it almost disappeared from the diary, replaced by reports of the progress of Roy's illness. Although the text includes no overt expression of emotion, the tension nonetheless mounts, peaking on 18 March, when the doctor made his dire prediction and Roy's sickroom became a hive of activity. Some readers might conclude that emotion is not at the centre of his grandmother's account; others would argue that emotion is at the very centre of her account.[54] A historical consciousness can alert us to the latter possibility. For although we cannot know the depth of Lucy Morrison's feelings during those tense days in March 1884, we do know that it would be unwise to make assumptions based on the matter-of-fact record typical of the nineteenth-century diarist.

Situating the individual within a broader context, Lucy Morrison's diaries tell the story of a middle-aged, middle-class matron, loyal wife, and loving mother of six boys, who, for her own good and sufficient reasons, turned her long-time gardening hobby into a thriving business. Literally thousands of celery plants each spring and thousands of heads of celery, professionally packed in sand for preservation purposes, each autumn, supplied a demand that has left no trace in the public record. Flowers for weddings, teas, and balls, wreathes for funerals, all flowed out of a business for which Lucy's diaries are the only extant record. Each morning, orders of plants, fruits, and flowers were sent off by train to the Saint John market. And plants for Fredericton and Marysville gardens were supplied each spring. Lucy Morrison's experience raises questions about the extent of nineteenth-century New Brunswick's "underground" economy and women's role within it.[55] And her diary, like Martha Ballard's diary, like Emma Chadwick Stretch's diary or like Jacobina Campbell's diary (where rural women are found not only shearing their own sheep, but shearing for their neighbours as well), awakens us to the possibilities that await the reader in the seemingly mundane diaries women chose to keep.

But whether terse and apparently mundane or discursive and apparently self-reflective, a diary is an edited version of a life. In reading, researching, and publishing diaries, historians seek to expand their own and their readers' understanding of the past, while at the same time recognizing that expanded understanding as an interpretive construction, rather than a definitive reconstruction. The gaps and mysteries that remain are what keep historians and, we hope, our readers intrigued, curious, and engaged. Taken together, the twenty-eight women diarists whose writing is central to the interpretation of nineteenth-century New Brunswick women's experience presented in this book can expand our understanding of the past. But questions remain, and the diaries are open to other interpretations.

Moreover, while this volume seeks to provide a composite portrait of women's experience in 19th-century New Brunswick, it does not represent the experiences of all New Brunswick women. By providing a demographic overview based on a life-course analysis that takes the mid-nineteenth century as its point of departure, the next chapter provides a backdrop against which our twenty-eight diarists can be viewed.

Chapter 3

The Life Course in Demographic Context: Women's Experience

Before focussing on the particular women whose individual and collective experiences are the subject of this book, it is useful to step back, out of the range of their distant, yet insistent, voices, to consider the broad picture. During the period spanned by their diaries, New Brunswick's population increased almost fivefold, from nearly 75,000 in 1824 to more than 350,000 in 1911.[1] Three panoramic views, based on aggregate censuses, capture some basic characteristics of the nineteenth-century population as a whole in the middle of our period, and will provide the background for a series of collective profiles that focus on the nature of the life course in New Brunswick.[2] The first, dated 1851, portrays a significant majority of native-born New Brunswickers – now 79 per cent of the nearly 194,000 New Brunswickers counted that year – flanked by a much smaller group of British-born immigrants, with the Irish, at 15 per cent of the whole, prominent among them. Ten years on, in a second panoramic portrait, the population is grouped according to their responses to a newly introduced census question on religion. As the Protestants – two-thirds of the population – come into focus, we can discern four distinct, often competing denominational groups: the Baptists, at 23 per cent, are the largest, followed by the Anglicans at 17 per cent, the Presbyterians at 15 per cent, and the Methodists at 10 per cent. The remaining 34 per cent, all Roman Catholics, and very largely Acadian and Irish, stand together somewhat uneasily, for here, too, competition occurred.[3] That scene remained largely unchanged in 1871,[4] but a question on ethnic origins makes it possible to bring the New Brunswick–born portion of the population – now 83 per cent of a total population of nearly 286,000 – into sharper focus, and to identify the Acadians among them as nearly one-sixth (16 per cent) of the provincial population.⁵ By mid-century, the population had moved well beyond the pioneer stage, achieving the maturity characterized by gender balance. Despite this demographic stability, New Brunswick remained a youthful society with 55 per cent of its population under the age of twenty-one.⁶ And it remained a predominantly rural society. Most New Brunswickers – still some 80 per cent by 1871 – lived in the countryside, a situation which did not change much, even by the end of the century.⁷

A demographic framework, achieved through the development of collective profiles of New Brunswick girls and women at each stage of the life course, provides the basis for a consideration of the extent to which the diarists shared the experiences of their contemporaries who left behind no written record. Comparisons are made with the Acadian experience, because, though the contact of our diarists with their francophone neighbours may have been limited, the two groups were part of the same, relatively small, shared "world"; they contributed to the same polity and the same economy. While demographic profiles cannot capture the entire range of women's experience, they can provide a backdrop against which to view the individual experience. Collective profiles based on manuscript census returns – in this case, mainly from the 1851 census, the first to record information on individual family members – and other routinely generated government sources are like a series of snapshots taken at particular stages in the life course. In most, individuals are just a little blurred, blending anonymously into the larger group. More sharply focussed snapshots of smaller groups capture contrasting experiences and shifting trends over the course of the century.

In almost every snapshot, girls and boys, women and men, appear in mixed groups, which is not to say that their experiences were the same – though they could be – or that they understood their experiences in the same way – though they might have. Demographic analysis cannot address such issues, but does permit the creation of an inclusive framework, and provides the opportunity for suggestive comparisons between the status of girls and women and that of their male counterparts. Widening the lens to capture the broader scene, viewing women alongside men, situating both women and men within their families, their communities, and their society, results in a complex and intriguing picture with the experiences of girls and boys, men and women, converging and diverging during the course of the life cycle. Age, class, marital status, and culture, no less than gender, proved significant determinants of patterns of dependence, independence, and interdependence.[8]

As we might expect, the subjects of the first two demographic profiles – children under the age of eleven and adolescents under the age of sixteen – proved overwhelmingly dependent. More than 95 per cent of New Brunswick girls and boys lived with their parents or parent during their first decade of life. By the time children reached the age of fifteen, the pattern had not changed much: more than 90 per cent of adolescents under the age of sixteen lived with their parents and siblings. A further 5 per cent lived in the home of a member of their nuclear or extended family. Blended families were common, just as they are today, but with death rather than divorce as the underlying cause. The probability of losing a parent or a sibling before reaching the age of sixteen was high. While few family circles remained unbroken until all children were grown, families were nonetheless large by today's standards, with an average of six to seven children surviving infancy. These relatively large families lived in comparatively small houses, precluding the possibility of the kind of privacy now idealized.[9] Siblings shared beds as well as bedrooms, no doubt a much-appreciated practice on cold winter nights. Separated from their siblings by an average age gap of just two years, children grew up in close-knit families that functioned as both social and economic units.

Yet a child's world extended well beyond the family circle. By the second half of the nineteenth century, most New Brunswick children were gaining some experience of school. Common schools, also called parish schools, were partially supported by government subsidies from the beginning of the century.[10] It was only decades later, by the Free Schools Act of 1871, that the government made schooling free and non-sectarian, and, in 1906, it made schooling compulsory. While differences between and within regions, counties, and parishes persisted, total enrollments for the province increased steadily. A series of sharply focussed snapshots can illustrate both the range of children's experiences of school, and change over time. The world of the schoolyard and the classroom was dominated by children between the ages of eight and thirteen. The parish of St Stephen, in Charlotte County, which included town and rural children in almost equal numbers, was fairly typical. There, by 1861, 68 per cent of children in this age group were enrolled in the common schools, with girls less likely than their brothers to be enrolled (65 per cent vs. 71 per cent). But what of the more than 30 per cent of children missing from this picture? There is compelling evidence that the majority of those children who did not attend local schools in 1861 were excluded by poverty rather than a lack of interest in education; a decade later, following the introduction of free schooling, enrollments rose significantly. By the 1870s, no fewer than 86 per cent of children between the ages of eight and thirteen in St Stephen were enrolled in the common schools, with the proportion of girls now slightly exceeding the proportion of boys (87 per cent vs. 85 per cent).[11] The trend was a general one. In ten of the province's fourteen counties, enrollment increased in the wake of the 1871 legislation.[12] In Roman Catholic districts, and particularly in Acadian districts, enrollments began to increase only in 1875, following the resolution of a crisis involving temporary school closures and the withholding of taxes.[13] Attendance, much to the chagrin of school reformers, rarely matched enrollments, however. It remained irregular in Protestant and Catholic, and English and French districts alike, to the end of our period. But if schooling did not become a habit, it did become the common experience of the majority of the province's children.[14]

Until the age of sixteen, then, the overwhelming majority of girls and boys lived with their parents and siblings, sharing, as they grew old enough, in household tasks that were normally gender-specific. A significant majority attended local parish schools, although their attendance was often irregular, dependent on the weather, the economic resources of the family, the rhythms of the household, the health of the child, and the distance from the school. Among the older children, a small number – no more than five per cent of the total – worked in the homes of others, sometimes as apprentices, more often as domestic servants. Like their counterparts at home with their parents and siblings, they, too, were considered "dependent children," with arrangements for their care as well as for their employment negotiated by their parents or by local parish officials. In some cases, these arrangements included an agreement to send the child to school. But whatever their circumstances, the majority of children who enrolled in the common schools did not continue in school beyond the age of thirteen or fourteen.[15]

The experiences of adolescents began to diverge after they reached the age of sixteen, with young women usually leaving home at an earlier age than their brothers. A demographic profile of this age cohort finds slightly more than 75 per cent of young women and 85 per cent of young men aged sixteen to twenty living at home with their parents. Sometimes young women left home to further their education, but more often they left to prepare for marriage by entering the paid labour force. This frequently meant working at one of the few jobs open to them: as servants in the homes of others. Approximately 5 per cent of all the young women in this age group were servants, with the proportion rising to 8 to 10 per cent among both Acadians and recent Irish Catholic immigrants.[16] A further 5 per cent of anglophone women and between 8 and 10 per cent of francophone women had left home to marry. The young women in this cohort had very varied experiences, not only in comparison with their brothers but also in comparison with each other. A series of snapshots brings the range of experience into sharper focus.

Gender, ethnic, and class divides proved particularly stark in Saint John, the province's largest urban centre, where the proportion of young women working as servants peaked. For children in the city's poorest families, the process of coming of age started early, with one twelve-year-old girl in fourteen enumerated as a live-in servant in 1851. For sixteen-year-olds, the ratio was one in four, while, by age twenty, some 42 per cent of women in Saint John worked in other people's homes. The majority were fatherless immigrants or children of immigrants. While two-thirds of Saint John's New Brunswick-born girls between the ages of sixteen and twenty lived at home with their parents, two-thirds of their Irish-born counterparts worked as live-in servants.[17] The brothers of these working-class immigrants proved likely to leave the city in search of work, and, as in other cities of the period, young women in this age group significantly outnumbered their male counterparts.[18] Over time, the declining proportion of immigrants in the population changed patterns of employment and, by the 1890s, Saint John's servants were largely New Brunswick–born.[19] But throughout the century, whatever their family's ethnic background or economic status, in both urban and rural settings, the turnover rate among servants was high. It would seem that young women who worked as servants between school-leaving and marriage could change places readily and that few women chose domestic service as a career.[20]

Although "servant" continued, until the end of the nineteenth century, to be the most common occupation for women, those entering the workforce increasingly looked for other options.[21] The thriving Saint John garment industry, for example, depended largely on the work of young single women: in 1871, 83 per cent of the city's female garment workers were between the ages of fifteen and twenty-five; 86 per cent were single.[22] The growth of manufacturing, further stimulated by the implementation of the National Policy in 1879, created new opportunities for women as well as for men.[23] Textile mills in particular attracted young women workers, and, by 1885, the Maritime region, with less than one-fifth of Canada's population, housed eight of the twenty-three Canadian cotton mills, seven of them built after 1879.[24] A demographic snapshot of women at Alexander Gibson's Marysville mill, one of the two largest cotton mills in the Maritimes, is suggestive of women's response to such opportunities. The manufacture of cotton in Marysville began in the spring of 1885; by 1887, "Boss" Gibson's cotton mill, which, like his lumber mill, ran ten hours per day, achieved an annual production level of 1,860,000 lbs of cloth.[25] In 1881, 24 per cent of Marysville's young women aged sixteen to twenty had been employed; of those, nearly 60 per cent (14 per cent of all young women in this age cohort) worked as servants. In 1888, the Marysville cotton mill employed 425 workers, of whom two-thirds were women. Fully, 106 of the 115 employees in the spinning room were women.[26] The Marysville workforce had been transformed. By 1891, 79 per cent of Marysville's young women aged sixteen to twenty were employed, 72 per cent of them in the cotton mill; less than 5 per cent were working as servants.

In opening up new opportunities for young women, the cotton mill also transformed family life in the community. Ten years earlier, young women had been required at home to help in household textile production that was labour-intensive and the equivalent of a cottage industry. From sheep shearing through carding, spinning, and dyeing the wool, to weaving it into cloth and fashioning it into garments, adolescent girls worked alongside their mothers and sisters in home production. Of Marysville's young people between the ages of sixteen and twenty living at home with their parents in 1881, just 13 per cent of adolescent girls, as compared to 50 per cent of adolescent boys, worked for wages outside the home.[27] In 1891, in contrast, 69 per cent of daughters in this age cohort and 95 per cent of their brothers reported that they were working for wages. The majority of these young women, along with many of their brothers, worked at the cotton mill. The cotton mill was, moreover, drawing young women from the countryside into the town to take up jobs: 28 per cent of the adolescent girls working at the mill, as compared to just 13 per cent of the adolescent boys, were lodgers.[28] Cotton mills in St Stephen, Moncton, and Saint John also attracted young women from the surrounding rural areas during this period.[29]

Middle- and upper-class youth of the same age left home not to work but to pursue their education beyond the level offered in the local common schools. As in the case of working-class youth, their experiences were shaped by gender. With limited access to the state-sponsored county grammar schools, which offered boys a classical education, young women and their parents looked for other options. When the Baptists established a coeducational seminary in Fredericton in 1836, girls eagerly registered; in the first two years, 94 young women joined 109 young men in the mixed classes offered at the school.[30] Nearly two decades later, in 1854, Mount Allison opened its female academy to a similarly enthusiastic response. With seventy boarders, the building was filled to capacity by its second week of operation, and accommodated twenty-nine day scholars as well. By the end of the first term, enrollment reached 118, exceeding that of the male academy.[31] By the 1860s, convent schools operated by the Sisters of Charity at St Basile and Newcastle offered advanced courses for young women, and by 1871, the Collège St-Joseph in Memramcook had also opened a girls' academy. By 1880, convent schools offering courses in both French and English were operating in Bathurst, Buctouche, Caraquet, Chatham, St Louis, and Tracadie as well. As in the case of the Protestant academies, enrollments in the convent schools grew steadily.[32]

Young women seeking professional qualifications had few options. School teaching was one of them. By 1852, just four years after New Brunswick's first normal school[33] opened its doors, forty-nine of the school's ninety-two students were women, an ascendency which female students never lost.[34] Tuition was free but students seeking admission required a solid scholarly foundation to pass the entrance examination. Of 303 applicants in 1880, sixty-five failed the exam.[35] In that year, women constituted 72 per cent (198 students) of a class of 274. Two years later, women made up 80 per cent (145 students) of a class of 181. Female students, with a median age of just seventeen, were about two years younger than their male counterparts.[36] Among 115 women (76 per cent of the 150 students) enrolled in the provincial normal school's summer session of 1877, many travelled some distance to attend, encouraged by a government subsidy. In addition to free tuition, the government offered 5 cents per mile travelling expenses to and from the normal school, as an inducement to students. In the winter session of 1877–8, 91 per cent of women students and 82 per cent of men students collected travel allowances.[37] In return for the free tuition and travel subsidy, students undertook to teach in a New Brunswick school within two years or pay $20 for each session in which they had attended the normal school.[38]

The majority of young women graduates did take up teaching, for a time at least. Predictably, women constituted a growing proportion of the teachers in the common schools of the province, increasing from just 20 per cent of the teaching force in the period before the establishment of the normal school, to a majority by 1871. As one young woman who attended the normal school in 1877 proudly informed her mother, her second-class teaching licence afforded her "a means of earning my living and being independent."[39] Like hundreds of other New Brunswick women teachers, she accepted a teaching position that required she board away from home. Although Acadian women gained ground more slowly than their anglophone counterparts, as early as 1864, the district school inspector reported that seventeen graduates of the St Basile convent were teaching across the border in Maine, where local school officials preferred them to teachers trained in the United States because they were fluent in both French and English.[40]

Whether they left home to become domestic servants, garment trade workers, factory hands, students, or teachers, young women launched themselves into the world with as much alacrity as their brothers. That they did so in significant numbers implies a confident independence that belies our image of nineteenth-century adolescent girls as sheltered and chaperoned. Young single women, like their brothers, sought work where they could find it. In some cases, this meant moving from farms to towns or cities within the province; in other cases, it meant crossing the border into Nova Scotia, and in still others, it meant travelling to the "Boston States." By mid-century, such migration patterns were well entrenched.[41] Many of those living in borderlands regions had friends and relatives on both sides of the line. The border continued to be very porous throughout the nineteenth century, permitting out-migration, whether temporary or permanent, by the coasting trade as well as by regular packet service to Portland, Maine.[42] At the same time, for young people of the second and third generations, who "belonged" in New Brunswick, family ties in the province remained strong, offering a social safety net when necessary.[43]

As young people came of age, the experiences of women and men continued to diverge. A demographic profile of young adults between the ages of twenty and thirty reveals that just 45 per cent of women and 65 per cent of men in the twenty-one to twenty-five age cohort were still living with their parents. Of this cohort, 41 per cent of the young women were married, compared to just 14 per cent of their male counterparts. More men married during their late twenties, but they could scarcely keep pace with the young women. While 70 per cent of young women aged twenty-six to thirty were married, just 49 per cent of their male counterparts had taken the plunge.[44] Yet there is little evidence that the remaining 51 per cent of young men were more likely than their unmarried sisters to be travelling, trying new experiences, and savouring their independence before settling down to the routine of married life: 69 per cent of unmarried men in this age cohort, as compared to 70 per cent of unmarried women, were still living in their parents' homes.[45]

The patterns are clear. Young women left home at an earlier age than their brothers, and took on the responsibilities of marriage and childrearing at an earlier stage in the life course. While the reasons for individual decisions cannot be determined, the underlying explanation for the trend lies in women's own expectations, driven both by societal attitudes and norms and also by a dearth of viable career options. During young adulthood, when their brothers were embarking on lifetime careers, young women were marking time between school-leaving and marriage. Following the familiar pattern established for them by their fathers, uncles, and older brothers, young men moved from school or apprenticeship into a career in which they would advance to the stage where they were earning enough money to marry and begin raising families of their own. Young women followed an equally familiar pattern established for them by their mothers, aunts, and older sisters, accepting lower pay than their brothers, for work which was valued less because they were expected neither to remain long in the workforce nor to require a family wage.

A series of focussed snapshots reveals the striking similarity in the experiences of women in this cohort, regardless of their economic background. While young men could find older male role models in whatever career they pursued, older role models for young women beyond the very significant career of home production were rare. There were virtually none in domestic service. There, adolescent girls and young women put the skills learned at their mother's knee to good use, working alone as the sole servant in their employer's household, rather than under the supervision of more senior domestic staff; although in Saint John, at least, the average age of female servants gradually increased, they still had no one ahead of them.[46] Nor were young women working in factories alongside other women likely to find mature role models to emulate. Thus, while sisters and brothers might begin factory work at the same time, and sometimes even in the same factory, women's career patterns differed from men's. The experience of the Bubar family was typical. In 1891, Lois, Florence, and their older brother, Ernest, all worked at the Marysville cotton mill. In 1896, at age twenty-one, Lois married a fellow mill worker. In 1901, her husband and her brother Ernest were still working at the mill, while Lois remained at home, caring for her two small children. Following her older sister's example, Florence, too, had, by 1901, abandoned mill work for marriage and motherhood, marrying a fellow mill worker who continued to work at the mill.[47] The statistics reflect this common pattern. While 72 per cent of Marysville's adolescent girls aged sixteen to twenty were employed at the cotton mill in 1891, just 41 per cent of women aged twenty-one to twenty-five were so employed. More than 30 per cent of Marysville women in the latter age cohort had married, the working women among them normally abandoning the paid labour force when they did so.[48] Their male counterparts, in contrast, continued working at the mill. The cotton mill employed 67 per cent of male adolescents between the ages of sixteen and twenty, and 69 per cent of males aged twenty-one to twenty-five. At the same time, those who remained there beyond the age of twenty, regardless of gender, were much more likely than their adolescent counterparts to be lodgers, young people drawn to the community by the prospect of mill work.[49]

The experience of young women in the teaching profession was, in some ways, similar to that of young female factory workers. After 1867, women constituted a majority of the province's teachers, but, despite a significant number of career teachers among them, the workforce remained young, for women rarely continued to teach after they married. The majority of women teachers taught in one-room schoolhouses, but also became part of a network of women teachers engaged in professional development. They attended and sometimes presented papers at annual teachers' institutes sponsored by the Department of Education and were as prepared as men for professional advancement. At such events, male administrators were the major speakers.[50] The trustees who hired teachers and the inspectors who assessed their performance, invariably men, viewed female teachers as temporary workers destined, as in the case of women factory workers, to leave the workforce upon marriage, regardless of their previous achievements. By the late 1880s, women constituted more than two-thirds of the province's teachers, yet male administrators continued to appoint other men, not women, as principals in the growing number of consolidated schools being established in the province.[51] Ironically, young men – even the principals among them – proved almost as likely as young women to to leave the profession. But while young women left teaching upon marriage, sometimes because school trustees required they do so, young men left to attend university or take up more lucrative employment.[52] Late in the century, a few women, following the example of male colleagues, were also able to abandon teaching for university.[53]

That small minority of women who attended university had limited career options, though their academic qualifications were equal to men's. With their small faculties, universities of the period offered a limited number of programs, which meant that women and men pursuing arts degrees took a wide range of subjects, among them mathematics and science (which included philosophy). In these fields, as well as in languages and literature, women competed successfully with men, consistently achieving top honours and regularly earning some of the most prestigious academic prizes. University-educated women were, as opponents of higher education for women had foreseen, less likely to marry than other women, perhaps because they had invested more time being educated, but possibly, as well, because women teachers in women's academies provided models for an independent life.[54] New Brunswick women who wanted to become doctors had to travel beyond the borders of the province for training; the majority of them, like men who took up medicine, looked southward. Only a tiny minority of young people – less than 1 per cent – attended university in the nineteenth century, however, and a significant proportion of the women among them would eventually marry, and abandon careers when they did so.[55]

Once they had reached their late twenties, then, the majority of young women had already embarked on the career that at least 85 per cent of all women were destined to pursue, and the only career for which young women had very many mature role models. For women, marriage meant a career in household production and reproduction. For most, it also meant following a familiar pattern established by their mothers, aunts, and older sisters: settling down on a family farm. Together with their husbands, they exhibited the specialized skills necessary to establish and maintain a viable family economy – skills that had been learned and honed in their childhood homes. Although the husband was identified as the farmer, the success of the venture was equally dependent on the labour of the farm wife. Thus, marriage, which normally took women out of the waged labour force, did not end their participation in the larger economy.[56] Married women were integral to the community network of barter and exchange that was so essential a part of the early New Brunswick economy. Significant numbers of them, especially spinners and weavers, seamstresses, dressmakers, and milliners, continued to ply their artisanal trades as self-employed business women. But few married women could maintain high levels of production during the period when they had very small children.[57]

For nineteenth-century women, marriage meant "a prolonged period of child bearing."[58] By mid-century, a married woman who survived to the end of her childbearing years could expect to give birth to approximately seven children and spend more than five years of her life pregnant.[59] Another series of snapshots, based on an analysis of age-specific fertility rates in two New Brunswick counties reveals that, at mid-century, women who married before the age of twenty-five were likely to have three children under the age of six by the time they reached thirty. Even those who married after the age of twenty-six, the average age at first marriage for women, were likely to have borne four children by the time they were thirty-five and five by the time they reached forty. Married women in the forty-one to forty-five age cohort, at peak marital fertility, had, on average, six dependent children.[60] Conforming to a pattern common in other regions, rural New Brunswick women tended to have more children than their urban counterparts, though the differential decreased over time.[61] Consistent with a broad British North American pattern, marital fertility was also slightly higher in francophone than in anglophone communities.[62] At mid-century, Acadian mothers, who tended to marry earlier, were likely to have five small children by the age of thirty-five and six by age forty. By age forty-five, their families at or nearing completion, Acadian women commonly had seven children to care for, the youngest often a babe in arms.

Whether they lived in rural or urban settings, and whatever their religion or ethnic background, some women eagerly looked forward to motherhood, while others, cognizant of the dangers involved, dreaded the prospect.[63] While such fears were not groundless, the majority of the women – approximately one in five – who did not survive their childbearing years did not die in childbirth.[64] Tuberculosis, which claimed so many young people in the nineteenth century, levied a greater toll.[65] Even so, because most people knew or had heard stories about a mother who had died in childbirth, pregnancy brought a certain level of anxiety, and women commonly referred to their confinement as a period of illness.[66]

While nothing in the written record implies that New Brunswick women consciously attempted to limit the size of their families, in the latter half of the nineteenth century, New Brunswickers did participate in a demographic transition characterized by declining marital fertility.[67] Fewer births were accompanied by declining infant and maternal mortality rates.[68] Explanations for this fertility transition include urbanization and the higher cost of raising children in an urban environment, the growing scarcity of good agricultural land, and the increasing value placed on education. But above all, shifts in marital fertility were associated with changing nuptiality patterns.[69] New Brunswick women were agents in these changing trends, delaying marriage, perhaps as a result of prolonging both schooling and their time in the workforce. By 1901, the majority of married women gave birth to no more than two children by the age of thirty, three by age thirty-five, and four by age forty, with completed family size now peaking at four children. Acadian women, too, though continuing to marry slightly earlier than other New Brunswick women, were beginning their families later and bearing fewer children. The majority of Acadian mothers gave birth to three children by age thirty, four by age thirty-five, and five by age forty, with completed family size peaking at five children.[70] By the end of the century, New Brunswick women were spending less time in childbearing and, concomitantly, in childrearing. But however large their completed family, married women were likely to be surrounded by young children and fully occupied with their care during their first decade of married life. Consequently, the majority of married women listed in the census as having an occupation were well over the age of thirty.

A demographic profile of New Brunswickers between the ages of thirty and thirty-nine reveals that, by the time they reached their thirties, men's and women's lives had begun to converge again. Married women in this cohort still outnumbered married men: 85 per cent as compared to 73 per cent. And 11 per cent of men in their thirties continued to live in a household headed by a parent or parents, compared to 7 per cent of women still living at home. That pattern of convergence peaked by the time people reached their forties, as the demographic profile of this age cohort demonstrates: 85 per cent of women and 84 per cent of men were married, while close to 15 per cent of each group remained single.[71]

In this primarily rural society, the majority of married couples lived on farms, for, important as lumbering, shipping, fishing, and even manufacturing were to the provincial economy, the most common male occupation throughout the nineteenth century remained that of the farmer. The farm economy depended on the farm family and, although rarely recorded in the census as having an occupation, the female members made a significant contribution to the family economy. A few focussed snapshots reveal the extent of their prodigious industry. In 1851, the more than 6,200 women in Albert, Charlotte, and Sunbury counties churned 689,000 lbs of butter and wove 94,000 yards of cloth on their hand looms – this, along with milking cows, making cheese, raising chickens for eggs and meat, tending kitchen gardens, making soap and candles, and caring for the needs of their 14,600 children.[72] Their production regularly exceeded the needs of their families, for, like their husbands, they were producing food and goods for the market as well as for home consumption. Provincial butter and cheese production was valued at $955,000 by 1860, while cloth produced was valued at $711,000.[73]

Home-based cloth production was a major economic activity for women, handloom weaving having long been primarily a woman's occupation. In 1871, women dominated commercial textile production in Charlotte County, where more than 100 weavers had small weaving businesses. Most of these artisan weavers were middle-aged married women who spent an average of two and a half months a year producing cloth. And these were not the only Charlotte County women producing significant amounts of cloth: a further 1,000 households reported textile production on the agricultural schedule of the census taken that year. Similarly, in Botsford Parish in Westmorland County, no women identified themselves as weavers, yet more than 80 per cent of households reported homespun cloth production on the agricultural schedules in 1871.[74] Within the network of community exchange, women weavers in Sunbury County bartered with both neighbours and local merchants for a range of goods and services. Like the women of Botsford Parish, none of the women listed in merchants' account ledgers was recorded in the census as a weaver.[75] Yet they were clearly busy contributing to the family economy, perhaps out of sheer necessity, perhaps to give themselves some measure of independence.[76] Given this background, it is not surprising that women – albeit young women – outnumbered men among the weavers in the cotton mills established in the 1880s.

As the life cycle advanced, demographic patterns for women and men, which had converged by the time they were in their forties, began to diverge once more. A demographic profile of men and women in their fifties demonstrates that the proportion of married women had dipped from 85 per cent to 78 per cent, while the proportion of married men remained stable at 84 per cent. A further 14 per cent of women had been widowed, compared to just 3 per cent of men. A demographic profile of those over the age of sixty reveals that 73 per cent of men were married and a further 9 per cent were widowers. In contrast, just 48 per cent of women in the same age cohort were married; 37 per cent were widows. More than longevity on the part of women was involved: the rate of remarriage for widowers was generally higher than the rate of remarriage for widows in every age cohort.[77]

Although the majority of widows and widowers were over the age of fifty, women and men of all ages and at all stages of their adult life course could experience the death of a spouse. If we consider widows and widowers as a separate cohort, it seems clear that widows, whatever their age, were more vulnerable than widowers. This situation arose not only because of dower regulations, which guaranteed a woman a life interest in only one-third of her husband's real estate upon his death, but also because women's skills, while vital to the family economy, were worth less than a man's in the marketplace. Unless they controlled significant real and moveable property, women lacked the earning power to support a family. While working-class widows, whose husbands had no property to bequeath, struggled to make ends meet, the experience of middle-class and other widows whose husbands had been wealthy, particularly those whose husbands' deaths meant the resumption of control over their own extensive property, could be very different. For such women, much depended on the nature of their husbands' testamentary instructions. While some men, in their wills, expressed their entire confidence in their wives, naming them as both sole legatee and sole executrix, others used the same medium to exercise what one scholar has termed "patriarchy from the grave," both restricting their wives' freedom of action, and also stipulating that widows' benefits should continue only "so long as she remain my widow."[78] Yet the meaning and impact of such bequests could be more complex than the statistics and language of the wills suggest.[79]

A series of snapshots illustrates the wide range of women's experience in a single county. The experience of the 151 women in Charlotte County whose husbands' wills were written and probated between 1845 and 1875 indicates that, far from restricting women's rights and independence, husbands and fathers more often sought, through their wills, to provide a security for their widows and minor children that would have been denied under the letter of the law.[80] Of these men, 36 per cent demonstrated confidence in their wives' abilities and business acumen by naming them as sole or co-executrix.[81] Yet even women appointed as sole executrix did not necessarily enjoy full control of the estate. Only 26 per cent of testators bequeathed their entire estates to their wives, with no conditions. These included fifteen of the twenty-one men who mentioned no children in their wills.[82] Still, these cases account for little more than a third of the forty women awarded full control of their husband's estate. More unusual were the ten widows whose husbands gave them full control of their property during their lifetime and the power to devise the estate to their "heirs and assigns" as they saw fit. At the opposite end of the spectrum were twenty-seven widows (18 per cent of the total) whose husbands awarded them full or partial control of their estate so long as they did not remarry. In fifteen of those cases, the couples' children were minors when their fathers died. In considering the intent of these wills, it is noteworthy that three of the widows were appointed as an executrix of their husband's will. Whether wives had participated in the framing of these wills or not, this and other evidence suggests that wives understood the laws of coverture, and the risks to their children's legacy, should they remarry.[83] By stipulating that a widow who remarried would forfeit control of that legacy, such wills ensured that no future husband would gain control of property accumulated during her previous marriage. In agreeing to and enforcing such clauses, women demonstrated that they were no more anxious than their husbands to alienate their children's inheritance.[84]

However they disposed of their estate, husbands sought, through their wills, to protect the most vulnerable family members – their widows and minor children.[85] When one or more of a couple's adult children had already taken over the management of the farm, widows were normally awarded a life interest in a portion of the estate, sometimes including specific living space and support.[86] In twenty-two of the 105 wills in which women were awarded a life interest, the son (or, in one case, daughter) who inherited the home farm was made responsible for supporting an aging mother and younger, unmarried siblings.[87] Whether such mothers had helped to frame husbands' wills is impossible to determine, but when widows came to write their own wills, they, too, sought ways to protect those most vulnerable under the law.[88] Moreover, it would seem that the "life interest" most commonly awarded widows (in 69 per cent of the cases) provided many women with an important degree of independence. In Charlotte County, widows bequeathed a life interest were just as likely to head households as those bequeathed an unencumbered estate.

Wills, however interpreted, tell only part of the story. A significant majority of men died intestate. When this happened, the widow was legally entitled only to her dower interest in her husband's estate: a one-third life interest in his "real property only." The remainder of the estate was to be divided "equally amongst his children or their legal representatives." Given these conditions, women whose husbands left wills usually had a clear advantage over those whose husbands died intestate. Demonstrating a good deal of initiative as well as considerable business acumen, some widows found ways to increase already significant incomes. A few took over the management of the marital property or of businesses established by their husbands. A greater number invested their capital in mortgages, lending money to various members of their communities and taking the deed to the land as security for the debt.[89] Many became investors, putting their money in bank and insurance stocks, which paid regular dividends.[90] In their wills, such women often attempted to ensure greater independence for others of their sex.[91]

Working-class widows whose husbands had no property to bequeath had to seek other means of support. Those who sought employment were most likely to find it in domestic service, and thereby to come full circle, as some had been servants in their youth. Widows worked as house servants, laundresses, washerwomen, cooks, and housekeepers. Some of the better educated sought employment as teachers. Others, trained in traditional women's artisanal occupations, might earn a living as seamstresses, milliners, or dressmakers. Still others established small businesses or continued to operate businesses established before the husband's death. There are examples of widowed women operating small grocery stores. A fortunate few were granted licences to sell liquor.[92] Poor widows unable to earn a wage or establish a business often relied upon the contributions of their employed children to balance the household budget.[93] But such arrangements were precarious and those with many dependent children to support, or who were aged or infirm, often faced destitution. Some turned to their extended family for support. Those without a support network sometimes managed to create one by joining forces, blending two or more families to make ends meet. Turning to community officials for relief was a last resort, reserved for the most desperate.[94] Aging widows proved more successful than their male counterparts at avoiding this fate, and were less likely to become almshouse inmates.[95]

A final series of demographic snapshots focussing on Charlotte County in 1871 sheds light on the intriguing issue of whether widows were more or less likely than widowers to avoid becoming dependent on either their families or the state. If independence can be defined, provisionally at least, as achieving the status of household head, close to half of the 694 widows resident in Charlotte County when the census was taken in 1871 qualify as independent.[96] The 335 widows who headed households constituted 8 per cent of the county's 4,174 household heads. While over half their male counterparts were household heads, widowers were less numerous, comprising less than 5 per cent (202) of the county's household heads. Widows and widowers in the age cohorts forty to forty-nine and fifty to fifty-nine were the most likely to be heading their own households (63 per cent of the widows and 69 per cent of the widowers). Among those below the age of forty, just 31 per cent of widows and 39 per cent of widowers were household heads, and, while a slight majority of widowers aged sixty and over (58 per cent) headed their own households, widows of the same age were less likely to do so (42 per cent). Among widows of all ages, those who headed households were more likely to be located in the county's towns and villages than in the rural areas, but this pattern did not hold true for widowers.[97] Whether located in town or country, the majority of widows and widowers who did not head their own households resided in the households of other family members, usually with one of their children.

Widowhood did not, then, mean retirement. For nineteenth-century New Brunswickers, whether single, married, or widowed, retirement, unless necessitated by infirmity, was not possible. Nor was it a concept many would have understood.[98] Aging New Brunswick women continued to direct and participate in household production. Indeed, household production often peaked when the farm wife reached her mid-fifties and had two or three unmarried daughters working alongside her. Some older women became even more involved in work outside the home than previously. Careers in midwifery, for example, which took women away from their homes overnight or for days at a time, normally reached their zenith when women were in late middle-age and could be continued through widowhood into old age. Although only a handful of midwives can be identified in the censuses, a systematic sample drawn from provincial birth registration records indicates that at least eighty-five midwives were active in the province from 1870 to 1900.[99] Their counterparts were the male doctors who increasingly practised obstetrics and delivered babies. But it is not apparent that the case loads of these male medics increased as they grew older, for physicians could usually afford to reduce their practices with the onset of old age.

Over the course of the life cycle, the experiences of women and men in nineteenth-century New Brunswick were characterized by converging and diverging patterns of dependence, independence, and interdependence. Those patterns were determined as much by age and marital status as by gender, class, and culture. In a society that offered them limited career choices, the majority of women – more than 85 per cent – chose marriage. But then, so did the majority of men. Households headed by a single male were as rare as households headed by a single female. The experiences of the girls and women who wrote the diaries cited in the following chapters should be viewed against this broad demographic backdrop. The extent to which the diaries of three generations of women, whose experiences span an entire century, captured the changing nature of New Brunswick life is the topic of the next chapter. For while our diarists were women of their own time and place, their world was by no means static and they were also women with their own opinions about their changing society.[100] And if our diarists are any guide, girls growing up in nineteenth-century New Brunswick did not share our modern perceptions about the limited nature of their choices.

Chapter 4

Three Generations: Women of Their Time and Place

The expectations and experiences of the three generations of women whose diaries are at the core of this volume varied widely, but in every generation, our subjects recorded, commented on, and responded to the social, economic, and political changes taking place in their society. They sought to understand those changes, discussing the implications for their families and for their communities and adjusting their expectations to accommodate new realities. When they deemed it either necessary or expedient, they took action, sometimes as individuals, sometimes working in concert with people of like mind, to lobby governments and establish voluntary associations. Taking advantage of new opportunities when these were offered, they participated in initiating as well as ameliorating change, thereby engaging in the process of state building.

Established as a separate colony in 1784, following the arrival of approximately 14,000 Loyalists, New Brunswick was, at the beginning of the nineteenth century, a society still in the process of formation. One-third of the diarists were descended from those Loyalists. Although they had come to a land rich in timber, the Loyalist settlers, few of whom had either the requisite capital or the expertise to break into world markets, occupied themselves with establishing productive farms on the fertile lands along the province's major rivers. The timber trade did not begin to boom until 1810, when Britain, facing a shortage of wood, facilitated the development of the industry by giving preference to timber imported from its North American colonies. By the 1820s, farmers could count on a ready market for their timber, and regularly spent a large part of the winter in the woods. The first generation of diarists, women like Jacobina Campbell and Marjory and

Isabella Grant, helped to ensure the continued smooth functioning of the household economy while their absent brothers contributed to the family income by logging in winter and rafting their logs to market in the spring.[1]

During the first few generations of settlement, lumber camps were not far from home, as men who began to think of themselves as farmers/lumbermen took the opportunity to clear more land for planting, stock up on fuel for their own fires, and pile their surplus to await the spring freshet.[2] In February 1827, the men in the Grant family, like many other New Brunswick farmers, spent much of their time at their lumber camp, which was close enough to allow them to return home regularly, to deliver wood, replenish their supplies and, occasionally, help with chores. Much involved in a family economy that depended on lumbering as well as on farming, Marjory Grant took note of the amount of wood harvested, the sharing of resources, and the precise nature and quantity of supplies taken to the lumber camp to sustain both the men and their animals. On 1 February, a clear, cold day, she recorded that her older brother William "took two bushel of oats from here and a barrel of flower for to take to the woods and a load of hay from his barn and went out as far as James Buchanan's in the afternoon." And on 9 February, when her brother Charles came in from the woods, she noted and that he and their father "went to the store in the afternoon with the steers and sled. Charles got 4 bushel of meal and 2 gallons of rum from Wm Porter – he got 3 axes fixt. Father took a crock of butter down to Mrs. Marks with 20 pounds in it." The distinction in this entry is significant. William Porter, a prominent lumber merchant, ran a store associated with his lumbering business and no doubt supplied the needs of the Grants' lumber camp on credit, in the expectation that they, in turn, would deliver their surplus logs to him come spring. In contrast, the family sold their farm produce, including her mother's butter, to Mrs Marks, whose husband, Nehemiah, had an import-export business and general store. The Grants chose to accumulate credit at the Marks' store, where they regularly shopped.[3] By late February, William had, with the help of his own oxen and his father's steers, hauled several loads of wood home for use in his parents' household as well as his own.[4] Returning to the camp on 26 February, he took a load of hay, "77 pounds of flour from here and 78 pounds from his house." The men were still in the woods on 5 March, when Isabella, as keen an observer as her older sister, recorded that "Mother took out 2 quarts of rum out of Cha's kegg that he took to the woods."

If the seasonality of lumbering and farming could be seen as complementary in summer and winter, both required attention as winter turned to spring. On 17 March 1827, with his married brothers turning to the demands of their farms, Charles "moved in from the woods." But unlike his father and older brothers, he was marking time, waiting for the spring freshet, which would bring rising waters, allowing men to raft their surplus logs to market. In the Grant family, this role fell to twenty-three-year-old Charles. Isabella recorded his movements, noting on 3 April that "Charles went to the woods along with Wm Hitchings to see his logs." He returned home two days later, but on 6 April was off again, this time with James Mitchell, "and they started to go a river driving." As Isabella's father and younger brother, with the help of a neighbour, began mending fences, picking rocks from their fields, harrowing, and ploughing, Charles disappears from her diary. On 1 May, he "came in from river driving" for the first time, but was soon off again, returning on 17 May for another brief visit. He left again five days later, but was back in time to help with the planting. With the work of the farm at its height, women and men worked in tandem. Isabella's diary provides a glimpse of the nature of farm life, including the exchange of goods with extended kin and neighbours, and the benign influence of the weather on springtime activities during this early period.

Thursday 17 May 1827. Clear and worm and my father soed three bushell of oats and Absalom was haroing and Charles came in from river driveing and we had a thunder shower.

Friday 18. Clear and warm – and my father soed a half a bushell oats and Absalom haroing and Charles went to the shore and my mother let Alexander's wife have two pound of butter and we had a thunder shower.

Saturday 19. Cloudy and my father was out to the back field and Absalom was haroing in the forenoon and Charles went out to John Milberys and got two 100 hay. Mrs McMolen got a half a bushel of potatoes May 17.

Sunday 20. Warm and some cloudy and my father went to church and my mother had the sik head ake.

Monday 21. Clear and warm and Jinnet and Marjory came in and father and Absalom was haling and Charles was to the shore.

Tuesday 22. Clear and warm. Charles went a-river driveing and father and Absalom haling dung and plowing and I lost my three goslans. William's got seven bushell of potatoes.

> *Wednesday 23. Overcast. My mother went to Oak Hill and father and Absalom haling dung and I saw the first cherry and plum blossoms.*
>
> *Thursday 24. Dull and rainy – and Absalom went to the shore and got a gallon of molasses from Alexander's and my father planted some potatoes in the garden for the first and Charles home from river driveing and we began to make garden. Father got half a gallon rum from William.*
>
> *Friday 25. Cloudy with some wind. My father and Absalom was planting corn and beans. Charles went to the shore. When he came back he was helping them.*
>
> *Saturday 26. Warm and clear – and father and Charles and Absalom was haling dung and me and little Mary planted two rows of cabbage seed.[5] Mrs. McMolen got a half a bushel potatoes.*
>
> *Sunday 27. Very warm – and my mother came in from Oak Hill and Jinnett came in with her and took Mary out.*
>
> *Monday 28. Clear – and Marjory came in and went to the shore and father and Charles was plowing in the fournoon and in the afternoon they went to the store and father got a pound of tea.*
>
> *Tuesday 29. Clear and warm – and Marjory came up from the shore and we sheared the sheep and father was diging the garden. Charles came up from the shore.*
>
> *Wednesday 30. Fair and clear – and father was giting his lines run A.M., and P.M. they plowing and we was washing the wool.*

Those few farmer/lumbermen who could afford to do so established sawmills; for another first generation diarist, Janet MacDonald, the family sawmill both supplemented the farm income and made it possible for three of her six sons to remain on the land.[6]

A burgeoning economy and cheap land attracted waves of immigration from the British Isles, changing the demography of the colony between 1815 and 1850. Almost half the diarists were descended from British immigrants who arrived during that period. By the late 1840s, these new immigrants had shifted the demographic balance, giving New Brunswick a character that had become more British than Loyalist, although the British tended to absorb rather than to displace the Loyalist population.[7] It seems ironic that, just at this time, England, moving towards a *laissez-faire* approach to international trade, began to dismantle the preferential tariffs that had promoted the province's seaward economy.

The removal of trade preferences created a panic among exporters of timber, resulting in a contraction of business that sent shockwaves through communities that relied on the industry. This initiated a pattern of out-migration in response to economic downturns that would come to characterize life in New Brunswick communities.[8] For the youth of Ann Eliza Rogers's community of Hopewell Hill, that commonly meant taking passage on a local sailing vessel bound for any number of New England ports.[9] In the late spring and early summer of 1854, Ann Eliza reported not only who was visiting home, but also how long they had been away. On 3 June, the "Schr Peerless arrived from Boston. Alada McAlmon came in her from Portland. She has been there three or four years." A week later, the "Schr Resolution sailed for Eastport. Mrs Towse & Mary went in her on a visit. James Bishop came home from California. He has been gone five years. Paul Moore came home from New York. He has been gone five years." And on 8 July, "Martha Archibald came home from Portland. She has been gone three or four years." As a teenager, Ann Eliza watched both sailing vessels and steamers come and go, recording the destinations of the local ships in her diary. But she occasionally reported more general activity, noting on 25 April 1852, "Nine vessels came up the bay today." Although this activity in the Bay of Fundy signalled the revival of trade, which was further stimulated by a reciprocity treaty with the United States in 1854, the toing and froing of young people in search of work had become an established pattern, familiar to the second generation of women, and one Ann Eliza Rogers and Mary Wolhaupter would participate in, in their turn. This pattern was facilitated by the increasing number of New Brunswick ships involved in the coasting trade.

Between 1840 and 1870, the lumber trade, which surpassed and all but replaced the timber trade during this period, fostered the development of a flourishing shipbuilding industry.[10] Just as the province's farm families were almost certain to have more than a passing familiarity with the lumbering industry, so, too, families in coastal communities were almost certain to have some connection to the shipping industry. Many among the second and third generation of women had such connections. Ann Eliza Rogers noted on 20 August 1852 that "John Russel (my cousin) had a brig launched. They called her *The Sarah.*" Seagoing diarist Amelia Holder came from a family of shipbuilders who established a successful shipping concern. The father of Amelia's cousin, diarist Emma Alice Pitt, was also involved in the family shipbuilding and shipping enterprises and two of Emma's three older brothers were mariners. Sons of merchants and farmers as well as sons of sea captains and shipbuilders in coastal communities often went to sea for a time between school-leaving and marriage, and daughters regularly married into seagoing families. Maggie Loggie, the daughter of a merchant, married sea captain William Valentine in 1873 and sailed with him regularly over the next two decades. Josephine Reid and her younger sister Orpah, daughters of a house joiner, also married sea captains. In the mid-1860s, when the Holders' shipping business was at its height, Maritime shipbuilding was at its zenith, and Maritime ships were world renowned.[11]

This was the Victorian era, the age of industry, "progress," and education. That separate-spheres ideology and the notion of woman as moral arbiter emerged at the same time as the new industrial ethic[12] has perhaps blurred our vision of women's enthusiasm for the age of progress. The study of women's relationship to science and technology is a relative latecomer to the study of women's history, at least partly because science has long been, and, to some extent, remains, a gendered enterprise, presenting systemic barriers to women's participation. Yet nineteenth-century women, like their fathers, brothers, and husbands, were fascinated by the unusual natural phenomena apparent in the world around them. In late September 1858, as the recently discovered Donati's comet, with its highly visible dust tail, achieved its brightest magnitude, Janet MacDonald went out every evening "to look at it."[13] Ann Eliza Gallacher commented with interest on 8 March 1866, "The papers speak of February as a moonless month, that is it had no full moon, January had two and March two. The like never happened before since the Creation of the World and cannot happen again for two million years." And Mary Wolhaupter lamented on 27 January 1869, "There was an eclipse on the moon this evening. I did not see it untill it was nearly off. I would like to have seen it very much indeed." Such women would instill in their daughters and granddaughters not only a respect for nature but a natural curiosity as well. Founded in 1862, the Natural History Society of New Brunswick further encouraged that curiosity, promoting a school science curriculum based on close and careful observation of nature that was meant to instill in all students, female as well as male, an appreciation of and identification with their region and its natural resources.[14]

Nonetheless, in the first half of the nineteenth century, whether at community-based schools or at boarding schools far from home, young women were denied access to the kind of formal scientific training routinely offered to their brothers. In New Brunswick, with its shipbuilding and seagoing tradition, "navigation" was a core subject in the government-subsidized grammar schools. But even in those grammar schools that admitted girls in the period prior to the Free Schools Act of 1871, navigation was a subject reserved for boys.[15] This did not necessarily mean that girls were denied such training. Amelia Holder's father drew no gender distinctions when, in 1869, during his fourteen-year-old daughter's third voyage, he taught her, as well as her older brother, Tommy, the technical skills necessary to navigate a sailing ship. On 11 December, a day when they "came across the Calms of Cancer without any calms," Amelia reported that "Pa and I take sights now, I take the time by the chronometer while he is taking the sun and I am learning to work them up." On the 16th, she noted, "I worked the eights up to-day alone. Tommy is learning to work them up too, he can take the sun at noon." By the 20th, aided by a fair wind, they were up to Maury's navigation track.[16] Three days later, having just weathered a squall and with no sun to guide them, Edwin Holder took the opportunity to teach his children a new skill. Amelia was enthusiastic: "Pa has to find where the vessel is by dead reckoning and he is teaching Tommy and me. Navigation is a great study. I like to learn it very much." Given the opportunity to study navigation in a practical setting, seagoing women like Amelia Holder often demonstrated both a keen interest in and a facility with the concepts involved.[17]

Although few New Brunswick women learned the intricacies of navigation, many developed a vast store of practical scientific knowledge in those subjects, such as botany, deemed more suitable than navigation for study by girls and women. Some turned their knowledge to good account in developing extensive private gardens. Lucy Morrison had greater ambitions and hired John Bebbington, a trained market gardener, who taught her a good deal in the two years he worked for her. Lucy extended her land under cultivation and, with two heated greenhouses, increased her production of fruits and vegetables for local and regional sale and provided flowers to a wide market year round. Other women combined the study of botany with the study of art, choosing botanical subjects.[18] The extension of women's interest from plants to butterflies and insects was not unusual, although the vast majority of those who pursued such an interest remained in the realm of the gifted amateur.[19] But in the first half of the nineteenth century, science was still very much the purview of the gifted amateur, particularly fields which had a clear practical application: botany, entomology, geology, and astronomy.[20] Partly because of those gifted amateurs, by the 1880s students like sixteen-year-old Laura Fullerton "had the pleasure of looking at different species of butterflies from India" under a microscope in their physiology classes.[21] Such specimens often made their way into New Brunswick classrooms as donations from missionary collectors, women as well as men.[22] Women thus contributed to the diffusion of scientific knowledge and promoted not only the study but also the popularization of science.

By the middle of the nineteenth century, natural history societies and mechanics' institutes were sponsoring lectures that proved popular with women as well as with men. Such lectures were most frequent and most spectacular in urban centres like Saint John, where the latest equipment was available,[23] but itinerant lecturers also visited rural communities. On 26 March 1853, fifteen-year-old Ann Eliza Rogers reported in her diary that "Mr Fenwick from Kings County lectured on electricity." Ann Eliza's interest in this new technology was not fleeting. Seven years later, now married and the mother of two, she noted that she "was to a lecture on electricity last night."[24] In their fascination with popular science and their attendance at such demonstrations, New Brunswick women were part of a trend then sweeping the Western world.[25] Colonial leaders encouraged this interest, seeking first to promote scientific and technological innovation at the local and provincial levels and then to publicize their particular colony's achievements in an international forum: the increasingly popular world exhibition.

The earliest local and provincial exhibitions were designed to promote innovation and progress in the kind of resource-based activities upon which colonial economies were built: grain growing, cattle breeding, and ploughing. But by mid-century, driven partly by audience demand and partly by new imperatives inherent in the "age of progress," organizers of provincial and even local fairs were seeking to appeal to an ever-widening spectrum of colonial society. The success of exhibitions, at whatever level, depended on attendance, and organizers soon discovered that displays of women's handiwork attracted many viewers. At both the local and provincial levels, displays of exclusively women's work, ranging from woollens and linens through embroidered handkerchiefs and straw hats to waxed fruit, also gained a firm foothold. Thus did women make their power as an audience felt.²⁶ Many of those who exhibited handiwork were farm women, who also exhibited produce ranging from cheese and butter to flowers and vegetables. The women in Lottie Reid's family regularly exhibited both handiwork and produce at the local fair, and in 1880, Lucinda Reid, the matriarch of the family, won first prize for her cheese. At provincial exhibitions, the manufacturing interest vied with the farming interest for control. In October 1869, Lucy Morrison had noted in her diary that she "received $8 for prizes at Exhibition, received $10.40 for garden produce," yet once she established her business, she had little time and perhaps no need to enter her produce into competition at the annual Fredericton Exhibition. But some businesswomen, especially manufacturers, did enter their wares, and, when successful, sought to capitalize on the recognition they received at such exhibitions.²⁷

One scholar has characterized exhibiting as "an act of self-assertion and, thus, a political act,"²⁸ particularly in the case of women who entered their work for exhibition at World Fairs, thereby gaining an international audience. Visiting England in 1862, "Mrs R. Wilmot" took the opportunity to attend the third World's Fair, the Great London Exposition. Colonials like Susan Wilmot, who was born and raised in New Brunswick, had a strong regional identity, and while she viewed the English exhibits with a critical eye, in commenting on Nova Scotia's exhibit, she noted that "as is natural I thought everything in it beautiful."²⁹ Mrs Wilmot's travel diary reflects both the tension inherent in the colonial relationship and also the self-identification with the broader Maritime region that would facilitate the transition to Confederation.³⁰

A regional colonial consciousness did not necessarily translate into a transcontinental consciousness, however, and, given the strength of Maritime economies in the early 1860s, it is scarcely surprising that the issue of Confederation proved controversial. New Brunswickers proved ambivalent, electing an anti-confederate government, which numbered Susan Wilmot's husband among its members, in 1865.³¹ And although some proponents of Confederation raised the spectre of a Fenian invasion in their efforts to convince people of the advantages of union, many avid readers of newspapers, Ann Eliza Rogers Gallacher among them, understood the international context. In her diary entry for 5 March 1866, Ann Eliza reported that the suspension of the Habeas Corpus Act in Ireland had reverberated half a world away, with a call for action from John O Mahoney of the "Head Quarters Fenian Brotherhood, New York." Claiming that "our brothers are being arrested by hundreds and thrown in gaol," he had instructed his followers thus:

"Call your circles together immediately. Send us all the aid in your power at once and in God's name let us start for our destination." Recording that "the papers say the Call was responded to by largely attended meetings," Ann Eliza further noted that "the news caused great excitement in St. John and the Provinces. Their destination is not known but fears are entertained that there will be trouble." Observing that "people around the lower end of the County are getting somewhat alarmed," she went on to explain that "there appears to be something unusual going on in New Ireland. Lights are seen in the Chappel after midnight and all sorts of suspicious things going on." Perhaps seeking further information, she visited her sister Mary the next day. "Israel Peck was there, he says the people at Hopewell Corner are very much alarmed. Have formed a Volunteer Company one hundred and twenty men. They keep on a guard at night." Newspapers, too, were sounding the alarm, claiming that "there are five hundred thousand armed fenians in New York, one hundred thousand of them are federal troops." A week later, on 13 March, the British Consul in New York weighed in, warning that "the Fenians were going to attack Campobello Island near Eastport on the borders between United States and Province of New Brunswick. Its population is about one thousand." Refusing to succumb to this growing panic, Ann Eliza remained skeptical, noting on St Patrick's Day, "It has been feared there would be some stir among the Fenians but all is quiet yet." But if the fear of a Fenian invasion was not enough to convince New Brunswickers of the need for Confederation, the failure of the anti-confederation government to renegotiate reciprocity with the United States and the promise of the Intercolonial Railway turned the tide against the anti-confederates in 1866, and in May a pro-confederation government was elected.

The railway age in New Brunswick did not, of course, begin in 1867. The mania for railway construction dated from the 1830s, although construction did not begin in a serious way until the 1840s, with several different lines vying for precedence. Visiting Saint John in 1853, Ann Eliza Rogers reported that, on 14 September, "We got up early to see the Rwy procession walk about 6 o'clock, the general procession of all trades walked about noon through the principal streets, then out to the valley where the first sod of the first railroad in the Province was turned by Lady Head and wheeled away by the Lieutenant Governor Sir E. Head. There was fireworks in the evening." But although Saint John was central to early railway construction in the province, the Intercolonial, built as a condition of Confederation, created new patterns of distribution, and, in the eyes of many New Brunswick businessmen, was not an unqualified success. The Maritime terminus of the railway would be Halifax, dashing hopes that Saint John would become Canada's winter port. Nonetheless, the coming of the railway did bring new opportunities, opening new worlds for women as well as for men. Rail travel not only brought communities closer together, but also made interprovincial travel more accessible. And thus it was in the third generation that women found a new freedom of movement that would make the public sphere more visibly the contested terrain it had always been.

The train was the ready means by which Laura Fullerton travelled to Mount Allison Ladies' Academy in Sackville from her home in Cumberland County, Nova Scotia, in the 1880s. Another of our diarists, Alva Estabrooks, travelled by train, as well as by steamer, from her home in Carleton County to the Ladies' Seminary in Wolfville, Nova Scotia, in the 1890s. Both young women travelled unaccompanied. During that same period, other women were boarding trains to attend the universities with which those ladies' colleges were affiliated. Mount Allison opened its degree program to women in 1872, the first university in Canada to do so. This was too late for Annie Trueman, who graduated that year and was, therefore, eligible only for the lesser diploma of mistress of arts. Yet, as she recorded in her diary, "our classes recited in the College – with the Profs & the Doctors of Divinity for teachers & the gentlemen for classmates."[32] Grace Annie Lockhart, a contemporary of Annie and Laura Trueman at the Mount Allison Ladies' Academy, went on to register at the university, graduating in 1875 with a bachelor of science and English literature, the first woman in the British Empire to earn a bachelor's degree.

As Grace Annie Lockhart embarked upon her bachelor's degree, the Western world was plunging into the Depression, which began in 1873. Responding to the downturn in the economy, young New Brunswickers, women as well as men, again boarded ships bound for that familiar region of New England they called the "Boston States" in pursuit of employment. The Depression accelerated a pattern that had, as the experience of Mary Wolhaupter and others suggests, remained in place since it was first established in the late 1840s. As the mechanical loom and the sewing machine transformed women's work, New Brunswick women had risen to the challenges, eschewing domestic service in favour of factory work whenever they had the opportunity to do so. After 1878, when the introduction of the Sir John A. Macdonald government's National Policy stimulated manufacturing of all sorts,

New Brunswick women were well positioned to take up work in cotton mills, shoe factories, and other manufacturing enterprises established by local entrepreneurs, the same kind of work their mothers and grandmothers had, in past times, travelled to New England to pursue.

But such initiatives lost momentum as control of finance and industry became centralized in Montreal and Toronto.[33] And so the cycle of outmigration would begin anew.[34] Thus, when middle-class women of the third generation began travelling to New England centres in increasing numbers for the purpose of pursuing new educational opportunities, they found themselves on well-trodden paths. During the final quarter of the nineteenth century, New England nursing programs began recruiting Maritime women, and many New Brunswickers responded to the call.[35] When some women were not prepared to accept the lesser role of nurse, and sought training as doctors, they too headed to the United States, where medical colleges had long been open to women.[36] Elizabeth Smith Secord was one such woman. Born on a farm in Blissville, Sunbury County, the fourth of nine children, Elizabeth was a young widow by the time she embarked upon medical studies. Upon her return to New Brunswick in 1883, she became the first woman to be granted a licence to practise medicine in the province.[37]

Meanwhile, by the 1880s, sail was losing ground to steam and sailing voyages were becoming longer as steamships were often used on the shorter runs.[38] The age of sail was drawing to a close, and women knew it. Women at sea well understood the changing nature of international trade as the world moved from the age of wood and wind to the age of iron and steam. Nowhere is this more clearly illustrated than in Josephine Turner's letters to her sister Lottie during the early 1880s. Writing from Antwerp, Belgium, in March 1881, she reported, "We are going to New York again, I think we would have gone to St. John this time if deal freights had not been so awfully low. We may go there next time, as the ceiling will likely have to come out of the vessel then. The vessel is chartered to carry 350 tons of railroad iron at 5s per ton, and then fill up with empty barrels at 6d per barrel, there will not be much made of it, but it will save buying ballast which is expensive here."[39] Two months later found them in New York where "there are any number of N.B. captains here now, it is a dull time for freight. The 'S.B. Meldon' has been here over two months and is not chartered yet, the 'Lewis Smith' and 'Lizzie Wright' are also here."[40] The Turners considered themselves fortunate to avoid such a long layover, but it was at some sacrifice, as Jo reported to her sister: "We are going to Germany again, James chartered the vessel yesterday for Lubeck. It is a far off port, and we get a low freight, but it is hard to tell when times will be any better for shipping, and this is a very expensive port to stop in very long, every day counts. We are to carry grain (corn) at 4s 6d per quarter."[41] By 20 October, James's vessel, the *Kesmark*, was back in New York, having returned from Lubeck "in ballast for the first time." And the shipping prospects were not improving. Writing to her sister at the end of October, she had "no news to write excepting that our vessel is chartered, we are going to Santander this time, a port in the North of Spain, we take a cargo of petroleum in cases, two boxes in a case each box contains five gallons, it is the best kind of oil to carry. We bring back iron ore, either to N.Y. or Baltimore, freights are still very low, and but little prospect of them being any better for some time yet."[42] Three years later, they were still struggling and, having taken cargo to Buenos Aires, were forced to return in ballast.

Monday, March 31, 1884 – They have nearly finished discharging cargo, cannot take quite all out until they get in a little ballast – for shifting. We have spent the evening onboard "The Maggie Dart." My cold is better.

Tuesday, April 1 – It seems quite like autumn today, the weather is so cool, it would be pleasant to spend a winter in this fine climate, but we will soon be travelling toward the tropics again.

Wednesday, April 2 – Finished discharging cargo today, and have taken in 40 tons of ballast, the vessel will probably be towed to the ballast wharf tomorrow to rec. the remaining 200 tons. James took letters to town to mail today. I wrote to Pa, also to Miss Hopkins. I have owed her a letter for a good while.

Thursday, April 3 – Rainy in the forenoon, the vessel was towed down to the ballast wharf this afternoon, there are very many vessels here as nearly all leave in ballast. We will not be ready for sea this week.

Friday, April 4 – I have spent this day onshore or at least part of it, took dinner onboard "The Maggie Dart" in the afternoon. Mrs. Dart and I went downtown, did some shopping, had no trouble going around, found we were pretty good pilots.

Saturday, April 5 – A beautiful sunshiny day but I have not been out anywhere, I got more cold yesterday and my head has pained me very badly all day, but guess a good night's rest will cure it. (Memorandum)

We did not get off to sea this week but the ballast is now about half in, will likely finish by the middle of next week when the vessel will go out in the roads to take in water, get sails, &c. I do not think I will go in her, will stop on shore a day or two while James is setting up.

Sunday, April 6 – A beautiful day, the weather is very cool. Now that the autumn season has set in, I should like to spend a winter in this fine climate yet very many are complaining at present of colds, probably owing to the sudden change in the weather.

Monday, April 7 – Too cold today that thin overcoats found to be very serviceable. A quick mail left here today for Europe, by which we sent quite a number of home letters I wrote four.

Through such letters, people at home participated in a discourse about the impact of changing trends in world trade that had also precipitated a decline in the wooden shipbuilding industry so fundamental to the local economies of the province's coastal communities.

At least partly in response to the precariousness of local economies, women's expectations and societal expectations about women changed in significant ways. By the closing decades of the nineteenth century, the world of our third generation of diarists – when young women like Sadie Harper, Violet Goldsmith, and Kate Miles were coming of age – increasing numbers of adolescent girls were attending high school, even if, like Kate, they had to board in town through the week in order to do so. With the emergence of the modern high school curriculum, girls and boys studied the same subjects, including geometry, chemistry, French, Latin, history, and literature: a curriculum designed not only to prepare students for a changing workforce, but also to prepare increasing numbers to enter normal school and a privileged few to enter university. In sixteen-year-old Kate Miles, we also see the modern adolescent emerging, with time spent in the classroom balanced against time spent in the company of friends, often downtown.

Wednesday, May 1, 1901. Lovely day and perfect to-night. I had a Geom. Sup. this morning.[43] Annie sick in bed. I was up to Sade's after tea. Played ball. Mr. Smith here to-night. I made 77 in my French sup.[44]

Thursday, May 2. Very windy to-day and dusty. Raining hard to-night. Edgar came up this morning. Sade, Ellie and I were down town after school. Mabel Smith in to-night after school.

Friday, May 3. Terribly windy and cold. Father came up for us. He got two gasoline lamps to-day. Got one fixed and put it up in upper parlor. Burns very well with nice white light. Charlie Charters, wife and her little sister are in other house.

Saturday, May 4. Still very windy. Mama and Father went to town. Aunt Mame went down the road after dinner. Mr. Harry DeVelier came up with her and spent the evening.

Sunday, May 5. Raining to-day. I read nearly all day.

Monday, May 6. Dark in morning but cleared off. Aunt Mame brought us up. We were up in Assembly Hall after school selecting songs. Mr. and Mrs. Johnson had musicle here to-night. E & I didn't go down. They brought us up nice lunch.

Tuesday, May 7. Dull day. We had Chem. exam this morning. Quite hard. I made 82 in Latin and 76 in History. Edgar is through until Friday. Jean didn't come for him though. Annie is in bed to-day.

Wednesday, May 8. Still dull in morning and cleared off in afternoon. We stayed after school to practise. I was up to Mrs. Waycott's after tea for quite a while. Annie got up this afternoon.

Thursday, May 9. Lovely day but very warm. They stayed to practise to-night but I didn't stay. I went out about 5:30. Coni went down town to price cotton. Gertrude and I out for a ride to-night. Sade in to study.

Friday, May 10. Another perfect day. Edgar drove up this morning. He had a drafting exam. Mrs. O.P. Brown here to tea. I sat out on back veranda and read after tea. Lovely out there.

Saturday, May 11. Raining all day. I walked up to Mrs. Foster's this afternoon. Took up waist for Bessie to make. Just poured when I was coming home.

Sunday, May 12. Dark but lovely out. Captain Banks' baby buried to-day. First body ever taken in the new Baptist Church.

Monday, May 13. Dark. Father brought me up. I was late. Annie & Edgar and I were up to Mrs. Waycott's to-night. Annie's hand played up. She went to the doctor. Edgar & I stayed until quite late.

Tuesday, May 14. Nice day but turned cold to-night. Went down town after school with committee meeting. Annie in bed to-day. Had Dr. Crocket.

Wednesday, May 15. Lovely day. Had a practise after school. Then committee meeting. Got picture of Bruce to-night. Very good. Annie up to-day. Out for a ride with Gertrude to-night.

Thursday, May 16. Fine day. Got note from Mama to-day saying to ask Miss Nieolson down. Edgar went home this afternoon. Mr. and Mrs. Johnson out to tea. Mabel S. and Sade in to tea to-night. Studied afterward.

Friday, May 17. Lovely day. Edgar drove up for me. Miss Nieolson didn't go down. Father got home to-night. He has been up to Oromocto for a few days. Grandpa and Aunt Mame gone.

Saturday, May 18. Very windy. Edgar had to go up for an exam. Gertrude came down with him. I had bad headache but slept it off some. Father, Mama and Baby down road. I had to write composition to-day.

Sunday, May 19. Nice but windy. Expected Uncle Harry & Aunt Annie over but they didn't come. Mama, Father and Baby were down below. Stayed to tea. Grandpa and Aunt Mame settled in new kitchen.

Monday, May 20. Lovely day. Edgar drove Gertrude and me up. Went right back. Father and Mr. Mc Fadger went to Keswick. We had a great practise after school.

Tuesday, May 21. Very, very hot. Edgar drove up and had French exam. Theo. and I got curtains for Assembly Hall. Up to Sade's before tea. Out for a ride with Olive Wallace after tea.

Wednesday, May 22. Warmer than yesterday. Father and Edgar up to-day. Hemmed curtains first hour this afternoon. Worked up in Hall until 6 o'clock. Got tickets and distributed some. Over on Windsor Hall veranda to-night.

Thursday, May 23. Rainy. Very hot at noon but turned very cold about 6 p.m. Empire Day. Had addresses at school in afternoon. Edgar came up. He, Sade and I went to opera house to see Little Minister. Edgar and I drove home afterward.

Friday, May 24. Cold and dark. Mrs. Barker was here to spend the day. Edgar went to town. College sports came off.

Saturday, May 25. Nice day. Mama, Edgar & Baby were to town in afternoon. Aunt Mame up in afternoon. Susie over to dinner. Mr and Mrs. Charters away.

Sunday, May 26. Perfect day. Aunt Annie and Uncle Harry were over. We were to Baptist Church in afternoon and down to B. Church in evening. Mr. Brown farewell sermon.

Monday, May 27. Dark and rainy. Holiday. Edgar brought me up. Very busy all day getting ready for concert to-night. It was a success, made about $35.

Tuesday, May 28. Rained hard all day. Had to stay in an hour after school with Miss Thorne. Sade and I were down town afterward. Met Edgar.

Wednesday, May 29. Dark and windy. Met Gertrude and Nan Clark at noon. Was down town after school paying bills for Dr. Clow. Daisy Van Nuke and Sade were with me.

Thursday, May 30. Still raining. Sade and I were down town after school and out for a ride after tea. Sade and Dick have a new wheel. Miss Rivers came to-day. Edgar was up to-day.

Leaving home to attend a public high school, the normal school, or the university really did mean striking out on one's own, for, unlike ladies' academies, these institutions did not have women's residences. Like young working-class women who migrated to the province's towns and cities in search of employment, middle-class women students also became boarders, and a familiar sight on Fredericton streets, travelling both singly and in groups, on their way to school or to work, to shops or to skating rinks, to prayer meetings or to parties, among other events.[45] In the province's towns and cities, young single women melded into a much broader social milieu.

While women remained largely participant observers in parades and public celebrations,[46] in philanthropy, social reform, and politics, they found their own unique voice and set their own priorities. Their philanthropic efforts undertaken through ladies' auxiliary organizations funded orphanages, hospitals, and church building projects.[47] Social reformers among them increasingly left female auxiliaries behind, choosing instead to establish their own separate organizations. The Woman's Christian Temperance Union, international in scope, became the most powerful voice of the continuing temperance crusade, while denominational women's missionary societies became the major fund raisers for the missionary movement, sending hundreds of female missionaries to foreign lands. At universities, normal schools, and high schools, participation in the emerging YWCA movement prepared young women for such social activism. Women's political activism resulted in a suffrage movement that reached its prewar peak in the final decade of the century, gaining the support of the majority of the province's newspaper editors, if not the majority of its politicians.[48] In all these endeavours, nineteenth-century New Brunswick women must be viewed against a backdrop of Western women on the move, part of an international intermingling of ideas and activities that would take the province into the twentieth century.

Over the course of the nineteenth century, successive generations of New Brunswick women, born into a new and evolving province, shaped by their physical surroundings as much as by their times, helped to define and redefine the conventions and mores of their society in response to shifting social, economic, and political realities. Yet women's experience, as reflected in their diaries, demonstrates significant continuity even in the midst of momentous change. Embedded within a web of family relationships, our diarists moved outward from the security of their nuclear family, into neighbourhoods that often included networks of extended kin, to position themselves within a range of community networks that extended beyond their immediate neighbourhoods and often beyond the geographic boundaries of their larger communities. From this vantage point – that is, the milieu in which they lived and functioned – they formulated their understanding of the broader society. Using this framework, the remaining chapters blend a thematic and a life-course approach. Taking advantage of what diaries as records of life in process can reveal about individuals' thinking at various stages of the life course, the following chapter focuses on the youngest diarists, as they begin to contemplate the future possibility of forming families of their own.

Chapter 5

From Innocent Flirtation to Formal Courtship

In the nineteenth century, as in our own day, adolescence signalled a new phase in young people's lives as their glances shifted more and more towards each other. Young people increasingly sought the company of their peers as they began to look to the future. What young women wrote in their diaries reflects this shift in gaze, as they reported not only their activities but sometimes their discussions with sisters and friends, their views of and interchanges with young men, their feelings as relationships evolved, and their turmoil and distress when their own feelings were not reciprocated. Their tentative posturing, innocent flirtation, and youthful crushes often emerge much more clearly in diaries than does the evolution of the more serious formal courtship that culminated in marriage.

Focussing largely on the experiences of the middle and upper classes, and the period of formal courtship that led to marriage, historians studying the history of courtship rituals in nineteenth-century British North America have portrayed young women as constrained by social mores that circumscribed their activities. In particular, the young women featured in descriptions of courtship in the early part of the century were almost always chaperoned when venturing abroad, only rarely appearing alone in public settings, and then usually in defiance of custom and without parental approval.[1] Yet, not all historians agree with this characterization, even for the early period.[2] The diaries of young single New Brunswick women imply that they had a good deal of freedom to come and go as they wished, which allowed them to enter into relationships without their parents' prior approval, or even knowledge.

Nineteenth-century New Brunswick was a youthful society, and young women, embedded in families and neighbourhoods overflowing with young people of all ages, had rich social lives. Innocent flirtation might or might not evolve into courtship and courtship might or might not culminate in marriage. During the late 1870s and early 1880s, Lucy Morrison's sons brought home young women, their future wives among them, for croquet parties or for supper. Sometimes the couples travelled alone, sometimes in a mixed group of young people, sometimes from nearby, sometimes from a distance. Courtship occurred in casual as well as formal settings and involved only the couple or peer groups as often as it involved family or supervised church or community events. The New Brunswick experience suggests an intermediary stage for young women no less than young men: a period of innocent flirtation during which adolescents slipped into and out of more tentative informal relationships that prepared the way for, and conditioned their attitudes about, formal courtship. From innocent flirtation to formal courtship, and from courtship to marriage, New Brunswick women exhibited a significant degree of independence.[3]

Perhaps taking their cue from contemporary novels rather than from advice literature, even quite young women travelled alone relatively freely, and this from an early period.[4] In 1823, Sarah Upton, then twenty-two, travelled from St Stephen to Boston, from whence she wrote airily to her parents, "I have been no where yet except to church ... I am in hopes that I shall go into the country this week. All that I have mentioned it to tell me that they would not hesitate to take so short a journey alone." Her parents, who did not hear from her for a full eight weeks, regretted their decision to allow her to go to Boston, but she came to no harm.[5] Two decades later, Sarah sent her own daughter, Mary Hill, to a boarding school in South Boston. At such schools, parents might expect that their teenaged daughters would be carefully supervised, yet Mary's reports of fortnightly balls that went on until 3 a.m. may well have given the mature Sarah pause.[6] Back in St Stephen, adolescents were rarely monitored more closely, however. The relative freedom Mary and her peers enjoyed at home is captured in an entry in her eighteen-year-old brother's diary: "Sunday, Feb. 3rd: Went to the Baptist House (Calais) to meeting in the evening. An account of the Siamese Mission was given by the Rev. Mr. Dexter – Afterwards two bona fide idols, taken from a Chinese Junk which had been sunk in the river, were exhibited by Noah Smith Esq. – went with the B'hogs and came home with the G'hals." Thus, while church-sponsored events provided the opportunity for young men and women to meet in a supervised public setting, that supervision did not always extend beyond the meeting-house door.[7]

At about the same time, in Hopewell Hill in Albert County, another teenager, Ann Eliza Rogers, was travelling about the countryside, sometimes on horseback, sometimes by horse and buggy, running errands for her mother, conveying friends and relatives around the county, often on her own, sometimes in the company of her younger sister or a friend. This freedom allowed Ann Eliza to initiate a courtship very much of her own choosing. Her future husband makes his first appearance in her diary on 21 May 1854: "Mr Gallacher came here from Boston. He is going to superintend a chemical works that is to be built by Mr Jim & John Steadman and some others on the back road near a Manganese Mine ... He was here about a month ago with Mr John Steadman and looked at the place." Her interest aroused, by July we find seventeen-year-old Ann Eliza riding alone on horseback to the site of the proposed chemical works in the hope of catching a glimpse of this new man in the community. The story of their courtship can be traced through occasional references embedded in her diary entries, although the main events, recorded well after the fact, are left to the imagination. On 8 August comes the first hint that Ann Eliza's interest may have been reciprocated: "There was a picnic at Caledonia today ... I went out with Mr Gallacher ... I enjoyed my drive very much. Mr Gallacher is very good company." In late September, they attended church together, a sure signal of the growing seriousness of the relationship between Miss Rogers and Mr Gallacher. As the year drew to a close, Ann Eliza confided to her diary, "I have been engaged to be married for some time past to John McAuly Gallacher. He has become very dear to me. We expect to be married in the spring. He is a native of Glasgow Scotland, has been in the States for some years. He is thirty-six years old."[8]

Because young men and women were so often in one another's company, serious courtship can easily be missed in reading young women's diaries.[9] Marjory Grant's marriage to William Buchanan on 4 March 1827 comes as a surprise to the reader of her diary. And even a careful re-reading yields few enough clues about preparations for the marriage, and none at all about the nature of the courtship. On 2 February, Marjory's younger brother Absalom was sent to the store to purchase "a half dozen buttons to put on Mr Buchanan's waistcoat," suggesting that Marjory may have been making the groom a new waistcoat to wear at the ceremony. Absalom purchased porringers on the same occasion, perhaps for the new household that would soon be established. But there is no direct reference to the upcoming event in Marjory's diary. Rather, she reports travelling around the countryside with her younger sister Isabella, visiting relatives and friends. On one occasion, they stayed overnight at the shore with their sister-in-law, Jannet Grant, visiting friends in the afternoon and attending a singing school in the evening. Another time, Marjory visited an older sister, Jannet Buchanan, in Oak Hill, where her fiancé, William Buchanan, also lived, though she does not mention him. Instead, she reports that she got a ride home with Thomas Fraser in his sleigh. The final two entries in her diary do indicate that some sort of celebration was in the wind. On 27 February, "Father and Mother and John's wife was down to the shore. Father got three gallons of rum and a cheese. Mother and Ann got some things over the river."[10] The following day, the family began to gather, and more supplies were purchased: "Charles came home in the evening ... and our Jannet came in with him and brought in her baby with her – Absalom went to the shore and got one lb Tea and seven lbs sugar from Mrs Marks."[11] But it was left to Isabella, taking over her sister's diary, to announce, on 4 March, that "Marjory got married" and record the family celebration the next day: "Alexander and his wife came up,[12] eat dinner with us and James Buchanan and his wife[13] and little Mary went home and Charles went to the woods and Wm R.B. took Marjory and me to the shore and brought us up in the evening." On 6 March, "Marjory moved out to Oak Hill."

Diarists themselves were sometimes taken by surprise, implying just how private a courtship might be. This seems to have been the case for Lottie Reid, when, in August 1879, her sister Jo married sea captain James Turner, the son of a neighbour and the older brother of one of Lottie's friends. James, who had become "quite a stranger around these parts," arrived home in early May, and paid his first visit to the Reids a week later. But not until July did he begin to visit regularly, Lottie noting, "He calls around quite often."[14] Although Lottie made no mention of her sister's plans to marry Captain Turner, it seems clear that they were well underway by 13 August, when she accompanied Josephine to see Mrs McCally, a dressmaker, who would spend the next week with them. On 25 August, two days before the wedding, Lottie reported that "Wat left this morning for Salmon River, Pa took him down. He is going in the 'Kesmark' (Capt. Turner's master) this trip, as carpenter. She is loading down in Salmon River. They expect her to be ready for sea the last of the week. We will be very lonely here when Wat and

Jo both leave." The following day, she commented that "Mrs McCally is here sewing again today. She is helping Josephine get ready to go away." Then, on 27 August, "Just a splendid day," she reported: "This has been a kind of bustling day for can it really be so, Josephine and Capt. Turner were married this morning by Mr. Hughes. There was no one in to see her except Mr. Turner's folk, Eleanor, and Willie's folk. As soon as the ceremony was over, after having taken a lunch, the bride and groom left for Salmon River accompanied by Anna and Abner."[15] On 29 August, commenting that "we have felt so lonesome today with Wat and Jo both away, we hardly know what to do with ourselves," Lottie admitted that the marriage had taken her by surprise: "I cannot fully realize that Josephine is really married yet, the affair seemed to come off with such a short notice." And two days later, when Wat, Josephine, and James came up for a brief visit before setting sail, she confided, "I cannot yet realize that Josephine has changed her name and is going to try a voyage on the water but suppose it must be so."

If the rituals of formal courtship are often difficult to identify in women's diaries, discussion of that intermediate stage of innocent flirtation is more common. In 1873, seventeen-year-old Amelia Holder, enjoying what was to be her final voyage with her sea-captain father, was accompanied by her younger sister Agnes. On the homeward journey, the ship carried three passengers bound for New York: the American Consul, his wife, and their adolescent daughter, Linney. The three girls looked forward to a stopover in Barbados and the opportunities for flirtation it might afford, with Amelia noting in her diary on 28 February, "We have been talking about what we are going to do when we get to Barbadoes. We are going to try and get introduced to some nice man or a rich old one and try and marry them." Meanwhile, they practised their feminine wiles, with but limited success. Thus, one evening when the first mate, Amelia's Uncle Charles, asked the two older girls, who were heading for their favourite spot on top of the cabin, if they were "going on the house," Amelia replied, "Yes, I expect we will blow away when we get up there." And Linney teased, "You'll jump over for us won't you if we fall overboard?" When Charles replied in the negative, Linney turned to the second mate and asked, "You will won't you Mr Lowry?" Mr Lowry said yes and when Amelia took up the question and "asked who was going to jump after me ... he said he'd jump after both of us." But Charles continued to demur, telling them that "that was the way young girls deceive young men, get them to jump over after them and then leave them to drown." Their efforts proved more successful during their anxiously awaited stopover in Barbados. On 8 March, Amelia reported, "We have had our dresses out to-day and our hats and everything else and are getting them ready to wear in Barbadoes. To-night we got our hair ready. Aggie put hers in paper, it makes her awfully cross, I braided mine." Two days later, when they went ashore, Mr Holly, the United States consul, took them shopping. Upon their return, they made a brief stop at his office, which overlooked the quay, and were delighted to catch sight of "some handsome young officers landing. They looked at us and we looked at them." From there they travelled in a cab "to Mr Holly's just out of town, a lovely place." Presumably, Linney's father assumed that the girls would be in safe hands with the American consul. Amelia was surprised as well as pleased by their visit, reporting in her diary, "I thought Mr Holly was a married man but now found he was a bachelor. A young man came in and was introduced to us as Mr Snell. Had blue eyes, a red face and a pretty large nose, had some signs of a coming mustache. Went to lunch, while there another young man came in and seemed quite at home, he played on the piano beautifully, afterwards heard he was a professor of music. He got acquainted with us very quickly, Mr Snell was bashful. About half past four Pa came and we went to the quay and when we got a little way off Linney and I bowed to them three times and they bowed to us, a little further off they waved to us and we nearly waved our bouquets to pieces, we got bouquets from Mr H.'s garden."[16]

Adolescents engaged in innocent flirtation in the hopes of attracting the attention of the object of their youthful crushes. When their tentative posturing went unnoticed or their feelings were not reciprocated, they felt the pangs of unrequited love. Emma Pitt, the only daughter in a family of seafaring men, was feeling those pangs when the *Lydia*, carrying her cousins, Amelia and Agnes Holder, arrived in Saint John on 23 April 1873. At sixteen, Emma had a serious crush on Fred Hatheway (referred to as "F." in her diary), a young man whose father operated the steamers that plied the St John River. In the company of her cousins, she looked around for other possible suitors, reporting a "splendid day, went over to the *Lydia* and had a stunning time. There was a whole lot of us and a Mr Saunders was there, he's very nice ... We staid on board all night and came home in the morning ... We went into Mr Vrooms comming home and was introduced to Mr Arnold, he's very nice too."[17] But she had not forgotten Fred, and some months later, on 12 June, she recorded that "A. and I went out walking and Fred passed us. That is the first time I have seen him for 7 months." Travelling upriver on

15 July, she saw him on the boat and commented that "F. looked awful sad when the boat started. I was looking at him all the time." Returning home the following week, she "had quite an adventure with a nice looking man," but if she was hoping thereby to make Fred jealous, her hopes were dashed, "for he never looked up at all." In September, taking the steamers back and forth to visit her cousins in Holderville, Emma reported a flirtation with another male passenger, recording that she had taken "a great notion to a young man on the steamer and he followed us all around." Nonetheless, she continued to pine for Fred, hoping to see him when she went to meeting of a Sunday, and lamenting, "I am lonesome and I can truly say I know not why I love thee! For I don't ever see him." The following Sunday, when she saw "F. pass by walking with B.E.," she confided in anguish, "Oh! heavens I thought I should die."[18]

Back at home in Holderville that winter, Amelia Holder, too, suffered the pangs of an unrequited adolescent crush. Christmas day 1873 was a milestone for Amelia, "the first Christmas I have been home for seven years. In the evening there were a lot of young folks and we enjoyed ourselves very well. I am eighteen today. How old that seems. Pa says I am of age. I wonder where we will drift to by next Christmas. R's 26th." Things for Amelia did not "drift" in the direction she had hoped. On 19 January 1874, she confided dramatically, "My heart is broke. I shall go stick, stark, staring mad. He is going to Tyber. It was in our paper Friday. I had great hope that he was coming here ... when the first thing strikes my eye is sailed for Tyber. I don't know exactly where that is but I think it is in the East Indies. I suppose I must give him up now, so farewell my dreams and hopes and let us plow on in the dreary sameness of this life."

Yet perhaps we should not take such passions too seriously, for their unrequited love did not, apparently, prevent either Emma Pitt or Amelia Holder from enjoying social events.[19] Amelia's younger sister Aggie reported on 22 February 1874 that "we have been having gay times lately, that is this last week. Tuesday Pa & I went to St John stayed all night, in the morning came up, brought Emma Pitt up with us, got home about twelve o'clock, started at half past three for the Hall at Carters first to a tea meeting, had a very pleasant time only no beaus: that was a dreadful drawback to our enjoyment of course, especially Emma & Meal."[20]

Even the most innocent of flirtations had the potential to arouse unintended jealousies among young women. In the summer of 1872, when her parents took in a boarder, Jennie Maddock, Laura Trueman enjoyed the novelty. "I dont think we could hardly have any one who was as nice to have as Jennie," she noted in her diary on 1 July. "There are some things of course which we would wish otherwise, but there is no one without some little failing. We get along together pretty well." Yet, as Laura's diary illustrates, three young women in the same household did create friction, especially when Annie and Laura's cousin, Josie Wood, began taking a greater interest in Laura, or perhaps in Jennie. Things began with a family fishing expedition.

July 10th, 1872. We are all pretty tired today. Mr Burwash has all along been trying to get up a trip to the Joggins but yesterday morning he & Clifford went up to the Head of the lakes to reconnoitre and see if it would not be better for us all to go up there and fish. Also yesterday morning Josie came in and asked us all to go up to Migie so we planned it up and went, we had a nice drive up. Jennie and I drove with Josie. When we got up there we went to John Oulton's, the man whose house we went to the time we were up with Prof. Spencer. She was very kind to us and after resting a little while we started for the Lake. We went a quarter of a mile thro' a most delightful little path in the woods, thus we came to a bog. Still we went on but found that if you went out to fish you must go in a boat and there was only one little one that would only hold 3 men so Pa and Josie and Al went out in it. They got 3 trout and then we went up off of the bog into the woods and chose ourselves a dining room in true camping style, the carpets had a ground-work of moss strewn with graceful ferns while our chairs were stumps and felled logs and we were surrounded with columns made after the style of Nature's architecture. We had a nice time over tea, then the men went back to fish while we went back to Mrs Oulton. She had a nice tea ready and after the men came home we ate a second tea, and then started for home with 10 fish, the result of our fishing expedition to Migie. Josie took Jennie & I to Amherst the other day for a drive, we had a very pleasant time and he asked us yesterday to go to Baie de Verte with him. He is so odd, Annie is too old for him to take much notice of, and it made me feel awfully bad this morning because Annie thought I kind of slighted her company for Jennie's & I am sure such an appearance was altogether unintentional, for God knows it is the furthest from the feelings of my heart. It does seem funny now since Jennie has come for Josie to take a crotchet to take us for a drive sometimes. I did not enjoy the one to Amherst very much for Jennie did not act a bit nice – she is so free with young men and I am sure it cannot proceed from pure-mindedness for there is none of that virtue in her for it to proceed from. Only 4 weeks now before school will begin! This vacation has slipped away almost imperceptably and when school begins I must go to studying hard again. I hope I will get on well. Yes, this really delightful vacation is almost gone and with it its deeds of evil & good. How few good I fear for me.

Laura's initial enthusiasm about their new boarder continued to fade, and on 24 July, the day Jennie left, she confided to her diary, "Jennie ... did not seem to feel bad at leaving us, she does not seem to be possessed of much feeling and does not make much impression on one, one way or another." Yet Jennie was not entirely devoid of "feeling," for Laura further commented, "She is sick after Josie. I don't wonder she likes him. I guess everyone does (but Mrs Alder). Annie and I think as much of him as we possibly could of a big brother and just feel toward him in the same way – he gets lovelier every time one sees him." It is unlikely that the Trueman parents or Jennie Maddock suspected that in inviting the two younger women to join him on outings, Josie, at twenty-nine, might be courting sixteen-year-old Laura. We cannot know Laura's own feelings, but her comment that "Annie and I think as much of him as we possibly could of a big brother" juxtaposed with her earlier observation that Annie, at twenty, "is too old for him to take much notice of," suggest a certain ambivalence in her own feelings at this stage in their relationship. That ambivalence had disappeared by 1874, when Laura married Josiah Wood.

Even in the carefully supervised setting of a Methodist ladies' academy, youthful flirtation could not be suppressed. The Mount Allison Ladies' Academy was, after all, adjacent to the Male Academy and College, and although unsupervised meetings between male and female students were strictly prohibited, such rules proved difficult to enforce. Laura Fullerton, writing in 1886, recorded several instances of infractions. On Tuesday 12 May, she noted that some of the young men from the Male Academy had been "under Min Rice's window, talking to the girls," a common enough practice, though a risky one. The following day, Laura reported that "Mr Borden had Ella & Ada Bowyer down in his office last evening, about talking from the windows and attracting attention, and this morning he had Ada Fraser and Berta Ross to his office." But the practice was too widespread to occasion very serious penalties, as implied by Mrs Archibald's injunction to all those who "had talked from window and waved to the boys ... to come to her room immediately after closing and report themselves."[21] In an effort to monitor evolving relationships between students, the administration at Mount Allison organized mixed social events and even "Private Receptions" were regularly scheduled. In some cases, young love blossomed, and sixteen-year-old Laura regularly reported on budding courtships in her diary. If supervised settings could not preclude flirtation, neither could they prevent the rivalries and complications often associated with first love. Nor could the school's supervision follow students as they ranged beyond the walls of the institution. Laura Fullerton, who had not yet given her heart to any young man, became inadvertently embroiled in something of a love triangle during her Easter holiday, which she spent with relatives at Point de Bute. She had travelled by train to Aulac with a fellow student, Min Curran. There, May (with whom Min was staying) and Laura's Uncle Douglas met them. As Mr Nash, who had been courting Min at various college-sponsored social events, was also among the students spending the holidays with friends or relatives at Point de Bute, Laura was not surprised to find him among the guests when she accepted an invitation to spend the evening with May and Min. Nor was she surprised when he was kind enough to escort her home at the end of the evening. Over the course of the holidays, she spent a good deal of time with May, Min, and Mr Nash, even taking them all for a drive one afternoon when her Uncle Douglas gave her his horse and carriage. But she was discomfited when it came time to return to school and, rather than taking care of Min, "Mr N took my satchel and assisted me into the train, found a seat and sat with me coming over, took my valise from the train, seen me safe in the carriage, and then left. All results in Min being in the background and Mr N. all attentions to me. Min feels it very much, too." Laura enjoyed Mr Nash's company, and he led her to believe that Min had lost interest in him, but she was not entirely convinced, confiding to her diary that "although I had a very lovely time I was not happy. It all bothered me in a way I cannot describe. Sleep was disturbed and rest gone. One thing I am glad the holidays are over." Her worries were not without foundation, for less than two weeks later she noted in her diary that "Mr Nash and Min have made up again I think, after all he said about her too. When we got back from P. de B. he wrote her to know if she did not wish to go with him anymore, if so he wanted her to say so, and not fool him any longer. I do not know what she answered, but anyway he came over this afternoon and had Private Reception with her. So I guess they have made up again." But things did not end there.

Reflecting the unavoidable emotional undercurrents circulating among young people in even the most carefully supervised settings, the situation evolved in a fairly predictable way. After evening reception on 9 May, Laura reported that "Nash was with Min, but the girls said he would have come up to me had I bowed. However I did not and he went with Miss Curran." A few days later, the tensions bubbled to the surface. When she received a letter from Mr Nash asking for her company at the next reception, Laura, assuming that Min had broken her connection with him, agreed. However, that evening "Min came up to my room and accused me of telling Nash things about her, which thing I never did. She says she is never going with Nash again. She does not think now that I told Nash anything about her." The following afternoon, "Mr N ... had Private Reception with Min," and the next day Laura attended a baseball match on the Academy Grounds, "mostly to see how Mr N would conduct himself. He went with Min. After a time Miss Dobson, Bell Townsend and Ada Fraser and I came home." Laura's dilemma upon discovering that Min and Mr Nash were still courting was resolved when she sought advice from Miss Black, her piano teacher. "She was so very kind and told me what to do. I was so glad I went to her. I am going to write to him, break the engagement. Miss B said she would get it over for me all right ... I wish I had never seen him. The affair bothers me." But Laura was unsure as to what kind of letter to write, "whether to be pleasant or to be cross and let him know what I think of him. I am inclined to be pleasant, but the girls advise me not be." We do not know what kind of letter Laura sent, but the following day she reported that she "wrote to Mr N today, cancelled the engagement. I gave the letter to Miss Black." On 18 May, she received a reply from Mr N, "answered it after school and sent it by Geo. Inglis ... I hope he will not reply."[22] Such early adolescent relationships rarely led to marriage, but the expectation of exclusivity when one was "going with" a young man set the stage for the potential shift to more formal courtship.

Perhaps diarists who, like Aggie Holder and Sadie Harper, had older sisters learned by example to deal with flirtation and infatuation with greater equanimity. Sadie Harper's diary strongly suggests that Sadie was smitten with Fred Henderson, a young railway employee who had become a favourite guest in the Harper home during a summer when he was stationed in Shediac. When Fred was posted to Moncton, the Harper young people wrote to him regularly, but he proved a poor correspondent. Sadie's bitter disappointment often spilled onto the pages of her diary. Her entry of 19 April 1895 was typical: "Fred H. hasn't written us for ages. He has been too mean for anything this winter, leaving off his old friends for new."[23] Although he rarely wrote, Fred did occasionally visit the Harpers, and on one such visit Sadie reported that he was "looking as nice and cute as ever and just as comical."[24] A few weeks later, longing to see him again, she confided her fears to her diary. Noting, "there he is in Moncton, so near and never comes over to see us or writes to us," she added, "I don't understand, except it must be true about him having a young lady." Yet although she gave no hint either that he singled her out for special attention during his infrequent visits to Shediac, or that she wished him to do so, she did not lose interest and was delighted to accept an invitation to accompany him to the opera when she was visiting her aunt in Moncton. She clearly saw Fred as someone who would fit well into her warm and affective family, "so jolly and just like one of us."[25] Nonetheless, even as she was confiding to her diary how very much she wished that Fred Henderson would write to her – "It's the same wish over and over again, but I can't help it. I would love to hear from him" – twenty-year-old Sadie Harper was encouraging the attentions of another young man.[26]

Certainly it is true that by the time most young women reached their late teens the prospect of marriage was much on their minds. Some were ambivalent, not at all anxious to give up a freedom they recognized would be constrained by marriage. Writing home in 1846, seventeen-year-old Mary Hill, having received news of a friend's recent marriage, commented that "it makes one feel old, to see all the playmates and companions of their childhood married. I am glad there is no news of Mary or Hannah Bixby's getting married. I should grow desperate on my return home and should wish to emigrate to a less precocious place where people do not instantly change from wild boys and girls, to sedate married persons, if they should. Is there no rumour of Achsah's getting married, so much the better.[27] I shall find some companions when I return. Hers will ever be a fresh and youthful spirit, fitted for single blessedness. The Rose will bloom on her cheek long after it has faded on those who have chosen a less carefree lot (there, is not that poetical)."[28]

Although young women themselves often grew anxious with the passing years, parents rarely encouraged early marriage.[29] Responding to her daughter's expressed concerns, Sarah Hill retorted tartly, "You must not fancy because some of your young friends are marrying at eighteen and nineteen, that you must leave school at eighteen." Telling

Mary that "if your improvement should answer our expectation, and you wish it I hope your father will allow you to remain another winter at school," Sarah sought to assuage her daughter's fears, informing her that "Mary Todd who is near two years older than you, is intending to go to Jamaica Plains in the Spring to school."[30] When eighteen-year-old Ann Eliza Rogers made her plans to marry a man nearly twenty years her senior, we cannot know whether either her parents or her fiancé had doubts, but for whatever reason, the marriage was registered not in the spring of 1855, as Ann Eliza had planned, but in October, by which time she was well into her third trimester of pregnancy.

At thirty, Sophy Bliss was old enough to know her own mind, yet her family and friends were, at best, ambivalent about her decision to wed William Carman, a fifty-five-year-old widower. In this case, a surviving letter from Sophy's mother, Sarah, written on the day before her daughter's marriage, provides a poignant glimpse of a family struggling to come to terms with Sophy's decision. Admitting that "*All I feel would fill sheets and a task I could not get through with very well, for you have been my support and my comforter so long that I hardly know how to resign you and give up my right to you my good excellent daughter,*" she went on to assure Sophy that "you have your mother's blessing." Speaking for Sophy's sisters, among others, Sarah reassured her daughter, "You must not expect your friends to *rejoice that they have to give you up* but you will have the warmest wishes for your welfare & happiness."[31] Indeed, no diarist's record suggests that parental pressure played any role in a daughter's decision to marry.

Nonetheless, as young women came of age, they began to seek more serious relationships, shifting from flirtation to courtship. Lillie Williamson's diary, which records the ups and downs of various family flirtations and courtships, including her own, illustrated this transition. In 1882, when the diary begins, her younger brother Fred was working as a machinist in Saint John and boarding with the Wightman family. Visiting the city that summer, Lillie observed that her brother had a new love interest, reporting on 4 August that "I was at Mr. Wightman's to dinner on Sunday and to tea on Monday, & I went to church twice Sunday with Fred Wightman ... Our Fred has grown pretty sweet on Carrie Wightman. I think she has pretty well taken the place of the girl with the 'passionless pale cold face' who gave him the cold shoulder up here." Lillie proved an astute observer, as her entry for 2 November demonstrated: "I got a letter from *Fred* saying that he was engaged to Carrie Wightman ... She is a lovely girl; a whole woman, perhaps not quite so exquisite and finished looking as his former love, but the soul is there." In Lillie's entry for 18 January, we learn the name of that "former love."

January 18, 1883. Things do turn out strangely sometimes. Maud Belyea and her Aunt and Uncle called down here on New Years day, evidently altogether on Fred's account, thinking he was home yet. It was just last New years day that she cut him the first time. I guess he thought then that it would be many a day before he would care for another, but strange to say, he met Carrie for the first time when he went down that time and although he did not take any fancy to her at first was engaged to her in six months from that time. I feel very sorry for poor Maud, but it was entirely her own fault. They gave us a pressing invitation down there when our boys came home. I think they were taken aback to see Carrie's picture & Fred's together in the album.

Joe and Sam arrived home last week. Sam on Monday, Joe Tuesday. Joe went away Monday to St. John and expects to go to Camden next Monday. He has bought out the jewelry and watch making part of the business from M & C & is going to set up for himself. It will cost $800. He has over $400 in the bank. He has grown to look like a regular Yankee since he has been living in the States and a very good looking one too. He made Ma a Xmas present of a lovely glass tea set, also a gold brooch, Kate a pair of cuff studs & me a dear little gold ring with three stones, and Sam a blue silk handkerchief.

I should not wonder if Joe gets engaged before he leaves the city too. It will be funny if the youngest and the oldest get engaged first, though Joe was kind of engaged once before, but it did not last long. Our hens are laying from 10 to 14 eggs a day.

Fred is getting $4.50 a week now and has to pay $3.00 for board. It is the highest he has got yet. He says he will be able to save $4.00 a week. I think there is a pretty good prospect for Carrie I hope so. I have missed Fred very much since he went away. The two Freds and Carrie talk of coming up some Saturday, perhaps next & stay over Sunday. They expect to drive.

Abrams & Kerr were not burned so badly as we heard at first.

Kate and I and the boys were down to <u>Mr. Sam Belyea's</u> to tea when Joe was up. Maud was over. She did not take to Joe as I thought she would.

Sunday, January 21. We looked yesterday evening for the two boys and Carrie, to drive up from the city, but they did not come, and it is just as well now for it has been raining hard so far since morning. We have had almost an unbroken succession of stormy Sundays since the Winter began, only one real fine one. I hope it will keep on now til it takes the snow all off the ice.

February 2. We had a regular overflow last Sunday. We had gone out to Meeting morning and afternoon and when we came home the second time we found the house full of young men. Our Fred and Fred and Avard Wightman, and Mr. Bane. They drove up from town a double sleigh. They were coming up Saturday evening but it stormed. We had a splendid time. In the evening we all went up to meeting, Fred Wightman went with me and Mr. Bane with Kate. There was an awful sight of staring done at us from all quarters. The house was pretty full. Fred W says the people here look just like a city congregation. They all went away again Monday morning waving hats, handkerchiefs & whips to us in the door. Our Fred has grown to be a splendid looking young man. It would be a tie to know which is the best looking he or Fred Wightman. If our Fred had the curly hair I think he would be the handsomest.

Tuesday, February 20. We have been having pretty gay times lately. A week ago last Saturday Sam drove me to town. I stayed til the next Wednesday and had a splendid time. I was out four times on Sunday. Fred Wightman went with me to church in the evening. I was at a party at Mr. Wightman's on Tuesday evening. They had recitations, readings, a dialogue, and singing, and games. They have such a party at the five houses belonging to their set. One every fortnight. Sam came down for me on Wednesday and Carrie came up with me. Saturday night about eleven the two Freds drove up. We were expecting them but had just given them up for that night and gone to bed when Carrie called out, there they are and we all got up and dressed and were down before they got in the house. We had a splendid time Sunday. There was Baptist meeting morning and evening, and we all went both times, we made quite a formidable crowd. Fred Wightman escorted me both times, and Carrie and Fred went together of course. They had to go down Sunday night, as our Fred was obliged to be at his work Monday morning. Mr. Bane has gone away to Toronto or he's left yesterday. Kate and I went for a skate the first of the season, but it was very poor skating. Father and Sam went to town today.

Following up on her comment that she expected her brother Joe to get engaged before he left Saint John, Lillie noted on 26 February: "I am pretty sure he got engaged to Miss Lawson before he left the city.

I saw her when I was down to town ... she is a very stylish looking little lady. I should think she and Joe would make a very cute looking couple." Confirming this assessment, she noted that Joe had sent them "two splendid photographs of himself and Miss Lawson. It is the best he has ever had taken, he looks just as if he would speak." Then, almost as an afterthought, or perhaps as an expression of her own hopes for the future, she added, "Fred Wightman gave me his photo when I was in town."

On 1 June, Lillie confided to her diary that her hopes had been realized: "Fred Wightman came up on the 24th and stayed till Monday. Last 24th of May was the first time he was ever here. I did not have much idea then that a year from that time we would be engaged. But it is even so. How much a year may bring forth; and about that time I was feeling as though I was getting to be an old maid, and that no one would ever take a fancy to me again.[32] I don't dare to write down here what I think of him for fear someone else might read it, but he is just my ideal man, even to being handsome, & I have always had a weakness for good looks." Hesitant in committing her own views to paper, Lillie took pleasure in reporting on 21 June that "the girls around here seem to be badly smitten with Fred Wightman even to Maud B. I am not the only one who thinks him handsome. It is the general opinion."

Like Lillie Williamson, Sadie Harper's interests also shifted from flirtation to courtship during the course of her diary. Frank Allen, the young schoolteacher whom Sadie would later marry, made his first appearance in her diary in August 1895. Soon Sadie was not only singing with him in the choir, but taking German lessons from him as well. Gradually, Mr Allen was incorporated into the Harper household's broad circle, and in early January 1896, Sadie reported, "About five o'clock Mr Allen came up then Nell, Blois, Mr Allen and myself practised some quartettes for Lodge. He stayed to tea ... Nell went to prayer meeting with Mama and Blois. Mr Allen and I went to Lodge where a pleasant evening was spent."[33] By March, Sadie was participating in some mild flirtation, and her diary entries suggest that Mr Allen's interest was piqued.[34] On 2 April, she reported that "Mr Allen came in on his way down from Ted's where he had been to tea, and he spent the rest of the evening here. He hadn't intended staying as he just called to leave a book for me from Ted. But he got talking and talking, and time slipped by so quickly." On 19 April, "after church Mr Allen came up again for a wonder. I don't know what struck him I'm sure. He got talking again about college life and it was after eleven when he went." Yet, while

Sadie enjoyed Mr Allen's company, she gave no hint that he enjoyed any special place in her affections. When the school semester ended, Mr Allen disappeared not only from Shediac, but also from Sadie's diary. And when he reappeared, at choir practice, on 15 August, her reference to him was almost offhand: "Mr Allen is back and as bashful as ever, but it's good to have a tenor again." Even as Mr Allen embarked upon a formal courtship that becomes ever clearer to the reader of her diary, Sadie, seemingly, did not immediately recognize his intent. Thus, noting on 15 November that "Mr Allen" had asked her "to go to hear Albani with him in Moncton," she confided only, "My but I was glad as I didn't want to take my own money but rather than not hear her I would do so. It is very kind of him, I think."[35]

Because her diary for 1897 is not extant, we cannot know at what stage Sadie became as serious about the courtship as Mr Allen. But perhaps that evening was a turning point, for on 25 November, she reported, "Mr Allen and I had splendid seats ... and oh, but I'll never forget that concert. Albani was something to dream about. She was just perfection ... I never imagined anything like it, and tho' I couldn't understand the Italian ... to hear her tone was enough ... It was grand GRAND ... That night I shall never forget, and I surely felt grateful to Mr Allen for giving me such a treat." Whatever the timing, by 1898, her heart was won and Mr Allen had become Frank. Well beyond schoolgirl crushes, at the "pretty ancient" age of twenty-three, Sadie, reporting private walks and private talks, reveals not only her feelings but also the tension between the desire for privacy and the desire to maintain a certain level of Victorian propriety.

Fri. Feb. 4, 1898. Nice and fine again. I sewed for most of the day. We had choir practice for a short time before tea. After tea since it had got beautiful and mild and was simply a perfect moonlight night I went and got Lena to come for a snowshoe tramp. So we had a very enjoyable one, just downtown over the drifts. After we both got home again, I practised some solos for a while. Then Blois came in from a hockey match and brot Frank in with him. So Nell and Duff played Crokino against the Professor and me and we had a lot of fun over it. Before he left that evening we had one of our pleasant sweet little confidential talks just by ourselves. He is such a dear good fellow.

Sun. Feb. 6. Sunday was a lovely day and quite mild. Mr Matthews did not have service this morning as he did not feel well enough for two services, so thot he would take the evening one. In the afternoon we went to S.S. as usual and then had choir practice and after that Frank and I went down the track for a walk and as it was such a beautiful afternoon we enjoyed our walk so much and when we got home he came in to tea. It was his 24th birthday so he is not quite a year older than I am. Out to service in the evening and after we came home we sat and talked in the parlour for a while, while Ted and Herb and the rest of them in the house here amused themselves in the other room. Of course they teased us well for going off by ourselves but Ted's been there before often and I don't care what any of them say.

Wed. Feb. 9. Wednesday was quite fine, tho it looked threatening. Ted called for me this afternoon and we went out together. She invested in some chocolates and off we went and walked away up to call on the MacDougalls. We had a splendid walk and were pretty tired when we got home. After tea Percy came up to play Whist with May and Bea.[36] I went down to prayer meeting. Afterwards I saw Laura McFadgen for a few mins and she invited Ted and me for tea on Friday. Frank walked up with me and he, too, treated me to chocolates. When we got home we found that Percy hadn't stayed for Whist but he and Bea and Blois and Lena had walked over to spend the evening at Pully's,[37] so Frank came in and we had fun over Crokino and then he and I had one of our confidential little talks before Blois and Bea came home. My but he is such a dear good fellow.

Thurs. Feb. 10. Thursday was fine again. Ted sent down for me to go up to dinner so I got leave of absence and went and the afternoon passed so quickly that it was half past four before I knew it. Then Ted came down with me to tea, and as it was my night home from the rink, all of the others went. Mrs Deacon brot her work down and we had a nice cosy pleasant evening of it and then when Nell came in from Lodge, Frank came and Ted and Nell played Crokino against Frank and me and we had such fun over it and played until eleven.

Fri. Feb. 11. Friday was first beautiful and fine and the storm that seemed pending never came so far. I was busy at one thing or another until it was time to go over to Laura's, so then I went up to call for Ted and Herb had sent up word he would drive us over, so he soon came along and off we went. Ted did the driving and just for me she took in every slough and pitch and dip she came to. My but we did some laughing among ourselves and landed safely after it all and had a very nice time indeed. Pully was there, too, then Herb's team took us home again. The Grammar School *team Duff is on played against one of the Town teams of small boys this evening and the Grammar School won. I guess the boys played very well and Frank said he felt proud of them. After the game he gave them all an oyster supper, and one can imagine how glad he made their hearts and he said it did him good to see how much they all enjoyed themselves.*

Sun. Feb. 13. Sunday was lovely and fine again and the walking not too bad at all. So as Mr Matthews was not having service again in the morning, Nell and I went down and heard Mr Smith preach. Frank walked up home with me afterwards and he said he was told to bring one of us back to dinner with him and as I had been up there just lately to dinner, Nell went with him this time. So we got Mr Deacon to stay with us for dinner as he had been in all morning talking to Papa. In the afternoon out to S.S. as usual and then choir practice, and afterwards Frank and I went for a lovely walk again down the track. In the evening out to church and after church as the evening was so perfect we went for a walk and when we came home we finished our talk in the parlour. As long as Mama doesn't mind, it doesn't matter a little bit to me what the other girls say.

While recognizing some intriguing, and perhaps surprising, continuities over time, the tensions both explicit and implicit in various diaries imply that shifts in attitudes and mores were subtle and required the encouragement and support of parents. But whether diarists were, like Mary Hill, reluctant to relinquish their freedom or, like Lillie Williamson, anxious to marry, young women contemplating a life of "single blessedness" had fewer career options open to them than did young men. At the same time, while the goal of courtship for both parties was marriage, the decision to wed often meant a much more significant transition for young women than for their male counterparts. For the teachers among them, it almost always meant giving up the autonomy an independent income could afford, as very few married women were employed outside the home. Yet, first betrothal, and then marriage, also brought a new status, which implied a different kind of autonomy, a transition so tellingly characterized by Mary Hill as "instantly" changing "wild boys and girls" into "sedate married persons."[38] By the end of the century, the custom of referring to one's betrothed by the formal titles of "Mr" and "Miss," which had, in the past, represented only the manifestation of this transition, was, as Lillie Williamson's and Sadie Harper's diaries suggest, going out of fashion.[39] Preparations for marriage further reflected the transition, as quilts and carpets were carefully sewn and silver and linens just as carefully chosen, in readiness for the day when the young couple would "go to housekeeping." No less important were the preparation and selection of a trousseau, a wardrobe befitting the mistress of a household. Whether or not girls were raised to become "a perfect farmer's wife,"[40] whether their destiny was to be married by eighteen or thirty-three or perhaps not at all, in this era, when companionate marriage was perceived as the ideal conjugal relationship, young women generally looked forward to the prospect of embarking upon a lifelong partnership. In the next chapter, we will turn to a consideration of family formation, family evolution, and the nature of family life.

Chapter 6

The World of the Family

The "world of the family" conjures up a picture of parents and children, a useful point of departure since, as successive censuses demonstrate, the majority of nineteenth-century New Brunswick households were comprised nuclear families. Censuses also offer evidence of the way households were configured and reconfigured during the life course of individuals and families, however, obliging us to recognize the limitations of the census in developing an understanding of the nature of family life. Over the course of their lives, individuals might experience life in a nuclear family, a single-parent family, a blended family, or an extended family household. And many individuals lived, for a time, apart from their families, sometimes at school, sometimes as a boarder or servant on the edge of someone else's family, or, more rarely, sometimes as an independent householder. But few indeed were alone in the world.

The diversity of women's experience of family life is reflected in the spectrum of living arrangements among our twenty-eight diarists at the time they began their diaries. Thirteen of the twenty-eight lived in a family that included their father as well as their mother, one lived with a widowed mother and stepfather, three lived with a widowed mother, one with a widowed father, five were married, two were widowed, and three were living independently of their families. In four cases, members of their extended family also lived in the household. Seven households included servants and six included boarders who were not family members. Two of those boarders were among our diarists. The diversity becomes even greater if the analysis is extended to consider how diarists' living arrangements changed during the course of their diary keeping: one lost her mother, five left home to attend school, while two more left home to teach school. Four returned home after a time at school, while three returned home after teaching school for a term. Five married, one separated from her husband, and three were widowed. The analysis undertaken in this chapter, then, examines family life from a variety of vantage points, reflecting the diversity of family relationships and suggesting how those relationships changed over time.

Historically, in New Brunswick, as in Canada as a whole, more than 85 per cent of women married, and a large majority of those women had children. Women's undoubtedly central influence in the domestic sphere, which was promoted in the prescriptive literature of the day, must also be viewed against the backdrop of the institution of the patriarchal family, and this, in turn, must be juxtaposed with what we can know of women's lived experience. Marriage really began when the couple "went to housekeeping," often some days or even weeks after the ceremony. Only then could they begin to define the nature of their conjugal relationship. The ideal promoted in both advice literature and popular novels of the day was a companionate marriage, characterized by a kind of interdependence between husband and wife.[1] The extent to which couples achieved such a balance, dependent as it was on their individual personalities and expectations, as well as on their particular situation, proves difficult to gauge from diaries alone, but the glimpses they offer can suggest a good deal about the nature of the conjugal relationship.

Establishing and maintaining a companionate marital relationship in the face of frequent and lengthy separations was a challenge faced by many New Brunswick couples, but few had the extra obstacle of an eighteen-year age gap. When the chemical works that brought him to Hopewell did not develop as the entrepreneurs who established them had envisioned, John Gallacher sought opportunities elsewhere. In January 1856, when he and Ann Eliza Rogers had been married for less than a year and their first child was less than two months old, he returned to the United States in search of work and his wife returned to her parents' home. Ann Eliza's diary during this period reflects the loneliness many couples felt when they were apart. On 3 February, she lamented, "How I wish he was here. He has been gone one week, it seems a month, the time goes so slow." Yet she was not unrealistic in her expectations, commenting on 17 February, "How I should like to see him, but I expect he will be gone all winter." Her poignant entry the following day indicated how lonely a young wife could feel, even in the bosom of her natal family: "Snowing very fast about 18 inches has fallen. It is night. I am alone. Baby is sleeping. She grows very fast. 'Tis now I feel as if alone. I miss my husband's company very much. If he was here I should feel very happy. He is all & all to me." When renewed hopes for the chemical works brought John's return in early April, the couple again established their own household and, eventually, purchased a house. But the chemical works were not, after all, destined for success.

On 21 September 1858, Ann Eliza reported that John had been "sent for to go to Philadelphia to a chemical works. I am very sorry to have him go away again, but he can do much better there." They decided to rent their house and, once again, Ann Eliza returned to her parents' home. There, on 26 September, the couple's second daughter, Ella Frances, was born. By November, John was urging Ann Eliza to join him in Philadelphia, yet she demurred, concluding on 11 November that "it is too late to take the baby," even as she admitted, "I am very lonely without him. It will be a long winter for us both." Nor could she be persuaded to change her decision, recording on 14 December, "I got a letter from John. He is well but very lonely but not more so than I am. I spend many many lonely hours. No one knows how long and lonely the hours are when our loved ones are away but they that have had the trial and he poor dear away among strangers. It seems very long to think we shall not see each other until Spring. Oh solitude where are thy charms." The wait would be even longer than Ann Eliza had anticipated. Not until the end of September 1859 did John return to Hopewell, meeting his second daughter for the first time two days after her first birthday.

Finding little work in Hopewell, in January 1860, John left again, this time heading to Boston. In June, he sent for his wife and daughters, and this time Ann Eliza agreed to go. Her maternal grandmother, along with a number of her aunts and uncles, lived in Boston, and her mother accompanied her on the journey. But, with no indication that she had consulted John, Ann Eliza noted that she had decided to take only four-year-old Isabelle, leaving Ella, who was not yet two, in the care of her father and sisters. In Boston, she again settled into family life, noting with satisfaction on New Year's Day, 1861, "My husband & I have been seperated part of the last year but we are together now and in very comfortable circumstances." Yet her satisfaction was tempered: "But we are still a broken family, our second girl is in New Brunswick with father & mother." Nor were they likely to send for Ella soon, for

Ann Eliza was pregnant again. In February, her sister Mary Susan joined them, and on 1 June, Ann Eliza reported, "I have not written any for a month on account of being sick. We have an addition to our family of a son born May 8th, he is a fine boy quite good most of the time." Despite an extraordinarily disrupted family life, Ann Eliza Rogers and John Gallacher achieved a marriage in which a much younger wife could mature and thrive, making important family decisions: a companionate marriage.

Not all women were so fortunate in their marital relationships. Annie T. Johnston's decision to marry Richard Claude Waltham, a young music teacher who had recently immigrated to New Brunswick, not only changed the dynamic in a household that included Annie's daughter and two sisters, but also introduced an unexpected element of fear when Waltham turned out to be physically abusive.[2] Although Annie's family relationships were always somewhat fraught – partly because she controlled the finances for her sisters' inheritance as well as her own – her second marriage, in January 1872, threw her life into unprecedented turmoil. Her new husband not only proved demanding and quarrelsome but was also an alcoholic. The downward spiral of the marital relationship was well underway before the year was out. On 15 December, she had "an awful day – quarreling and scolding all day." The following day she reported, "A miserable day – scolding and storming. Mr Waltham has a toothache and seems to think we all ought to suffer the torments of Hell – besides working like dogs – to add to all in the evening he fell at the back door and hurt himself and we were all consigned to perdition in consequence – I slept in the back bed room with Annie." On 28 December, it was "just as cold and wretched as possible. A miserable week indeed ... Mr Waltham complaining of being sick seems to think no one else has any feeling or deserves any consideration – God help such an unreasonable being! God knows how I have tried to please him – how hard I have worked – and how I have been abused in return!" The pattern established, ensuing years brought more of the same. Nor did things improve following the birth of their baby in 1875: on 26 January 1876, she reported, "A most awful quarrel at night – baby's crib broken – God help such a lunatic and tyrant."

Robert Waltham's status as family patriarch, achieved through his marriage to Annie Johnston, further allowed him to exercise a legal authority which, under other circumstances, she would have welcomed, for she was tired of bearing the burden of managing the various investments of her extended family. Waltham, however, had neither financial experience nor business acumen, and, being some years younger than Annie, was perhaps too proud to seek her advice about the family's business affairs, which she had successfully managed for over a decade. With the family's economic status as well as her own physical well-being at risk, Annie Waltham was left with few avenues of escape from a disastrous marriage. Yet while the conjugal relationship, which set the pattern for family relationships, vested legal authority in the husband, the Waltham marriage proved the exception and, for the most part, the patriarchal family did not prove a repressive institution for our diarists, either as wives or as daughters.[3] Indeed, six of the eight New Brunswick women diarists who kept diaries during the course of their marriage could be said to have achieved companionate marriage relationships.

In considering the role of the family in shaping women's worlds in nineteenth-century America, scholars have pointed to the importance of the mother-daughter relationship.[4] Because the prescriptive literature of the period placed the burden of responsibility for determining a child's nature squarely on the shoulders of the mother, the mother-daughter relationship remains a significant theme for those seeking to understand nineteenth-century women's experience.[5] Sophy Carman, raised from the age of seven in a single-parent family, retained a strong bond to her widowed mother, Sarah Wetmore Bliss, visiting her several times a week, bringing her tempting delicacies such as oysters when she was sick, and otherwise undertaking some of the responsibility for her care. Sarah and her youngest daughter, Jean, lived in her son George's household, but in April 1872, when George and his family were preparing to move, Sarah temporarily joined Sophy's household, staying until mid-June, when her room in the new house was finally ready. Although George's new house was close to Sophy and William's home, this did not preclude extended visits, and November found Sarah and Jean staying with Sophy. They returned to George's on 10 January 1873, "after a visit of two months." All this can be gleaned from Sophy's diary. However, although diaries provide a window on family life, the view through that window cannot capture what is going on just outside the frame. The limits thereby imposed tantalize the reader, inviting speculation, cloaked in a consideration of both what the documents reveal and what they omit. Sophy Carman had a very close relationship with her mother and younger sister, yet she rarely mentions her brother George or his wife in her diary, implying not only that Sarah and Jean likely had quite private accommodation in their home, but also that Sophy's relationship with her brother and sister-in-law was not particularly close.[6]

Although mother-daughter relationships, as revealed in diaries, were typically close, they were rarely entirely free of tension.[7] In her diary, Mary Wolhaupter both recorded and lamented her sometimes fraught relationship with her mother, Emily. Returning home after two months away teaching and boarding in a nearby community, Mary, finding it difficult to settle into the routine of family life, often regretted her own "fractiousness." On 27 March 1869, she confided, "I acted very unwisely a while this afternoon, that is, I was not as pleasant with Ma and Carrie as I ought to have been. I have hurt myself a great deal pretending to be very much out of humour when I was not. I do hope I may in the future have grace to keep me from such folly." Mary sympathized with her mother, and wanted to please her, noting in one entry, "Ma is a very smart woman of her age and one who has gone through a great deal of hardship in her time, yes even since I can remember. I hope I may ever be a very good girl towards her. I have been rather uncomfortable sometimes because I was not the kind amiable girl I should be, but I never could bear any praise. This morning Ma went to praise me and I did not feel flattered at all."[8]

As her daughter's diary reveals, that year was a difficult one for Emily Wolhaupter. By mid-summer, the health of her aging parents seemed increasingly precarious. Meanwhile, her daughter Haddie was several months into an increasingly difficult pregnancy. Then, in August, Emily received a letter from her eldest child, Charles, then teaching in Maine, informing her that things were not going well and he was sending his pregnant wife, Maggie, and daughter Gertrude home to New Brunswick. Mary, recently returned from an extended sojourn sewing for relatives in Houlton, Maine, observed, "Ma feels badly about Charles. I do not wonder that she does for he is near and dear to her. A mother's love never grows cold and my mother seems to have very strong love and attachment for her children."[9] Yet Mary's empathy did not extend to patience when Emily, who must have been pushed to the very limits of her endurance, appeared distracted. The day after her return home, she reported, "I felt very sorry at dinner time for I hurt Ma's feelings a good deal. She took up a dish that was dirty and was wiping it on the tablecloth and I took it from her and washed it saying, 'do let me have it, that is no way to clean it.' I hope I may be a great deal more careful of peoples feelings especially my mother's."

Perhaps because she had not seen Haddie for some time, Mary did not realize the seriousness of her sister's condition, and Emily's increasing concern aroused jealousy rather than sympathy in her older daughter. A few days after Mary's return home, on a morning when Haddie's husband, George Nye, was busy haying, Emily and Carrie, her youngest daughter, went to see Haddie. Mary, who had been "real sick" that morning, felt recovered enough to undertake some spinning in the afternoon. But when both Carrie and her mother stayed at Haddie's all day, she began to feel resentful: "I spun late and felt very tired and provoked at [Carrie] for staying so late but come to find out Ma told her to stay untill Geo. got back." Although the following day passed pleasantly enough, with Mary and Carrie spinning and picking raspberries together, while their mother prepared first tea and then supper, Mary perhaps misread her mother's mood when she concluded that "I scolded some and so did Ma so I guess there was no harm done," for the next day she reported, "Ma gave me quite a sitting down about not going to see Haddie before, but it was unnecessary for me to go sooner and it appears that all the care or thought Ma has is for Haddie. Everything that is spoken of must be for H. no matter what it is."[10] The mother-daughter relationship between Emily and Mary Wolhaupter as portrayed in Mary's diary was undoubtedly fraught, but theirs was, nonetheless, a very close bond.

When they exist, letters can complement diaries in offering insight into the nature and variety of family relationships.[11] Even more than diaries, correspondence provides insight into the relationships between mothers and their daughters, particularly when it is possible to follow the interaction over a series of letters. In the extant correspondence between our New Brunswick diarists and their mothers, some common and predictable patterns emerge. Mothers regularly offered advice to their daughters, especially when those daughters were quite young. As daughters matured, a greater sense of interdependence developed. This pattern is especially obvious in the Trueman correspondence.[12] Correspondence collections are not always available, however, and diaries, especially those used as confidantes, remain an indispensable source for those who would understand the evolution of the mother-daughter relationship in all its variety, for they provide our only insight into the relationship between mothers and daughters who lived together, or whose contact with one another was so frequent that there was no need for an exchange of letters. In the case of Annie and Laura Trueman, their diaries serve to confirm the warm and affective relationship with their mother that is revealed in their correspondence. But as the Trueman correspondence – as well as Sophy Carman's and Mary Wolhaupter's diaries – aptly demonstrate, for women, the world of the family extended not only beyond the mother-daughter relationship but also beyond the confines of the household.

Nor was the private sphere of the family dominated by women. The seven mothers among our diarists were as often the mothers of sons as of daughters. For them, husbands and sons were also central to family life. Parenting was a cooperative project and the nature and character of the relationships between parents and their children were very much influenced by the nature and character of the relationship between a wife and her husband. Diarists Annie and Laura Trueman, along with their younger brother Albert, thrived intellectually in a household where their views, like those of their mother, Rebecca, were respected by a gentle and supportive husband and father. His time taken up with the business of the family farm, Thompson Trueman often chose to remain at home, while the toing and froing of his wife and children swirled on around him. In contrast, Sarah Upton Hill's husband George, a member of the provincial legislature, was regularly absent from home for long periods during the legislative sessions. Nonetheless, his daughter, diarist Mary Whitney Hill, and her eight siblings developed a warm and loving relationship with both parents. For the Truemans and the Hills, marital relationships built on interdependence and mutual respect nurtured close family relationships.[13]

The private world of the large and lively Hill family is revealed first in letters between Sarah and George and later in correspondence between the couple and their teenaged children. During the early years, when the children were small, we see the family largely through Sarah's eyes, as she reported their progress to her politician husband in Fredericton. In the winter of 1836–7, the couple had five children, the eldest not yet ten and the youngest a babe in arms. Coping on her own, Sarah had little time for writing, but although she bore by far the greater burden of childcare, her letters demonstrate that she viewed parenting as a partnership. In response to George's query about their family's health, and his teasing question – "Is the little *un-named* well and troublesome as ever?"[14] – Sarah replied with some asperity: "Augusta, or the 'little unnamed,' as you *will* call her, is unwell, the first real sickness that she has had. She was taken with vomiting on Tuesday, has been feverish and restless these two nights, is not very cross through the day if I hold her in my arms and rock her, but lays with her eyes shut, and does not wish to be disturbed." Then, her irritation dissipating, she reassured her husband that "I do not feel uneasy about her, as her illness is doubtless occasioned by her cutting teeth." Continuing her letter the following day, Sarah, noting that one of Augusta's teeth was now cut through, admitted that "I feel more anxiety about the children when you are gone, and it appears lonely not to have you coming in, and pitying poor baby." The children, too, missed George, with nine-year-old Upton "teasing" his mother to help him write a letter to his father "by telling him what he should write about," seven-year-old Mary begging Sarah to read her what she had written, and four-year-old George urging her to "tell Pa that he was a good boy." Even Isa (Hesediah), who was not yet three, "tells the baby very often, since she has been sick, that Pa will come and buy her some honey, and some medicine to make her well." But Sarah's own view of marriage and parenting as a partnership comes through most clearly in her closing comment: "Surrounded by the children, and my time at present devoted to them, I need not, while writing to their father, I think, make an excuse for speaking chiefly of them."[15]

Like many fathers of his generation, George Hill took his parenting responsibilities seriously, and, over time, he and his wife developed different, yet complementary parenting styles. Their individual styles were effectively captured in the joint letters sent to their children when the latter were away at school. George's contribution was generally perfunctory, limited mainly to instructions and admonitions. Sarah leavened her advice with home news, serving to soften the tone. In one such letter, written in 1846, after telling his daughter Mary that her younger cousin, who was attending the same school, would be returning home for the summer vacation, George informed her, "We intend to keep you there until next Spring," and added that "we suppose you have no particular desire to come home ... during the next vacation." Urging her on the one hand to "relax from close application and take plenty of exercise" during the vacation period, he admonished her as well to "let general reading alone, and apply yourself to the Studies in hand, and not dissipate the time in desultory reading which ought to be applied in acquiring the elements of knowledge." Sarah, just as anxious as her husband to keep her daughter at school for another year, took a more empathetic approach: "I hope, dear Mary, that you will not be disappointed at the prospect of not returning home, till spring. Perhaps you may have a visit from your uncle Upton in July, but he is undecided yet."[16] With their complementary parenting styles, Sarah Upton and George Hill encouraged their children to become both independent thinkers and independent actors.

Sophy Carman's diary records that her husband William shared some of the responsibility for childcare when their children were small. On Easter Sunday, 31 March 1872, a day "Cold as Christmas," she was

> up at 6, had a quiet time to read and get ready for early service. W[illiam] & I went to early celebration, 70 present, walked with Fishers ... Had a cheerful breakfast, children enjoyed their eggs. Mrs Lee sent them coloured ones. I went up and stayed with Mother while Jean went to 11 o'clock. W & Bliss went to 11, Murray not out. The day turned dull and cold, children did lessons as usual and I read to them. Bliss and M[urray] went for a walk with their father, I had a quiet time at home. Mae went out to tea, we had tea at 5. I went to evening service. W stayed home with the children, Jean and I sat together, low down. Bishop gave a powerful sermon, singing good, cathedral full. B[isho]p went to see Mother.

When summer came, Sophy, William, ten-year-old Bliss, and eight-year-old Murray set off for a holiday near Bay Shore, on the Fundy coast. In this case, William did not prove of much help in keeping track of either the children or the luggage, and Sophy no doubt regretted their decision to set out for their holiday on Dominion Day. That morning, she was "up at 5, left for St John in afternoon train. Great crowd, hot and dirty. Missed Murray in hoard, arrived in rain, lost chair, things got wet, trunk did not come, bags went astray." At the shore, she was left in charge, with William joining the family at weekends. The following day, "W[illiam] went to St John to stay. I took a book and went on rocks with Murray. Lovely evening, Clara took a bath. B[liss] in boat." The days settled into a pleasant routine. On 3 July, she "wrote to Mother and Jean. Murray went in bathing. H Boyd called. [I] miss W so much." Despite missing her husband, she reported the next day that she was "enjoying 'Retreat,' spent morning indoors, went on rocks with Murray, took my book 'Daily Readings' and read ... Found it cool, had strawberries for tea. Commenced reading 'Hannah.'" On 5 July, "Bliss went fishing with Charlie & the chief Engineer." Sophy "went to service at St George's" where she met up with William. They called on his adult daughter Annie on their way back to Bay Shore. The next day, a Saturday, brought a round of visits, and ended with leisurely pursuits: "After tea had a stroll on railroad, lovely evening. W & I went for a pail of tide water. Letter from Mother and Jean, all well at home."

Adolescence and young adulthood brought the negotiation of a new relationship between parents and their children. Sophy Carman's diaries and letters written in the early 1880s offer readers a glimpse of the nature of that process. After the completion of his bachelor's degree at the University of New Brunswick in 1881, Bliss Carman and his parents followed the advice of his teacher and mentor, George Parkin, who urged that he be sent to England to continue his education at Oxford. Arriving in England in 1882, twenty-one-year-old Bliss failed to gain entry to Oxford; instead, he enrolled at the University of Edinburgh, but soon became homesick. Sophy, suffering from recurring bouts of eczema that kept her virtually housebound,[17] worried about her son, privately recording the depth of her distress in her diary. On New Year's Eve 1882, "Murray and Minnie went to mid-night service. I did not go to bed until after 12. Prayed the old year out (much for my boy. He is all my thoughts at these times – & at all times)." On 7 January, "Mr Parkin came to talk over Bliss's future plans and we think he had better not come home till August." Mr Parkin was in again on 15 January, a day when Sophy had a "long letter from B, 1 to his grandmother and card – his letter makes me sad, fear he is pining for home." And Sophy, for her part, was longing to see him. On 21 January, a cold and stormy day, she reported, "Feel very dull and wanting my boy. Suffering with my old skin trouble – no comfort in anything – sat in my boy's room and cried." As her affliction prevented her from getting out, on 5 March, "Mr A came at 11:30, administered H[oly] C[ommunion] to J, M & self in B's room. Beautiful & peaceful, felt very happy & as if my sins are really forgiven. 1 year today since I last heard a sermon in the Cathe'l ... in bad health – a cross laid upon me." Sophy had other reasons to think about crosses laid upon her that day. Innuendos aimed at William had caused the legislative assembly to consider the propriety of one man being both clerk of the pleas and clerk in equity, positions William Carman had held for thirty-one years. While staunchly supporting her aging husband, Sophy accepted the decision of the legislature with stoicism: "C Allen came to tell W he must give up his Office – hard to bear – but we must do it – & be thankful too." And, despite their somewhat straitened circumstances, the couple remained determined to continue funding Bliss's sojourn in Britain. So life went on: 15 March was spent "writing to B. Em in, got me some cards, had talk in my room. Jule[18] in after tea. Sent note to Jean. 6 months today since I saw my bonny Boy."

At nineteen, Muriel – no longer Murray – was also becoming more independent, attending events with friends rather than with her parents, choosing to remain in Fredericton when her parents made their annual summer pilgrimage to Bay Shore, and travelling on her own to visit relatives and friends within the province and beyond. Her mother's concern about Bliss during his long sojourn in Britain apparently occasioned comment from Muriel, for when she was away in June, Sophy noted in a letter that "I would like to see my own bright cheery Muriel again – Mother has been much worried about her little girl this spring, more so than said little girl dreams of – am not so full of 'the boy' as to forget the girl – 'see'?" But the correspondence between mother and daughter also makes clear their great affection for one another with Sophy regularly using pet salutations, like "Muriel mine," "Sweet Muriel," or "Puss." And Sophy was as open and amusing in letters to her daughter as Muriel was in her letters to her mother, reporting in one letter, "Dadsy & I went for a little gad. The Bishop came to see us on Monday after din. I came down with my hat on, so he wld not stay long, we walked together as far as Cameron's Corner."[19]

Situating the relationship between mothers and their adult daughters within the broader context of family life suggests the nuances and complexities of that relationship. Certainly it would seem that the tensions in the relationship between Emily Wolhaupter and her daughter Mary may have had as much to do with looming family crises as with generational differences. In August 1869, Emily, busy enough in her own household – which, besides herself and her husband, included two adult daughters and two adult sons – spent part of each day also seeing to the needs of the household of her pregnant daughter Haddie and son-in-law George. By 19 August, this task had become almost overwhelming and Emily was becoming increasingly impatient. As her daughter Mary reported in her diary, "Ma felt very much vexed at noon today about the inconvenience about the house and scolded considerable but the men all thought she was to blame and Benjamin said some rash things and so did Ma, that Benjamin thought rather hard. Well I suppose all familys have some jars but I think people might get along in a little more quietude if they were of the mind to try a little harder." But the family tensions that boiled to the surface that day in August involved rather more than any mere "inconvenience about the house," threatening, the following morning, to tear the family asunder. According to Mary, "Benjamin talked of leaving this morning but we all persuaded him to stay. He seemed to have a very restless night last night. I felt worried about him in fact we all did. He told us this morning that he intended to marry Phebe if anyone. Poor Sam seemed to feel very badly about him. He wept like a child so we all did. We had a very sorrowful time for a while but we felt better after a while." It seems doubtful, however, that Emily Wolhaupter and her husband Hanford felt very much "better," for the next day, as expected, their eldest son Charles's pregnant wife Maggie and two-year-old daughter "arrived in Monticello ... in the stage." Commenting, "I do not know what is to become of the poor creatures but I suppose God will provide," Mary concluded that Charles "must be very down hearted." As Emily and Hanford no doubt realized, it would be Charles's and Maggie's parents who would be called upon to provide. On 22 August, Mary reported that "Pa went over after Maggie after dinner and she came over with him. Little Gertrude seems to be a poor frail little creature but Maggie looks well." Thus, while we cannot know the precise nature of the "rash things" that Emily and her youngest son had said to one another in their argument four days earlier, the evidence might lead us to speculate that her words may have been sparked by the fear that, should twenty-one-year-old Benjamin marry, her own responsibilities would increase rather than decrease. Perhaps Emily was worried about the possibility of having yet another pregnant young woman to care for. Yet despite the difficulties occasioned when young adult children, and sometimes their families, returned to the nest, they were rarely turned away.

As Mary Wolhaupter had recognized, no matter the age of the child, "a mother's love never grows cold." For parents, large families were more often than not sources of comfort and satisfaction, and nineteenth-century mothers recorded in their diaries how much they missed their children once they had left home. Such entries were especially common during the holiday season. To the modern reader, Janet MacDonald's 1864 diary reveals a woman embedded within a large and expansive family. Janet and Alexander MacDonald's son James, his wife Sally, and their five youngsters lived with them on the home farm. Yet, as Janet's diary entries demonstrate, today's so-called empty-nest syndrome must be redefined in light of nineteenth-century perceptions. On 24 December, she noted wistfully, "This is Christmas Eve but there is a good many vacant seats. It don't seem like old times, nothing is as it used to be with me, I have changed and all is changed in the world, a great deal not for the better. We are alone tonight, very dull times." And on the following day she reported, "A dull Christmas. No one here. Donald and Mary[20] took dinner with us. Only two now to take dinner with us, there used to be seven children. All scattered about in different places [now].[21] My heart is sad today."[22]

Diarists also missed their siblings when they were apart from them for extended periods. All but two diarists had at least one sister, and most recognized the importance of their sisters in their lives.[23] Annie Trueman was the most explicit: "O! dear Laura I am just longing to have a good talk with you. There is nothing special you know, or nothing to worry me, but I should so dearly love to have just the talk that one can have with a sister, & with a sister only."[24] Twenty-seven of the twenty-eight diarists had at least one brother, and though few professed the same intimacy they shared with their sisters, they did miss their brothers when they were apart, particularly when they were close in age. For instance, although her older sister Kate was still at home, Lillie Williamson found life lonely indeed when her younger brother Fred went to Saint John to find work.

Siblings as well as parents eagerly awaited the arrival of family members returning after a long absence. When Lottie Reid's older sister Orpah went sailing with her sea-captain husband, Alden West, she took her baby daughter Jo (Josephine) with her. By the time they returned, in February 1879, Jo was a year and a half, and Lottie recorded several family celebrations.

Wednesday, February 26, 1879 – Not very pleasant, rained some towards night. Orpah and Alden and little Jo arrived home tonight about four o'clock. We were very very glad to see them back again. Jo has grown to be a great big girl, she would not have anything to say to any of us at first but seemed to get acquainted after a while.

Thursday, February 27 – Quite dull and stormy. Alden and Orpah went down to Mrs West's to dinner and staid all night. I think that is all I have to say, will leave the rest for another day. So no more this time, goodnight.

Friday, February 28 – Very pleasant. This has been a kind of bustling. We had a goose cooked and Mary, Willie and family, Annie, Alden, Orpah and little Jo helped us eat it. We were glad to have them all here. Jo and Wat went to the Xenium[25] tonight and I guess they are going to stay all night.

Saturday, March 1 – A splendid day. We are having very quiet times here tonight. Ma and Pa, Orpah and Alden, Willie's folk and I don't know how many more are down to Mrs. Downie's visiting, expect they will have a fine time. I was down skating a while this afternoon, made out some better than I did the last time I tried it. The ice is grand.

Sunday, March 2 – Dull in the morning but cleared off very pleasant in afternoon. Wat and I, also Alden and Orpah were over to Hopewell to baptism this afternoon. Mr Chipman held forth, assisted by Mr Keith from Sussex. There were eight baptized. We did not stop to the evening meeting. Mr Blackaddor baptized five today also, Edith Coonan being one of the number.

Monday, March 3 – Very pleasant. We were all up very early this morning, as Alden left for St. John, and we were up to see him off. Ernest [?] left also, he is going with Alden this trip. Mrs Watson was in to see us a while, also Elisha R and Albert Smith. There is quite a crowd on the marsh skating tonight. It is so fine I would like to go too as I and some few others had an invitation, but guess I can't this time.

The world of the family extended like a web, encompassing relatives who lived not only within the near neighbourhood but also many miles away. Family relationships were maintained and nurtured through correspondence and regular contact, and not only with siblings. As one historian has commented, "the clean lines that distinguish the generations ... that set apart members of the nuclear household from first cousins, aunts, uncles, even grandparents, were inconceivable in most eighteenth- and nineteenth-century homes."[26] So it was in nineteenth-century New Brunswick. Grandmothers, sisters, aunts, and cousins offered young women alternative maternal, marital, and sometimes career models to emulate and relationships with these family members could prove almost as important as the relationship with one's mother.[27] Certainly Jacobina Campbell and Annie Trueman "mothered" nieces and nephews who were in and out of their homes regularly. As teenagers, Annie and Laura Trueman frequently made extended visits to aunts and older cousins.[28] And other diarists regularly visited siblings or aunts, cousins and nieces, who lived nearby. Then, too, women who travelled with their husbands regularly left children behind, in the care of other adult women, often for lengthy periods. Laura Trueman Wood left her children with her parents and sister when she travelled to Ottawa to be with her husband, a Member of Parliament, during the parliamentary session. Ann Eliza Gallacher left one or more of her children in the care of her parents and sisters whenever she followed her husband to a new home. And Amelia Holder's mother, Hannah Parrett, left her younger children in the care of an unmarried sister when she went to sea with her husband.[29] In all these cases, older female relatives mediated the influence of the mother in shaping the identity of younger relatives.

Like Ann Eliza and John Gallacher, Hannah and Edwin Holder longed to be together when they were apart. Edwin also very much missed his children, and treasured their "little letters," reading them "over and over" while he was at sea. Finally, in early February of 1867, he declared that he could not bear to go to sea again "without some of you with me."[30] Although Hannah believed that it was her responsibility to remain on shore to care for their young children, she acceded to his wish, in the hopes of improving her own failing health. So it was that the diarist Amelia Holder embarked on her first sea voyage, taken along to help care for her mother. Amelia took readily to the seafaring life, noting on 16 October, "I am not homesick but sometimes think of home and what nice times they will have, but I think after all I will have a very nice time of it." In the years following her mother's death in 1868, much of Amelia's family life was experienced on-board ship, for she continued to sail with her father, always in the company of a younger sibling. On her second voyage, her sister Agnes came along; on her third, her seven-year-old brother Eddie accompanied them. A loving father, Edwin demonstrated a level of sensitivity that is rarely associated with nineteenth-century widowers. On 10 December 1869, in preparation for his daughter's fourteenth birthday on the 25th, and no doubt in recognition of the young woman she was fast becoming, he obliged her by piercing her ears. On her birthday, Amelia reported, "Pa put my earings in yesterday. They went in very easy. This afternoon it is very still. Pa is sleeping on the lounge and Eddie is in the bed and I am thinking of home. I suppose they are at church or meeting now. When I think of Aggie, I almost wish she was here or I there. I think more of her because we have been together so long. I have been reading in this book about the time we were together in the Mediterranean." But Amelia loved the seafaring life, commenting on 20 December, "There is more wind than there was yesterday and the sea looks so blue and I think, how can anybody be sick at sea, it seems so exhilarating to see it and feel the fresh breeze in your face that comes off no swamp or smoky city, but from the salt sea." And for her and her widowed father, that life was very much the world of her family. On 6 January 1870, heading for Buenos Aires, Amelia reported, "This evening we are all up on deck enjoying ourselves, Eddie is climbing up the rigging and Pa is playing he is a bear." And on 18 January, she noted, "I have been sewing a good deal and heard Eddie's lessons. Eddie has made a boat and I made some signal flags and the boat is towing astern." On her fourth voyage, this time with ten-year-old Ada along, stockings were hung as usual on Christmas eve, though, in reporting on "Christmas at Sea on Board the Brigantine Mina in the Year of Our Lord 1870," Amelia noted that "we were divided in opinion whether Santa Claus would visit us south of The Line ... but we hung up our stockings just to see if he would come or not. We jumped up as soon as we woke up and got our stockings and there, sure enough, Santa Claus had filled them quite full. Ada never believed in Santa Claus before, but now she does."

In contrast to Amelia Holder's experience, Ida MacDonald's record of the companionable sociability of evenings at home on a New Brunswick farm appears to offers a compelling example of the idyllic world historians often dismiss as romantic nostalgia, when it is described in novels or by popular historians. Yet, like Amelia Holder, Ida did not inhabit the traditional nuclear family with which this chapter began. Ida's world of the family included her widowed paternal grandmother, her widowed mother, three older sisters, two older brothers, and a maternal aunt. Inclusive rather than exclusive, family life for Ida further extended to sundry "visitors," among them two shoemakers who boarded with the family during the fall and winter of 1881–2.

> *October 1st 1881. A.D. Several months have elapsed since I last wrote in my diary. I take up my pen tonight to try and write some. This is a lovely night, still & quite warm. Mr Oram is here. Fred, Robbie, John, Sis & Ella are to Lodge – Black also – he came down yesterday. Dan Fitzgerald is going to join tonight; he is shoemaking here.[31] It is nearly nine o'clock. Grandma is reading. I am just going to get "Campbell's Poems" to read, so I will not write any more.*
>
> *Oct. 2nd. Sunday. Mr Oram had meeting at the school house this morning – there was Sunday School this afternoon & service again this evening. Laura, Annie & Bertie were here this afternoon. Fred went over with them tonight. There were several in here tonight.*
>
> *Oct. 3rd. It has been quite cool today. Fred & Black were over the Lake. Robbie went to Fredericton this morning with John Belyea. I was up to the "Office" this afternoon. Mr Oram is here tonight.[32]*
>
> *Oct. 4th. It has been very cold today & raining most of the day. Black went home this afternoon. Uncle Macky was here to tea. Ella is sick tonight.*

John & Dan have moved into the kitchen tonight to work. We have all been out watching them.

Oct. 5th. There was a very heavy frost last night – killed everything. It has been fearful cold today – snowed some this afternoon. Rob got home this afternoon about 3 o'clock. Mr Oram had meeting at the schoolhouse this evening. We were all up.

Oct. 6th. It has been very cold today. Fred, Robert & Sis are up to John Belyea's tonight. They are going to have a sing.

Oct. 7th. This has been a beautiful day, quite warm. Grandma was down to Melvin's all day. I was up to the Office tonight. Fred went to St John this morn. Robbie, John & Dan are over to the Hall to meeting this evening. Mr Oram is here. Uncle Macky was here this afternoon.

Oct. 8th. This is a beautiful evening. The "boys" and Ella are to Lodge. Mr Oram is here. Fred came home this afternoon.

Oct. 9th. Sunday. This has been a beautiful day, very warm. Mr Oram preached at the school house this morning. Sunday School this afternoon. This evening we all went over to the Hall to meeting. Mr Oram preached his "farewell" sermon. He is going away.

Oct. 10th. It has been raining today, snowing tonight. Mr Oram is here. Fred went over the Lake today. I was to the Office this afternoon. Will is here helping Robbie today.

Oct. 11th. There was quite a snow storm last night – about half an inch fell – it has all gone off now. They moved the "Well-house" this afternoon. They are going to make a shoe-shop out of it. Mr Oram & Mrs Belyea are here tonight. Mr & Mrs Mott, Mrs Courser, J. McD. Belyea & George Clark were here this evening. Mr Wortman died last night.

Oct. 12th. This has been quite a cold day. Mr Oram left this morning. Mr Lewis had meeting at the school house this evening.

Oct 13th. This has been a very nice day   looked some like rain this morning. We were all up to Jemseg this afternoon to the Exhibition – we went in the "farm wagon." Mr Lewis is here – he went up with us.

Oct. 14th. This has been a cold day. Mr Wortman was buried today. Fred was to the funeral. Uncle Alexander preached. Frank & George stayed here till he came back – they went home tonight. Mrs Belyea went away today.

Oct. 15th. It has been raining hard today, raining & blowing hard tonight. Grandma was up to George Macdonald's today visiting. Fred was up the Lake, has just got home. We have just had a game of "Logomachy."[33] *They did not go to Lodge.*

Oct. 16th. Sunday. This has been a nice day. The "boys" were all over to the Cove this morn to meeting. Mr Lewis had meeting up at the school house this afternoon. We were all over to the Hall tonight.

Oct. 17th. It has been very cold today. Will was here working. Hanford Macdonald was here today. He was up to David Gilchrist's. They have got the diphtheria. Fred was over the Lake. I was up to the Office tonight. John & Dan are playing checkers, Sis reading.

Oct. 18th. This has been a stormy day – raining & snowing. Gilbert Pugsley & Howard were here this forenoon. Fred was to the Narrows this afternoon, went up in the boat. Robb is writing, Ella reading, the rest sitting round the fire.

Oct. 19th. It has been raining most all day. Fred was over the Lake. This is Ella's birthday. Brad Leonard was here this afternoon. The kitchen is full of men tonight – getting shoemaking done.

Oct. 20th. This has been a nice day but quite cold. John went to Grand Lake today, has not come back yet. They gathered some of the apples today. I was husking corn this afternoon. George Clark in here this evening.

Through the lens Ida MacDonald trained on her family of an evening, we catch snapshots of her brother Rob playing his violin, of family members popping corn, or of someone reading aloud.[34] Some snapshots include visitors, while in others we see the family and their boarders. But whatever the configuration, it is a companionable group and we picture the family, as Ida did on the evening of 26 October, "all sitting round the fireplace talking and laughing." In the next chapter, we shall consider how young women raised in such settings, drawing on their own clear understanding and experience of how society worked, emerged as independent actors when necessary, and interdependent actors by choice.

Chapter 7

Households of Independent Women

The still-popular custom of a father giving away a daughter in marriage is rooted in the traditional assumption that women were, from the cradle to the grave, dependent creatures. Yet, as the demographic analysis in chapter 3 demonstrated, the reality was infinitely more complex. Nineteenth-century New Brunswick women did live in a society in which patriarchal norms had the full weight of legal sanction. At the beginning of the century, marital property laws vested control of a couple's real property in the husband and inheritance laws guaranteed the wife no more than a life interest in one-third of that property should she survive her spouse. Such laws made married women legally dependent on their husbands. That neither women nor men entirely accepted the implications of these laws, however, is evidenced by the provisions of some wills, written even before the introduction of the first Married Women's Property Act. Writing in 1845, for example, after bequeathing two "houses and premises" in St Andrews, including one "occupied by James W. Street, merchant," to her three widowed sisters, Harriet Clarke added the following: "After the death of my sister Charlotte, I give and devise her undivided ... share ... unto her daughter Mrs Street, wife of the said James W. Street, to have and to hold the same in fee simple in common with my said two sisters, but independently for her sole use and benefit and not subject to the debts or control of her said husband."[1] In New Brunswick, this kind of subversion of the law, while by no means a universal practice, occurred often enough to suggest that the perception of women as dependent from the cradle to the grave requires revision.[2]

Even so, women – and, in particular, married women – remained constrained by the law. As was the case in other provinces, New

Brunswick's Married Women's Property Acts, passed in 1851, 1877, and 1895, proved, at best, halting steps towards women's legal equality.[3] The 1851 act, designed largely to protect deserted wives, was also the first such act in British North America to include a clause aimed at protecting propertied widows from a penniless old age, should a husband's debts exceed his assets upon his death.[4] Yet the act did not give a married woman the power to act as a *feme sole*, except in the case of desertion by her husband. Nor did the 1877 act, which provided clarification of details, extend married women's rights far beyond the 1851 act.[5] Even the 1895 act, which might be considered egalitarian legislation in so far as it gave married women the right to act as a *feme sole* with respect to their real or personal property, as well as the right to control their own wages and personal earnings, did not imply equal status for women under the law.[6] But it did open up new opportunities for women, and women who had, like Harriet Clarke and others, long found ways around the law were well placed to take advantage of those opportunities.[7] Nonetheless, in the nineteenth century, when family members worked together to ensure the stability of the family economy, which often meant the success of the family farm, few women would have understood our modern notions of independence. Setting aside those modern sensibilities and definitions, this chapter considers the kind of independence required of and exhibited by our diarists and their contemporaries.

Although one is struck, in reading nineteenth-century women's and men's diaries, by ubiquitous references to men's activities in women's diaries compared to the relative dearth of references to women's activities in men's diaries,[8] a close reading of most New Brunswick farm diaries reveals that men were often absent from home for extended periods. In the winter months, many New Brunswick men went off to lumber camps, leaving their wives to cope with the problems of wintering livestock and ensuring a constant supply of food and fuel, sometimes, but by no means always, with the help of elderly men and young boys as well as girls and other women. As land was cleared the industry moved inland, taking men further from home.[9] Nor was lumbering the only occupation that took New Brunswick men away from their households for extended periods. In communities like Holderville, which were built on the seafaring industry, independence was both expected and required of women like Hannah Parrett Holder, mother of diarist Amelia Holder, who spent many months each year waiting for the return of her husband.[10] As the author of one study of the nineteenth-century

New Brunswick seafaring experience has argued, seafarers' families, in times when the mariner was absent, "had to be willing to move house, leave home, share finances and food and look after each others' children."[11] Hannah Holder often had difficulty making ends meet when her husband, Edwin, was at sea.[12] In a region as dependent on the sea as New Brunswick, Hannah's dilemma was not uncommon.

Although her husband was not a mariner, Ann Eliza Gallacher's situation was not so very different from that of Hannah Holder. In January 1865, her husband John again in the United States looking for work, Ann Eliza was living on Eliott Row in Saint John. Although accustomed to such separations, this one must have been particularly difficult: the previous May they had lost their five-year-old daughter, Ella Frances, to complications following the measles, and just six months later, Ann Eliza had given birth to another daughter. Now her husband's absence left her in a situation similar to that of many other women in the city. And Ann Eliza numbered several women whose husbands spent long months at sea among her closest friends. On 1 February, she "spent the day with Mrs Thomas McFee. Mrs Willson was there too." A few days later, she reported, "Mrs Gallagher & Mrs Cameron called this evening." On 6 February, "Mary Carlisle & Mrs McFee here for tea" and the following week she "took the children and spent the day with Mrs. Tom McFee."[13] On Saturday, 18 February, "Edith & Maggie McFee & Annie Cameron came to spend the afternoon with [nine-year-old] Isabella. Mrs. Williamson called." The next day, Mrs Tom McFee sent her daughter Maggie to invite Ann Eliza "to go up tomorrow to look at a house on Leinster Street." By Wednesday, the women had decided "to take a house .... It is large enough for Mrs. Tom & William McFee & myself." Having made the decision, the families became even closer, although they would not actually make the move for several months. Thus, on the following Sunday, Ann Eliza reported, "I went to Mrs. Tom McFee's last night. Stoped all night. Olivia McFee & I went to Church." On Tuesday, 28 February, "Mrs. McFee & I went to Mrs Gallagher's and spent the afternoon & evening. Had a pleasant time." And on Sunday, 5 March, Ann Eliza "went up to Mrs. T. McFee's. She kept baby while Olivia & I went to meeting. Stoped for dinner. Mary Carlisle called." Living as a single parent in Saint John, then, Ann Eliza developed a strong network of women who supported each other in various ways. On 9 March, she "went with Mrs. Huestus to buy her a carpet. When we got home Mrs. McFee & her girls were here. They stoped for tea." On Sunday, 12 March, "Mrs McFee called for me to go to church. Mrs Huestus said she would keep baby so we went to hear Mr. McKewan. Mr. Reid called, says Mr. Wilson is going to Boston in the morning, will see John. I will send letters. Edith McFee got a letter from her father (Capt John McFee). He is in Philadelphia. His wife (Edith's stepmother) lives in England. Fred Wilbur was in today. He has been to sea all winter." Two weeks later, she went with Mrs William McFee to Zion Church. The following day, Monday, 27 March, she reported that Mrs T. McFee, who was pregnant, was "quite sick. I will stop with her a few days." Finally, on 1 May, a day when it was "raining hard," "I moved on Leinster St. Mrs. McFee moved in the same house."

Unlike the wives of mariners and industrial workers, the wives of politicians rarely seemed short of money to run their households when their husbands were absent. Moreover, unlike those women waiting for their husbands in port towns, they remained at home, where they were embedded in a network of extended kin, even as they acted as independent agents while their husbands were away. Sarah Upton, daughter of a prominent Charlotte County family, married George Stillman Hill in 1825 when she was twenty-four and he was thirty. Five years later, Sarah, by then the mother of two small children, witnessed the election of her husband to the legislative assembly. Thus began a pattern that continued throughout their married life. In early January of each year, George departed for Fredericton, from whence he would return in late March. The couple corresponded regularly when George was away from home, and it is through that correspondence that we catch a glimpse of Sarah Upton Hill's self-sufficiency and independence. During the 1830s and 1840s, when her nine children were young, not only did Sarah run her large household alone while the legislature was in session, but her husband also expected her to act as his political agent, ensuring that his constituents were kept informed of his activities.[14] George was absent for the births of at least three of the couple's seven children born after 1830. Decades later, in the 1880s, diarist Laura Trueman Wood followed a similar pattern when her husband, Josie, a member of the federal House of Commons, was away in Ottawa.[15] Surrounded and supported by strong kin networks, Sarah Hill and Laura Wood, like other New Brunswick women, acted as independent agents in the absence of their husbands.

Widows, in particular, relied on strong kin networks.[16] After the death of her first husband, Ann Eliza Gallacher returned to Hopewell Cape and her parents' home. Agnes Estabrooks, mother of diarists Alva and Hannah Estabrooks, and Sally MacDonald, mother of diarist Ida

MacDonald, were, like many rural widows of their generation, not only surrounded by family, but also embedded in an extended and mutually supportive family economy. Indeed, Sally and her husband, James, the eldest son of Janet and Alexander MacDonald, had lived on the home farm with James's parents throughout their marriage. Sally's two young adult sons took over their father's work both at the mill and on the family farm their father had run, supervised, no doubt, by their mother and grandmother, as well as by their grandfather and several uncles.[17]

After her husband's death in 1859, Annie Johnston and her baby daughter had returned to her family home to live with her widowed mother and two unmarried sisters, Fannie and Lucretia Gilbert. Following her mother's death a year later, it was Annie, as the most experienced of the three, who took over the management of the family's business affairs. As well as administering the various family properties, Annie, like other women of her day, sought to build her capital by holding mortgages. Although James Curry, her local lawyer, proved a source of constant frustration, by 1870, she had learned a good deal about the law and how to make it work to her advantage, becoming a shrewd businesswoman, capable of tough talk and decisive action.[18]

> *Thursday, January 20, 1870. Sun shines very bright. No snow on the ground, Annie went to School in Dickie's wagon. I think I'll make an effort and go and see Curry today and get his accounts, the miserable fellow. I suppose I'll have bother I feel so poorly. I sent my letter to Lizzie Smith to the post office. I went down in the afternoon, he was not in. I went to McDermot's, saw Will and Phoebe, heard about the municipal corporation, bought some lozenges, musk and paid Will $5.50 for four [?]. Curry came into McDermot's for me and I went up to his office. Accounts in very mixed up state, he could not give me a copy of them and I could not assertain how much we owe him. He promised to copy them out properly at once. I gave him a written notice to give up the Loder farm on the first of May 1870 and he promised the Hobens should be notified. I felt poorly – very feverish and slept little during the night.*
>
> *Friday, January 21. Dark morning, no snow yet. Annie went to School with Mr Dickie this morning. I feel gloomy and depressed but hope I shall be able to bear up. It's hard to struggle through such repeated trials of faith. I went to Gagetown to Curry's office, went over accounts and he promised to bring them up to me in evening – got a "London Society" from the mail for Lucretia.*

Saturday, January 22. Curry came bringing accounts saying a balance due him of $200. Eliza[19] came in with Fannie & Annie who had been up there. She was disappointed about the account and I feel much worried.

Sunday, January 23. Rain – did not go to Church.

Monday, January 24. Sunny morning. I went to Mr. Curry's office and showed him errors in account, he rectified all, then gave me receipted accounts for each of my sisters of their private accounts and I signed on the book a receipt and he marked his off and I gave him a due bill for $120 and made all square. He comes up this evening and I've promised to pay him. I trust I may be kept from getting any farther in debt. Oh how many cares beset me, but if the Lord be on my side I have nothing to fear from my enemies, Jesus is able to subdue all things under him. Oh God grant me grace to persevere. In the afternoon James Curry came and I paid him $120 and he gave me the due bill. Lucretia paid me her share in $120 – being $45.

Tuesday, January 25. When I arose this morning much surprised to find the ground covered with snow – and the snow storm increasing – Dickie had gone away at night and so there was no one to take Annie to School. Quite a heavy snowstorm today. When yesterday I drove to Gagetown in an open wagon with the sun shining warmly – afternoon Mr Dickie came in and said Susan was poorly. I went down and stayed to tea. After tea Dr Black came. Susan seemed better and I came home – quite a heavy snowstorm.

Wednesday, January 26. Great crust on the snow. Annie could not go to School.

Thursday, January 27. Eliza and I have been examining Curry's accounts and memorandum of money received. Dr Black called a few minutes on his way home. I have explained matters to Eliza and she has expressed herself [satisfied] with my [re]presentation of facts. I've explained the money paid to Wiggins and by giving her credit for Tapley money, money received by me and not paid into her [accounts] I find only due me on the principal of Wiggins money 37 pounds 1s.

Friday, January 28. I wrote to Curry asking for an explanation of the Justin [E] Wright matter. Fanny and Lucretia went to Gagetown.

Saturday, January 29. Annie and I went to Burton with Mr Dickie, went to Wm Gilbert's – then to Mr Hubbard's, then to Wm Gilbert's to dinner then to Hubbard's where I got a copy of the [deed/mortgage?] to sell the Swan Creek land for which I paid $1 then called at Sam Gilbert's.

> *Mrs Curry wanted me to come to a large party on Tuesday – then called at Capt Weston's. Lucretia said Curry called while I was away but did not leave any papers for me.*
>
> *Sunday, January 30. Storm in the morning – afternoon Eliza [Clowes] & baby called. We all went to Church. Received a letter for [?].*
>
> *Monday, January 31. Wrote Charley Stockton regarding payment of the 1st note – received notice from Allison that insurance would expire on the 2nd, find the receipt says the 4th Feb – wrote to Mr Allison. Went to Gagetown and got a money order for $30. Lucretia paid her share which I enclosed to Mr Allison. Called at the Peters', blew Annie Wetmore sky high – then called at the Neales – felt very poorly – came home feeling awfully sick, and passed a dreadful night.*
>
> *Tuesday, February 1. I felt much better this morning, the dreadful fever had abated – and about 12 o'clock noon I rose and dressed myself – it's storming fearfully – Annie went to School. Mr. Dickie went to St. John – O what will this month bring to me – Oh God help me – if thou wilt not help me no one else will!*

February brought more unpleasant dealings with Mr Curry. On 4 February, informed that he would be going to Saint John the following week, Annie asked him to collect their rents; he agreed to do so "for 3 percentage." The following day brought "a great disappointment in the shape of a letter from Charley Stockton saying they can't pay the money when it becomes due." On Friday, 11 February, she went to Curry's office in Gagetown only to discover that he had not, after all, gone to Saint John. When he then told her about a mistake he had discovered in the accounts, "settled of course in his favor," she reported that "we had some high words." Perhaps in an effort to mollify a client he did not wish to lose, he promised to go to Saint John on Monday, and further reported that he had spoken to two of her tenants on her behalf. But Annie was more irritated than mollified, confiding to her diary that "Curry is such a mean man it is a great trial to do business with him." Upon his return from Saint John on 17 February Curry paid her $165.62, the rent collected for one of the family's farms, of which she owed Lucretia $61.70 as her share, Eliza $41.40, and Curry his 3 per cent ($5.12). She also authorized Curry to sue for collection of the note now due from Sidney and Charley Stockton.

The following year found Annie still frustrated with her lawyer, but relieved that he had managed to negotiate an out of court settlement with the Stocktons. On 16 February 1871, she reported the following:

> At noon two men drove to the house whom I found to be Sid & Charley Stockton. Soon Curry came – after a good deal of talking, I had the satisfaction of getting for Fannie $110 and paid Curry $2.30 coin. She gave her receipt to Sidney, then we had a noisy discussion about my claim. I refused to admit Gerow's bill for repairs on the Island, $58, and when they paid me one Thousand dollars in Bank of New Brunswick money I refused to take Nova Scotia money for the balance and they promised to deposit Eight hundred and Eleven dollars & 38 cts in the Bank of New Brunswick to my credit one week from next Saturday, making the 25th Feb. I paid Curry all his costs except the cost on the judgement. I asked Curry if he had received the rent from Burke. He said he had three quarters on hand, $45, but he wanted his costs on the judgement. I gave him some pretty rough talk. Lucretia says her share in the $45 may go towards paying for the affidavits I have had to make from time to time before Col. Peters ... Truly the Lord has been very good to me to-day. I am saved from the horror of a law-suit for Fannie's claim and have rec[eived] the greater part of mine & I am thankful.

Widows like Annie Johnston often demonstrated resourcefulness and ability in managing their own and their family's affairs.

For Bertha Frost Jones, a King's County widow who was forty-nine years old in 1893, when her extant diary begins, her modest independence was hard won. The owner of a small farm, she hired young men to plough, plant, and harvest the fields, paying them out of the proceeds from the sale of the crops. But Bertha Jones oversaw the field work as well as undertaking the tasks more usually thought of as "women's work." In her diary, farm work blends with community life to suggest the network of friendship and support that was so central to the maintenance of rural communities. The backbreaking nature of household labour was mitigated by the friendly offer of a drive, a neighbour dropping by to chop wood or a brief interruption for tea and a chat. Then, too, the hard labour paid dividends as the needs of her family were met and home and market economies intersected as peas were harvested both for home use and for sale, and "ten or eleven new boys," potential boarders, were promised. She and her daughters, fifteen-year-old Ada and twelve-year-old Alma, planted an extensive garden, selling whatever surplus they had. The surplus was not large, for Bertha had turned her farmhouse, which was near the Saint John River, into a boarding house as well as a stopping place for travellers, and much of the garden produce went to feed her paying guests and her young family, which included six-year-old Hildrick as well as the two girls. The boarders, young men who had come to work at the nearby skate factory, provided a useful supplement to the modest income from the farm.

July 13th, 1893 – Finished killing potato bugs for a few days. Warm & dry. Picked 6 boxes strawberries.

14th. Fine. Mrs B. Belyea to dinner. Ten or eleven new boys. Rudly came & chopped wood for us.

15th. Still fine & dry, grass seems to be parched. Ada and I were killing potato bugs. I started to walk to Mr Marley's to ask his advice about getting a horse. Dot met me & drove me there & back. Mr Marley fell out of wagon & cut his head. The Eagles came up to stay over Sunday.

16th. Lovely rain, did not get to church until evening. Went to Sunday school in the afternoon. Ada walked to O.P.

17th. Monday, very fine. A & I put out a large wash. Mr & Mrs Geo. Fowler called in the morning.

18th. Fine, dry and warm. Mrs D. Whelpley & Miss Hanson called. I was picking strawberries. Alma came home.

19th. Mrs Eagles went home. A very heavy shower with thunder & lightning about noon. A letter from Mr Daw [from] the upper Island. Nelson & John commenced mowing this morning.

21st. Dry, fine & warm. I walked up to Mr Marley's after dinner & back before tea time.

22nd. Nelson working in the factory as the day was dull. Willie left at noon. I walked & was weeding the beans. Willie hoed the corn in the morning.

23rd. Ada & I walked up to church. Went to S.S. in the afternoon. Mr Edwards, Alma Robins called, found the house locked.

24th. I weeded the strawberries while the girls washed.

25th. I am still at the strawberries.

26th. Cloudy. Nelson here to breakfast. Willie hauled wood to the wood house. Charlie Bacon called to see if I wanted beef. I finished a pair of stockings for Ettie.

27th. Alma went to the Rectory, joined Myllie B. Then Myllie took tea with me. Mrs D. Whelpley & Miss Hanson took tea with me.

28th. Alma went for raspberries with [?]. I was very busy as Nelson was haying in the afternoon, nearly finished.

29th. Sold peas to Mrs D. Whelpley and Mrs F. W. Gave Nelson ½ peck.

30th. Sunday. Dull in the morning, we did not go to the service. S.S. in the afternoon, service in the evening.

31st. Fine. Ada went to spend afternoon with Bessie Richards – Nelson & Joseph W. got in the last of the hay, took a load to Dr Gilchrist. I cleaned the room that Norman [was] in.

Yet the income the farm and garden provided was precarious, and Bertha supplemented it by spinning for others. Thus, the first day of August found her washing "one fleece of wool in the weeks wash." The fleece was "very fine packing wool" and by 4 August, a day when "two men came for tea & remained all night," as well as caring for their needs, she was busy "coloring wool black." The next day, she "had a large washing. Got breakfast about 9 for the two men," who "gave $1.00." On 9 August, she reported "lovely weather for haying," and by the following day her hired men "had got in 13 loads of hay." But dry weather had disadvantages as well, for on 11 August she noted that "the factory men are worried for fear the factory will be closed for want of water. I do hope that will not be as I will lose my boarders." And she needed the money they provided. On 12 August, she "paid C.W. Bacon $3.45 for beef" and on 15 August she sent her daughter Ada "to Mr [...] to pay $20.00 on note." By 12 November, she was having trouble making ends meet, recording in her diary that when her boarder "Neal laid the rent on my table at night, $1.50, I was so thankful as I had not one cent ... for collection on this first day of the week." Having put $.50 in the collection plate Sunday, on Monday she "paid out my dollar to Johan P. for heavy feed got in Sep. and 50/100 in necessaries for my table." Thursday found her "spinning to fill an order," and she noted, "Alma is learning to spin." But later that day, Alma "went down to see Aunt May."[20] The following day, Bertha, still busy spinning, had no time to attend "the Social & Concert in meeting house. They have all gone, even my boy. An agent came to stay all night." Finally, on Tuesday, 21 November, she reported, "finished spinning today." That evening she went to service, and after that "went with Miss J. Packett to the Rectory for a few minutes. Invited them to tea next eve."

When faced with the death of a spouse or left as a grass widow when husbands went to the woods, to sea, to the United States, or to the legislature to work for months at a time, New Brunswick women had no choice but to act as independent agents in the public sphere. None of the women who had such an experience chose independence over dependence, yet they embraced independence naturally, and few enough families were untouched by the necessity for it. In a province with such a history, women who had become accustomed to assuming responsibility for the welfare of their families raised their daughters to be independent. Independent mothers, whether consciously or unconsciously, served as role models for their daughters.

Certainly the young women among the diarists emerge from the page as strong of mind and spirit. Like their counterparts who did not write diaries, the teachers among them usually left home at age seventeen or eighteen to attend the normal school in Fredericton or to begin their teaching careers without such training. Independent young women, they found their own jobs and, when offered more than one school, made their own decisions about which offer to accept. Although most trained teachers found positions in schools not far from their local communities, few managed to find a school near enough home to obviate the necessity of boarding in the homes of strangers. A good deal younger, on average, than their male counterparts, many were not much older than the eldest of their pupils. Yet, while twenty-one-year-old Kate Loggie confided to her diary her worries about how best to handle the "big boys," she gained the respect of the trustees, who sought to hire her for a further term. And twenty-two-year-old Violet Goldsmith boldly confronted a stranger whose dog caused an incident in her schoolyard.[21] Both young women were living and teaching not far from their home communities.

Some of their counterparts travelled further afield in their search for paid employment. Like many young, single Maritime women of her generation, Mary Wolhaupter travelled to Lynn, Massachusetts, probably to work in a shoe factory there for a time, before returning to her home community of Bloomfield in Carleton County. There, she sometimes taught school, boarding away from home, and sometimes looked to other money-making ventures.[22] During the periods when she was without a teaching position and living at home with her parents and three younger siblings, Mary not only did her share of the daily chores, but also found ways to maintain her own financial independence, while contributing to the family economy. Her strategies for doing so ranged widely, and extended well beyond home production. Mary's careful accounts of her monthly cash receipts and purchases, itemized at the back of her diary, reveal her as an astute manager of her relatively modest income. These accounts, coupled with the occasional cryptic references in her diary, indicate that one of her strategies for making a modest profit was through loaning money to family and friends. The first such note came on 28 November 1868, just before her brothers left for a winter sojourn in the woods: "I leant brother Benjamin $33.37cts." The purchases listed in Mary's accounts were normally under a dollar. Her January purchases included her diary, for which she paid 65 cents. The amounts received, though rarer, were generally more significant, and usually involved repayment of loans. A diary entry for 9 March 1869 makes reference to a loan she had made to a neighbour: "I went up to Chas Alterton's[23] this forenoon to get some money but he is not prepared to take up the note that is due." At the end of that month, Benjamin, now returned from the woods, repaid his note, and in early April, Charles Alterton, who had borrowed $20.00, repaid his.[24] Having received repayment of both loans, on 9 April, Mary, with cash on hand, made a loan to her brother-in-law. It would seem that Mary did not always seek to profit from her loans, for she made a special note when she lent money "on interest." Living, as she did, in a borderlands region, she kept supplies of American as well as provincial cash on hand. Her loan to her brother-in-law, George Nye, for example, was listed as "$20.00 American money." On 14 July, she "lent Ma $1.00 American money" and a few days later, on 19 July, she "let Pa have $33.00 Province money on interest." The majority of her loans were for modest amounts, and some, at least, may have been paid back in kind. Thus, on 13 September, she lent her sister-in-law Maggie $3.55 American money, and on 22 September reported that "Maggie gave me a nice bunch of black dress binding." Three days later, Maggie gave her a "half quire note paper." Major loans were generally repaid in cash, sometimes in installments: "George Nye paid me $8.06 province money Friday, October 8th on the 20 American." The following month, she lent her sister Carry $28.00 American money.[25]

Beyond loaning money to her family and sometimes to her neighbours, Mary engaged in a number of other entrepreneurial activities. On 11 September, she reported that she had "bought a nice looking little black cow of Will Cluff this forenoon, paid him $18.50 cts. Proving money for her I let George Nye take her.[26] I hope she will do well." Perhaps Mary saw the cow as a potentially risky speculation, for her only other purchase recorded that month was 5 cents worth of candy. For the most part, Mary's personal purchases included food, sewing goods, or items of apparel, though occasionally there were other expenditures. In October, her "Paid" column included both $1.00 for the Missionary Cause and 24 cents for a half-pint of Brandy. But the cow was not her only speculative purchase that year. Her November purchases are dominated by a single item, referred to in her diary entry for 3 November: "Mrs. London and Willard came up just before tea, want me to go down with them and Willard will bring me home with my butter. I guess I will for I do not know of any other way of getting it up." It is scarcely surprising that Mary required help bringing her butter home as she purchased no less than 86 lbs, at a total cost of $19.78. We can only assume that she was using it as an item of trade. In December, Mary's major purchase was a much-needed "pair of Lazarus and Morris spectacles," for which she paid a significant $2.50. By the end of the year, her receipts exceeded her expenditures, and she still had a number of outstanding loans for which she could expect repayment during the coming year. Through her financial acumen, Mary Wolhaupter helped to maintain the balance in a sometimes unstable family economy and also achieved the economic independence upon which she placed such a very high value.

Not all young single women had the advantage of an education that would allow them to obtain a teaching position or engage in entrepreneurial activities. Many of those who lived in seafaring communities engaged in the coasting trade travelled to the "Boston States" in search of work. Ann Eliza Gallacher's diary provides a record of a number of such women, including Direxy Carlisle, who, responding to an invitation from Ann Eliza, sailed with a sea-captain relative from Albert County to Boston in November 1861. In Boston, Direxy joined Ann Eliza's family. In January 1862, she took advantage of an opportunity to learn to operate a sewing machine and was soon employed in a vest-making establishment. Back at home in Albert County the following year, Direxy could find only domestic employment, working as a housekeeper before her marriage in 1865. Hannah Estabrooks had a different experience, but one which became increasingly common for young New Brunswick women who sought work in New England. Hannah worked as a housekeeper during her sojourn in Maine at the turn of the century, but as a store clerk upon her return to New Brunswick.[27] Like Direxy Carlisle, most young single women married and, once married, shifted from the paid to the unpaid – or invisible – workforce.

But some diarists were among the 15 per cent of New Brunswick women who did not marry. Mary Whitney Hill, having completed her education at a private academy near Boston, returned to her parents' home in St Stephen. Like her unmarried sisters and brothers, she remained in her mother's household after the death of her father in 1858. For nearly twenty years, she found employment teaching school on both sides of the St Croix River, in Calais, Maine, as well as in St Stephen. But sometime following her mother's death in 1874, Mary Hill left St Stephen, and, in the late 1870s, unmarried and in her late forties, was living independently in St Andrews, renting a house from another single woman, Miss Morrison. Relying largely on the investment dividends from her modest inheritance, Mary managed her small annual income carefully, supplementing it by teaching music. In so doing, she was drawing on her long-ago training at Mrs Burrill's academy, demonstrating that she had not, as some members of her family had feared, been "throwing away her time" in pursuing the study of music.[28] Mary lived frugally, keeping careful accounts of even the smallest purchases. In St Andrews, she developed a network of friends, patronized the local shops and became an active member of the Methodist Church. She regularly hired Mr Kezar, a local truckman, to haul her wood and coal, and undertake other heavy jobs. When she purchased a new stove in 1878, it was Mr Kezar who not only delivered it but also set it up for her.

Thursday, Nov. 21st, 1878. Cloudy all day. At F.C.'s store, saw Mrs C. and got some sausages. She thinks the rain is not over yet, and will recommence before clearing. Got letter from Henry at P.O. with bank draft for $25.[29] Cashed at Campbell's Nov. 22nd.

Fri. Nov. 22nd. Morning cloudy, began to rain about 4 P.M. Went to P.O. this morning and got my Courier with Dowd-Ward case reported in it. Went to Campbell's and cashed draft and paid my debts to him in full, 92 cts, also paid Mr Swift 56 cts and paid Mr Stevenson $3.00 for wood, ½ hard and ½ soft. Owing to Mr Swift 70 cts now for 5 ½ lb sugar and 1 pk apples. All other debts paid except Kezar. In hand 20 dollars and 40 cts. Mr Swift and another man of name unknown to me, think prisoners in D. case ought not to be hung, seems barbarous.[30] Went to Church last evening (Thanksgiving).[31] Prayer meeting. Very few there. Mr Harrison made a few remarks from the Text "Praise the Lord Oh my soul all that is within me bless His Holy Name," mentioned the Pestilence at the South[32] and our greater freedom from Calamity – very appropriate. Nights very dark and streets dreadfully muddy.

Sat. Nov. 23rd. Day cloudy, evening dark.

Sunday, Nov. 24th. Day clear and bright. Went to Service Morning and evening and Sunday School in afternoon. Mr H. preached in the morning from Acts first, and ver. 8th: put ten cts in box for widows fund.

Monday, Nov. 25th. Day fine evening sleety. Ida in the evening in; 20 cts beef from McLangle paid; I called on K. Shaw and Mrs Hunt on Sat.

Tuesday, Nov. 26th. Day cool, cloud and sunshine; evening bright starlight; new moon not visible to night; Kezar brought me a dollar's worth of wood; paid when brought this morning; bought and paid for ½ gal molasses at Campbells also paid Swift to night 70 cts for apples and sugar sent up Nov 22. M. Brien in and went shopping with me this evening. Miss Hawkins in. No others in. Freezing to night for the first time in several nights. I went to Society at Mrs Stentiford's and saw no one else there but her and Mrs Harison; brought home white apron to make.

Wednesday, Nov 27th. Miss Hawkins called, wanted me to see about coal; called on Katy Shaw and went with her to Mr Chase's house: he has no coal, and Ross, sole holder has some which is not good – Spring hill; heard Maria sing "the dying Nun," came home by nine, ground frozen, moon still up then and visible. Day was fine and sunny all day: began to rain in the night. Mrs Baker, Mrs Harper and daughter called, and Miss McLean in the evening.

Thursday, Nov. 28th. Raining hard all the morning, not out; stopped raining in the afternoon but cloudy; Mrs Baker and Miss Hawkins in towards night.

Friday Nov. 29th. Bright and sunny and not cold all day, ground not froze. Went to P.O. for my paper and spent 16 cents at Black's for Indian meal and Onions. Mrs Baker sent for me in the evening, went over and found her, Mr Mowatt and Lizzie. Miss H. out; she came in before nine, been to see Miss Amy Campbell who is poorly; (Mem. to call there) Embroidered a handkerchief for M. B. while there. Came home by nine.

Spent for I. Mo. 12 Onions 4   4 × 0.12 = 16 cts.

Sat. Nov 30th. Morning bright and sunny and not cold for the season, ground not frozen, but quite muddy. Went to Odells in the Afternoon and spent 37 cts for flowers and 12 cts for braid and 5 cts for spool of black thread. Trimmed my hat in the evening; no callers; clear moon light in the evening, not out. Spent at Odells 05 cts.

Sun. Dec. 1st. Weather sunny and bright all day, but much colder, ground frozen; but quite pleasant. Heard Mr Harrison preach in the morning, read Chapter from Hebrews, text Psalm 84.10 on public worship; went to Sunday school in afternoon and taught from last chapter of Luke; to service in Evening. Mr H. preached from Hosea 14th Chap., 2nd ver. Called after School at Mary Breen's, sick with cold, not out all day. At Miss Hawkins' in the evening. Not out to service – she or Mrs B. No one in; clear moonlight tonight. 3 cts in Box.

Monday, Dec. 2nd. Cloudy and windy, looks like rain. Went in the morning with Miss Hawkins to Foundry to see stove. To Ross to see coal. To Odells and bought gloves, pins. To Mrs Harvey's and saw rugs, to Lorimer's and bought buckwheat. To Miss Morrison's, to Hatheway's. To Kezar to order stove brought up. Miss H. and Mrs Baker in in afternoon. Mrs B. invites me to a sing there. Ida and Abbert in in the evening. Began to blow and rain hard about ten P.M.

Spent at Odell and Lorimer 46 cts.

Tuesday, Dec. 3rd. Stopped raining about daylight, but cloudy and misty till late in the day, bright moon light in the evening. Wait yet at home for Kezar to set stove, he did not come, missed the sing, no callers today. McLean got my paper of 27th ult. Letter from Louise brought by Hattie. Abbie [Beth?].

Wednesday, Dec. 4th. Raining hard all day till late in the night, a warm rain. Kezar came and set stove at one o'clock P.M. in kitchen. Parlor stove not set, no suitable pipe. Wasn't out all day. Miss Hawkins, Mrs Baker and Miss Morrison in to see stove, which they much admire. Mary Breen in in the afternoon, came back after dark and brought me some yeast. Mrs Harrison called in the afternoon, found me washing up the kitchen floor, is better of her rheumatic attack.

Owing for stove $8.00

Thursday, Dec 5th. Cloudy and very dark all day and very warm for the season, horribly muddy. Miss Hawkins in and invites me to a sing at Mrs Baker's which was put off till to night; later: went to sing, Mrs and Mr Rigby there. Spent a pleasant eve. Came home at 10 ½.

Friday, 6th. Cloudy, much colder, ground frozen, water thinly frozen. Went to P.O. and got my paper of 4th with description of Jenny Whitlock's wedding in it. Married in Church at 7 A.M. on Wednesday, Dec. 4th, St Andrews. Went to Kezar at noon and sent him to Ross for coal, ½ ton, filled a barrel myself. Kezar filled 4, borrowed two from Miss Morrison. Paid Mrs Stinson by her little girl 25 cts for milk and stopped taking.

Owing for coal	$2.00
paid for milk	.25
paid McLaughlan - mutton and Beef	.70
Paid girl for Butter of Mr J. Wren	$0.48

February of 1881 found Mary still living on her own in St Andrews and still calling upon Mr Kezar for much of her heavy work. In Mr Kezar, Mary Hill had a workman she could trust. But when she sent him to Mr Chase, a coal merchant, on her behalf that winter, Chase insisted that his own man would deliver the coal. Dissatisfied with the coal delivered, Mary informed Mr Chase that she would not keep it. However, he refused to take it back, and when she persisted and told him that she would not pay for it, he threatened to sue not her but Kezar. Writing to her brother George some months later, she explained: "I didn't like the idea of sheltering myself behind a truckman, so I paid the bill but under protest." No doubt Mr Chase believed that would be the end of the matter, but Mary Hill was an independent woman who was not to be trifled with. Irritated that she was unable to "put on a shovel full as it stood and was obliged to sort coal out of dirt and stones all winter, for the dirt put the fire out and the exploding stones were dangerous to the stove and one," when she could find no further coal herself, she "hired a man to sort the coal out of the dirt, he got several barrels of refuse which came by weight and which I sue in damages for as it came to me." Advised by Mr Hatheway, a local Justice of the Peace, that having paid the bill, she would be able to recover nothing, Mary wrote to George, a trained, though not a practising, lawyer, to consult him on this legal point. Confiding that "I would drop the case if I could in justice to myself and others, or if I could use what is left; for the gaining of the suit will not repay me for the bother or the loss of more than a year's coal which was all gone in less than three months," she concluded that, "while I have that refuse, it would be too cowardly to throw it away and do nothing." Having stated her determination to pursue the matter, she had devised a "plan which I did not tell Mr H. as he is the friend of Chase: I have that stuff that is left, put into a cart, weighed, brought to the office for the Jury to see, summon the blacksmith who tried it, said he couldn't use it, and the man who sorted it to prove what I say. Now what in law and justice can prevent my getting damages from any honest Jury? " She asked George whether he might be able to send her "any book or pamphlet ... that would explain the law in such cases," which she could offer as a "reference, not wishing of course to mention as authority any *people* who have advised when the time comes to decide." Although Mr Hatheway had promised to try to negotiate a compromise, Mary was not optimistic, noting "I know the crocodile wont. I tried that." Commenting that "Mr Hatheway says I must pay first, and if I gain, it is refunded," she asked, "Is that right? it seems strange. I never heard of it before. Have I 30 days to pay in if I lose?"[33] We do not know either how her brother answered or the outcome of the potential court case, but Mary's letter offers both a compelling example of the ways New Brunswick women exerted their independence and confirmation of the continuing significance of kin networks.

Embedded in a strong network of family and friends, the majority of New Brunswick– born women enjoyed security in the kind of interdependence that makes such independence possible. Ann Eliza Rogers travelled well beyond her rural community with her first husband, John Gallacher, living, by times, in Boston, Saint John, and Philadelphia. But whenever John was out of work for an extended period, Ann Eliza came home to Hopewell Hill. Often this meant a reunion not only with her parents and siblings, but also with one of her own children who had been left behind in the care of her parents.[34] Similarly, Hannah Parrett Holder, left behind in Saint John when her husband went to sea, soon made her way back to family and friends on the Long Reach on the Kingston Peninsula.[35] The comfort of such networks made up, in some measure, for the absence of husbands and fathers. Yet for the wife and mother waiting at home, the responsibility for maintaining the family and for making decisions about where and how to live remained hers alone.

The glue that held together those neighbourhood and community networks, so important to women's lives and experience, was simple sociability. And sociability, the topic of the next chapter, also provided the underpinning for a culture of mutual aid and support that was central to nineteenth-century life.

Chapter 8

Sociability and Social Networks

When we remember how hard our ancestors worked, we often imagine that, aside from Sundays, when friends and neighbours met at church, they had little time for sociability. Yet to anyone reading their diaries, nineteenth-century New Brunswick women's lives sometimes seem like an endless round of visiting and being visited. Not only was this the case for women in towns, or for women of leisure; nineteenth-century New Brunswick farms were far from isolated and, for some women at least, a day with no visitors was rare enough to occasion comment.[1]

The nuclear family at the centre of an individual diarist's world was embedded in a web of interwoven households, connected to it by ties of both family and function. As the nuclear family expanded and contracted, so too was the web woven and re-woven. In 1830, Jacobina Campbell, living with two younger brothers and a younger sister in a nuclear family headed by her widowed mother, visited back and forth with her sister-in-law, Caroline, though no more often than she visited her near neighbour, Sarah Young. Ties of family and friendship were cemented by ties of function. Thus Caroline sheared her own sheep, and generally brought the wool to Jacobina's household to be spun. Over the years, Jacobina's household contracted as her brothers established their own households, and expanded again as nephews moved in and out of it. But her network of women remained the stable core of her social life.[2] Similarly, a contemporary of Jacobina's, Janet Hendry MacDonald, wife and mother of six sons and a daughter, would see her household contract and expand until, in late middle age, she came to depend on her daughters-in-law, not only to help with wool production, quilting, and gardening, but also to reshape and maintain a domestic world of comfortable sociability.[3]

For sisters Marjory and Isabella Grant, February, viewed by many New Brunswickers today as a cold and inhospitable month, was a season for socializing. As Marjory's diary entries for February 1827 demonstrate, while their brothers were busy in the woods, she and Isabella enjoyed a round of visiting with family and friends.

Monday 12th February, 1827. Clear and cold with a high wind and drift. Alex and his wife was here to dinner coming from Oak Hill. Charles and Wm started for the woods and went as far as Oak Hill. They got their hay out of Duncan Barber's barn.

Tuesday 13th. Cloudy with some snow in the afternoon. Father and Absalom was out to John's trying to fix a sheep pen – our Caty and Nancy McDonald was here visiting.

Wednesday 14th. Clear and cold with a high wind and drift. James Buchanan and Mr. Haycock was here to breakfast.

Thursday 15th. Fair and clear – Father was choping wood at the door – Isabella and me was out to John's in the afternoon and to Caty's in the evening – it snowed in the night. Mrs Grimmer was visiting here in the afternoon.

Friday 16th. Quite moderate with considerable rain, turned colder at night with wind.

Saturday 17th. Some cloudy with wind – Father and Absalom was cutting wood at the door.

Sunday 18th. Cloudy with some snow in the forenoon, turned warmer in the afternoon with some drops of rain. Isabella and me was to meeting.

Monday 19th. Cloudy and cool – Father was out cuting some wood.

Tuesday 20th. Clear and cold with a very high wind. Father was out getting wood. Wm hauled one load of wood here and one to his house with our steers and his oxen – Isabella and me went to the shore and staid all night. Jannet Grant and us was up to Mr Crabtree's in the afternoon und to the singing school in the evening.[4]

Wednesday 21st. Fair and clear in the forenoon but clouded over in the afternoon. Father was to the shore – John Simpson brought us and Hesadiah up in the evening in his sleigh.

Thursday 22nd. Cloudy with some wind – Father was over to mill all day but did not get his grain ground – Ann was here visiting.

Friday 23rd. Fair and clear – Father went over to mill and got his grist in the forenoon and in the afternoon he was out getting wood. Wm hauled one load of wood here with his oxen and our steers. Mother was visiting to Wm McDonald's – Absalom went down and got one gallon of molasses from Mr Marks.

Saturday 24th. Some cloudy but pleasant – Father was out to the woods. Wm hauled one load here and one to his house.

Sunday 25th. Fair and clear – John and his wife was here to dinner. Jannet Grant came up with the horse and sleigh and took Hesadiah home.

When her sister Marjory married and moved to Oak Hill, some little distance away, Isabella Grant's social life underwent a fundamental shift, for the sisters had spent little time apart, whether working together at home or travelling the countryside together to visit family and friends. Adjusting to the new relationship, Isabella soon began travelling on her own, making her first independent visit to Oak Hill on 22 March 1827, a few weeks after her sister's marriage. She returned home two days later. On 31 March, Marjory, in her turn, "came from Oak Hill and went to the shore," probably to purchase supplies. She stayed two nights with her parents, returning home on 2 April, a busy day in the Grant household, with their mother "making sap," their brother Charles off to the shore, and Isabella "baken" a pie for Charles. Absalom, their youngest brother, accompanied Marjory to take out her cow. With the sap running, spring was in the air, and on 4 April, a day when her mother was "out to John's helping" her daughter-in-law "Ann to make sape," Isabella "saw a flock of robins." The following day, out visiting on her own, she reported yet another sign of spring: "I was over to Mr Hunters and I herd the frogs a-singing." Young women like Marjory and Isabella Grant regularly travelled significant distances to visit family and friends. Several decades later, Ann Eliza Rogers and her sisters similarly roamed the countryside, sometimes on horseback, visiting friends who lived at some distance.[5] Maintaining ties of family and friendship, such visits helped to define the boundaries of neighbourhood.[6]

Women's social networks emanated outward from the domestic world of home and family. Grounded in their households, but not bounded by them, women of all ages regularly visited back and forth with family and friends who lived in their immediate neighbourhoods. Sometimes such visits had a work-centred purpose: two or three women gathered at the house of a fourth, to make a quilt or a carpet. Women came together more formally in denominational sewing circles, usually held at a member's home. But more often, family and friends gathered informally. Sharing one's mid-afternoon tea with neighbours and friends was a ritual that was by no means confined to middle-class urban women. And, although for some women – as for Lucy Everett Morrison when her flower and vegetable business was at its height – calling on or entertaining friends could sometimes become more duty than pleasure,[7] many busy women were happy enough to make time for a visit.

Individuals who lived outside the context of a nuclear family, while rare in the nineteenth century, formed their own social networks, within the broader networks of neighbourhood and community. Mary Whitney Hill, living on her own in a rented house in the little seaside town of St Andrews in 1878, established a circle of friends, the closest of whom were, like herself, single. Rare was the day when no one dropped in. On 12 November, "Miss Hawkins made a short call." Later that day, when Wallace McLean came by to return the *Saint Croix Courier*, which he regularly borrowed from her, she "had a talk with him about the affair of Esther Cox reported there; neither of us know what to believe about such spiritual manifestations; nor is the rest of the world much wiser, but I expect some day such things will be better understood."[8]

Evenings brought a different kind of sociability. Frequently, music was involved – the piano, "fiddle," or some other musical instrument. When extended families gathered, or friends came in of an evening, someone might suggest a "sing." Mary Hill often enjoyed such evenings with her friends. On 15 November, she "went to Fannie's in the evening. 8 ladies, 7 gents, very pleasant. Danced to Henry's and Fred's singing. Took a mince pie. Pound party. Came home after midnight." And on the following day, she herself entertained a few friends, reporting a quieter, but no less sociable evening: "8 p.m. just struck; Abbert ... came in again with Maria, Anne, Ida & George Pye. I played them a few tunes on the piano; they have just gone."

Music and games, particularly literary games – Authors or Logomachy – transcended generations in their popularity.[9] On the evening of 18 April 1895, the younger generation of Harpers, along with their houseguest, Fred Clarke, had been invited to a party at a friend's and, despite treacherous road conditions, Sadie reported that "Win, Fred, Blois, Helen, Mr Borden and I drove in our carriage ... We had a nice evening with games and music and started for home after eleven. Both going and coming we had to walk the horse as the roads were in a terrible condition. The mud was over half a foot thick most of the way and the rest was slush. However, we got home all safe and sound." On the following evening, it was the Harpers' turn to entertain, which involved significant preparation, as Sadie explained in her diary: "A beautiful beautiful day. As we were going to have company in tonight there was an awful lot of work to do. I went down to Aunt Deanie's right after breakfast and then back again to do some shopping. May and Fred went out to do the inviting. Helen and Aunt Kate were here all day. I don't know what we should have done without them ... We are just having the young people tonight as we wanted to have the party while Fred was here, so we didn't have much time to get things ready." In all, their guests included ten women and nine men. Reporting that "I think they all enjoyed themselves," Sadie added, "Fred C. is just a beautiful dancer. All the girls were just crazy about his waltzing. It was after three o'clock when we all got to bed, so of course we all had a late breakfast this morning."

Women functioned within complex social networks that often extended far beyond the close-knit communities in which they lived.[10] In a society where geographical mobility was common, almost everyone had relatives and friends who lived at some distance. In the Campbell household, as in many other rural households of the time, the rhythms of the farm economy shaped the rhythms of sociability. As well as the frequent toing and froing with family and neighbours who lived nearby, Jacobina Campbell made several trips into town – Fredericton – each year. Most such trips were short, rarely taking her away from the farm for more than two days. But in late September and early October, when the autumn colours were at their most glorious and the harvest was gathered in, Jacobina found time for more prolonged visits with members of her extended family or with friends in town. Between 1825 and 1835, these annual sojourns often began with a trip up the St John River to Douglas to visit her cousin Susan Dayton and her Aunt McGibbon, her mother's sister. In later years, the autumn trips became shorter and less regular, probably because of increased household responsibilities as the older Jacobina relinquished her place to the younger. But on a Thursday morning in late September 1826, following Wednesday's Methodist class meeting, which she rarely missed, twenty-nine-year-old Jacobina borrowed a neighbour's horse and set off with her brother Patrick to visit their cousins.[11] Jacobina spent five days with her cousin Susan, canoeing to Fredericton one day, and accompanying her to meeting on Sunday. During the ten days following her return home, she made four visits and received six visitors, her McLean relatives prominent among them.[12] On 9 October, her cousin Archy stayed all night, possibly because he had been helping "get in the last hay." On 11 October, her sister Ann stayed overnight at the McLeans' and the next day Jacobina noted, "Aunt Mc[Lean] comes up & stays all night."

The following year, Jacobina chose not to include Douglas in her autumn excursion, but instead enjoyed visiting friends in town. On 25 September, she went "to town with Patrick. Go to meeting, stay at Mrs Clark's." She spent the next day shopping "for things to send by Patrick," who returned home on 27 September, while Jacobina embarked upon a round of visits. That day she dined at Mr Strong's; on the 28th she drank tea at Mrs McBeath's and attended "Prayer meeting at Mr C"; on the 29th she reported, "Dine with Miss Gaynor. Drink tea at Mrs Barker's." She attended meeting the following day, and stayed at Mr Strong's that night. On 1 October, she had "breakfast with Mrs Blair" and visited Mrs Till. Her brother Ludlow and Sally, their hired girl, came to town on 2 October and Jacobina returned home with them the next day.[13]

Jacobina Campbell's experience was by no means unique. Diarists who lived on farms regularly made trips to visit friends and relatives, often in nearby towns. In May 1883, Lillie Williamson travelled to Saint John "to spend the centennial, see the landing of the Loyalists and all the grand doings. I could not begin to tell what did take place. I think the mock landing of the Loyalists was the most interesting part. Then there were the polymorphians,[14] and the bands playing, and an old log cabin with people in and around it, and lots of other things too numerous to mention ... I had a grand time altogether." By this time, Lillie and Fred were courting in a serious way, and she noted that "on Saturday I went over to town with Fred Wightman and got some photos taken. I think they will be very good. I will not get them till the last of this week ... We were to Watch Night meeting in the Centenary Thursday night, got home about 1 A.M. and had to get up at about 4:30 to get ready to go to the landing etc. ... I have not written much of an account of all that took place, but my head is not very clear yet."[15]

Extended visits from, as well as to, friends – or, more often, relatives – also provided the occasion for much toing and froing about the neighbourhood and more than the usual amount of entertaining. Visits from cousins who were around her own age always gave Ida MacDonald great pleasure. Probably her most frequent and favourite visitor was her cousin Jennie, the daughter of her Uncle Alexander. Jennie was a year older than Ida and a year younger than her sister Ella. But without doubt the most lively of Ida's visitors was Georgie Wetmore, another more distant cousin, whose visits always meant good fun.

> *Sep. 18th 1880. This has been a lovely day. Uncle Malcolm was here to tea. Georgie Wetmore came up this afternoon. They are all to Lodge tonight.*
>
> *Sep. 19th. Sunday. This has been a beautiful day – quite warm. Mr Oram had meeting to the school house this morning. There was a "Praise Meeting" over to the Hall tonight. We were all over.*
>
> *Sep. 20th. This has been a rainy day. I was to school. Calvin, Georgie & I were over the lake tonight. We had a boss time.*
>
> *Sep. 21st. Raining again today. Uncle Alex & Aunt Mima were here today. Fred & Rob are up to the Narrows tonight to a lecture. Grandma, Ma, Mary, Geo. Clark, Mary Jane, Ella, Georgie & I are all sitting around the table eating apples.*
>
> *Sep. 22nd. This has been a lovely day. I was to school. Sophia, Will, Ella, Georgie & I were over to the shop tonight.*
>
> *Sep. 23rd. I was to school today. Came home at 3 o'clock. Mary Jane, Georgie & I went up to Delilah's to get sumach berries, we got tea there. Howard is here. It is very cold tonight.*
>
> *Sep. 25th. Ma, Ella, Georgie & I went down to Aunt Eleanor Ann's yesterday, came up tonight in the boat. Ella & Georgie went on to the Narrows. Emerson came home today. Asa Wetmore is here.*
>
> *Sep. 26th. Sunday. This has been a dark, cloudy day. Fred went up to the Narrows this morning. Ella & Georgie came home with him tonight. Howard is here.*
>
> *Sep. 27th. I was to school today. It is raining some tonight. Fred took Asa up to Mr Scovil's this afternoon.*
>
> *Sep. 28th. Raining hard tonight. John & Calvin are here. Mary Jane, Ella, Georgie & Calvin were over the lake this afternoon.*
>
> *Sep. 29th. I was to school today. Fred went to town tonight in the night boat. Robt took him up to Mr Slipp's.*

Sep. 30th. This has been a lovely day. We had a "husking party" tonight: about 30 here. Emerson & Jennie are here. They came down this afternoon.

October 1st 1880 A.D. This has been a nice day. Emerson & Jennie went home this afternoon. Robert went to town this morning. Fred is sick tonight. Georgie had a fit tonight Ha! Ha! Ha!

Oct. 2nd. This has been a beautiful day. Ma & Mary Jane were over to the shop this afternoon. Howard was here to tea. We were all out to the barn tonight husking corn. John & Calvin were here.

Oct. 3rd. Sunday. This has been a lovely day. Mr Oram had meeting to the school house this morning. Calvin was here this afternoon. Howard is here this evening.

Oct. 4th. Fred, George, Mary Jane & Ella went down to St John this morning to the Exhibition. Mr Mott was here this evening.

Oct. 5th. Howard & Robt went to town tonight. Mr Oram is here. Georgie & I were up to the shop this afternoon.

Oct. 6th. This has been a lovely day. Geo came up today. Mr Oram is here tonight.

Oct. 7th. Quite cool today. Grandma was down to Melvin's today. Mr Oram here tonight.

Oct. 8th. A beautiful day. Emerson was here to tea.

Oct. 9th. This has been a beautiful day. They came home tonight from the Exhibition. Georgie went away today.

Extended visits to relatives and friends took women of all ages not only to other New Brunswick communities, but also beyond the province's boundaries. Eleanor Rogers's mother and siblings lived in Boston and, in 1860, when her daughter, diarist Ann Eliza Gallacher, and granddaughter were travelling to Boston to join Ann Eliza's husband, who had found work there, Eleanor accompanied them, partly to help her daughter, but with a clear view to visiting other members of her family. Almost a decade later, shortly before embarking on her second marriage, the widowed Ann Eliza made a trip to Saint John to visit old friends there.[16] As teenagers during the same period, Annie and Laura Trueman of Sackville visited relatives at Richibucto and in Saint John, making extended visits each time. In 1882, Annie Trueman travelled to Somerville, Massachusetts, to assuage her mother's worries about the health of her younger brother, who was working there, and stayed on to visit friends and relatives there and in Watertown. The following year, Rebecca Trueman, then over sixty years old, travelled with her son-in-law to Ottawa to pay her sister and brother-in-law a visit, abandoning her husband and family for over two months. From home, her daughters revelled in the adventures described in her lively letters, and urged her to enjoy herself.[17] As those letters suggest, abroad as well as at home, women's social activities reflected women's particular interests but also intersected with men's social activities when these interests overlapped.

Many New Brunswick women were members of seafaring families, and a significant number of those who married sea captains accompanied their husbands on at least one voyage. When women went to sea with their husbands or fathers, they assuaged the loneliness of the long sea voyage for the men they were accompanying, but, except in ports of call, opportunities for sociability were rare. Like the majority of seagoing women, Jo Turner, travelling with her sea-captain husband, socialized almost exclusively with other shipboard families while in port. There was always a lively sense of community among those families. In February 1884, when the Turners arrived in Buenos Aires, they found the bustling harbour particularly busy, with Jo reporting, "I never before saw such a number of vessels laying so closely together and it being feast day or carnival, the flags of all nations were flying from the farest of masts." The couple knew a number of the other captains and their families, and a few days later Jo noted, "We had company this evening and lots of music. Capt. Johnson and Capt. Davis and his son were here, they brought their violin which Capt. Davis plays very nicely and his son played on the organ. They are both good singers and willing to sing."[18] Jo was especially pleased to discover "the Barque 'Albuera'" in a nearby berth, and commented that "the Capt. (Gilmore) has been on board to see us, his wife and two children are with him." A few days later, Capt. Gilmore, his wife and little girl came to tea. Jo and James spent the following evening "onboard 'McDermot.' Capt. Davis and his son gave us any amount of music, they have an organ, banjo, and violin on board." And "a lovely moonlight evening" was spent "onboard the brig 'Herman,' now laying outside of our vessel, so we can step from one to the other, Capt. Hichborn has his wife with him." Friends continued to arrive, and on 10 March, Jo reported, "We have been onboard the 'Maggie Dart' this evening, there was quite a company of captains and their wives." The following day, "a very warm day, with any quantity of dust flying about, James and I took tea onboard the 'Albuera' this evening, spent the afternoon there, had a pleasant time."[19] By 27 March, when they had been there over a month, they began to venture further afield. That day, Jo recorded that "James and I and Capt. Gilmore and his wife were out to Palermo Park this afternoon, had a pleasant time although it rained, thundered and lightened before we got home again, and took tea at the Hotel de [Seondre]."

When Alexander and Catherine Loggie decided to send their youngest daughter, Jessie, on a sea voyage to improve her health, they turned to their daughter Maggie, who regularly sailed with her husband, sea captain William Valentine. In the summer of 1887, Maggie returned to Burnt Church to accompany Jessie to Liverpool, where they would join William on a voyage to Calcutta aboard his sailing vessel, the *Muncaster Castle*. The sisters travelled from Rimouski to Liverpool, not on a sailing ship, but aboard the *Parisian*, a steamer owned by the Allan line. Maggie reported that on the last day of July, their first Sunday at sea, they "had preaching, services conducted by a Church of England bishop. Doct. Nevill presided at the piano. Mr Crowe, a Halifax gentleman, has been very attentive and kind to us. In the evening some of us gathered round the piano and had some singing which I think we all enjoyed." Both women were impressed with the facilities aboard the steamship, with Maggie commenting, "What a beautiful boat the Parisian is. The music and drawing saloon is so nice and airy and the dining saloon is large and beautifully done up. Much finer than any of the other Allan boats." They were equally impressed with the quality of the company, Maggie noting on 1 August that "last night Jessie had quite a religious discussion with a young gentleman." Picking up the narrative the following day, Jessie confirmed that "last evening a gentleman from P.E.I. proved very entertaining to me while Maggie was having a promenade on deck with a gentleman. I think life on board a steamer is quite enjoyable when a person is well." Unfortunately for Jessie, she was often laid low with what her sister referred to as "mal de mer." That very day, following "a turn on the deck with a Mr Beer, a fine looking gentleman, who loaned me a book titled Ben Hur," she "sat reading for a while and was suddenly seized with seasickness … In the meantime Maggie was enjoying herself by having a game of quoits[20] and another game the name of which I forget … After dinner last evening had a walk with Mr Crowe and afterwards some music in the music room while Maggie had a game of whist in the saloon." Intrigued by "all the different characters a person meets on a trip like this," Jessie lamented the prevalence of seasickness, commenting, "When a lady and gentleman meet, the first question on his side is 'did you eat anything for your dinner?' and the next is 'did you keep it?' I have not coughed any since I left home and if it was not for seasickness would be enjoying myself first-class. We are seated in the saloon at one of the long tables. Some are playing cards, some checkers, while others are reading."[21]

By Sunday, 7 August, they were in England, and about to embark on a lively social life there. Jessie reported that "in the evening Maggie went up to Mr. Pearson's and Mr. Pearson and Jessie returned with her. They invited us up to tea for the next p.m. Yesterday the 8th we went over to Liverpool, saw through some of the swell shops, purchased a bonnet, jacket and parasol ... Came home in the 5 o'clock boat and as we were due at the Pearsons by six, had to dress pretty hurriedly and rush off. While at tea who should arrive but Capt. Valentine. The rejoicing was general." The following week, Jessie paid her first visit to the *Muncaster Castle*, the ship that was to be her home for the next several months. She was impressed, noting that "it quite puts to shame our Michie ships.[22] After investigating every nook and corner in the captain's end of the ship, and finding all so cosy, we all retired to the dining saloon where we enjoyed a hearty repast to which was added claret and champagne. Jessie Pearson arrived on the scene soon after when we all went to town. Got home in good time for tea." Having entertained callers late into the evening, they arose the next day and went off "to hear a Mr somebody preach ... Was more charmed with the music than edified by the sermon. Bad condition to be in."

In Jessie's record of the voyage across the Atlantic, the visit in Liverpool, and the time spent in Calcutta, the reader meets three distinct "social circles" and gets a clear sense of "women abroad" in the late-nineteenth century. In Calcutta, like Jo Turner, Jessie and Maggie spent most of their time in the company of other sea captains and their families, playing at being tourists while the sailors and dockworkers unloaded and reloaded the ship. On 3 March 1888, Jessie reported,

> Will, Maggie and I spent the day on board the Loch Carron with Capt. Clarke. Our last day in Calcutta. In the p.m. we all went driving ... Returned to the Loch Carron in time for dinner and then we all proceeded to the Gardens for the last time. Heard the Viceroy's band and then said goodbye to all our friends. Mr and Mrs Berhand, Captains Tickle, Williams, Shimmons and Hawthorne. Capt. Clarke drove down to Garden

Reach with us and on our way ... called at the ship and got a bottle of champagne, glass and corkscrew and before we parted there was none of it left. Left our friend on the landing stage wiping his eyes and nose, and we wiped our eyes and noses in sympathy. Such is life.

Whether they lived in rural communities, towns, or cities, whether they were at home or thousands of miles away, on Sundays, whenever possible, girls and women, boys and men, met and mingled at church services. For young people, attending church as a couple often signalled a budding courtship. Not only church services, but also a wide variety of church-sponsored events provided opportunities for young women to mingle freely in mixed company. Singing schools, often taught by itinerant ministers hoping to improve the quality of church music, were very popular in nineteenth-century New Brunswick. These schools, which involved both women and men, usually began with instruction in sight reading and rapidly progressed to the elements of harmony.[23] Among our diarists, Jacobina Campbell, Marjory and Isabella Grant, the young people in Janet MacDonald's family, and Avaretta Estabrooks all attended singing schools. Annual church picnics brought young and old together, while pie and box socials were often designed to bring young men and women together as well as to raise funds. Kate Miles attended one such event on an evening in February 1901: "Down to pie social in upper hall in evening. Will Cox got my basket, Miss Mineill ate with us. They made 48 dollars."[24]

While churches undoubtedly served as social as well as spiritual institutions, young women in nineteenth-century New Brunswick had many other opportunities to mix with young men in formal and informal social settings. Young and old came together in a wide range of community activities, including temperance lodges, educational lectures, concerts, fairs, and school exhibitions. And, as Sadie Harper's and Ida MacDonald's diaries attest, young women regularly worked with young men in planning entertainments to raise money for various good causes. In Lottie Reid's rural community, the young people organized a social club that met during the winter months. On 20 April 1881, Lottie reported that she had been "to a big candy spree this evening up to Mr. John Reid's, it was gotten up by the Xenium Club. We put away a large amount of candy & sugar. Had quite a nice time there. There was considerable dancing done ... We got home quite early in the morning. Edith stayed here all night, or until daylight." And again on 30 April, she "was up to the Xenium this evening. It met for the last time, until another winter. Had a gay time ... There was lots of mints, candy &c flying around, the floor was not left as clean as it was found."

For the majority of children, going to school took them beyond the purview of their parents for the first time, offering a public space they could claim as their own. Girls attended the common schools with their brothers, and as the diaries of schoolgirls and young women demonstrate, school was very much a social experience.[25] Although some children hurried home to help with chores at the end of the school day, others had time to enjoy the company of friends. Ida MacDonald often stopped to play croquet at the home of a school friend.[26] And Kate Miles, boarding in Fredericton during the week to attend high school, regularly reported that her friend "Sade [Waycott] and I were down town after school."[27]

Boarding in the same household as her older brother Edgar in 1901, sixteen-year-old Kate Miles enjoyed a significant degree of independence, yet her socializing often involved her parents and other relatives, who frequently came to Fredericton to visit, shop, or attend various cultural events. Thus, on Monday, 18 February, Kate reported, "Edgar & I were up to Mrs. Waycott's to-night. Had great fun. Didn't get [in] untill nearly twelve." The following day she "got an invitation to a tea by the King's Daughters.[28] Lots of girls got them. Sade & I were down town after four." On Wednesday, "Father & Aunt Mame were up ... Fred Miles up for the day. Gertrude invited Sade & me to go to opera house with her to hear Cox to-morrow night. Father got seats next ours for Mama, E, & himself." When they arrived the following day, her parents "brought my new dress up which I wore to tea and theatre. Both splendid. Mama, Father, Edgar, Gertrude, Sade & I had one row at hall. At Home was good too." The following Monday, Kate once again reported, "Edgar and I up to Mrs. Waycott's to-night. Gertrude there and Barry Allen. Great fun with him. Sade & Edgar & I are invited to Gertrude's 27th."

Parents who sent their daughters to private boarding schools expected stricter supervision than placing them in a private home would afford. Yet in the mid-1880s, when Laura Fullerton was a student there, Mount Allison Ladies' Academy was a place of exuberant sociability. Rare attempts to curb that sociability could not dampen normal adolescent high spirits for long and, as Laura's diary demonstrates, the girls often had their way in the end. On Saturday, 1 May 1886, she noted,

> Although my name did not come among the ones allowed to go out shopping, I got Ada Bowyer's place, and she had Mary MacNutt's place.

Mrs Archibald made a fuss about it when we started but after we came back Ada & I went in and explained. Ada & I asked Mr B. if we could go out for a walk in the afternoon, but old Miss Freeman was there and she had to put in a word where she had no business. She says, "It is not generally allowed; is it?" I could have struck her. We did not say any more but left the office. I stayed up in Ada's room all the afternoon.

That evening, one of the regularly scheduled receptions, held to allow young men and women to meet in a supervised setting, was held: "Ella got a ticket and a letter from George Inglis but returned it. Ada got one from MacCan. We had some fun with the boys tonight .... Several girls were away mayflowering today, got quite a few." That evening Laura reported that "Ada came up to sleep with me." However, the next night, "Ella and I asked Mrs Archibald if Ella could sleep with me tonight, but she said when one chose to room alone it was contrary to rules to allow anyone to be excused to sleep with another. Afterwards she came up to Ella's room and told her she could come to sleep with me." Despite Mrs Archibald's half-hearted attempt to invoke the rules, Laura regularly had friends "come up" to sleep in her room, both before and after this incident. And even at the Methodist college, attending church was not an exclusively spiritual outing. On Sunday 2 May, after attending the Methodist Church in the morning, Laura and her friends Ella B., Ada B., and Ada Fraser went to the Church of England in the evening. "Ada B came home with McAnn. She rec'd a ticket from him yesterday, but he did not mention it coming home this evening." Clearly, it is necessary to look beyond the official rules and regulations to gain any real sense of academy life. At such schools, girls used the social skills they had learned at home to develop social networks that would, in many cases, last a lifetime.[29]

Outside of school, young people engaged in many seasonal activities. Popular winter pursuits included skating, tobogganing, and snowshoeing. At sixteen, Emma Pitt, though often complaining of loneliness, enjoyed many opportunities for sociability, particularly in the company of members of her extended family network. On 7 March 1873, a "lovely" though snowy day, she reported, "We went down to Uncle Sam's in the eve and went coasting and nearly broke our necks."[30] The next day was Saturday, and although "it blew heavy in the evening ... a whole lot of us went down to Uncle Ed's and we had a jolly time. We had some fun comming home." On Sunday, "there was no meeting so we staid in the house. The old folks and Mina went away so we spent a lively afternoon. Had quite a concert, for we had an organ." Sociability in the company of relatives regularly extended beyond the family, as it did for Emma on the evening of 12 March when "a lot of us went down to the concert and we had the greatest fun comming back imaginable." April brought the first signs of spring, with the sap beginning to flow, and young and old looked forward to trips to the sugar bush. In New Brunswick, spring was the season when young people went mayflowering, with the tiny, fragrant blossoms bringing the anticipation of summer picnics and riverboat excursions.

For young people living along the banks of the St John River in the 1880s, summer was a time for steamboat excursions. Ida Macdonald's family lived on the shores of Washademoak Lake, very near the St John River. In the summer, her family travelled up and down the river by steamboat and, at least once a summer, they joined in one of the excursions offered by the steamboat company. Ida's diary provides clear evidence of the popularity of such excursions.

1880: June 29th. Excursion.

June 30th. It has been very hot today. Thermometer up to 90° – Fred & Rob are over the Lake. Mary-Jane went up to Martha's to stay all night. There was a moon-light excursion in the Soulanges last night – from the Island to Thompson's wharf. We all went. There were 22 got aboard here. There were over 300 passengers on board. We had a splendid time. It was 2 o'clock when we got home.

July 1st, 1880 A.D. Dominion Day. This has been a beautiful day. There was an excursion in the Soulanges today to the Narrows. Lou Wiley and Eleanor Wilson are here tonight. Robert & Lou were up to Jemseg this afternoon to a bazaar.

July 2nd. This has been a nice day. Lou went away this afternoon. Calvin was here this evening.

July 3rd. There was a heavy shower this afternoon. Fred & Grandma went up to the Narrows. Mr Harris & John Thorn were here to dinner. Mrs Porter came ashore this afternoon; she is going to stay to Martha Straight's till Monday.

During summer holidays spent at the sea shore near Saint John, Sophy Carman welcomed a continual round of visitors with whom she made frequent trips "to town" to shop, to attend church and to visit

William's daughter Annie as well as any number of friends. On 25 July 1872, Sophy was expecting the arrival of her younger sister Jean.

Thursday, July 25, 1872. St James Day. Fine & bright. W & Bliss in town. Expect Jean, did not come.

Friday, July 26. Letter from Mother. Jean came in evening train. W, Bliss & self went to town in the morning, took lunch at Sparrow's. Murray and 2 Lees went to Bay shore.

Saturday, July 27. Coys came. Jean & I went to see "Boyd & Son." Wrote to Mother. W in town. Mrs Cougle came to see Jean. We all went on board of the Lady Heart.

Sunday, July 28. Fine. Went to Ch[urch] 3 times. Mr Brown preached & addressed the children. Mr Dowling preached in evening.

Monday, July 29. Not very fine. W, Jean, Milly Coy and self went for a walk, called at Mrs Dowling's. Mrs D came to see Mr Carman. Mrs & Miss Richards arrived.

Tuesday, July 30. Heavy rain last night, cleared off. W went to town, theatre, stayed all night. Jean, Cassie Coy & I took a long walk. Got a book from Annie. Had some music and fun after tea. Letters from Mother to Jean.

Wednesday, July 31. Fine. W came home after breakfast. We went to see Miss Stratton, very tired – [?] After dinner we all dressed and went to town. W dined at Mr Thomson's. We took tea at Uncle Wright's. Pleasant evening. Lovely coming home.

Thursday, August 1. Beautiful day. Wrote to Mother. Mrs C. Coster came to see me, brought Murray a book. W returned with Mrs C. Jean went to sit with H. Boyd. Murray at picnic with Mrs Richey. Mrs Hunt & family arrived.

Friday, August 2. Fine. W, Jean & I went to town in the forenoon, lunched at Sparrow's – got toilet set & 3 [?]. Came home tired. After tea went to prayers.

Saturday, August 3. Hot day, passed it in our room. Mrs Cougle came to see Jean. I did some packing. Letter from Mother.

Sunday, August 4. Dull, we all went to 11 o'clock. Mr Dowling preached on "Worship." W, Jean & I stayed to the Celebration. Louisa Hunt sat with us, Portia Robinson with the Dowlings. Jean & I & children went to catechizing. Jean and Murray took tea at Mrs Coster's. W went to Valley to Ch & tea. Sat with Mrs Coy while the rest were at Ch.

Monday, August 5. Beautiful day. Bazaar at Hall. We went at 2. W left from there & went home. Got some useful articles of clothing for children. Spent about £3. Went again after tea with Cassie Coy and Mrs Richey.

Tuesday, August 6. Fog came in very thick about 3. Went to Bazaar and Depository. Must not get any more books at present. Mrs Coleman came to see us. Went to Concert and Bazaar.

Wednesday, August 7. Foggy morning. Jean & I went to Valley Ch at 5, Prayers. Lost in Fog, did not go to S. Robinson's. Lightning very bright, thunder & rain. Annie & Janie came to see me.

Thursday, August 8. Fog & rain. Wrote to Mother and W. Passed afternoon at H Boyd's.

Friday, August 9. Beautiful day. Jean & I went to town, paid 7 visits, had no dinner, came home. Dressed in hurry to go to Annie's, did not go after all. I went to Prayers.

Saturday, August 10. Fine. Mrs Jack's 5 children arrived. Making dress for Coleman baby. Letter from W. W & Mr Richey came in the evening train. All went to Annie's to tea.

Sunday, August 11. Wet morning – cleared off. We all went to morning service, (dull). Took children to 3 o'clock. Rosa Louisa baptized. Jean & M went to Mrs Coster's to tea. The [?] Allen came last night. W. & I walked up to R.C. Chapel to hear fine music.

Monday, August 12. Hot. W & I went to town, lunched at Sparrow's. W gave me a sweet little chain. Carrie Dowling & Mrs Coster came, W & Jean went home, left us homesick – lovely evening.

Then, as now, on high days and holy days, celebration and sociability intersected, often in community- or church-sponsored events. On Christmas Eve, 1878, Mary Hill participated in a wider, community celebration, reporting that she "went in evening to see Tree …. Lots of children, very noisy, delighted with their presents. Called off a quadrille, danced to singing, played with children." Like Mary Hill, Bertha Jones, a widow and single parent whose siblings and other relatives lived some distance away, found a strong social support network among her neighbours, and particularly those in her faith community, the Church of England in this case. On 23 February 1894, with the help of her fifteen-year-old daughter Ada, her friends organized a special celebration for her. That day, Bertha woke to a very cold morning, a soft snow having fallen during the night. She had been invited to the Rectory and, upon arrival, found a party waiting for her: "Mr. Neal handed me an apron to remember my Birthday," she reported in her diary later that day, and "when dinner was announced I was much surprised when Mr. P. took me out to dinner, in honour of my Birthday (he said, I was not going to mention it). After dinner I was again surprised when Mrs P. handed me an envelope containing a nice handkerchief and Dot a handsome calendar on which was the Lords Prayer ... I was still more surprised when Mr P. handed me a parcel (as he was delivering the mail to the rest). It contained a large bunch of stationary." This was a milestone birthday for Bertha, and she was grateful to her friends for marking the occasion. "It is my 50th Birthday," she wrote, "and such a pleasant surprise to me. For countless mercies my Father make me truly thankful. Ada came for me – the snow had drifted and it was so very cold."

Our subjects' diaries and correspondence touch on all these many levels of sociability, demonstrating the breadth and depth of nineteenth-century New Brunswick women's social networks. By providing a window on women's experience at various stages of the life course, they allow for a consideration of how social networks evolved and were sustained, suggesting not only the centrality of family to women's lives, but also the centrality of women to community life. Above all, the modern reader will be struck by the sheer number of people encompassed within the circumference of an individual woman's social circle.

In the early years of the century, local communities, forged through social networks, established their own social institutions, beginning with schools and churches. Parents came together to establish schools, providing a schoolroom, often in someone's home, and raising the requisite monies to match the provincial subsidy that would allow them to hire a teacher. Over time, the provincial government became increasingly involved, exacting control in return for the subsidy and, by mid-century, establishing a provincial training school for teachers. It is to the evolution of this social institution and women's roles in that evolution that we now turn.

Chapter 9

Schooling and Scholars

Although women's names are not found among the nineteenth-century New Brunswick school promoters identified in history books,[1] women did play key roles as school promoters at every stage of the transformation in public education that occurred during the course of the nineteenth century. Women put theory into practice, working within the system when possible and outside it when necessary, rejecting its limits and adapting it to their needs. Women were instrumental in establishing schools in the early-nineteenth century. Some established private venture schools, usually for girls, running them from their homes and earning a meagre living by doing so.[2] Others taught in the Madras schools, which were underwritten by the missionary arm of the Church of England. Many more, like Jacobina Campbell of York County, worked to raise the monies necessary to establish parish schools in their local communities.[3]

Under the Schools Act of 1802, which introduced subsidies for local parish schools, schooling was neither free nor compulsory. The responsibility for establishing a school fell to local initiative, with parents required to subscribe an amount equal to the subsidy.[4] There were no prescribed textbooks and no standardized curriculum, and teachers who taught in the parish schools rarely had any formal training, were generally poorly paid, and might have five students one day and twenty-five the next. Even among children whose parents enrolled them in the local common schools and supported those schools by paying the required tuition, regular attendance was rare.[5]

Thinking mainly of the education of their own sons beyond the level of the common school, in 1805 legislators passed the province's first Grammar School Act, providing a subsidy for the establishment of a grammar school in each county. Parents who sought education for their daughters beyond the parish school level faced greater challenges than did those who sought further education for their sons, for although the act stipulated that the grammar schools would be open to both sexes, the curriculum offered was specifically designed to provide boys with a classical education. Not until the 1820s – and then only in the more rural, less populous counties, struggling to bolster enrollments – did grammar schools regularly admit girls.[6] And even in those schools boys remained an overwhelming majority. In the most densely populated counties, the grammar schools remained an all-male preserve.[7]

The majority of young women who continued their education beyond the parish school level attended private girls' schools where they were exposed to a curriculum that reflected the separate-spheres ideology of the day. The "female accomplishments curriculum" had been exported to the colonies as part of the cultural baggage of British women who then established private-venture schools.[8] Along with the basics of reading, writing, and arithmetic, the early ladies' academies offered a variety of ornamental studies ranging from fancy needlework to drawing, painting, and music. While their brothers studied the classical languages, girls studied French and other modern languages. The product of this curriculum, characterized by one historian as "the woman at the piano" – the accomplished woman, the model of femininity – was educated for intelligent companionship rather than for autonomy.[9] Yet for the diarists of the second and particularly the third generations who attended ladies' academies, education extended well beyond the traditional "female accomplishments."

The impetus towards increasing academic rigour was encouraged by parents who perceived that, in times that seemed uncertain at best, their daughters may be required to support themselves. In 1846, Mary Hill was attending the Hawes Institute in South Boston, where she sought to pursue her talent for music. But her father had other ideas. In 1844, George Hill had enjoined his eldest son, then at school in Maine, to study "the work connected with mathematics ... natural philosophy, chemistry, & mineralogy, and also botany & physiology, etc." Now he told his daughter, "You had better commence the study of Chemistry, Botany, and Natural Philosophy, and pursue them in succession," adding that "the Sciences are a great deal too much neglected, especially by females – Your arithmetic you will not neglect."[10] But his daughter proved to be an independent young woman who charted her own course of studies, reporting to her younger sister the following year that "Mrs. Burrill is forming a class in Botany but I do not mean to join. You and I will study it after I go home and find specimens in the woods to classify and study together, won't we?"[11]

By the early 1840s, New Brunswick legislators had become concerned about the quality of the schools they were subsidizing. No doubt some, like George Hill, who had chosen to send his eldest son, as well as his daughter, to a private academy, had been dissatisfied with the local subsidized parish schools in their communities. An inspection of all licensed schools in the colony, undertaken in 1844, confirmed their fears: all too often schoolrooms were makeshift, books and equipment inadequate, and teachers unqualified. By the Schools Act of 1847, the government, seeking both to improve the qualifications of the province's current teachers and to guarantee a continued supply of trained teachers, made provision for the establishment of a normal school. In the event, not one, but two normal schools were established, one in Fredericton, the other in Saint John. Ironically, although a growing proportion of teachers in New Brunswick's parish schools were women and the government appointed inspectors had noted that many of those women, like their male counterparts, would benefit from professional training, only one woman, Rachel Martin, was admitted to the Fredericton training school when it opened in 1848, and only one, Margaret Jagoe, was admitted the following year. Already highly regarded teachers, both were mature women.[12]

Thrust to the margins, New Brunswick women refused to remain there. No clause in the legislation establishing the normal schools had excluded female students, and, when Training Master Edmund Duval initially resisted admitting women to the Saint John normal school, applicant Martha Hamm Lewis appealed to the Lieutenant Governor. The Lieutenant Governor-in-Council ruled in her favour, and, undeterred by the stipulations that Duval imposed to ensure that strict propriety be observed, in 1849, Martha Lewis entered as a member of the first class in Saint John.[13] Other women, poised to take advantage of the opportunity for further education and training, followed in the footsteps of these three pioneers. Among them was nineteen-year-old Huldah Turnbull. Unlike Martha Lewis, who had been educated by private tutors and in boarding school, Huldah had received her education in the Albert County Grammar School, for the school trustees in Albert, whether because they were particularly enlightened, or because they needed the fees, had opened that county's grammar school to girls. Huldah Turnbull attended the Saint

John Normal School in 1851, the last year when men outnumbered women among the students.[14]

Whatever the explanation for the decision to admit female pupils to the Albert County Grammar School, Huldah Turnbull was fortunate in her county of origin. Daughters of parents of modest means in Charlotte, St John, and York Counties did not have the option of continuing their education at a grammar school subsidized by the government. Parents who could afford the tuition fees might send their daughters to a private ladies' academy, but those looking to educate daughters within the province had few enough options: a coeducational Baptist Seminary which operated sporadically in Fredericton, Saint John, and St Martins between 1836 and 1895; Mount Allison Ladies' Academy in Sackville, which opened in 1854; a number of convent schools, including two operated by The Sisters of Charity (opened in 1858 in St Basile de Madawaska and in 1864 in Newcastle) and two operated by The Congrégation de Notre Dame (opened in 1869 in Bathurst and in 1870 in Newcastle); and a girls boarding school associated with the Holy Cross Fathers' College of St Joseph in Memramcook, which opened in 1871.[15]

Some parents, like the Hills, sent their daughters to private academies in the United States, but even for the wealthiest among them, choices often had to be made. The Hills were comfortably off, yet they had seven children by the time they sent their eldest son to boarding school, and, responding to his queries about when they were going to send Mary away to school, Sarah, commenting in one letter that "means were wanting," confided in another that "it has never been the fashion in the family of Hills that the females are much cared for."[16] Although her fears that George might prove unwilling to give their daughters the same opportunities as their sons proved unfounded, even the Hills could afford to send only one child at a time. Partly in response to parental demand for subsidized education for their daughters beyond the common school level, a new School Act in 1858 provided funding for a new category of school, the coeducational superior school, allowing one such school per parish.[17] Yet because the superior schools, like the grammar schools, and, later, the high schools, were centrally located in towns and villages, the cost of board remained a major consideration.[18] Paying for a child to board in town, which also meant losing that child's labour at home, was not an option for most rural families – and more than 80 per cent of New Brunswick families were rural.[19]

The School Act of 1858 brought further reforms. Under its provisions, the school trustees who presided over the administration of schools in each parish were to be elected rather than appointed, and local school committees assumed a new level of responsibility. Standardized textbooks were also introduced. But compulsory taxation in support of schools would come only in the Free Schools Act of 1871, and the new tier of male administrative authority did little to improve working conditions for women teachers. Teachers like Mary Wolhaupter, who would be thirty-three by the time the Free Schools Act was passed, spent their careers "boarding around," sometimes sharing beds as well as bedrooms in the households of strangers, and teaching in often inadequate rooms in people's houses. Such teachers worked very hard to ensure they had the minimum enrollment to make them eligible for the provincial subsidy. They regularly visited families, especially mothers of families, to urge them to send their children to school. These were the real school promoters, self-interested to be sure, but dedicated to a cause as well.

After 1871, schooling, at least at the elementary level, became free for all New Brunswick children in nonsectarian public schools supported by taxation rather than fees. Taxation in support of education came late to New Brunswick, and mothers like Ann Eliza Moore of Hopewell Hill, Albert County, understood its significance for their own families. On 8 May 1871, Ann Eliza noted in her diary, "Dull all day. This is Frank's 10th birthday. A Bill has passed the House of Assembly to tax the County of Albert $60,000 to build a railway, also one has passed to have free school." Ann Eliza had good reason to take note of the new Schools Act, for Frank was just one of three children from her first marriage who would be attending school in the coming year. Widowed in 1867, at the age of thirty, she had remarried and, with her new husband, Lemuel Moore, had begun a second family. The new law came into effect in January 1872, and, on the 13th, Ann Eliza duly recorded, "Fine. Lemuel has been chosen one of the school trustees with Mr Thomas E. Peck & Gilbert Peck under the new law. We are to have free schools now."

Although educational administrators and politicians had hoped that "free schools" would result in universal education for all New Brunswick children, their insistence on a rigid application of the nonsectarian principle made this goal impossible in districts that depended on state support for parish schools established and run by congregations of women religious.[20] But in Ann Eliza Moore's home county of Albert, as in many largely Protestant counties, the law posed no threat to existing schools. In her diary entry for 28 May 1874, Ann Eliza, a Methodist, summarized the situation as she saw it:

> There is to be a General Election in the Province of New Brunswick. The Question will be Free Non-Sectarian or Separate schools. The Catholics are determined to have separate schools & the Prodestarians are equally determined not to. It will be shall Prodistant or Catholic rule. There is not much said by either in this County as there are very few Catholics here.[21]

Both sides were indeed determined, and not until a crisis had been precipitated and blood spilled would the government seek a compromise in response to Acadian and Irish Roman Catholic objections to the discrimination inherent in the original bill.[22] Moreover, while the advent of free schools did result in the registration of a higher proportion of the province's eligible students, accessibility did not solve the problem of irregular attendance.

By the time Kate Loggie attended the normal school and embarked upon her teaching career, schooling in New Brunswick was free, though not yet compulsory, and the majority of teachers in the common schools were women. Young women teachers such as Kate Loggie provided role models for the girls in their classrooms. Many, like Kate, participated in the Teachers' Institutes, sponsored by the provincial government to promote good teaching and provide the opportunity for continued professional development. Teachers, as well as administrators, delivered papers, and in August 1880, Kate "commenced a paper on geography," which she planned to present at the next meeting. On 16 September, with the date of the Institute fast approaching, she commented tersely, "Feel bothered about my paper for the Institute." She feared that she had been wasting her time on less worthy occupations, noting, "Have a feeling of idleness. Troubled with sleeplessness. Read, this evening, *History of Mary Queen of Scotts* & other reading from *Harper's Magazine*, not so profitable. No work done." Two days later, however, she seemed more sanguine, reporting that she had "looked over essay on Geography. Finished *History of Mary Queen Scotts*. 'Uneasy is the head that wears a crown' is true of her." Some weeks later, she reported that she had been "up to the Institute since last I wrote. Read my paper on Geography. Was complimented on it. Hope all were sincere." Kate Loggie had received her academic preparation at the provincial normal school, graduating with a first-class licence.[23]

Certainly Ida MacDonald saw her teachers, particularly those who boarded with her family, as role models, and was eager to attend the local school, announcing on 20 November 1879, in her first diary entry, "I am going to school to Miss Nettie Belyea. Came home to night in a great snow storm. The snow was up to my knees." The following day, a Friday, "awful cold day: snowing and drifting, George Clark came up with the oxen to bring me home." On Monday, she was again off to school, reporting in her diary, "I haven't missed a day yet and dont want to if I can help it." On 3 December, her older sister Ella began to attend as well. The MacDonald family valued education and, at fourteen, Ida was articulate and well read, having been well served by her teachers, both at home and at school. But although she clearly enjoyed school, occasionally noting that they had "great fun to school to day," her diary entries are silent on the curriculum.

At fifteen, Sadie Harper, like Ida MacDonald, enjoyed school, but her diary also suggests some of the reasons why the Free Schools Act of 1871 did not solve the problem of irregular attendance. For many children, the obstacles preventing regular attendance were practical and substantive: the availability of a school, a family's economic status, the weather, and so on. But in other cases, the obstacles proved more abstract and, therefore, more difficult to combat, for they were grounded in traditional attitudes. The Harpers were a solidly middle-class family who could afford to send their daughters to Mount Allison Ladies' Academy, yet even for their daughters, schooling was a luxury rather than a necessity.[24] In early January 1890, the coldest weather in years did not prevent Sadie from going to school, but later that month, with her mother ill and the family with "no girl" to help with the chores, school took second place. On 23 January, a day when her older sister Winnie, who had been ill with "La Grippe" had recovered enough to accompany her father to his shoe factory where she worked in the office, Sadie did not go to school "but stayed home to work and work I did. I don't know how many times I didn't wish to be back in school, only that I had not my lesson prepared, as it was Latin and Roman History ... Mama is feeling very well today. She is sitting up in her bedroom having her tea and the tea table here is waiting for me to clear it off." The following day, a Friday, she "did not go to school today as we have no girl yet and no hopes of one. I think it is dreadful. It is run here and there, keeping pots from going dry and not letting things burn and so on. I think I am getting to be quite a cook and I like it quite well. Today I cooked the meat for dinner."

On Monday, Sadie was back at school, her return coinciding with that of a number of her friends who, like her sister Winnie, had been ill with "La Grippe," and their delight in seeing one another again appears to have taken precedence over their lessons. As Sadie reported, "It seemed like old times again for us all to be back. Mr Belyea was quite cross, telling us that whoever talked would have twenty lines to write after school, so we talked a little less than usual." Indeed, the social aspects of school generally took precedence in Sadie's diary. On Tuesday, she reported that she and her friends "had quite a lot of fun making paper boxes from our drawing book this morning, and in the afternoon bookkeeping was what Mr Belyea told us to do, but not many of us did much of it as we took our boxes and passed them around so that the girls would write their names in them and any little saying they wanted us to remember." On the whole, however, Sadie's school attendance was more regular than that of many of her contemporaries. Until a compulsory school law was passed in 1906, New Brunswick children's experience of schooling, like that of children in other parts of the country, while increasingly universal, remained erratic and relatively brief, not generally extending much beyond the age of fourteen.[25]

If a large majority of New Brunswick children had some experience of "going to school," only a small minority had any experience beyond the parish, or elementary, level. Nonetheless, a growing population and changing attitudes made necessary the establishment of more secondary institutions, the expansion of the curriculum, and the admission of girls. The proportion of the province's students who attended those institutions remained very small throughout the long nineteenth century, although that proportion was gradually increasing, with the admission of girls on the same basis and into the same courses as boys helping to swell the numbers. Increasingly, as well, trustees in the most ambitious rural school districts sought to hire teachers with first-class or superior school licences, who would be able to deliver the basics of a high school curriculum.[26]

By 1901, the majority of the province's teachers were graduates of the provincial normal school, and the majority of those graduates were women. Only a relatively small minority held a first-class licence, however, as the school's academic standards were rigorous. On 12 April 1902, Violet Goldsmith, who was very much hoping to earn that coveted first-class licence, reported,

> Last Tuesday we got our marks for the Easter Exams. I made 65 in Reading, 68 in Science, 70 in Professional Theory, 71 in Mathematics, & 94 in

> Literature. My Literature was the highest mark made in the Junior division of the class ... When I went up to see my marks, Mr. Creed said "This is the 94 paper" & the class applauded. Poor Edna James has been put back to Second Class, and I feel almost as sorry for her as I would for myself. Of course it would have been more disgrace for me to fail, for Edna never studied the Science & Math before, & I did. There were seven put back & three left in conditionally.

Then, as now, teacher training involved practice teaching, and, at the turn of the century, student teachers fulfilled this requirement by teaching in the "Model School," established for the purpose of training teachers. Violet completed her practice teaching in her second and final term. On the same day she reported her grades, she further noted:

> I have my teaching in the Model School over too. I taught "Limonite" to Grade VIII.[27] They all say I did very well. It was the last hour of the day & just after Recess, so the children were tired & restless; the steam was escaping from the radiator; some of the Observers were whispering; so everything was against me. Mr. Brittain was amused with the way I stuck to it. He said I improved very much as the lesson proceeded, & got & held the attention well.

A week later she recorded, with some relief, the news that the students who had been put back to second class, including her friend Edna, had been allowed to go into first again, and would be allowed to take the final. In the end, Violet achieved her goal, reporting on 1 August, "My marks came to hand this morning. I made 94 in Practical Mathematics which gives me a Superior License."

At private ladies' academies, women's education was also at the crossroads. Students attending Mount Allison Ladies' Academy, no matter what their particular interest, received a solid academic grounding. Sixteen-year-old Laura Fullerton's experience provides a case in point. On the one hand, Laura, a talented pianist, who enjoyed the challenge of learning new and difficult pieces, was delighted, if a little nervous, when she was selected to perform at one of Mount Allison's major public concerts. But she equally enjoyed the challenge of learning new and difficult concepts in mathematics and science, earning grades of 98 in geometry and 82 in physiology. When in May 1886, Professor Burwash invited her physiology class "to come over to see an experiment performed on a frog," a fascinated Laura recorded the demonstration in meticulous detail in her diary:

> *He had the frog in a glass of water and after taking it out in his hand and wrapping it in his pocket handkerchief, he stretched its claws on a board so that the web of its foot would be seen, he then placed it under the magnifying glass. It was very interesting to see the blood circulating through the capillaries. After we had all seen that experiment, he gave the frog ether to make him unconscious, then he destroyed the cerebral hemisphere. Then he cut it open to show us the heart beating. He even took the heart from the frog and laid it on a glass but still it contracted as before. The auricular and ventricular contractions were easily seen.*[28]

Her intense interest in the experiment is reflected in the precision of her description. It is not surprising that this young musician also revelled in mathematics. But she did not enjoy composition, another required course.

> *Wednesday – 10th March 1886. Got along nicely with my recitations today. Wrote a composition on Temperance tonight. I wish I could get excused from writing them. I find it hard to get the time. We had a nice prayer meeting tonight. Mr Bordon having asked me I led in prayer. I felt very weak but in God's strength spoke. I looked in vain for a letter from home today. It is a fortnight tomorrow since I have had a letter.*

> *Thursday – 11th. To-day was just charming, it was more like a day in May than March. Several of the girls went out for exercise after breakfast. I took my music lesson this morning, took my first lesson in second Czerny, it is not as hard as I thought it would be. Still no word from home. What is the reason they do not write? Ada Frazer's father came today. I was in her room at recess, she gave me a lovely orange and some candy. Mr & Mrs Bordon went to Amherst this afternoon. Several of the girls were invited to Mrs Wood's to tea tonight, and some to Captain Read's.*[29]

> *Friday – 12th. Went through the usual routine of work today. We have written examination in Geometry Monday. I reviewed about forty exercises and studied a little Physiology this evening. I went out calling after school, intending calling on Ida Trenholm but she and a Miss Ford were just starting for the Rink so I did not go in. Went into Uncle Jessie Bent's, stayed over half an hour got back about five. Uncle Douglass did not come for me tonight either. I guess he does not intend to come until*

Pa comes. I had my usual Friday night's bath. Mrs Archibald conducted the prayer meeting tonight Mr Bordon being away. Quite a number were there, and we had a nice meeting. Tonight being singing class evening, Proff and wife were here to tea.

Saturday – 13th. I was down shopping this morning, bought a key ring and a few other things. Studied with Julia Sayre this afternoon, learned considerable Literature. We had Reception this evening, but dull. Mr and Mrs Bordon are away to Moncton, went yesterday will not be back until Tuesday. Mrs Archibald was away today to dinner and Miss Freeman and Miss Black, leaving only Mrs Townsend, and Miss Bishop, so the girls had a pretty livly time. Mr Inch was here to tea and stayed to Reception. I had a long letter from home today. From what Ma said I think Pa will be up about next week. I asked Miss Freeman to excuse Annie to sleep with me tonight and she refused. Oh, I was cross! Weather soft.

Sunday – 14th. I was out to meeting this morning. Proff. Burwash preached an exceedingly nice sermon from the text, "Keep thyself unspotted from the world." I did not go to College this afternoon. Read a sermon delivered by Spurgeon in London, then I wrote most of a letter home. We had Bible Reading in Tina Ferguson's room and afterwards in Nett Phase's room. Nett was not well and so could not leave her room. We had Reading and Singing in the Drawing Room this evening. Mr Bordon is away so we could not go out to Church. I want to get up early in the morning to study. We have a written examination in Geometry in the morning.

Monday – 15th. I got along nicely in my Geometry examination this morning, answered all the questions. We did not have it two periods as we thought of first, but are to have another tomorrow morning. Miss Black gave me a piece of Music today, it is hard but I think will be pretty. I have practised four hours and a half today. There is some pleasure in practicing when that which you are playing is pretty. I had a letter from Aunt Nellie today, saying Uncle D. would be over for Annie & I on Friday if it did not storm. I wrote a long letter home today, also answered Aunt Nellie's letter in the affirmative. Hope it will be fine, anticipate a good time. We had our usual Monday night prayer meeting. Alice Knight led. Mr B. came home today. Mrs. B. is not coming back until the last of the week. I was down in the Hosp.

Tuesday – 16th. We had our last semi-terminal examination in Geometry this morning. I answered all but one. That I did not have time to answer. It has stormed fast all day. The announcement was made at school closing that the Band would be here tonight but at tea Mr B said it had been delayed. This is the sixth time it has intended to come but failed every time. Sent my letter home this morning and also the card to Aunt Nellie. I am very sleepy tonight, must get to bed.

Although Laura was much less confident about English literature than she was about geometry and physiology, she spent the weekend before that examination visiting her Aunt and Uncle at Point de Bute, returning only on Monday morning. As she reported that day, "We had the written examination in English Literature this morning. I am afraid I did not do very well, not having studied it on Saturday and the names are so hard to remember." While she did not expect to do well in literature, she did expect to do well in geometry and resented the result when she misinterpreted a question on a test, confiding to her diary on 20 April, "In my written paper in Geometry yesterday, I mistook one of the exercises for another and so took twenty from my paper. All the others were perfect; I was cross. I think Mrs A might have let it go when she knew I could do the other as well as the one I did."

Laura Fullerton's experience at Mount Allison Ladies' Academy may usefully be compared to Alvaretta Estabrooks's experience at Acadia Ladies' Seminary a few years later. While Alva went to Acadia mainly to study music, she, too, was required to take a full range of courses. At twenty-two, Alva was older than many of her fellow students and had not attended school for some years. Perhaps as a result, she took her studies somewhat more seriously and was somewhat more critical in her assessment of her teachers – and of college food – than our adolescent student diarists.[30]

September 16th, 1891. Wed. Arose at 5. The lessons keep me in a hurry all the time. Was disappointed in not getting a letter from home. Went walking with Miss Henigar. Retired at 10.

17th. Thur. Arose at 5. Studied until breakfast time. Was in class all morn. Took vocal lesson. Went walking with Lottie Burns. Studied my history lesson from ten to eleven by moonlight.

18th. Fri. Arose at half past 5. Studied untill breakfast time. Took music lesson. Went walking with Miss Eton & Miss Henigar. A very heavy wind, rain, thunder and lightening. Eve, got letters from Uncle Amos and Hannah. Retired at 10.

19th. Sat. Arose at half past 5. Cleaned out my room before breakfast. Practised 2 hours, studied some. The other girls went to Canning to see a ship launched. Was here in my room nearly all day alone. Was very lonesome at night. The Pierian Society of the Sem. met eve in the Reception room.[31]

20th. Sun. Arose at half past five. Wrote a letter to Uncle Amos. Went to Bible class & to meeting A.M. Wrote to Nellie Cormier, Arthur & Mother, and Ella Harmon, did not go to meeting eve. This has been a very long day. Have had the blues all day but feel some better now. Retired at 10.

21st. Mon. Arose at 5. Studied until breakfast. Knew my lesson quite well. Rhetoric excepted. Retired at ten. Rain.

22nd. Tues. Arose at 5. Studied all morn. Went walking with Lottie Burns P.M. Met Mr Shaw on the street, he was just on his way from train to College. He called eve, brought me a parcel Uncle Amos sent to me. Miss Graves[32] *would not let him see me. Retired at 10.*

23rd. Wed. Arose at 5. Studied morn, did not know my Rhetoric as usual. Miss Graves very cross. She asked me what I got in the box last night. I just thought it was none of her affairs but did not say so. Walked with Miss Henigar today. Retired at 10. Miss Chute sick with a cold. Got letters from Uncle Amos and Ralph & Ella Wolhaupter.

24th. Thur. Arose at half past five. Studied morn. Knew lessons. Went out walking with Miss MacKenzie. Retired at 10.

25th. Fri. Arose at half past 5. Studied all morn. Knew lessons. Went walking with Miss Henigar, called at a Miss Kempton's. Got a letter from Ella Harmon & Arthur. Eve, we were all called down to Reception room and were treated to pears which a Mr Wallace had sent up to the Sem. girls. Three cheers for Wallace whoever you might be. Retired at 10.

When Alva returned to school the following year, Acadia was a familiar and comfortable environment. Yet learning a new instrument made her a little nervous.

October 14, 1892. Fri. Arose at 6. I thought this morning I would not be able to get through my lessons, I knew them so poor, but I am still living. Went walking with Lottie. We had a pleasant time. Look for a letter from Arthur to-night but it did not come. Fine.

16. Sun. Arose at 7. Went to Church morn & eve. Dr Higgins preached both times. Wrote to Hannah, Arthur & Uncle Amos and read some. Very fine.

17. Mon. Arose at 5:45. Knew my lessons well to-day, so got through all right. Went walking with Nellie Belcher. A lovely afternoon, the hills look lovely now in their autumn dress. Fine. Mailed letters to Uncle Amos and Arthur.

18. Tues. Arose at 6. Knew my lesson all right. Went walking with Carrie. Went to girls prayer meeting eve. Led the meeting, which was quite a hard thing for me to do. Fine.

19. Wed. Arose at 6. Got along fine to-day. Went shopping but did not go any farther than Miss Rands. Went to prayer meeting eve. There was a very good meeting. Cloudy. Had letters from Uncle Amos & Arthur.

20. Thur. Arose at 5:30. Lessons. Practice &c. took up the day. Went walking with Lottie.

21. Fri. Arose at 6. Began taking violin lessons. I don't know how I will make out. I feel kind of "shaky" about it. A lecture in the college gymnasium. Lottie went, I did not. Went walking with Lottie. Cloudy.

22. Sat. Arose at 6:30. We did our room work before breakfast. From 5 to 10 practised violin. 10 to 11, studied. 11-12, Chorus sing. 12-1, study. After dinner, 2-3, Miss Dodge had a music class in Chapel. 3-4, worked Arithmetic. 4-5 practised violin. 5-6, took a bath and got ready for tea. After tea, 6:30-7, practised violin. 7-7:30, took violin lesson. 7:30-8:30, practised on Piano. 8:30 to 9:30, worked at arithmetic. 9:30-10, wrote in this (Miss Dodge was in about 10 minutes) and got ready for bed. Wrote to Arthur. Cold, windy.

Fortunately for Alva, the regimen outlined for 22 October was not one she was required to adhere to, and on many days she, like other diarists who attended private academies, found time for shopping, went for walks, participated in prayer meetings and missionary meetings, went to concerts and lectures, and enjoyed receptions that included students from the men's seminary.

Although at mid-century the majority of young women who continued their studies beyond the common school level attended private academies, by the time Laura Fullerton, Alva Estabrooks, and Sadie Harper were pursuing specialized programs in music and art at the ladies' academies associated with Mount Allison and Acadia, a growing proportion of their contemporaries were enrolling in the public high schools. Kate Miles's record of her experiences at Fredericton

High School, written in 1901, would not sound so very alien to today's sixteen-year-olds. Kate took her school work seriously enough to study regularly and to record the marks she earned. But, like Sadie Harper, she also very much enjoyed the social aspects of school, and was an enthusiastic member of the decorating committee for graduation. Thus, on Monday, 7 January, returning to school after the Christmas holiday, Kate reported, "Started Chemistry. I made 56 in Latin. Sade & I downtown at noon and after school." The following day, she recorded more grades from the previous term – 71 in literature and 96 in history – and further noted that her class had "started Enoch Arden for Literature.[33] Down town after school." After school on Wednesday, 16 January, "Dick, Sade, Hal McM and I were out for a snowshoe .... Only went over as far as the mouth of the Nashwaaksis. A big storm came up. Sade and I were downtown afterwards." On Thursday she "had to stay in for French to-night. Came home and studied an hour before tea and then from 6:30 until 10 o'clock." Again on Friday, she "had to stay in an hour after four for history but Mr. Mae let me off." Despite being required to stay in occasionally, Kate clearly enjoyed school and sometimes even chose to stay late. On 5 March, a day when they "were out snow balling at recess," she "did an experiment after school up in laboratory. Stayed until nearly 6. Then down town." On 6 March, she again "had to stay in to-night for French" and the following day "had a lot of studying to do," yet she enjoyed outings with her friends on both days. On Friday, 12 April, she "came up to Sade's after school to stay over Sunday." That weekend, the two friends mixed work and pleasure, beginning on Friday, when they "read some and studied some Latin in evening for Lat. Sup. on Monday." On Saturday, they went "down town in morning ... Ruth E. came to Sade's at 11 and we did some Latin. Sade and I had our pictures taken in afternoon." On Sunday, "We were to St. Anne's in morning[34] ... and to Methodist in evening. First time I was ever to Methodist Church. Mr. Campbell preached good sermon." On Monday, Kate and Ruth "had our Latin Sup. Quite hard. Sade and I were to see Gertrude after school. I got my wheel out to-night from Burt's." The following week, on 23 April, they "formed Decorating Committee ... for graduation ... I am sec-tres. We went to Mrs. Gibson's in evening. Had very nice time. Didn't get home until after 1." By 21 May, the decorating committee had begun its work in earnest and by June studying and decorating consumed almost all her time. On Friday, 21 June, she "had Grammar and Geometry exam ... Worked up in Assembly Hall until 5:30 crimping crepe paper to put up as streamers." On Monday, she "had Latin exam ... Up stairs first hour working, last hour singing. Made 80 in History. Wheeled over bridge after tea with Sade. Sade in to study." Tuesday it was "Botany in morning. Worked up stairs in afternoon until six." On Wednesday, Kate "had French exam this afternoon. I made 60 in Latin, and 46 out of 75 in Botany. Worked upstairs after school. Out for ride after tea. Sade is to sleep with me." On Thursday, "We worked up in Assembly Hall all day. Sade & I didn't go home to dinner. Annie brought me some strawberries." Finally, the day she had been working towards arrived: "Friday, June 28: Dark and warm. Bruce, Edgar, Mama and I up to closing this morning. It was fine and hall looked very nice indeed. Mama and I were up to Mrs Waycott's to dinner." And so ended another school year.

Once Mary Kingsley Tibbits of Fredericton had entered the University of New Brunswick in 1886, the way was opened for women to vie with men for scholarships.[35] Less than a decade after UNB opened its doors to women, Annie Ross entered with a county scholarship in hand; similarly, in 1903, Violet Goldsmith entered as the holder of the Gloucester County scholarship. Such equal competition signalled a change in societal attitudes and expectations. Although women, to greater or lesser extent, occupied "a little sphere all their own"[36] on university campuses, women and men soon began to negotiate another kind of relationship. Male students increasingly adopted a "flirtatious and often teasing manner" and female students sometimes responded in kind.[37] At the same time, higher education gave women an altogether new kind of independence. An 1895 survey of American women graduates found that fully half remained single, and the case in the Maritimes was similar. This development confirmed men's worst fears and fed the continuing debates about the suitability of education for women.[38] As reported by Violet Goldsmith, who soon joined the Delta Rho, the Women's Debating Society at the University of New Brunswick, women themselves participated in the debate on that as well as other significant issues of the day. The first debate, held in November, dealt with one aspect of the larger issue: "'Resolved that old bachelors are more use in the world than old maids.' Ina Mersereau affirmative, Hattie Irvin negative. I spoke (very briefly) on negative."[39] In the second term, Violet played a more active role, becoming a leading member of the Debating Society.

Sat Feb 27, 1904. I heard from Edna James this week, the first time she wrote since her father's death. I got half a dozen photos today like the one for the Encaenia picture. There was a meeting of delegates to the Women's council yesterday. Julia, Ina and I went from our Y.W.C.A. Miss Thorne was chairman, and when one lady started to give her opinion the chairman struck the desk and said "Address the Chair please." I was out to Mrs Colter's this afternoon. Hattie was with me. I gave her one of my photos. I led the affirmative at Debate last Monday, and Jessie Weyman led the negative and won 21 to 13 points. Subject: "Resolved that coeducation is a benefit to U.N.B." I thoroughly enjoyed it, and was not so nervous as I feared I would be.

Friday March 18. Last evening we had a Debate at Mrs Colter's. "Resolved that compulsory education would be a benefit to New Brunswick." Edith Davis, leader of the affirmative. Gertrude Coulthard of negative. I spoke on negative. There were 16 of us there, and Mrs Colter presided. It was the best I have been at yet. At Y.W.C.A. this evening Hattie presided and Clara Robins led. Last Saturday we had the Juniors "At Home." I took ice water wafers and a cake. I was on the invitation committee and helped print souvenir cards. They were red with black ribbon bow on the corner, and a quotation from Shakespeare printed on them, one for each of the Seniors. It was a perfect success. I helped wait on the table. I went to the Home Department Social at the Parsonage on Monday night, to College to Dr Hannay's lecture on "How Britannia Rules the Waves," on Tuesday night, to Ina's to write a Latin exercise on Wed night, debate last night, and prayer meeting tonight. It think that is pretty good for one week.

Sat March 19. I was weighted today, and weight 122 lbs, a loss of ½ lb since last of January. I have started today giving up eating dinner. I do not know how long it will last. The U.N.B. boys, Richards, Pugsley, and McCarthy, were defeated by Mt A in Debate last night.

Monday March 21. I nearly starved this afternoon, and have decided to eat my dinner after this, after trying the new plan for three days. I read my paper on Abnormal Imagination today and Dr Riley said it was good. Last night was a memorable night. About 2:15 a.m. there was a severe earthquake. There were two shocks, the first much nearer than the second. The house rocked, doors rattled, and the latch on my trunk made an extra noise. It seems strange that none of us got up, or called to each other. Two of the girls did not wake. I am glad I was awake. Dr Rogers preached last evening on "Remember Lot's wife," and spoke of the destruction of Sodom, Pompeii, etc. etc. and his words seem to have been prophetic. Bella McEwen said she did not know what it was, but it seemed to be only in her room and she was afraid to move for fear she would "set it up again." Some people who woke in a hurry thought there were burglars in their houses and grasped revolvers, etc. Edith Davis got up and looked at the graveyard to see if the dead were rising from their graves. She was sure the judgement day had come.

Thursday, March 24. I was at a general social in the Methodist Church last evening. There was a nice crowd there, and I had a good time. We girls had a banquet today given by the Freshmen and it was splendid. After the banquet we had a debate on "Resolved that it is preferable for a man to marry a girl with a good Cooking School Education than a graduate from a good Arts College." I was on the negative & it is the first time I have been on the winning side. Clara Robinson & Edna Bell were the leaders.

F'ton, Thurs., April 14. I went home for Easter on March 30. It was after 3 a.m. March 31 when I got there. I slept till twelve, then got up and went for a drive with Papa down to the points to see sick people. Aunt Maggie was sick all the time with rheumatism so I was scarcely out of the house all the time. Miss Kerr spent last Sunday night with us. I came back on Tuesday, and my trunk came by St. John. I did not know where it was till this morning, and it arrived here this evening. I had quite a fight with the Canada Eastern people about it. I was at Debate tonight. Subject Heredity versus Environment. I was chairman. Affirmative won. Last evening I went to College expecting to see some radium. By some mistake we had to go down to Parliament Buildings, & then we did not see radium but zinc sulphide illuminated by radium.

Friday, April 15. This was an eventful morning. We had a visit from Mrs Nation.[40] All the students assembled in the Library, and she gave us a splendid address on liquor and tobacco, cigarettes, etc., and turned to us girls and lectured us on our influence. She shook hands with us. Dr. Riley took her into the Laboratory & put her through those wonderful physical and mental tests. I read my paper on "The Golden Rule" at Y.W.C.A. this evening, and the girls thought it was good.

While Violet pursued her Bachelor of Arts degree, another young woman, Mabel Penery French, born and raised in Saint John, pursued a Bachelor of Civil Laws degree at King's College School of Law in Saint John. When, following her graduation in 1905, the Barristers' Society of New Brunswick refused to admit her to the bar on the grounds that women were not persons under the law, Mabel contested this decision. Although the Supreme Court of New Brunswick upheld the Society's ruling, in 1906, the provincial legislature ruled that women were persons, and in 1907 Mabel French became the first woman admitted to New Brunswick bar, the fourth woman to be called to the bar in Canada, and the first woman admitted outside of Ontario.[41]

As demonstrated in their diaries and letters, women participated in the evolution of education in New Brunswick. As school promoters, teachers, and students, they sought to shape the system to meet their needs and used it to their ends. While the appointed school trustees were invariably men, women like Jacobina Campbell were just as often the driving force in establishing rural schools. Women teachers such as Mary Wolhaupter and Kate Loggie struggled to convince mothers of the importance of education. Young farm women such as Ann Eliza Rogers, Lottie Reid, and Ida MacDonald took advantage of whatever schooling was on offer in their communities. More privileged young women, such as Mary Hill, Annie and Laura Trueman, Laura Fullerton, Sadie Harper, and Alvaretta Estabrooks, given the opportunity to continue their education at ladies' academies, "improved their time," as their mothers would have said, by preparing themselves to earn money by teaching music or painting. By the turn of the century, more and more young women were, like Kate Miles, attending high school, even if it meant boarding in town. Significant numbers attended the provincial normal school each year. And a few, like Violet Goldsmith, were entering university. Women's responses to New Brunswick's evolving educational system can thus be traced through the medium of their experience.

Women were, perhaps, even more active in their churches, institutions that were central to the social and intellectual as well as the spiritual dimensions of nineteenth-century life. The next chapter examines the nature and manifestation of women's sustaining faith.

Chapter 10

A Sustaining Faith

The significance of Christian faith and practice in women's lives emerges clearly in the diaries of girls and women. Ubiquitous references to ministers, "meetings," Sunday school, missionary societies, and sewing circles, to say nothing of church socials, bazaars, and picnics, provide evidence of the rich religious life central to the experience of our diarists. Even the most laconic of diaries reflect patterns of regular church attendance. Yet for those mature diarists whom other sources have identified as leaders in their faith communities, daily entries offer few enough insights into the nature and depth of that experience. It would seem that a mature, sustaining faith is manifested in the lived life and appears only fleetingly in the written record.

The often oblique references in Jacobina Campbell's terse daily entries demand careful assiduity and imaginative detective work of those seeking to identify her role within her faith community through the pages of her diary.[1] Yet taken together with other sources, the diary reveals Jacobina as a Methodist activist, a sponsor of the women's class meetings, which waxed and waned in her community during the nineteen-year period encompassed by her diary. She was instrumental in arranging for itinerant preachers or leading Fredericton Methodists to make the weekly trip up the Nashwaak to conduct Sunday meetings. Those meetings provided her with intellectual as well as spiritual stimulation. The upsurge in religious activity in late 1840, followed by a revival in early 1841, is reflected in Jacobina's diary entries. "Singing School begins," she reported on 30 November 1840. Thereafter, Mr Kemp travelled up the Nashwaak regularly to lead the singing school, staying "all night" with the Campbells on two occasions. The first hint that the singing school might be attracting ministers comes on 14 December, when "Miller & Brown bring Mr Kemp." The following day, Jacobina reported that "Mr Troop preaches & stays all night," and on 16 December she went "up with them to Frasers." Although winter storms brought occasional cancellations, the singing school continued meeting once, and sometimes twice, a week into 1841, culminating in the arrival of a group of American preachers on 25 March.[2] At the height of the religious fervour, the workaday world almost disappeared from Jacobina's diary. On 26 March, she went "to Meeting at Urquharts' Morng & Evng." And ministers continued to arrive: On 28 March, "Mr Shepherd up"; on 29 March, "D Brown up with Mr K."; on 30 March, "Mr McMartin here to dinner"; and on 1 April, "Mr McMartin preaches & stays all night." On 4 April, they had a "house full of people to our meeting," and on 5 April, "Mr Kidder stays all night." By mid-April, the normal farm routine had re-emerged in Jacobina's diary, but local enthusiasm remained strong and regular class meetings continued through the summer. Nevertheless, while Jacobina's diary testifies to the significance of religion in her daily life, it provides no information about the nature of the sermons she heard or the discussions in the class meetings she attended. Nor is Jacobina Campbell's diary unusual in this regard.

While diaries provide compelling evidence of the centrality of religious practice to nineteenth-century life, glimpses rarely extend beyond the concrete manifestation of that practice and it is often only through the care with which diarists have chosen to record the comings and goings of their ministers that we can gauge the importance they themselves accorded their spiritual experience. The search for a new minster for St Paul's Presbyterian Church in Fredericton in 1875–6 is carefully documented in Lucy Everett Morrison's diary, for example. And, although one can infer from Jacobina Campbell's diary her own centrality to Methodist life in her community of Taymouth, Janet MacDonald's diary offers no hint to alert us that she had been instrumental in the founding of the Second Baptist Church of Wickham, in Queens County.[3]

During the final months of 1858, however, Janet and Alexander MacDonald, as pillars of their local Baptist community, had much to celebrate. In October, Alexander Black Jr, their fourth son, was ordained as a Baptist minister. Then, in December, Janet rejoiced to see a stirring among the young people in her community, including her two youngest sons, William and Malcolm, and a granddaughter. In all, twenty-two "willing converts" were baptized that month. In her chronicle of the progress of the revival, Janet gives expression to her own strong faith.

December 3rd 1858, Fri. Wind, cloudy, quite moderate today. They have been hauling wood from the mill. Father chopping some. Donald painting. Malcolm come home tonight and John Trimble and him went up the lake to meeting. Started at six o'clock. Donald has gone to singing school.[4] *Father was at George's this evening. Last night William, Malcolm and James McAlpine skated from the Portage to Amos Mott's. Donald started yesterday to go to George MacDonald's but there was no skating above Amos Mott's. It is snowing some now, it wants twenty minutes of ten. Father and I is alone, the rest is gone to bed, but D has not got home yet from school.*

4th, Sat. N.W. wind, clear and quite cold. James and George hauling slabs from the mill. Donald working in the shop. Father was up to see Beckah Bulyea this afternoon. She is very poorly, she is failing fast. This evening James and Sally and Fred has gone to see her. William Hendry and his wife and Thomas is at George's this evening. William has just got home from Mr McAlpine's, fifteen minutes after nine. Mrs McAlpine is very low. Sally stopped at Mr Bulyea's all night. About eleven o'clock Malcolm and John Trimble come home from up the lake where they had been to meeting, and told us he was going to be baptized on Sabbath after meeting. They both prayed then went to bed.

5th, Sun. N.E. wind, clear and cold this morning. James went after Sally before breakfast. Father, Donald, William, Malcolm, John, Beckah[5] *and myself went up to the meeting house to meeting. Mr Skinner preached. Text was from the III Chapter, First Epistle of John, first part of the 14th verse.*[6] *There was prayer meeting in the morning. After meeting we all went to the water at Mr Ephraim Briggs' landing, and there Malcolm was buried with Christian Baptism by the Rev Joseph C. Skinner. There was a large congregation and very solemn. There is a goodly number appears to be inquiring the way to Zion. Then we went to different places and took dinner. Beckah, Malcolm and I got dinner at George MacDonald's and tea. We all stayed to night meeting. Joseph Blakney preached in the evening from 1st Corinthians, XV Chapter and last clause of the 31st verse.*[7] *Before dark it began to snow. It was the worst storm we have had this season. It was after ten when we got home and it was snowing hard and very cold then. The text was "I die daily."*

6th, Mon. N.W. wind, clear and cold, blowing hard. James took the children to school with the oxen, then went to Mr Cameron's after a barrel of flour. The rest is working at different things. I was washing today. Beckah is here this afternoon.

7th, Tues. N.W. wind, very little, clear and fine. Yet very cold. James and George hauling coal edges from the mill. Donald skated up the lake today. Father and I was down to Joseph Hendry's today. They sent for us this afternoon. The two Mr Blakneys, Allen MacDonald, and Alexander McClarey was here to tea. They had prayer meeting at the school-house. They had a great meeting. A good many spoke and prayed. There are a good many inquiring minds now. After meeting Uncle Lewis and Mr Keith come home with them. Mrs Merigold is here today. Sally washed some today. It is a lovely evening. The moonlight nights is just commencing. It is beautiful travelling on the land road. The ice is not fit to go on yet.

8th, Wed. N.E. wind and snowing. Then it commenced to hail and rain a little and froze as it fell. In the afternoon Father and I was to see Mrs McAlpine. She is very low: going fast. She is prepared to go. This afternoon the wind is N.W. James is shoemaking. Donald working in the shop. This evening George, Beckah, Father and I was up to Mr Bulyea's to see Beckah. She is going fast. William and John Trimble went to Mrs Blizzard's funeral today. She died with a cancer in her breast. Mr Crandel preached.

9th, Thurs. N.W. wind, clear and very cold. James and George hauling wood from the mill. Donald and father working at different things. There is a prayer-meeting at the school-house. They are all gone but Mary, the children and myself. They had a good meeting. There was a good many spoke in the meeting. There seems to be a deep work going on amongst the young people. I hope it may continue until they are all brought into the fold of Christ. It was ten o'clock when they got home. This is washing day.

10th, Fri. N.W. wind, clear and cold. They are hauling wood. George hauling hay for Mrs Watts. Mr Blakney is here to dinner, then he went up to the other meeting house. There is prayer meeting there tonight. Beckah is here this afternoon. They are ironing today. Thomas McCray died tonight.

11th, Sat. W. wind, cloudy and cold. James was down to Mr Case's. [?], Donald and George went after hay, but could not get across the creek. They brought some hay for Mrs Straight from Mr Colwell's. In the afternoon he hauled a load of wood. Father was up through the neighbourhood getting signers for Mr Blakney. He made out very well. This evening there is prayer meeting at the school-house. Father, James and I went up, but could not get in, there was such a crowd of people. The rest got in. We were rather late, so come home again. After meeting, Judson Blakney, Delilah and Susan McDonald come home with them. It was midnight when they got home.

12th, Sun. N.W. wind, clear and very cold. There was meeting at the meeting house today. Mr Keith preached from the II Chapter of Galations, first clause of the 13th verse.[8] The two Mr Blakneys was there and took part in the services. After meeting we all repaired down to the water at the lake shore and there was five converts baptized by Elder Keith. They were William Mott, and Ann Mott, his daughter, Joseph and James Mott, and Mary Mott,[9] children of Amos Mott. It was a solemn time then. Uncle John MacDonald, Aunt Sally and Charlotte and Elinor and Sarah McClary come home with us to dinner. Then Father, Donald, William, Malcolm and John all went up to the other meeting house to meeting. Yesterday the first team crossed from the Point over to the Portage and today the first team crossed from the Point over this way. Mac stayed at Mr Bulyea's all night.

13th, Mon. N.W. wind, clear and cold. James and George was down to the marsh after hay. This morning father went to the barn to feed the cattle and the ladder slipped and he fell and sprained his foot. He is quite lame. There is prayer meeting at Mr Colwell's this evening. There was nobody down from here. This evening the wind is N.E. and is storming snow and hail.

14th, Tues. Still this morning and foggy all day. In the afternoon southerly wind, very little. James and Donald hauling hay. Just as they was getting ready James Mott come after George to go and stay with William Mott till they went after Dr Peters. He is quite deranged. In the afternoon I was up there to see him. He is very bad. The doctor come while I was there and bled him. Joseph Blakney was here when I come home and Margaret Watts. The doctor called here to see Mary. This evening there is prayer meeting at the school-house. We was all up but Sally and Mary. We went with the horse and sleigh, Father and children and I. We had a good meeting.

15th, Wed. Still foggy and raining. The first rain we have had since the 7th of November. It did not thaw much. It did not take all the snow off. The travelling on the land is not hurt. James is shoe making. Donald was up to see William Mott tonight. He is very bad. They dare not *leave him alone. He is entirely out of his mind. The doctor thinks it is the brain fever.*[10] *Prayer meeting at William Colwell's. Father and John Trimble went down with the horse and sleigh. They had a good meeting.*

16th, Thurs. N.W. wind, clear and quite cold. Donald painting the other sleigh. James chopping wood at the school house. He was at W. Mott's, he was no better. This afternoon I was up to see him. The doctor came this evening to see him. He called here. There is prayer meeting at the school house this evening. They are all up. This is washing day.

17th, Fri. N.W. clear and cold. James chopping in the woods, Donald painting. Father is quite lame yet. George and Beckah was over the lake. Judson Blakney is here to dinner, then went over the lake. There is prayer meeting at S. Wetmore's. After meeting William and Alexander Hendry came home. James Hendry come in the afternoon, then he went up the lake.

18th, Sat. N.W. wind, clear and cold. James has gone after Dr Peters for William Mott. He is no better. Mr Keith and Uncle Lewis is here to dinner and Mr Blakney. William is home today. This evening there is conference at the meeting house. The men is all gone but James. Him and Sally is gone to see Mr Mott. The doctor come while they was there. He thought him a little better this afternoon. Mr Duval come and went to meeting with them, then come and stayed all night, and Mr Blakney.

19th, Sun. N.W. wind, clear and very cold this morning. Mr Duval and Mr Blakney has gone to their appointments. Mr Duval to the Narrows, and Mr Blakney to the Skinner meeting house. There was no meeting here today. Mrs John McAlpine was buried today. Donald, Malcolm and John Trimble was over at the funeral. Mr Perry preached. William is not well today. She died Thursday morning at seven o'clock of consumption. This afternoon I was up to see Mr Mott. He is no better to all appearances. I road down with Thomas Earl and Susan.[11] *They had been to see Beckah Bulyea. She is failing fast. James was after the doctor, did not come. He sent medicine. Mr London and his wife was here this evening. There is meeting at the meeting house. Judson Blakney preached. They had a good time. A good many spoke and prayed afterwards. There is good times here now.*

20th, Mon. Southerly wind and snowing hard. About eight o'clock it stopped snowing. Then the wind came from the [?].W. with quite a snow squall. Then it cleared off and was quite pleasant. There is meeting at the meeting house at 10 A. M. We was all down but Mary, the baby and Marthy Stewart.[12] *There was a large congregation. Mr Duval preached. His text was the VIII Chapter of the Acts of the Apostles, last clause of the 39th verse: "and he went on his way rejoicing." Then we all repaired to the lake shore and there the Rev. Joseph C. Skinner baptized twelve willing converts. It was a solemn time. They were Joseph Hendry and his daughter Ruth, William Colwell and his wife, Amelia and Diadamy Holder, William Straight and Willet Worden, Malissa Mott and Emaline McDonald, my grand-daughter,[13] and my own dear William L. MacDonald and John Trimble. I rode down with James Hendry. After meeting Mr Duval come here with us and Mrs Joseph Mott, and Malissa and Allen MacDonald was here to dinner. This afternoon George killed a hog. He is going to St John in the morning.*

As the year drew to a close, Janet MacDonald looked back with pleasure and forward with hope:

This is New Year's Eve. What changes since last New Year's eve. How many has gone the way of all the earth since then, and oh! what a change in this place. How many young people now is rejoicing and praising the Lord that this time last year did not appear to think about religion, and others inquiring the way to Zion. Oh! it is a good time here. Now I do hope it will continue on till all may come to Christ from the least to the greatest.

She was by no means alone in this hope. In late 1858, the editors of and writers to Baptist and Methodist newspapers, as well as some of the organizers of local revivals in the Maritimes, saw these as part of an international revival, one that is now considered the last large-scale Anglo-American transatlantic revival. The MacDonalds, voracious readers, subscribed to at least one Baptist newspaper, and Janet may well have had this wider context in mind as she recorded her reflections on the previous year.[14]

In contrast to older women, who were secure in their faith, the diaries of younger women provide insight into the often remarkable level of intellectual exploration and analysis involved in the evolution and maturation of faith. A comparison of women's various paths in their quest to achieve a sustaining faith reveals a diversity of experiences, reflecting not only a diversity of attitudes and outlooks but also a critical engagement with theological questions and issues. In the early-nineteenth century, young women were encouraged to use their diaries as an expression of faith and a means of self-discipline.[15] And for some of the younger diarists, struggling with questions of belief and feeling angst about the state of their souls, diaries provided a place to confide their innermost thoughts. Both Mary Wolhaupter's and Kate Loggie's diaries seem to confirm the contention that "the resolutions sprinkled throughout diaries suggest that exhortations to self-denial and service were not simply the stuff of advice manuals, but made their way into girls' own self-expectations."[16] Yet Mary's and Kate's "self-expectations" were very different.

Certainly Mary Wolhaupter's diary exemplifies the view "that the goal of being good required the suppression of self and the subordination of girls to their mothers."[17] Thus, on leaving home to return to her school on 21 January 1869, she reported that, having kissed her, "Ma told me to be a good girl. I hope I may be a good Christian girl." But, in her own view, Mary regularly fell short of that goal. Following her return home in February, she often perceived herself to be ill-tempered and sulky and prayed to be "better." Hoping to profit from a sermon heard on Sunday, 2 May, she reminded herself that "I am the oldest child at home and ought at all times to be setting good examples. God grant that I may for it is very important that I should." And on 22 December, a day when she "did not feel very well" but had been "very sullen and wicked, not pleasant to Ma," she prayed: "Lord grant that I may grow wiser and do different from what I generally do for it is very wicked not to be pleasant with ones mother."[18]

In contrast, Kate Loggie's spiritual angst had little to do with either "the suppression of self" or obedience to her mother. Raised a Presbyterian, Kate found herself drawn to Methodism, partly, no doubt, because her friend Fanny McLeod was a Methodist, and she was contemplating conversion.[19] But her decision did not turn on friendship. During an era when churches competed for souls, Mr Mason, recently appointed Presbyterian minister in Burnt Church, made a concerted effort to retain Kate's loyalty, visiting her at her school on at least three occasions in November 1880.[20] Kate could not be swayed by such pressure, but she was impressed by his sermon: on Sunday, 7 November, she "went up to preaching in the school-house at three o'clock. Mr Mason preached. Text Job 3: 'Will he always call upon God?' Liked the sermon very much." In contrast, Mr Wells, the Methodist minister, failed to impress: "Went to hear Mr Wells at half past six. Tried to go in a right spirit but still did not care for the sermon, though from text, 'I go to prepare a place for you,' a precious promise. Scarcely think I'll go back again." Nonetheless, Kate's preoccupation with the state of her soul persisted. On 10 January 1881, a Sunday when the Methodist minister "did not get up," she "had very uneasy thoughts all the evening. Wish that I could feel assured that I am converted. Know my heart is very forgetful of God. Am much inclined to murmur at my situation. O Lord teach me for Jesus sake. Yesterday read the Gospel according to John." When the minister again failed to arrive the following Sunday, Kate once more pursued her own Bible study, reading "Judges & Ruth & two chapters in the Young Christian." On Monday evening, Kate attended the Methodist class meeting, led by Mr. Quinn, noting, "Hope I have learned something. Text Isaiah 55 chap. & 1st clauses of the 10th & 11th verses."[21] At home the following weekend, she attended the Presbyterian communion service with her family, but after her return to her boarding place confided in her diary, "Fear I do not enjoy communion as much as I should." There she looked to her Methodist class leader for intellectual as well as spiritual guidance: "Have been reading Woodstock, but cannot help thinking I am wrong, although Mr. Quinn approves." Despite his approval, in a spirit of self-denial, she "set it aside today," but then "spent nearly the whole evening over Castle Daly. I think it is a good story but fear I have devoted too much time to it." And she continued to agonize over the state of her soul: "All have gone to bed & I do not feel prepared to go. Is it because there is a cloud between me & my Master? Fear I am holding the world with too tight a hold."[22]

Yet Kate did not doubt her ability to hold her own in discussions of issues of faith, reporting on Sunday that her landlord "Mr. Grattan came from the woods tonight. We had a conversation on religion. Hope it may prove profitable to both. Oh Lord enable me to grow in grace. Let me constantly press forward to those things which are before. For Jesus sake Amen."[23] In her diary, Kate Loggie, like Mary Wolhaupter, recorded her inner struggles with questions of theology and belief. In their search for affirmation and direction, both women sought answers in Bible passages and published sermons, and attended church regularly. Yet their spiritual struggles were fundamentally different.

Other women travelled a road to spiritual maturation that was less fraught, recording no crises of faith or inner spiritual struggles in the pages of their diaries. Growing up in a devout Methodist family, Annie Trueman was raised in an atmosphere that promoted discussion and critical appraisals of seasoned as well as apprenticing ministers. Yet, as her 1871 diary illustrates, at nineteen, Annie questioned neither the tenets of Methodist faith nor the nature of her own belief.

Sunday [Jan. 29], 1871. We were all out this morning to listen to a searching sermon full of sound doctrine, from Dr. Stewart. In the afternoon

Mr. Laurence came and stayed to tea. He seems to be a fine young man who is determined to make his mark in the world – a hard student he is a relative of ours. I do not know if he is a Christian.

Tuesday [Jan. 31]. Mamma & Papa went over the Marsh today. Yesterday we spent a very pleasant evening at Mr. Woods.

Thursday [Feb. 2]. The concert came off this eve: the hall was crowded to its utmost. We managed to get a very poor seat. Prof's instrument was the best feature of the whole proceeding, the music he brought from it was perfectly charming in some parts. The tone is much softer than the piano. The result of the affair was 100 dollars.

Sat. [Feb. 4] Extreme cold. How many poor creatures are suffering tonight from hunger & cold & I have everything to make me comfortable. The lines are indeed fallen to me in pleasant places. I have everything to be thankful for. O Lord give me a more grateful heart.

Sunday, Feb. 5th. A holy Christian Sabbath evening! What a delightful time is this, when father, mother, brother and sisters gather around the glowing fire and talk of holy things: of words of cheer & warning spoken by the earnest soldier of the cross. A Christian home who can tell the influence of these Sabbath evening talks? This day has been a very long one to us for we have not been able to listen to the preaching of the Gospel, on account of such severely cold weather. We have been reading a good deal. Papa has been out three times today. I have felt an increased desire today that I might be the instrument in the hands of God of bringing some soul to Christ. What joy would this be!

Monday [Feb. 6]. A glorious morning. The full orbed moon is shining so brightly and looks down so sadly at us, while the glittering stars twinkle so gaily and pale. Aurora playfully dances in the North. When contemplating such a night as this one might for a time almost think that our earth is some delightful Paradise, that we live in some Golden age when everything is beautiful and our whole lives calm, peaceful and serene, but we are soon aroused to the fact that even if all Nature is beautiful around us yet man is vile and blights our lovely earth with his wickedness that in every place Satan finds some whom he leads captive at his will. It seems to me that the masterpiece of Satan's machinations is the Rum traffic, even in our own Sackville there are six places where the horrid beverage of Hell is sold. Some people feel the strong desire to save their fellow creatures from a drunkard's life and a drunkard's hell, and these are working diligently. This evening we all (excepting Mamma)

> attended a Temperance meeting where we listened to a very able speech by Prof. D. Allison, which I am sure ought to do us a great deal of good. Mr. James & Mr. Murphy also offered some earnest remarks. There is so little philanthropic feeling here that these meetings are poorly attended.
>
> Tuesday [Feb.7]. We walked down this eve to the vestry and listened to a very nice little sermon from J.W. Doull. He bids fair to be a useful minister one of these days. The subject was Christ our foundation.

Annie's diary entry the following Sunday (12 February) illustrates her faith in the power of God's word: "Mr. Brettle preached a searching and impressive sermon from the words 'And the hail shall sweep away their refuge of lies.' Hallett one of the rumsellers who is an infidel listened to the earnest declaration of the truth. Surely he could not go away unmoved. Surely the thought that 'after all the Bible may be true' will haunt him all this week." In later years, Annie's desire to be "the instrument in the hands of God of bringing some soul to Christ" and her convictions about the evils of the rum traffic found practical expression in social action, as a member of both the Methodist Women's Missionary Society and the Woman's Christian Temperance Union.

In the case of the Trueman sisters, the evolution of their Methodist faith can be traced by reading their diaries in conjunction with their correspondence. The extensive correspondence between Rebecca Trueman and her two daughters, Annie and Laura, provides evidence of an increasingly sophisticated intellectual conversation about ministers, their sermons, and matters of faith. Through the medium of this conversation, Rebecca encouraged her daughters not to suppress their own views, but rather to develop strong critical minds. Living in Sackville, the training ground for Methodist ministers, from a young age Annie and Laura Trueman had high standards when it came to preaching. Visiting cousins in Saint John when she was about seventeen, Laura reported to her mother, "We went out this morning to Lion's Church to hear Mr. Brecken, but to our intense disappointment *Mr. Anguin* preached, and you know that I would rather listen to any minister in the Methodist Conference than him. I suppose you had the supreme happiness of listening to *Wesley*."[24] While Rebecca did not refute Laura's assessment of Mr Anguin, in responding she subtly encouraged her daughters to turn their critical eyes on Wesley as well, confirming that she had, indeed, heard him on Sunday:

> He preached yesterday from the words Man that is born of a woman &c, a real funeral sermon & had funeral hymns. After the service was over a

stranger accosted Pa at the door with the question "Has any distinguished person died lately, that the young man was preaching a funeral sermon?" He (W.) seemed to have exhausted the hymn book for all the dirge like quotations he cd find ... Was it not too bad you had to go to church in St. John to hear Mr. A. preach.[25]

A few months later, Annie and Laura made a second trip to Lyon's Church, but seemed destined to miss Brecken, with Annie reporting, "We have been out to church once & expect to go to Germain St. in the evening. There was a stranger in Lion's church this morning. We went hoping to hear Brecken." Annie judged the sermon "a pretty poor attempt, like the average sermons of the Sackville students, much Mr. James' style in appearance, & mind too I rather think – one of the young Englishmen. I tried to get some crumbs of good, but I dont know as I succeeded. Maybe the fault was in myself. I thought of the delightful sermons we are privileged to hear at home – & that you would be listening to this morning."[26] It seems likely that Violet Goldsmith's widowed father, himself a Methodist minister, had similar conversations with his daughter, who emerges in her diary as firm in her faith but independent in her judgment. And, if the comments of diarists Sadie Harper, Laura Fullerton, and Alvaretta Estabrooks may be taken as representative, ladies' academies associated with theological colleges encouraged a critical approach when it came to evaluating lectures and sermons by male seminarians.[27]

Nor did women lose their critical edge as they matured in their faith. Rather, they continued to discuss their experiences and exchange views not only about the sermons and styles of local ministers but also about the fundamentals of belief and the nature of practice. Reporting on a Baptist revival in Albert County in 1879, Lottie Reid, at twenty, emerges as an acute and somewhat skeptical observer.[28] Her family were Baptists, but, as was common in rural communities dependent on itinerant ministers, they also attended Methodist and Presbyterian services. Like the Truemans, Lottie was a well-informed and critical listener, commenting on the ministers and their sermons as well as on the progress of the revival. On Sunday, 2 February, she noted in her diary that "there were several baptized at Hopewell this afternoon. A good many went over from this way." The snow, which "began to fall thick and fast" the following Sunday, did not prevent Lottie, her brother Wat, and sister Jo from going "to Hopewell to baptizing ... Mr. Chipman baptized nine. There were a great crowd, altogether to the water. We then went to hear Mr. C preach in the hall at Riverside. Heard a very good sermon. The hall was filled to overflowing." Over the next several weeks, the religious excitement continued, peaking on Sunday, 9 March, when Lottie reported that "Merritt, Wat and Jo have been away all day attending meetings and baptizing at Hopewell. Mr. Chipman baptized 16 today at the Hill." Lottie was a loyal Baptist, yet her final comment – "There can't be many bad ones left over that way" – sounded a skeptical note. Following the progress of the revival, the younger generation of Reids ranged widely, attending services in a variety of neighbouring communities. On 13 April, with the "roads fearfully bad," they stayed close to home, where "Brother Blackaddor baptized seven." The following Sunday, "Susan Reid and Watson went ... to baptizing and meeting at New [Horton]. Mr. Keith baptized 5, they are having great meetings there. Brother Blackaddor keeps working away ... But I think he has to work pretty hard now." On 27 April, Lottie, Wat, and Susan "went to New Horton again to meeting and baptism. Heard a loud and able sermon from Mr. Keith." Baptisms continued into May, though the numbers, as Lottie had predicted, dwindled.

Lottie Reid's comments and critique, though more subtle than those of the Trueman sisters, proved no less sharp. On 12 May, Lottie and Merritt were to Riverside where they heard "a short but pretty fair sermon." On 25 May, she noted, "There was quite a crowd out considering that Brother Blackaddor held forth as well." On 1 June, perhaps to avoid Brother Blackaddor, "the boys and I were up to Methodist meeting ... Mr. Lodge preached in Mr. Wilson's place. He is stationed at Salisbury I think." They returned the following week to hear Mr. Wilson. "His subject was on baptism. There was quite a turnout." On 22 June, she did not name the minister, but reported, "Merritt and I ... heard a pretty dry old sermon. There was a large crowd out though." And on 6 July, "Merritt, Wat and I were up to hear a sermon given by Mr. Miner Cleveland which was very good considering it was his first attempt to preach." Travelling further afield on 20 July, "Ma, Pa and I were over to Hopewell Corner this morning to hear the Rev. Mr. Hogg, the Presbyterian minister of Moncton. Heard a very good sermon." Travelling to nearby communities to hear sermons delivered by ministers of different denominations gave Lottie Reid a sound basis for her evaluations.

When they were far from home, women often took the opportunity to attend church services, and their reports on their experience to family and friends reflect judgments that were both thoughtful and astute. Writing to her mother and sister from New York in 1881, twenty-five-year-old Laura Truman Wood provided a discerning and intellectually sophisticated analysis of the nature of the appeal of two church services aimed at very different audiences, which she attended on a single Sunday. Of the first, "a missionary sermon preached in St. Paul's M[ethodist] E[piscopal] Church by Dr. Chapman," she declared, "I am sure I never enjoyed a service better ... It was such a soul stirring sermon, so full withal of Christ's love & praise & comfort for the believer." But Laura further recognized that the surroundings and the music played an equally significant role in stirring the soul, offering a compelling argument in her evocative description:

> And Oh! in these elegant churches there is so much wrought on the feelings through the senses ... I wept as I heard the Angelic voice of the soprano pleading in the words of the lovely hymn (read it, I never knew it before to be so full of meaning) "Jesus my strength my hope, On thee I cast my cares." Oh! I wish you could have heard her sing the line "Bold to take up firm to sustain"; I never can forget it. Away up in a beautiful niche somewhere behind us. It seemed to me like the song of a soul that had reached a higher plane than those below, and that we were now striving after. Then what perfection the art of painting churches has arrived at. The background for the minister seems really to glorify him at the same time giving miraculous rest and comfort to tired eyes.

Laura's account of the second service was no less evocative. Knowing that her mother and sister would share her excitement, she wrote, "Guess who we went to hear ... I happened to see that O'Connor's name in the Herald, and remembered how your 'Witness' was full of him." His church being within walking distance, she and her husband attended the evening service. "The congregation," she observed, "was a pretty rough looking one composed I should think of reformed Irish Catholics & a few strangers who went from curiosity. It was not an immense audience ... & a great many kept coming & going at the door." Of the service itself, she noted,

> The meeting opened by singing "I am so glad that Jesus loves me" & "Sweet Hour of Prayer." It was all conducted very informally ... After the singing ... O'C called on Bro Parker to pray – He said Bro. P. had been converted "both from *Rum & Rome*" & he said they generally went together ... Well this Bro P's prayer was a regular Irish prayer, just pleading over & over in the garrulous Irish fashion Dear Jesus Loving Jesus Have mercy O God. Strengthen us O God &c ... but it came right from the heart & I enjoyed it.

Laura was less impressed by Father O'Connor, "a man of rather ordinary ability ... intersperses what he says with ... puns & jokes." Indeed, she rather sympathized with the Roman Catholic critique of him, illustrating her point with one of his jokes: "He said 'You Rom. Cath'lics think the priests & the Bishops & the Pope have grace & power to hand you up into heaven no matter what you do, but I think their hands would have to be well graced (greased) to do it.' All such jokes as this – and I dont wonder he was mobbed some time he uses such strong expressions about the Pope & the Rom. religion, & we all know how excitable & touchy the Irish are in regard to their religion. However," she concluded, "I have no doubt he is just the man for the work."[29] Laura Wood's implicit advocacy of proselytization, despite her recognition of its potential to create tensions within communities that included diverse ethnic and religious groups, is a measure both of people's engagement with theological distinctions and of the depth of their convictions.

Occasionally, the competition for souls that characterized nineteenth-century religion caused serious rifts within otherwise cooperative communities. Like many rural parishes, Greenwich, in Kings County, depended on itinerant ministers of different denominations alternating in shared space. In 1882, Lillie Williamson's father, who served as a lay minister for the Wesleyan Methodists, was instrumental in furnishing and overseeing the management of a new church hall. But the Anglicans – "the Church party" – perhaps because they had a more permanent minister, soon staked an exclusive claim to the space, creating something of a crisis for the Methodists. Watching events unfold, Lillie confided her view of the situation to her diary on 26 February 1883:

> There has been a great deal happening about church affairs ... ever since the hall was built, which I have not written, because I dislike to write about anything of that sort. Father made the great blunder of letting Parson Pickett in to preach, and there have been nothing but rows in consequence, and now the rowdy party have actually taken possession and taken it out of Father's hands. He could have a trustee meeting, and outvote them, but he thinks he has stood in the foreground long enough, and unless the conference takes hold, I guess they will be allowed to keep it. It would be far too long to write particulars but anyone who has ever worked with the Church party could guess them pretty well.

By 8 March, the Methodists had decided to do nothing until spring, when Mr Currie, the leading Methodist minister in the province, could get up the river to convene a meeting. In the meantime the Church Hall had temporarily fallen into disuse, possibly because Lillie's father "had taken the organ, lamps, stove, and pipe out of the hall; which was all his own property over and above his subscription." By 1 April, however, the "Church people" had installed their own stove with a view to holding services there. And for Lillie, the results of the trustee meeting, reported in her diary on 1 June, proved less than satisfactory: "There were no results, except that father took back the furniture, of course we did not want it and were glad to get it out of the house."

The dispute between the Anglicans and Methodists opened the way for the Baptists to step into the breach. According to Lillie, the Methodists, deprived of the use of the hall, were dependent on "a Mr. McKenzie a Baptist minister [who] comes to the Flat occasionally to preach or we would stagnate all together I think." Listening to Baptist sermons did not shake Lillie's firm Methodist convictions, and late that autumn as a Baptist revival got underway, she voiced her strong disapproval of the Baptist "rage for dipping" – adult baptism that involved total immersion, sometimes at the height of winter. On 8 December, she reported, "The Baptists are having a revival at noon. The minister, Mr. Trafton is fully connected, but still I think he is a good man and is doing some good. He has very nice meetings, and does not bring in the dipping in his preaching." Mr Opie, the newly appointed Methodist minister, held his first meeting that morning, and the Williamsons "of course ... went to our own meeting," but, perhaps because there were only a handful in attendance, the meeting ended early, and Lillie and her family were able to go to the baptism. "There was a crowd of the Baptists. Mrs. Charlie Gorman, Dave McNiel, and Maud Belyea were the ones who were immersed. I did not care for the others but it made me mad to see them put Maud under the ice and snow. It is well that she is not Fred's girl. I think he would have left her if she had been." With the revival underway, Lillie soon lost all respect for Mr Trafton, noting on 7 January 1884, "Like all Baptist ministers Mr. Trafton was very quiet about the dipping at first, but grows bolder as he goes on, especially when he finds that every one does not go in with him." Noting that "he preaches regularly on both Mr. Opie's and Mr. Pickett's appointments," Lillie now dismissed him as "very bigoted," yet shrewdly observed that "as he is the only earnest preacher, and the only one who has attempted to hold revival meetings for so long he of course reaps what other ministers have sown. There has been a dipping every Sunday but one since he came." The third, when three converts were baptized, "was the most cruelly bitterly cold day that ever comes in a winter. We heard that their clothes froze on them as soon as they were out of the water." Although she did not indicate whether there were any former Methodists among those baptized, Lillie took no little satisfaction in recording that

> the fourth was [Wilber] Belyea, formerly a good Churchman, and last Sunday Will Day also a good Churchman, and Cady Johnson. The Church people are just as mad as they can be. They have never had so many of their flock picked off before. They have something else to talk of now besides Williamson's bad doings. I expect it would be quite rich to hear Parson Pickett preach now. Mr. Trafton gets great crowds. Last Sunday there was scarcely room to find seats at all.

Over the next few months, Lillie followed the progress of Mr Trafton's revival, although she did not continue to attend his services. On 16 February, she reported that "Mr. Trafton is holding meetings over the river now." Closer to home, Methodists appeared to be returning to the fold: "Mr. Opie received Mr. and Mrs. Harvey in the church last Sunday. We had a regular old time crowd. We had quite a nice prayer meeting at the end of service." Yet by 29 March, Mr Trafton's Baptist revival was still gaining converts. Finally, on 31 May, came some good news: "We had the great Revd. D.D. Currie last Sunday evening in the hall. He preaches a splendid sermon. Mr. Trafton preaches here every fortnight but his congregation has decreased a great deal."

Often the mainstays of their faith communities, women attended church more regularly and in greater numbers than their male counterparts. Among other contributions, including significant fund raising, women's church activism involved a good deal of unremarked, though by no means unremarkable, domestic labour. Such practical activism has often been the focus of discussions of women's contributions to their faith communities, and not without reason. For the women in the Reid family, the annual Baptist Association meeting meant household upheaval when it met in Harvey in 1881. Writing to her sister Lottie on 14 May, Jo Turner commented,

> I don't wonder that you are dreading the Association; I expect you will have a crowded house all the time, and you will all work yourselves half to death. I hope Ma will get someone to help her for a while, if she does not I fear you and her both will get sick cooking and working around in such hot weather. I think the best thing that could be done, would be to shut up

the house for a week or so and go off on a cruise somewhere. Mary will have a house full too, she won't surely try to get along alone ... I am afraid she is doing too much.[30]

Two months later, with the meeting looming, their brother Wat also spared a thought for his mother and sisters, noting in a letter dated 10 July, "I suppose when you receive this the association will be in full blast and you will all be up to your ears in work with the home all upside down and all filled with ministers, etc. I hope they will be a little moderate and not make too much work for you and Ma and Mary."[31] Lottie recorded the details of that busy period in her diary. On 12 July, "Mr Kelly and wife got dinner here today, also Mr Truman Steeves. Hope we will not have a very big crowd here. Pa, Ma and Josie went up to the meeting this afternoon." Two days later, she noted, "We have had quite a crowd here yesterday & today. The association closed this evening. I was there for the first time." On Friday, 15 July, she was "glad all the strangers took their leave this morning." Lottie scarcely had time to remark on the outcome of the meeting, but her sister Jo, writing from Germany on 30 July to beg for information about the results, reminds us of women's roles as audience as well as workers: "We are anxious to hear how it came off. If it will only be the means of Mr. Blackadar's leaving Harvey it would be a good thing." Mr Blackadar did not immediately leave Harvey, but if he continued to preach, Lottie did not attend his sermons.

Women thought about, discussed, and debated theological questions. Far from feeling constrained by a system of beliefs that demanded self-denial and the suppression of the self, some women found a kind of freedom, and even a degree of independence through faith.[32] More commonly, young women, though denied the formal theological training available to young men, sought intellectual stimulation in sermons and religious texts that were widely circulated. Jacobina Campbell nourished her faith and developed her intellect through the medium of the Methodist class meeting[33] and the keeping of a commonplace book into which she copied quotations, summaries of sermons, and various commentaries, as well as excerpts from published spiritual writings. This commonplace book offers a rare insight into the breadth and depth of one woman's knowledge of the religious writers and thinkers of her day, and into the sophistication of the sermons preached in one rural community on the Nashwaak River during the first quarter of the nineteenth century.[34] Further, Jacobina's commonplace book, in which she both recorded and reflected upon biblical passages, sermons, and other religious commentaries, offers an unusual opportunity to gain insight into the mind of "a thinking woman" as she embarked upon a lifelong spiritual journey. Although we cannot know for certain, it seems likely that her commonplace book also reflected subjects discussed at Methodist class meetings.

Whether or not women debated theological issues at Methodist class meetings, they undoubtedly discussed them in other contexts. Writing from England to her sister Annie in 1882, Laura Wood reported, "I have been doing some grand reading 'The Nemesis of Faith' by Froude, 'Sartor Resartus' by Carlyle & now I am going to read Emerson's Essays. These books are all mine, & you shall have them." Through her promise to share her reading material, Laura held out to her sister an invitation to engage in discussion and debate. Citing a letter Annie had written, she noted,

> It quite seemed to be a reflection on me ... that you spoke about the Church members having deviated so much from their old faith. I have been reading these heterodox works but they have not filled me with doubts because I will not doubt, – but I think every one must have their little wonderings we might call it, but they don't touch the root of the matter Annie. I think I shall like to read some of these things with you.[35]

Similarly, Sophy Carman drew both strength and sustenance from her Anglican faith. Particularly, though not only, during Lent, her daily religious rituals were woven seamlessly into the routine of family life. But like other diarists, her faith was informed by reading. Sophy was good friends with Margaret Medley, the Bishop's wife, and they enjoyed sharing books with one another. On 12 March 1872, Sophy reported that she "read Lecture No. 1 ... on 'Tradition'" that Mrs Medley had lent her. The following day she read Lecture No. 2. And on New Year's Day, 1873, she noted that "Mrs Medley gave me a little book by 'Goulburn.'" Edward M. Goulburn was an English churchman and scholar, and the book in question was very likely *Thoughts on Personal Religion* or *The Pursuit of Holiness*.[36] Informed and thoughtful, women sought the depth of understanding necessary to sustain their faith.

Religion and religious observance permeated almost every aspect of nineteenth-century life. In times of trouble, women looked to their sustaining faith, drawing upon it to help them bear the loss of a parent, a child, or a husband. And they called upon that faith as they sought to improve and reform their society in voluntary organizations ranging from maternal associations to temperance lodges.[37] Women sustained their churches, becoming key fund raisers, organizing bazaars, teas, picnics, and musical evenings that brought the entire community together. Churches sustained communities just as faith sustained individual women. And undertaking the kind of work that is generally omitted in routinely generated statistical calculations of productivity, women sustained both their faith and their churches by regularly entertaining ministers in their homes.[38] The following chapter considers the productive nature of women's work in the home.

Chapter 11

Work in the Home

Integral to both the smooth functioning of individual households and the smooth functioning of the local economy, women's work, though often overlooked or subsumed in calculations of men's production by census enumerators, is so important that it cannot be treated as a single category.[1] This chapter will, therefore, focus on women's work in and around the home that was generally, though by no means always, "unpaid" work, while chapter 12 will consider women's "paid" work that was generally, though by no means always, undertaken outside the home. In situating women's contributions in each category within the context of both the family economy and the market economy, these chapters focus on the complex nature of the nineteenth-century gendered division of labour and its relationship to the spatial organization of private and public life. In revising our understanding of men's roles in the private sphere, historians of masculinity have effectively demonstrated that public and private space cannot be neatly divided when people are living in both.[2] Neither can family and market economies be neatly separated when people are functioning in both.[3]

Intersecting and overlapping roles both in the private world of the family and in the public world of the community characterized the lives of women and men in the nineteenth-century farm family. In contrast to their male counterparts, whose descriptions of work tend to focus on their own activities, rural women diarists provide a picture of the household economy at work, allowing us to situate their activities within the context of a broader extended family and even community economy.[4] The nature of those activities changed with the seasons.[5] On the farm, women's seasonal round began, as did men's, as winter turned to spring. Like the Grants and so many other second-generation New

Brunswick women, Jacobina Campbell was a member of an extended farm family with siblings living on contiguous or neighbouring farms. And each year, as spring advanced and the seasonal round of farm production began anew, Jacobina's diary reflected the sometimes separate, sometimes intersecting nature of women's and men's work, with the rhythm of male and female activities appearing in bold relief in her terse entries. When the men began rafting logs to market, the women were taken up with boiling sap. In April 1830, Jacobina's brother Ludlow found time for ploughing, and her nephew Tommy, the eldest son of her brother Sandy, came to "make the garden," but the women were on their own when their cows calved. By May, however, the men were home and planting fields and garden proceeded in tandem.

1830: April 8: Patrick goes to the woods.
9: Good Friday. Go to see Mrs Ross.
10: Ludlow goes up the Tay with Sam Casey.
11: Make cabbage beds. Patrick at Aunt McLean's. Surveying the Property.
13: Patrick goes to Mr Harrison's. Ann to Slasons.
14: Mr Harrison up to sign some deeds.
15: Patrick goes to Cain's River[6] to run timber.
16: Go to see Sandy who is sick. Caroline comes over.
17: Boiling sap up the Tay. Ludlow & Sam Casey there.
19: Sewing hats. Ann at Youngs.
20: Boiling up the Tay. Ludlow ploughing.
21: Caroline over. Little Ludlow goes to school.
22: Ludlow ploughing for early potatoes. Thunder & lightening.
23: Ludlow goes down with a raft. Liney has a calf.
24: Go to Sam Casey's. Ludlow comes home.
25: Sandy & Caroline here. Benn comes to tea.
26: Make a hat for Mary. Ludlow clear[in]g wheat ground.
27: Mrs Slason here, sister here.
28: Go up to McLagans. Thomas comes to make the garden.
29: Tommy goes to Mr Harrison's for potatoes.
30: Plant early potatoes.
May 2: Go up to Sunday school. Cherry has a pied heifer.
3: Go to Urquharts for rye.
4: Go to Aunt McLean's. Sandy sews our wheat.
5: Class meeting here. Plant potatoes & peas in the garden.
6: Tommy & Sally go to town. Sew beets & carrots.
7: Tommy goes down with Benn's horses.

9: Mr Bunnil up. Go up to Frasers in the afternoon.
10: Ludlow goes to town about Sandy.
11: He comes home without him.
12: Go up to McLeods. Meeting at McDonalds.
13: Shear sheep. Benn gets to old man [?].

As on the Campbell farms, on most New Brunswick farms, sheep shearing took place in May and, in this task, the work of the men, who raised the sheep, and the women, who prepared the wool, intersected. Thus Jacobina Campbell reported in 1826 that "W. Abernethy comes to shear," and in 1827 that "Mrs A[bernethy?] comes to shear." But for the Campbells, at least, the production of wool, from the sheep shearing to the homespun cloth, was a market in which women, more often than men, sold and exchanged their labour. In 1828, Mrs Welsh did the shearing and in 1829 Peggy Casey helped to shear the sheep on the home farm while Jacobina's sister-in-law Caroline sheared her own. In succeeding years, Jacobina and Caroline, usually with the help of other women, sheared their own sheep.[7] The Grants also raised sheep, and in their family, too, the women took responsibility for the shearing.[8] In other families, the men sheared the sheep. On 1 May 1861, Janet MacDonald, summarizing the day's work in her diary, noted "Donald and Andy sawing, James and George shearing the sheep. We are washing." And on 14 May 1889, Alvaretta Estabrooks reported that her stepfather, Mr Else, "sheared the sheep." If men's and women's work intersected in the shearing of the sheep, the time-consuming processing of the wool was left to the women: two days after shearing the sheep, Isabella Grant reported, "P.M. they plowing and we was washing the wool."

Janet Hendry MacDonald, a contemporary of Jacobina Campbell, provides a window on the nature of life on a well-established New Brunswick farm thirty years on. By 1860, five of Janet and Alexander's seven children had married. While their daughter and her husband lived on a neighbouring farm and their three youngest sons had left the farm to pursue professional careers, they had the help of their three eldest sons, James, Donald, and George, as well as two daughters-in-law, James's wife Sally and George's wife Beckah, during this period, when the production of their farm was at its height. Janet's diary entries evoke the cadences as well as the routines of farm work: women and men – "we" and "they" – work in tandem, the nature of the work changing with the seasons. For the men, the combination of farming and lumbering continued, but by the time Janet was writing, her husband and adult sons operated their own sawmill.⁹ For the women, the home production of wool and cloth continued, and although her married daughter lived some distance away, for Janet, the help of daughters-in-law and near neighbours ensured the continued companionability and cooperation that typified women's as well as men's work. At the junction of the St John and the Washademoak in the 1850s and 1860s, the production of wool began much as it had at the junction of the Nashwaak and the Tay in the 1820s and 1830s, with the shearing of the sheep.

April 25th, 1861, Thurs. Still today and cloudy. In the afternoon it cleared off beautiful and warm. They are sawing. Father is sick today. I am spinning flax. There was a thunder shower on Tuesday night.

May 1st, Wed. Southerly wind and raining. Donald and Andy sawing, James and George shearing the sheep. We are washing. Uncle Joseph and Charlotte is here. The wind is west this afternoon, partly clear and cold.

2nd, Thurs. W. wind, clear and very cold; froze hard last night. They are sawing but it is most too cold. The sheep won't go out today at all. It freezes all day. The wind blows hard. We washed wool today. It is almost a match for the 1st of May 1837. I think it did not freeze quite so hard as it did then.

3rd, Fri. W. wind, partly clear and very cold. Froze hard last night; the ground is hard. It is wonderful weather for May, it don't look like farming. There is plenty of snow to be seen yet. Up the River St. John the snow is three or four feet deep yet, and I do not know but what it is more than that. They are sawing. We let the sheep out this forenoon and had to get them in the barn again as soon as we could. They would soon have chilled to death.

4th, Sat. W. wind, clear and not quite so cold as it has been. They are sawing. Emaline and Janet is over. Today it is quite pleasant. Mr. Harris come today. This afternoon I was at George's picking wool and at Mrs. Stewart's. This evening they are at prayer-meeting at the school-house. The wind is south west this evening. Coloured black today.

5th, Sun. South wind and clear. The men has all gone to meeting at the meeting-house. Mr. Harris preached. This afternoon he preached at the school house. We was all there but Mary. The Sabbath School commenced today.

6th, Mon. Still and clear. This is a fine pleasant morning. They are sawing. George ploughing. Father and I was over to Mr. Wright's to get shoes made. Mr. Harris is here. He is not well. Mrs. Stewart is here picking wool. This afternoon southerly wind. Washing day. Washed the black wool today.

7th, Tues. [?] wind and cloudy. They are sawing. It rained today. Mr. Harris is here. We are picking wool. Beckah is helping.

8th, Wed. South wind. Finished picking wool today. It is clear and warm. They are sawing. George ploughing.

14th, Tues. Southerly wind, clear. They are planting potatoes today. They can't saw now it is back water, the freshet is so high. We are washing today. Picking stone in the garden.

15th, Wed. Still today and cloudy; some showers. It rained Tuesday night. Father covering potatoes. Gilbert picking stones in the garden. Donald working at the mill. James and all his family went below today, he took the wool to Thompson's. Sally went to Lake's store a trading some. Mr. Farris, the candidate for Queen's was here to tea. This evening it is clear and fine. Mary and the little girls stayed. Donald MacDonald went up the lake today.

Each spring, Janet waited anxiously for the ice to clear and the weather to turn so that planting could begin. Then the men planted the field crops, while the women planted the kitchen garden. The products of that garden, like the field crops, not only fed the farm household, but also brought in income. Janet noted on 27 July 1857, "We have been picking peas for market this morning." The gardening season extended from the first planting in late April or early May to the end of the harvest in October.

Throughout the spring and summer months, planting, maintaining and harvesting the garden; raising chicks, ducklings and goslings; gathering eggs; cleaning; washing and making soft soap; churning butter; and processing wool proceeded in tandem with other activities. Although Lucy Morrison was the wife of a mill owner rather than a farmer, her diary entries in the years before she turned to commercial gardening provide a sense of the rhythm of the work as well as the satisfaction involved in planting, maintaining, and harvesting a kitchen garden intended mainly to feed and sustain the family. In early June each year, Lucy, with some help from a hired man, planted the pole beans, "rodded" the peas, and "set out" the tomatoes."[10] In mid-June, she "set out" her cabbage. By that time, the peas were "in pod," the tomatoes "in blossom," and the cucumbers "ready for the table."[11] In late June, she served first wild strawberries and then "our own strawberries" for tea.[12] By early July, when the beans were "in blossom," she could serve "green peas for dinner."[13] In mid-July when the corn was "in tassel" and the currants ripening, Lucy was serving "raspberries for tea" and "green beans for dinner."[14] By that time, in the relatively short New Brunswick growing season, the garden was beginning to peak, and the family enjoyed its bounty, with Lucy commenting proudly on 18 July 1872, "Colonel & Mrs. Inches here to dinner. Peas, beans, carrots, Beets & coucumbers on the table." Similarly, on 23 July 1873, she reported serving "new potatoes for dinner. Picked currants for jelly." By late July, when the corn was "in silk,"[15] Lucy and her housekeeper were already busy preserving fruit: 29 July 1873 found "Agnes preserving raspberries," and two days later, having managed to get cherries from St Stephen, Lucy "made 6 pots of preserves of them." Not until mid-August did tomatoes and corn ripen.[16] Although there were some regional variations, at this stage in its evolution, Lucy Morrison's kitchen garden was fairly typical.

By the time Janet MacDonald's grandchildren were teenagers and young adults, the MacDonald farm was very much a family enterprise, with all hands participating in various aspects of the work. On 24 July 1882, her granddaughter Ida, then sixteen, reported, "We sent a crate of cultivated strawberries to St John this morning." No doubt she, her cousin Jennie and their boarder, Emily Blatch (the school and piano teacher) had helped to harvest them. Two days later, and again on 2 August, Ida noted that they had "sent a crate of strawberries away this morning." The significance of strawberries to the family economy is implied in Ida's diary entry for Monday 9 July the following year: "Did not go to school this morning – had to stay home to help pick strawberries to go by boat." And on Friday, 13 July that same year, she noted that "after breakfast we all went over to the other house to pick strawberries – & then the boys went over the Lake."

All hands were called to help in other aspects of the farm work as well. On 26 July 1882, a "very, very hot" day, while the women were busy ensuring that the strawberries were sent off, the "'boys' commenced haying. After breakfast," Ida reported, "Emily, Jennie & I went down to the spring & got a 'turn' of water. Emily & I took some down in the field to the 'boys.'[17] Then we pulled carraway till we blistered our hands, came to the house got our dinners. After dinner we all went out to the barn to help get the raking machine down – Fun ... Minnie & Emily washed the wagon this P.M." And on 4 August, another hot day, with the "thermometer at 90°, Emily and I were out this P.M.

turning over hay for Fred. We were nearly cooked when we came in. We got something cool on, & Emily lay down & entertained us by reading aloud from Harper's Magazine. After tea we went down to the 'old house' & picked all the English Cherries." Not all young women had either the time or the inclination to participate in field work. On 18 July 1889, a day when her brother Arthur "commenced to hay," nineteen-year-old Alva Estabrooks "helped to pick the wool." And on 31 July, the day Arthur finished haying, Alva "churned, scrubbed and helped iron A.M. Went to quilting at A.W.E.'s, had quite a nice time. Practised 2 hours. Went to bed at 11." Nor was Alva as cheerful as Ida when occasionally called upon to help with fieldwork, reporting on 30 August, a day when her mother was "poorly," that "I had to do all the work," including helping Arthur "take in a load of oats."[18]

In autumn, women harvested the remains of their kitchen gardens, storing some fruits and vegetables and preserving others in preparation for the long winter ahead. On 11 September 1871, with only a few late vegetables remaining in the garden, Lucy Morrison was busy "sorting & putting up garden peas." The following day, she served the "first squash" for dinner. But "frost killed squash vines & coucumbers" on 18 September that year, though not until 22 September did she report that the tomatoes were "all gathered." In 1889, Alva Estabrooks reported that she "started to make tomato pickles" on 25 September. By 30 September 1871, Lucy Morrison's onions and beans had been "gathered & put in hotbeds to dry," and her squashes were "all in." By 3 October, she had her seeds "sorted & put away." But the garden would not be entirely put to bed until she could report "roots in pit" as she did on 16 October 1871, or "carrots, beets & mangles put into cellar" as she did on 26 October 1872.

Like other farm work, the processing of wool, extending from spring through the winter, was part of the seasonal rhythm of the farm routine. Carding was usually done in July, then spinning commenced. Although Janet MacDonald did her own carding, some women paid others to do this task for them. The Campbell women sometimes did their own carding, sometimes paid other women to do it, and occasionally sent their wool to the carding mill. Spinning began in mid-to late summer and continued into the autumn. In 1889, Alva Estabrooks first reported spinning in late August, but not until early October did spinning begin to consume the bulk of her time. Even on days such as 1 October, when she reported that she had "spun all day," she found time for two to three hours of piano practice. Perhaps she did so by skimping on sleep, generally going to bed at 10 p.m. and rising at 5 a.m. On 3 October, she not only "spun ... Churned after tea [and] ... took the dahlias roots up," but also managed two hours practice. On 8 October, she "spun ply" and three days later "finished spinning. Mother helped the last two days." Wool processing did not, of course, end with spinning. On Tuesday, 15 October, Alva "finished twisting yarn," and on 16 and 17 October, "helped colour yarn." For the majority of women on farms with sheep, spinning continued well into the fall.

The processing of wool could bring in a useful income as well as provide thread to be woven into cloth and knitting yarn to be transformed into sweaters, hats, and mittens for the household. The 1871 census returns indicate that the proportion of handlooms reported by individual households was considerably higher in New Brunswick than in other regions, implying that New Brunswick women continued to produce cloth on their handlooms for at least a generation after cloth manufacturing in Ontario and New England had shifted to factory production. Yet such statistics, which are dependent on the way census enumerators interpreted sometimes confusing instructions, can be misleading.[19] An investigation of individual women's particular experience demonstrates that even women who spun their own yarn employed neighbours to weave their wool into homespun, and this from an early period. In Jacobina Campbell's community, Nancy Casey was the weaver, with yarn being delivered to her in September or October and the homespun picked up the following month. Meanwhile, Jacobina continued spinning, this time for mittens, and started a quilt.

> 1830: October 1: *Begin to dig potatoes.*
> 2: *Sprain my back.*
> 3: *They all go to school.*
> 4: *Aunt McLean here & Mr Stokoe.*
> 5: *Sally & Ann Nevers here.*
> 6: *They go up the creek.*
> 7: *Mr Busby gets up. Meeting in the chapel & at Youngs.*
> 8: *He goes down. Ludlow at Aunt McLean's. Patrick at Cain's River. Send the yarn to N. Casey.*
> 9: *He gets home. Go over to Caroline's.*
> 10: *Go with Patrick to the school.*
> 11: *He goes to town.*
> 13: *Sandy & Ludlow go to town.*
> 14: *Saul brings up his waggon. Ludlow goes up to Smiths.*

15: Buy Saul's waggon for £16.
16: Sam ploughing here.
17: Go to church. Dr Jacob comes up. Preaches and stays all night.
18: He goes down. Sally & Tommy go to Douglas.
19: Rain. They cannot get away.
20: They go on to Miramichi. Spin for Caroline.
21: Sally & Tommy get home. Mr Busby comes. Preaches.
22: Go down to meeting. Stay at Browns.
23: Rain. Tommy comes to meet me. Sandy McGibbon gets up.
24: Go to church but are disappointed. McLeans and Harley come to tea.
25: Sandy goes down.
27: Ann & Sally go to Mrs Boobair's to quilt.
28: Jenny Cameron married.
29: Ann & I go to Mr Harrison's in the waggon.
1830: November 1: Spin for mittens. Men ploughing.
2: Election at Youngs. J. McDonald dines there.
3: Tommy goes to mill in the waggon.
4: Expect Mr Busby. He comes late. Rain. No meeting.
5: Go up with him to Frasers. He goes to the school house.
6: McLeans up.
7: Go to see little Mary.
8: Put in the quilt.
9: Pick the wool off old Croppy.
10: Tommy gets the homespun from N. Casey.

Jacobina reported spinning "the last of the wool" on 16 December and finishing "Tommy's double mittens" on 31 December.

As fall turned to winter, with field crops harvested, many men departed for the woods to harvest lumber, leaving the women to manage the farm in their absence. In the winter of 1827, while Marjory Grant's father and brothers were busy cutting and hauling wood, the women of the family spent a good deal of time together, working, visiting, and exchanging goods. On 3 February, the same day her brother William "came in from the woods," Marjory "came in from Oak Hill" where she had been visiting her sister Jannet, who "sent in two geese and a gander." And Marjory reported that on 6 February, before he returned to the woods, "our Wm, Will McDonald and James Milbery was here helping to kill the old sow in the forenoon." William's wife Betsy was also "here visiting. Wm came and cut up the meat in the evening and John Barber came with him and staid to supper."

Women left on their own during a New Brunswick winter, welcomed visitors, but whatever the season, family and friends found reasons to gather in each other's homes. Like Jacobina Campbell's sister Ann and Sally, the Campbells' hired girl, who, on 27 November 1830, went to Mrs Boobair's to quilt, women often combined work with sociability, helping each other stitch quilts or carpets, enjoying companionship, and offering one another encouragement and support in good times and bad.[20] Sewing for the household was a routine part of "women's work" that contributed to the family economy. And whatever their social status, women found pleasure as well as useful activity in denominational sewing circles, in some cases trading their talent for money which they then contributed to the upkeep of churches or the support of missionaries.[21] The same women combined work and sociability in less organized ways, in occasional quilting bees and knitting parties. Mary Wolhaupter's sister-in-law, Maggie, living on her own in November of 1869, and in need of wood, decided to hold a bee in order to replenish her supply. In the event, she managed to combine a quilting bee with a chopping bee, as Mary reported in her diary on 2 November: "Carrie and I were up to Maggies this afternoon. There were two or three more girls there and we quilted an old quilt for her and there was quite a number of men there and they got her up a nice lot of wood. I am really pleased with the job she got done and it all passed off nicely." Thus it was often quite literal threads that stitched together women's social, spiritual, and working lives into a patchwork of labour and leisure, family and community.

A consideration of both the concrete and symbolic threads of women's lives demonstrates the inextricable connection between the family and market economies, and serves as a metaphor for women's fluid movement between private and public spaces. Women traded or sold butter, eggs, and homespun cloth at the counter of the general store, just as men traded or sold the products of their fields and forests. The butter produced by the women in the Grant family sometimes brought in welcome cash and at other times served as a medium of exchange at the local store. On 2 February, Marjory reported that her "Mother sold five dollars worth of butter to Mrs. Christie and got the money." Like many farm women of the period, Catherine Grant not only sold her butter to friends like Mrs Christie, whom she visited regularly, but also marketed it through Mrs Marks at the general store, accumulating credit for the purpose of purchasing staples such as tea and sugar, which she could not produce herself. On 9 February, her husband had taken a crock of butter "down to Mrs. Marks with 20 pounds in it." Some months later, on 14 May, Isabella reported that "my mother ... setld with Mrs. Marks and thar was two and threpence coming."[22] On New Brunswick farms, then, women and men shared a cooperative and interdependent working relationship, each contributing their specialized skills to the maintenance of the family economy.

Women's diaries reveal women as partners in production, their ostensibly unpaid labour – though reported in censuses only obliquely (as, for example, the aggregate amounts of butter churned or cloth woven) – intersecting with that of men's in contributing in very material ways to the family economy. Yet in both historical and contemporary analyses of the workforce, women appear in the foreground only when accorded an occupational designation by census enumerators, a rare enough occurrence for married women in past times, no matter how significant their contribution to family or market economies. We cannot know what inspired Nancy Casey to take up weaving as an occupation in her community along the Tay, nor can we discern the importance of her contribution to her family's economy. But we do know that, although there are certainly examples of women taking up weaving when their husband's business faltered or disaster struck, the majority of New Brunswick's nineteenth-century women weavers were not listed as such in the decennial censuses.[23] Yet the homespun cloth they produced, characterized by one researcher as "the denim of the 19th century," was much in demand. Merchants supplying lumbermen heading into the New Brunswick woods regularly advertised "homespun shirts, pants and drawers, camp blankets, grey, check and white homespun as well as socks and mitts."[24] Entering the informal rather than the formal market economy, the women who produced the homespun cloth exchanged their labour for goods or cash, sometimes to help stabilize a precarious family economy.[25] And some women, the Wolhaupters among them, entered the formal economy, procuring quantities of homespun to ship to American markets.[26]

Lucy Morrison's contribution to her family's economy proves more difficult to categorize. Although she did not, even in her diary, confide her reasons for turning her passion for gardening into a profitable business, it seems highly unlikely that the fact that the transition began soon after her husband's lumber mill was destroyed by fire in 1872 was entirely coincidental. Lucy, who had long overseen both their kitchen and ornamental gardens, began overwintering plants and nurturing seedlings in the house well before the construction of the first of her two greenhouses in 1874. In her diary, she had always referred to the garden as hers, and the seeds she ordered each year as "my" seeds, and by 1881, when her gardening business reached its peak, she consistently used the same proprietary adjective when referring not only to the produce – from the flowers to the fruits and vegetables – but also to the greenhouses.[27] Yet her business – for it was certainly that – can be situated within the context of work in the home not only because it, like her husband's mill, was located on their home property, but also because the 1881 census enumerator listed no occupation for Lucy Morrison. Although Lucy's business was a year-round enterprise, it is instructive to consider her diary for April, when both she and her husband were preparing for the busiest season in their respective businesses. As John headed to Woodstock to negotiate the purchase of logs, Lucy and her four employees got to work.

Friday, 1 April 1881: I repotted out of box pansies in small pots. Ditto verbenas out of saucer. Sent Mrs George 28 pots of her plants. Radcliffe repotting plants all day, Dave washing pots. Cloudy and warm, no current in the river on account of water being so low. If there was [the] ice would have run out. Got George to take boxes out of one hot bed & put lath edgings under them & put part of boxes in another bed & give air on account of sweating.

Saturday, 2 April: Ice made another start & stopped, blew a gale of wind today. Cold. Father went to Woodstock. I was fixing up front of green house most of the day. Full of bloom, a great many roses both on climbers & in bed, pot ones not doing much now. 80 small pansies in pots back of smilax. 6 azalias in bloom, not many carnations. Sent Mrs. Sampson & Mrs. G. Gregory boquets.

Sunday, 3 April: Frank spent the day here. He gave me a cabinet likeness of himself. Very cold high wind all day. I went out & fixed green house fires 2:30 a.m. Green house has not looked better this winter than it does now. 4 Pelargoniums in bloom, 2 Mrs. Braun, 1 Mrs. Gibson, 1 King of the blacks.

Monday, 4 April: Weather still very cold, ice wasting none. I put in 1 paper of White Phlox Drummondii & one paper of Portulacca seed. Put in a saucer of verbena cuttings. Young plants in pots, holding their own. I put 3 saucers of alternantherus cuttings into 3 boxes, ditto dew plant into one box. Hot beds proving very satisfactory so far but on account of cold weather we have put in no more boxes. George looked over all the rose bushes in the pots potted, some ditto fuchsias. Davy preparing soil & putting in boxes. Ferry boat crossing, also persons on the ice.

Tuesday, 5 April: I put in 6 saucers of celery seed, 1 of Tomato Perfection, put in more boxes of alternantherus, achyranthus, sedums & Phlox Drummondii into hotbed, also pots of tuberous rooted begonias & Dracenas. Filled 6 boxes with 24 pots of verbenas in each box, filled round them with sand after dipping them into Tobacco water & left them in small green house while it was smoked. Put in a saucer of Guaphalium cuttings, potted a saucer of coleus cuttings. Cold high wind all day. Father got home.

Wednesday, 6 April: Cold morning, fine & sunny. Put 6 boxes of verbenas in pots in hotbed. A great many roses & other bloom. George put Tomato plants out of boxes, 80 into pots & set them in hotbed. George manuring rheubarb & putting barrels round it, preparing a bed for cabbage & sowed the seed. Planted 1 row of peas, American Wonder. I transplanted 2 saucers of stocks into 2 boxes. Ice hard & fast in the river. Made a boquet to day of La Marque Glorie de Dijon, Bon Silene Saffrane Pink & Crimson tea roses, Pinks Heliotrope, &c.

Thursday, 7 April: Cold last night, fine today, ice moved a little. I filled 3 more boxes of Pyrethrum seedlings & 2 of stocks, put in more seed of both. Put in two boxes rooted Guaphalium, potted young Heliotropes, 30 in all. Have a nice stock & variety of Geraniums in bloom. Azalias still making a good show, sweet alysseum in bloom. Duetsias have not flowered well this year but eupatorium is still in full bloom.

Friday, 8 April: High cold wind, ice running in the river. I put in a saucer of verbena cuttings, then put old plants into hot bed. I potted some carnation cuttings & put in more. We never had as much bloom in the green houses before with as much variety. Lots of roses, not so many carnations.

Saturday, 9 April: Ice ran out of river to day, milder weather. I put in ameranthus seedlings into boxes, also stocks & more pyretherum & put them in hot beds. Sowed 3 saucers of red Dwf celery & 1 saucer of Early cluster cucumbers. It did not come up. Took up Canna seed & poured boiling water on them. I have two hot beds full of boxes, the 3rd has 80 pots of Tomato plants 8 do. of pansies & 144 of young verbenas & of old plants.

Sunday, 10 April: Mother & Frank here spending the day. Mr Mowet ill, no service in Kirk. A lovely day. River open.

Monday, 11 April: Fine day. George raked off croquet side of lawn, cleaned all up that side of small green house. Thomson has all cleaned up the kitchen side. Mill got up steam & sawed one log. I was in house all the afternoon making green house blind. Have orders for $6 worth of Easter flowers. Smoked small house. I filled one lot of alternantherus, 3 of Pyrethrum & 1 of achyranthus, put some Pollock geraniums in hot bed. Orders coming in for Easter.

Tuesday, 12 April: I sold two dozen Pollock & two do. silver leaves. I then seperated some where two were in pots & took cuttings off then re-potted them. Looked over coleus bed. Took down & washed Stephanato & Rhyncospernum. Weather raw & cold today. George digging parsnips. They are a good size.

13 April: I had a very sore throat & chest almost preventing my speaking. 5 a.m. got on a mustard poultice & pepper tea which helped me amazingly. Getting in orders for Easter, 6 so far, amount $8.50. I filled boxes of Pyretherum & stocks, Phlox Drummondi &c & put them in hot bed. Sowed 5 saucers of Tomato seed in place of those that did not come up. George dug all the parsnip barrel, opened carnation pit. 4 hot beds filled with boxes, raked over & cleaned up rose bed.

14 April: Cold rain, not much. Father & Jack went to Gibsons. I cleaned up & tied carnations, looking over & arranging plants in small green house. George took leaves off rose bed & piled up boughs. Got the 5 barrels of parsnips ready for St John. Kate got me a Calla Lily from Miss Clifford. White was here & promised me one.

Good Friday, 15 April: A very cold easterly storm, snow, sleet & rain. Father went to St John. Sold my parsnips here. I sent $3 worth of flowers to Chatham & 1 to Bebbington. George cleaned under staging & washed off English Ivey leaves & cleaned up smilax bed. I was looking over the plants in small green house, took off & put in a good many cuttings in geranium & centaura maritima. Roses not coming out as well on account of cold weather. Our hot beds never done better.

Saturday, 16 April: I must have picked 100 roses today. Was rushed til 1:30 p.m. getting flowers off to St John, then cleaned up front & was surprised to have left such a good show of bloom. I scarcely miss the 6 boxes sent away. Rained off & on all day, warmer. George put Dahlias & Gladiolas in boxes. Father came home.

Sunday 17 April: None of us at church. Fine day, travelling bad. A great deal of bloom in green house.

Monday, 18 April: Raw cold wind to day. I made up 4 boquets for friends. A great many roses out as well as other bloom. I potted some carnation cuttings & put in more, also geranium ditto, transplanted Phlox drummondi & stocks into boxes. Got Carters seeds. Carnation pit opened, plants looking well. George raked off grass in flower garden, hauled away boughs, got leaves off rose & other beds. Peonies & other things in that bed coming up.

Tuesday, 19 April: Sowed asters & Phlox of Carters seed. Transplanted 1 box of celery plants out of saucer, sent a friend 2 boquets. Helen Jack married. Weather raw & cold in the morning, warmer after dinner, snowed during night. Water has risen a little. Carnations in the pit looking very well.

Wednesday, 20 April: I put in achyranthus cuttings & filled 4 boxes with celery plants & sowed 3 saucers with German stocks. Thomson got hogshead ready for Lily of the Valley, boughs all hauled away. George trimmed roses, sowed 2 double rows of early premium Gem Peas & getting ground ready for onions. Lawrence digging weeds out of strawberries & other ground. Fine sunny day. Water falling. I got 10 doz pots here.

Thursday, 21 April: Transplanted celery & stocks into boxes, sowed stocks, Petunias & Cockscomb in saucers, potted silver leaves into No. 4 pots. Lawrence weeding strawberries. George trimmed gooseberries & transplanted some raspberries. Flurries of snow all day. Afternoon turned very cold. Sent a customer 2 boquets. Cabbage coming up in cold bed that has glass on. Agnes got 2 leech barrels up & is washing dishes in the large pantry. X Paid Agnes up to date.

Friday, 22 April: Heavy white frost this morning, sun came out strong. George planted onions & beets. I was in the house all the afternoon. Lawrence away. I put balance of silver leaves in larger pots, set out a good many geranium cuttings, also roses.

Saturday, 23 April: Sent 3 boquets & box of flowers to friends. Heavy white frost last night, bright sunny day. I got up both blinds in small green house. Rearranging plants most of today. George planted migionette & sweet peas.

Sunday, 24 April: Mother & Frank here all day. Warmest day yet. Made no fire in green house.

Monday, 25 April: High wind from the North. George took all the verbenas out of hot bed & put them in small cold frame. I was in the house *all the afternoon, no callers. Bovardias full of green fly, scaly bug & red spider. George has not been syringing it as he ought to have done. The ones I potted have never recovered. A number of fuchsias in bloom & lots of climbing roses. Got kitchen pump fixed.*

26 April: Sunny morning, rainy afternoon. George planted Potato Onions, moved & set out some raspberry bushes, got ground ready for parsnips. Transplanting celery plants from saucer into boxes, have 16 boxes not in hotbed, 84 in a box. Smoked verbenas in hot bed. Got order for $7 worth of cut flowers for Miss Burpee's wedding & order from 8 for flowers for Government House Ball on Thursday.

Wednesday, 27 April: All the morning getting flowers ready to send to St. John for Miss Burpee's wedding. In the afternoon cleaning up front. Less bloom left than I have had for months. Climbers full of roses, carnations making a start into bloom & looking well. Mrs Glasier & Blanch called here & saw me in greenhouse. Very warm today. George planted parsnip seed. Water rising. Gibson sawing with 5 gates.

Thursday, 28 April: In the morning making boquets & getting flowers ordered sent away. Ball at Government house. Afternoon put in more Phlox & celery seed, transplanted celery & Tomato plants, put in a number of cuttings of geranium. Showery. Carrots sowed. Father in bed all day. Carnation bed all opened.

Friday, 29 April: Cloudy & rainy all day. I was potting cuttings & plants, looking over rose bushes & coleus. Smoked large green house & got 3 dozen plants packed ready for Indian Town. Lawrence hoed round strawberries, got walks cleaned in far garden. Peas up & cabbage plants sowed outside. George working at hotbed, preparing to make another. Thomson has walks cleared from barn to the house.

Saturday, 30 April: All day cleaning up & arranging plants. High cold wind. Lawrence putting in glass in hotbed frames. Davy getting boxes ready for transplanting. Fire in green house tonight, none in it for the past week. Logs came to the mill. Father has been in bed last 3 days. Water has risen a good deal. Sorted & arranged rose & fuchsias. Rose bed & carnations doing well now. Gladiolus & dahlias set in hot bed.

In contributing to her family economy, Lucy Morrison became fully engaged in the market economy, managing her own business from the purchase of seeds through the hiring of staff to the filling of orders.

In Lucy Morrison's gardening operation, then, we see the intersection of women's work in the home and women's work for pay outside the home, which is the subject of the next chapter. In their respective contributions to the family economy, Lucy and John Morrison formed an interdependent partnership, which afforded them a comfortable middle-class income and lifestyle, but in establishing her own separate business, Lucy entered the market economy as an independent, rather than an interdependent, actor.

Farm women, engaged with their husbands and brothers in a cooperative enterprise, were interdependent actors in both family and market economies. As active participants in that cooperative enterprise that was the family farm, they played a significant role in ensuring the stability of the market economy of their communities: in the sale of their farm produce and manufactured goods; in their patronage of carding and weaving mills, grist and flour mills, and soap factories; and in their purchases of tea, cloth, shoes, and sundry other items. Their seasonal round began when the sap began flowing in the spring and the smells and sounds of the sugar bush filled the air. It is the rhythms of life, rather than the drudgery of the daily grind, that emerge as the main theme in most New Brunswick farm women's diaries. Farm women worked hard, and their work was difficult and never-ending, yet they worked in tandem with, if not precisely alongside, husbands, fathers, and brothers. The rhythm and companionability of farm work can be heard as well as felt in Janet MacDonald's lilting diary entry: "They are sawing, we are quilting."[28] And, while the "typical farm woman" may well have "laboured ten hours a day in winter and thirteen in summer,"[29] her work was varied, and not without its satisfactions as well as diversions.

Chapter 12

Beyond the Bounds of Family: Paid Work

Analyses of nineteenth-century women's work in the home effectively demonstrate that, quite aside from their major responsibilities for child-rearing and health care, women contributed to the family economy by cooking and cleaning, making soap and candles, spinning wool and flax, weaving cloth, and making clothing, quilts, and blankets. They produced food for the table by growing fruits and vegetables, maintaining dairies, and raising poultry. Women's work in the home intersected with the market economy when they took their wool to carding mills, provided eggs and poultry for other women's tables, sent their garden produce to market, undertook carding, spinning, sewing, and weaving for others, or appeared at the counter of the general store to exchange butter, eggs, wool, and cloth for goods or cash.[1] Yet by most calculations, women's contributions remained largely outside the market economy, subsumed, if counted at all, under their husbands' or fathers' names. Then, too, as the example of Lucy Morrison demonstrates, it is often difficult to determine where the family economy begins and ends.

At what stage do we judge women to have moved beyond the bounds of family? Had young women working for wages and boarding away from home, but often returning on weekends, moved beyond the bounds of family? Historians tend to credit young men in parallel situations with greater personal and economic independence than they recognize in their female counterparts. But were such young men really less dependent on their families? Lucy Morrison's sons embarked upon careers while remaining safe within the bonds and bounds of family. Lucy's eldest son, Tom, moved to Saint John to take a job in his Uncle Luke Stewart's shipping firm. A few years later, he married a niece of that same uncle, the husband of Lucy's sister Belle. Another son,

Julius, entered the same firm. A third, Jack, went into business with his father, eventually taking over the mill. Frank and Stewart, the two youngest, went to work for another uncle, Julius Inches, the husband of Lucy's sister Jane. Frank would eventually take over the insurance firm Julius had founded, while Stewart would run his dry goods store. Only Lucy's second son, William, who apprenticed with a local druggist, followed a career that would take him beyond the bonds as well as bounds of family. Young women who, in striking out on their own as domestic servants, mill workers, seamstresses, nurses, and teachers, physically distanced themselves from their homes were not as well paid as their male counterparts, but their movement into the workforce demonstrated no less independence and was just as surely a transition from the private world of family to the public world of the marketplace where they exchanged their labour for wages.

The experiences of the majority of working women, like the experiences of the majority of working men, went largely undocumented, except in routinely generated sources such as censuses, though even there women workers were under-represented.[2] Domestic servants remained the largest category of women in the paid workforce throughout the nineteenth century, followed by various categories of seamstresses and factory workers. We occasionally catch glimpses of domestic servants in the diaries of the women who employed them, but learn little about their feelings or attitudes. Juliana Ewing, the wife of a British army officer posted to the garrison at Fredericton in 1867, complained of the quality of domestic servants in New Brunswick, who, it would seem, were not so biddable as servants in England, perhaps because the demand for servants in the province greatly exceeded the supply.[3] Yet despite often rapid turnover, our New Brunswick–born women diarists rarely complained about either the work or the work habits of their hired "girls." Sadie Harper's family seemed unable to retain their servants, who were often Acadian, but there is no way to determine whether this problem was the result of cultural differences or, as seems more likely, merely a manifestation of the common pattern of young women working briefly during the period between school leaving and marriage.[4] Lucy Morrison employed Agnes McNabb for over 25 years, yet she also employed sundry other local women, who came and went with startling regularity.

Although self-employed, the majority of seamstresses, like domestic servants, worked in other people's homes. Some, like Lavinia McLauchlan, the wife of a Fredericton shoemaker, were contributing to their family's income by continuing to ply their trade after marriage. Lucy Morrison was one of Mrs McLaughlan's loyal clients.[5] Seamstresses came somewhat less regularly to the homes of diarists Annie and Laura Trueman, Sadie Harper and Lottie Reid, who also reported sewing their own clothes. Indeed, Lottie Reid's older sister Anna had herself worked as a seamstress prior to her marriage. When Mary Wolhaupter, looking to earn some money in July 1869, accepted an invitation from her Aunt Sarah Johnson in Houlton Maine to "go out and sew some for her and make a visit," she discovered that mixing business with pleasure had certain disadvantages. Just four days after her arrival, Mary complained: "Have been sewing all day. I felt hurt this morning to see Aunt and Miss Grace out playing Croquet and me sitting sewing but so it is I suppose." The next day, after "sewing most all day," she reported that "my eyes seem to fail me some. They feel pretty bad tonight." Although her eyes continued to trouble her, she felt considerably cheered a few days later when, after sewing "most all day," she had her "first game at Croquet with five others. Got an introduction to Mr. Holland, Attorney at law, and Mr. Stockbridge, the freewill Baptist minister, and played Croquet with them. I enjoy myself nicely out here."[6] Nonetheless, sewing for another of her aunts at the end of August, Mary concluded, "I do not like much going out to sew for it is rather hard work."

By the late nineteenth century, many of Saint John's seamstresses and milliners worked in factories, although, as was the case in other urban centres, some established their own businesses, hiring other women to help them with the work. By 1871, 214 of Saint John's 634 dressmakers and milliners were plying their trade in factories employing more than ten workers.[7] The majority were young single women, a significant number of whom had moved to the city from the surrounding rural communities in search of work. Other young women looked further afield, but found similar opportunities. Direxy Carlisle and Lizzie Stiles, whom we meet in the pages of Ann Eliza Gallacher's diary, travelled from Hopewell Cape to Boston, where they boarded with the Gallachers and found work as vest makers. Both remained friends with Ann Eliza, keeping in touch with her as they moved in and out of the paid workforce, on both sides of the border.[8]

Women factory workers became increasingly common in New Brunswick, as elsewhere, throughout the course of the nineteenth century. A number of such women, friends, and neighbours of diarist Ann Eliza Rogers travelled with some regularity between their work in towns in Maine or Massachusetts and their families in Albert County. Before turning to teaching, Mary Wolhaupter had left her Carleton County home to travel to Lynn, Massachusetts, to work, probably in the shoemaking industry, which drew many young New Brunswickers to that town. Although women also worked in garment and textile factories, boot and shoe factories, confectionary factories, and fish-packing plants in New Brunswick, our diarists rarely mentioned either factories or factory workers. Yet they undoubtedly knew such women. As early as 1871, almost 20 per cent of Saint John's single women between the ages of sixteen and forty-one worked in the garment industry.[9] Sadie Harper's father was co-owner of a shoe factory, and his children very likely had classmates who left school as soon as they were old enough to work there. And, especially after the establishment of a number of textile mills in the province in the 1880s, young New Brunswick women whose mothers had worked as domestic servants prior to marriage chose factory work instead.

As was the case elsewhere, independent businesswomen constituted a significant proportion of working women in nineteenth-century New Brunswick.[10] Many of these worked in the garment and textile industries, most often following a model not unlike the example of Lavinia McLauchlan: women seeking to supplement a precarious family income by turning their own skills to good account. In the early-nineteenth century, Mary Bradley "notified her neighbours" when she decided to "take up the business of weaving."[11] Other women had greater ambitions. No less than twenty of the thirty-seven Saint John businesses associated with the garment industry listed in the 1871 census were owned by women.[12] Some offered their owners only a precarious independence; others became highly profitable. In Fredericton, Sarah Grace Young abandoned a teaching career and, in partnership with her sister Eve, established a millinery business in the early 1880s. Grace continued in the business even after her marriage and, by 1900, she and Eve employed up to ten milliners and made regular trips abroad to purchase materials.[13] While women who ran shops and factories were listed in business directories and advertised in local newspapers, like Lavinia McLauchlan, most self-employed women depended on word of mouth to build a client base.

Those women who served as community nurses or midwives also depended on word of mouth, but, unlike seamstresses, dressmakers, and milliners, who were usually identified in decennial censuses, they are almost invisible in routinely generated government records.[14] And although some did keep diaries, even there it is often impossible to distinguish between neighbourly, perhaps mutually exchanged, assistance and paid employment.[15] The journal of Elizabeth Innes, a well-known Saint John midwife, who served her community from the 1830s to the 1850s, contains only two fleeting references to her role as a midwife: "Nursing – I have nursed in my time 168 women in their Confinement and 157 Labour;" and "Bees wax, honey, sweet oil, Rosin for sore nipples."[16] Nor were nurses and midwives generally identified in other women's diaries. Viewed as women's natural roles, nurturing and care-giving were so common, so widely accepted and so expected, that they tended to be taken for granted. And because health care occurred almost exclusively within the home, the nature and extent of nursing as an occupation – as paid employment – during the period before professionalization prove impossible to document.[17] Thus, while Bishop John Medley has been the subject of a good deal of research, his wife has been overlooked. Yet, as Juliana Ewing informed her mother,

> Mrs. M. is almost as great a character as he is – & in a way as clever. She is a great gardener & a botanist – & lithographs a little ... But besides – she has nursed in English and foreign hospitals for 20 years, though I do not think she has ever belonged to any order of Sisters ... She nursed in the King's Cross Hospital in London – the Hotel de Dieu in Paris – & somewhere else abroad – I have forgotten where.[18]

Most women care-givers were not as professional as Margaret Medley, yet by the latter half of the nineteenth century, increasing numbers of women were choosing nursing as a career and seeking professional training. Many Maritime women pursued that training in the "Boston States," where nursing programs were multiplying and seeking ever more recruits.[19] If New Brunswick was relatively late in introducing professional training for nurses, the province was an early entry into the field of professional training for teachers.[20]

Although women had long been teachers of children, both in the home and in private-venture and church-sponsored schools, not until the mid-nineteenth century did they begin to rival men in numbers as teachers in government-sponsored schools. And until the introduction of taxation in support of schools, parents in rural areas struggled to provide the requisite schoolroom, and the teachers they hired struggled to enroll the requisite number of students to qualify for government subsidies. January 1869 found Mary Wolhaupter boarding with the

Kitchens, who had four school-aged children, and teaching in a room in their home. By 8 January, with few students, Mary was already feeling discouraged, confiding to her diary her view that "a person who is obliged to work for a living has many discouraging seasons and is much confined to their work. I like freedom, but I am afraid that I like money better. I hope I do not love it well enough to injure my health or soul by getting it. God forbid that I should." Things did not improve despite Mary's best efforts to encourage parents to send their children.

Tuesday, February 2, 1869. Windy and sunshiny. In school today. I do not feel very well this forenoon, my head aches. I have not recovered from my cold yet and I am a good deal discouraged about my school; it is so small. I was very foolish that I did not stay home this winter. Mama and Carrie both warned me too but I thought best to keep school for a while. Father & Mother were down here this evening & a while in the afternoon. They made us rather a nice visit. I was pleased to see them. I suppose it will not be long at the longest that we will enjoy each others company therefore we ought to prize it very highly.

Wednesday, February 3. Cloudy. In school again to-day half sick & discouraged by having so few scholars. I do not know what people mean that they are not more punctual about sending to school. It has been snowing this afternoon. I do seem to have a dreadful cold in my head. I heard this afternoon that Mrs. Guion's children[21] were sick which is the reason they have not been to school this week. Mr. Kitchen has been reading this evening in Wm. Lighton.[22] It seems to be a very good book, a great deal of information in it. I hope I may profit from the reading of it.

Thursday, February 4. Storms. I am in school today with but four scholars and it is snowing and blowing considerably and I do not feel well so upon the whole it is rather gloomy looking as Phebe said when she came upstairs. There has not been a person passing here today and the snow is pretty deep. It snowed all night and most all day. It is thought to be the heaviest fall of snow we have had this winter and I think it is. I do feel that there is great need of me being a much better girl than I am. I hope I may be led to ask for help and assistance which I know will be granted if I ask aright.

Friday, February 5. Snow. In school with only the four Kitchens. It still continues to snow and no passers by yet which makes things pretty dull. And me having so few scholars gives me a good chance for reflection. I have been looking back to the time I kept school above Florenceville.

What a good time I had there for a while and have been thinking too that perhaps it was a mercy that I did not settle myself up there for to all appearances I had a chance. The people have turned out this afternoon to break roads, it has drifted nearly over again. Fred has gone up to my house, I do not know how he will get back.

Saturday, February 6. Very pleasant. In school again today. Carrie came down with Fred yesterday afternoon – was much pleased to see her for the storm had been so great that we had not seen any one for some time. There seems to be considerable travelling this afternoon. We finished reading Wm. Lighton last evening. It was not so interesting as we supposed it would be. I expect Fred will take Carrie and I home this evening. We went home but the travelling was very bad.

18 Riches and honour are with me; yea durable riches and righteousness.

19 My fruit is better yea than fine gold; and my revenue than choice silver.

Sunday, February 7. Pleasant. At home untill about three. Father brought me down to my school. Travelling is still bad. Pa went over for Haddie in the forenoon so that she and George were there to dinner, H was there when I left. I felt a good deal downhearted this afternoon and evening. I do not know what ails me. Every good and perfect gift cometh from above. May the Lord bless me and all that belong to me is my most humble prayer. Amen

20 I lead in the way of righteousness in the midst of the paths of judgement.

Monday, February 8. Pleasant. In school again with a very few scholars. I went down to Mr. Cowperthwaites at noon to see what kept them at home, they say they are coming again soon.[23] I hope they will and I was into Mrs. Guion's and Mrs. London[24] came there while I was there. I have been looking over the books of Job today. I hope I may search the scriptures daily and I hope I may have my eyes opened that I may behold wondrous things out of the law of God.

21 That I may cause those that love me to inherit substance, and I will fill their treasures.

Finally, on 24 February, deeming it not worth her while to continue, Mary gave up her school.

By 1871, women comprised nearly 56 per cent of New Brunswick's licensed teachers, compared to 47 per cent for Nova Scotia and 50 per cent for Ontario.[25] An increase in the number of pupils registered in the common schools of New Brunswick after the Free Schools Act came into force required a concomitant increase in the number of teachers. This meant that graduates of the normal school had more opportunities than ever before. Partly because women regularly outnumbered men among the normal school graduates, and partly because pay scales for women teachers were significantly below those of their male counterparts, the feminization of teaching proceeded apace. Although they commanded less pay than their male colleagues, young women such as Leila DeWolfe, who earned her second-class teaching licence in 1877, soon discovered that, in a sellers' market, pay was often negotiable.[26] Still, the male prerogative prevailed and was generally accepted. Even Kate Loggie, who held a first-class licence, received less pay than young men with the same qualifications. And although women generally taught the younger children in consolidated town schools, in the one-room schools attended by the majority of the province's children, women were expected to teach pupils of all ages. Moreover, unlike their male colleagues, female teachers could also be expected to take responsibility for domestic tasks ranging from keeping the school clean to making the curtains.

In January 1881, Kate Loggie, returning to her teaching position in Tabusintac, reported, "Mother drove me down here on Monday. I am back to Mrs Grattan's again. Have my own bed this time." Unlike Mary Wolhaupter, she also had her own schoolhouse. In her diary, Kate confided worries that young women embarking on a career in teaching today would understand: discipline problems and inspectors' visits. She also faced a number of challenges that today's teachers could scarcely contemplate: taking responsibility for making blinds for her schoolroom or ensuring that when an itinerant minister used her schoolhouse the men in his audience would not leave traces of their chewing tobacco behind. But although she, like Mary, was frustrated by fluctuating attendance, for her, the issue was not low student numbers.

1881: March 16th. Since I last wrote the McKenzies & I spent an evening at Mrs. Simon Simpson's, Neguac. It rained very heavily that evening, & all next day, still I had a very good attendance at school. Sunday I spent at Mrs. Grattan's & had my little Sunday school with Maggie. Monday evening received notice from Inspector that he would visit my school on Tuesday, the next day, or yesterday. That evening I also got another letter for which I had cause to be thankful that God had kept my darling sister safe through her long voyage for the letter was from Maggie. I felt more occasion for thanks after learning from it that a vessel had sunk a short distance from Shanghai, & that Capt., his wife & others were drowned. How many unseen dangers we pass through. How we should watch & pray continually, that our call come not unawares. The letter contained some very interesting information about the Chinese. We have great reason to be thankful for the gospel. Enclosed was a photo for Mary McKenzie. Yesterday the inspection came off. Not very well I fear. Mr. Cox took tea at Mrs. Grattan's. Mr. Stymist & Mr. Alex. McKenzie, Trustees, were present at the exam. Also a few others. Had only one long session today, on account of pupils being kept so late last evening. Cut out blinds for the school this afternoon. Mr. Stymist brought the material this morning. Since I last wrote have finished Life of Sir William Wallace by Rev. Mr. Glass.[27] Not entirely pleased with it or with the style. It appeared to be a continual scene of blood shed. It is indeed a sad tale. Finished The Young Christian, & from it got some hints on reading & improvement by writing.[28] Wish to act on them. Think it an excellent book. Wrote tonight to Mary Russell.

March. 18th. We are having very fine weather. Have lots of scholars this week. And 29 these two days. Miss J. McLeod & I spent the evening at Mrs. McKenzie's. Mr. M. drove us home. They have just received a picture from Bella. Disappointed in not getting home today. Have no reading matter on hand just now.

March 19th. Finished my tidy with birds today.[29] Hemming blinds for school. Finished Woodstock by Sir Walter Scott.[30] Like his writings. Began the book early in the winter, but conscience forbade me reading it. Fear it must have been owing to indulging in it too strongly. Hope I may have wisdom in my choice of reading. That I may be taught from on High.

Tabusintac, March 25th. Spent last Sunday [20th] here at Mrs. G.'s. Read a sermon on revision of Bible to Mrs. Grattan. Sermon by Rev. Gavin Lang. Read Bible & some parts of Witness until 2:30 P.M., when I had my little Sunday School. Had Susan & little Isabella Ross in it that day. Subject: Jesus coming to teach his own people. Tried to impress on class, they ought to be kind & obliging to friends at home. In evening went to school to hear Mr. Wells preach. His text was II Kings 6.5 – "Alas, master, it was borrowed." Substance of remarks that our time & all else we have here are borrowed from God. Spoke of cultivation of soul & intellect. Made me rather agitated by instead of cautioning audience against spitting tobacco, as requested by trustees, spoke only of disarranging seats, an article that never is disarranged. Laid all blame on teacher. Tuesday evening [22nd] visited Mrs. Coltart & Mrs Kenny. Annie Kenny sick. Mrs. K. appeared very grateful for the boots I gave Annie. Hope that seeing others so void of comforts is making me more thankful for my own comfortable home. Pray it may be long spared to me. Willie L. came down with me, for some pills I was to send Annie. Wed. [23rd] New scholars still coming in, makes it very discouraging for me. It is impossible to succeed. Had a call from Mary McKenzie & went down & stayed all night with her. Gave her the picture Maggie sent for her. They all thought very much of her doing so. (Little acts sometimes give so much pleasure.) Am thinking of applying for another school. Hope I am guided in what ever I do. Wish my will to be that of my Master['s]. Had a lovely walk back on the crust. Thursday morning. [24th] Thurs. evening detained class A for History lesson. It seems the only way to get some of them to learn & yet it is not a pleasant way. Find the big boys very rude & rough. Mr. G. & men came from woods. At Mr. McLeod's to try & get word from home. Fannie & Mrs. McL. complaining of health. Here it is Friday [25th] again & still no one has come for me; but I have a hope that if it keeps fine & frosty Mr. M. McKenzie will drive me up tomorrow. I am to go down there tonight. Had rather a discouraging hour at recitation today. This school week has had its trials, but on the whole it has been tolerable. Little Peter Stymist has come back. He appears a little more tractable now than last summer. I think I could love him now. It will soon be a fortnight since the world, but especially Europe was startled by the news that the Czar of Russia had been assassinated. How true is "Uneasy is the head that wears a crown." The unfortunate Emperor died on Sunday, March 13.

March 30th. We are having very fine weather. Frosty nights & sunny days. On Friday 25th went down to Mrs. McKenzie's & on Sat. morning Mr. McK. & I started for B[urnt] C[hurch]. Went up in an hour & 40 min. Got up at 8:25. Jessie the only one of the family at home & she was very glad to see me. Mrs. Quinn still there. Spent the day, chiefly in talk, some of it profitable & some not. Gave Maggie's letter to read & got her log in return. In afternoon, Misses Nellie & Maggie Young from Tracadie came up with their brother John who stayed at Donald's. After tea Mrs. Q., the Misses Young & I went up to Anderson's store. I had to get some things for Mrs. J. McKenzie. Also got mail. Mother & Father came home about dusk; they had been at Chatham & Oak Point. Mary at O.P. Donald, Mr. Young & Stuart & Alex Davidson spent evening at house. Had some music & singing. Sang Beula Land. Sunday after breakfast the Youngs left. I went over to Donald's with them. The children just getting over Scarlet rash. Came home & dressed, had dinner & started for Tabusintac. Stuart drove me down. Spent a very idle Sunday. Did my own work. Mon. morning [28th] got letter from Mary Russell about Douglastown school. I think I would like it & Father wishes me to take it; though Mother would rather I not teach next summer. Tues. had rather a hard time in school. Big boys rather rough. Fear I do not know how to manage boys, not rough ones any way. Spent night with Mary McKenzie. Very sad at parting with Mrs Edmonds who went away. Mon. morning sent in my resignation of this school. This morning, Wed., had a pleasant walk on crust from McKenzie's. Do not think I enjoy walking this spring. Not lonely ones any way. Must prepare for school. Wish I could go with an humble heart or spirit.

The problem of how best to "manage the big boys" was particularly pressing, for they made up fully one-quarter of her thirty-nine students. Their erratic attendance only exacerbated the problem.[31] Yet despite her concerns and her worries about the inspector, as a teacher, Kate Loggie was much in demand, and had her choice of schools each term.

Over the course of the nineteenth century, teaching became an increasingly attractive career path for young women.[32] And by the last quarter of the century, those who, like Kate Loggie, aspired to teach in the province's public schools enrolled in the normal school in Fredericton, seeking the qualification that was increasingly demanded by school trustees. Having achieved their teaching licence, graduates of the normal school, whether they pursued teaching for a short time before marriage or as a lifelong career, took their profession seriously. Many attended the Teachers' Institutes and, like Kate Loggie, occasionally presented papers at district institute meetings. In one-room schools across the province, such women provided the majority of their pupils with the only formal education they would receive before entering the broader "public" world of work outside the home.

Born the year the Free Schools Act was introduced, Hannah Estabrooks had completed her schooling before the era of compulsory education. But while it was the skills learned at home that she used to support herself during her time spent working as a domestic servant in Lewiston, Maine, the solid grounding in arithmetic that she received in the common schools of Carleton County stood her in good stead when she returned home to work in the general store managed by her older brother Arthur. After the turn of the century, increasing numbers of women began moving into clerical work, a relatively new field for women.[33] In 1903, Hannah, then thirty-one, sometimes boarded in the village of Rockland with her brother's family, but more often slept "down home" on the farm with her mother, even though she found the walk back and forth daunting in winter. Clearly very competent, Hannah managed the store when her brother was absent, yet viewed her work as a job rather than as a career. On the whole, a sense of lassitude, restlessness, and general malaise permeates Hannah's record.

Coldstream, Carleton County, N.B., 1903: Jan. 1st: Jan. has started in quite warm. I have made no new resolutions for this year except to keep a journal which I shall break about as soon as if it was something important. I don't feel very spry today so not at work.

2nd: Arthur and Nellie went to Woodstock and I had to go to store. A long day. Mr Wetmore and family took tea with Frank. Arthur came after I had closed the store, said Nellie got her teeth out all right.[34]

3rd: Snowing today. Nothing of interest happened. Got a chance home with George Hayward.[35] Every thing moves on in the same old quiet way. Beatrice Nevers is visiting at A.W.E.'s for two weeks; sewing circle there. I went over and got my supper.

18th: Sunday, a wild blustering day. I did not go to church. Frank and Arthur and family down, went home about dark. Arthur wanted me to go too but I had not the courage. After we had our supper we ate nuts and read until late bed time. A very cold windy night.

19th: Monday – I walked to the store this morning and nearly frose. Was so cold I turned sick before I got to the F[ree] B[aptist] Church, but braved it out and got there alive.

Tue. 20: Last night was very cold. It was 29 below this morning but with no wind. Arthur went to Ashland and the forenoon dragged slowly away. Arthur came back about two and the P.M. was shorter.

Wed. 21: Rained hard all day when it was not snowing. Prayer meeting supposed to be at A.W.E. but there was only two there. Mr. Wetmore took tea at Mrs. Shaws but did not come over.

Thu. 22: A beautiful day. I bottled oil all of the forenoon. Nellie came up P.M. and staid untill dark and I came down home with her. Ray McClean here working for a few days getting wood. Arthur finished books and began posting. I feel limp tonight.

Sun. 25: Very cold. Nellie and I did not go to S.S. as we did not know what time it was when we got up. Read and cracked nuts and ate all day. Arthur came down about dark and finished work. Stayed to supper. Nellie and I went up to Meeting. Mr. Wetmore preached. Walked home. Very cold. I got too tired or cold, turned faint and funny, but the cold has served me just such a trick once or twice before this winter.

Mon. 26: Did not go to store untill noon as I felt so weak, then walked up. Put in a hard time and came home after my work was done feeling about used up.

Tue. 27: Geo. Shaw came to work the team and Nellie went to Rockland and got a chance to Hartland en. route for Florenceville. Jodie and children came down. I laid up for a spell.

Wed. 28: Warmer, snowed some. I am feeling some better. Geo Shaw here to dinner.

Thu. 29: Warm all day. Jodie and children here yet. We churned. I knit some, peeled apples evening. George Shaw here and cleaned stables, here to dinner.

Friday 30: Rained, Snowed, Sleeted, blowed all day. I made cookies and knit some. We cooked mince meat.

Sat. 31: A very cold rough day. I intended going to the store but it was too cold and rough. George Shaw came down and took Jodie and children up to Rockland, brought a letter down for me from C.M.G.H., S.A.D., also Nellie's pictures.

February, Sun. 1st: A warm bright day. I did not go to church or Sunday School. Have felt limp all day and my head has acked and felt as though loaded with lead. Read, slept, helped with barn work, drank sage tea and am now going to bed. I dread getting to Rockland in the morning but see no way out.

Mon. 2nd: Quite cold. Snow all day. I walked to Rockland, not much going on.

Tue. 3rd: Snowed all day with some wind. I walked down and stayed with Mother all night. Snow pretty deep.

> *Wed. 4th: Snowing harder than ever and blowing, every thing blocked up. I could not get home. Very quiet time in the store.*
>
> *Thu. 5: Snowing yet and blowing. Nothing going on, no mail today, roads blocked up.*
>
> *Friday 6: Snowed some forenoon, cleared P.M., but windy. A little more going on in the trade line. Arthur and I packed bottles for shipping. I came home at night and stayed with mother. Walking very bad. People are beginning to break out the roads today. Yesterday's mail got here tonight at dark.*

Two years later found Hannah still working in the store, but no happier in the job. In particular, she did not enjoy the kind of men's camaraderie often associated with general stores, confiding to her diary on 19 February 1905 that "cheap stories, swearing, smoking, spitting and a surly Boss have made the time seem long and dreary ... I cannot make myself believe I like the work. I get so tired of tobacco and cheapness generally."[36]

While Hannah Estabrooks, who, like Mary Wolhaupter, was obliged to work for a living, had limited career options, her sister Alva used her musical talent to chart her own path. Alvaretta Estabrooks had launched herself on a teaching career even before she was given the opportunity to attend Acadia Ladies' Seminary, where she further honed her musical skills. In November 1889, having learned everything the piano teachers in her home community could offer her, Alva began travelling to Florenceville to take more advanced lessons. After her uncle, Rev Amos Hayward, was posted to Florenceville in 1890, she made the trip twice a month, staying overnight with her Uncle Amos and Aunt Lucretia, enabling her to take two lessons per trip. By August, she felt confident enough to try her hand at teaching in her local community, though well beyond her immediate neighbourhood. As Alva's diary entries demonstrate, establishing oneself as a music teacher required entrepreneurial initiative as well as musical talent. On 25 August, she reported, "Mr. Newcomb, Aunt & I went up Windsor ... I am try[ing] to get up a class to teach music to. We got dinner at Mr. Conolley's. Nora is a going to take lessons. Stoped at several places. Annie Orser will also take. Took tea at Ezra Estabrooks's. We called at Eb. Foster's. Went down to see Abbie about taking lessons too but they were all away. Got home about 8 o'clock eve." The following day, she "drove up Coldstream to see about getting scholars," but did not get any. By early September, she had a few pupils, but was struggling to find more. On 5 September, she "went out Ashland p.m. to see about getting scholars. Got Jodie Boone & Miss Davis." By 18 September, she was spending her days travelling to give lessons: "Rose at 6. Gave Abbie Nevers & Emily Foster lesson a.m. Got dinner at Fosters. Nora Conolly & Annie Orser lessons p.m. Tea at Conollys. Got home after dark." Again on 3 October, she "arose at 6. Gave Abbie lesson, A.M. ... Gave Miss Davis lesson P.M. & Jod. Boone. Walked out Ashland. Got tea at John Clark's." As an itinerant music teacher, Alva Estabrooks gained a measure of independence and perhaps helped to fund her further training at Acadia Ladies' Seminary the following year.

Other young women who received training in the fine arts at ladies' academies – diarists Mary Hill, Annie Trueman, and Sadie Harper among them – turned their talents and training to good account in teaching music and art. Rebecca Trueman, writing to her daughter in the mid-1870s, wondered, "Dont you want some music pupils when you come home? Did Laura tell you that Amelia has twelve? Maggie Fitch gives lessons at two dollars per qr has pupils like John Delaney &c. Dont you think that brings it down a little?"[37] Annie did follow her mother's suggestion, reporting in an 1877 letter, "I went out and gave a music lesson in the afternoon for I have a few pupils now – Ella Fawcett & Johnny Fleming now, Alice Cole commences in a week & Mrs Albion Estabrook's little girl in about a month – with the prospect of at least one more, perhaps two – 6 dollars a quarter, that is quite fair for a beginning dont you think?"[38]

Teaching music in an institutional setting removed the entrepreneurial imperative and provided a secure salary. By the early 1880s, Annie Trueman was teaching at Mount Allison Ladies' Academy. Some flavour of the life of a teacher in the Academy can be gleaned from a letter written to her sister on an evening when she was in charge of supervising the students who lived in residence: "I have just finished the 9 o'clock round of visits to the girls' rooms – have said goodnight to some seventy-odd young damsels and, returning to the charge room conclude to spend the remaining minutes of the evening with you." Annie's letter suggests that she enjoyed the work and confirms that young women at Mount Allison Academy were encouraged to think for themselves:

> This evening has been rather a lively evg with our girls, as they, a number of them, got into politics tonight and actually got so excited over it that

they ended by getting quite angry at each other, a few of them. I was glad when the time came for the first study bell. About a half dozen of them came up to me, "Now Miss Trueman are you a grit or a Conservative? Which side are you on?" I assured them I was on the side of those who were quick on the halls. I thought I would not tell them in their state of excitement. You would laugh to hear Edna Chapman talk politics. She is pretty well up too.

At the Academy, Annie had more pupils than she could find for herself: "My classes still increase, one numbering 35 now."[39] Unlike Mary Wolhaupter and Hannah and Alva Estabrooks, Annie Trueman was not obliged by circumstance to work for a living, and, in 1884, her sister Laura Wood commented cryptically in her journal, "Dear Nan's second year of teaching in the Academy. I think she will not teach anymore."[40]

Perhaps Annie enjoyed either teaching or the independence it afforded more than Laura realized, however, for she was still working in 1886. Her diary entries for that year indicate that while she did not look forward to the responsibility of supervising all the girls on "charge days," she generally enjoyed not only her students and her classes but also her colleagues.[41] On 20 August, the day after the Academy opened, Annie "went down to school. Found 35 students with few familiar faces as yet. Called first on Mrs Archibald, Miss M Bishop, Miss L. Black, Miss Darcy, Miss Freeman.[42] No work done today." Although Monday dawned "dark and dreary" and "nothing seemed to go easily or cheerfully," she noted that "many old students greeted me this morning. All of them are most welcome to me. The charge day looms up rather unpleasantly, but then we live the days 'one by one' and strength will be given for their time of need." Her first charge day, 25 August, "proved very wearisome. After a hard day's teaching, this is a considerable ordeal. However, in many ways it was more pleasant than I had anticipated."

Nor were single women and working-class married women the only women who were engaged in paid work outside the home. Some middle-class married women, seeking greater security for their families than their husbands were able to provide, gained an independent identity by establishing their own businesses.[43] As suggested in the previous chapter, diarist Lucy Morrison was one such woman. In the mid-1870s, spurred by recurring crises in her husband John's sawmilling operations, Lucy moved decisively into the business of market gardening, building a greenhouse to overwinter her plants and hiring a trained gardener to assist her.⁴⁴ Like Lucy's business, the independent business established by that gardener two years later shared the same grounds as his home, but while he was listed as a gardener in the 1881 census, she was not. Lucy Everett Morrison's diaries, in which she kept a comprehensive record of her commercial enterprise, provide unique insight into the seasonal round of a successful nursery business that, at its height in the early 1880s, employed six gardeners and supplied flowers, fruits, and vegetables to retailers as well as to individual customers in both Fredericton and Saint John. A brief survey of that round for 1881 effectively illustrates both the nature of her business and the extent of its reach. January found Lucy busy putting in cuttings, fertilizing carnations and roses with manure water, and dipping cinneraras in tobacco water. By 22 February, with the legislature in session and the social life that came with it in full swing, she was "making up boquets & button holes," until, by the end of that day, the greenhouse began to look "bare of bloom." Three days later, she faced a minor disaster when the youngest of her helpers "took some button holes to Barker house.⁴⁵ They were all frozen when he got there." By mid-March, with the demand for cut flowers still high, both Lucy and her customers had begun planning for spring planting. On 17 March, a customer left her "an order for plants," and she sent an "order to Henderson for seed."⁴⁶ That same day, she received money from Hannington Bros. in Saint John for flowers she had supplied, and three days later filled a large order for flowers from J. Murray Kay, the manager of the Saint John and Maine Railway.⁴⁷ Outdoor planting began with the preparation of the hotbeds in late March and continued well into May. On 12 May, when Daniel Kenny, one of her competitors, held "an auction sale of flowers," Lucy was busy "putting in celery in boxes, over 4000 transplanted."⁴⁸ Lucy generally hired women to help carry out the design of her ornamental gardens, while the men did the heavy work, and on 27 May reported, "Miss Perley here all day helping me set out flower garden. Lawrence cutting & hauling sods. George & he sodding. I & boys potted balsams & put in boxes asters, Phlox &c. We set out 6 beds ... filled 4 heart beds & 1 oval." A few days later found Miss Perley drawing patterns of scrolls, crests and hearts. They "got two crests & 2 scrolls sodded & filled. Also 2 more heart beds." Like the greenhouses and vegetable gardens, the flower gardens required constant maintenance. They were well worth the effort for Lucy Morrison's ornamental gardens were famous, attracting the attention not only of visitors and potential customers, but also of passengers on the train that regularly crossed the nearby railway bridge.[49] Meanwhile, her customers were planting their own gardens and, on 6 June alone, she sold 525 cabbage plants. On 14 June, she "was up 4 a.m. making boquets, then sending away plants." On 28 June, she hired Jane Gordon to help her clean the greenhouses, and the following day reported "a good shew of bloom." Even after James Gibson arrived and "got a lot more plants, reducing bloom some, on the whole," she noted, the "house looks very nice." On 6 July, the labour-intensive cultivation of Lucy's major crop began, Lawrence having "5 long trenches dug for celery & 9 half length ones," while customers who preferred to cultivate their own began picking up plants. By 8 July, she had sent away 1,281 celery plants and had 350 more "engaged." At the same time, Lucy and her gardeners were busy harvesting and selling gooseberries, strawberries, and currants. On 9 July, she started selling bouquets and buttonholes as well as strawberries through John Wiley, a Fredericton druggist. By 18 August, Lawrence and George were "moulding up celery plants" and on 2 September George was "molding up celery the 2nd time." In late September, they started bringing plants inside, finishing the job by 6 October, with the greenhouse "very full of plants ... Carrots all in the cellar, onions still out but covered nights." The following day found the "men moulding up celery for the last time." In anticipation of the winter trade in cut flowers, Lucy ordered $55 worth of roses and other plants from Dingee Conrad & Company on 1 October; her order arrived on 12 October, and the following day she potted them, noting that the roses "came in good order, Carnations not much." On 14 October, she "sent an order to Henderson for plants, also one to Harris of Halifax." On 28 October, the men packed 800 heads of celery in sixteen barrels of sand. Lucy already had orders for 500 heads. November was a slow month, spent keeping the fires going in the greenhouses and nurturing the plants. On 30 November, she sent away the last of her celery. Regretting that she had had only one rose to put in the bouquet for the St Andrews dinner, Lucy noted on 1 December that "a great mistake was made in George cutting down the Bovardias when bringing them in. The spring is the time to do that. Let them grow up in the fall & get into bloom as soon as possible." The following day she commented that the Dingee and Conrad "carnations are not coming on as they should ... My own are better." In Saint John for her son Tom's wedding on 7 December, she took the opportunity to visit local greenhouses and purchase plants. That Christmas she sold all her flowers to Bebbington, who told her that "he never had his flowers blooming so badly." Lucy's situation was similar, with "very little bloom this Xmas."

In comparing herself to other gardeners, Lucy Everett Morrison clearly identified with the professionals. Comparing her ornamental garden to those of two well-known amateur city gardeners – Fenety and Ray[50] – she commented, "They both looked splendid, throwing mine all in the shade." In contrast, comparing herself to Fredericton's two professional gardeners, her comments were more competitive: "Kenny's garden & green house not looking well, his onions beats ours. Beb's about same as ours. Our celery beats them both & our garden & green house quite up to Beb's."[51] Lucy Morrison not only saw herself as an independent businesswoman but also judged herself a match for the other major commercial gardeners in the city.

Whether they were single or married, whether they were contributing to their family's income, seeking to maintain a precarious independence, or running a successful business, over the course of the nineteenth century, women became increasingly visible in the public sphere of paid employment. Implicitly recognizing that women who entered the realm of paid work were integral to the smooth functioning of New Brunswick's economy, both men and women defended the trend. In examining contemporary responses to and justifications of a changing reality, historians have analysed the continuing pervasiveness of the domesticity discourse that characterized the prescriptive literature of the period, noting that women no less than men unselfconsciously identified sewing and weaving in factory settings, as well as nursing and teaching as suitable female occupations, perceiving such work to be an extension of women's work in the domestic sphere. In some instances, such as in the response of midwives as doctors moved into the field of obstetrical care, the discourse, which risked becoming defensive, may well have proven conciliatory and even cooperative in New Brunswick, where an analysis of birth registers identified eighty-five midwives who were active between 1870 and 1900, often in concert with doctors.[52] In other instances, such as in response to the inexorable feminization of teaching, the discourse was offensive rather than defensive, part of a generally successful attempt to mediate resistance to change.[53] In both cases, women argued that, in seeking training to enter the workforce as nurses and teachers, they were acquiring skills for which they were deemed, as women, to be particularly well suited, for they were capitalizing on skills they had learned at their mother's knee. Male educational administrators also justified the feminization of teaching on the grounds that the care and nurturing of young children came naturally to women. In calling upon the domesticity discourse to support their arguments, women, like men, contributed to the tendency to undervalue women's skills by "naturalizing" them, even as they claimed space for women in the public sphere.

Viewed from another perspective, it would seem that the belief in the notion of a "natural" division of labour, which had worked well in the pre-industrial era, remained intact. New realities demanded adjustments to the interstices of that division, extending fields of intersection and overlap, and involving minor, rather than major, shifts in attitudes. In politics, too, new realities called for adjustments in women's and men's intersecting and overlapping political activities as, seeking to improve society, women sought new ways to make their voices heard. The next chapter considers the changing nature of women's political engagement.

Chapter 13

Politics and Social Reform

In myriad ways, nineteenth-century women participated in shaping and reshaping community and societal norms and values.[1] Reflecting the values of their families and faith communities, and acting both as individuals and in concert with others of like mind, they made their influence felt well beyond their families and even their churches. Fully engaged in community life, women read both local and denominational newspapers and participated in a public discourse on issues ranging from the cost of railroads to the treatment of the poor. Often working through the medium of an expanding number of voluntary associations, New Brunswick women played a significant public role in their society as political actors and social reformers, influencing public policy and helping to establish a range of charitable institutions.

Although not generally associated with electoral politics, New Brunswick women were among the first in the field. Until a legislative amendment in 1843 denied them the franchise, propertied New Brunswick women were legally entitled to vote. And, in the early-nineteenth century, a number of those women did exercise their franchise, though in the two documented cases – involving forty-three Kings County women in 1827 and thirty-nine Sunbury County women in 1839 – their votes were subsequently struck off the rolls.[2] Like their male counterparts, the women who voted in those elections were propertied household heads. Like their male counterparts, they demonstrated their interest in and knowledge about electoral politics by their participation in the system, going to the polls to support the candidates of their choice. Conditioned by British and North American custom, and sharing the social mores of their day, women did not publicly question the amendment that disenfranchised them.[3]

But they had not lost interest in politics. Instead, after 1843, propertied women, like women who did not own property, found other ways to involve themselves directly in politics. They could and did seek to influence the men elected to the legislative assembly, particularly in the era that preceded the establishment of formal political parties, when ordinary folk, voters and non-voters, women and men, routinely used the petitioning process to speak to and through their local representatives.

From the founding of the province, petitioning was an integral part of the formal political system. Loyalists petitioned the government for land in compensation for their loyalty and for the losses they had endured as a result of that loyalty. Soldiers and their widows were required to submit petitions requesting the government pension they were entitled to under the law. Jacobina Campbell's mother was among those widows who received such a pension. Following the establishment of schools, teachers were paid the government subsidy to which they were entitled only upon the submission of a petition. Individuals as well as local officials petitioned for government funding for public works projects. Businesses, voluntary associations, and even towns seeking incorporation made their application by petition. These are just a few of the many and varied kinds of requests for which a petition to the government was required. This is to say nothing of the use of the petition, by members of a society much accustomed to the process, to seek individual aid or redress or as a means to lobby governments in concert with others of like mind. Members of the legislative assembly received all manner of petitions from their constituents, and duly presented those petitions to the legislature. Local and provincial governments responded, often favourably, to petitions, whether they were from individuals seeking some form of personal redress, a local committee seeking support for a proposed public works project, or a group of people seeking legislative change.[4]

Women, like men, sought legislative change through the petitioning process. Women, like men, could be passionate about their political views, and women's political activism was too ubiquitous to be regarded as extraordinary. Over the course of the nineteenth century, their political passions tended to emerge from a common set of social priorities. Married, middle-class, and often middle-aged women were among the strongest advocates of temperance legislation in the mid-nineteenth century, and thousands of women across the province took up their pens in the cause. In 1854, women representing nearly one-third of the families in Sunbury County were among those signing petitions calling for a prohibitory liquor act.⁵ And legislators paid attention. In 1852, George Hatheway, a representative for York County, argued that women's signatures on petitions were "a sufficient reason" for passing the liquor bill then before the House. Noting that a politician needed "the good opinion of the fair portion of the community," he acknowledged women's political influence, declaring that he "would always rather have one lady canvasser than a dozen men."⁶ New Brunswick's liquor law, the first in British North America, though short-lived, demonstrated both women's ability to mobilize effectively and the extent of their engagement in politics and the political system.⁷ Although the petitioning process proved a useful way for women and men to join forces in lobbying their government for social change, even before Confederation removed the major seat of government to Ottawa, the emergence of party government in the mid-1850s combined with the sheer volume of petitions submitted in each legislative session led to a restructuring of the administration of government. The result was to make petitioning less satisfactory and less effective as a means of political activism.

When the petition became a less efficacious tool following the emergence of political parties, women as well as men became partisans, attending political rallies and promoting as well as supporting the party of their choice. In 1883, twenty-four-year-old Lottie Reid noted in her diary that "Pa and I were over to hear Sir Leonard Tilley give a political discourse at Hopewell this afternoon. The Hall was packed full."⁸ Tilley, a pre-Confederation New Brunswick premier and staunch temperance advocate, was a Reformer who, when elected to the House of Commons in 1867, joined Conservative John A. Macdonald's coalition government. As finance minister in Macdonald's cabinet, Tilley had been the architect of the National Policy that returned the Conservatives to power in 1878.⁹ This policy was, no doubt, much discussed in the Reid household, as Lottie's brother-in-law, Senator Abner McClelan, a member of Tilley's Reform administration in the decade before Confederation, had remained a Liberal and, convinced that the protective tariffs introduced in the National Policy would prove detrimental to the smaller provinces by the sea, continued to favour free trade.¹⁰

Laura Trueman would become a firm supporter of her husband Josiah Wood's political ambitions. But on 10 May 1878, when he was running as a Liberal candidate in the provincial election, she admitted in her Journal of Everyday Affairs, "Josie has gone to Shediac today. He is a candidate for the House of Assembly. I did not feel as if I wanted him to at first, but I am quite reconciled to it now. He has been urged to it by his friends." This required no small sacrifice for Laura, who at twenty-two, with two small children to care for, recognized that "Josie will be very busy until the election is over, scarcely has time to speak to me. I must try to take all the care I can off his shoulders in connection with the house providing & the garden also." By 5 June, she was fully engaged, reporting that "Martha was here and had brought me an armful of rhubarb. I gave her two little white dresses and canvassed her for her husband's vote." Although Josie lost that election, four years later, attracted to both the Conservative Party and federal politics by the National Policy, he was victorious in his bid for a seat in the federal House of Commons, unseating a longtime incumbent, a member of the opposition Liberal Party.[11] Describing the local victory celebration in her journal, an elated Laura, who had again canvassed on her husband's behalf during the campaign, demonstrated her knowledge about the nature of electoral politics.

> *June 21st 1882. Yesterday was the proudest day of my life in a worldly sense. All day it rained and I felt quite dejected. No one could tell anything about how the day was going and Father came in to dinner looking rather downhearted. He thought so many of the people were working against Josie. But after we were through tea we sat and talked a few minutes and then there was a ring at the doorbell. George Ford with some returns, enough to make Josie's election sure. I danced and screamed and jumped. Dora and all the house caught up the refrain.[12] Edward Clifford came, then Mr and Mrs McCurdy and Mrs Wiggins and Lucy Milner, Mrs Milner and Seaford. As I had been sewing all day to drown my anxiety, I had on my old blue cotton. But about this time I began to realise that I might see some company, so I flew up and changed my dress. As soon as I got down the rush commenced Pa rl[?], Dr Weldon, Mr Burwash being the first. The house was soon filled. Then they lit a ferocious bonfire on the road in front of the house. We all went out to watch it but were glad to make our escape as we saw a big crowd swaying along the street screaming hurrahs and carrying Josie in the midst on a chair. He arrived in time to watch them come in in the lurid light of the fire. Josie spoke a few words, they even cheered me, to cheers on the doorstep. Then while the crowd sang, the church bells rang, whistles [blew]. They played the piano in the house and all stood and watched the magnificent light of the bonfire. It was the greatest rejoicing Sackville ever saw. They say it was glorious in Moncton, which*

gave Josie a 300 majority. Tilley had 270 majority in Saint John and the Dominion returned a 70 majority of government supporters. It was a grand Liberal Conservative victory and something wonderful for Josie, who defeats a man who has been so long in power, who has spent such a fearful amount of money and who has an immense deal of influence over a large class of people. I could not keep the tears back as I stood and watched the bonfire and thought of my life, how it has been fraught with blessing. What should I ask for that I had not? Seldom is it the lot of one to be so richly blessed as I have been. The darlings got up and watched the bonfire in their nightdresses from Auntie's window.[13] People said they looked so sweet there. Today people have been in all day with their congratulations, and tonight I feel tired.

Even at seventeen, Sadie Harper demonstrated an avid interest in electoral politics, following the 1892 provincial election campaign in the newspaper, attending political meetings and formulating clear and decided opinions. "Everything is election just now. I do hate these times so much as there is always so much drinking," she noted in her diary on 10 October. But that did not mean that she had no interest in politics, for she went on to add, "Wednesday evening there is to be a political meeting in the hall and I want to go if possible as I like to hear the speeches." Although Sadie did not get to go to that meeting, her older sisters, May and Win, attended. There was another political meeting scheduled for the following week, Sadie noting in her diary on Monday that "the Blair men are going to have their meeting tomorrow night. John Smith is going to speak, and I would very much like to hear him as he is young and this is his first appearance in politics."[14] This time, she did attend, summarizing the meeting in her diary.

Tues. Oct. 18. It was a beautiful day today. I went to school as usual. After school I went for a long walk with Minnie Lawson and we both enjoyed it very much. After tea I trimmed my last winter's hat over, and then Win, Nell and I went down to the political meeting. The hall was packed, so to speak. We had a good deal of work getting through the crowd at the door and then we had hard work to get seats. We enjoyed it very much. I thought Mr Woodbury Wells spoke best, he also spoke first. Then came J.W.Y. Smith. He called himself the Baby Politician and gave a short comical speech. Then came the Hon. Mr Richard. Well, he was a lawyer. If anyone ever told fibs, I think he did. Oh, he went for Mr Powell and Mr Melanson in fine shape, calling them I don't know what all. Then Mr McQueen spoke. He gave just a short address. I suppose by Saturday evening one side or the other will be in it or snowed under as the political term is. But I hope our side, which is the opposition, will be in it. This evening Aunt Deanie and Winnie Campbell were up for a while. Aunt Deanie's finger is getting better.

Thurs. Oct. 20. Was kind of cloudy in the morning, nice and fine in the afternoon. I went to school as ususal. After school I went for my lesson. After tea I went to Lodge for a while. We do not intend to hold it in the schoolhouse any more I think, as one of the teachers wants that room fixed up for her. So we will have to look around for another. Mr Bailey was up and spent the evening. After I came in, Win and I against Nell and Mr Bailey played Tiddlywinks and we beat them a good deal. Then Blois and Winnie against Mr Bailey and I played Pedro, and then Mr B. and I were the losers.[15]

Fri. Oct. 21. Quite fine in the morning, but not in the afternoon. I went to school and everything went on as usual. We have lots of fun nowadays dancing the Militaire, nearly every girl can dance it in our room and lots in other rooms, too. We are having all the blackboards in the school fixed over. So I suppose our room won't have any school when they fix the ones in this room. After school I sewed on my blue skirt quite a bit and practised some. Tomorrow is election day. May is coming home on Monday in the evening train. "Don't vote for the Baby."

Sat. Oct. 22. It was lovely and fine all day, especially in the afternoon. I did my Saturday's work in the morning, then worked up in the henhouse for quite a while getting it ready for winter, putting lots of hay in the nests and pasting paper here and there over cracks and so forth. Then I practised some, and before tea I went down to Aunt Kate's with Mama for a while. There were lots of people on the streets, of course, as by that time nearly all had come back from the polling booth in Barachois. After tea, Winnie and I went down to practise, as Nell could not go because nearly all week she has been suffering dreadfully with toothache. Only Mr Bailey came so we did not practise long. Blue news about the election. In this parish the oppositionists were away ahead, but taking all of New Brunswick, the Government were ahead.[16] Moncton spoilt this county. The money that was floating around Moncton was awful. Oh, but the Government would go ahead in the money line every time. So it took a good deal out of them if nothing else. I think it is terrible the way elections are carried on here. By both sides. I do hope Richard won't get in anyway and I hope Melanson will.

Women of all ages took a lively interest in partisan electoral politics, participating in discussions of both candidates and party platforms. But, perhaps because the issues – particularly the social issues – that most concerned them were seldom reflected in party platforms, they also sought other ways to make their voices heard. Thus, while women did canvass on behalf of the candidates and party they supported, many more canvassed on behalf of voluntary organizations.

Young women followed their mothers into the ranks of voluntary associations, beginning their apprenticeship at around the age of sixteen. The first organizations they joined were usually denominational associations, most often women's sewing circles, which supported their local churches in a variety of ways. In St Stephen, for example, while a few leading businessmen were the major donors in support of the Methodist churches, female "circles" or "societies" of members and adherents served as the regular fundraisers for each chapel.[17] Such activities, were not, of course, limited to Methodist women. Whatever their denomination, women, working through voluntary organizations, supported their churches in very practical ways, raising money for repairs, new buildings, furnishings, and decorations. They also undertook charity work, sustaining the poor in their particular communities of faith and often well beyond.[18] As women's voluntary associations proliferated, benevolence became a basis for social reform. Refusing to blame the poor – especially the women and children among them – for their plight, women urged their churches and governments towards a more compassionate society, and took positive action to ensure the success of their efforts. Without the work of women, who raised the money to fund hospitals, orphans' homes, and similar charitable institutions, such institutions would not have been established in many communities.[19] Coming together for such purposes, women helped to build the foundations of civil society.[20]

In claiming authority as they entered the public discourse on issues involving the need for social reforms and social infrastructure, women often spoke from first-hand knowledge, gleaned from their observation of a wide variety of social institutions, and this from an early age. At school in Boston, in 1846, seventeen-year-old Mary Hill reported to her mother that "our teacher Miss Lydia took the girls to see the state prison on Saturday." Describing the experience, she admitted "a slight emotion of fear when we first went in ... and found ourselves in the midst of the prisoners watched only by one or two men." Commenting that the superintendent was "celebrated for his humanity and kindness to the prisoners," Mary nonetheless viewed the institution with a critical and compassionate eye, noting that "the rooms are not larger than one man could entirely fill," and observing, "I should think they would die in summer."[21] Such visits to prisons and other institutions by women as well as men were common in the nineteenth century. In Philadelphia in March 1867, Ann Eliza Gallacher visited both the penitentiary and "the house of refuge for bad children," where trades were taught to "over 400 boys & 80 girles." While she did not offer an opinion about either of these institutions, she much admired Gerard College, established for the purpose of educating orphan boys born in Philadelphia. And while twelve-year-old Isabelle did not accompany her on these visits, Ann Eliza did take her daughter to visit "the blind asylum," where they saw the children "work & sing," and were impressed to discover that one boy, who could neither see nor hear, "could read and had done some bead work."[22] During a period when a wide variety of charitable institutions were being established, and people were increasingly recognizing the need for prison reform, women gained invaluable knowledge through such visits.

For women, social reform activism and political activism were often integrally connected. And for many, social activism and membership in voluntary societies went hand in hand. New Brunswick women had, from very early in the nineteenth century, been active in mixed gender voluntary associations, with temperance lodges being perhaps the most common.[23] Ann Eliza Rogers's parents were both strong advocates of temperance, and Ann Eliza, in her turn, became a lifelong temperance advocate. Returning to New Brunswick following the death of her first husband in 1867, she soon became active in the temperance lodge. There she met a local bachelor, a man she had known since childhood, and, with his encouragement, gained an effective voice, noting in her diary on 15 January 1869, "I wrote a piece for the division paper. Lemuel is Editor." Before the year was out, Ann Eliza and Lemuel Moore were married. Two years later, her eldest daughter, sixteen-year-old Isabelle, joined the lodge. As well as writing articles for the division paper, Ann Eliza was an active fund raiser for the cause. In 1874, when the "ladies" of her community met to discuss plans to form "a Society to raise money to assist in building a Temperance hall," Ann Eliza, now the mother of five, and her sister Maggie played leading roles. On 5 March, she reported, "Mrs Alexander Rogers & I were appointed to draw up some rules for the Society." Four days later, they met again, "adopted the Rules and appointed Officers, Maggie

Rogers is President. Mary Bacon & Julia Peck vice Presidents, Florance Moore Secretary,[24] Mrs A. Rogers financial secretary, Mrs James Rogers Treasurer. Mrs A Rogers & I are to get work." Like Isabelle, Ann Eliza's remaining children followed their parents into the movement, joining the local division of the temperance lodge when they turned sixteen.

The decision to establish specifically women's organizations required leadership as well as cooperation. During the course of the nineteenth century, New Brunswick women imported and established a wide variety of such voluntary associations, ranging from denominational women's auxiliaries, sewing circles, maternal associations, and missionary societies through literary societies, art clubs, temperance societies, Local Councils of Women, enfranchisement associations, the Young Women's Christian Association, alumnae associations, the Imperial Order of Daughters of the Empire, to that quintessential Canadian contribution, the Women's Institute. In the mid-nineteenth century, when women's voluntary societies began to proliferate, it was largely middle-class women who made up the membership of those societies.[25] Some historians have argued that, in organizing for the purpose of reforming society, the middle classes – men and women alike – were seeking to achieve the hegemony of their own values. Others explain the overrepresentation of the middle classes among the membership as a function of greater leisure time, allowing them the luxury not only to think about social issues, but also to establish organizations through which they could respond more effectively to those issues.[26] Yet, in the rural areas, at least, while middle-class women predominated among the membership, voluntary organizations attracted members from a broad cross-section of society.

In the final quarter of the nineteenth-century, increasing numbers of women who had, in the past, worked alongside men in local temperance lodges, or perhaps in women's auxiliaries of men's temperance organizations, joined the Woman's Christian Temperance Union (WCTU). Founded in New York in 1874, the WCTU crossed the border into Ontario the same year. Women in Moncton established the first Maritime branch in 1875 and the movement quickly spread.[27] Women had long participated in the temperance crusade, but it took on a new life with the founding of the WCTU. Within two decades, the movement had spread across Canada and almost every community of any size had a local branch.

Some of the reasons why women who had long been involved in mixed-member temperance organizations found the WCTU so attractive are revealed in Laura Wood's Journal of Everyday Affairs. On 18 March 1878, a day when the "great storm of blustering snow" might well have prevented people from attending any meeting, Laura confided in her journal that she felt "very much disappointed about the Temperance Meeting." Worried that dwindling attendance presaged "the death of the Reform Club in Sackville," she admitted that she thought that "it was never taken hold of here, as it was in other places." Significantly, she blamed the male leaders and organizers, noting that "the meeting for tonight was never given out until Saturday evening in church where on account of the dreadful state of the roads but few were present." But she believed, in any case, that "a special invitation seems more pressing than a general one," and expressed her frustration at "C.B.," who, "as usual wants great things done in the cause of Temperance but oversteps the bounds of common-sense and makes himself ridiculous." Obliquely hinting that men might not be as sensitive as women in recognizing family problems, she noted that she had "heard again from Mollie, just after Josie left. J says they seem very comfortably situated but H still looks as if he drank. Poor man!" Like many women who would make the transition to the WCTU, Laura Wood was convinced that "if Prohibition were possible and surely it is how certain it is that half at least of the misery in the world might be prevented." She further noted that she was "struck in seeing notices of crime in the newspapers at the great majority being directly or indirectly traceable to intoxication."

Five years later, in 1883, Laura Wood and her sister Annie Trueman were instrumental in organizing a Sackville WCTU branch. As interest in establishing a branch of the WCTU in Sackville grew, Annie and Laura sought advice from their mother, who was then in Ottawa, visiting her sister. Writing to her on 12 February, Annie reported that "Mrs Powell is perfectly enthused with the idea of getting up a coffee & reading room for the young people here, as effective temperance work. She is really in earnest about temperance & wants to get up a W.C.T.U." Knowing that Ottawa had a branch, she sought Rebecca's advice: "We dont know how to go about to form one. Does [Cousin] Minnie belong to one?" Annie was convinced that they "could not get such a thing as a reading room etc. in operation without first having a well organised W.C.T.U." and urged her mother to help them: "If there was any little pamphlet with directions – It would be so good if we could have one here in Sackville."[28] Writing to Laura on 20 February, Rebecca declared herself "delighted to hear that there is a revival in temperance in Sackville" and added that "if I can serve Mrs Powell in any way, either by printed matter or asking questions about the conduct of the meetings of the W.C.T.U., I shall be only too happy to do so." Offering some very practical advice, she further suggested, "There will be a nice chance for Miss Wood [Josie's aunt] to show her interest in the cause by giving liberally of her means to sustain the organisation, for as Bella Flint remarked, there must be money supplied, for we cannot do much without the sinews of war. I cd send some tracts to be read in meeting if you wd like to have them. I invested 25¢ in temp. literature."[29]

While the Trueman sisters looked to their relatives in Ontario for advice, Mrs Powell and others consulted the women who had established the first Maritime branch and on 20 March, Laura reported to her mother that "Mrs. Pickard & Mrs. Powell came in to say Mrs. Crandall was coming from Moncton tomorrow to start our Union." Guided by her own view that special invitations seemed more pressing than general ones, Laura "went to see the Baptist Minister's wife, & ask her to join. She was pleased & will come."[30] Determined to be inclusive – that is, interdenominational – the Sackville organizers early learned the necessity of compromise. When twenty-one women, including Methodists, Baptists, and Episcopalians among their number, assembled at the home of Mrs Powell, disagreements on apparently minor issues reflected denominational differences. Which pledge to adopt? They had three examples before them: Moncton's, Saint John's, and Ottawa's. Annie described the meeting in a letter to her mother: "Mrs. Crandall read the minutes of the inauguration of Moncton's W.C.T.U. which, by the way, happens to be the oldest in the Province – then read their pledge & the St. John pledge, also the one Minnie sent by you. Of the three Mrs. C. & we all liked best the one Minnie sent which we adopted as ours." But controversy arose when some members proposed including a clause from the Moncton pledge that excluded the use of liquor for cooking purposes. According to Annie, who supported the proposal, "there was quite a discussion on this point, as the majority wished to have that inserted in our pledge. Finally a vote was taken & all the episcopal people with Mrs. Prof. Smith voted against & although we had the majority, still we thought it better to leave it there." In compromising, the group adopted a pledge which the Methodist and Baptist members saw as "a total abstinence pledge," but which allowed the Episcopalians some flexibility in interpretation. Annie's account, tinged with humour, as well as a certain level of incredulity, suggests that coming together in common cause required much more than mere good will:

> Mrs. Cogswell said "Why how could you make mince pies Mrs. Crandall?" To which she made answer by giving her the recipe which she used. Of course you know Prof. Smith could not do without it in his food. Just fancy their expecting to pledge to give up their cups & they were not willing even to do without it in mince pies! where it will make so little difference in the taste. Well they all signed, episcopal & all. Laura is President much to her distress of mind. Lucy Milner, Mrs. McDonald & Mrs. Powell Vice Presidents. I am Secretary. Mrs. C.A. Bowser Treasurer.[31]

In writing to Laura, who had confirmed her distress at being made president, "the youngest one among them all & totally incompetent,"[32] Rebecca offered reassurance. Declaring herself both "very much pleased & rather surprised that the CWTU was taken up so in S," she admitted that she "did not suppose that the E. church people wd have any thing to do with it." Recognizing the level of negotiation involved, she commented that "it was a grand idea to have three denominations represented in the vice-presidents and you must feel your position as Pres. to be a rather responsible one & one which you will need more than human assistance to help you to fill." But she expressed confidence that Laura would "grow into it as in every good work and you will be helped, if you ask aright for guidance. It is never too young to begin to work for the cause of God & humanity, there is nothing like beginning young."[33]

The WCTU lobbied not only for temperance legislation but also for a variety of other moral and social reforms, and succeeded in its campaign to introduce temperance education in schools. Although their activism focussed on social reform rather than on the issue of rights for women, as the advent of the party system and the decline of local authority combined to make legislators less amenable and less vulnerable to public pressure, members of the WCTU began to turn their attention to issues of suffrage and other kinds of systemic discrimination. Writing to her daughters from Ottawa in 1883, Rebecca Trueman had noted that several of the WCTU speakers she had heard there "advocated 'woman suffrage,'" adding, "I suppose they thought to encourage the women to clamor for this privilege." While Rebecca did not imply that she herself was likely to clamour for this privilege, neither did she suggest that she was opposed to the idea, commenting only that she "was surprised to find Mrs Tilton shrank from the idea, and she an American."[34] In New Brunswick, WCTU branches in some regions did lobby the government in favour of women's enfranchisement. Leading the way, in February 1888, the Eastern New Brunswick WCTU submitted nine petitions to the New Brunswick legislature urging the House of Assembly to confer "upon all females ... who ... possess the qualifications ... now necessary in the case of male persons ... the right to vote at the elections of Members of Municipal Councils throughout the province."[35] At its annual convention that year, the Eastern New Brunswick WCTU endorsed a petition recommending full suffrage for women.[36] But the Maritime WCTU was divided on this issue, and, although many supporters' husbands joined their wives in signing the 1888 petitions, the legislators did not act on these calls for women's enfranchisement.

Possibly frustrated that the WCTU remained divided in their support for suffrage, eighteen members of the Saint John branch came together in 1894 to establish a separate Women's Enfranchisement Association (WEA). Although women in other communities did not follow their lead, the WCTU did add suffrage to its provincial platform the following year, and, over the next four years these two voluntary associations organized a number of petition- and letter-writing campaigns. Their impressive lobbying resulted in four women's suffrage bills, but despite significant media support they failed to win over a majority of legislators. In 1898, both organizations shifted their attention to other reform issues.[37] Both Emma Fiske, a widow who was elected as the WEA's second president in 1898, and Ella Hatheway, secretary-treasurer of the WEA and the wife of businessman and social reform activist Frank Hatheway, were also very involved in a range of other social reform initiatives.[38] Ella Hatheway became a member of the committee for enacting free daycare, and the WEA initiated the idea of a children's aid society.[39] Under Emma Fiske's leadership, the WEA, in concert with other voluntary societies, became involved in campaigns to promote compulsory schooling and lobby for the passage of factory laws. And in 1904, when the government appointed a factory commission to tour the province's leading industrial communities to gather evidence, Emma Fiske was selected as a member of that commission. Unlike the unsuccessful suffrage campaign, both the campaign for a compulsory school law and the campaign for a factory law culminated in legislation. Yet the achievement of women's enfranchisement remained a fundamental goal for both the WEA and the WCTU. Shifting the campaign to a grassroots level, Emma Fiske, in her capacity as both suffrage club organizer and head of the provincial WCTU's suffrage department, travelled throughout the province seeking to educate both men and women on the subject of equal rights.[40]

Even as WCTU branches multiplied and expanded their mandate far beyond temperance, the traditional mixed-member temperance lodges continued to flourish, particularly in rural communities, with women playing an active role in maintaining them. For young people, especially, these were social as well as political organizations, as is apparent in the diaries of Ida MacDonald and Sadie Harper. On 19 November 1881, a few weeks before her sixteenth birthday, Ida Macdonald reported in her diary, "I joined the Lodge tonight; there were four others joined also." Raised in a devout Baptist household, Ida, the youngest member of her family, believed in the temperance cause. Yet to adolescents like Ida, joining the lodge meant something more than a pledge of active support for that cause. As her diary demonstrates, "Lodge," held once a week, was as integral as Sunday meeting to the social life of the young people of the community. This mixture of pleasure and politics is captured in her diary entries for March 1883, when the young people were planning an "Entertainment" to raise money for the Lodge. On 1 March, Ida noted, "We were all up to the school house tonight to practise. Cal & I skated." On Saturday, 3 March, "we were all to Lodge ... Inglewood, George & Cal here after." On 7 March, they were off to "'Thorn Town' to County Lodge ... 9 of us went ... We went to Mr Worden's to tea. There was a great crowd to the public meeting in the evening. We had a good time coming home, but it was pretty cold. It was 2 o'clock when we got here. Inglewood & Calvin came with us." On Friday, she reported, "George & Cal. here this evening. Practice night." Another Practice, on 13 March, found "Inglewood, Howard, Geo. Mott, Geo. Mac & Calvin here." The next day, Ida noted, "Rehearsal tonight. Howard & Geo Mott, Georgie, Calvin & Geo. Mac here. After rehearsal they had a business meeting to see about tickets. Mr Mercer wrote them & Pres. signed them ... They have decided to have the Entertainment on this coming Saturday." On Friday afternoon, "they took the 'piano' up to the school house ... We were all up to the school house tonight. Rehearsal. Ing, George & Calvin here." The entertainment, held on "St Patrick's Day ... came off better than we expected. Mr Mercer's playing was the best of it. Quite a little crowd there."

Like many other women diarists, Sadie Harper was both a loyal Methodist and a strong advocate for the temperance cause. Like her parents and siblings, she was a member of the temperance lodge and, like Ida MacDonald, she enjoyed the social aspects of lodge membership. Indeed, on 1 February 1895, noting that "our Lodge seems to be growing," she added, "I hope it will be found interesting to the boys whom we want to keep in." Laura Wood, who identified Annie Inch as "my model girl – so cool is she to young men," would have had little sympathy with this sentiment. In the spring of 1878, Laura, commenting on a meeting of the Mount Allison Euchetorian, which she considered "execrable," dismissed the debate on protection vs. free trade as "an utter failure" and pronounced an essay on man's slate "incoherent, & slighting to women," giving it as her opinion that "young men should think of their mothers when they are speaking of our sex instead of the school girls here whose heads seem to be full of beaus & dress to the exclusion of every thing sensible."[41]

Although she would not have met the standard of Annie Inch with reference to her attitude towards young men, at seventeen, Sadie Harper was not only committed to temperance reform but also very knowledgeable about the underlying politics involved. The winter of 1895 brought renewed interest in the temperance cause in Shediac, perhaps in response to the appointment of a Royal Commission on the Effects of the Liquor Traffic, which reported, later that year, that although jurisdictions in ten of the province's fifteen counties had voted to implement the Canada Temperance Act, the trade in alcoholic beverages continued to be conducted quite openly, even in those districts.[42] Despite the strong support for temperance among the Methodists, Sadie realized that the Scott Act was unlikely to win majority approval in Shediac.

> 1896: Mon. Jan. 6. Last night Mr Matthews gave simply a grand sermon on the way one should vote at the election today. Oh, he made everything so plain and clear, and he dealt with everything so well that I'm sure no one of that congregation could of a clear conscience vote any other way than for the Canadian Temperance Act. Well, I hope it will go all right today. In this parish it is almost sure to be hard as this is a holy day with the French, and of course they will all be sure to come and vote for license as Father Ouellett is opposed to the Scott Act and of course they go with the priest. It is bitterly cold out today again, and it looks as if it might snow, I wish it would.[43]

The Catholic hierarchy opposed the Scott Act not because they did not support the temperance cause but because they believed that the Church, not the state, should dictate morals.

Women who were members of temperance societies were often also members of missionary societies and, just as many women found reasons to shift from mixed-member to exclusively women's temperance organizations, so, too, increasing numbers of women shifted their support from mixed-member to exclusively women's missionary societies. Annie Trueman became a very active member not only of the interdenominational WCTU but also of the Methodist women's missionary society, noting in her diary on 21 August 1886, "Went to Mrs Humphreys and attended to WCTU business ... In the afternoon wrote a report of our Women's missionary society for our delegate, Hattie Stuart, to read at convention in Charlottetown." While not overtly or conventionally political, the missionary movement must be counted as a political movement in so far as it fostered as well as reflected Western imperialism. By the 1890s, it rivalled the temperance movement in its appeal to women. Although that appeal was broadly based, the movement was especially successful on college campuses. Inspired by Hannah Maria Norris, a young instructor at Acadia Ladies' Seminary, Maritime Baptist women established Canada's first separate women's missionary societies in 1870. Within the year, Norris, funded by those new societies, became a member of the first contingent of single women missionaries. Many young graduates of the Acadia Ladies' Seminary would follow her example, as would many Mount Allison graduates; many more would, like Alva Estabrooks and Annie Trueman, join women's missionary societies.[44] By the turn of the century, not only Baptist but also Methodist and Presbyterian women's missionary societies would be acting independently of their male counterparts, raising money to sponsor female missionaries.[45]

In the YWCA, popular on university campuses across the country, the missionary and temperance causes intersected within a single organization.[46] Like many of the young women of her generation who attended normal schools and universities, Violet Goldsmith was a member of the YWCA. Noting in her diary on 10 December 1901 that "the girls had a meeting to organise a Y.W.C.A. for the Normal School in the afternoon," she added, "I was very sorry I could not attend." But she was among those present on 15 December, when they held the first meeting, in the parlour of the Baptist church. Violet renewed her membership in the YWCA when she returned to Fredericton to attend the University of New Brunswick the following year. On 2 May 1904, she noted that they had elected their officers for the coming academic year and that she had been "unanimously elected President. I feel that it is a great responsibility, but I am glad of the privilege of doing the work for the year. May God grant that I shall be faithful." In the autumn, returning for her final year at university, as well as taking a full course load and paying for her board by helping with the cooking, cleaning, and ironing, Violet took up her post as president of the YWCA, reporting in her diary on 10 October, "I am taking Greek, Latin, English, Physics and Philosophy. Yesterday afternoon we had our first meeting of Y.W.C.A. It was quite encouraging. I welcomed the new girls and explained to them about the Association, especially about the Bible Study, then Hattie talked Mission Study." The following spring, giving her final address at the Association's Seniors' Farewell, Violet, "speaking of the changefulness of life ... spoke on the words 'Jesus Christ, the same yesterday, today and forever,' then of the opportunities of the College girl. 'Behold, I set before you an open door.'"[47] In describing the members of the class of 1905, *The University Monthly* characterized her as "a pillar of the Y.W.C.A." Given her busy schedule, it is impressive that Violet was also able to report, on 31 May 1905, "I have graduated in 1st Division after all. I made 1st in Greek, Latin & English, & 2nd in Philosophy & Physics."

New Brunswick women did not exist on the margins of society, but claimed a central and active role, engaging in debates on social and political issues and lobbying governments on a regular and ongoing basis. Accepting their role as the centre around which family life revolved, women taught their daughters as well as their sons to stand and speak, leading them into a plethora of both mixed-member and single-sex voluntary organizations seeking to improve society. Through the medium of those organizations, women made their voices heard, helping to lay the foundations and build the infrastructure of civil society. Political actors and social reformers, women fit social activism into lives that were often very full of other, sometimes more mundane, sometimes more pressing, duties and concerns. Although few married women had jobs outside the home, as well as caring for their children, many were not only engaged in home production but were also busy producing goods for the market. Thus, once voluntary organizations were established, attendance could rarely be maintained at the initial high levels, and individual women's activity reflected the particular rhythms of their own lives. Yet, as early school reformers discovered, irregular attendance does not necessarily mean a lack of interest or commitment, and even the busiest of women could be motivated to act, drawing energy as well as inspiration from those who had kept the faith when they themselves had fallen by the wayside. As the diaries and letters of New Brunswick women attest, there is, after all, only one thing more powerful than a woman with a purpose: a group of women with the same purpose.

Women's political purpose was most often the promotion of social reform. And while their priorities and focus tended to centre on social reform aimed at improving family life, the broader significance of the temperance cause in nineteenth-century society begs for a redefinition of politics and political activism to include the politics of the family. For it is in the politics of the family writ large that we find the basis for the priorities in which our social and political systems are grounded. Significantly, too, the causes that most engaged women reached beyond local, provincial, and national boundaries, as did the reach of many of the voluntary organizations they joined. New Brunswick women's opinions and attitudes were grounded in a cosmopolitan outlook. It is the origins and nature of that outlook that are the subject of the next chapter.

Chapter 14

A Cosmopolitan Outlook

Nineteenth-century New Brunswick women were members of a cosmopolitan society. Living, as they did, in a seaward-facing province, dependent on world markets and international trade, New Brunswick women, like the men in their families, were aware of, and took an interest in, life well beyond provincial borders. Women raised in the farming and lumbering communities dotted along the province's rivers and streams well understood the economic significance of log booms that clogged local waterways, awaiting the spring freshet that would take them to mills or to market at the end of the winter lumbering season. Women who lived in port cities and towns could scarcely avoid wharves crowded with merchant vessels; even less could women in coastal towns and villages ignore harbours filled with the sights and sounds of a shipbuilding industry that was world-renowned. Yet before the end of the century, they would watch the decline of these resource-based industries as markets for both lumber and wooden ships contracted. And they would embrace the rise of a new manufacturing economy, hopeful that New Brunswick's cotton mills, garment industry, shoe factories, sugar refineries, fish canneries, foundries, rolling mills, and railway car plants would prove as successful as those in New England.[1]

New Brunswick women were as familiar with the New England economy as they were with their own, for people and goods moved back and forth across the border in a very casual way.[2] Women looked to American markets to purchase goods ranging from seeds to fashion accessories. And, as Lucy Morrison's experience demonstrates, they knew the market for people as well as for goods. In developing her garden, Lucy Morrison shopped internationally, not only for seeds, which she ordered by mail, but also for gardeners. In 1874, her husband,

John, travelled to Boston on Lucy's behalf to recruit John Bebbington, an English gardener who had spent some time in Fredericton a few years earlier. Two years later, when Bebbington decided to establish his own business, Lucy again looked to Boston, this time travelling to the port city herself, not only to hire a gardener, but also to visit the various market gardens that regularly filled her orders for seeds and plants, and to attend the Boston Horticultural Fair.

Like British-born John Bebbington, many native-born New Brunswickers, female as well as male, travelled back and forth across the border following job opportunities. Many of the women among them were, like Mary Wolhaupter and Hannah Estabrooks, single women. Others, like Ann Eliza Gallacher, went to be with husbands who had found work. Attuned to job markets, Ann Eliza had long observed the comings and goings of her contemporaries between New Brunswick and the "Boston States." Living in Roxbury[3] in the 1860s, she encouraged that migration, inviting young single friends to come to Boston and providing a home for them while they established themselves. Some such migrants would, like Ann Eliza, be sojourners; others, like her eldest daughter, would become permanent residents.[4]

By the late nineteenth century, New Brunswickers, like other Maritimers, were moving further afield when they left the province.[5] The extension of railways to the Pacific coast, first in the United States and then in the new Dominion of Canada, facilitated these later migrations. Ann Eliza Gallacher Moore reported the departure of significant numbers of her neighbours, en route to California, beginning with a trickle during the depression of the mid-1870s, and becoming a steady stream during the downturn of the late 1880s.[6] Patterns of chain migration meant that, just as New Brunswickers had followed neighbours and kin to the "Boston States" in an earlier era, people soon began joining friends and family in the far West, including British Columbia as well as California. Ann Eliza's son Frank and her sister Mary were among that second wave of Albert County emigrants. Lottie Reid's brothers, like many others, moved westward by degrees: to Wisconsin, to Winnipeg, and, finally, on to California. After 1896, when Canada's newly elected Liberal government initiated an aggressive campaign to attract settlers to the "Last Best West," Maritimers joined British, American, and European immigrants on the Canadian Prairies and in the interior of British Columbia. For young single women, the demand for trained teachers and the prospect of significantly higher wages proved particularly attractive.[7] Violet Goldsmith was among those taking advantage of this burgeoning job market, although she (along with her Aunt Maggie and sister Mabel) headed for Saskatchewan, mainly because her father had left the ministry to take up homesteading there. Like her four friends who accompanied them on the westward journey, Violet had applied for a teaching position before leaving New Brunswick. Two of the four stopped in Winnipeg, while their companions travelled on to Regina. There, Violet "registered in the Teachers' Agency" before heading to Lumsden to join her father. But within a week, she was off to the small community of Stockholm, to take up a teaching position.[8]

Knowledge about and participation in national and international job markets reflected a depth and breadth of understanding of the world and the way it worked that historians rarely recognize in nineteenth-century women.[9] Women were fully engaged in the political and economic as well as in the social and spiritual life of their society. They read newspapers, following current events with a critical eye, formulating opinions and regularly expressing their views. While they informed themselves about federal as well as provincial politics, their interests, like their connections, were also transnational. Educated in the common schools of Albert County and imbedded in a family with close kin connections to the wider world – her father had siblings in Nova Scotia, her mother had siblings in Boston, and she had married a Scot – Ann Eliza Rogers Gallacher took a keen interest in current events. During the 1860s, Ann Eliza followed the progress of the American Civil War in newspapers on both sides of the border, as she and her first husband, John Gallacher, moved back and forth across the line.

Ann Eliza's Civil War narrative captures the essence of the relationship between the Maritimes and New England, which, for many New Brunswickers, had become, by the mid-1860s, something of a borderlands community of integrated families. "At home" on both sides of the divide, migrants nonetheless understood clearly where they "belonged." Ann Eliza's diary exemplifies the dual perspective shared by many of her contemporaries – that of a disinterested observer who "belonged to New Brunswick" and an interested party who had relatives at the front. April 1861 found Ann Eliza and John, two of their three children, and Ann Eliza's younger sister Mary living in Massachusetts. On 18 April, she noted in her diary, "The Northern & Southern States are about going to war. There is great excitement all over the Union. They are getting up volunteer troops." By 23 April, the fighting had begun: "Five States seceded from the Union. Colours are hoisted most every day." By early June, her cousin, Simon Hiscock, and uncle,

John Gibbs, had enlisted. On the 4th of July, Independence Day, Ann Eliza's mood was sombre: "The war is still going on, regiments are still ordered South. It is feared there will be a hard war before peace is again declared." No doubt her mood reflected the concern felt by countless women whose relatives had enlisted. On 1 November, with "the war ... still going on," Ann Eliza recorded the impact on the Boston branch of her family: "Uncle J. Gibbs got sick and came home. Aunt Emeline has three sons at the war. Aunt Mary Packard's son Wallace was down South before the war. He started to come home, they have heard nothing from him since, are very anxious about him." By 4 December, Wallace Packard had arrived home, but Simon Hiscock was in Washington, mortally ill. Having "worked for three days in the rain" helping to "carry off the wounded and bury the dead ... he ... took the lung fever, is not expected to get well."

Ann Eliza's interest in the war extended to its international reverberations. On 17 December, she noted the particulars of the Trent affair, demonstrating her grasp of the significance of the cotton trade in swaying British sympathies: "The Northerners have taken two Southern men out of an English steamer.[10] It is not according to the Law. The English are very mad about it. They have almost declared war. They have threatened to open a southern front and open a cotton trade. The North will not give them up under any consideration." By 21 December, British pressure had not abated and there was "great excitement about Mason & Slidell. The English have demanded their release or they will be taken by force." Five days later came the denouement: "Mason & Slidell will be given up rather than have war with England."

Perhaps the fear that "they will have to draft," reported in Ann Eliza's diary entry for 21 May 1862, played a role in the Gallachers' decision to return to Hopewell in June, for a few months later, when John made a brief trip to Boston, "he had a good deal of trouble to get away from the States on account of there being a talk of a draft."[11] But the following year, with few employment opportunities in Hopewell, John and Ann Eliza returned to Boston. By that time, some men had begun returning from the front. On 10 June 1863, Ann Eliza "saw in the morning papers the 44th regiment had got home from war. Mrs Corcoran's brother is in it." The next day they "went with Mrs Corcoran to see her mother ... Her brother looks well, only sunburnt. They were nine months men."[12] Later that day, she visited her Aunt Emeline and discovered that "two of her sons are home from the war. They are both lame." But the war was far from over and "a call for 100,000 men" on 16 June having failed in its objective, on 7 July Ann Eliza reported, "drafting is going on. Everyone in fear." Following the progress of the draft with no little interest, on 10 July she noted that "Mr Richie has escaped" and that "Sam Curren's name is among the drafted. But as he has a British protection he hopes to get clear. He belongs to Albert County, New Brunswick." The following day, she saw the name of Tom Young, another friend, among those drafted. On 13 July, she observed that in New York "they are resisting it. The mob has rose. They are trying to burn the City." The next day, "the Riot ... commenced in Boston. Several policemen have been killed at North-East. My Cousin Liberty Packard has been drafted." On 16 July, taking her small daughter with her, she went to South Boston to visit the Packards and learned that "Mrs Packard has been sick. He has been drafted but by paying three hundred dollars will get clear." John joined them there for tea. Walking back to Roxbury, they found everything quiet, but observed that "soldiers are placed all over the city. Martial law has been put in force. No man is allowed to leave the city." Four days later, Ann Eliza visited another friend whose husband had been drafted, though he had "hopes of being exempt on account of a lame hand." On 24 July, they "went over to Charleston to Mr Tom Young's, stoped for dinner & tea. Mr Young was drafted but is not an American. He is a Scotchman." And on 26 July, visitors from home reported that the American husbands of two of Ann Eliza's old school friends had been drafted "but are going to try and get substitutes." Again, Ann Eliza and John Gallacher, who was, like his friend Tom Young, "a Scotchman," found it prudent to return to New Brunswick.

A decade later, when her second husband, Lemuel Moore, who already "takes the Toronto Globe and Canadian Messenger" decided "to take the Dominion Monthly, a Canadian pamphlet," Ann Eliza commented drily, "There is a good deal of reading."[13] But she remained an avid reader of newspapers and a shrewd observer of her society. In this, she was not unique. Young women, no less than young men, were encouraged to read newspapers, with their parents sending them local papers when they were away at school.[14] And, like Ann Eliza, many other women who had relatives living in the United States took an interest in events in that country. Women also followed events in Europe through the pages of their local newspapers, while articles in denominational periodicals offered an introduction to unfamiliar cultures in faraway lands. Among those writing such articles were women missionaries, many of them graduates of ladies' academies, normal schools, or universities in the Maritimes.[15]

Not only were New Brunswick women attuned to a transatlantic world, but throughout the nineteenth century, that wider world penetrated their local experience through the medium of literature of all kinds. Our diarists read popular periodicals, newspapers, philosophy, sermon literature, and popular fiction, as well as history and biography.[16] Their records of what they were reading demonstrate that nineteenth-century New Brunswick women were as well-informed and well-read as educated women in Britain and the United States. In her commonplace book, kept between 1817 and 1825, Jacobina Campbell copied, occasionally with commentary, excerpts from sermons and philosophical discourses written by leading theologians and religious thinkers.[17] Half a century later, Sophy Carman read and exchanged sermon literature and other philosophical and theological works with Mrs Medley, the wife of the Anglican Bishop.[18] Like other women of their day, a number of the inveterate readers among our diarists professed the desire to read for the purpose of self-improvement, even as they were drawn to popular fiction.[19]

While some diarists saw reading fiction as something of a guilty pleasure, others plunged voraciously into an eclectic array of novels, reading them alone or aloud to other family members.[20] In general, the books they chose included a mixture of British classics, major popular works of the period, and semi-sensational low-brow novels. The fact that the modern novels they read often carried a Christian message reflected their times as much as their tastes. The majority were written by British authors, supplemented, in later years, by increasing numbers of American authors, as well as by the occasional Canadian. Sir Walter Scott and Charles Dickens proved the most ubiquitous authors, mentioned by the majority of diarists who recorded the books they read. Although Sophy Carman also read works by American novelists Wilkie Collins and Nathaniel Hawthorne, beyond Scott and Dickens, her taste ran mainly to women and included, among others, the English novelists Charlotte Brontë, Maria M. Grant, Jean Ingelow, and Charlotte Mary Yonge, as well as the Scottish novelist Margaret Oliphant. The light reading that made its way into in the MacDonald household was somewhat more eclectic, including, along with a selection from Scott and Dickens, works by American temperance crusader Timothy Arthur Shay, American playwright Howard Bronson, an American Baptist Society publication by Ada C. Chaplin, as well as novels by the prolific English novelist Dinah Maria Mulock Craik, the noted American authors Harriet Beacher Stowe, Augusta Jane Evans, and Mark Twain, and the more sensationalist Charles Frothingham. Authors mentioned by other diarists included English novelists Beatrice May Butt, Annie Keary, Katherine Sarah (Gadsten) MacQuoid, and J. Jackson Wray; Scottish novelist Winifred Taylor; Irish novelist Charles James Lever; American novelists Mrs Ann S. Stephens, Susan Warner and Lew Wallace; and Canadian novelists Norman MacLeod and Ralph Connor. Although the majority read contemporary novels, Daniel Defoe's *Robinson Crusoe* (1719) and John Bunyan's *Pilgrim's Progress* (1678) found their way to Amelia Holder, perhaps standard fare for a "seaman's library." Many women read Shakespeare with pleasure. The works of Tennyson in particular, but also of Keats and Byron, were popular.[21] Novels – especially, but not only, those written by contemporary women novelists – while often sentimental, frequently portrayed women as self-reliant and strong-willed, not dependent and submissive.[22] Many contained more than a minor element of social commentary; a significant proportion of novelists sought to raise readers' awareness of social ills. Indeed, nineteenth-century novelists legitimated social activism.

Reading in all its forms – fiction no less than non-fiction – served to arouse women to social and political activism, which increasingly found expression in membership in voluntary organizations. Many such organizations had originated in the United States. The sheer number and variety of voluntary organizations that "crossed the border" demonstrate the extent to which British North Americans shared concerns with their counterparts on the other side of the line. In this case, the migration was almost exclusively northward. American organizations were enthusiastically taken up by New Brunswickers, particularly in borderlands regions, where residents often had relatives or friends in the United States. Of course, some social issues had global implications and inspired international social movements. Abolitionism was one such movement, temperance another, that existed in Europe as well as in North America.

As our diarists' experiences demonstrate, New Brunswickers were not isolated on their farms or in their communities. Steamboats plied the St John River until freeze-up each year, and women as well as men regularly travelled that and other river "highways." Regular sailings and regular steam packets to international ports of call meant that Boston was readily accessible, as was Portland, Maine, and other destinations along coastal British North America and the United States.

Women and men of all classes travelled such routes. Significant numbers who could not afford to book passage on the faster passenger lines had relatives involved in the coasting trade who were willing to ferry them back and forth to the "Boston States." Then, too, New Brunswick sailing vessels crossed the Atlantic regularly. Women were often among those on board. Meanwhile, waiting at home, mothers, wives, daughters, and sisters, who saw loved ones set sail on voyages that could take months rather than weeks, followed the progress of local vessels with both interest and anxiety, as they sailed the oceans of the world.[23]

Josephine Reid and her sea-captain husband, James Turner, regularly sailed out of New York, and writing home from that port, Jo kept her sister Lottie updated on the latest fashion trends. In May 1881, she wrote:

> Almost anything you can wear is in style, hoop skirts are not worn so large as they were last summer. Polonaise are not so much worn as basks and overskirts, in fact they are almost out of style here, the overskirts are quite short especially in the front, the little short circular capes are all the rage, some are very small, mostly covered with bead trimming and fringe.[24] The hats and bonnets are of every shape and size, but the courser the straw the nicer the hat is considered. I got me one this week. I have a feather on each side the only trimming, flowers are but little worn here this season.[25]

In England, Liverpool served as home port to many shipping lines. Ships originating in Maritime ports regularly took on or exchanged crew members there, and many women and their sea-captain husbands settled permanently in that port. They welcomed visitors from home into an expatriate colonial community abroad, comprised of the families of sea captains, shipbuilders, and shipping agents.[26] Some New Brunswick women who settled in Liverpool after years of sailing with their husbands never returned to the land of their birth.[27] Others, like Maggie Loggie Valentine, whose British-born husband was among those captains who sailed out of Liverpool, did make periodic visits home.

Many New Brunswick women – especially, but by no means only, the wives and daughters of sea captains – travelled widely. In their diaries and letters, they recorded their experiences, both for their own future reference and for a home audience. Travel diaries are, in many ways, a separate genre. And, as one analyst has pointed out, "while some ... offer spellbinding descriptions of landscapes and local customs, and others offer penetrating glimpses of a personal psyche engaged with the Other, many more provide a banal recitation of miles traversed, mountains or paintings viewed, and bad hotels suffered, in texts remarkable primarily for their repetitiveness."[28] In travel diaries, which were generally meant to be shared, style becomes significant, for while repetitiveness in an ordinary diary can suggest a certain daily rhythm, and repetitiveness in a diary of a voyage can suggest the rhythms of shipboard life, it is out of place in the kind of "logs" and journal letters that Maggie Valentine and her sister Jessie Loggie regularly sent to their parents and siblings.

In her lively accounts of her travels, Maggie Valentine shared her adventures with her family, introducing them to lands they would never visit. In 1885, leaving her husband busy loading his vessel, the *Muncaster Castle*, Maggie, in the company of a female companion, embarked upon a trip into the interior of Norway. She described that trip in a "journal letter" to her mother, which she playfully "dedicated to her Highness Lady Alex Loggie of the City of B[urnt] Church." Setting the tone for the account that followed, she noted that she and Miss Shultz "left Fredrikstad on the morning of July 11th ... for a short tour ... my time being limited. I had to return in ten days if I wished to accompany the Muncaster C. To Melbourne." Among "the little group assembled to see us off ... was my sailor husband looking with glad eyes at his departing spouse, I mean enjoying the anticipation of my pleasure as much as if he was to be the sharer." She confessed to being a little startled when the mother of her companion "presented ... a pained Miss Shultz a small dagger in a case to hang at her side, which I thought looked rather formidable & was inwardly wondering if we were to be placed in any position where it would be necessary to defend ourselves." On the train, the two women "settled down to reconsider our route." In search of the picturesque, like so many tourists of their day, they chose Kavenuset as their first destination. To this end, they left the first train at Moss and "crossed over by boat to Horten, the principal Naval Port of Norway." There they caught the train for Skien where they boarded another boat to Hitterdal, arriving at 10 p.m. The next day being Sunday, they toured the surrounding area, attending a service at one of the oldest churches in Norway and visiting "the Tin Falls or Foss."

> *1885 [On Monday] we left at seven in the morning for Ulefoss. It was damp & rainy but it cleared by 8 o'clock & everything was so pretty*

bright & fresh in its ever changing beauty. The little hills & mountains are so well wooded. There are a few houses here & there. Now the scene broadens & the landscape is lovely while the water is studded with little islands & points of land stretching into the water, nothing but nature without artificial adornments. Those are the Saude waters we are sailing in today retracing a part of Saturday's journey to reach Ulefoss where we took a gig after bargaining how much he would drive us through Strengen for. And a most lovely drive it was, the road running & winding a little above & close along the clear swiftly running river most all the way & as it had been raining the previous day everything was fresh and lovely, not a particle of dust on anything to mar our pleasure. The water was remarkably clear as I could see the bottom all along. Our driver was very chatty & pleasant & Miss Shultz gained considerable information about the place & intended route & although I could not understand yet it was not unpleasant listening to their voices. I don't think I ever had a more enjoyable drive. We had some doughnuts the steward had baked for me & we partook of some of those, Miss S especially enjoying them immensely. I have not mentioned the surroundings of Ulefoss which were pretty, the little Castle upon the hill had a most lovely & extensive view. One young Norwegian Gentleman who came in the same boat last Saturday & to-day and who was travelling through to Bergen on his bycicle & was on ahead of us, was causing quite an excitement & the people would come to their doors & say you'll have to go faster or he'll be there first, & he's got a horse of his own etc. Eventually we came to Strengen where the boats were waiting to take passengers on to Ialen, a small place at the head of Ialen waters. It was a long distance & very cheap, there were two steamboats running in opposition. The water to there lies between the high mountains & as we neared our destination we could see the snow peaks in the distance on a mountain which heads the waters. We arrived at six o'clock & ordered horses immediately for Kavenuset. I forgot to mention that Miss Shultz met a friend (a Lawyer) on the boat & as the boat touched at his house his wife & sister came down to meet the boat, the latter joining us to see Kavenuset. So to start with we could only get one saddle the other two having to go in a conveyance, no there were two saddles but the two girls went in a gig as far as the road went & then were to take the saddle time about. The mountain saddles for ladies are a kind of chair you sit quite on one side, baskets as they are called, only they are made of leather & quite strong. So off we started, to reach the top of the mountain. One could not imagine how till you were rightly started as the road winds across & across each turn taking you higher, the road lined or studded here & there with bowlders to form a kind of fence. Sitting on the high horse one was almost afraid to take your eyes off – to take a downward glance. On we wound till we reached the top as it were, when the road had a more gradual slope & we came & dismounted at a curious little old church which has some little history. Here the other horse was saddled as there was nothing before us but a foot path. The two guides either leading or walking beside the horses. Such a path I never trod before & many a time I was afraid my horse would fall, especially where the steep places were covered with smooth hard stone & my fat nag was not nearly so nice as the other pony, or so sure footed, the reason I afterwards learned, was because there was something the matter with her shoes, and she had a little foal that followed us all the way & had a knack of getting in the wrong places. Well after going up hill & down dale, we came to our destination, tied up the horses some distance in case this precious foal might fall over the precipice as of course we did not know very well what we were to see – But a few steps brought us to Kavenuset which is an immense ravine 180 feet deep. We cautiously went close up there, laid down on the overhanging rocks & looked down into the narrow rushing waters below. I can not explain the grandeur of this sight. It was awfully grand. The high mountains on each side, & far down the narrow seething waters below. It fully repaid one for our tedious journey up the mountain. We threw stones down & the guides bits of logs which were crushed to pieces & I don't know how many we counted before it reached the bottom. 30 Miss S said. Just as we were preparing to take our departure the young gent with bycicle came along (poor soul such a mount as he had, of course his guide with his assistance had to roll it all the way). So we took the opportunity of returning with him to take a last look at this thrilling scene. He burst forth with so many exclamations, went into ecstasy over it saying I never! No, I never! I have travelled all over. I have been here, I have been there, & I have never seen anything to compare with this. He admired us for our perseverance in coming up at that hour of the evening after our long day's travelling. He sometimes wrote for a paper & would mention meeting two so courageous ladies, as it was a quarter past one in the morning when we got back to the little Inn in which we spent the remaining night.

Armed with a knapsack containing a "flask of port & brandy in case of extra fatigue," Maggie and Miss Shultz travelled further inland on horseback. Leaving the more settled and familiar territory behind, they soon found themselves negotiating with peasants to supply them with food and beds as well as a guide and fresh horses. Reflecting on their adventure, Maggie rather agreed with the young man, whom she had found so amusing earlier in her trip, commenting that "I must admit to feeling a little curious at being placed in such a strait & the conclusion we came to between ourselves was that we were two very courageous & clever women to have undertaken & planned this route ourselves without the help of any of the sterner sex to assist – or rather to make a fuss & jumble matters."[29]

Travel encouraged women not only to view their own familiar landscapes within a broader context but also to juxtapose their own culture against another, more or less familiar and sometimes quite exotic, culture. The result was a re-vision of their understanding of the world.[30] Whether attempting to assimilate new experiences or revising previously held assumptions, women drew comparisons between the familiar and the unfamiliar, situating their own experience within a global context. Sailing through the Straits of Messina, twelve-year-old Amelia Holder was awed by the scenery, confiding to her diary that "one mountain with its top covered with snow is away up in the clouds. I was frightened almost when I first saw it." But she drew on her New Brunswick experience to make the awesome familiar: "The snow on the top reminded me of home."[31] By her fourth voyage, Amelia, at fifteen, was a seasoned traveller. In Buenos Aires with their father, she and her sister Ada attended the annual Carnival,[32] despite the threat of yellow fever hovering over the town. In her account of that event, Amelia demonstrated her recognition of and appreciation for different cultural mores in the countries she visited.

> *Friday, 24 February 1871. We staid on shore until after Carnival. They have great times on that occasion. The streets were all hung with flags and Chinese lamps, they made a splendid appearance in the evening. Pa and Ada and I went for a walk. It was in the English newspaper that there was to be no water thrown this Carnival, but when we went out we were scented through. They have little scent bottles made of tin and paper and when you squeeze them the scent comes out. We stood in the door awhile the first evening and all the different kinds of maskers passed. One band represented Italians, another Portenas or people that are born in this country, another the English, almost every nation was represented. There were the Turks too, but what took my attention most was the Salamancas, they were all dressed in black velvet and looked*

splendid. Each company had a standard borne before them with the name of the nation they represented. After them came a long string of coaches with ladies and gentlemen in them. There were some maskers that did not represent anything. One cart full was very funny, one had the face of a cat, and another had a great broad hat on with a bottle on top. The ladies stand in the balconies or sit in the front windows or stand in the street door and the maskers as they pass throw little paper bags of candy up to them. We saw one scene that was quite funny, a couple of maskers were passing along the street opposite, when they stopped a little below us and began talking to some people gathered around them. Just opposite them were some ladies in a balcony. The maskers talked awhile and then one of them walked on, seeming to expect his friend to follow. But he looked behind and there he was still, so he went back and gave him a touch with a long stick he had in his hand and seemed to be telling him to come on, but the other one talked with him a little while and then pointed to one of the ladies in the balcony. The one that had walked on pointed with his stick as much as to say "Is that the one," the other one nodded his head and it was ludicrous to see him take out his handkerchief and pretend to be wiping the tears off of his face. He had a very ugly mask on and that made him look funnier. By and bye he went out in the street and knelt on one knee and threw a kiss to her and then he and his friend went away, but it seemed very hard work for him to get away. I suppose young ladies in our country would be offended, but the ladies do not get offended here because it is the custom of the place. The second night of the Carnival a Capt. Young and his wife and Pa and Ada and I went out for a walk. The streets were so crowded we had to push along all the time and sometimes had to go in the middle of the street. At first when they squirted scent on Mrs Young she would give a little scream and then they would laugh and squirt more on her. After awhile we went into a shop and got a dozen of the little scent bottles and squirted them on any one that squirted them on us. The last night of Carnival was the grandest of all. It was not man's work that made it so, but God's. Great flashes of blue lightning spread over the sky and showed the clouds that looked like mountains and valleys. We went out for a little walk but the streets were so crowded we came back again and it came on to rain down in torrents just as we came in. So the Carnival ended grandly with water thrown on everyone. Carnival lasts three days, ladies go out with masks and suits on and that protects them from all harm. A lady is safer to go out with a mask on than one without, for a lady without a mask is wet through, but they dare not throw anything on a masker.

> The yellow fever is in some parts of Buenos Ayres now. It is in the low and poor parts but they fear it will spread all over the town.

The Holders went on board two days after Carnival and sailed the following week.[33]

A keen observer of the customs of other cultures, who regretted her inability to speak the language of the people in the ports she visited, Josephine Reid Turner regularly shared her observations, especially about women, with family back home. In an 1881 letter to her sister Lottie, sent from Antwerp, Belgium, where they were "discharging a cargo of wheat," she wrote, "It is amusing to watch the Belgians in their red or blue jackets, working away jabbering in Flemish all the time, the women come on board and work as well as the men, indeed they are bosses here, the men let them look after business affairs and they (the men) do the light work in the house, such as washing potatoes, dishes, etc." These "hardy looking" women, she continued, "nearly all go bare-headed on the streets, except on Sunday, they are the queerest lot I ever saw. There is quite a little village of Lighters[34] here in the Dock, they are packed almost solid together, are used as store houses for grain, whole families live on board of them and seem to put in a happy time of it, the little young ones play around on top of them and have no fear of tumbling overboard."[35] Writing from Santander, Spain, later that year, Josephine portrayed the role reversal in the gendered division of labour there in a much less favourable light, perhaps because she perceived the Spanish women as exploited by their husbands and the Belgian women as controlling the household finances. "Santander," she wrote, "is not much of a town ... The work is mostly done by the women, they even load the vessels with iron ore which they carry in baskets on their heads about one hundred weight at a time and it is surprising to see how quick they will go up the stage with it. They work all day this way for about one Peseta (equal to about 20 cents) while their husbands are loafing around the streets ready to receive their money when it is so hardly earned. It is too bad isn't it, but there are strange people in the world."[36]

Even as travel broadened women, cultural comparisons also often confirmed them in their imperial prejudices. Like colonial men, colonial women who traced their roots to Loyalist and British immigrants saw themselves as part of the British Empire, and their observations about other cultures and their customs reflected a decidedly imperialist outlook. Their "imperial gaze" emerges most clearly in their descriptions of "exotic" lands. Accompanying her sister and brother-in-law on a sea voyage to India in 1887, twenty-eight-year-old Jessie Loggie entered the wider world she had been reading about for over a decade in her sister Maggie's letters and logs. Now it was her turn to provide information about the natives of India, who, although "not at all like I imagined they would be,"[37] remained, in her description, the unfamiliar, colonized "other," whose place in the Empire was very different from her own.[38] In a "journal letter" to her family, Jessie Loggie revised her own, and their, perceptions about India, her tone shifting from naive excitement to an attempt at disinterested observation. As early as the day of her arrival in India, on 26 December 1887, she began to revise her preconceived notions:

> Just wish you could see the natives in the tugboat. I think they are real nice looking. Not at all like I imagined they would be ... Three boats came down to us this evening full of natives ... They are small boned and featured and quite nice looking and the poor wretches have nothing on but a diaper, while some have a piece of cotton they draw over their shoulders. I was standing on the bridge as they came over the side ... I turned tail and fled, much to amusement. They came along and salaamed to us to the poop. It was amusement enough for me to watch them for awhile.

Despite her "re-vision," the Indian people remained, for Jessie, part of the "picturesque," to be viewed, quite literally, from a height and "captured' on paper."[39] In Calcutta, however, she saw a different face of India, and once again revised her view.

> *27th December. For breakfast this morning we had fish called Bumlow. They were just delicious. We have just been out watching the Panorama. It is the most interesting scene I have ever beheld. The verdure is quite green with palm trees interspersed here and there. Passed a native village, huts composed of clay with hay stacks for variation. Passed some dinghy boats propelled by almost naked natives quite brown. Some came on board with papers which they offered to me, but I referred them to the Captain. They are not at all repulsive looking as I imagined they would be. I forgot to mention the Buffalow we saw at the village and with which they cultivate the land, and which also give milk. They look something like cows.*
>
> *28th December. Yesterday at noon we came to anchor at Diamond Harbour where we still are. Mr Laish, the Pilot, Mr Jonas, Maggie and*

I went ashore and had a long walk. Saw an abundance of palm trees, cocoanut trees with cocoanuts hanging on them. Parrots were flying about, also some other pretty birds. Passed the oddest looking cemetry with tombstones that looked almost like mountains. We could not get in as it was locked, so did not examine very closely. The native houses or huts are built of mud divided into two apartments, one of which is occupied by the Buffalow which is their cow. I picked a bunch of flowers but they were not much to look at. We were followed by a bodyguard of natives and which made some of us feel ten inches taller. We got back in time for tea and which we were all ready for. We got a supply of oranges, yams, pumlows[40] and two cocoanuts and lots of eggs, so we have been just feasting. Every one I ate I just begrudged that you home folks couldn't get a share. The cabin looks just sweet now and all the ornaments are not yet out. There are lots of natives on board now. You can't form any idea of how they look, some are all rolled in rags always displaying a back view of bare legs. How I wish Mary you could see them – I know you would have a hearty laugh. I followed them round this morning trying to get a sketch of them, but just as soon as I would get the back of a head done he would turn his face round, and as it was particularly a back view I wanted t'was no go. Eventually I captured one old man on a spar and seating myself immediately in front proceeded to reproduce him on paper much to the interest of the others who gathered round. The old man kept asking me for (?) all through the performance, but I was conveniently deaf just about then. I need not say that the picture was not as satisfactory as one would wish, for you know my sketching of old. Letters, letters, letters is what we are all most anxious for now. Think I will cry if there is not one from at least Mary and Alexander.

29th. In Calcutta at last. Got in before five last evening. The ship was not moored until a crowd of Baboas came on board looking for work to do for the ship. Some were very nice looking men and very nice mannered. The doctor also paid us a visit. Mr Baring arrived this morning and invited Maggie and I up to breakfast which invitation was accepted for some day next week. Captain is away up to the office this morning and we have not got our letters yet and I am all impatience. The natives are a great source of amusement to me.

30th December. We are getting more fruit now than we can use. Oranges, pumlows, pomegranates, grapes sweet as sugar, paupas, leeches, banannas, guavas, etc. Cocoanuts, other kinds of nuts, a small whitish kind of raisin. I have eaten fruit this morning until I couldn't eat any more. How I wish you could all share it. We got our letters yesterday and all the dear home letters. What a dreadful thing about the Sewells. We got Mary's letter just before sailing and were shocked to hear of dear Janie's and George's deaths, and then to think that Willie has gone since. It is very hard to realize. How glad I am Mother was so kind to them. Poor dear Mrs Sewell my heart is sore for her, and I intend writing to her. Last evening Will, Maggie and I went ashore, took a ticker garry and had a drive away up the miadan up to the Eden Gardens, and past the Government House.[41] I did not imagine Calcutta was half as grand a place as it is. We passed a good deal of statuary in the grounds, saw a fountain playing, but as it was after dark have not a very bright idea of it all. Got a large bunch of flowers yesterday and today, so the cabin looks quite gay. The weather is quite cool. We sleep with a blanket, and it is almost too cool for thin dresses. Almost the whole morning has been spent in looking over chicken [Chikan] work which a Mahomaden was exhibiting in the cabin. There was one beautiful ecrue silk embroidered in white silk – very rich and also a beautiful price. Will offered him twenty-five dollars for it, but he would not give it for that.*

Like many colonials and Europeans, Jessie had difficulty assimilating what she observed, noting on 2 January 1888, "I never get used to the native dresses. You see so many different kinds. Saw a native Prince Sat. evening who was dressed in a green changeable silk robe. They are quite good looking and as straight as arrows. Calcutta is a very showy place. Everyone drives in carriages with drivers and footmen in liveries. Of course the servants are all natives and some of the natives have the handsomest carriages."

Jo Turner, like Jessie Loggie, did not so much long for home as for her family to be with her, to share her experience of other lands. Writing to her sister Lottie from Belgium in 1881, she commented, "I wish you could see the farmers wagons, you would think them a novelty I know, but they have fine horses here. I wish we had some like them in our country, the Flemish horses are handsome great big famous looking fellows, and some of them such a pretty colour. Dogs are used here nearly as much as horses, they harness them up and you would be surprised to see what heavy loads they draw." She particularly enjoyed the cultural attractions:

There are some fine cathedrals …We are going tomorrow to visit the one for which Antwerp is famous, there is a chance to ascend to the top of the steeple, which ranks fourth in height to any in the world; there are over 400 steps. I wish you were here to go with us, I know you would enjoy it. The museum is a fine building and the oil paintings there are magnificent, you know oil paintings originate in Belgium, and it has been the birthplace of the most distinguished painters in the world ... Vandyke, Rubens and Teniers were all born in Antwerp, and the statues erected to their memories are splendid. Rubens Palace is a fine building.[42]

For Amelia Holder, Josephine Turner, Maggie Valentine, Jessie Loggie, and many other New Brunswick women, the opportunity to travel the world on trading vessels changed their lives.[43] For their relatives and friends who remained ashore, these travellers opened a window on a wider world.

As the great era of sailing ships drew to a close, New Brunswick women were more likely to get their information about the people and cultures of Asia and Africa through letters from Maritime missionaries, often published in national denominational papers. By the end of the nineteenth century, a majority of those in the mission field were women, funded by female missionary societies.[44] From an early stage, New Brunswick women answered the call with alacrity. In a seaward-looking province, in which religious faith played such a significant role in people's lives, young women did not hesitate to enter the mission field. New Brunswick's single women missionaries were among the best-educated people of their generation. The majority had graduated from a normal school, a ladies' seminary, or a university. A few were medical doctors. But whatever their level of education, Maritime women were over-represented among Canadian missionaries on foreign mission fields.[45] The New Brunswickers among them sent back a variety of reports, for a variety of audiences: private letters to family and friends at home, less personal correspondence designed for publication in denominational papers, and confidential reports to the missionary societies that were funding them. Home on furlough, they toured the province, often armed with artifacts, giving presentations to raise money for the cause. Through all these mediums, New Brunswickers gained a further perspective on the wider world.

New Brunswick women were cosmopolitan in their outlook at the same time as they were very much women of their particular time and place. Whether they gained their knowledge of the world through personal experience, letters, newspapers, or books, our subjects shared an imperial vision. Perceiving themselves as part of the great

British Empire, they believed they had a role to play in that Empire and beyond. Firm in the conviction that theirs was a superior culture, they shared the world view of a generation of Westerners who mingled politics and religious faith. Their understanding of their temporal, physical, and spiritual worlds shaped their particular colonial identities and conditioned their responses not only to life but also to death. The final chapter explores evolving societal responses to death as reflected in our diarists' experiences.

Chapter 15

In the Midst of Life

In 1846, writing to her seventeen-year-old daughter Mary, who was at school in Boston, Sarah Upton Hill enumerated no fewer than seven friends or acquaintances who were ill or dying. Six of the seven were young people, four of them victims of that great nineteenth-century killer, consumption. Sarah's letter, written in response to Mary's expressed desire for news of home, was not meant to depress her daughter. Indeed, Sarah noted that "I wish I had something pleasant to communicate, which would contrast with what is already written. But this does not offer at present."[1] Like Sarah Hill's letter, nineteenth-century women's diaries are full of reports of illness and death; yet, as her comment implies, these were often juxtaposed with accounts of happier events.

Life and death intersect in women's daily records, with deaths and marriages occasionally noted in the same entry, almost always amidst the routine reports of ordinary activities, usually with little or no comment. Thus, on 29 December 1859, Ann Eliza Gallacher noted, "Rather warmer. We came home, stoped at Mr Lyons' for dinner. Stoped a little while at Uncle Clark's. Got home very well. Mr Stephen Stiles died yesterday. Mr McNay had a child died in Meamull [Memel]. Thomas Brigham of Massachusetts married Sarah Vergie a few days ago." Similarly, on 30 December 1864, Janet MacDonald inserted a sad note in the midst of an otherwise routine entry: "Friday. N.W. wind, clear and freezing. James at the mill cutting slabs. Donald fixing the bob-sled. Father busy as usual. Anna and Douglass Mott at Donald's. James and Counsel Hendry here tonight. Heard of Joseph McAlpine's death tonight; died yesterday afternoon. The young folks singing some this evening; Donald, Emma, Mary J., Susan and Anna Mott and James and

Counsel Hendry. Sam London shoeing the oxen." And on Monday, 15 March 1880, in the midst of her daily record of the progress of her gardening, Lucy Morrison inserted a jarring note: "Fine day. Aunty & Miss Skinner here for tea. Was very busy watering all the spare time I had. Rev. Mr. Stevens died. George pegging down rose cuttings in pots." While such entries offer little insight into the diarists' attitudes towards death and dying, they do inspire our curiosity.

Reports of death and funerary rituals figured prominently in nineteenth-century diaries, reflecting a society in which, despite declining mortality rates, few escaped being touched by death at an early age.[2] This did not mean, as modern readers of nineteenth-century diaries have sometimes assumed, that people were either obsessed with or inured to death. In a study of death in early America, one historian has argued that modern Americans misperceive their ancestors' frequent and unselfconscious references to death and dying as an obsession with death only because, for them, death has replaced sex as the major taboo, with the current practice of removing the dying to hospital a reflection of that taboo. In contrast, people in past times had more contact with death. People were buried from their homes, and public funerary rituals brought communities together to offer support and solace.[3]

Historians of religion who have tracked changing attitudes towards death through an analysis of sermon literature argue that, in the early-nineteenth century, evangelical Protestant ministers in particular enjoined those gathered to listen to funeral sermons to prepare for death, warning the unregenerate that "unless ... [they] converted ... they would surely be cast into hell forever."[4] Nor was the subject of death confined to funeral sermons. Rather, the uncertainty of life and the unpredictability of death were frequent themes in the early- to mid-nineteenth-century sermon literature. Such sermons undoubtedly had an impact on audiences, especially during periods of heightened religious enthusiasm, and one historian has persuasively argued that New Brunswick diarist Alexander Machum's careful catalogue of the deaths in his community in the late 1840s reflected "a popular preoccupation with death that was ... fuelled by the millenarian enthusiasm then sweeping the northeastern portion of the continent."[5] Yet the frequent references to death and dying in women's diaries both well before and for decades beyond the 1840s reflect the close-knit nature of their communities, rather than a preoccupation with death.

Our nineteenth-century New Brunswick women diarists had all had personal experiences with the uncertainty of life and the unpredictability of death, often at an early age. Jacobina Campbell had been faced with the death of her father when she was thirteen. Sophy Bliss (Carman) had lost her father when she was just seven years old. Amelia Holder was twelve when her mother died of tuberculosis. Ida MacDonald, like Jacobina Campbell, lost her father at the age of thirteen. Alva and Hannah Estabrooks were fourteen and twelve when their father died. And Violet Goldsmith was six when her mother died. Diarist Bertha Jones, who had married a widower with five children, was left with three young children of her own to support when he died sixteen years later.[6] Annie Johnston had lost both her first husband and an older sister in a drowning accident, when she was just twenty-five. Ann Eliza Gallacher's first husband also died tragically, in an industrial accident, leaving her a widow at thirty. Ann Eliza was no stranger to death, for her two younger brothers as well as her own second daughter died before reaching the age of ten. Others among our diarists had also lost children. Ida MacDonald's father, James, was the eldest son of diarist Janet MacDonald. By the time James died, at the age of fifty-eight, Janet had already lost two other grown children: a younger son, George, who drowned at thirty-three, and her eldest child and only daughter, Susan, who died at forty-eight.[7] Lucy Morrison's first grandchild survived less than a year. This must have been especially difficult for Lucy, who had lost her own firstborn as an infant.[8] A decade after Sarah Hill's letter was written, Mary would watch, with her parents and younger siblings, as her older brother Upton wasted away and died at the age of twenty-seven, yet another victim of tuberculosis.[9] Marjory and Isabella Grant and the Loggie sisters had also lost siblings. John Loggie, the captain of his father's fishing schooner, drowned at sea when he was just twenty-five.[10] The seafaring life, so important to the New Brunswick economy, was particularly dangerous, and few families involved in it escaped unscathed. Amelia Holder and her cousin Emma Pitt had already lost two uncles, an aunt, and three cousins by the time two of Emma's three older brothers were lost at sea.[11]

It is in their reports of death that we get the most intimate glimpses of our diarists. And although their diaries remind us that this was a world in which it was not only appropriate, but also necessary, to speak of death, it is here that the modern reader truly feels like a voyeur, prying into emotions that our own society views as private. People acknowledged the uncertainty of life and well understood the general ineffectiveness of medicine, particularly against communicable diseases, yet their grief at the loss of loved ones, especially young people struck down in the prime of life, was no less than our own. And that sense of loss is palpable, no matter what the nature of their diary.

Reminders of their own mortality – of the fact that, as Sarah Hill put it in her letter to her daughter Mary, "neither youth, nor health, is any security against death"[12] – proved unavoidable for young people. At sixteen, Ann Eliza Rogers and Harriet Towse were near neighbours and the best of friends, with Ann Eliza's diary entry for 25 June 1853 capturing the school girl camaraderie they shared: "Rainy day. I went to take Hariet Towse to Salmon River. She teaches school there. We got some wet." The two girls spent the next day exploring Salmon River together, and on 27 June, having seen Harriet settled in her boarding place, Ann Eliza set off for home. This was the last such trip the two girls would make together. By the following March, Harriet was too ill to teach. The final stages of her illness can be traced through the pages of her friend's diary. On the 27th, Ann Eliza reported, "Harriet Towse very sick. Her people are afraid she will not get better." And on 16 April, Easter Sunday, noting, "James Lee died of consumption," she added, "Harriet Towse very bad." On the 28th, she again reported, "Harriet very bad, do not think she will live long." Recording her friend's death the following day, Ann Eliza's words, with their undercurrent of contained emotion, convey both the helplessness of family and friends in the face of this disease for which there was no known cure, and her own deep sense of loss: "Died of consumption, Harriet Ann Towse, aged 17 years and 4 months. She has been very sick for 5 weeks. She was taken with a cough about the last of January, was very bad a while but got better, was able to go out. Her people thought she would get well until about five weeks ago she took to bleeding at the lungs, from that time she continued to get worse very fast until she died. I shall miss her very much. We have been friends for a long time." On 1 May, a foggy, rainy day, Mr Bent chose, as the text of his funeral sermon, "A good name is better than precious ointment; and the day of death than the day of one's birth" (Ecclesiastes 7, 1st verse), offering Harriet's grieving friends and relatives the consolation of a future of life everlasting for a young woman who was a member of the church. But there was little comfort for Ann Eliza, who, on the day of Harriet's funeral, "got word that Mrs John McFee died very sudenly at Sackville last Saturday." She went on to further record that Mrs John McFee "was 19 years old last March. She has left a little girl baby. She was another of my schoolmates and very dear friend." In this close-knit community, perhaps others recognized that the loss of two school friends in a single week was a great deal for a sixteen-year-old to bear. Or perhaps it was some other impulse that led Harriet's grieving father to give his daughter's diary to her friend to read. "It is very nice," Ann Eliza reported in her own diary. "She speaks of the time she was converted and joined the church."[13] Mr Towse's decision to share his daughter's diary may indicate that he, too, consoled himself with the thought of Harriet's conversion, but more likely it was offered in the recognition of a shared grief. Funeral sermons like Mr Bent's, offering solace to grieving family and friends, became increasingly common over the course of the century, but were relatively rare at mid-century.

Required by conditions of life to accept death, many, including ministers, regarded it as a test of faith.[14] Eleanor and John Rogers surely faced such a test when, in February 1858, their second and only surviving son died tragically. As their daughter Ann Eliza recorded it in her diary, "This has been a sad day to us. Brother Howe went to school this morning. When he came home at noon Tom Brown was with him. He did not come in the house but went and got his sled, to slide down hill between the road. The horse had just been turned out, one that has been about for many years, kicked him in the forehead. His nose was cut right open, he was picked up for dead but lived about four hours but never spoke or noticed any one. He died about 15 minutes to 4 oclock. He is seven years and one month old." No doubt recognizing that such terrible tragedies can test the faith of even the most devout, two days later, at the child's funeral, "Mr Hughs preached from Job, 13th chapter and 15th verse," a powerful passage: "Though he slay me, yet will I trust in him: but I will maintain mine own ways before him." Life would go on for Ann Eliza Gallacher and her family, but things would not be the same. The day after the funeral, she confided, "We are left alone again. We miss him so much." And the following Sunday, "We are very lonely today. We miss Howe so much, he was always here doing or saying something."[15]

Moreover, for families who faced the sudden tragic death of a loved one, the sense of loss persisted. On 29 October, 1861, Janet MacDonald's third son, George, who was born on the tenth anniversary of her marriage, died in a drowning accident, leaving behind not only his parents and siblings to mourn his loss, but also a pregnant wife and two small children. Though her strong faith undoubtedly helped Janet to cope with the loss, it did not serve to lessen her grief. Nor did the pain of loss abate over time. Each year, on the anniversary of George's death, her anguish surfaced anew. On the first anniversary, she noted in her diary,

"This day year poor George was drowned. Oh dear, what a scene. What news! What news that was. Oh! How dreadful it seems to me now, how fresh everything is to my mind now, and ever will be." And in 1863, she again recorded this tragic anniversary: "October 29th. This day two years poor George was drowned. Oh dear, how dreadful it seems yet to me. How fresh everything about it seems."

The experience of watching friends, siblings, and children die did not make death any easier to bear or diminish the sense of loss. Nor could a recognition of the fragility of life prepare one for an unexpected death. January 1867 found Ann Eliza Rogers, her husband, John Gallacher, and two of their three young children living in Camden, New Jersey, just across the river from Philadelphia, Pennsylvania, where John worked. On 14 January, he went to work as usual. Ann Eliza's moving account of the days that followed, while filled with anguish, suggests her strength of character as she struggled to maintain her equilibrium during this terrible time.

Camden, New Jersey, January 1867

14th: Fine. John went away very early this morning, he thought he would come home tonight but has not come yet.

15th: Tuesday. When I got the paper this morning I see there was an explosion at the works where John is and that he was scalded bad but the paper says not dangerous. I went right into Mr Davis's, he offered to go over with me so we went to Mrs Whitehead's but he was not there, heard he was at the hospital. Mr Davis went up to see if I could get in. He soon came back. I went up with him. But Oh what a sight I beheld. My poor husband was scalded nearly all over. They say he is not very dangerous. But I am very much afraid he will never get better. He knew me, said he was glad to see me and wanted me to kiss him. His head was very bad scalded and both hands and arms, one leg was very much bruised and scalded too. He slept most of the time. They gave him a good deal of morphine. When I came away the door keeper said I could not get in tomorrow without a permit. It was too late in the day to get one so I did not know what to do. There was one man killed on the spot and five others taken to the hospital, two died today. I came home, will go over and try to get in tomorrow.

16th: Mr Davis went in to see if I can get in and how John was. The paper says he is sinking fast. Last night the paper said they did not think he would live through the night. I cannot think it true. Mr Davis got back about a little after noon. He says my dear husband died about 10 oclock last night. Oh what news. What shall I do – to have him die there alone with no one to speak to. What shall I do without him. My poor dear John, he was so good & kind to me. He was 47 years old last Saturday. Oh how awfully sudden to leave home so well and meet death so soon. Mr Atkinson & Miss Hartley came over for me to go over to Mrs Whitehead's. I went with them, took my poor fatherless children with me. Mr McIntire called this evening, he is an old friend of John's.

17th: Very cold. Mr Patton called. He said he would do all and see to every thing that was needed to be done. Feels very bad.

18th: Very cold. Mr Preastly & McIntire called this forenoon. This afternoon at two oclock the funeral of my poor husband took place. He was buried from the undertakers. Oh what a sight to see his poor face so disfigured one would scarcely know him. I do not know how to give him up, to think that I never shall see him again. He is buried in Mount Moriah Cemetery. There he must lie until the resurrection morn. I know he is in the hands of a merciful God.

20th: Sunday. Cold, snow in the afternoon I went to Church. Oh what a lonely Sunday. My dear John was always home on Sunday. We have spent such happy Sundays together this winter and to think he will never come again. I can scarcely face the thought. All alone. Mr McRay got back last Thursday. He called today.

Devastated by her husband's death, and forced to vacate the house they had been renting, Ann Eliza took time to consider her options. Despite letters from her father and younger sister Maggie, urging her to "go right home," she refused to make any hasty decisions, remaining in Philadelphia for over three months. When, in March, she decided that she would go home, Mr McRay helped her to make the arrangements. Yet while Mr McRay and Mr Patton, who were both associated with the company that had employed John, provided her with financial support, it was to Mrs Whitehead and Mrs Jennings, the women with whom she boarded following her husband's funeral, that she turned for emotional support. As she made plans to leave, she mourned her loss, confiding to her diary on 8 March, "How much I miss my dear husband. When I came before he was with me. Now I am alone, no one to speak to, no loving arm to lean on. No one give a kind word of advice, all alone."

On 6 April, two weeks before leaving Philadelphia behind, Ann Eliza "went to Mount Moriah cemetery to see my husband's grave. I feel very bad to go away and leave him alone with no one to care for him, but I know his grave will not be lost sight of for he is buried in a lot belonging to the Scotch St Andrews & Thistle Society. It is hedged around with cedar shrubs. It is on what is called the New ground in Mount Moriah Cemetery, joining is a lot belonging to the Methodist Conference. I took Isabella with me. Miss Jennings went too." Yet despite so many losses in her own life, Ann Eliza never became preoccupied by death.

Other women, faced with the loss of a loved one or a sudden rise in the number of deaths in their communities, did confront their own mortality. On 3 March 1869, following the death of her aunt, Mary Wolhaupter reflected that "death is ever on our track, it shows us how we ought always to be prepared to meet death." Two years later, on 22 January 1871, commenting on the "many deaths" that had occurred in her community since the New Year, fifteen-year-old Laura Trueman, who may well have been recalling the message of funeral sermons she had recently heard, wrote, "What a warning it should be to the living to prepare for the great change which all must meet with: when we consider the *eternal* misery and *eternal* joy, how small the trivial things of this life appear to us." Although sermons that included such warnings did, no doubt, result in some deathbed conversions, they likely had their greatest impact on those who, like Laura Trueman, were already believers, while providing but little comfort for the grief-stricken.

As the century progressed, ministers engaged in a competition for the souls of the living increasingly sought ways to offer comfort to their bereaved parishioners. Funeral sermons focussed less and less on divine judgment and eternal damnation, and more and more on the concept of the "good death."[16] Advances in medical knowledge did not bring miraculous cures, but by the late-nineteenth century, medical intervention could achieve a less painful and more peaceful death, thereby facilitating the "good death" typified by acceptance and even relief. The "good death" served as a sign of redemption and life everlasting. By the late-nineteenth century, this greater emphasis on the promise of life everlasting for the devout Christian made possible "the celebration of death as a passage to perfect happiness and fulfilment in a heavenly paradise."[17] As ministers seeking to comfort and reassure grieving families increasingly began to emphasize this promise in funeral sermons, romantic notions of the afterlife permeated the popular culture.[18]

Changing attitudes to death over the course of the century are reflected in the writings of nineteenth-century diarists and their families. Yet some, at least, retained a certain skepticism, recognizing the mixed signals inherent in a "good death." Mary Wolhaupter's report of the "good death" of one of her contemporaries effectively captures the difficulty in distinguishing between the longing to be called home and the longing for relief from one's suffering: "Heard this afternoon that Elisha Briggs died last night. Poor fellow, he has suffered long & much, but I suppose he has met with a happy change for he has been a very good living boy & man and has been longing for the day to come when he would be called home, that is, since he has been sick."[19] In contrast, Annie Trueman's report of a beloved cousin's death reflected popular romantic notions and illustrates what one historian has referred to as "the Evangelical ideal of the 'good death.'"[20] "Last night at 11½ o'clock," she wrote, "our darling cousin Mary Allison passed away from earth to that bright home where there is no night and where sorrow and sighing are forever fled away. She has seen the Lamb in all His glory – our blessed Saviour who died for us. Peacefully and calmly she took her upward flight; death had no terrors to her ... Why need we fear to go down into the dark valley if the Captain of our salvation is with us & a convoy of angels to conduct us *Home*." According to Annie, Mary Allison's death was "so peaceful that the watching friends could scarcely tell when the gentle spirit left its tenement of clay! ... her voice now joins in the grand choir of the church triumphant. Her eyes have opened upon those glories which no mortal eyes have seen." But did Annie miss something, even as she faithfully recorded her cousin's words? What, the reader wonders, did Mary, who had suffered for months, mean when she declared "what a mercy that I sought my Saviour in health for I never could seek religion now and I never could find it"?[21] Certainly the belief that, if in life there was rather too much death, in death there was yet life in the promise of life everlasting did provide consolation to grieving families. Yet whether they were writing in the early-, mid-, or late-nineteenth century, our diarists rarely expressed the kind of romantic notions of the afterlife found in funeral sermons or in obituaries in denominational papers.

Moreover, while the notion of a "good death" could bring comfort to the relatives and friends of those who had been "great sufferers," people who suffered great pain, often dying slow, lingering deaths, the concept offered no solace in cases of tragic accidents, or the death of a child.[22] The loss of one's child, at any age, was particularly traumatic.

Despite assumptions that in past times, when infant mortality rates were particularly high, parents resisted becoming attached to newborns until they were sure they were going to survive, the evidence in diaries belies such arguments. Sophy Carman's youngest child died within two weeks of his birth. Seventeen years later, writing to her daughter about the recent death of a relative's baby, she reflected, "Some think the loss of a *babe* is *nothing*, & one should not grieve, but *I know better.*"[23] Even before they had names, newborns captured hearts. When her sister-in-law, Lott, gave birth to "a baby girl, the damndest thing you ever saw," fifteen-year-old Emma Pitt was intrigued by the notion of becoming an aunt, reporting in her diary on Saturday 10 May 1873, "I was up to see the baby it is a wonder to be sure. It dident know its Aunt Emma I presume for it dident speak to me." Indeed, she was so entranced that the following Saturday, she admitted that she had missed seeing her brother Ed, the baby's father, before he left to join their brother Abe aboard their ship, which was about to sail: "We were all up stairs making fun of the baby." By August the baby had a name and Emma was getting to know her. Tragically, death intervened. And by the time little Katie died, Emma, despite her father's optimism, was becoming daily more certain that her older brothers Abe and Ed were lost at sea.

August 7,1873, Thursday. Fine day I took little Katie out in the yard and we had a nice time.

8 Friday. Fine day. Little Katie is very sick. I went for the Doctor. Maria Holder came down and I went with her. She was here to tea.

9 Saturday. Fine day. Baby is still worse. We don't expect her to live. The Doctor was here twice. Pa heard today that the boys are lost for certain.

10 Sunday. Lovely day. Little Katie died this morning at 10 minutes after three. I didn't see her die for I had to stay with Ma but I went after a while.

11 Monday. Fine day. There were a great many people in to see her. G.H. was in too, and Miss Baisley and Mrs. were here. The coffin wasen't bought till 6 o'clock.

12 Tuesday. Fine day. The funeral was at half past seven and then they went up to Hampton to bury her. Maria and Lott C. were here.

14 Thursday. Fine day. Pa heard to day the boys might have been saved, that it wasen't so bad as Hunt made out.

16. Saturday. Raining pretty hard for a while. Lott C went up home.

17 Sunday. Lovely fine day. I did not go out anywhere. There was not any person here and I am very lonesome. It is just a week since Katy died.

18. Monday. Cloudy day. I haven't anything particular to write. Lott is very sick. Sent for the doctor.

19 Tuesday. Raining very hard. I am nearly distracted we haven't heard from the boys yet. I wish we would.

20. Wednesday. Fine day. The Church picnic was today. I did not go to it. Lott S came down and E.

21. Thursday. Fine day. Pa heard today that the boys might have been saved or that it wasn't so bad as Hunt told it.

22 Friday. Fine day. Pa went over to a fortune teller and she told him the boys were living and a whole lot of other things and she said he would get a letter.

23 Saturday. Fine day. Stormed awful in the evening. Pa got a letter with money in it. I am very lonesome tonight.

24 Sunday. The dreadfullest storm that ever was known. It is fearful. Getting worse every hour. I expect to see the old tree blow over every minute.

25 Monday. Cloudy day. It was so dreadful last night that I had to come down stairs at twelve oclock and sleep in Ma's bed.

27 Wednesday. Fine day. J. E. Kendall was over here and I went only before they did and had my fortune told and she told me a lot of trash.

29 Friday. Fine day. In the evening J. E. Kendall was here and took Ma's picture. He is splendid I think but he is married. I burnt my fingers fearfully.

30. Saturday. Fine day. I went in to Aunt Jane's awhile and I saw the Count and Countess pass in a carriage. We heard that Mr Brat died last night.

31 Sunday. Lovely day the last Sunday in summer. How solemn it seems to me. I feel like crying, the church bells seem so solemn too.

Over a century later, readers of Emma Pitt's diary and those of other relatives of seafaring men and women can feel an undercurrent of tension when loved ones were sailing the high seas and the release of that tension when word came that they had arrived at their destination. Although Emma's diary entries are spare, the undertone of distress, as no word came, is clear throughout. Attempting to suppress her fears about her brothers, Emma nonetheless found herself "nearly distracted" by worry, clinging to every shred of hope her father offered despite the fact that she did not share his faith in fortune tellers. As summer turned to autumn with still no word, her hope faded. Finally, on 17 October she confided, "This is the day that we expect the boys home. But they diden't come and I don't think they ever will." Sadly, Emma's fears were well founded. While Emma's diary does provide evidence of her father's difficulty accepting the probability that his sons had perished at sea, it does not provide any insight into how her sister-in-law was managing to cope with the loss of her husband so soon after the death of their baby daughter.

Lottie Reid's diary for March and April 1879 portrays a family plunged first into grief and then into despair when her sea-captain brother-in-law Alden West, husband of her sister Orpah, was shipwrecked. On 3 March, Alden left for Saint John and the whole family was up very early to see him off. Although Orpah had, in the past, sailed with him, this time he left her and their small daughter Josie behind. On 7 March, Lottie reported, "Alden left St. John for Dublin Wednesday the 5th, hope he may have a pleasant voyage." But that was not to be. Lottie's moving account of the dual tragedy that struck her family in the weeks that followed takes us into the heart of a family in the midst of life – a family that had, as recently as 26 February, welcomed Orpah, Alden, and their two-year-old daughter home.

Monday, March 10, 1879 – Not very pleasant, storming a little. Saw by the days paper some very very bad news. Alden's vessel went ashore at Big Rock near Grandmanan and was a total wreck and worse than all Alden with seven of the men were lost. This occurred on Friday morning the 7th. It does not seem possible that such can really be the case, just one week ago this morning he left home so well and in such good spirits.

Tuesday, March 11 – Dull raining a little. It is really so about Alden being lost. At least that is the word today. Although it hardly seems as if it could be. It is only a week yesterday since he left us, and little we thought then it was his last visit home. But it seems it was. What sad news a few days may bring around. Anna and Elenor took dinner with us today, there were also several others in.

Wednesday, March 12 – Dull, some appearance of rain. A good many callers and visitors, all of which sympathized deeply with Orpah on her sad bereavement. Annie was over a while. Mrs. Murphy, Mrs. Steeves, Mary, Eliza Reid and Susan took tea with us. But for all of the many callers, the days seem sad and gloomy. We little thought when Alden started with us on that Monday morning that it was the last time we should see him here but such is life. Woe cannot look for [help].

Thursday, March 13 – Windy but quite pleasant. A big boat left St. John this morning for Big Rock Island to bring up the remaining crew from the wreck, if Alden had only have been among those who were saved what joy it would have been to his many friends and relatives. But suppose we cannot have the least hope of this.

Friday, March 14 – Very warm and pleasant. 16 of the crew arrived in St. John today. Suppose there will be an investigation before they leave. None of the bodies of those lost have been found yet except that of the cook. Hope they will not fail in finding poor Alden's. Just a week ago this morning since this sad event took place.

Saturday, March 15 – Cloudy and dull, rained hard last night. Willie and Ernest arrived home today.[24] They have not brought much later news regarding poor Alden, no more bodies have been found. They are afraid that no more will be found. If Alden's body could be found it would be a little satisfaction, but the sad loss can never be made up.

Sunday, March 16 – Cool and pleasant. A fortnight ago today poor Alden was with us well and happy. Oh! What sad, sad changes in that short space of time, but I suppose all things were ordered for the best, though it seems hard to think so sometimes. Wat and I were over to [?] a while this afternoon.

Monday, March 17 – Pleasant in forenoon but in afternoon it snowed. This I suppose is St Patrick's Day, and it is not an unusual thing to have a storm on that day. It is Josephine's birthday also. Anna was over to see us a while. No more this time, goodnight.

Tuesday, March 18 – Warm and quite pleasant. Everything today seems dull and quiet. This evening Adelia Smith and Mary called in a while to see us, and so ended another day. The Reverend Mr. Chipman has a donation at the hill tonight. Heard since he got $175, quite a donation. Orpah is sick tonight.

Wednesday, March 19 – Just as warm and pleasant as can be. Orpah went down to see Mrs. West a while today. This evening John Brewster called in for a short time. I have no more to write this time. It is now about bedtime so adieu.

Thursday, March 20 – Cool and pleasant. Orpah sick today, Dr. Perdy over tonight to see her, hope she will be better soon. Poor Ma is almost sick herself she has to be around so much she is nearly tired out. We have so much company. Today Charlotte was down and spent the day. Mrs. Ed Bishop was in a while, Anna also spent the day with us, were glad to have her.

Friday, March 21 – Fine. Orpah no better. Dr. Perdy and Lady called over today to see her. I hope she will be better soon. I am afraid Ma will be down sick if she has to be around so much. Carrie Casey and Mrs. Coonan were in a while, it was nothing but company, company all the time.

Saturday, March 22 – A nice day. Orpah worse if anything. I wish she could get something to help her. And poor Ma is so lame she can hardly get around. Callers today as usual. Squire Stevens died today very suddenly, only sick about an hour. He had been having an arbitration and it is thought his excitement over it brought on apoplexy.

Sunday, March 23 – Stormed some in morning but cleared off quite fine in afternoon. Poor Alden's funeral sermon was preached this afternoon by Mr. Hughes, but neither Orpah nor Mrs. West were able to attend. The house was pretty much filled but I think that more would have been there had it been fine. Suppose poor Alden's body will never be found.

Monday, March 24 – Pleasant. Orpah seemed to be better in morning, but worse again at night, she is very sick indeed yet we all hope she may get better again soon. Dr. Perdy is attending her, he calls to see her every day and is trying to do all he can.

Tuesday, March 25 – Quite pleasant. Orpah no better, worse if anything. This morning very early Drs. Coleman, Jump and Perdy were all here to see her. They left her some medicine which I hope may help her. We are all anxious to see a change for the better.

Wednesday, March 26 – Fine. Am sorry to say there is not much change in Orpah, she is little or no better, very low indeed. We do hope she will be better soon. We all feel very anxious about her. Ma is laid up also with lame feet, a kind of rheumatism, she can't go about all day.

Thursday, March 27 – Quite pleasant. Orpah still continues about the same. We all try to do all we can for her, although it does not seem as though we can do much still we hope for the best. Mrs. Maybe sat up with her tonight. Mrs. Myles was in a while this evening also.

Friday, March 28 – A lovely day. We are in hopes Orpah is a little better, but she is very weak. We are all greatly in hopes she will improve now, keep getting better everyday. Susan Reid is here, she has been helping us do up the work, we got quite a washing out for one thing. We have been very busy this week, that is all who are able to work.

Saturday, March 29 – Quite fine and warm. Poor Orpah does not get much if any better, Oh! If we could only get something to restore her to helth again but I suppose that lies beyond human power. We can only do what we can and hope that she may be better soon.

Sunday, March 30 – Storming some, but very warm. Orpah seemed about the same until about ten o'clock when she dropped off in what seemed to be a sound sleep, and has remained in this way all day. We are afraid it is a change for the worst. Susan Reid and I went up to baptizing this morning, Mr. Blackaddor baptized 17 in the river up back of Mr. Vernon.

Monday, March 31 – Quite fine, roads fearfully muddy. Orpah still remains in the same way we fear, yet we cannot give up all hopes, that she will never wake again. Oh! I hardly feel like writing on anything else. To think that we may be forced to part with our darling sister whom we all love so well. Dr. Jump was here this evening but thinks it a hard case.

Tuesday, April 1 – Oh! The saddest day that we have yet known. Death has for the first time entered our home and snatched dear sister from us. At about ¼ after 10 o'clock our precious sister passed away. Only three short weeks ago she was with us in her usual health. We know she has left this world of trouble to dwell in a better land, that she is now happy. But Oh! It is so hard to part with those who are so dear to our hearts. How can we give her up.

Wednesday, April, 2 – We are all sad sad indeed today. Oh! I can hardly realize that our darling sister has gone from us, never to meet us again *in this world. Yet all things I suffer are ordered right though it may be hard for us to think so. Poor James does not yet know that we have been forced to part with our loved one.*[25] *Granville [Aggarth] died today, poor Anna is the last one left of the family.*

Thursday, April 3 – That one chair in the home circle is now vacant. We had been in hopes that we should all meet together in one unbroken family under the old homestead roof once again, but Oh! This, alas, can never be, yet her name by us shall never be forgotten; we will cherish her memory forever. She was loved by us all so much. She was taken to her last resting place today. Mr. Hughes preached her burial sermon. The text was Proverb 18 ch 10 v.

Friday, April 4 – Our home is sad and lonely. It seems as though there was no more joy or pleasure for us, all our fond hopes seem shattered. Poor little Josie is now left in this cold world without either father or mother. Oh! Can it be so? It all seems like a dream. We cannot tell what a few days may bring forth such sad changes in so short a time.

Saturday, April 5 – The days are sad and dreary we feel lonelier every day. To think that we shall never hear dear Orpah's voice again; that she has gone from us forever. But though we may never meet her again in this world, we will hope, sooner or later to meet her, on the other shore never to part again.

Although Mr Hughes's text – "The name of the Lord is a strong tower: the righteous runneth into it and is safe" – was designed to offer the consolation of life everlasting, for Lottie the reality of her sister's death, following so rapidly and so inexplicably upon that of her husband, remained almost incomprehensible. While she echoed the consolation of the faithful – "we know that she has left this world of trouble to dwell in a better land, that she is now happy" – Lottie, finding it "hard to part with those who are so dear to our hearts," admitted that she found it difficult to think that "all things were ordered for the best." Across the centuries, the reader can feel her anguish.

Even those diaries that are not as forthcoming in their expressions of grief can provide useful insight into the way families coped with the experience of death and dying. On 21 April 1890, Alva Estabrooks reported that her eldest brother, George, a twenty-four-year-old widower, "got hurt very badly tonight by being kicked by a horse. They came after mother. Arthur went to Hartland for Doctor." But although doctors were summoned at such times, and did what they could, it was then left to the family, and, most particularly, to the women, to provide the day-to-day care. Alva's references to George, and to her role in his care, over the course of the two and a half weeks he clung to life are cryptic, yet they provide a poignant record of a close and caring family's bedside vigil. While his mother stayed with him throughout the period, his younger siblings took turns travelling to the "bridge" each day, with the two eldest regularly taking the night shift to allow their mother time to sleep.[26] On 22 April, Alva and her younger sister Hannah "went to Rockland ... to see George. He is very bad. Arthur stayed last night. He and mother sat up with him. Arthur went up again tonight." The next day Alva was again in to see George, and found him no better. On the 24th, she went up to George's at 11 and stayed all night, returning home at noon, when George "seemed a little easy." But if Alva's hopes were raised, they were dashed on the 26th, when she went to the "bridge" in the morning and stayed with George all day and through the night, reporting that he was "not any better." In the morning, a Sunday, she went to church, then went home to dinner and slept all afternoon. That night Arthur went to the bridge, but Alva went back again on the 28th, and "sat up with Geo," returning at tea time the next day. On 30 April, she again "stayed with Geo. all night," but this time she did not go home the following day, instead staying "with Geo all day and part of night," and returning home on the morning of 2 May, to be replaced by her younger sister Hannah. On 3 May, Alva again "went to bridge eve." She spent the following day, Sunday, with friends, but on 5 May reported, "Arthur and I went to bridge eve. and up with George." By 7 May, George was "very low. Hannah stays tonight." But "Geo. Else came down for us about 2 o'clock A.M.[27] They thought Geo. was dying." George did not die that day, nor the next night, although Alva remained with him, returning home in the morning, a Friday. She went back "to bridge about 5 o'clock. George died half past 6 P.M." Following the common practice of sitting with the body until the funeral, Alva "went to bridge eve" again the next day and "stayed all night." She remained there until the next evening, when someone else took over. George was buried on Monday afternoon, 12 May, with their Uncle Amos Hayward preaching the funeral sermon. In her diary, then, Alva Estabrooks did not express her feelings for her brother in words, but in her record of his family's bedside vigil we have eloquent testimony of their love.

In the experience of the diarists, at least, one's nearest and dearest rarely died the "good" death that Annie Trueman had described, but not watched in 1871. When Annie's father, Thompson Trueman, died in 1904, his eldest daughter, who was with him and her mother during his final days, described his death quite differently. Writing to her sister Laura, who was abroad at the time, Annie reported that their father had been well until 21 March, when, "on rising from ... prayers he was seized with a terrible pain in his chest." When the pain returned the following afternoon, braving a snowstorm, Annie went out to ask a neighbour to go for the doctor, who came and gave him some tablets. But after what he termed "the longest night he ever spent," Thompson became progressively worse, although, Annie assured her sister, "he did not suffer constantly." Once again called, the doctor "made another thorough examination, gave new medicine, ordered mustard for the pain in region of heart, and left us." Thompson Trueman died while Annie and her mother were making the mustard poultice. "We poured ammonia into his lips, held hot cloths to his heart, but to no avail. It was night and we were alone with our dead ... At last I said one of us must go for help ... & I went out into the darkness." Finding some neighbours passing, she sent them for the doctor, and for Laura's young adult sons, Herbert & Willie. "It seemed too dreadful to be true & you so far away ... If I wrote you reams of paper, I could not tell you all that came in endless terrible days." Annie Trueman's anguished cry to her sister – "Oh, it is a tremendous revelation to look into the face of a dead loved one. I know now I never knew how to sympathize. We cannot know"[28] – surely strikes a chord with those among us who have ever lost a parent or a partner, a child or a sibling. Perhaps, after all, grief is the one universal sentiment that transcends cultures and time.

Breaking the rhythm of the matter-of-fact entries, the detailed report of the death of a loved one, overlaid with emotion, comes almost as a shock. But even the fleeting reference, in an otherwise routine entry, can remind us that the pain of loss, stoically endured and rarely mentioned, remained: "Very cold day. Mr & Mrs Hetherington & Mr & Mrs Jones were here. Emily, Susie & Nett were up to Geo. Macdonald's to tea. Fred was over the Lake today – bought a new horse. The Bible Meeting was held at the school house tonight. The meeting was addressed by Mr Wright, J.A. Belyea & James Macdonald. Inglewood drove Susie & Ella & I home. Ella got a letter from George tonight. Grandma got one from Uncle Willie & the 'Boys' got Xmas cards from Mrs Beal. It is four years today since Pa died."[29] Similarly, although her sister Orpah's name rarely appears in her diary in the months following her death, Orpah remained much in Lottie Reid's thoughts, surfacing in entries such as that for a beautiful sunshiny day in May 1879: "A year ago tonight James, Merritt and I were spending the evening in Saint John. Oh! What sad changes since then. We little thought then that a year could make such a change in our home circle."[30] In other cases, the writer's empathy for another's loss is distilled but clear and often the more moving for its simplicity: "N.E. wind, blowing very hard and hailing all night. It was a dreadful night ... There has not been anything like it this winter ... There was a funeral today up the lake. William Straight's child. It died on Monday morning. It is only a month since he lost his wife."[31]

In reminding her daughter that "neither youth, nor health, is any security against death," Sarah Hill was preparing Mary not for death but for life – a life in which pregnancy carried with it significant risks for the mother, newborn "little strangers" could not be counted upon to "stay," and many men's occupations were fraught with danger – during a time when it was usually left to women to care for and comfort the sick and dying. Our diarists who were in the midst of life did not exhibit a morbid obsession with death. And although reports and rituals of death were so embedded in family and community practice as to appear routine, we may not assume that an individual's grief at the loss of a loved one was any less poignant than our own. In the end, it is empathy that we feel for these women who inhabited that foreign country which is the past.

Conclusion

Viewed within a broad context, records of individual lives can offer a window into the past. But we should not assume that we have gained entry into any diary writer's innermost thoughts or even her boldest actions, for, at best, a diary is an edited version of a life. Shaped by their families, their communities, and the broader nineteenth-century society in which they lived, the twenty-eight women whose diaries are at the core of this book reflect both continuity and change in the attitudes and outlooks of the dominant sector of New Brunswick society that was anglophone, Protestant, and white. As Ann Eliza Rogers might have put it, all twenty-eight women "belonged to the Maritimes"; twenty-six of the twenty-eight "belonged to New Brunswick." To "belong" meant much more than to be a Maritimer or a New Brunswicker by birth. The multi-layered levels of belonging extended along a continuum from family to community to society. Our subjects were profoundly of this place, belonging to and understanding it in a way not possible for an immigrant. Such a level of belonging provided a sure and strong support network in times of trouble.

The diarists' world was the world of a North American settler society, well beyond the pioneer stage by the time our lens is turned upon it. The women in that society shared much of the world view of other women in similar circumstances. Their education and religious experience was similar to that of their counterparts in Nova Scotia or Ontario. But there were significant distinctions as well. The wider maritime economy introduced a cosmopolitanism that set the diarists apart from their Ontario counterparts and determined that they had more in common with women in Maine and Massachusetts. They read the same books and the same sermon literature as women throughout the English-speaking world. Their local economy, whether land- or sea-based, was conditioned by the seasons. Given New Brunswick's extensive river system, they were far from isolated, at the same time as they enjoyed many more connections with the wider world in the seasons when the waterways were open than in those when they were not.

And although, from a twenty-first-century perspective, these nineteenth-century women's lives may seem narrow and circumscribed, their horizons were not. Nineteenth-century New Brunswick women's reach, as well as their vision, extended beyond their families and communities, into the far corners of the world. In their diaries, we see their construction of themselves as individuals, their place as building blocks of their families and communities, and their contributions in shaping their society, in directing its outward gaze, and in envisioning its future. My ultimate purpose in this volume has been to throw light on New Brunswick women's experience and to offer the basis for a comparative framework that can be used by scholars and general readers alike in developing a composite picture of women's worlds in nineteenth-century North America.

In situating women within their families and in framing their experience, I chose to confront rather than to dismiss the private/public sphere dichotomy, replacing it with a continuum that moves from family to community to society. This continuum, envisioned as three concentric circles, provided a framework that allowed scope for an analysis of the complexity of women's lived experience. The women whose diaries provided the basis for that analysis may be regarded as fairly conventional, at the same time as they did do remarkable things. If they were not radical or subversive, they were sometimes innovative and often thoughtful and inclined to arrive at diverse, imaginative solutions to their problems.

Within the domestic sphere of the household, mothers taught their daughters to sew and to knit, to spin and to weave, to make quilts, clothes, and carpets, and to produce butter and cheese. Together, girls and women did all these things. As well, they raised chickens and geese, milked cows, and sheared sheep. They planted and harvested household gardens. They prepared meals, washed clothes, and cleaned house. But they also read books, painted, and played the piano and other musical instruments. They worked hard, but usually work was shared by many hands. During the day, they found time for visiting and for receiving callers. In the evening, their daily tasks complete, they were rarely too exhausted to participate in lively conversation, share a book, write letters or record the day's events in their diaries, have a "sing" or attend a meeting. They regularly entertained overnight guests and few among them did not make their own extended visits to family and friends. Through regular correspondence, they kept in touch with family and friends who had left their communities, and often New Brunswick, behind. If their lives revolved around the rhythms of the household, those rhythms included time for thinking as well as doing, for sociability as well as work.

Ensconced within a supportive network of kith and kin, our New Brunswick women diarists, whether single, married, or widowed, exhibited a strong sense of self. At the same time, the pattern of women's life course, like the pattern of men's life course, proved predictable enough. Young women exhibited the restlessness associated with youth in any society, a sense that they were waiting for life to begin. Solitude held few charms for the young, and those who imagined a future of "single-blessedness" and an independent career were rare indeed.[1] The majority saw marriage as a goal to be attained, but, in their pursuit of the "ideal man," women sought a partner rather than a patriarch. The married women, both among the diarists and among those they portrayed, who appeared most content with their lot were those in companionate marriages. When such a partnership ended in the death of one of its members, widows, like widowers, used a variety of strategies to maintain the balance of the family economy. And, because they were less likely than their male counterparts to remarry, many widows, including the mothers of several of our diarists, raised their families as single parents. Mothers, whatever their marital status, took particular pleasure in their children, watching them with pride as well as with trepidation as they entered the wider world to "begin" their own lives. And in their roles as daughters, sisters, wives, mothers, or widows, women were sometimes dependent, sometimes independent, and, above all, interdependent.

The three generations of New Brunswick women who came of age during the course of the nineteenth century were grounded not only in their families, but also in their communities and in their society. Their work lives and their social lives extended well beyond the domestic space of the household. Our subjects were to be seen out and about in the community as often as were their husbands, fathers, and brothers. The community as well as the household was women's space. From an early age, girls mixed and mingled with their male counterparts. They lived in what one historian has referred to as a heterosocial society.[2] Along with their brothers, they attended local coeducational schools. The majority continued to attend such schools into their teenage years. They participated in school examinations during which they performed publicly, judged not only by their teachers, but also by school inspectors and local school trustees, before an audience of parents and other interested community members. Young and old attended local fairs where women, like men, showed their wares and competed for prizes. The young were perhaps more likely than their parents to attend the travelling circuses that occasionally made the rounds of the province's major towns. Parades and public celebrations of all kinds attracted an audience of women and girls along with men and boys. In summer, young people in particular enjoyed planning and participating in picnics and steamboat excursions. Some enjoyed boating and a few went swimming. Croquet offered pleasant and genteel recreation. By the end of the century, bicycling had become popular with young women as well as with young men. In winter, young people of all ages enjoyed tobogganing and skating. Indeed, schools sometimes had "skating holidays" when the ice was particularly fine.[3] And in all seasons, both private and public parties often began in early evening with various kinds of games and other entertainment, followed by a meal or other refreshments, in preparation for the dancing that continued into the early hours of the morning. In all of these activities, men and women met and mingled, enjoying time spent in one another's company in places that were more often public than private.

The church, while generally accepted as an institution central to nineteenth-century community life, continues, in much of the historiography, to sit awkwardly at the intersection of private and public spheres, belonging to neither or belonging to both. The reason for this ambivalence on the part of scholars is clear. On the whole, religion has been viewed as a conservative influence in women's lives. Throughout the nineteenth century, many church leaders, both in published sermons and in articles in denominational newspapers, stressed the critical significance of the mother as moral arbiter, extolled the virtues of domesticity, criticized the very notion of women moving into the public sphere, and resisted the growing influence of women within their own institutions.[4] At the same time, viewed as public institutions, churches can serve as a useful indicator of the extent of women's public presence in their communities. Families attended church together. And, like church services, many church-sponsored activities were multi-generational in character, attended by people of all ages. Sunday School picnics and other church-sponsored social events may have offered "respectable" places for young people to meet and mingle, but they were, nonetheless, chaotic affairs, which did not provide the level of supervision we so often associate with nineteenth-century courtship. Singing schools, church choirs, pie or box socials, and even revivals all provided neutral public space where young single women and men could meet. They also gave courting couples opportunities to spend private time together, occasionally to slip away from the crowd without being missed, more often to walk home together in the company of a friend who might discreetly disappear along the way.

More significantly, as public institutions, churches played a critical role in ensuring their communities' social as well as spiritual welfare. Women often took the lead in initiating, as well as in facilitating, this role. Over the course of the nineteenth century, women of all ages became increasingly active within their churches. The majority of such activities, including women's class meetings, sewing circles, maternal associations, women's auxiliaries, and women's missionary societies, involved meeting together with other women. But participation in church-sponsored voluntary associations also involved organizing entertainments, speakers, bazaars, teas, garden parties, and a variety of other fund-raising events designed to appeal to men as well as to women. Women proved eminently successful in such fund-raising efforts, regularly providing more money than their male counterparts to support causes ranging from the provision of relief for the poor through the construction and repair of church buildings to staffing foreign mission fields.[5] As members of church-sponsored voluntary organizations, women inculcated, reinforced, and transformed religious and community values through their own example. By providing necessary funds for diverse local projects, church women's voluntary organizations indirectly both supported and stimulated the local economy. And, in so far as they decided on which causes to support, the members of such organizations played a significant role in determining the direction, nature, and extent of social activism both within and well beyond their communities. By the end of the century, women's insistence on directing the bulk of the monies collected by their separate women's missionary societies towards the support of women missionaries had effected a shift not only in the gender balance but also in the focus of the missionary movement, as trained ministers began to be outnumbered by trained teachers and health care workers.[6]

As individuals, women's participation in both formal and informal market economies took them into the many and varied public spaces of their neighbourhoods and communities. Like their male relatives, women regularly visited local shops and other businesses, including lawyers' offices. At the counter of the general store, farm women exchanged their eggs and butter, cheese and cloth for a variety of necessities and the occasional luxury item. A few established contacts that allowed them to distribute their goods to a wider market in the towns and cities of New Brunswick, and sometimes to the neighbouring American states. Many more travelled to those towns and cities themselves, where they sold their skills rather than their goods.

By the end of the century, women had taken charge of the majority of one-room schools in the province, where they equipped children with the basic reading and numeracy skills necessary to run not only households but also farms and small businesses. Some prepared their students to pursue further education at grammar schools, private academies, or even the provincial normal school. Though attendance was voluntary, such women did regularly attend the government-sponsored Teachers' Institutes, the equivalent of today's professional development. Still other women earned a living as itinerant music teachers. Some women worked as itinerant seamstresses, while others established their own shops. Women founded a variety of other retail businesses, including millinery shops and grocery stores. They applied for, and received, tavern licences. And, of course, women ran boarding houses, entering the wider world by opening their homes to strangers. Women even entered the world of financial speculation; they held mortgages and owned and rented land. They also held and sometimes themselves purchased bank stocks, supporting the same banks by depositing their money in savings accounts. Certainly it is true that men in nineteenth-century society had far greater earning capacity than women. But if men played the leading roles in the economy, women nonetheless shared the stage. The same was true for the political and, increasingly, the intellectual spheres.

Women's political and intellectual interests extended far beyond the household. Women were to be found listening attentively to a wide range of travelling lecturers at church and community halls, lyceums and Mechanics' Institutes. Whether the subject was natural history, temperance, the abolition of slavery, Christian missions in foreign lands, astronomy, or electricity, women helped to swell the audience. At academies and universities, women as well as men engaged in debates on topics ranging from free trade to the value of education for women. After graduation, the same women retained their interest in intellectual pursuits. As members of voluntary organizations, they promoted education in various ways, providing educational materials to schools, attending academic presentations, and funding awards for academic achievement. Intellectual debate often reflected ideological differences, and for women, as for men, ideological differences found an outlet in partisan politics. Political rallies were crowded with women who could not vote, along with men who could.[7] Aware of and interested in the major issues of their day, women expressed their political views not only in private conversation and correspondence but also through the medium of public petition. Indeed, if women were at the heart of the family, they were also at the heart of the community, passing judgment on politicians and political platforms and lecturers and lectures, as well as ministers and sermons.[8]

Women's engagement in the affairs of their community and of their society is perhaps most clearly illustrated in the nature and number of the voluntary societies they established and joined.[9] Throughout the nineteenth century, the temperance cause attracted both men and women to its ranks, reflecting the significance of alcohol as a broadly recognized societal problem. While many New Brunswick women who supported the cause joined the WCTU after its arrival in the province in 1875, others remained loyal to their mixed-member temperance lodges. Yet, whatever their preference, women played a leading role in the temperance movement, promoting the inclusion of education on the dangers of alcohol and tobacco in the schools, providing prizes for essays on the subject by schoolchildren, hosting temperance teas, and sponsoring speakers. But as was the case with women's missionary societies, the shift to an exclusively women's temperance organization gave members not only control of their own funds, but also the flexibility to choose their own direction. Moving beyond a narrow focus on liquor and tobacco, by the late 1880s, many WCTU branches had established suffrage committees, and had begun lobbying for local and provincial women's enfranchisement. While the suffrage campaign signalled women's desire for a stronger voice in public affairs, the call for women's enfranchisement reflected a continuing rather than a new engagement in the public life of their communities and their society.

Whether they were from the province's towns and cities or from rural farming and fishing communities, nineteenth-century New Brunswick women were cosmopolitan in their outlook and experience. Living, as they did, in a province that faced seaward and traded in global markets, like the men in their lives, they followed the vicissitudes of world trade with a practised eye. During the period when the wooden shipbuilding industry was at its height, many took advantage of the opportunity to travel offered by locally built vessels engaged in the coasting trade. Some sailed the high seas with their husbands or fathers, sharing their adventures with their families through the medium of letters or logs. With the construction of the Intercolonial Railway in the years immediately following Confederation, and later the Canadian Pacific Railway, women, like men, travelled westward to visit family members who had left the province.

Women's reading reflected their involvement in their society. They kept up to date with the latest news from both home and abroad, subscribing to local, national, and denominational papers. New Brunswick women diarists also found time to read the latest British, American, and Canadian novels. Yet although, like us, our diarists might have identified with the subjects of the newspaper articles and books they read, their own experience was unique to their time and unique to New Brunswick at that particular time. Neither they nor the men who shared their lives and times viewed the world as we do. They saw themselves and their actions from the perspective of a rapidly evolving present, moving forward into a future they could imagine but not quite discern. In one sense, the nineteenth-century New Brunswick women who wrote diaries may, nonetheless, be compared to many of the readers of this book. They, too, were people who had the time to think, the time to read, and the time to write.

Afterword

Diarists' lives do not end with the last page of their diaries. Looking beyond the diaries – and looking beyond the scope of this volume – we are left wondering what the future held for our twenty-eight women diarists. What happened to them after they made their last diary entries? A few pieces of the puzzle are provided below.

1. Janet Hendry MacDonald (1795–1887) and her granddaughter,

2. Ida MacDonald (1865–1883)

We learn something of Janet Hendry MacDonald's life in the years following her diary from her granddaughter Ida's diary. By 1879, when Ida began keeping a diary, Janet and her husband Alexander had lost a third child – their eldest son and Ida's father, James (d. 1878). Alexander died the following year, on 29 March 1880. The 1881 census describes the household as headed by eighty-five-year-old Janet MacDonald, rather than, as we might have expected, her fifty-seven-year-old daughter-in-law, Sally, or her grandsons, twenty-seven-year-old Fred or twenty-four-year-old Robert, who were managing the family farm and sawmill. In the summer of 1883, in the closing pages of her diary, Ida reports a silent and anxious household: her older brother Fred was gravely ill, having contracted typhoid fever. Ida's diary ends abruptly in September of 1883, when she, too, fell ill. Fred recovered, but, tragically, Ida and her eldest sister, Mary Jane, did not. Ida died on 26 October, less than a month before her eighteenth birthday.[1] Her grandmother, Janet Hendry MacDonald, died four years later, on 27 April 1887, at the age of ninety-two, having lived a rich, full life on the Hendry/ MacDonald farm on the shores of Washademoak Lake in the lower St John River Valley. As she so often put it in her diary, "O what changes" she had seen.

3. Jacobina Campbell (circa 1797–185?)

By 1843, when her diary ends, Jacobina Campbell's three brothers had all established their own farms, carved out of the 580 acres their father had been granted at the junction of the Tay and Nashwaak Rivers. Neither Jacobina nor her younger sister Ann married; following their mother's death, they inherited the home farm. The Campbell farms did not prosper and by 1851 Jacobina's eldest brother, Sandy, his wife, Caroline, and their family had moved to Upper Canada. In that year, Jacobina and her sister Ann were living in Fredericton. Only Ludlow continued to farm along the Tay. Patrick, who was listed as a surveyor in the 1861 census, did not marry until 1865. Whether Jacobina and Ann followed their brother Sandy and his family to Upper Canada is unclear. Certainly they disappeared from the New Brunswick record, and left no record of their deaths.[2]

4. Marjory Grant Buchanan (1800–187?) and her sister,

5. Isabella Grant Christie (1807–186?)

Marjory Grant finished her part of the diary, married William R. Buchanan in 1827, and moved to Oak Hill. Sometime in the early 1830s, Isabella married Robert Christie, the son of a neighbouring farmer. By 1851, Isabella's family was complete: she and Robert had six children aged four to seventeen. The 1861 census finds Marjory, at sixty-one, living not in Saint James, but in Lower St Stephen. A widow, she headed her own household, which included a twenty-one-year-old female lodger who was teaching school in the district. Isabella did not outlive her husband. In 1871, her widower, Robert Christie, lived in St Stephen Parish, the head of a household made up of their son William, daughters Henrietta and Jannet, as well as a thirteen-year-old adopted son.[3] Marjorie, at seventy-one, continued to head her own household in 1871, but disappears from the records after that.

6. Lucy Everett Morrison (1823–1893)

On Sunday, 28 May 1893, Lucy Morrison recorded the death of her husband, who had fallen ill on 1 April. Two full months of nursing him had undoubtedly taken their toll on Lucy, who died six weeks later, on 11 July. She was sixty-nine. Her obituary was a model of those written to commemorate the lives of upper middle-class matrons. Thus, although John A. Morrison's obituary had much to say about his business enterprises, Lucy's did not mention hers. Indeed, following the custom of the day, it did not even mention her given name. Mrs John A Morrison was described only as "a very amiable and kind-hearted lady" and "a member of St Paul's Presbyterian Church."[4] Yet John Morrison had been well aware of her competence. In his will, he had named his wife, Lucy Morrison, an executrix.[5] She had earned the respect of the community as well, and her funeral "was very largely attended ... the employees of the mill attended ... in a body." Whether any of the men and, in later years, women, who had worked for Lucy as gardeners, the women who had been employed by her as seamstresses, or the women who had worked in her household were among those in attendance is not recorded. Certain it was that her longtime housekeeper, Agnes McNabb, was among the mourners.

7. Sophy (Sophia) Bliss Carman (1828–1886)

In January 1886, less than a year after her husband's death, Sophy Carman reported another bedside vigil in her diary, as her Mother grew weaker and weaker.[6] Her son Bliss's diary for 23 January states, "Dear Mother's mother died this morning." The following morning, a Sunday, he and Sophy attended High Communion for the last time together. Sophy's mother's funeral was held two days later, on 25 January. Then, on 2 February, Sophy attended the Feast of Purification service alone and "went to bed that night with a cold." She died a few days later. Bliss's diary entry for 10 February reflects the shock he and his sister felt: "Who shall say – what pain we all felt? This day at sunset the Hand of God came to lead unto Himself one of the most beautiful spirits we shall ever see ... Merciful Father, thou hast crowned Thy servant not with length of days but with a short waiting [that] soon very soon she might follow her darling ... But it is so hard for us, Jesu Mercy."[7] Sophy Bliss Carman was fifty-seven.

8. Mary Whitney Hill (1829–189?)

When her diary closed in 1879, Mary Hill was unwilling to renew her lease for another year because she was uncertain if she wished to remain in St Andrews. Yet she remained for at least two more years; in 1881, she was still living in the seaside town.[8] But by 1891, Mary had returned to her home town of St Stephen, where, at sixty-one, she continued to live on her own, although surrounded by family and, no doubt, by old friends as well.[9] Sadly, 1892 brought the death of two of her three younger sisters. Louisa, who, like Mary, had never married, died in October 1892, at the age of fifty-eight. Augusta, a widow, died less than two months later, at fifty-six. By the time the 1901 census was taken, Mary, like her sisters, had disappeared from the record.[10]

9. Annie Gilbert Johnston Waltham (1833–1882)

Tragically, Annie Waltham did not enjoy her newly established independence for long. Nor would she ever return to New Brunswick. During the months following her separation from Waltham, Annie was plagued by constant money worries, frequent nightmares, and an often overwhelming sadness. Her health deteriorated rapidly, and by June 1882, the number of recorded visits from the doctor increased markedly. In her final entry, on 16 June, she noted that she felt "very poorly" and that her daughter Annie "was quite ill all day yesterday." But she continued to look to the future, reporting that "Annie commenced a new course of music lessons." By that time, twenty-three-year-old Annie had begun to share the financial responsibilities with her mother. Had her mother been preparing her for a role she would be required to play all too soon? Annie Gilbert Johnston Waltham died in September 1882, in London, at the age of forty-nine, leaving her daughter Annie Johnston in charge not only of the family finances, but of her nine-year-old sister, Lena, as well. Perhaps seeking to gain control of the estate, Richard Waltham returned to New Brunswick, where he died in June of 1883, without realizing that purpose.[11]

10. Ann Eliza Rogers Gallacher Moore (1837–1896)

An anomalous statement by her daughter, placed after Ann Eliza's diary entry of 1 September 1888, both offers insight into the nature of her diary keeping, and prepares the reader for her death: "Aug. 21,

1898. I have decided to finish copying from small pieces of paper the remainder of Mother's Diary as she died July 16, 1896 before completing the copying. [Signed:] Ella Moore."[12] Ann Eliza's second husband, Lemuel Moore, had died on 16 April 1895, following a three-month illness. "How we shall miss him," Ann Eliza wrote on the day of his funeral. "He was 52 years old last November."[13] Ann Eliza, five years his senior, did miss him, especially as her remaining children began to leave home. On 4 January 1896, she reported, "Archibald & Donald both went away this morning, Art to his school, Don went to Halifax, is going to the Business College." Two days later, when her daughter Ellie left for the Lower Cape to teach school, she confided, "Dodge & I are alone & I will be very lonely." But Ellie visited regularly, and Ann Eliza visited Jennie and kept in touch with her remaining five adult children through regular correspondence.[14] Indeed, in her final diary entry, made on 9 March 1896, Ann Eliza reported writing a letter to her eldest son: "Fine but cold. The Dr came up this forenoon to see me, says I have a very bad cold, does not think it will last long. I wrote to Frank, Dodge wrote part of it." Some time before she penned that last entry, Ann Eliza had apparently decided to leave a fair copy of her diaries for her children and grandchildren. At her death, she was in the process of recopying into notebooks diaries which, in later years at least, she had kept largely on salvaged paper. We are fortunate that her daughter Ella completed the task.

11. Mary Isoline Wolhaupter Watters (1838–1920)

At the time the 1871 census was taken, Mary Wolhaupter, at thirty-three, was still living at home, and once again employed as a teacher. But on 2 May of that year, Mary married George Watters, a widower not mentioned in the 1869 diary. Perhaps her decision to marry was foreshadowed in her oblique reference to the "chance" she had not taken to "settle" in Florenceville when she was teaching there.[15] The couple's first child, Hanford, was born in 1872, followed, at two-year intervals, by Lottie, Allan, Hattie, and Isoline. At age forty-one, with five children under the age of ten, it is likely that Mary Wolhaupter Watters had need of a sustaining faith. In 1901, four of George and Mary's children – Hanford, Allan, Hattie, and Issie – were still living at home. Within the next few years, Allan began courting Nellie Estabrooks, the younger sister of Alvaretta and Hannah. By 1911, only thirty-nine-year-old Hanford and an eight-year-old granddaughter were living on the home farm with

George and Mary, both by then in their seventies. Mary "Issie" Watters, by now a widow, died on 10 April 1920, at age eighty-two. Her death was reported by her son Hanford.[16]

12. Emma Bertha Frost Jones (1843–1925)

In the 1901 census, fifty-seven-year-old Bertha Jones was listed as a farmer. Ada (twenty-three), Alma (twenty), and fourteen-year-old Hildrick were still living at home.[17] Bertha employed one farm hand, and she had one boarder, Hiram W. Coady, a young Church of England clergyman, who, in time, became a well-known New Brunswick novelist. By the time the 1911 census was taken, both Bertha's daughters had left home, and her twenty-four-year-old son, Hildrick, was listed as the head of the household, which, as well as his widowed mother, included seven-year-old Benjamin Burns, who had emigrated from England in 1910, and forty-seven-year-old Charles Edgett, a lodger who was teaching at the local public school.[18] Bertha Jones died on 20 May 1925, at eighty-one. In reporting her death, her son Hildrick did not mention her years running the farm, but noted that she had, in earlier days, been a teacher.[19]

13. Jo (Josephine) Reid Turner (1849–1884) and her sister,

14. Lottie (Charlotte) Reid Turner (1859–1889)

By the end of March 1884, Josephine Turner and her sea-captain husband had been in the port city of Buenos Aires for more than five weeks. As the unloading of cargo was completed, and preparations to take on ballast commenced, Josephine did some last-minute shopping with another sea captain's wife. On the whole, she had enjoyed this trip to Buenos Aires, a port to which she and her husband planned to return with another cargo. But she could not shake a nagging cold, which she attributed to the sudden change in the weather.[20] On Monday, 7 April, she noted that "a quick mail left here today for Europe, by which we sent quite a number of home letters. I wrote four." These would be the last home letters her family received, for Josephine Turner died of typhoid fever on 22 April.[21] Married just five years, and already an established member of the seafaring community, like so many other seafaring New Brunswickers, she died far from her beloved home. She was thirty-five years old.

Lottie remained at home in those years. William Reid died in February 1885, causing sons James and Wat to return to Harvey. In a letter to his sister Lottie in May, Merritt, married and living in Evansville, Indiana, wrote, "I hear you are talking of going to St John to school which I think is a good idea. All the rest of the girls had a chance to go to school away from home and I think you ought to too, and you will enjoy it I know."[22] By October, Lottie was in Saint John furthering her education, and her brother Wat was managing the family farm and working as a builder in the local community. But if Lottie worked outside the home after the completion of her studies, she did not do so for long. As an 1887 letter from her eldest brother, James, reveals, she had plans to marry. "Dear Lot," he wrote,

> Thought I'd add a few lines to the public document enclosed to tell you how glad and sorry I am at the same time that you have [decided to] set sail on the sea of matrimony ... I hope you will be very happy and believe you will for I think the Capt. is as noble hearted a fellow as ever lived and I don't know of but one fault that you have ... a fault that will be corrected as you mix with the world – the lack of self-assurance ... I have only one regret that you are going to get married and that is that someone else is to show you the world. I had figured on a trip we would take together some time here, there and everywhere. But my ship didn't get in on time you see.[23]

On 6 July 1887, at her mother's home, Charlotte Reid married her dead sister's husband, James Brewster Turner, captain of the *G.P. Sherwood* and the *Kesmark*.[24] James and Lottie had even less time together than James had had with Josephine, however. On 25 December 1889, Ann Eliza Rogers noted in her diary, "Mrs James Turner died at Harvey this morning."[25] Lottie was just thirty years old.

15. Annie Trueman (1851–1914) and her sister,

16. Laura Trueman Wood (1856–1934)

Annie, the elder, and probably more delicate of the Trueman sisters, never married. She remained at home with her parents and, as her correspondence demonstrates, remained active in her community, holding executive positions in the Methodist Women's Missionary Society and the WCTU, as well as teaching Sunday school. Like many unmarried daughters, Annie took on greater family responsibilities as her parents aged. Thompson Trueman died in 1904, at the age of eighty-eight. In 1911, Annie, at fifty-nine, was living in a household headed by her ninety-four-year-old mother.[26] Rebecca Trueman died the following year. Annie, perhaps as a result of the rheumatic fever she had contracted as a young woman, was not as long-lived as her parents. Involved as she was in her community, her life had revolved around her parents' household, and the family home must have been very lonely without them. Annie Trueman died in November 1914, at just sixty-three.[27]

Laura Trueman Wood, who normally remained in Sackville when her husband travelled to Ottawa to attend parliamentary sessions, also became a community activist. Partly because she was married to a prominent politician, various voluntary groups sought her patronage. But by the time Josie was appointed Lieutenant Governor of New Brunswick, in 1912, his wife Laura had gained a reputation in her own right.[28] Committed both to Mount Allison University and to its affiliated Ladies' College, Laura played a philanthropic and then an administrative role in the support of those institutions. She gave her time as well as her money, often entertaining students and guests of the College in her home, and eventually becoming a member of the university's Board of Regents.[29] In 1934, Laura Trueman Wood, by then a widow, was named a commander in the Order of the British Empire in recognition of her long service to her community and to her province. She died later that year, at age seventy-eight.

17. Maggie (Margaret) Loggie Valentine (1852–1893) and her sisters,

18. Kate (Catherine) Loggie (1857–?) and

19. Jessie Loggie (1859–1892)

It is from a note appended to Maggie Valentine's journal letter from Norway of 30 November 1885, sent to their mother, that we learn a little of Kate's life after her diary ends in 1881. Kate had been gravely ill, but her family now had reason to hope that she would recover: "I got Jessie's letter ... I need not say how grieved I was to hear such sad accounts of dear Kate but hope the doctor has made a mistake & that she will be long spared to us yet. The last account was more cheering as the change in N. York seems to have benefited her very much."[30]

To speed her convalescence, a change of scenery had, apparently, been deemed desirable, and, given her destination, it seems likely that Kate had been sent to her sister Ellen Lamont, then living in New York. Kate's sojourn in the United States did not, however, end in New York. A brief addendum to her own diary finds her in Hendersonville, North Carolina. It suggests that she had been away from home for some time and was not expecting to return any time soon.[31]

Jessie's health had also been a cause for worry in 1885 and 1887, when their parents had enlisted Maggie's aid in providing the curative change in scenery and climate that seemed to cause Jessie's health to improve. By 1891, both Jessie and Kate had returned from their travels and, along with their older, unmarried sister Mary, were living with their parents.[32] It is very likely that Jessie was by then losing ground; she died in 1892, at the age of thirty-three.

In 1894, the *Muncaster Castle*, which had taken Jessie to India and in which Maggie and her husband William had, for over a decade, travelled the world together, was sold. Was this a practical decision, taken as the age of sail was drawing to a close? Or was it that William Valentine could no longer bear to sail in her? In December 1893, after an absence of twenty years, Captain Valentine returned to Burnt Church, but without Maggie, who had died three months earlier at the age of forty-one.[33] When Alexander Loggie died in 1897, in his eighty-fourth year, he was survived by his widow, his son, and longtime business partner Donald, and two unmarried daughters, Kate and Mary, who were all with him at the time of his death. Kate may have been living elsewhere, and may have returned home when she learned of her father's illness. She disappears from the record after that time. In 1901, only Mary was living at home with their widowed mother.[34]

20. Amelia Holder Henderson (Diaries 1855–1936) and her cousin,

21. Emma Alice Pitt Brown (1857–circa 1910)

Amelia Holder's days of sailing with her father ended when her Aunt Mary Ann Parrett left their household in 1874. Five years later, Edwin Holder moved his family to Portland. By the time he died, in 1884, he, too, had given up the seafaring life. Two years later, Amelia, then thirty, married Benjamin Henderson, the brother of her Aunt Angeline Holder, widow of her father's youngest brother. Given her clear penchant for shipboard life, it is scarcely surprising that Amelia married a seafaring man. But, unlike her mother, Amelia did not go to sea with her husband. Nonetheless, she never forgot her voyages with her father, and left her record of those voyages as a legacy for her three children: Thurlow Benjamin (b. 1889), Oliver Raymond (b. 1892), and Marjorie Agnes (b. 1898). Amelia's sister Agnes married Erastus P. Calder, a Methodist minister, in 1891. Like Amelia and Benjamin, Aggie and Erastus had three children: Ada (b. 1894), Benjamin Raymond (b. 1896), and Lila Belle (b. 1899). Amelia's youngest sister, Ada, the other sometime diarist in the family, died in 1889, at the age of twenty-nine.[35] In 1892, Amelia and Aggie lost a second sibling; their older brother Tommy, a sea captain like their father, died in Santos of yellow fever, leaving behind a wife and three children.[36] His obituary noted his superior navigational skills, perhaps recalling to Amelia their father's lessons when the three of them sailed together. Amelia Holder Henderson died in 1936, at the age of eighty, having outlived her husband by eight years. Her sister Aggie Holder Crawford died in 1953, at age ninety-four.[37]

Emma Pitt's story resembled that of her cousins Amelia and Aggie Holder, who, as teenagers, had very much enjoyed the company of young men, but who married late. Emma's father died in 1877; her only surviving brother, David L. Pitt, married in the same year. In 1881, Emma, at twenty-six, and her sixty-three-year-old mother, were living in Saint John, with Emma's brother and his young family. Four years later, when David, a merchant, moved his family to Florenceville, Emma and her mother went with them. Then, in 1890, the family moved to Woodstock.[38] And a decade later, Emma, then forty-two years old, married George H. Brown, a farmer. The couple, as well as Emma's mother Catherine, settled on a farm in Greenwich Parish, Kings County. Catherine died in 1909, at the age of ninety. Her daughter did not long outlive her. By the time the 1911 census was taken, Emma, too, had died.[39]

22. Lillie (Lillian) Williamson Wightman (1861–1891)

Fred Wightman went on to become the Methodist minister he had aspired to be, and Lillie supported him in his endeavours. On 13 August 1890, following his ordination, their seven-year courtship ended in their long-planned wedding. Rev Frederick A. Wightman, Methodist Minister of Weldford, and Lillian Williamson were married by Lillie's uncle, Rev Steven Teed, husband of her mother's sister Rachel.[40] Sadly, Lillie enjoyed her long-anticipated marriage for less than a year. A brief entry in the *Moncton Times* on 7 April 1891 reported that Lillie Wightman, "the wife of Rev F.A. Wightman, age 29, of Weldford (Kent Co.) ... [died] at that place Sunday [5 April] of convulsions. The remains passed through Moncton yesterday, en route to Greenwich (Kings Co), former home of the deceased. Mr and Mrs Wightman had only been married about eight months. A child, prematurely born, is living."[41]

23. Alva (Alvaretta) Estabrooks (1869–1941) and her sister,

24. Hannah Estabrooks (1871–1950)

Alva Estabrooks returned to her studies at Acadia Ladies' Seminary, graduating in 1896. She put her qualifications to good use, supporting herself by teaching music in and around Florenceville, where she lived with her Aunt Lucretia and Uncle Amos Hayward. She visited her mother and her sister Hannah regularly, as did their sister Nellie, who, after qualifying as a teacher, taught in various nearby communities. Nellie was teaching school when she met Mary Wolhaupter Watters's son Allan, who, by 1905, had begun courting her.[42] By the time of the 1911 census, Agnes Estabrooks had died, and Allan and Nellie Watters, by then the parents of two small children, had settled on the family farm. Hannah, who lived with them, continued to work in the local store, but now as bookkeeper, earning more for her labour than her sister Alva, then living with her widowed Aunt Lucretia in Florenceville, earned as a music teacher.[43] Neither Alva nor Hannah married. After the death of their Aunt Lucretia, the two sisters lived together in Hartland. Alva continued to teach music until 1940, and died on 19 July 1941, at the age of seventy-two.[44] After Alva's death, Hannah moved to Fredericton, where Nellie and Allan were then living. She died there on 28 October 1950, at seventy-nine, leaving close to $10,000 in savings to her sister Nellie.[45]

25. Laura Cynthia Fullerton Fawcett (1870–1953)

After completing her schooling, Laura returned home to Mill Village, in Cumberland County, Nova Scotia, where she contributed to the family income by teaching music.[46] She married Bliss Milligan Fawcett, a widower with two children, in 1901, when she was thirty-one years old. She and Bliss had three more children: Carman Bliss, Margaret Rosamund, and Agnes Maude. Bliss, a cattle breeder and strawberry grower, was active in the Sackville Agricultural Society and served as president of the Farmers' and Dairymen's Association of New Brunswick and as director of the Maritime Stock Breeders' Association.[47] After her husband's death in 1915, Laura raised her children as a single mother, continuing to live on the home farm in Middle Sackville. In later life, she lived with the elder of her two daughters, Margaret R. Norrie, and her family in Truro, Nova Scotia, where she died, in 1953, at the age of eighty-three.[48] Laura was the grandmother of Margaret Norrie McCain, a graduate of Mount Allison University and Lieutenant Governor of New Brunswick, 1994–7.

26. Sadie (Sarah) Harper Allen (1875–1915)

When Frank Allen began courting Sadie Harper, he was teaching school in Shediac. But Frank had higher ambitions. Like many other young men of his generation and beyond, he had begun teaching school to finance his university studies. "The professor," as he would soon be nicknamed, earned a doctorate in physics from Cornell University before he and Sadie married in 1903. They settled in Winnipeg where Frank had been offered a position as professor of physics at the new University of Manitoba. The couple had three children: Lillian (b. 1905), John (b. 1908), and William (b. 1914). In 1912, leaving Lillian and John with Sadie's family in Shediac, they travelled to London and Zurich. Back home in Winnipeg, Sadie established her own niche in the community. However, she would not live to watch her children grow to adulthood. As a child, Sadie had had rheumatic fever and it had, apparently, left her with a damaged heart. In 1915, in the midst of spring cleaning, she suffered a heart attack and died. She was forty years old.[49]

27. Violet Goldsmith Brown (1880–1964)

On 4 December 1905, Violet Goldsmith, then teaching in Stockholm, Saskatchewan, noted in her diary that she had met Rev John Brown at her school on 2 November and that, though this was very much "out of my plan," they had become engaged on 30 November. Recognizing this development as part of God's plan, she prayed for his blessing and that she might be a "faithful wife."[50] Thus the daughter of a Methodist minister recorded her decision to marry a Presbyterian minister. In the newly established and sparsely populated provinces of Saskatchewan and Alberta, communities found it difficult to support a minister, however, and the young couple decided to become homesteaders, settling in Verdant Valley, Alberta. There they raised their five children: Margaret, Hugh, twins Art and Bert, and Bill. Violet later recalled the experience: "After we had a few acres broken we still had no seeder. I drove the wagon up and down the field, Margaret and Hugh asleep at my feet, while my husband broadcast the seed from the back. He harrowed it, walking behind the harrows. I don't remember whether it was wheat or oats, but it grew." Hard work was supplemented by intellectual and spiritual stimulation. Violet remembered that one winter "we had a Literary Society ... It met every two weeks, and people came to it for miles around ... We had good programs and some real good debates." And John Brown "continued to preach at the country schools." After the Second World War, their son Art took over the farm and Violet and John retired to Drumheller. John died just a year later, in 1946. Violet survived him by close to two decades. She died in 1964 at the age of eighty-four.[51]

28. Kate (Katherine) Miles (1885–1963)

By 1907, twenty-two-year-old Kate Miles was on a train, heading west to visit her older brothers. Edgar was working in Saskatchewan at the time, while Bruce had just established a dental practice in Cranbrook, British Columbia. Kate must have liked what she saw, for by 1911 she was living in Regina with her cousin Blanche Dibblee, a stenographer, and another woman friend. The three flatmates regularly enjoyed food parcels from Kate's parents' productive New Brunswick farm. When the First World War broke out, Kate was editor of the "Ladies' Page" of the Regina *Evening Province and Standard*. She left that position, however, to work for the Regina Red Cross. Among other duties, she organized shipments for the Halifax disaster relief. After the war, Kate left Regina for points east, working, for a time, for the *Toronto Star*, before heading home to New Brunswick. She returned to Regina in time for the cyclone of 30 June 1923, but did not settle there permanently. After another sojourn in New Brunswick during the late 1920s and early 1930s, she departed for Ontario, where her older brother Edgar had settled. There, she worked as a journalist before settling on a farm with a woman friend. Kate Hawes Miles died in March 1963 at the age of seventy-eight. She is buried in Sutton West, Ontario.[52]

Appendix

Table 1. New Brunswick Population Statistics to 1911

County	1824*	1834	1840	1851	1861	1871	1881	1891	1901	1911
Albert				6313	9444	10671	12329	10971	10925	9691
Carleton		9493	13381	11108	16373	19938	23365	22529	21621	21446
Charlotte		15852	18178	19938	23663	25882	26087	23752	22415	21147
Gloucester		8323	7751	11704	15076	18810	21614	24895	27936	32662
Kent	9267	6031	7477	11410	15854	19101	22618	23845	23958	24376
Kings	7930	12195	14464	18842	23283	24593	25617	23087	21655	20594
Madawaska				3361	4786	7234	8676	10512	12311	16678
Northum	15829	11170	14620	15064	18801	20116	25109	25713	28543	31194
Queens	4741	7204	8232	10634	13359	13847	14017	12152	11177	10897
Restig			3161	4161	4874	5575	7058	8308	10586	15687
St John	12907	20668	32957	38475	48922	52120	52966	49574	51759	53572
Sunbury	3227	3838	4260	5301	6057	6824	6651	5762	5729	6219
Victoria				2047	2915	4407	7010	7705	8825	11544
Westmor	9303	14205	17686	17814	25247	29335	37719	41477	42060	44621
York	10972	10478	13995	17628	23393	27140	30397	30979	31620	31561
Totals	74176	119457	156162	193800	252047	285594	321233	321263	331120	351889

*The population of New Brunswick after the arrival of the Loyalists in 1783 has been estimated at between 14,000 and 15,000, and in 1806 at 35,000, but these figures are approximations at best.

Source: Tables 1 to 4 are based on New Brunswick census returns for the years 1840 (which contains the figures for 1824 and 1834) and 1851 to 1921.

Table 2. Acadians as a Proportion of the Total Population 1871–1911*

Year	Proportion	Number
1871	15.7 %	44907
1881	17.6 %	56635
1901	24.2 %	79979
1911	28.0 %	98795

*Information not available for 1891.

Table 3. Rural-Urban Distribution 1851–1921

Year	Total Population	Urban	Rural	Percent Urban	PercentRural
1851	193800	27203	166597	14	86
1861	252047	32969	219078	13	87
1871	285594	50213	235381	18	82
1881	321233	59092	262141	18	82
1891	321263	65608	255655	20	80
1901	331120	77285	253835	23	77
1911	351889	99547	252342	28	72
1921	387876	124444	263432	32	68

Table 4a. Protestant-Catholic Distribution 1861

County	Population	Percent Protestant*	Percent Catholic*
Albert	9444	91	9.35
Carleton	16373	87	13.24
Charlotte	23663	85	15.19
Gloucester	15076	17	83.20
Kent	15854	35	65.35
Kings	23283	84	16.33
Northumberland	18801	54	46.31
Queens	13359	89	11.06
Restigouche	4874	60	39.58
Saint John	48922	61	39.35
Sunbury	6057	85	15.49
Victoria**	7701	32	68.37
Westmorland	25247	62	38.28
York	23393	81	19.19
Totals	252047	66	34

* Percent Protestant and Percent Catholic usually do not add up to 100 because of rounding and because no religion was recorded for a small number of New Brunswickers. Furthermore, there were a very few non-Christians.
**The future Madawaska County was still part of Victoria County in 1861.

Table 4b. Protestant-Catholic Distribution 1871

County	Population	Percent Protestant*	Percent Catholic*
Albert	10671	92.15	7.62
Carleton	19938	87.83	12.11
Charlotte	25882	84.41	15.17
Gloucester	18810	14.49	85.47
Kent	19101	30.79	68.91
Kings	24593	84.91	14.84
Northumberland	20116	55.01	44.90
Queens	13847	90.40	9.53
Restigouche	5575	58.92	40.87
Saint John	52120	65.59	34.20
Sunbury	6824	84.87	15.10
Victoria**	11641	28.79	71.04
Westmorland	29335	59.41	40.23
York	27140	83.58	16.16
Totals	285594	66.17	33.61

*Percent Protestant and Percent Catholic do not add up to 100 because of rounding and the presence in New Brunswick of 48 Jews, 76 people for whom "No Religion" was indicated, and 392 for whom no information was provided, all of whom are omitted from this table. Nor are the 59 Mormons included, as, whatever their status as Protestants in our own era, they were not widely regarded as Christians in the nineteenth century.
** Includes information for the 7,234 soon-to-be residents of Madawaska County, created out of the northern part of Victoria County in 1871.

Notes

Preface

1 These include the Centre d'études acadiennes at the Université de Moncton, where we found memoirs, but no diaries for the period.
2 The total here is thirty, as different diaries by two diarists are held at two separate repositories.

Introduction: "I wish to keep a record"

1 Catherine Loggie Diary, 1880–1881, Loggie Collection, Burnt Church, NB, MG H 128, No. 1, University of New Brunswick Archives (hereafter cited as UNBA).
2 "The past is a foreign country: they do things differently there" is the opening line of Hartley, *The Go-Between*.
3 In the past two decades, the term "historical consciousness" has been redefined in new ways. Here I am using an older, or more traditional definition, but one that also finds resonance in the recent work of Phillips, "History, Memory, and Historical Distance."
4 While numerous fine studies have focussed specifically on the immigrant experience, we still tend to conflate the experience of British and American immigrants with that of second- and third-generation British North American women. The nineteenth-century "Canadian" women whose experience we know most about were mainly immigrants, the best known being Susanna Moodie and Catherine Parr Traill. Besides their own publications, see Gray, *Sisters in the Wilderness*. A significant proportion of nineteenth-century Ontario women and the majority of nineteenth-century Western

women whose diaries have been published were, like Moodie and Parr Traill, immigrant women.
5 Women from these groups may certainly have kept diaries in the nineteenth century, but I was unable to locate any at the province's major archival repositories.
6 By the mid-nineteenth century, a significant majority of New Brunswickers were born in the province (79 per cent by 1851).
7 Ann Eliza Rogers Diary, MC260, Provincial Archives of New Brunswick (hereafter cited as PANB). For references to people "belonging" in Nova Scotia, see 9 December 1852, 30 June 1853; for references to people "belonging" in New Brunswick, see 4 November 1856, 10 July 1863.
8 Parr, "Notes for a More Sensuous History," 720–45.
9 Harris, "The Spaces of Early Canada," raises the issue of place not only in shaping experience but also in shaping values, and, noting different settlement patterns in different provinces, concludes that "in these circumstances, people in different places told quite different stories" (725–59, quote p. 750).
10 As Nussbaum has pointed out, diaries and journals proliferated in the late seventeenth century, emerging particularly "from the Dissenting groups of Quakers, Methodists and Baptists who urged conversion narratives on their members" ("Eighteenth-Century Women's Autobiographical Commonplaces,"153). In nineteenth-century New Brunswick, moreover, among Protestant denominations, the more evangelical Baptists and Methodists were in the ascendancy throughout the century, while Anglicans and Presbyterians were in decline.
11 Carter, *The Small Details of Life*; Conrad, Laidlaw, and Smyth, *No Place Like Home*; Barman, *Sojourning Sisters*; Noël, *Family Life and Sociability*; Van Die, *Religion, Family and Community*.
12 Occasional clarifications of transcriptions are indicated by square brackets.
13 Compare Rendall, "Women and the Public Sphere," 482. For alternative definitions of "community," see Walsh and High, "Rethinking the Concept of Community," 255–73.
14 Women students did, of course, also consort with their male counterparts; see Marks and Gaffield, "Women at Queen's University," and Prentice, "'Friendly Atoms in Chemistry.'"
15 See Habermas, "The Public Sphere," 49–55. Although this is to use Habermas's conception of the public sphere as "a realm of our social life in which something approaching public opinion can be formed," I recognize that his concept of the public sphere is essentially ahistorical, and has little in common with the public sphere as conceived of by the authors of

the nineteenth-century prescriptive literature promoting an ideology of separate male/female, public/private spheres.

16 For two useful discussions of the inadequacies of the separate spheres framework in analysing women's experience, see Kerber, "Separate Spheres," and Vickery, "Golden Age to Separate Spheres?" For a perceptive analysis of the intersecting, overlapping, and shared lives of one Ontario family, see Van Die, *Religion, Family and Community*.

17 As the editors of a collection of essays on Maritime women's history have noted, and as the documents in this volume will attest, "the ideology of separate spheres was neither a blueprint for the daily reality of 19th-century Maritime women nor the basis for a uniform women's culture or a universal sisterhood" (Guildford and Morton, eds., *Separate Spheres*, 10). Even Davidoff and Hall, whose book *Family Fortunes* became the main focus of the critique of separate spheres, did not claim that their analysis and conclusions extended far beyond the middle class in industrialized English cities.

18 See, for example, Buss, "A Feminist Revision of New Historicism," and Huff, "Textual Boundaries."

19 See, Tosh, *A Man's Place*; Little, "Gender and Gentility," and "The Fireside Kingdom."

20 Arguing that "a single version of the public sphere is insufficient to allow us to understand the complicated variety of ways in which women might identify with communities which stretch far beyond the borders – whatever those were – of home and family," Rendall notes that "Habermas's highly secularised version of the public sphere, for instance, pays very little attention to the understanding of religious identities" ("Women and the Public Sphere," 482–3).

21 On expanding definitions or understandings of the public sphere, see Rendall, "Women and the Public Sphere," 480–3. For the continuing relevance of the debate over "the public/private divide," see Davidoff, "Gender and the Great Divide," who argues that "the debate over separate spheres has become complicated and the terms slippery" (11). For the use of "civil society," see Kelley, *Learning to Stand & Speak*; for the use of "the social," see Hansen, *A Very Social Time*.

1. The Diarists

1 Janet MacDonald Diary, MG H 108, UNBA. A highly edited and abridged version of this diary has been published in Reicker, *Those Days Are Gone Away*, 118–52.

2 Ida MacDonald Diaries, privately held. I thank Alice Taylor for permission to use them.
3 Although George Hendry was born in Scotland, his family had immigrated to America in 1776. Caught in the vortex of a revolutionary war, they waited out the conflict in New York and sailed to Saint John, New Brunswick, with the Loyalists in 1783.
4 A common practice in early-nineteenth-century New Brunswick, this resulted in what Wynn has referred to as "the ubiquitous scatter of small mills serving local demand" (Wynn, "The Rise of Sawmills," chap. 4 in *Timber Colony*, 110).
5 Greenwood, *The Early Baptists of Cambridge Parish*, 43.
6 Information on birth years was calculated based on the 1871 manuscript census returns for Central Cambridge, Queens County, New Brunswick.
7 See 1881 manuscript census returns for Central Cambridge, Queens County, New Brunswick.
8 Jacobina Campbell Diary, York-Sunbury Historical Collection, MC300, MS23/1, PANB. A transcription of this diary has been published in *A Calendar of Life*, edited and introduced by Young and Campbell.
9 Young, "A Calendar of Life in a Narrow Valley." All information about Jacobina Campbell and her family is taken from this source.
10 [Marjory and Isabella] Grant Diary, MC285, PANB.
11 While the identity of the author or authors of the Grant Diary is impossible to confirm, in part because the diary deposited at the Provincial Archives is a transcription of the original, there is much internal evidence that the diarists were Marjory and Isabella. Marjory is not referred to in the diary until the day of her marriage, after which she appears regularly; Isabella, on the other hand, is referred to regularly until the end of February, after which she disappears. The diarists' parents and other siblings are mentioned throughout. Subtle changes in style further support the "two diarists" theory, the most obvious involving a shift in nomenclature from "Mother" and "Father" to "my Mother" and "my Father." The two "voices" do blend into a coherent single whole, for the second diarist closely followed the style established by the first. Its characterization in the PANB finding aid as "the Grant diary" is suitable. I shall refer to the two halves as the Marjory Grant Diary and the Isabella Grant Diary, because I find the internal evidence compelling.
12 Genealogical information on the Grant family drawn from Family Histories, MC1, PANB.
13 Lucy Everett Morrison Diaries, MC1958, PANB.

14 The genealogical and family information provided here owes a good deal to the very fine unpublished genealogical profile of the family written by Patricia Morrison, Lucy's great granddaughter, and deposited with the diaries in the Provincial Archives of New Brunswick (see MC1958, PANB).
15 Sophia Carman Diaries, William F. Ganong Papers, 3456 5 F218-4, F516-S225, New Brunswick Museum Archives (hereafter cited as NBMA). Information from Sophy Carman's diaries was supplemented by correspondence and other documents in the William F. Ganong Papers, 3436 5 F218 LE2, NBMA.
16 Sophy regularly ordered plants from Lucy Morrison; see Sophia Carman Receipt Files for 1884, William F. Ganong Papers, 3436 5 F511, NBMA.
17 Mary Whitney Hill Diary, George Stillman Hill Manuscript Collection, MC1001, MS3E4, PANB.
18 Based on information drawn from the 1851 manuscript census returns for St Stephen, Charlotte County, New Brunswick.
19 The George Stillman Hill Manuscript Collection (MC1001, PANB) deals mainly, but not exclusively, with the political affairs and business correspondence of Mary Hill's father. Fortunately for the historian interested in the history of women and the family, the collection also includes personal papers, particularly an extensive body of correspondence.
20 The first record of Mary teaching school appears in her brother George's diary, written in 1850, when he was eighteen years old. At that time, Mary was teaching across the border in Calais, Maine (see George F. Hill Diary, George Stillman Hill Manuscript Collection, MC1001, MS6/34, PANB). In 1861, Mary was listed as a teacher in the census (see manuscript census returns for St Stephen, New Brunswick, 1861). And in March of 1867, Miss Hill's school, the Church School House near Christ Church, was among the St Stephen schools listed in an article in the *Saint Croix Courier* (St Stephen, 15 March 1867).
21 Will of George Stillman Hill, written 2 March 1857, Probate Records for Charlotte County, 1858, RG 7, RS 63, PANB. George Hill named his wife, Sarah, his sole executrix, devising to her "the use, income, and profits of all my real estate ... during her natural life, for the purpose of ... the nurture, support and education of our family."
22 In 1861, Sarah Hill's household included all eight of her surviving children. By 1871, Sarah, at seventy, headed a household that included six of the eight: Mary, then forty-one; George, thirty-eight; Louisa, thirty-six; Arthur, twenty-nine; Joanna, twenty-four; and Henry, twenty-two, Augusta and

Edgar having married and left home (see manuscript census returns for St Stephen, New Brunswick, 1861 and 1871).
23 I am grateful to Twila Buttimer of the Provincial Archives of New Brunswick for bringing this previously unattributed diary to my attention. Internal evidence made it possible to confirm that the diary was written by Mary Hill.
24 For the opportunities Methodism offered women for leadership, community, and voice, see Lane, "'Wife, Mother, Sister, Friend,'" 113–16.
25 Annie T. Johnston Waltham Diaries, Marianne Grey Otty Papers, S119, NBMA.
26 Thomas Gilbert was a member first of the New Brunswick House of Assembly and, later, of the legislative council. Gilbert, Thomas (Hon), Queens County, MC1156, Vol. 8, part 2, PANB.
27 For a fuller analysis of Annie Waltham's diaries and unfortunate second marriage, see Hutchinson, "'God Help Me for No One Else Can,'" 72–89. Unless otherwise cited, background information on the family also comes from this source.
28 Ann Eliza Rogers Diaries, MC260, PANB.
29 Information calculated from the 1881 manuscript census returns for Hopewell Parish, Albert County, New Brunswick.
30 Mary Isoline Wolhaupter Diary, Marjorie Watters MacMullin fonds, MG H 174, UNBA.
31 Information calculated from the 1851 manuscript census returns for West Simonds/ Wilmot Parish, Carleton County.
32 Given Mary Wolhaupter's focus on "profitable" employment, more than chance may have led her to choose Lynn over the textile towns in Massachusetts. Wages for shoe fitters and stitchers were higher than wages for cotton textile operatives. See Beattie, "'Going Up to Lynn,'" 66.
33 Diary of a King's County Widow (1893–1894), F806, PANB (the Bertha Jones Diary). Identified in the finding aid at the Provincial Archives only as the "Diary of a King's County Widow," this diary offered few clues as to the widow's identity: her farm was situated along a river, probably on the edge of a village, since there was a skate factory nearby, affording her the opportunity to take in boarders. Internal evidence suggests that she had two daughters, Ada and Alma, and one son, Hildrick. But whether Norman, who was planning to leave when the diary opened, was a son or stepson is unclear. Using the diary both to identify other family members and to locate the diarist's community in reference to other places mentioned, the author was identified as Emma Bertha Frost Jones of Greenwich Parish. My thanks to Dorothy Bennett,

research assistant *extraordinaire*, who identified this "King's County Widow."
34 Based on information drawn from the 1851 and 1861 manuscript census returns for Norton, Kings County, New Brunswick.
35 Bertha Frost was listed as a schoolteacher in the 1871 manuscript census returns for Greenwich Parish, Kings County, New Brunswick.
36 See 1891 manuscript census returns for Greenwich Parish, Kings County, New Brunswick. Further information comes from the probated will of Zebulon Jones, 1892, Greenwich Parish, King's County, RG 7, RS 66, [F11718], PANB.
37 Josephine Turner Diary while in Buenos Aires, February–April [1884], Turner Family Papers, 5024 12 S208-1, F34, NBMA.
38 Charlotte Reid Diaries, Turner Family Papers, 5024 12 S208-1, F46-1, NBMA.
39 Based on information drawn from both the diary and the 1871 and 1881 manuscript census returns for Harvey Parish, Albert County, New Brunswick.
40 Josephine Turner Correspondence, Turner Family Papers, 5024 12 S208-1, F43, NBMA.
41 See Turner Family Papers, 5024 12 S208-1, F46 Le-2, NBMA.
42 Annie Trueman Diary (1871–1872), Josiah Wood Manuscript Collection, MC218/6, PANB. See also Laura Trueman's Notebook (1885), Wood Family Papers, 8914/7, Mount Allison University Archives (hereafter cited as MAUA). Although catalogued as "Laura Trueman's Notebook," it was Annie who kept it as a diary for brief periods in 1885, 1886, and 1888. It will, therefore, be cited here as "Annie Trueman Diary (1885, 1886, 1888)."
43 Laura S. Trueman Diary, 1868–1873, Wood Family Papers, 8914/5/1; Laura Trueman Wood Journal of Everyday Affairs, 1878 & 1885, Wood Family Papers, 8510/1/4; Laura Trueman Wood Diary, 1898–1900, Wood Family Papers, 9542, MAUA.
44 See extensive correspondence in the Josiah Wood Manuscript Collection, MC218, PANB.
45 Margaret Loggie Valentine Journal Letter, Loggie Collection, Burnt Church, NB, MG H 128, No. 2, UNBA.
46 Catherine Loggie Diary, 1880–1881, Loggie Collection, Burnt Church, NB, MG H 128, No.1, UNBA. Although this diary was first attributed to Jessie Loggie, the diarist's references to Jessie provide clear evidence that she was not the author. Study of the 1871 and 1881 manuscript census returns for Alnwick Parish, Northumberland County, and a careful reading of the

diary, which mentions sisters Mary and Maggie, confirm that the writer must be the fourth sister – Kate.
47 Jessie Loggie Diary, Loggie Collection, Burnt Church, NB, MG H 128, No. 4, UNBA; Jessie Loggie Journal Letter, Loggie Collection, Burnt Church, NB, MG H 128, No. 3, UNBA.
48 Information from the 1861 manuscript census returns for Alnwick Parish, Northumberland County, New Brunswick.
49 They owned a lobster-canning factory at Big Tracadie, but also dealt in dried cod, herring, smelt, and, above all, fresh salmon. As lumber merchants, they conducted extensive woods operations on the Burnt Church and Tabusintac Rivers, supplying logs for the J.B. Snowball Company at Chatham (Hamilton, "Loggie, Alexander"). According to his obituary, Alexander Loggie was "one of the substantial old-time merchants of the Miramichi ... distinguished for his geniality no less than for his integrity" ("Death of Alex. Loggie, Esq.," *Miramichi Advance*, 6 May 1897, cited in Daniel F. Johnson's New Brunswick Newspaper Vital Statistics, PANB).
50 See Trustees' Returns, 1880, McRobbie's Road, School District 8, Alnwick Parish, Northumberland County, RS657, PANB.
51 *The World* (Chatham), 20 December 1893. Maggie Loggie and William Valentine married on 5 May 1873. *Union Advocate* (Newcastle), 14 May 1873, cited in Daniel F. Johnson's New Brunswick Newspaper Vital Statistics, PANB.
52 Margaret Loggie Valentine to Mrs Alexander Loggie, Journal Letter (1885).
53 The search for the picturesque began to emerge as an aesthetic movement as early as the mid-eighteenth century. For a discussion of this phenomenon, see Ghose, *Women Travellers*, 38–42, and Pratt, *Imperial Eyes*, 10, 201–8.
54 Amelia Holder Diaries, MC665, MS1 [Microfilm: F569], PANB. Amelia Holder's diary of her second voyage, "September 1868–March 1869," when her sister Agnes and brother Abram were also on board, is published with an introduction by Joanne Ritchie in Carter, ed., *The Small Details of Life*, 95–115.
55 Emma Alice Pitt Diary, MC827, PANB. A very lightly edited version of this diary is published in McGahan, ed., *Whispers from the Past*, 79–91.
56 Insight into the family's life on-shore during Edwin's absences is afforded through various letters in Bannister, Fullerton, Holder, Duplisea, Titus, Duplisea, Barnett, and Quigley, compilers, "Sea Going Days," MC80.1723, PANB. For a contextualized discussion of this pattern in seagoing families,

see Clayton, "Maintaining the Mariner's Family at Home," chap. 3 of "'A Long Voyage Before Us.'"
57 Druett found, for example, that about half of all merchant captains took their families with them in the last half of the nineteenth and early-twentieth centuries. *Hen Frigates*, 90.
58 This summary owes a great deal to Clayton, "'A Long Voyage Before Us.'"
59 Amelia's shore-based diaries cover the periods 17–19 August 1873, 15 October 1873–25 December 1874 (not continuous), 3–24 August 1875, 30 November 1875, 18, 25, and 31 December 1875, 30 October 1877, and 1–5 January 1879. Aggie's sporadic entries date from 1–2 April 1873 (arriving home after a voyage with her father and Amelia), 11 June and 20 July 1873, and 22 February 1874. And Ada's brief periods of diary keeping occurred between 3 November 1872 and 18 April 1873, 24 January 1874, 17 February 1874, and 1–4 March 1874. See MC665, MS1 [Microfilm: F569], PANB.
60 Calder, *All Our Born Days*, 126.
61 Lillian Williamson Diary, S155-6, NBMA.
62 Information from 1871 manuscript census returns for Greenwich Parish, Kings County, New Brunswick.
63 Alvaretta Estabrooks Diary, 1889, MC259, MS1A, PANB; Alvaretta Estabrooks Diaries, 1890–91, 1892–93, Marjorie Watters MacMullin fonds, MG H 174, UNBA.
64 Hannah Estabrooks Diary, Marjorie Watters MacMullin fonds, MG H 174, UNBA.
65 *Christian Visitor* (Saint John), 10 October 1883 (cited in Daniel F. Johnson's New Brunswick Newspaper Vital Statistics, PANB).
66 For the death of George Else's wife, see *The Daily Telegraph* (Saint John), 30 July 1884. For the marriage of Mrs Agnes E. Estabrooks and George E. Else, see *Carleton Sentinel* (Woodstock), 16 May 1886 (cited in Daniel F. Johnson's New Brunswick Newspaper Vital Statistics, PANB).
67 In 1891, George Else was listed as the head of a household which included Agnes and her three daughters, but neither of her sons (1891 Manuscript Census returns for Simonds Parish, Carleton County, PANB). For George Else's death see *Christian Messenger and Visitor* (Saint John), 11 September 1895 (cited in Daniel F. Johnson's New Brunswick Newspaper Vital Statistics, PANB).
68 Marriage Record of George C. Estabrooks, Rockland, and Sarah Jane Else, Rockland, 24 January 1888, RS141, B1a [F13378], PANB.
69 By the opening pages of Alva's 1889 diary, it would appear that George was a widower, the father of a baby who would not long outlive its mother. For George's baby, see Alvaretta Estabrooks Diary, 11–15 January

1889. For George's death, see Alvaretta Estabrooks Diary, April–May, 1890. There is no mention of George's wife in these entries.
70 In the 1891 manuscript census, Arthur is recorded as living in the household of Charles Harmon, a merchant in nearby Peel Parish. His occupation is recorded as "clerk." See 1891 manuscript census returns for Peel Parish, Carleton County, PANB.
71 The information in this paragraph is drawn largely from Hayward, *Pioneer Families*, 17–18. That Alva divided her time between the two homes is clear in her 1891 diary entries and also in the manuscript census, where she is listed in both the Hayward household and the Else/Estabrooks household. See diary of Alvaretta Estabrooks, 1891, and the manuscript census returns for Simonds Parish, Carleton County and Brighton Parish, Carleton County, PANB.
72 Information from 1901 manuscript census returns for Brighton Parish, Carleton County, New Brunswick.
73 Information from 1900 manuscript census returns for Lewiston, Maine, USA (online).
74 Laura Cynthia Fullerton Diary, 1886, 630, 8021, MAUA.
75 Information from 1881 and 1891 manuscript census returns for Mill Village, Cumberland County, Nova Scotia.
76 As cited in Reid, *Mount Allison University*, 140.
77 See, for example, Peck, ed., *A Full House and Fine Singing*. Similarly, Selles, *Methodists & Women's Education*, argues that students' behaviour was closely monitored and their time tightly scheduled. See, especially, chap. 5.
78 Sadie Harper Diaries, MC286, PANB. An edited version of Sadie Harper Allen's diaries and letters has already been published, and the excerpts included in this book provide only the merest glimpse of this prolific diarist. Readers are encouraged to consult Mary Biggar Peck's text for the full range of Sadie's experience; see Peck, ed., *A Full House and Fine Singing*.
79 Information from 1891 manuscript census returns for Shediac, Westmorland County, New Brunswick.
80 Violet Goldsmith Diary, MG H 133, UNBA.
81 Much of the information on Violet's early life comes from http://www.alittlehistory.com/Vi-schol.htm. Charlotte Stewart, the housekeeper Violet would remember most fondly as having been "a real mother to us," was still living with the family when the census was taken in 1891. John Goldsmith's younger sister Maggie, who had lived with the family when Violet was a baby, joined them again in 1895 or 1896 according to Violet's later memoir. See also the 1881 manuscript census returns for Township 13

(Tyne Valley) District 1, Prince Edward Island, and 1891 manuscript census returns for 133 Kings Division, District 1, Prince Edward Island (online).
82 A superior school licence would allow Violet to prepare students for normal school and university entrance examinations, making her eligible for a higher rate of pay.
83 "Class of 1905," *The University Monthly*, Vol. 25, no. 1 (University of New Brunswick), UA RG84, UNBA.
84 Katherine Miles Diary, MC1145, MS2, PANB.
85 Information from 1891 and 1901 manuscript census returns for Maugerville, Sunbury County, New Brunswick.
86 Sade Waycott was Kate's best friend.

2. Reading Nineteenth-Century Diaries

1 Conrad, "'Sundays always make me think of home,'" and "Recording Angels."
2 Compare, for example, Mallon, *A Book of One's Own*, which went through six editions between 1984 and 1995, and Bunkers and Huff, eds., *Inscribing the Daily*.
3 Blodgett, "Preserving the Moment," 167, 156. Blodgett critiques the work of Culley, *A Day at a Time*, and Lensink, "Expanding the Boundaries of Criticism," as having blurred this significant distinction. Nussbaum, *The Autobiographical Subject*, shares this tendency.
4 Blodgett, "Preserving the Moment," 168.
5 This definition of historical consciousness and, in particular, the articulation of the concept of distance-consciousness, owes a good deal to Phillips, "History, Memory, and Historical Distance," 89–99 (quote p. 99). In the introduction to *Theorizing Historical Consciousness*, Seixas offers a broader definition, which I have also drawn on: Seixas defines distance-consciousness as "individual and collective understandings of the past, the cognitive and cultural factors that shape those understandings, as well as the relations of historical understandings to those of the present and the future" (10).
6 The clearest example in Canadian historical writing of the potential impact of what might be considered historical voyeurism is the popular reappraisal of Prime Minister Mackenzie King following the publication of Stacey's *A Very Double Life*.
7 Huff made this argument and went on to assert that diaries are "accessible not exclusive, comprehensible not arcane, and in their very accessibility they establish ties between the reader and the writer, between one human

being and another" ("'That Profoundly Female, and Feminist Genre,'" 6). A decade later, however, Huff herself revised this statement, having recognized that "learning how to read manuscript diaries is complicated detective work, a labor of frustration and love, which allows us much latitude for interpretation yet often gives us few clues" ("Reading as Re-Vision," 506).

8 Mallon makes precisely this assertion in *A Book of One's Own*, xvii.
9 Laura Cynthia Fullerton Diary, 1886.
10 Mr Borden was the principal of the Ladies' Academy. He also taught composition.
11 Luke 19:41–2: "And when he was come near, he beheld the city, and wept over it, Saying, If thou hadst known, even thou, at least in this thy day, the things *which belong* unto thy peace! but now they are hid from thine eyes."
12 Mrs (Mary Mellish) Archibald, a widow, served as preceptress and vice-principal of the Ladies' Academy from 1885 to 1901 (d. 1901). She taught geometry, physiology, and even composition.
13 Galatians 1:4: "Who gave himself for our sins, that he might deliver us from this present evil world, according to the will of God and our Father."
14 Huff, "'That Profoundly Female, and Feminist Genre,'" 6.
15 Jacobina Campbell Diary, 1825.
16 "Whitetop" is probably *Erigeron strigosus*, or daisy fleabane, which flowers in August; its use is not known. I thank Dr Mary Young for this information.
17 See Motz, "Folk Expression, of Time and Place." Jacobina Campbell's diary, while typical of the kind of diary Motz characterizes as "folk diaries," does not "represent an attempt to find patterns in even the least controllable and predictable aspects of life, weather, and death" (145).
18 Young, "A Calendar of Life."
19 Cottam, "Diaries and Journals," 268.
20 For a discussion of the ubiquity and limitations of printed pocket diaries, see McCarthy, "A Pocketful of Days," 274–96.
21 Emma received her diary in 1873 and maintained it for a single year. Kate Miles had likewise received her diary as a gift; she used it to record her daily activities throughout 1901, when she was attending Fredericton High School, boarding in town through the week and spending weekends and holidays at home.
22 I am indebted to Gwen Davies for the information on the Sarah Frost diaries and to Jenny Clayton for the information on the two versions of Amelia Holder's diaries. See also Davies, "The Diary of Sarah Frost, 1783," 57–69.

23 The definitive clue signalling this change is the disappearance of Isabella's name and the appearance of Marjory's name in particular entries.
24 Used as the title for Hutchinson's article, "'God Help Me for No One Else Can,'" which focusses on the diarist's relationship with her second husband, it should be noted that this was a *cri de coeur* Annie Gilbert Johnston used regularly even before her disastrous marriage to Mr Waltham. See Annie T. Johnston Waltham Diaries, 1 and 13 February 1870.
25 For an example of the very best of such analysis, see Ulrich, *A Midwife's Tale*. See also Carter's perceptive analysis in "An Economy of Words."
26 Smyth, "'Thinking Back Through Our Mothers,'" 19.
27 Charlotte Reid Diaries, 4, 6, and 9 January 1879.
28 Bloom, "Adolescence and Life Writing," 6.
29 Laura Trueman Wood Journal of Everyday Affairs, 1878 & 1885. See also Laura Trueman Wood, "Biographical Note," n.d., Josiah Wood Manuscript Collection, MC218/5, PANB.
30 Hannah Estabrooks was not recorded in the 1901 New Brunswick census, but was located in the 1900 census for Lewiston, Androscoggin County, Maine. Then twenty-nine years old, Hannah was working as a housekeeper in a household that included a forty-three-year-old travelling salesman, his wife and small child, and a sixty-nine-year-old mill worker. In 1901, her older brother Arthur, along with his wife and small daughter, was living at home on the family farm with their mother and younger sister Nellie, a school teacher. At that time, his occupation was listed as "farmer," but by 1903, Arthur and his family had moved to Rockland, where he served as bookkeeper and manager in the store where Hannah worked. First settled as a farming community in the 1820s, Rockland had been renamed Coldstream when the post office was created in 1852, but it would appear from the Estabrooks diaries that the local population continued to use both names, giving their address as Coldstream, but referring to the village as Rockland.
31 Hannah Estabrooks Diary, 5 November 1905.
32 See Hannah Estabrooks Diary, entry for 4 May 1903, reporting on a friend who was planning to return to the United States to work: "I almost wish I could go back with her but I think I am better here."
33 Probated will of George S. Hill, 1858, RG 7, RS 63, PANB. For a case study of the significance and extent of women's investment income in late-nineteenth-century Canada, see Baskerville, "Women and Investment," 191–218.
34 For a good discussion of the difficulties in maintaining such an independence for one group of nineteenth-century businesswomen, see Gamber,

"A Precarious Independence." For New Brunswick, see Larocque, "'The Work Being Chiefly Performed by Women,'" 139–65. Of the thirty-seven businesses he located, twenty-two were owned and operated by women (157).
35 Mary Hill's age, reported as forty-one in 1871 when she was still living in her mother's household in St Stephen, was recorded as forty-five in the 1881 census when she was living on her own in St Andrews. Annie Trueman, whose age was recorded as twenty-eight in the Sackville census for 1881 was reported as age thirty-two in the 1891 census. In both years, she was living in her parents' household.
36 Mary Isoline Wolhaupter Diary, 13 March 1869.
37 Hannah Estabrooks Diary, 25 February 1903.
38 Lillian Williamson Diary, 1 June 1883.
39 Annie T. Johnston Waltham Diaries, 26 October 1880. See also Hutchinson, "'God Help Me for No One Else Can.'"
40 E. Bertha Frost Jones Diary. See also probated Will of Zebulon Jones, 1892, Greenwich Parish, King's County, RG 7, RS 66, [F11718], PANB.
41 Sophia Carman Diaries, March–April 1883.
42 Janet Hendry MacDonald Diary, 15 October 1857, 28 September 1858. Donati's comet was discovered by Giovanni Donati in June of 1858.
43 Ulrich, *A Midwife's Tale*, 8–9.
44 Ulrich, *A Midwife's Tale*, 25.
45 Carter, "An Economy of Words," 56.
46 Carter, "An Economy of Words," 44.
47 Carter, "An Economy of Words," 50–1. Lejeune also assumes that every diary is interesting, arguing that "they don't have to be evaluated like literary works, which they are not," and further noting that "a historian does not have to select material" ("The 'Journal de Jeune Fille,'" 112).
48 James Robb to Jane Robb, 26 February 1839, in Bailey, ed., *The Letters of James and Ellen Robb*, 26. King's College would, of course, become the University of New Brunswick.
49 The "Boston States" referred to New England in general and, for New Brunswickers, to Massachusetts and Maine in particular.
50 Huff, "Reading as Re-Vision," 514.
51 Patrocinio Schweickart, cited in Huff, "Reading as Re-Vision," 521–2.
52 See Patricia Morrison's unpublished genealogy, MC 1958, PANB. I am grateful to the Morrisons for their generosity in talking to me and sharing their knowledge of their great grandmother with me.
53 "Father" is a reference to Lucy's husband John.
54 Consider, for example, the differing interpretations of Carter, in analysing Emma Chadwick Stretch's description of her baby's illness and Ulrich in

explaining the fleeting reference Martha Ballard makes to her daughter's birthday in the middle of dealing with an epidemic; see Carter, "An Economy of Words," 52–3, and Ulrich, *A Midwife's Tale*, 36, 43, as well as the more extensive discussion in the film based on Ulrich's book.
55 For an exploration of the financial contribution made by middle-class matrons to the family economy, see Guildford, "'Whate'er the duty of the hour demands,'" 1–20.

3. The Life Course in Demographic Context

1 Rounding has been used for convenience. For the precise numbers, see Appendix, Table 1.
2 The aggregate and manuscript censuses, as well as other government documentation, which have provided much of the demographic information used in this study, are unreliable with regard to the comparatively small groups of First Nations peoples and Blacks in New Brunswick. It has therefore seemed advisable not to try to include these groups in this analysis.
3 The proportion of native-born remained steady in that decade, at 79 per cent.
4 Although individuals changed allegiance fairly regularly, the denominational breakdown shifted only minimally between 1861 and 1871, when the distribution was 24 per cent Baptist, 16 per cent Anglican, 14 per cent Presbyterian, 10 per cent Methodist, and 34 per cent Roman Catholic.
5 Acadians are not distinguished from other native-born New Brunswickers in earlier decennial censuses, and even this figure – also used in Roy, "Settlement and Population Growth," 170 – is based on the assumption that those who self-identified as French were overwhelmingly Acadian. The Acadian proportion of the population increased steadily, reaching 28 per cent by 1911 (see Appendix, Table 2).
6 From 1851 through 1871, the gender balance remained stable at 51 per cent male and 49 per cent female.
7 See Appendix, Table 3, for the rural-urban distribution by census year. In 1871, just 18 per cent of New Brunswickers lived in centres with more than 1,000 inhabitants. This was below the national average of 23 per cent. By 1891, the national average had risen to 33 per cent, but the New Brunswick average had risen to only 20 per cent. For New Brunswick, see *Historical Statistics of New Brunswick*, 21–2; for Canada, see Measner and Hampson, "The Canadian Population, 1871, 1891," Plate 29.

8 The demographic snapshots presented in this chapter are largely drawn from my own research and, unless otherwise noted, are based on a quantitative analysis of manuscript census returns for the entire population of three New Brunswick counties – Albert, Charlotte, and Sunbury – for 1851, 1861, and 1871, supplemented by 1851 manuscript census returns for at least one parish population from each of the remaining nine counties for which the 1851 manuscript census returns are extant. The 1851 manuscript returns provided the basis for the calculations of converging and diverging patterns. Taken together, the returns used include 25 per cent of New Brunswick's population in 1851. Of those included in the analysis, 13 per cent were Acadian, an approximate representation of the Acadian proportion of the population in 1851. Under-enumeration was not a significant problem in the mid-nineteenth century with regard to the dominant populations, though First Nations and transient workers (such as railroad navvies), certainly were under-enumerated. The problem of multiple recording of names is addressed in this analysis by the use of the manuscript rather than the aggregate census (compare Curtis, *The Politics of Population*, 17).
9 For the changing nature of domestic privacy, see Ward, *A History of Domestic Space*.
10 "Parish" and "common" were used interchangeably in nineteenth-century New Brunswick, to describe what we would today call public elementary schools.
11 In his comparison of an urban and a rural school district in Saint John City and County, Caplan, "'A Law Unto Oneself,'" found a similar pattern, although attendance in the rural district remained considerably lower than in the urban district. Moreover, the St Stephen pattern mirrors that of Ontario, where enrollments rose from 61 per cent of the school-aged population in 1851 to 86 per cent in 1871 (Houston and Prentice, *Schooling and Scholars*, 200).
12 MacNaughton, *The Development of the Theory and Practice of Education*, 200, shows that, as a result of the 1871 legislation, in Gloucester enrollment declined significantly and in Kent, Northumberland, and Victoria it remained stationary.
13 Andrew, *The Development of Elites*, 84–5. Catholics, protesting the withdrawal of subsidies under the Free Schools Act, refused to pay school taxes and in some cases Acadian local officials refused to collect taxes for the secular system (see also Andrew, "Selling Education," 19–21). Some 16 per cent of New Brunswick's population was Acadian in 1871; 34 per cent was Roman Catholic. However, the proportion of Roman Catholics

ranged from a low of 8 per cent in Albert County to a high of 85 per cent in Gloucester (Migneault, *Les Acadiens du Nouveau-Brunswick*, 56). For a breakdown of the percentage of Roman Catholics for all counties, see Appendix, Table 4.

14 The experience of being taught in the parish schools of the province changed with the generations. In the 1840s, teacher training was introduced, and in the 1850s, the province moved towards standardization of the curriculum. In 1841, 80 per cent of the teachers in the parish schools were men; by 1901, 80 per cent of the teachers were women.

15 In 1871, 86 per cent of thirteen-year-olds in St Andrews, New Brunswick, were enrolled in schools; by age fourteen, the proportion dropped to 66 per cent, and by age sixteen, to 28 per cent. The pattern proved similar on the national level. As late as 1901, although 86 per cent of Canadian ten-year-olds and 82 per cent of twelve-year-olds were enrolled in school, the proportion dropped to 73 per cent by age thirteen, 57 per cent by age fourteen, and 29 per cent by age sixteen (see Mandeville, "'What a gap that leaf may make,'" 23, and "Who Went to School?," 41).

16 Young Acadian men were at least as likely as their sisters to be listed as "servants" in the census, though they were undoubtedly farm hands, while their sisters were domestics.

17 Acheson, *Saint John*, 238–9.

18 Acheson, *Saint John*, 239. For Montreal, see Cross, "The Neglected Majority," 67–71.

19 Biggs, "Domestic Service," 125–7.

20 Biggs, "Domestic Service," 154–9. See also Lacelle, *Urban Domestic Servants*.

21 For Saint John, see Biggs, "Domestic Service," 167.

22 LaRocque, "'The Work Being Chiefly Performed by Women,'" 150–3.

23 For the response of Maritime entrepreneurs to the opportunities offered by the National Policy, which introduced protective tariffs to encourage the establishment and growth of a wide range of manufacturing industries, see Acheson, "The National Policy."

24 Acheson, "The National Policy," 14.

25 Pond, *The History of Marysville*, 27.

26 Cited in Pond, *The History of Marysville*, 28.

27 Significant numbers of those adolescent boys were employed in Gibson's lumber operations.

28 Figures calculated from the 1881 and 1891 manuscript censuses for Marysville, York County, including, for 1881, the census district.

29 For St Stephen/Milltown, see DeLottinville, "Trouble in the Hives of Industry,"106. For New Brunswick Acadian workers in mills

in Amherst, Nova Scotia, see Muise, "The Industrial Context of Inequality."
30 Financial difficulties caused the closure of the female department between 1843 and 1857, and again in 1872. The seminary closed entirely two years later. In 1882, the Baptist seminary was re-established as a coeducational institution in Saint John. In 1888, it was relocated to St Martins. Plagued by debt despite attracting significant numbers of students, it closed definitively in 1895. (Trites, "The New Brunswick Baptist Seminary").
31 Reid, "The Education of Women at Mount Allison," 6.
32 The New Brunswick census reported seventeen Acadian girls over the age of sixteen enrolled in school in 1861, thirty in 1871, and eighty-two in 1881. Students over the age of sixteen were, of course, only a very tiny fraction of girls attending the province's convent schools. The school at Buctouche, for example, had 118 girls enrolled in 1880, the year it opened (Andrew, "Selling Education," 17–23).
33 The provincial teacher-training institution. The first normal school opened in Fredericton in February 1848, and, before the year was out, a second one opened in Saint John. Although the Saint John normal school had no permanent building, when the Fredericton school burned to the ground in 1850, the Saint John school became the only provincial normal school. A second normal school was established in Chatham in 1867, and the two schools operated until 1870, when the government decided to establish and operate a single normal school in Fredericton (Picot, *A Brief History of Teacher Training in New Brunswick*, 13–34).
34 MacNaughton, *The Development of the Theory and Practice of Education*, 141.
35 "Report of the Principal of the Normal School," *Journals of the House of Assembly of the Province of New Brunswick* (hereafter cited as *JHA*), 1880.
36 On the normal school students of 1882–3, see Thorne, "Higher Education for New Brunswick Women." The normal school held two sessions that year, with twenty-nine men and 137 women in the nine-month session and seven men and eight women in the three-month session (designed for teachers seeking to upgrade licences). Thorne's findings parallel those of Prentice, "'Friendly Atoms in Chemistry,'" and Bernard and Vinovskis, "The Female School Teacher."
37 "Report of the Principal of the Normal School," *JHA*, 1878.
38 Declaration signed by all student-teachers prior to entering the Provincial Normal School, Chief Superintendent's Report, *JHA*, 1878.
39 Leila DeWolfe to Maria Moore DeWolfe, 11 November 1877, Moore-DeWolfe Collection, [F4249], PANB. Leila was eighteen.

40 Andrew, "Selling Education," 24–5. Many Acadian women continued to depend on the convent schools to prepare them for teaching, as the provincial normal school did not open a French department until 1878, and, until 1884, offered students in that department only a third-class licence. Picot, *A Brief History of Teacher Training in New Brunswick*, 41–3.
41 Even before 1800, immigrants who had come as Loyalists had begun drifting back, and those who stayed and could afford it often sent their children to private schools in the United States.
42 On out-migration in the later period, see Brookes, "Out-Migration," and Thornton, "The Problem of Out-Migration." For young New Brunswick women seeking work in Nova Scotia and New England, see Muise, "The Industrial Context of Inequality," and Beattie, "'Going up to Lynn.'"
43 For an example of farm family persistence in one New Brunswick community, despite consistent patterns of out-migration between 1851 and 1901, see Lewis, "Rooted in the Soil."
44 These marriage rates reflect the New Brunswick pattern as calculated by Gee in "Marriage in Nineteenth-Century Canada," 320. They also conform fairly closely to Medjuck's figures for Moncton during the same period ("Women's Response to Economic and Social Change," 14–15). Gee calculated the average marriage age for women to be 26 in 1871, 25.4 in 1881, and 26.3 in 1891, and the average age at marriage for men was 28.8 in 1871 and 29.4 in 1881 and 1891, respectively.
45 Or 21 per cent of all women and 35 per cent of all men in this age cohort.
46 The balance shifted slightly as the century progressed. Biggs reckons that the proportion of servants in Saint John in the sixteen to twenty-five age cohort declined from 67.8 per cent in 1851 to 58 per cent in 1891 (Biggs, "Domestic Service,"124).
47 Information on the Bubars comes from the manuscript census returns for 1891 and 1901 and from Daniel F. Johnson's New Brunswick Newspaper Vital Statistics, PANB website.
48 Fewer than ten married women were recorded as working at the Marysville cotton mill in the 1891 census. Similarly, although "marriage was not a bar to employment" at Ganong Bros. confectionary factory, the majority of female employees were young and single (McCallum, "Separate Spheres," 77).
49 While just 28 per cent of adolescent female mill workers were lodgers, 47 per cent of female mill workers in the twenty-one to twenty-five age category were lodgers. The contrast for men was even more stark: while just 13 per cent of adolescent male mill workers were lodgers, 43 per cent

of male workers in the twenty-one to twenty-five age cohort were living as lodgers (manuscript census for Marysville, 1891).
50 See various issues of the *Education Circular for the Province of New Brunswick* for reports of the teachers' institutes, including transcriptions of some of the speeches. For an account of the exceptional newspaper coverage of a speech at a teachers' institute meeting by one particularly gifted Acadian woman teacher, see Andrew, "Selling Education," 26.
51 For an analysis of the situation in Nova Scotia, see Guildford, "'Separate Spheres': The Feminization of Public School Teaching."
52 Sadie Harper's future husband served as both a teacher and a school principal in her community, saving money to attend university to prepare for a career in university teaching. Nonetheless, careers in teaching at the elementary school level were much more common than either contemporaries or scholars have claimed. See LaVorgna, "Lessons in Mid-Nineteenth-Century New Brunswick Teacher Careerism."
53 Mount Allison opened its doors to women in 1873, graduating its first woman with a bachelor's degree in 1875; the University of New Brunswick admitted women in 1886, graduating its first woman in 1889.
54 Field, "The First Generation of Women," and Hansen, *Those Certain Women*. For the first generation of Dalhousie women, see Fingard, "College, Career and Community." For the impact of role models and women's academies, see Kelley, *Learning to Stand & Speak*.
55 For an Ontario example, see Smith and Strong-Boag, "*A Woman With a Purpose*."
56 See Craig, *Backwoods Consumers*.
57 Catherine Kelly notes that, in nineteenth-century New England, women's participation in voluntary societies was similarly constrained by childbearing and childrearing, with "the most active members and officers ... frequently single women or middle-aged matrons" (Kelly, *In the New England Fashion*, 202).
58 Gagan, *Hopeful Travellers*, 86. Women in pre-Confederation Upper Canada "expected to become pregnant shortly after their wedding, and then again at approximately two to three year intervals thereafter until they reached menopause" (Errington, *Wives and Mothers, School Mistresses and Scullery Maids*, 58).
59 Mitchinson, *The Nature of Their Bodies*, 159. Apparently this average had not changed by 1870. See Allen, "Contextualizing Late-Nineteenth-Century Feminism," 35.
60 Charlotte and York counties were selected both because they were among the most densely populated and for their balance between town and

country. For the purposes of analysis, married women were divided into seven age cohorts: seventeen to twenty, twenty-one to twenty-five, twenty-six to thirty, thirty-one to thirty-five, thirty-six to forty, forty-one to forty-five, and forty-six to fifty. Women in second marriages and women who had been widowed before the age of fifty were eliminated from the calculations. While both means and medians were calculated, the median was used as the most accurate measure of central tendency as, unlike the mean, it cannot be distorted by outliers. "Peak marital fertility" refers to the age cohort during which women who survived childbearing completed their families. For women in both the previous (thirty-six to forty) and following (forty-six to fifty) cohorts, the median number of children was slightly lower (five). A median of six living children by age forty-five conforms with Mitchinson's findings, given the infant and child mortality rates during this period. In her study of Upper Canada, Jane Errington estimated that families could expect that at least one of their children would not reach adolescence (Errington, *Wives and Mothers*, 69).

61 Thus, while the median number of children for rural women in the forty-one to forty-five age cohort was six, the corresponding median for Fredericton women was four. By 1901, the medians had declined in both cases, to four in the case of rural women and to three in the case of Fredericton women. In nineteenth century Saint-Hyacinthe, fertility differentials between rural and urban communities were not great. See Gossage, *Families in Transition*, 156. See also McInnis, "The Population of Canada," 388–415.

62 Shediac Parish in Westmorland County, Dalhousie Parish in Restigouche County, and St-Basile and St-Léonard in Victoria County were selected to provide a basis for comparison between British and Acadian experiences. As in the case of Charlotte and York counties, calculations are based on an analysis of the 1851 and 1901 manuscript censuses; see also McInnis, "The Population of Canada."

63 Errington, *Wives and Mothers*, 54–61.

64 Gagan gives this one-in-five figure for women who married in Peel County in the 1840s and 1850s (*Hopeful Travellers*, 89). Mitchinson cautions about the difficulties of estimating maternal mortality rates. Moreover, statistics suggest that maternal mortality declined after mid-century. Statistics from the 1871 census indicate that maternal mortality accounted for only 8.1 per cent of the deaths of New Brunswick women during their childbearing years, which was lower than Ontario's rate of 10.8 per cent. As Mitchinson points out, however, the census figures were, no doubt, unrealistically low. For useful discussions of the difficulties estimating maternal mortality

rates, see Mitchinson, *The Nature of Their Bodies*, 224–9, and Emery, *Facts of Life*, 117–26.

65 Mitchinson, *The Nature of Their Bodies*, 54. Mitchinson further notes that in 1901, while women constituted 48 per cent of the population, they accounted for 56 per cent of deaths from tuberculosis, and that most of these deaths occurred in the childbearing years.

66 Hoffman and Taylor, *Much To Be Done*, 45. See also Errington, *Wives and Mothers*, 59–60.

67 For the fertility transition in Canada, see McInnis, "The Fertility Transition," Plate 30.

68 Allen, "Contextualizing Late-Nineteenth-Century Feminism," 35. Still, as Gossage found in his study of Saint-Hyacinthe, given the decline in infant mortality rates, even a 20 per cent decline in fertility rates between the 1850s and the 1880s did not necessarily mean fewer surviving children (*Families in Transition*, 158).

69 McInnis, "The Population of Canada," 393. For a fuller discussion of explanations for the fertility transition in Canada, see 388–415.

70 While the proportion of mothers under the age of thirty-one declined in both British and Acadian parishes between 1851 and 1901, Acadian levels in 1901 remained higher than British levels in 1851. Thus, while in Charlotte and York counties, the proportion of married women under the age of twenty-six declined from 16 per cent of the total to 12 per cent, in the four Acadian parishes the proportion declined from 22 per cent to 18 per cent. Similarly, while in Charlotte and York counties, the proportion of married women under the age of thirty-one declined from 34 per cent to 28 per cent, in the Acadian parishes, the proportion declined from 41 per cent to 33 per cent. It should be recalled that "the total" in each case refers to the total number of married women under the age of fifty-one, for whom this was a first marriage. Given these differentials, it is perhaps not surprising that the Acadian proportion of the population rose to 24 per cent by 1901 and 28 per cent by 1911.

71 Settled earlier than Ontario and the West, the Maritimes and Quebec had achieved a more even gender balance, leading to a convergence between the proportion of spinsters and bachelors. The closest balance was in New Brunswick, where, by 1881, the proportion of single people over the age of thirty-one had risen to 17 per cent of both women and men (Stairs, "Matthews and Marillas," 249–50).

72 Agricultural and industrial schedule for the manuscript censuses for Albert, Charlotte, and Sunbury Counties, 1851. See also Craig, *Backwoods Consumers*.

73 By comparison, potatoes produced for market in 1860 were valued at $1,697,000 (statistics from Acheson, "New Brunswick Agriculture," 13). Acheson estimates that over two-thirds of New Brunswick farms were producing marketable surpluses by 1860, including surpluses in butter, cheese, wool, and cloth.

74 Rygiel, "'Thread in Her Hands,'" 59–61. For a comparative analysis of the commercial significance of domestic textile production, which also includes a case study of Madawaska, New Brunswick, see Craig, Rygiel, and Turcotte, "The Homespun Paradox," 28–57.

75 Account Ledger, Hazen, White and Company, General Merchants, Oromocto, 1785–1821, and also Account Ledger for Nathaniel Hubbard, Burton, York-Sunbury Historical Society Collection, PANB. Although the weaving is credited to the accounts of the various family heads, it was no doubt the contribution of the women in the family to the household economy. Cited in Wallace-Casey, "'Providential Openings,'" (MA); and "'Providential Openings,'" 37. For a similar pattern in an earlier period see Mancke, "At the Counter of the General Store."

76 Craig and Rygiel, "Femmes, marchés et production textile," argue that it was profit, not poverty, that motivated women weavers.

77 Although based on an analysis of widowhood and remarriage in Albert, Charlotte, and Sunbury counties, this pattern has emerged in other studies as well. See Gossage, *Families in Transition*, 89, and Bradbury, "Surviving as a Widow," 149–50.

78 Davis, "'Patriarchy from the Grave,'" argues that men sought to exercise continuing control over their wives through their wills. Pickles, "Locating Widows," lends support to this view. But other scholars have painted a different picture. See chap. 2 of Baskerville, *A Silent Revolution?*, Elliott, *Irish Migrants in the Canadas*, 198–201, and Waciega, "A 'Man of Business,'" 40–64.

79 Only a focus on the experience of widows can reveal the variety of their experiences. See Bradbury, "Widowhood and Canadian Family History." This she has provided for Montreal in *Wife to Widow*, "Part 2: Individual Itineraries of Widowhood."

80 Charlotte County Probate Court Records, RG 7, RS 63, PANB. This is part of a larger analysis of more than 250 Charlotte County wills written and probated during this period. Testators included 151 husbands, 40 widowers, 21 widows, 36 bachelors and 5 spinsters. I am grateful to Michele Stairs and David Bent who transcribed half the wills examined for the purposes of this analysis. Wherever possible, decedents and their families were traced to the 1851, 1861, and 1871 manuscript censuses.

81 Fifty-four of the 151 husbands. Significantly, no other group of testators – widowers, bachelors, widows, or spinsters – appointed a higher percentage of women as executrix.
82 The failure to mention children did not necessarily mean that the couples were childless. Some had adult children who were already well established.
83 Although this underlying issue is not made explicit in such wills, it surfaces elsewhere. See, for example, the 1869 will of widower Neville Parker. Parker left £500, or $2,000, each to his daughters Jane, Julia, Mary, and Florence, along with an equal share with his four sons of the residue of his estate, but further stipulated that "the bequest to and share of the residue of any married daughter whose coverture may continue at the time of such distribution is to be invested in good securities ... to pay interest or dividends to such married daughter," but if she outlived her husband, she was to gain control of the whole and the right to dispose of the residue in her will.
84 For a similar view of the issue, though one which does not speculate on the wife's view, see Baskerville, *A Silent Revolution?* 60–1, and Elliott, *Irish Migrants in the Canadas*, 200.
85 Similarly, in her research on the transmission of property in the upper St John River valley, Craig found that parents sought to ensure their own economic security in old age, and that, in their wills, men gave priority to the security of their widows and minor children over the needs of their adult children ("La transmission des patrimoines fonciers," 220–6).
86 Often the son who inherited the farm (who might or might not be married himself) was already living in the homestead with his parents at the time of his father's death.
87 In three instances, the will specifically stipulated that if he failed to meet the standards of support outlined in the will, the farm would revert to his mother's entire control.
88 See, for example, the 1871 will of Anna B. Rose, which explicitly bequeathed to her married daughter Hannah Hutton "all and singular the lot of land upon which I now reside together with the buildings and erections thereon for the sole use and disposal of the said Hannah Hutton," or that of Eliza Waddell of St Stephen, written in 1874, in which she bequeathed "all my real estate and personal property of every nature and kind whatsoever" to her married daughter Alice Cullinen, "her heirs and assigns forever." To ensure Alice's control, her mother named her as sole executrix.
89 For examples of women holding mortgages, see Charlotte County Registry Office Records, 1846, Mortgage Deeds T/741 #975, U/53 #60, U/54 #1221,

U/60 #97, U/99 #156, V/31 #1370, V/233 #1371, and V/418 #1520, among others. See also chap. 5 of Baskerville, *A Silent Revolution?*

90 See Wills of Harriet Clarke, 1849, Matilda Stubbs, 1857, Ann Fitsimmons, 1858, Betsey Porter, 1870, and Elizabeth Atherton, 1874, Charlotte County Probate Court Records, RG 7, RS 63, PANB. See also chap. 3 of Baskerville, *A Silent Revolution?*

91 See, for example, Wills of Harriet Clark, 1849, Matilda Stubbs, 1857, Ann Hatch, 1859, Alice Wilson, 1860, Mary Ann Brown, 1865, Mary Porter, 1868, Betsey Porter, 1870, Anna B. Rose, 1871, Elizabeth Atherton, 1874, Jane Getty, 1874, and Eliza Waddell, 1874, Charlotte County Probate Court Records, RG 7, RS 63, PANB. For an American example of a similar pattern, see Lebsock, *The Free Women of Petersburg*.

92 Janice Cook found examples of women employed in all of these occupations in her analysis of "Saint John Widows, 1880–1900." In the period 1845–75, the only women granted tavern licences in Albert, Charlotte, and Sunbury counties were widows. Court of General Sessions for Albert, Charlotte and Sunbury Counties, 1845–75, RG18, RS146, RS148, and RS157, PANB.

93 For a discussion of the strategies employed by working-class widows, see McLean, "Single Again," and Bradbury, "Surviving as a Widow."

94 Reports of overseers of the poor sometimes offer insight into the plight of the most destitute widows. See, for example, the report for the lower district of St George Parish in Charlotte County for 1858, Court of General Sessions Records, RG18, RS148/B/1/36c, PANB.

95 An analysis of the inmates of the Saint John County Almshouse and Workhouse found that 48 per cent of inmates at the almshouse between 1855 and 1857 were female and 52 per cent were male, but among those over the age of fifty, just 29 per cent were female and 71 per cent were male (Cormier, "The Saint John County Almshouse and Workhouse"). An analysis of the Fredericton Poor House for 1861 and 1871 confirms this pattern: 26 per cent of inmates over the age of fifty were female and 74 per cent were male. Even more interesting, although the numbers are small, in 1871, widowers outnumbered widows by a ratio of almost 2:1 (manuscript census for Fredericton, Carleton Ward, 1861 and 1871). For a similar pattern in Ontario, see Stewart, "The Elderly Poor in Rural Ontario," 224.

96 Similarly, 90 per cent of native-born widows in Oneida County, New York, resided with their children, the majority as heads of households (Ryan, *Cradle of the Middle Class*, 192).

97 Acheson found that in 1851, one Saint John household in seven was headed by a woman, the majority of them widows. While the New

Brunswick–born among them enjoyed a comparatively high level of prosperity, those who were recent Irish immigrants headed households that were among the city's poorest (Acheson, *Saint John*, 233).
98 Only soldiers, their widows, and their minor children were eligible to receive a modest government pension, although, by the end of the century, career teachers and a few other groups had begun lobbying the government for pensions.
99 Some ninety-seven doctors reported delivering babies during the same period. In this transitional period, when doctors moved increasingly into the field, it seems likely that eighty-five is a conservative estimate of the number of midwives. See Rae, "Nineteenth-Century Midwifery," 85. The figures are based on a one-in-ten sample.
100 Compare Hoffman and Taylor, *Much To Be Done*, 6

4. Three Generations

1 For the best discussion of the New Brunswick timber trade in the colonial period, see Wynn, *Timber Colony*.
2 As late as the 1851 census, a significant proportion of New Brunswick male household heads identified themselves as having this or another dual occupation.
3 Similarly, in *Consumers in the* Bush, Douglas McCalla found that rural Upper Canadians could choose from among and regularly shopped at a variety of general stores.
4 See Marjory Grant Diary, 7, 23, and 24 February 1827.
5 "Little Mary" was Isabella's niece, the daughter of her sister Jannet.
6 For a similar pattern in Quebec, see Martin, "Colonisation et commerce."
7 Buckner, "Whatever happened to the British Empire?" 27.
8 This is not to suggest that there was no significant degree of out-migration prior to this time. When they discovered that fertile farmland was at a premium in the province, significant numbers of Loyalists had drifted back across the border, while later arrivals from Great Britain, taking advantage of the relatively cheap fares offered to passengers who served largely as ballast on returning timber ships, regularly used New Brunswick as a way station to the United States or Upper Canada. Such "out-migration" was not a response to a significant economic downturn, however. Nor did it involve significant numbers of the established population.
9 For a discussion of out-migration from another county during the same period, see Acheson, "A Study in the Historical Demography of a Loyalist

County." For a fuller discussion of out-migration in Ann Eliza Rogers's diary, see Little, "'I think I will go.'"

10 In this context, the timber trade refers to the trade in ton (or square) timber, that is, "timber hewn approximately square with an axe," while the lumber trade refers to the product of sawmills and includes deals (approximately 3 inches thick, 9–11 inches wide, and 10–24 feet in length), planks (approximately 2 inches thick, 7 inches wide, and at least 10 feet long), and boards (with minimum dimensions of 7/8 inches thick, 7 inches wide, and 10 feet long). These definitions come from Wynn, *Timber Colony*, 3–4, at footnote *.

11 At its zenith in 1878, the Canadian fleet was the fourth-largest merchant marine in the world, with 72 per cent of the tonnage registered along the Atlantic coast (Buckner, "The 1870s," 61).

12 For the argument that the emergence of the "cult of domesticity" was associated with the changes associated with the rise of capitalism and industrialization, see Ryan, *Cradle of the Middle Class*, and Davidoff and Hall, *Family Fortunes*.

13 Janet MacDonald Diary, 28 September 1858.

14 McTavish, "Learning to See in New Brunswick," suggests that society members hoped to encourage in adults as well as children "what might be called geographic citizenship, an identification both of and with the visual aspects of the landscape," 555.

15 At a time when schools were dependent on subscription and enrollments, girls were admitted to the grammar schools in smaller counties where their fees were needed. See Grammar School Records for Albert and Sunbury counties, PANB. For a similar pattern in Upper Canada, see Gidney and Millar, *Inventing Secondary Education*, 105–9.

16 Matthew Fontaine Maury, who began his career as a midshipman in the United States Navy, was assigned to the Depot of Charts and Instruments in Washington in 1842. There he developed the first track charts for the North Atlantic. These quickly became popular with sea captains and were in wide use by the time Amelia Holder was sailing with her father.

17 Amelia Holder Diaries, 3rd Voyage, 11, 16, 20, and 23 December 1869, See also Jessie Loggie Journal Letter, 30 November 1887.

18 Some of these women, too, went beyond the status of gifted amateur to develop their talent into careers. For a Nova Scotia example, see Guildford, "'Whate'er the duty of the hour demands.'"

19 While most women who joined the Ladies' Auxiliary of the New Brunswick Natural History Society confined their interests largely to the fields of botany and ornithology, Caroline Heustis, an entomologist,

presented reports on her insect research to the society as early as 1881, and provided the Natural History Museum in Saint John a catalogue of local insects the following year (McTavish, "Strategic Donations," 99).

20 Bogaard, "Introduction," 15–16; Hewitt, "Science, Popular Culture, and the Producer Alliance," 244; McTavish, "Learning to See," 576. Women proved "crucial in the identification and codification" of Australian flora and fauna (Theobald, "The Sin of Laura," 262).

21 Laura Cynthia Fullerton Diary, 28 January 1885.

22 See, for example, Smith, "Missionary as Collector,"102–3; for New Brunswick women, see "Offering Orientalism," chap. 3 of McTavish, *Defining the Modern Museum*, 80–5. For women's donations of local botanical specimens and, more unusual, a cariboo, for public display in New Brunswick's Natural History Museum, see McTavish, "Strategic Donations," 101.

23 For a discussion of this trend and a description of some of the most spectacular lectures, see Hewitt, "Science as Spectacle."

24 Ann Eliza Rogers Diary, 26 March 1853 and 8 June 1860.

25 In Tasmania, for example, Jane Williams, a contemporary of Ann Eliza Rogers, writing up her notes on a lecture on optics, commented with enthusiasm that "it is really astonishing to see such things in so young a settlement" (Theobald, "The Sin of Laura," 262).

26 Heaman has argued that "exhibitions provided women with a back door into the public sphere" ("Taking the World by Show," 599–631, quote p. 600). My discussion of fairs and exhibitions owes much to Heaman. Williamson's MA thesis, "From Agricultural Improvement to Industrial Affirmation," supports Heaman's argument regarding the evolution of local fairs and provincial exhibitions.

27 Thus Mrs Bourdillant, a manufacturer of "ladies and gents furs," advertised that she had been awarded "a diploma for excellency of workmanship" at the 1868 Industrial Exhibition in Halifax (Guildford, "'Whate'er the duty of the hour demands,'" 15).

28 Heaman, "Taking the World by Show," 631.

29 Mrs R. Wilmot Travel Diary, 8 and 10 July 1862. For further development of this theme in reference to Mrs Wilmot, see Campbell, "Nineteenth Century New Brunswick Women Travellers," 79–81. For a discussion of the kind of "national consciousness" promoted in the Canadas by international exhibitions in the mid-nineteenth century, see Murray, "Canadian Participation and National Representation."

30 Observers of the day agreed with Mrs Wilmot that exhibits from Maritime provinces, Nova Scotia especially, were particularly impressive (Heaman, *The Inglorious Arts of Peace*, 168).

31 Robert Duncan Wilmot, a Saint John businessman who had served as mayor of that city and as a member of the legislative assembly, was elected as an anti-confederate in 1865.
32 Annie Trueman Diary, 7 November 1872. According to her younger sister's diary, these classes included trigonometry and geology among six others (Laura S. Trueman Wood Diary, 20, 21, and 24 May 1872). Annie was an outstanding student and stood at the top of her class.
33 Acheson, "The National Policy."
34 For a discussion of Maritime women in one American factory town, see Beattie, "'Going up to Lynn.'" See also Brookes, "Out-Migration," and Thornton, "The Problem of Out-Migration."
35 Beattie, *Obligation and Opportunity*, 94–8. For a New Brunswick example of one such woman, see "Passing Through: Pictures from the Life of Mrs. W. Garland Foster (Nee Annie H. Ross)," Annie H. Ross Foster Hanley Memoir (1939), MG L7.3.4, UNBA.
36 Young New Brunswick men interested in pursuing careers in medicine similarly headed to the United States. Janet MacDonald's son William trained in Boston as a dentist, while Malcolm trained as a medical doctor. In a later generation, Kate Miles's older brother Bruce would also travel to Boston for training in dentistry.
37 Hacker, *The Indomitable Lady Doctors*, 70, 78–9. Elizabeth's two older brothers would follow their father into farming, while her older sister would become a teacher (1851 and 1871 manuscript censuses for Blissville, Sunbury County, New Brunswick).
38 Burton, "The Making of a Nineteenth-Century Profession," 106–8.
39 Josephine Reid Turner to Charlotte Reid, 15 March 1881, Turner Family Papers, S208-1, F46-1, NBMA.
40 Josephine Reid Turner to Charlotte Reid, 14 May 1881.
41 Josephine Reid Turner to Charlotte Reid, 3 June 1881.
42 Josephine Reid Turner to Charlotte Reid, 30 October 1881.
43 Kate had contracted measles and missed a number of her examinations as a result. She wrote "supplementary" examinations upon her return.
44 Edgar, Kate, and their cousin Annie, who was, like Kate, attending high school, boarded with the Johnsons. Sade Waycott was Kate's best friend.
45 For a discussion of women's expanding sphere during this period, see Marks, *Revivals and Roller Rinks*, especially 127–30, and Ward, *Courtship, Love, and Marriage*, 88.
46 Huskins, "The Ceremonial Space of Women."
47 See, for example, Godfrey, "'Into the Hands of the Ladies,'" and Marks, *Revivals and Roller Rinks*, 67. For American examples, see Ginzberg, *Women*

and the Work of Benevolence. Using a similar approach, the Ladies' Auxiliary of the New Brunswick Natural History Society funded the educational activities of the society (McTavish, "Strategic Donations," 95).
48 Clarke, "The Saint John Women's Enfranchisement Association."

5. From Innocent Flirtation to Formal Courtship

1 See, especially, Ward, *Courtship, Love, and Marriage*, which is the standard work on Canadian courtship. Hoffman and Taylor, *Much To Be Done*, 7–40, offer a similar view.
2 See "Courtship and Engagement," chap. 1 of Noël, *Family Life and Sociability*. The women cited do not appear to have been particularly troubled by either parental or societal constraints. For the United States, see Rothman, *Hands and Hearts*, who discusses the freedom young single people had to come and go as they wished. Like Rothman, Lystra, *Searching the Heart*, also focusses on the increasing significance of romantic love in shaping the experience of courtship during the course of the nineteenth century. Noël also focuses on the role of romantic love.
3 In her study of farm women in the Nanticoke Valley in New York, Nancy Osterud also found that "couples courted within an informal, gender-mixed milieu and enjoyed relative freedom from parental supervision; they interacted in flexible and intimate, rather than stiff and stereotypical ways" (*Bonds of Community*, 11).
4 For an analysis of nineteenth-century novels that idealized independent and self-reliant women, see McCall, "'Shall I Fetter Her Will?'" 95–113. And Kelley has argued that even for "the sentimentalists," for whom "piety involved more than an inner conviction," the "ideal woman" was "strong, active and independent" ("The Sentimentalists," 439–40). For the Canadian context, see Guildford, "Creating the Ideal Man."
5 Sally Upton to her parents, and Mary Whitney Upton to Sally Upton, 1823, George Stillman Hill Manuscript Collection, MC1001, PANB.
6 Mary W. Hill to her sister and mother, 15 December 1847, George Stillman Hill Manuscript Collection, MC1001, MS6/4, PANB. For a discussion of supervision and expectations of girls at female academies, see chap. 5 of Selles, *Methodists & Women's Education*.
7 George Hill Diary, 3 February 1850, George Stillman Hill Manuscript Collection, MC1001, MS6/34, PANB. George Hill and his friends clearly found the Protestant churches a very good place to meet young women, as would young men in small towns in Ontario a generation later. See Marks, *Revivals and Roller Rinks*, 36–7.

8 See Ann Eliza Rogers Diary, 21 May; 27 and 29 June; 3 and 8 July; 8 and 22 August; 20, 24, and 26 September; 1, 3, and 18 November; 16 and 31 December.
9 See also the discussion of the courtship of Louisa Collins in Conrad, Laidlaw, and Smyth, *No Place Like Home*, 61–80.
10 The reference here is to the shore of the Ste Croix River, where the village of St Stephen and the local store were located. John was Marjory's older brother; Ann was his wife.
11 Marjory Grant Diary, 2, 27, and 28 February 1827. Charles was Marjory's younger brother. "Our Jannet" is a reference to her older sister, who was married to James Buchanan, a brother of the groom. Jannet, who lived at Oak Hill, in St James Parish, would stay with her parents until after the wedding; James arrived a few days later.
12 Alexander, Marjory and Isabella's eldest brother, and his wife, Mary, also lived at Oak Hill.
13 The "our Jannet" referred to in Marjory's diary.
14 See Charlotte Reid Diaries, 7 and 14 May; 8, 15, 21, and 27 July 1879; quote from 27 July.
15 "Willie's folk" is a reference to her brother-in-law, William West, her older sister Mary, and their family. Anna and Abner are her older sister Anna and her husband, Abner Reid McClellan (one of the pro-confederation candidates elected in Albert County in 1866).
16 Amelia Holder Diaries, February–March 1873.
17 Emma Alice Pitt Diary, April 1873.
18 Emma Alice Pitt Diary, 27 September; 2, 4, and 9 November 1873.
19 For a somewhat different interpretation of Amelia's unrequited love, see Ward, *Courtship, Love, and Marriage*, 159.
20 Agnes Holder Diary, 22 February 1874.
21 Laura Cynthia Fullerton Diary, 12–13 May 1886.
22 Laura Cynthia Fullerton Diary, 26 April–18 May 1886.
23 Sadie Harper Diaries, 19 April 1895. See also entries for 12 January, 30 June, 13 and 31 August 1895; 14 March and 2 November 1896.
24 Sadie Harper Diaries, 2 August 1895.
25 Sadie Harper Diaries, 31 August, 19 September, and 14 December 1895.
26 Sadie Harper Diaries, 2 November 1896; on her encouragement of her new interest, Mr Allen, see entries for 9 January, 18 February, 9 March, 2 April, 19 April, 10 May, 15 August, 31 October, and 15 November 1896.
27 Although Achsah Upton was Mary's maternal aunt, the two young women were close in age and the best of friends.

28 Mary W. Hill to Friends at Home, 10 February 1846, George Stillman Hill Manuscript Collection, MC1001, MS6/1, PANB.
29 Chambers-Schiller, *Liberty, a Better Husband*, 17, argues that between 1800 and 1860 the view that women would be better off single than to enter into a bad marriage or compromise their integrity in exchange for a husband gained "widespread currency in newspapers, periodicals, fiction and advice books" in the United States.
30 Sarah Upton Hill to Mary W. Hill, 23 February 1846, George Stillman Hill Manuscript Collection, MC1001, PANB.
31 Sarah Bliss to Sophia Bliss, 31 May 1859, William F. Ganong Papers, 3436 5 F508, NBMA.
32 Like her brothers, Lillie, too, had had previous loves. On 29 November 1883, she reported, "My old beau Hedley White got married the other day to a Miss Smith. She is an only daughter, and he goes to her home to live."
33 Sadie Harper Diaries, 9 January 1896.
34 See, for example, Sadie Harper Diaries, 9 March 1896.
35 Born in Chambly, Lower Canada, Emma Albani trained in Europe, where she made her career. She returned to her native country regularly, on tours that took her across the country nine times between 1883 and 1906. Vachon, "Lajeunesse, Emma," *Dictionary of Canadian Biography* (hereafter cited as *DCB*).
36 Whist is a classic card game which was very popular in the nineteenth century. Like bridge, which displaced it in popularity in North America in the twentieth century, it is a trick-taking game played by four people, playing in two partnerships. Whist continues to be popular in Britain.
37 Fulvia Dickie, known as Pully, like Ted Deacon, was one of Sadie's closest friends (Peck, ed., *A Full House and Fine Singing*, 16).
38 Mary W. Hill to Friends at home, 10 February 1846, George Stillman Hill Manuscript Collection, MC1001, MS6/1, PANB. For an example of such a change, see "Rebecca Byles" in Conrad, Laidlaw, and Smyth, *No Place Like Home*.
39 Although it had not entirely disappeared. See Violet Goldsmith's diary entries for 4 December 1905, and 23 January, 5 February, and 15 March 1906.
40 Ball, "A Perfect Farmer's Wife."

6. The World of the Family

1 In discussing companionate marriage, I am using Bettina Bradbury's useful caveat, and considering the concept not as we might understand it today, but rather within the context of the common understanding of

the period as a "companionate patriarchy," thereby recognizing men's continuing legal authority. See Bradbury, *Wife to Widow*, 18, 62.

2 For an analysis of the Annie Waltham diary during the period of her marriage, see Hutchinson, "'God Help Me For No One Else Can,'" 72–89.
3 For a similar argument, see Noël, *Family Life and Sociability*, especially, but not only, chap. 8, "Parent-Child Relationships."
4 See, in particular, Smith-Rosenberg, *Disorderly Conduct*, who has cogently argued that "mother-daughter bonding served as the model for subsequent relations with other women" (32).
5 For a discussion of the emergence and promotion of the "cult of motherhood" in the Canadian context, see Backhouse, *Petticoats and Prejudice*, 201–3.
6 This speculation is confirmed in reading Sophy's diaries for the 1880s in concert with her letters to her daughter Muriel during the same period.
7 See, for example, Rosenzweig, *The Anchor of My Life*, who uses both diaries and correspondence in her analysis of mother-daughter relationships.
8 Mary Isoline Wolhaupter Diary, 3 April 1869.
9 Mary Isoline Wolhaupter Diary, 14 August 1869.
10 Mary Isoline Wolhaupter Diary, 16, 17, and 18 August 1869.
11 See Smith-Rosenberg, *Disorderly Conduct*, and Rosenzweig, *The Anchor of My Life*.
12 See Josiah Wood Manuscript Collection, MC218, PANB.
13 See Josiah Wood Manuscript Collection, MC218, PANB, and George Stillman Hill Manuscript Collection, MC1001, PANB.
14 George S. Hill to Sarah Upton Hill, 30 December 1836, George Stillman Hill Manuscript Collection, MC1001, PANB.
15 Sarah Upton Hill to George S. Hill, 5–6 January 1837, George Stillman Hill Manuscript Collection, MC1001, PANB.
16 George S. Hill and Sarah Upton Hill to Mary W. Hill, 24 June 1846, George Stillman Hill Manuscript Collection, MC1001, PANB.
17 On 2 January 1883, for example, Sophy recorded that she was "taking quinine – do not feel well" (Sophia Carman Diaries, 1883).
18 A reference to Julia Plant, the young woman who, for a time, seemed likely to marry Bliss.
19 Sophia Carman to Jean Muriel Carman, William F. Ganong Papers, 3436 5, NBMA, 7 June 1883, F511; 20 June 1883, F510, NBMA. See also an 1884 letter, when Bliss was back in New Brunswick: "We shall miss 'the Boy' dreadfully, but not as much as I missed the *girlie*, & not as we missed him last year – because it is for a short time" (Sophia to Muriel, 11 May 1884,

William F. Ganong Papers, 3436 5, F512, NBMA). Their letters are full of confidences and commentary on family and friends.
20 A reference to her son Donald and his wife, Mary Mott.
21 Susan, married to Thomas Earle McDonald, lived on a nearby farm; George had died three years earlier; Alexander and his wife, Jemima MacDonald, and their family lived at some little distance; William, his wife Emily Conant, and their family had settled in Boston; and Malcolm was also in Boston where he was completing his medical training.
22 Almost two decades later, Janet MacDonald's sentiments were echoed by another mother of grown sons, Lucy Everett Morrison: "25 December: Xmas 1881. I was sick in bed nearly all day. Jack & Kate went to her Fathers yesterday, stayed all night & till this evening. Mother, Morrison & Stewart dined alone. Six years ago to day my boys were all home, the last time I saw them all together." Jack was the fourth of Lucy's six sons; Stewart, not yet twenty, was the youngest.
23 For the significance of sisters in the lives of Maritime women, see Conrad, "'Sundays always make me think of home,'" 12–13.
24 Annie Trueman to Laura Trueman Wood, Greenville, Somerville, Mass. [1882], Josiah Wood Manuscript Collection, MC218/16 (517b), PANB.
25 A winter social club, organized by the young people of the community. The name of the club is intriguing and suggests a certain level of sophistication among the founders. "Xenium," derived from ancient Greek, referred to a present given to a guest or stranger, while the meaning of "xenial" is given in the *Concise Oxford Dictionary* as "of hospitality or relations between host and guest." Certainly the choice of name was appropriate for a group whose sole purpose seems to have been to extend hospitality to fellow members.
26 Smith-Rosenberg, *Disorderly Conduct*, 33–4.
27 Smith-Rosenberg argues, for example, that "as the young woman moved toward maturity, aunts, older sisters, and cousins functioned as caretakers, confidantes, playmates, and instructors" (*Disorderly Conduct*, 33–4).
28 See Jacobina Campbell Diary; Trueman Family Correspondence, Josiah Wood Manuscript Collection, MC 218, PANB.
29 See Josiah Wood Manuscript Collection, MC 218, PANB; Ann Eliza Rogers Diary; and Amelia Holder Diaries, 1867.
30 "'I wish you was with me': Connecting the Seafaring Family," chap. 4 of Clayton, "'A Long Voyage Before Us,'" quote p. 79. Compare with Fournier, "'Home Folks,'" 51–79.
31 Black was a cousin. At fifteen, Ida was too young to join the Temperance Lodge. She would join on 19 November, a little more than two weeks after her sixteenth birthday.

32 The "Office" is a reference to the post office.
33 Logomachy is a word game in which the object is to change a word into another word by moving the letters around. Originating in Cincinnati, Ohio, Logomachy was awarded a silver medal at the Cincinnati Industrial Exposition in 1874 as the "Best New Parlour Game." The game has something in common with the modern game of Scrabble, although it was played with cards rather than with tiles. "Prize" cards were those with the letters J, K, V, X, Q, and Z, with Z being a "double prize" card.
34 Ida MacDonald Diaries: see 1 and 3 March, 13 April, 21 September 1882, and 10 January 1883 for Rob playing the violin. See 5 and 27 April 1882 and 20 March 1883 for popping corn. For references to reading aloud, see 14 January 1881; 31 March, 4 and 6 August, 8 September, 17, 19, 20, 21, and 30 November, 1, 3, 10, 11, 12, 17, and 24 December 1882; 1, 7, 23, 24, and 26 January, 7 February, 5 March, 16, 17, and 20 April, 11 and 21 June 1883.

7. Households of Independent Women

1 Will of Harriet Clarke, probated 1849, Charlotte County Probate Court Records, RG 7, RS 63, PANB. Compare Lebsock, *The Free Women of Petersburg*. Osterud claims the nineteenth-century New York farm women she studied were "denied independent land ownership," and does not indicate whether they ever made wills in their own right (*Bonds of Community*, 64–5, 275).
2 See, for example, the 1845 wills of Robert Wilson and Archibald Heney, and the 1849 will of Joseph Clark, all of whom left land to married women relatives. See also that of Gordon Gilchrist of Saint Andrews in 1846, bequeathing Ann Berry £250 "for her separate use and benefit notwithstanding her Coverture" (Charlotte County Probate Court Records, RG 7, RS 63, PANB).
3 Compare Girard, "Married Women's Property," Girard and Veinott, "Married Women's Property Law," Chambers, *Married Women and Property Law*, and Baskerville, *A Silent Revolution?*
4 Backhouse, "Married Women's Property Law," 218–22. Specifically, the act stipulated that "the real and personal property belonging to a woman before, or accruing after marriage, except such as may be received from the husband while married, shall be owned as her separate property so as to exempt it from seizure or responsibility in any way for the debts or liabilities of her husband" (*The Revised Statutes of New Brunswick*, 1854, Chapter 114, Section 1).
5 Backhouse, "Married Women's Property Law," 229–30. Although the New Brunswick Married Women's Property Act of 1877 did leave open

the possibility of a broader interpretation, the majority of both provincial and federal judges agreed that "the intent of Married Women's Property Acts was that married women's property be protected not set at liberty [for women's separate use]." Arguing that judges, not legislators, were primarily responsible for delaying women's property law reform, Backhouse notes just three exceptions: two Ontario judges and one New Brunswick judge (Mr Frederic Eustache Barker of the New Brunswick Supreme Court).

6 Backhouse, "Married Women's Property Law," 211–57. Ontario passed the first Canadian act giving married women the right to act as a *feme sole* with respect to their separate real or personal property in 1884.

7 See the conclusion of Baskerville, *A Silent Revolution?*

8 Janet MacDonald's diary offers a much more well-rounded view of rural life than do those of James Brown, Thomas O. Miles, or David Wetmore. And this is not atypical (see Campbell, "Using Diaries"). For an analysis of Miles's diary, see Munro, "A Farm Community"; for Wetmore's diary, see Baxter, *Clifton Royal*. See also Osterud, *Bonds of Community*, 160.

9 For the significance of the lumbering industry in nineteenth-century New Brunswick, see Wynn, *Timber Colony*. In contrast to the early period, when Jacobina Campbell and Marjory and Isabella Grant were writing, by mid-century men were regularly away for months rather than weeks at a time. Mary Wolhaupter's brothers, who were already away in the woods when Mary's diary opens on 1 January 1869, did not return home until the end of February. For rural men who did not own their own woodlots, this became the more common pattern.

10 For women's experience in seafaring communities in Maine, see Fournier, "'Home Folks,'" 53–79. For a discussion of this phenomenon in a slightly different context, see Norling, "Ahab's Wife," 73–9. Norling argues that as the length of whaling voyages increased, mariners were forced to depend "upon women to sustain maritime families and communities ashore" (73).

11 Clayton, "'A Long Voyage Before Us,'" 54.

12 Ibid., 54–6.

13 Ann Eliza Rogers Diary, 15 February 1865.

14 As he noted in one letter, "I write for the information of *my constituents*, making you the medium of communication" (George S. Hill to Sarah Hill, 8 March 1835, George Stillman Hill Manuscript Collection, MC1001, PANB).

15 See various letters written during the 1880s by Laura Trueman Wood, Josiah Wood Manuscript Collection, MFC 218, PANB; also Laura Trueman Wood Diary, 1886, 1888.

16 Strong kin networks were equally important for widowers. Thus, following his wife's death, sea captain Edwin Holder depended on her unmarried sister, Mary Ann Parrett, to help his father manage the household and care for those of his children left behind when he went to sea (Clayton, "'A Long Voyage Before Us,'" 36). And although Violet Goldsmith's father hired housekeepers to care for his young daughters and infant son after his wife died, following the death of his son at age three, he turned to his sister to take over the management of his household.

17 Ann Eliza Rogers Diary, 1867; Hannah Estabrooks Diary, 1903–1906; Janet [Hendry] MacDonald Diary, 1857–1868; Ida MacDonald Diaries, 1879–1883.

18 Annie T. Johnston Waltham Diaries, 1869–1871. Gagetown barrister James R. Curry was listed in Lovell's Canadian Directory for 1871.

19 Eliza Clowes was Annie's older, married sister.

20 Aunt May may have been Bertha's younger sister, Mary.

21 Catherine Loggie Diary, March–April 1881; Violet Goldsmith Diaries, 30 November–5 December 1900. See also chapter 12 of this book.

22 Mary Isoline Wolhaupter Diary. That she looked to other opportunities is scarcely surprising, for she was obliged to wait until May to receive her "School Draft," a very modest $17.50, in payment for her teaching in January and February.

23 Charles Alterton was twenty-six in 1869. Listed as a farmer in the 1871 census, he was married to twenty-five-year-old Fanny and the couple had one son, Debert, who was just a year old in 1869. Like the Wolhaupters, the Altertons were Wesleyan Methodists.

24 Mary Isoline Wolhaupter Diary: "Monday, April 5, 1869.... Charles Alterton was here this evening. Took up a note I held against him." Mary recorded this repayment in her "Cash Account" record as well.

25 Mary Isoline Wolhaupter Diary: Accounts, Friday, 5 November 1869.

26 "Proving money for her" implies that the terms on which Mary "let George Nye [her brother-in-law] take" the cow she had purchased involved a promise that, should the cow "do well," he would pay her a higher price than she had paid for it (thereby "[im]proving" upon her money spent).

27 For Direxy Carlisle's story, see Ann Eliza Rogers Diary, 2 November 1861–15 June 1862, and 22 February–20 October 1865; Hannah Estabrooks Diary and the 1900 manuscript census for Lewiston, Maine. For Maritime women's experiences in the "Boston States," see Beattie, *Obligation and Opportunity*.

28 Mary Whitney Hill Diary, 1879. The quote cited is from a letter from Sarah Hill to Mary, 23 February 1846, also in the George Stillman Hill Manuscript Collection, MC 1001, PANB.

29 Mary's youngest brother, Henry, lived in St Stephen, where Mary's investments, including some stock in the St Stephen bank, were held.
30 A reference to an ongoing trial of Thomas Dowd for the murder of Thomas Ward, both of St Stephen.
31 From 1878 until 1898, Thanksgiving Day was celebrated on a Thursday in November. Not until 31 January 1957 was the second Monday in October officially designated as Thanksgiving Day in Canada.
32 This is a reference to the yellow fever epidemic at New Orleans and other places on the lower Mississippi River. Beginning soon after midsummer, it did not disappear until early November. In his "Second Annual Message," in December of 1878, President Rutherford B. Hayes reported that "Louisiana, Mississippi and Tennessee suffered severely – about 100,000 cases, 20,000 fatal, according to intelligent estimates." Not until the turn of the century did scientists discover that mosquitoes carried yellow fever. Hayes' speech cited from http://millercenter.org/president/hayes/speeches/speech-3749
33 Mary W. Hill to George F. Hill, 23 February 1881, George Stillman Hill Manuscript Collection, MC1001, MS6/13, PANB.
34 Ann Eliza Rogers Diary, 1856–1867.
35 Clayton, "'A Long Voyage Before Us,'" 54–6.

8. Sociability and Social Networks

1 See also Noël, *Family Life and Sociability*, and Hansen, *A Very Social Time*.
2 Jacobina Campbell Diary, August 1825–1843.
3 Janet [Hendry] MacDonald Diary, 1857–1868. For the role of kinship in developing a social network, see also Osterud, "Visiting with Folks and Friends," chap. 10 of *Bonds of Community*.
4 Hansen claims that in New England, singing schools "convened almost exclusively in December, January, and February," when winter weather brought a break from the "long intense hours of farm work" (*A Very Social Time*, 83).
5 Ann Eliza Rogers Diary, 1852–1856.
6 See Macdonald and Hansen, "Sociability and Gendered Spheres," and, in a related context, see also Wilson, "Reciprocal Work Bees."
7 Lucy Everett Morrison Diaries, especially those for the period 1878–85.
8 For a recent analysis of "the affair of Esther Cox," see Norris with Thompson, *Haunted Girl*. For other examples of Wallace McLean borrowing her newspaper, see 3 and 28 December 1878, and 4 January 1879.

9 Authors, invented in Massachusetts in the late 1850s, was a card game, the object of which was to collect sets of cards listing different works by famous authors (there were eleven authors in the deck and four cards for each).
10 For a discussion of this pattern in the American context, see Smith-Rosenberg, *Disorderly Conduct*, especially the chapter on "The Female World of Love and Ritual."
11 Jacobina Campbell Diary, 27 September–12 October 1826.
12 Another maternal aunt and her family, who lived much closer to the Campbells.
13 Jacobina Campbell Diary, 25 September–3 October 1827.
14 The Polymorphians were a quasi-service club, made up mainly of young men whose main activities involved the organization of public parades and entertainments. See Huskins, "Public Celebrations," 225–49.
15 Lillian Williamson Diary, 23 May 1883.
16 Ann Eliza Rogers Diary, August 1869.
17 Trueman Correspondence, 1883, Josiah Wood Manuscript Collection, MC218, PANB.
18 Josephine Turner Diary, 26 February, and 29 February 1884.
19 Josephine Turner Diary, 1 March, 4 March, 5 March, 7 March, 10 March, and 11 March 1884.
20 Originally, quoits was a lawn game, the object of which was to throw a metal ring over a pin some distance away. Here Jessie is referring to a variant, played on shipboard, and therefore sometimes called "deck quoits," involving the use of rope rings rather than metal rings.
21 Jessie Loggie Diary, 3 August 1887.
22 The reference here is to ships Jessie saw landing at Miramichi ports.
23 For singing schools, see Green and Vogan, *Music Education in Canada*, 18, 46, 90–1.
24 Katherine Miles Diary, 22 February 1901. See also Alvaretta Estabrooks Diaries, 3 August 1889: "Fixed for the basket social which we went to in the evening. Enoch got my basket. Went to bed at half past 11." For a comprehensive discussion of such activities, see Marks, "Strawberry Socials and Sacred Space," in *Revivals and Roller Rinks*, 75–80.
25 This comes through very clearly in Sadie Harper's diary (see Peck, ed., *A Full House and Fine Singing*, especially the early chapters).
26 Ida MacDonald Diaries, 1879–1883.
27 See, for example, Katherine Miles Diary, 19 and 26 February 1901.
28 The King's Daughters was founded in 1886 in New York City. Organized by ten Episcopal, Methodist, and Presbyterian women, its object being "the

366 Notes to pages 166–72

development of spiritual life and the stimulation of Christian activities," it soon became international in scope. Because it attracted men as well as women, in 1891 the name was changed to the King's Daughters and Sons. By 1896, Canada had 6,000 members (information from http://www.iokds.org). In the early-twentieth century, the Fredericton branch regularly invited young women attending high school, normal school, and university to attend entertainments and receptions.

29 For the importance of social networks established at female academies, see Kelley, *Learning to Stand & Speak*.
30 Today we would say "sledding" or "tobogganing" rather than "coasting."

9. Schooling and Scholars

1 The reference here is to those nineteenth-century educational reformers usually identified with school reforms such as the introduction of teacher training, regular government inspection of schools, tax supported public schools, and compulsory attendance. For New Brunswick, see MacNaughton, *The Development of the Theory and Practice of Education*; for the Ontario case, see Prentice, *The School Promoters*.
2 Such schools for girls were commonly called "dame schools." See, for example, Errington, "Ladies and Schoolmistresses."
3 Jacobina Campbell Diary, 1833.
4 For a detailed discussion of the development of New Brunswick's education system during the nineteenth century, see MacNaughton, *The Development of the Theory and Practice of Education*, which remains the standard source on the topic.
5 For a general overview of problems faced by nineteenth-century British North American teachers, see Axelrod, *The Promise of Schooling*. For a more detailed discussion of the Ontario example, see Curtis, "Struggles over School Attendance," chap. 5 of *Building the Educational State*.
6 Although the 1805 act had stipulated that the grammar schools would be open to both sexes, there was no reference to females in the second Grammar School Act, passed in 1816, and in the 1820s, when the trustees of Kings County admitted what appear to be the first female grammar school students, they requested and received the Lieutenant Governor's permission to do so (Preston, "A Study of the New Brunswick Grammar Schools," 76). For the significance of financial pressure in the decision to admit girls to grammar schools in Ontario, see Gidney and Millar, *Inventing Secondary Education*. Reid points to a similar pattern in facilitating the admission of women to Mount Allison, the first university in British

North America to grant a degree to a woman (Reid, "The Education of Women at Mount Allison").

7 Of the 219 students attending the province's seven grammar schools in operation in 1842, 192 were male and 27 were female (Preston, "A Study of the New Brunswick Grammar Schools," 77). By 1867, the number of grammar schools had increased, but the ratio of male to female students did not yet approach parity. Thus, for example, seventy-eight boys and just twenty-three girls attended the Sunbury County Grammar School, and while the differential was not as great in Albert County, with a ratio of 35:22, boys still outnumbered girls by more than three to two. Grammar School Records for Albert, Charlotte, and Sunbury Counties, 1845–1875, F647, F650, PANB.

8 For Upper Canada, see Errington, *Wives and Mothers, School Mistresses and Scullery Maids*, 209–32; for Australia, see Theobald, "The Sin of Laura," 259.

9 Theobald, "The Sin of Laura," 268.

10 George S. Hill to A. Upton Hill, 8 June 1844, and George S. Hill to Mary W. Hill, 24 June 1846, George Stillman Hill Manuscript Collection, MC1001, PANB.

11 Mary W. Hill to Hasadiah Louisa Hill, 28 May 1847, George Stillman Hill Manuscript Collection, MC1001, PANB.

12 LaVorgna, "Lessons in Nineteenth-Century New Brunswick Teacher Careerism," 210–15.

13 Although there is no official record of the nature of those stipulations, Martha Hamm Lewis herself later recalled that she was required to wear a veil, arrive ten minutes before class began, and leave five minutes before it ended (MacNaughton, *The Development of the Theory and Practice of Education*, 140–1).

14 Information on Huldah Turnbull was drawn from Ann Eliza Rogers Diary and the Albert County Grammar School Records, F647, PANB.

15 Trites, "The New Brunswick Baptist Seminary," 103–23; Reid, "The Education of Women at Mount Allison"; Andrew, "Selling Education," 17–21.

16 Sarah Upton Hill to Upton Hill, 30 April 1844; undated [1845], George Stillman Hill Manuscript Collection, MC1001, PANB.

17 MacNaughton, *The Development of the Theory and Practice of Education*, 168.

18 Following the 1858 act, grammar schools were supplemented by government-subsidized superior schools, with both grammar schools and superior schools eventually being transformed into high schools. For an excellent analysis of these and other issues with reference to Ontario, see Gidney and Millar, *Inventing Secondary Education*.

19 *Historical Statistics of New Brunswick*, 21–2. See also Appendix, Table 3.
20 At issue was the decree, in a period when women religious wore habits and taught in schoolrooms within the walls of the convent, that no religious symbols could be displayed in the classrooms of government-funded schools.
21 Roman Catholics constituted less than 10 per cent of the population in Albert County. See Appendix, Table 4.
22 For analysis of this controversy, see Baker, *Timothy Warren Anglin*; Toner, "New Brunswick Schools"; and Stanley, "The Caraquet Riots of 1875."
23 Catherine Loggie Diary, 30 August, 16 and 18 September, and 12 October 1880. For other young women teachers who served as role models for their students and participated in the Teachers' Institutes, see Ida MacDonald Diary, 1882 (references to Miss Blatch), and Ann Eliza Rogers Diary, September 1891 (references to her daughters Achsah and Ellie).
24 For Sadie's experience at Mount Allison, see part 2 of Peck, ed., *A Full House and Fine Singing*.
25 For a New Brunswick case study, see Caplan, "'A Law Unto Oneself.'" See also Axelrod, *The Promise of Schooling*; Davey, "The Rhythm of Work" and "Trends in Female School Attendance"; and Gaffield, *Language, Schooling and Cultural Conflict*.
26 Centralized provincial administration and regular inspections also insured a certain level of standardization across the province. See Quinn, "'Sympathetic and Practical Men'?"
27 Limonite is an ore mined for use in the production of iron.
28 Laura Cynthia Fullerton Diary, 11 May 1886.
29 "Mrs Wood" is a reference to diarist Laura Trueman Wood.
30 For a view of life at Mount Allison contemporary with Alva's experience at Acadia, see part 2 of Peck, ed., *A Full House and Fine Singing*.
31 A literary and musical society that held fortnightly meetings, Moody, "Graves, Mary Elizabeth," *DCB*.
32 Miss Graves, the principal of the female seminary, also taught rhetoric and literature. See Moody, "Graves, Mary Elizabeth." *DCB*.
33 "Enoch Arden" is a poem by Alfred, Lord Tennyson, published in 1864, when Tennyson was England's Poet Laurlate. The hero, a fisherman who becomes a merchant sailor in an attempt to support his wife and three children, is shipwrecked and, upon his return home ten years later, discovers that his wife, thinking him dead, has married his childhood rival.
34 St Ann's was one of Fredericton's two Anglican churches.
35 Women had had the right to attend Mount Allison University since 1872 and the University of New Brunswick since 1885, when arguments made

on behalf of Mary Kingsley Tibbits had caused the legislature to threaten to block university funding and the UNB Senate had given in. Grace Annie Lockhart, after several years at the Ladies' Academy, entered Mount Allison University for her final year and gained a Bachelor of Science and English literature degree in 1875. (See chapter 4 of this book.) Mary Tibbits gained her Bachelor of Arts degree in 1889 and went on to be a member of the first class of graduate students at Bryn Mawr.
36 Marks and Gaffield, "Women at Queen's University."
37 Burke, "New Women and Old Romans," 228. This certainly conforms with Annie Ross's experience when she arrived on the campus of the University of New Brunswick in the late 1890s (Annie H. Ross Foster Hanley Memoir, MG L7.3.4, UNBA).
38 Rayner-Canham and Rayner-Canham, *Harriet Brooks*, 8. Fingard found that about half of the women who attended Dalhousie between 1885 and 1900 also remained single, as compared to 10 to 15 per cent of the female population as a whole ("College, Career, and Community," 31).
39 Violet Goldsmith Diaries, 28 November 1903.
40 Carrie Nation was a radical American temperance activist.
41 Yorke, "Mabel Penery French."

10. A Sustaining Faith

1 Fortunately for me, I did not have to do that detective work, but was able to depend largely on Murray Young's engaging analytical introduction to the manuscript to guide me through the forest of multiple meanings underlying those terse daily entries ("A Calendar of Life").
2 See Jacobina Campbell Diary, 30 November 1840 through 25 March 1841.
3 For Janet MacDonald's role in the founding of the Second Baptist Church of Wickham, see Greenwood, *The Early Baptists of Cambridge Parish*.
4 Observing that singing schools "convened almost exclusively in December, January, and February," Hansen, *A Very Social Time* (83), does not mention whether they were often followed by revivals, as was the case along the Tay in 1840–1 and on the shores of Washademoak Lake in 1858.
5 A reference to her son George's wife, Beckah McDonald.
6 I John 3:14: "We know that we have passed from death unto life, because we love the brethren."
7 I Corinthians 15:31: "[I protest by your rejoicing which I have in Christ Jesus our Lord,] I die daily."
8 Galatians 2:13: "And the other Jews dissembled likewise with him [Peter]; [insomuch that Barnabus also was carried away with their dissimulation.]"

9 Mary Mott (b. 1840) would later marry Janet's son Donald.
10 The modern reader may be moved to wonder whether the "brain fever" William Mott suffered may have been caused by plunging into the icy waters of Washademoak Lake in mid-December. William Mott would eventually recover.
11 Janet's son-in-law and daughter.
12 The baby referred to is Janet's grandson Robert; Mary is the sister of Janet's daughter-in-law Sally, wife of James.
13 Emaline McDonald was the daughter of Janet's daughter Susan and her husband, Thomas Earle McDonald.
14 I am grateful to Hannah Lane for making this connection.
15 Hunter, "Inscribing the Self in the Heart of the Family," 51–2.
16 Ibid., 63.
17 Ibid., 61.
18 For more examples of Mary's resolutions and prayers to be a "good" or "better" girl, see, among other references, Mary Isoline Wolhaupter Diary, 20 and 28 January, 4 February, 6 and 30 April, 31 May, 15 November, and 13 December 1869.
19 For the prevalence of conversion, see Lane, "Tribalism, Proselytism, and Pluralism."
20 For a discussion of the concept of a "religious marketplace" and conversion experiences in antebellum New England, see Hansen, *A Very Social Time*, 153–9.
21 Isaiah 55:10–11: "For as the rain cometh down, and the snow from heaven, and returneth not thither, but watereth the earth, and maketh it bring forth and bud, that it may give seed to the sower, and bread to the eater:/ So shall my word be that goeth forth out of my mouth: it shall not return unto me void, but it shall accomplish that which I please, and it shall prosper in the thing whereto I sent it."
22 Catherine Loggie Diary, 26 January 1881. *Woodstock or The Cavalier: A Tale of the Year Sixteen Hundred and Fifty-one* (1826) is a historical novel by Sir Walter Scott. Set during the English Civil War, it deals with the escape of Charles II, during the Commonwealth, and his final triumphant entry into London. Praised for its balanced perspective, *Castle Daly: The Story of an Irish Home Thirty Years Ago*, in two volumes (1875) by Annie Keary was set in the days of the Famine and the Young Irelanders' Rising.
23 Catherine Loggie Diary, 30 January 1881.
24 Laura to Mother, Tuesday noon [July 1873?], Josiah Wood Manuscript Collection, MC218, MS 8 (145), PANB.
25 Rebecca Trueman to Annie & Laura, Monday Eveg. [July 1873?], Josiah Wood Manuscript Collection, MC218, MS 5, PANB.

26 Annie to Mother, Sunday Afternoon [Nov. 1873], Josiah Wood Manuscript Collection, MC218, MS 8 (39), PANB.
27 See especially Laura Cynthia Fullerton Diary and, to a lesser extent, Alvaretta Estabrooks Diaries. Hansen notes that women were more likely than men to comment on sermons (*A Very Social Time*, 141–5, 159–60).
28 For a somewhat different analysis, see Grant, "Young Women Who Tell a Different Story."
29 Laura to Mother and Annie, 16 January, 1881, Josiah Wood Manuscript Collection, MC218, MS 5 (60), PANB.
30 Josephine Turner to Charlotte Reid, 14 May 1881, Turner Family Papers S208-1, F46-1, NBMA.
31 Watson Reid to Charlotte Reid, 10 July 1881, Turner Family Papers, S308-2, F44-7, NBMA.
32 See, for example, Bradley, *A Narrative of the Life*, or, for a briefer consideration, "Mary Bradley's Reminiscences."
33 For an analysis of the significance of the class meeting, "a devotional and fellowship subgroup," and particularly private, all-female class meetings for women, see Lane, "'Wife, Mother, Sister, Friend.'"
34 Jacobina Campbell's Commonplace Book, 1817–1825, York-Sunbury Historical Collection, MC300, MS2/126, PANB. I am grateful to Dr D. Murray Young for pointing this source out to me.
35 Laura to Annie, 22 August 1882, Josiah Wood Manuscript Collection, MC218, MS 5 (68), PANB. The books which Laura was reading and proposing to share with Annie were classics of the debates which engaged intellectual supporters of the mainstream churches and skeptics at Oxford University in the mid-nineteenth century, and which were subsequently taken up by a widening range of intellectuals in Britain and eastern North America.
36 Edward Meyrick Goulburn (1818–1897), Dean of Norwich, whose *Thoughts on Personal Religion* (1862) had recently been reprinted. *The Pursuit of Holiness: A Sequel to "Thoughts on Personal Religion" Intended to Carry the Reader Somewhat Further Onward in the Spiritual Life* was first published in 1869.
37 See, for example, the Minutes of the Maternal Association of St Stephen-Milltown, Charlotte County, 1836: Maternal Association of St Stephen-Milltown Records, MC399, PANB; or the Minutes of Meetings of the Woodstock WCTU, 1888–1893, 1893–1899, New Brunswick Woman's Christian Temperance Union Collection, MC63, 3/2, 3/3, PANB.
38 On calculating productivity, see Folbre, "The Unproductive Housewife."

11. Work in the Home

1. Although Canadian historians of women have not specifically analysed the history of the way women's non-waged work has been reported in the census, such studies have been undertaken in other countries. For the United States, see Anderson, "The History of Women and the History of Statistics"; for a comparative analysis of England and the United States, see Folbre, "The Unproductive Housewife"; and for Australia, see Deacon, "Political Arithmetic."
2. Most studies of masculinity focus almost exclusively on men's roles; a notable exception is Tosh, *A Man's Place*.
3. Compare Bremer, "Australia: 18th- and 19th-Century Diaries and Letters," 66.
4. Campbell, "Using Diaries." Osterud, *Bonds of Community*, makes a similar point (160).
5. Osterud argues that New York farm women's work was more monotonous and much less seasonal than men's (*Bonds of Community*, 12, 161). This was not the case in New Brunswick.
6. A major tributary of the Miramichi. Patrick must have been lumbering there and was about to take part in "the drive."
7. Jacobina Campbell Diary, 18 May 1826, 21 May 1827, 21–2 May 1829, 13 May 1830, 1 June 1832, 28 May 1833, 26 May 1834, 2 June 1835, 24 May 1837, 21 May 1838, and 27 May 1839. At least one correspondent to the "Women's Column" in the *Maine Farmer* in the 1870s enumerated sheep shearing, along with haying and harvesting, as part of the farm woman's work (Brown, "Gender and Identity," 126).
8. Isabella Grant Diary, 29 May 1827.
9. See "The Rise of Sawmills," chap. 4 of Wynn, *Timber Colony*.
10. Lucy Everett Morrison Diaries, 2 June 1873, 3 and 5 June 1871, 7 June 1872, and 4 June 1873.
11. Lucy Everett Morrison Diaries, 7 and 13 June 1871, 22 June 1872, 23 June 1873, 13 June 1871, 15 June 1873, 23 June 1872, and 17 June 1873.
12. Lucy Everett Morrison Diaries, 24 and 28 June 1871, 29 June 1872, 30 June and 1 July 1873. On 28 June 1852, Ann Eliza Rogers reported, "Strawberries ripe and very thick."
13. Lucy Everett Morrison Diaries, 2 July 1871, 1 July 1872, 4 July 1873, and 6 July 1871.
14. Lucy Everett Morrison Diaries, 11 July 1871, 12 July 1872, 15 July 1873, 17 July 1871, 22 July 1873, 24 July 1871, 13 July 1872, and 18 July 1873.
15. Lucy Everett Morrison Diaries, 25 July 1871, 23 July 1872, and 21 July 1873.

16 Lucy Everett Morrison Diaries, 14 and 16 August 1871, 11 and 19 August 1872, 18 and 14 August 1873.
17 Ida's use of quotation marks very likely indicates expressions used by her mother and grandmother.
18 Osterud also found that the division of labour varied with families (*Bonds of Community*, 164).
19 See the discussion of this issue in Inwood and Wagg, "The Survival of Handloom Weaving," and Inwood, "The Representation of Industry."
20 See, for example, Macdonald and Hansen, "Sociability and Gendered Spheres." Women also participated in a wide variety of work bees, which brought neighbours together to share a particular task. See Wilson, "Reciprocal Work Bees."
21 Janet MacDonald and her younger relations were undoubtedly among the Baptist women who came together at McDonald's Corner and Wickham in August of 1870 to form two of the first women's missionary societies in Canada (see Clarke, *Sisters: Canada and India*, 23). For the significance of women's missionary societies in funding the activities of missionaries in the overseas missions, see "A Mind to Work: Maritime Women and Mission Societies," chap. 2 of Nelson, "Links in the Chain."
22 As well as the dates noted here, see Grant Diary, 28 February, 11 March, and 21 and 28 April 1827 for purchases made at the store and sales of butter to neighbours.
23 Nancy Casey, along with Peggy and Sally, may have been daughters of the Mrs Casey whose husband died in January 1826. Peggy helped to shear the Campbells' sheep in 1829 (21 May), the first year they sent their yarn to Nancy (19 September) (see also Bradley, "Mary Bradley's Reminiscences"). For a discussion of the "missing weavers," see Wallace-Casey, "'Providential Openings'" (MA report), and Rygiel, "'Thread in Her Hands – Cash in Her Pockets.'"
24 Rygiel, "'Thread in Her Hands – Cash in Her Pockets,'" 59–61.
25 Craig and Rygiel argue that profit, not poverty, drew women weavers into the market in New Brunswick. Their evidence that female weavers could expect to earn almost as much as male wage earners is compelling ("Femmes, marchés et production textile").
26 See reference in Mary Wolhaupter's diary, 10 May 1869, to letters from Mr Bates, Miss Mary Bates, and Mr John Little, "wishing us to make them a great quantity of home made cloth."
27 Significantly, too, Sophy Carman's Receipt Files include lists of plants purchased from Lucy Morrison and one receipt signed, "Received

payment, Lucy A. Morrison, With many thanks" ("Receipt Files," William F. Ganong Papers, F511, NBMA).
28 Janet [Hendry] MacDonald Diary, 15 October 1857.
29 These are the hours of labour cited by Cynthia Comacchio for the "typical farm woman" in 1900 (*The Infinite Bonds of Family*, 28).

12. Beyond the Bounds of Family

1 For a fuller discussion of the roles women played in the market economy as both producers and consumers, see Craig, *Backwoods Consumers*, and Mancke, "At the Counter of the General Store." While Mancke argues that, in the eighteenth century, women were consuming to produce, Craig argues that by the nineteenth century, women had shifted from the production of goods for the household to the production of goods for the market, and were now producing to consume. The majority of New Brunswick women diarists who were selling the goods they produced fall into the latter category of "homespun capitalists." For the extent to which "women's work was bound up with their household's relation to the market," see Kelly, "All the Work of the Family," chap. 2 of *In the New England Fashion*. See also Cohen, *Women's Work, Markets, and Economic Development*.
2 Although she cautions against interpreting major discrepancies between reported workforce participation by men and women simply as "a result of the under-enumeration of women's work by census takers," Bettina Bradbury also argues that historians using the census have given "little thought to kinds of work that are not clearly listed" (Bradbury, *Working Families*, 141–2). For under-representation of American women's occupations in censuses, see Anderson, "The History of Women and the History of Statistics."
3 Blom & Blom, eds., *Canada Home*, 24.
4 Peck, ed., *A Full House and Fine Singing*.
5 For Lavinia McLauchlan, see Lucy Everett Morrison Diaries, 1869–1893, and the manuscript censuses for Fredericton, 1871 and 1881. For a case study of two groups of self-employed seamstresses, see Gamber, "A Precarious Independence." See also Larocque, "'The Work Being Chiefly Performed by Women.'"
6 Mary Isoline Wolhaupter Diary, 17, 30, and 31 July, and 2 August 1869.
7 Larocque, "'The Work Being Chiefly Performed by Women,'" 158–61.

8 Ann Eliza Rogers Diary. For Direxy Carlisle, see various entries from November 1861 through December 1865. For Lizzie Stiles', see various entries from 1863 through 1870.
9 Larocque, "'The Work Being Chiefly Performed by Women,'" 161.
10 According to the 1870 United States census, businesswomen made up 10.5 per cent of all working women. In 1871, businesswomen made up 20 per cent of working women in Hamilton, Ontario, and Victoria, British Columbia (Taylor and Baskerville, *A Concise History of Business*, 240–1).
11 Bradley, "Mary Bradley's Reminiscences."
12 These were, to be sure, small businesses, employing between one and fifteen women (Larocque, "'The Work Being Chiefly Performed by Women,'" 158–9).
13 Jones and Jones, *Fredericton and Its People*, 81. The sisters were descendants of the neighbours so often mentioned in Jacobina Campbell's diary, and forebears of the historian D. Murray Young.
14 Rae made imaginative use of nineteenth-century New Brunswick birth registers to identify a number of midwives who were not listed in other records ("Nineteenth-Century Midwifery").
15 There is no New Brunswick equivalent of the diary maintained by Martha Ballard, the eighteenth-century Maine midwife whose life and career are analysed in Ulrich, *A Midwife's Tale*. Ann Eliza Rogers's diary is tantalizing on this question, as she does record being called to sit with women who were "ill," which meant staying overnight, and sometimes for several days. Quite often, though not always, this was related to a woman's confinement. Although this happened fairly regularly when Ann Eliza's husband John was working in the United States and she was left behind in New Brunswick, the diary does not reveal whether remuneration was involved.
16 Excerpts from Elizabeth Innes's Journal and Notebooks, which are held at the New Brunswick Museum in Saint John (cited in McGahan, *Whispers from the Past*, 150).
17 The first training program for nurses in Canada was established in 1874.
18 Blom & Blom, eds., *Canada Home*, 31–2. Margaret Medley was the Bishop's second wife and a good friend of Sophy Carman.
19 For a useful analysis of this phenomenon, see Beattie, *Obligation and Opportunity*.
20 Although Ontario claims leadership in this field, having established the first provincial normal school in 1847, New Brunswick followed a similar trajectory, establishing two normal schools, one in Fredericton and one in Saint John, in 1848 and 1849, respectively.

21 Eliza Guion, thirty-four, New Brunswick–born, and, like her thirty-eight-year-old farmer husband John, of French descent. Nonetheless, the Guions were adherents of the Church of England. Mrs Guion was pregnant with her seventh child (Mary) in 1869. Only her three eldest – Barzina (nine), Harry (eight), and Netta (six) – would have been old enough to attend Mary's school.
22 *Narrative of the Life and Sufferings of William B. Lighton (Minister of the Gospel)* (Boston: 1844).
23 William Cowperthwaite, fifty-eight, a farmer, and his fifty-six-year-old wife Mary, both New Brunswick–born Baptists, had three children: William (eighteen), Benjamin (sixteen), and Julia (fourteen). Certainly the two younger would have been candidates for Mary Wolhaupter's school.
24 Mrs London was probably the wife of Isaiah, thirty-nine, a New Brunswick–born farmer, and the mother of fourteen-year-old Willard. The Londons were Free Christian Baptists.
25 Prentice, "The Feminization of Teaching," 55.
26 Letter from Leila DeWolfe to Mrs Maria W. DeWolfe, 18 November 1877, Moore-DeWolfe Collection, F4249, PANB.
27 Reverend Charles Gordon Glass, *Stray Leaves from Scotch and English History with The Life of Sir William Wallace, Scotland's Patriot, Hero and Political Martyr* (Montreal: A.A. Stevenson, 1876). A Presbyterian minister, Glass was a Scottish immigrant to New Brunswick, who chartered a ship to bring immigrants to establish the community of Glassville in Carleton County. Sir William Wallace (circa 1270–1305) led the unsuccessful Scottish resistance to Edward I.
28 Designed to appeal to young people between the ages of fifteen and twenty-five, *The Young Christian: or, A Familiar Illustration of the Principles of Christian Duty* by Jacob Abbott (1803–1879) was first published by the American Tract Society in 1832.
29 A "tidy" is an ornamental cover for a chair back or table.
30 See chapter 10, note 22, in this book.
31 Trustees' Return, 1880, McRobbie's Road, School District 8, Alnwick Parish, Northumberland County, RS657, PANB.
32 By 1881, 60 per cent of teachers in New Brunswick and Nova Scotia were women, the highest proportion of any province except Quebec. The Maritime provinces also had the highest teacher-to-student ratios. And by the end of the nineteenth century, one in every eleven Canadian women who worked outside the household in a salaried occupation was a teacher (Sager, "Women Teachers in Canada, 1881–1901," 212, 204).

33 For women's gradual movement into this field, see England and Boyer, "Women's Work: The Feminization and Shifting Meaning of Clerical Work."
34 Frank was Arthur's wife. Nellie, Hannah and Arthur's younger sister, was a teacher. She left for her school on 27 January, but often came home at weekends.
35 The expression "to get a chance" refers to getting a ride with someone who is passing by chance, rather than arranging for a ride with someone.
36 Hannah Estabrooks Diary, 19 February 1905. It would seem that her brother, whom we may assume was the "surly Boss," may have agreed with her view of the men who used the store as a meeting place.
37 Rebecca Trueman to Annie, Josiah Wood Manuscript Collection, MC218, MS5/153, PANB.
38 Annie Trueman to Rebecca Trueman, 1 October 1877, Josiah Wood Manuscript Collection, MC218, MS8/50, PANB.
39 Annie Trueman to Laura Trueman Wood, Tuesday Evening [1884?], Josiah Wood Manuscript Collection, MC218, MS16/81, PANB.
40 Laura Trueman Wood Journal of Everyday Affairs, December 1884.
41 Annie Trueman Diary for 1886. This is catalogued in the Mount Allison University Archives as Laura Trueman's Notebook, but it is clear that Annie used it as a diary for a brief period in 1886 (Laura Trueman's Notebook, 1885, Wood Family Papers, 8914/7, MAUA).
42 All were mistresses at the Ladies' Academy in1886.
43 Guildford, "'Whate'er the duty of the hour demands.'"
44 Lucy Everett Morrison Diaries.
45 Fredericton's major hotel, where many members of the legislative assembly boarded when the House was in session.
46 Two days later, Lucy "sent away order to Carter for seed" (Lucy Everett Morrison Diaries, 19 March 1881).
47 The Hanington Brothers, druggists and apothecaries in Saint John, also sold flowers. For Hanington Brothers, see *McAlpine's Saint John City Directory* (St John: D. McAlpine & Co., 1878–9), 107; (1879–80), 122; (1880–1), 107. For J. Murray Kay, see *McAlpine's Saint John City Directory* (1880–1), 128.
48 Like Bebbington's, the gardening business run by Daniel Kenny and his son was listed in the census.
49 Ted Jones, "Bebbington's Gardens," *Daily Gleaner* (Fredericton), 10 June 2000.
50 The Fenetys and the Rays, like Lucy, maintained greenhouses and extensive gardens, though they did so for pleasure rather than for profit.

51 Lucy Everett Morrison Diaries, 12 August 1881.
52 Rae, "Nineteenth-Century Midwifery." For the increasing involvement of doctors in medical obstetrics and the impact on midwives, see Mitchinson, "The Emergence of Medical Obstetrics," chap. 6 of *The Nature of Their Bodies*, especially 162–7. While noting a decline in the number of midwives in Canada during the course of the nineteenth century, Mitchinson found that the decline was not as precipitous as in the United States, and that midwives certainly did not disappear, especially in rural areas.
53 For an excellent discussion of this process in relation to teaching, see Guildford, "'Separate Spheres': The Feminization of Public School Teaching."

13. Politics and Social Reform

1 This extended even to defining masculinity, as Janet Guildford has demonstrated. See Guildford, "Creating the Ideal Man."
2 Klein, "A 'Petticoat Polity'?" Both documented cases involved contested elections, because the margin of victory was so small. Women may well have voted in other ridings where the contests were not so close and in other elections but there is no way to calculate the extent to which propertied women may have exercised their right to the franchise prior to 1843 as no poll books are extant. However, the fact that the 1843 amendment occasioned no comment suggests that, by that time at least, women had ceased going to the polls.
3 The law brought New Brunswick law into line with British law as well as the law in other British North American provinces and in the United States during this period.
4 For New Brunswick women's use of the petitioning process during this period, see Campbell, "Disfranchised but not Quiescent." For the significance of petitioning in the American context, see Baker, "The Domestication of Politics." Among the diarists, Annie Johnston, in charge of protecting her family's property, petitioned the legislature to "fortify the banks of the canal" (Annie T. Johnston Waltham Diaries, 31 December 1870; 1 April, and 22–23 June 1871).
5 Campbell, "Disfranchised but not Quiescent," 39.
6 "Mr Hatheway," *Reports of the Debates and Proceedings of the House of Assembly of the Province of New Brunswick* (Fredericton: 1852), 101.
7 For similar arguments, see Ginzberg, *Untidy Origins*, and Zaeske, *Signatures of Citizenship*.
8 Charlotte Reid Diaries, 26 September 1883.

9 Wallace, "Tilley, Sir Samuel Leonard," *DCB*.
10 Rose, ed., *A Cyclopaedia of Canadian Biography*, 349. For a similar argument about political debates taking place around family tables, see Bradbury, *Wife to Widow*, 113–15.
11 For the role of the National Policy in attracting Josiah Wood to federal politics, see Godfrey, "Wood, Josiah," *DCB*.
12 Baby Dora was not quite a year old.
13 This is a reference to Josie's paternal aunt (Annie) and the couple's two older children, Daisy (seven) and Herbert (five).
14 Sadie Harper Diaries, Monday, 17 October 1892.
15 Pedro was a card game.
16 The editor of Sackville's *Chignecto Post* (27 October 1892) agreed with Sadie, declaring that "the defeat of Mssrs Melanson, Wilberforce Wells and Sumner in this county is to be regretted." But the results for Shediac belied Sadie's claim for her parish: Smith and Killam, both government men, led the polls there.
17 Lane, "'Wife, Mother, Sister, Friend,'" 102, and "Evangelicals, Church Financing, and Wealth-Holding," 116–18.
18 See Marks, *Revivals and Roller Rinks*, 64–9; Van Die, "Revisiting 'Separate Spheres,'" 242–50; Clarke, *Piety and Nationalism*, 84–7; and Liebenberg, "Handmaiden of the Church," 5–10.
19 See, for example, Godfrey, "'Into the Hands of the Ladies,'" 27–43.
20 For the significance of women's voluntary associations in shaping and reshaping civil society see Ryan, *Cradle of the Middle Class*, 97–103, and Kelley, *Learning to Stand & Speak*, 7–15.
21 Mary Whitney Hill to Sarah Hill, Sunday 26th [Mar 1846], George Stillman Hill Manuscript Collection, MC1001, MS6/4, PANB.
22 Ann Eliza Rogers Diary, 25–7 March 1867.
23 Jacobina Campbell first reported attending a temperance meeting in July 1832. But although she became active in this mixed-member movement, her diary entry for 13 February 1834 – "Boys do not go to temperance meeting" – hints that her brothers did not share her enthusiasm for the cause. Perhaps they, like the Grants and so many other men involved in New Brunswick's lumbering industry, depended on rum to keep them warm in the winter woods.
24 Florence Moore, a teacher, was Ann Eliza's sister-in-law.
25 For the argument that voluntary associations "laid the basis for women's claim to the public voice and intellectual authority necessary for the making of public opinion," see Kelley. *Learning to Stand & Speak*, 13–14.

26 For an early, largely social control approach to the analysis of perhaps the best-know women's voluntary society, the Woman's Christian Temperance Union, see Mitchinson, "The WCTU: 'For God, Home and Native Land'"; for a fuller and more nuanced analysis of the WCTU, see Cook, *"Through Sunshine and Shadow"*; for a useful discussion of the contrast in membership between mixed-gender temperance lodges and the WCTU, see Marks, *Revivals and Roller Rinks*.
27 Veer, "Feminist Forebears," 5–6.
28 Annie Trueman to Rebecca Trueman, 12 February 1883, Josiah Wood Manuscript Collection, MC218, MS 16 (71a), PANB.
29 Rebecca Trueman to Laura Trueman Wood, 20 February 1883, Josiah Wood Manuscript Collection, MC218, MS 16 (88), PANB.
30 Laura Trueman Wood to Rebecca Trueman, 20 March 1883, Josiah Wood Manuscript Collection, MC218, MS 16 (76), PANB.
31 Annie Trueman to Rebecca Trueman, 23 March 1883, Josiah Wood Manuscript Collection, MC218, MS 16 (77a), PANB.
32 Laura Trueman Wood to Rebecca Trueman, 26 March 1883, Josiah Wood Manuscript Collection, MC218, MS 16 (78), PANB.
33 Rebecca Trueman to Laura Trueman Wood, 28 March 1883, Josiah Wood Manuscript Collection, MC218, MS 16 (92), PANB.
34 Rebecca Trueman to Laura Trueman Wood, 20 February 1883, Josiah Wood Manuscript Collection, MC218, MS 16 (88), PANB.
35 The petitions came from Welford in Kent County, from Chatham and Newcastle in Northumberland County, and from Baie Verte, Dorchester, Petitcodiac, Port Elgin, Salisbury, and Upper Sackville in Westmorland County.
36 Veer, "Feminist Forebears,"195, and endnote 6.
37 For a full discussion of the WEA, see Clarke, "The Saint John Women's Enfranchisement Association." Not until 1919 would New Brunswick legislators pass a bill enfranchising women.
38 Emma Fiske was a member of the Saint John Art Club, the ladies' auxiliary of the Natural History Society, the Associated Charities of Saint John, the Woman's Christian Temperance Union, and the Red Cross Society (Cook, "Skinner, Emma Sophia (Fiske)," *DCB*).
39 McAdam, "In Search of Ella Hatheway," http://www.wfhathewaylabourexhibitcentre.ca/labour-history/in-search-of-ella-hatheway-social-reformer-in-early-20th-century-saint-john-new-brunswick/
40 Cook, "Skinner, Emma Sophia (Fiske)," *DCB*.
41 Laura Trueman Wood Journal of Everyday Affairs, 21–2 March 1878.

42 Couturier, "Prohibition or Regulation?,"145. The Canada Temperance Act, or Scott Act, passed by the federal government in 1878, allowed for local option. Moncton opted for a ban on alcoholic beverages in 1879, although, as Sadie's diary suggests, the Acadians had opposed it.
43 Having agreed to hold a national referendum on prohibition, Prime Minister Wilfrid Laurier's recently elected Liberal government, faced with the result – a majority of voters in every province but Quebec supported prohibition – determined that the Canada Temperance Act remained their least divisive option. Rejecting the results of the referendum on the grounds of low voter turnout, they returned the decision to local jurisdictions.
44 See Coops, "Living By Faith," and Nelson, "Links in the Chain."
45 For a discussion of this shift, see Brouwer, *New Women for God*, and Gagan, *A Sensitive Independence*. For Maritime Baptist women, see Ross, "Sharing a Vision."
46 For a discussion of the significance of the YWCA on university campuses, see Pederson, "'The Call to Service,'" 187–215.
47 Violet Goldsmith Diaries, Sunday, 21 May 1905.

14. A Cosmopolitan Outlook

1 Acheson, "The National Policy," outlines both the impact of the National Policy on New Brunswick and the ensuing decline. See also Nerbas, "Adapting to Decline," 151–60, for the response of the bourgeoisie to changing realities.
2 This was especially true in borderlands communities (see Davis, *An International Community*). See also Hornsby, Konrad, and Herlan, eds., *The Northeastern Borderlands*. The broader significance of "socio-economic, geopolitical and psychological" borders is addressed in Widdis, *With Scarcely a Ripple*.
3 A suburb of Boston.
4 For a contemporary assessment of these migrants, see Brookes, "The Provincials."
5 See Brookes, "Out-Migration," and Thornton, "The Problem of Out-Migration."
6 See Ann Eliza Rogers Diary, 5 March 1874, November 1875, and February–May 1889.
7 Barman, "Nova Scotia to British Columbia," chap. 3 of *Sojourning Sisters*.
8 Violet Goldsmith Diaries, 8–30 June 1905.
9 A notable exception is Kelly, *In the New England Fashion*.

10 On 8 November 1861, the *USS San Jacinto* intercepted the British mail packet *Trent* and removed two Confederate envoys, James Mason and John Slidell, who were bound for England and France hoping to press the Confederacy cause. Britain and the United States teetered on the brink of war until the Lincoln administration released the men and disavowed the action.
11 Ann Eliza Rogers Diary, 10 September 1862.
12 In May 1861, many men responded to President Lincoln's call to serve in the Union Army for a term of three years, or for the duration of the war. In August 1862, with enlistments falling, the president reduced the term of service to nine months – hence, nine months' men.
13 Ann Eliza Rogers Diary, 22 April 1873.
14 George Hill to Sarah Hill, 26 February 1846. George Stillman Hill Manuscript Collection, MC1001, MS 6, PANB, in which George noted that "Mary would like to receive papers frequently, and you will have enough to send her of extra papers, during the Session."
15 See, for example, the many letters and articles cited in Nelson, "Links in the Chain."
16 The families of a number of diarists subscribed to *Harpers*, and some diarists occasionally had access to *The Illustrated London News*. The most common denominational papers subscribed to were *The Christian Visitor* and *The Witness*. Biographies read by our diarists included, among others, the following: *Charles Kingsley, his Letters and Memoirs of His Life* (1877), written by his widow, Fanny Grenfell Kingsley; *History of Mary, Queen of Scots* (1878) by Jacob Abbot; and *Stray Leaves from Scotch and English History with the Life of Sir William Wallace, Scotland's Patriot Hero and Political Martyr* (Montreal: 1876), by Charles Gordon Glass. I am grateful to Andrew Lockhart, who undertook the preliminary research in identifying the specific works of fiction and non-fiction the diarists were reading. For a discussion of the eclectic range of reading material that led one nineteenth-century rural New Brunswick woman not only to embrace the dress reform and hydrotherapy movements but also to become actively involved in the movement to establish utopian communities, see Findon, *Seeking Our Eden*.
17 Jacobina Campbell's Commonplace Book, 1817–1825, York-Sunbury Historical Collection, MC300, MS 2/126, PANB.
18 In 1883 among a good many other books, Sophy recorded reading and enjoying *The Life Worth Living: Missionary Sermons* by Wilmot Buxton, published in London the previous year. Other diarists also enjoyed a variety of spiritual texts. Kate Loggie "thought very highly" of Rev Dr Newton's eighteenth-century *Letters to his Adopted Daughter* (first published in the

nineteenth century), while her sister Jessie added the Scottish evangelist and natural science lecturer Henry Drummond's *Natural Law in the Spiritual World* (1885) to her shipboard reading.

19 See especially Mary Wolhaupter and Kate Loggie's diaries. For a discussion of this view of reading fiction as a guilty pleasure – characterized by Kate Loggie as "idle reading" – in the American context, see Kelley, *Learning to Stand & Speak*, 179, 182–7.

20 Although diarists rarely mentioned the source of their supply of books, Sophy Carman frequented Hall's Bookstore in Fredericton (which continued to serve the people of that city for over a century).

21 Poetry read by Ida MacDonald included the poetry of Alfred Gibbs Campbell, an abolitionist, a temperance campaigner, and an advocate of women's rights (*Campbell's Poems*), and a poetry chapbook, *Mary, the Maid of the Inn* (1837), compiled by Robert Southey.

22 McCall, "'Shall I Fetter Her Will?'" 99–104. See also Kelley, "The Sentimentalists," 440. Guildford addresses this issue from a slightly different perspective in "Creating the Ideal Man."

23 See, for example, Lottie Reid's diary for 1879 as she followed the voyage of the *Kesmark*, carrying her newly married sister Josephine and her brother Watson.

24 A Polonaise was a coat-like dress with a fitted bodice and full skirt draped in front from the waist and caught up at the back so it fell in three loops. A "basque" refers to a short continuation of the bodice below the waist.

25 Josephine Reid Turner to Lottie Reid, 14 May 1881, Turner Family Papers, S208-1, F46-1, NBMA.

26 Baird, *Women at Sea*, 42–4.

27 See, for example, the story of Annie Parker Cochrane in Baird, *Women at Sea*, 46–56.

28 Steinitz, "Travel Diaries, Journals, Logbooks," 887.

29 Maggie Loggie Valentine Journal Letter, 1885, UNBA.

30 Huff argues that "for the growth of experience to thrive in diaries featuring travel women writers must review their personal and cultural identities by symbolically joining the places visited as well as the places left behind with a journey into the psyche" ("Writer at Large," 127).

31 Amelia Holder Diaries, 20 January 1868. For a similar tendency among British women travellers, see McEwan, *Gender, Geography and Empire*, 78–9.

32 The Buenos Aires Carnival (or Carnaval), an annual event, was traditionally held four days before Ash Wednesday, the day of fasting that marks the beginning of Lent.

33 Amelia later noted in her diary that at the height of the epidemic of yellow fever at this time, as many as 700 a day died.
34 Lighters are barges, usually flat bottomed, used in unloading (lightening) ships offshore.
35 Josephine Reid Turner to Lottie Reid, 15 March 1881, Turner Family Papers, S208-1, F46-1, NBMA.
36 Josephine Reid Turner to Lottie Reid, 11 December 1881, Turner Family Papers, S208-1, F46-1, NBMA.
37 Jessie Loggie Journal Letter, 26 December 1887.
38 Campbell, "Nineteenth Century New Brunswick Women Travellers."
39 On the search for the "picturesque," see Ghose, *Women Travellers in Colonial India*, 42.
40 "Pumlow" is almost certainly a misspelling of "pomelo," the largest of the citrus fruits.
41 The Maidan (literally, open field) is the largest urban park in the Indian state of West Bengal. It is a vast stretch of field, dotted with statues and other architectural features, but best known for its numerous play grounds, including the Eden Gardens, a famous cricketing venue.
42 Josephine Reid Turner to Lottie Reid, 15 March 1881, Turner Family Papers, S208-1, F46-1, NBMA.
43 Clayton, "'A Long Voyage Before Us,'" 95–6. Mann, "Travel Lesson," disputes the notion that travel was a broadening experience for women, but the evidence from New Brunswick women travellers does not accord with the experience of the Ontario women she cites (see Campbell, "New Brunswick Women Travellers").
44 Brouwer, *New Women For God*, and Gagan, *A Sensitive Independence*.
45 Nelson, "Links in the Chain," and Coops, "Living By Faith."

15. In the Midst of Life

1 Sarah Hill to Mary Hill, 23 February 1846, George Stillman Hill Manuscript Collection, MC1001, MS6/4, PANB. Consumption is, of course, today known today as tuberculosis.
2 While it is impossible to calculate death rates before mid-century, the annual Canadian death rate stood at 21.6 per 1,000 population for the period 1851–61, declining to 12.9 per 1,000 by the decade from 1901–11 (Urquhart and Buckley, eds., *Historical Statistics of Canada*, Series B 100–107, 44). By 1982, New Brunswick's annual death rate had declined to 7.4 per 1,000 population (*Historical Statistics of New Brunswick*, Table A-1, 6–7).

3 Vinovskis, "Angels' Heads and Weeping Willows." Rosenblatt offers a similar argument for the nineteenth century: "The great contact the diarists had with dying and the dead makes the apparent 'preoccupation' of people of the nineteenth century with death more understandable" (*Bitter, Bitter Tears*, 67).
4 Marshall, "'Death Abolished,'" 372.
5 Little, "Death in the Lower St. John River Valley," 126–7.
6 See marriage licence for Zebulon Jones and Bertha Frost, F-9100, #2241 (1875), PANB; manuscript census returns for Greenwich Parish, 1881, 1891, PANB.
7 For the first specific references to George MacDonald's date of death, see Janet MacDonald Diary, 31 December 1861; for Susan McDonald's death, see March 1867.
8 Interview with Frank Morrison, Lucy Morrison's great grandson, 2001.
9 For a record of Upton's death, see George E. Hill Diary, 16 November 1854, George Stillman Hill Manuscript Collection, MC1001, MS6/34, PANB: "My brother A. Upton Hill died this day."
10 See obituary, *The Daily Telegraph* (Saint John), 16 October 1876 (cited in Daniel F. Johnson's New Brunswick Newspaper Vital Statistics, PANB).
11 Clayton, "'A Long Voyage Before Us.'"
12 Sarah Hill to Mary Hill, 23 February 1846, George Stillman Hill Manuscript Collection, MC1001, MS6/4, PANB.
13 Ann Eliza Rogers Diary, 7 May 1854.
14 Marshall, "Death Abolished," 373–5.
15 Ann Eliza Rogers Diary, 6, 8, 9, and 14 February 1858.
16 Marshall, "Death Abolished," 372; see also Jalland, *Death in the Victorian Family*, 39–46.
17 Marshall, "Death Abolished," 372–9, quote p. 372.
18 Marshall, "Death Abolished," 378.
19 Mary Isoline Wolhaupter Diary, 25 March 1869.
20 For a discussion of the concept of "holy dying" and the changing "Evangelical ideal of the 'Good Death,'" see chap. 1 of Jalland, *Death in the Victorian Family*.
21 Annie Trueman Diary, 3 January 1871.
22 For a discussion of the "ideal of a good Christian death," particularly as it related to deaths from consumption (tuberculosis), see Jalland, *Death in the Victorian Family*, 39–46.
23 Sophia Carman to Muriel Carman, 11 August 1882, Correspondence Jean Murray Carman to Parents, 1882-83, F511, S225, William F. Ganong Papers, NBMA (emphasis Sophy's). Each year, on 25 August, Sophy recorded

Norman's birthday, noting, in 1885, "My Baby's 20th birth-day (had he lived)."
24 Willie is the brother of Alden and husband of Lottie's older sister Mary.
25 James, Lottie's eldest brother, was working away from home at the time of Orpah's death.
26 These were twenty-two-year-old Arthur, twenty-year-old Alva, and eighteen-year-old Hannah. The youngest, ten-year-old Nellie, was the only exception.
27 George Else Sr was married to Agnes Estabrooks by this stage. He was also George Estabrooks's father-in-law, though George's wife had died, probably in childbirth. The George Else referred to here was very likely George Jr, brother-in-law to George Estabrooks.
28 Annie Trueman to Laura Trueman Wood, Sackville, 2 April 1904, Josiah Wood Manuscript Collection, MC218/16 (276), PANB.
29 Ida MacDonald Diaries, 3 January 1883.
30 Charlotte Reid Diaries, 29 May 1879.
31 Janet MacDonald Diary, 22 December 1858.

Conclusion

1 Mary Hill was the only diarist who referred to the possible advantages of "single blessedness," and this as a witty, tongue-in-cheek comment in a letter written while she was still a teenager (Letter from Mary W. Hill to "Friends at Home," 10 February 1846, George Stillman Hill Manuscript Collection, MC1001, MS6, PANB). Nonetheless, whereas four of the thirteen single women diarists who later married expressed concern that they might not marry, of the seven diarists who lived beyond the age of thirty-five and did not marry, only one, Hannah Estabrooks, expressed the view in her diary that life had passed her by (Hannah Estabrooks Diary, 25 February 1903, Marjorie Watters MacMullin fonds, MG H 174, UNBA).
2 For an insightful analysis of "heterosociability" in nineteenth-century New England, see chap. 7 of Kelly, *In the New England Fashion*. Similarly, Noël argues that "the family life of the literate classes in the Canadas before 1870 was not located in the narrow private world of the domestic sphere but in a much broader social space shared by people of both genders and all ages" (*Family Life and Sociability*, 13). For yet another perspective on the heterosocial aspect of public life – in this case, in taverns – see Roberts, *In Mixed Company*.
3 However, some serious students might, like Violet Goldsmith, spend such holidays "'skating' through Physics, Psychology, etc." (Violet Goldsmith Diaries, 28 November 1903).

4 For an excellent analysis of the idealization of domesticity in denominational periodicals, see Marks, "'A Fragment of Heaven on Earth'?"
5 For women's success as fund raisers, see Godfrey, "'Into the Hands of the Ladies,'" and Nelson, "Links in the Chain."
6 Nelson, "Links in the Chain." See also Brouwer, *Modern Women, Modernizing Men*.
7 For women's political partisanship in New England during the same period, see Kelly, *In the New England Fashion*, 210–12.
8 For women's intellectual engagement during an earlier period, see Kelley, *Learning to Stand & Speak*, 30–1.
9 For a discussion of the significance of women's voluntary associations in nineteenth-century New England, see Kelly, *In the New England Fashion*, 199–202.

Afterword

1 *The Visitor* (Saint John, 28 November 1883), in Daniel F. Johnson's New Brunswick Newspaper Vital Statistics, PANB. Unless otherwise noted, all newspaper citations in this chapter come from this source.
2 D. Murray Young traced Sandy's family to Etobicoke Township, near Toronto, but did not find any record of other members of the family having settled there. According to Maxwell, *An Outline of the History of Central New Brunswick*, Patrick also immigrated to Upper Canada. She states that Jacobina and Ann are buried with their father in the Central Loyalist Cemetery in Fredericton, but this cannot be confirmed.
3 The information in this paragraph is drawn largely from the 1851, 1861, 1871, and 1881 manuscript census returns for St Stephen, Charlotte County, New Brunswick.
4 *The Daily Gleaner* (Fredericton, 12 July 1893). Lucy's son Willie, who left Fredericton seventeen years earlier, seems entirely forgotten by the authors of the obituary. Like his brothers Tom and Julius, William Morrison (a druggist) was working and raising his family in the United States at the time of his mother's death. Lucy's remaining sons – Jack, Frank, and Stewart – were all living in Fredericton.
5 In his will, John Morrison left "[the] mill, mill property and machinery owned and occupied by me" to his son John, who had been managing the business for some years. He bequeathed his remaining personal estate and "the Homestead and all other buildings in connection with my residence, together with the gardens, to be subject to the life interest of my wife, Lucy

A. Morrison, who shall have the absolute right to have and enjoy the same as she may think proper." After her death, these were to go to John (will of John A. Morrison, probated 5 June 1893, York County Probate Records, RG 7, RS 75 [F11762], PANB).
6 Sarah Bliss's decline began on Sunday, 10 January 1886. She died at 3 a.m. on the 23rd, according to Sophy Carman's diary entry for 22 January 1886.
7 Cited in Miller, *Bliss Carman*, 36–7.
8 Another family – a sixty-year-old Irish-born contractor, his wife, and three children – are recorded as living in the same house. Although the 1881 census does not list relationship to head of household, it would seem likely that, since Mary Hill was listed as a separate "family," before Peter Carroll and his family, the house was divided into two separate flats (manuscript census returns for St Andrews, New Brunswick, 1881).
9 Manuscript census returns for St Stephen, New Brunswick, 1891.
10 For Louisa and Augusta's deaths, see *Saint Croix Courier* (St Stephen, 6 October and 1 December 1892). There is no obituary for Mary Hill in Johnson's listing, which covers the period to 1896. As she is not in the 1901 census records, she must have died between 1895 and 1901.
11 For Richard Waltham's death, see *The Daily Telegraph* (Saint John, 30 June 1883).
12 Ann Eliza's own transcription had ended abruptly in the middle of the diary entry for 1 September 1888: "Rained very hard ..." Ella Moore's note follows that entry, and her transcription begins with that same entry.
13 Ann Eliza Rogers Diary, 18 April 1895.
14 Her eldest daughter, Isabelle, was married and living in Boston, while her eldest son, Frank, also married, was living in Laconner, Washington Territory.
15 Mary Isoline Wolhaupter Diary, Friday, 5 February 1869.
16 From the manuscript census returns for Carleton County, New Brunswick, 1871, 1881, 1901, and 1911, and Mary Watters's death certificate, filed in 1920.
17 Manuscript census returns for Greenwich Parish, King's County, New Brunswick, 1901.
18 Manuscript census returns for Greenwich Parish, Kings County, New Brunswick, 1911. Benjamin Burns may have been a British "home child." The word "adopted" was first entered, then crossed out and replaced with "domestic."
19 See death certificate for Bertha Jones, filed in 1925.
20 Josephine Turner Diary, 5 and 6 April 1884.
21 *The Daily Telegraph* (30 May 1884).

22 Merritt Reid to Charlotte Reid, 10 May 1885, Turner Family Papers, S208-1, F44-4, NBMA.
23 James Reid to Charlotte Reid, [June] 1887, Turner Family Papers, S208-1, F44-4, NBMA.
24 *Chignecto Post* (Sackville, 14 July 1887).
25 Ann Eliza Rogers Diary, 25 December 1889. *Messenger and Visitor* (Saint John, 1 January 1890), gives the date of death as 24 December.
26 Manuscript census returns for Sackville, Westmorland County, New Brunswick, 1911.
27 Laura Trueman Wood Correspondence, 1914, Josiah Wood Manuscript Collection, MC218, PANB.
28 Josiah Wood served in the House of Commons from 1882 to 1895. Appointed to the Senate of Canada in 1895, he served until 1912, when he was appointed Lieutenant Governor of New Brunswick, a post he held until his death in 1927.
29 Jobb, *The Life and Times of Josiah Wood*, 95–6.
30 Margaret Loggie Valentine Journal Letter, 30 November 1885.
31 Catherine Loggie Diary. Two undated entries, at the end of the diary, are dated 8 and 13 January. They can have been written no earlier than 1886 and no later than 1890.
32 Manuscript census returns for Alnwick Parish, Northumberland County, New Brunswick, 1891.
33 *The World* (Chatham, 20 December 1893). Launched in April of 1882, at the shipyard of W.H. Potter & Son, Liverpool, for the Lancaster Shipowners' Co., also of Liverpool, the *Muncaster Castle*, designated for use in the India jute trade, had always been captained by William Valentine.
34 Manuscript census returns for Alnwick Parish, Northumberland County, New Brunswick, 1901.
35 *The Daily Telegraph* (14 January 1889).
36 *The Daily Telegraph* (5 May 1892).
37 Unless otherwise noted, information on the Holders comes from Bannister, Fullerton, Holder, Duplisea, Titus, Duplisea, Barnett, and Quigley, compilers, "Sea Going Days," MC80.1723, PANB.
38 *Daily News* (Saint John, 16 April 1877); *The Daily Telegraph* (8 November 1877); *Carleton Sentinel* (Woodstock, 6 April 1889 and 17 May 1890).
39 Manuscript census returns for Saint John, New Brunswick, 1881, Woodstock, Carleton County, 1891, and for Greenwich, Kings County, 1901 and 1911, when George was listed as a widower.
40 *Chignecto Post* (21 August 1890).
41 *Moncton Times* (7 April 1891).

42 "Mr Waters" made his first appearance in Hannah Estabrooks's diary on 31 January 1905.
43 Manuscript census returns for Brighton and Florenceville, Carleton County, New Brunswick, 1911. Hannah reported earnings of $270, while Alva reported earnings of $250. It is likely that Arthur, also living in Brighton and listed as a self-employed "trader," now owned the store in which he and Hannah had previously worked and employed his sister as bookkeeper.
44 Information from the certificate of registration of death, Province of New Brunswick, filed by her sister Hannah. She was listed as a music teacher, who had last taught music in 1940, and who had practised her profession for twenty-five (sic) years.
45 Information drawn from Hannah Estabrooks's probated will, F6219, #106-8, PANB.
46 No occupation is listed for Laura in 1891, when both her parents were still alive. By 1901, their father having died, her younger brother Walter was managing the farm, and Laura was listed as a music teacher (manuscript census returns for Mill Village, Cumberland County, Nova Scotia, 1891 and 1901).
47 Lewis, "Agrarian Idealism."
48 All information on the period following Laura Fullerton's marriage is drawn from Lewis, *The Fawcetts of Sackville*, 178–9.
49 Peck, ed., *A Full House and Fine Singing*.
50 Violet Goldsmith Diaries, 4 December 1905.
51 Violet Goldsmith's memoir is cited from http://www.alittlehistory.com/Vi-schol.htm.
52 Information about Kate Miles's later life is mainly from Kate's letters to her mother, 1907 to 1923. Although Kate is listed in the 1911 manuscript census as living at home with her parents in Maugerville, her letters from that year indicate that she was not. Her letters are privately held, and I am grateful to Celia Munro, Kate's great niece, for sharing them with me and for providing the information on Kate's later life (from Charles Miles, son of Kate's younger brother, George).

Bibliography

Archival Collections

Mount Allison University Archives (MAUA)

DIARIES:
Fullerton: Laura Cynthia Fullerton Diary, 1886, 630, 8021.
Trueman: [Annie Trueman Diary (1885, 1886, 1888)] Laura Trueman's Notebook, 1885, Wood Family Papers, 8914/7.
Wood: Laura S. Trueman Diary, 1868–73, Wood Family Papers, 8914/5/1.
Wood: Laura Trueman Wood Journal of Everyday Affairs, 1878 & 1885, Wood Family Papers, 8510/1/4.
Wood: Laura Trueman Wood Diary, 1898–1900, Wood Family Papers, 9542.

New Brunswick Museum Archives (NBMA)

CORRESPONDENCE:
William F. Ganong Papers, 3436 5 F218, F520, LE2.
Josephine Turner Correspondence, Turner Family Papers, 5024 12 S208-1, F43.
Turner Family Papers, 5024 12 S208-1, F46 LE2.

DIARIES:
Carman: Sophia Carman Diaries, William F. Ganong Papers, 3436 5 F218-4, F516-S225.
Reid: Charlotte Reid Diaries, Turner Family Papers, 5024 12 S208-1, F46-1.
Turner: Josephine Turner Diary while in Buenos Aires, Turner Family Papers, 5024 12 S208-1, F34.

Waltham: Annie T. Johnston Waltham Diaries, Marianne Grey Otty Papers, S119.
Williamson: Lillian Williamson Diary, S155-6.

MISCELLANEOUS
Carman: Sophia Carman Receipt Files for 1884, William F. Ganong Papers, 3436 5 F511.

Provincial Archives of New Brunswick (PANB)

CORRESPONDENCE:
George Stillman Hill Manuscript Collection, MC1001.
Josiah Wood Manuscript Collection, MC218.
Moore-DeWolfe Collection, Microfilm: F4249

DIARIES:
Campbell: Jacobina Campbell Diary, York-Sunbury Historical Collection, MC300, MS23/1.
Estabrooks: Alvaretta Estabrooks Diary, 1889, MC259, MS1A
Grant: [Marjory and Isabella] Grant Diary, MC285
Harper: Sadie Harper Diaries, MC286.
Hill: George F. Hill Diary, George Stillman Hill Manuscript Collection (Hill Family Collection), MC1001, MS6/34.
Hill: Mary Whitney Hill Diary, George Stillman Hill Manuscript Collection (Hill Family Collection), MC1001, MS3E4.
Holder: Amelia Holder Diaries; also diaries of Aggie and Ada Holder, MC665, MS1 [Microfilm: F569].
Jones: [E. Bertha Frost Jones Diary] Diary of a King's County Widow, F806.
Miles: Katherine Miles Diary, MC1145, MS2.
Morrison: Lucy Everett Morrison Diaries, MC1958.
Pitt. Emma Alice Pitt Diary, MC827.
Rogers: Ann Eliza Rogers Diary, MC260.
Trueman: Annie Trueman Diary, Josiah Wood Manuscript Collection, MC218/6.

FAMILY HISTORIES: MC 1
Grant Family.

MANUSCRIPT CENSUSES:
Albert County: 1851, 1861, 1871, 1881, 1891.
Carleton County: 1851, 1861, 1871, 1881, 1891.
Charlotte County: 1851, 1861, 1871, 1881, 1891.
Kings County: 1851, 1861, 1871, 1881, 1891.
Northumberland County: 1861, 1871, 1881, 1891.
Queens County: 1851, 1861, 1871, 1881, 1891.
Restigouche County: 1851
Saint John County: 1851, 1881
Sunbury County: 1851, 1861, 1871, 1881, 1891.
Victoria County: 1851.
Westmorland County: 1851, 1891.
York County: 1851; Fredericton, 1861, 1871, 1881, 1891; Marysville, 1881, 1891.

MISCELLANEOUS GOVERNMENT RECORD COLLECTIONS:
Charlotte County Registry Office Records, 1846–1850.
Court of General Sessions for Albert, Charlotte and Sunbury Counties, 1845–75, RG18, RS146, RS148, and RS157.
Petitions to the Legislative Assembly of New Brunswick from WCTU branches in Welford in Kent County, from Chatham and Newcastle in Northumberland County, and from Baie Verte, Dorchester, Petitcodiac, Port Elgin, Salisbury, and Upper Sackville in Westmorland County.
Reports of the Debates and Proceedings of the House of Assembly of the Province of New Brunswick (Fredericton, 1852).

MARRIAGE RECORDS:
Marriage Registers, RS141, B1a [F13378].
Marriage Licence for Zebulon Jones and Bertha Frost, F-9100, #2241 (1875).

SCHOOL RECORDS:
Grammar School Records for Albert, Charlotte, and Sunbury Counties, 1845–1875, F647, F650, PANB.
Teachers and Trustees' Returns, 1880, McRobbie's Road, School District 8, Alnwick Parish, Northumberland County, RS657.

WILLS:
Charlotte County Probate Court Records. RG 7, RS 63.
Probated Will of Hannah Estabrooks, 1950, Fredericton, York County, F6219, #106-8.
Probated Will of John A. Morrison, 1893, Fredericton, York County, RG 7, RS 75 [F11762].

Probated Will of Zebulon Jones, 1892, Greenwich Parish, King's County, RG 7, RS 66, [F11718].

MISCELLANEOUS PRIVATE MANUSCRIPT COLLECTIONS:
Bannister, Marjory Henderson, Charlotte Henderson Fullerton, Jean Henderson Holder, Margaret Henderson Duplisea, Gladys Henderson Titus, Mark Duplisea, Cleadie Barnett, and Beth Titus Quigley, compilers, "Sea Going Days of the Holder Family, 1851–1878," unpublished manuscript, MC80.1723.
Jacobina Campbell's Commonplace Book, 1817-1825, York-Sunbury Historical Collection, MC300, MS2/126.
Gilbert, Thomas (Hon), Queens County, MC1156, Vol. 8, part 2.
Laura Trueman Wood, "Biographical Note," n.d., Josiah Wood Manuscript Collection, MC218/5, PANB.
Minutes of the Maternal Association of St Stephen-Milltown, Charlotte County, 1836: Maternal Association of St Stephen-Milltown Records, MC399
Minutes of Meetings of the Woodstock WCTU, 1888–1893, 1893–1899, New Brunswick Woman's Christian Temperance Union Collection, MC63, 3/2, 3/3.
Patricia Morrison, unpublished genealogy of the Morrison family, MC 1958.
Mrs R. Wilmot Travel Diary, 8 July 1862, MC300, MS23/3

ONLINE RESOURCES:
Daniel F. Johnson's New Brunswick Newspaper Vital Statistics.
Lovell's Canadian Directory for 1871.

University of New Brunswick Archives (UNBA)

DIARIES:
Estabrooks: Alvaretta Estabrooks Diaries, Marjorie Watters MacMullin fonds, MG H 174.
Estabrooks: Hannah Estabrooks Diary, Marjorie Watters MacMullin fonds, MG H 174.
Goldsmith: Violet Goldsmith Diaries, MG H 133.
Loggie: Catherine Loggie Diary, 1880–81, Loggie Collection, Burnt Church, NB, MG H 128, No. 1.
Loggie: Jessie Loggie Diary, Loggie Collection, Burnt Church, NB, MG H 128, No. 4.
Loggie: Jessie Loggie Journal Letter, Loggie Collection, Burnt Church, NB, MG H 128, No. 3.
Loggie Valentine: Margaret Loggie Valentine Journal Letter, Loggie Collection, Burnt Church, NB, MG H 128, No. 2.

MacDonald: Janet [Hendry] MacDonald Diary, MG H 108.
Wolhaupter: Mary Isoline Wolhaupter Diary, Marjorie Watters MacMullin fonds, MG H 174.

GOVERNMENT DOCUMENTS:
"Chief Superintendent's Report." *Journals of the House of Assembly of the Province of New Brunswick (JHA), 1878.* Fredericton: 1879.
"Report of the Principal of the Normal School." *JHA, 1878.* Fredericton: 1879.
"Report of the Principal of the Normal School." Appendix A. *JHA, 1880.* Fredericton: 1881.

MISCELLANEOUS:
"Class of 1905," *The University Monthly,* Vol. 25, no. 1 (University of New Brunswick), UA RG84.
Education Circular for the Province of New Brunswick [Microfiche].
"Passing Through: Pictures From the Life of Mrs. W. Garland Foster (Nee Annie H. Ross)," Annie H. Ross Foster Hanley Memoir (1939), MG L7.3.4.

NEWSPAPERS:
Carleton Sentinel (Woodstock, NB)
Chignecto Post (Sackville, NB)
Daily News (Saint John, NB)
The Daily Gleaner (Fredericton, NB)
The Daily Telegraph (Saint John, NB)
The Moncton Times (Moncton, NB)
Saint Croix Courier (St Stephen, NB)
The World (Chatham, NB)

ONLINE SOURCES:
Manuscript Censuses for 1901:
    Carleton County (also for 1911)
    Charlotte County
    Kings County (also for 1911)
    Northumberland County
    Queens County
    Restigouche County
    Sunbury County
    Victoria County
    Westmorland County (also for 1911)
    York County

Manuscript Census for Lewiston Maine, USA, 1900.
Manuscript Censuses for Mill Village, Cumberland County, Nova Scotia, 1881, 1891, 1901.
1881 Manuscript Census Records for Township 13 (Tyne Valley) District 1, Prince Edward Island, 1881.
Manuscript Census Records for 133 Kings Division, District 1, Prince Edward Island, 1891.
President Rutherford B. Hayes. "Second Annual Message," December of 1878. http://millercenter.org/president/hayes/speeches/speech-3749
McAdam, Susan, "In Search of Ella Hatheway, Social Reformer in Early 20th Century Saint John, New Brunswick." Frank and Ella Hatheway Labour Exhibit Centre. http://www.wfhathewaylabourexhibitcentre.ca/labour-history/in-search-of-ella-hatheway-social-reformer-in-early-20th-century-saint-john-new-brunswick/
On King's Daughters, http://www.iokds.org
On Violet Goldsmith, http://www.alittlehistory.com/Vi-schol.htm

Interviews

Frank Morrison (Lucy Everett Morrison's great grandson), 2001.
Dr D. Murray Young, 2000–14.

Privately Held Manuscripts

Diaries:

MacDonald: Ida MacDonald Diaries [property of Alice Taylor].

Primary Sources: Published

Bailey, Alfred Goldsworthy, ed. *The Letters of James and Ellen Robb: Portrait of a Fredericton Family in Early Victorian Times*. Fredericton: Acadiensis Press, 1983.
Blom, Margaret Howard, and Thomas E. Blom, eds. *Canada Home: Juliana Horatio Ewing's Fredericton Letters, 1867–1859*. Vancouver: UBC Press, 1983.
Bradley, Mary [Coy Morris]. *A Narrative of the Life and Christian Experience of Mrs Mary Bradley of Saint John, New Brunswick*. Boston: Strong and Broadhead, 1849.
Bradley, Mary [Coy Morris]. "Mary Bradley's Reminiscences: A Domestic Life in Colonial New Brunswick." *Atlantis* 7, no. 1 (Fall 1981): 92–101.

McAlpine's Saint John City Directory. St John: D. McAlpine, 1878–9; 1879–80; 1880–1.
The Revised Statutes of New Brunswick, Vol. 1. Chapter 114, Section 1. Fredericton: J. Simpson, Printer to the Queen's Most Excellent Majesty, 1854.

Secondary Sources: Published

Acheson, T.W. "The National Policy and the Industrialization of the Maritimes, 1880–1910." *Acadiensis* 1, no. 2 (Spring 1972): 3–28.
Acheson, T.W. "New Brunswick Agriculture at the End of the Colonial Era: A Reassessment." *Acadiensis* 22, no. 2 (Spring 1993): 5–26.
Acheson, T.W. *Saint John: The Making of a Colonial Urban Community.* Toronto: University of Toronto Press, 1985.
Acheson, T.W. "A Study in the Historical Demography of a Loyalist County." *Histoire sociale/Social History* 1, no. 1 (April 1968): 53–65.
Allen, Judith. "Contextualizing Late-Nineteenth-Century Feminism: Problems and Comparisons." *Journal of the Canadian Historical Association* 1, no. 1 (1990): 17–36.
Anderson, Margo. "The History of Women and the History of Statistics." *Journal of Women's History* 4, no. 1 (Spring 1992): 14–36.
Andrew, Sheila M. *The Development of Elites in Acadian New Brunswick, 1861–1881.* Montreal: McGill-Queen's University Press, 1996.
Andrew, Sheila. "Selling Education: The Problems of Convent Schools in Acadian New Brunswick, 1858–1886." *CCHA, Historical Studies* 62 (1996): 15–32.
Axelrod, Paul. *The Promise of Schooling: Education in Canada, 1800–1914.* Toronto: University of Toronto Press, 1997.
Backhouse, Constance B. "Married Women's Property Law in Nineteenth-Century Canada." *Law and History Review* 6, no. 2 (Autumn 1988): 211–57.
Backhouse, Constance B. *Petticoats and Prejudice: Women and Law in Nineteenth Century Canada.* Toronto: Osgoode Society and Women's Press, 1991.
Baird, Donal. *Women at Sea in the Age of Sail.* Halifax: Nimbus, 2001.
Baker, Paula. "The Domestication of Politics: Women and American Political Society, 1780–1920." *American Historical Review* 89, no. 3 (June 1984): 620–47.
Baker, William M. *Timothy Warren Anglin, 1822–1896, Irish Catholic Canadian.* Toronto: University of Toronto Press, 1977.
Ball, Rosemary. "A Perfect Farmer's Wife: Women in Nineteenth-Century Rural Ontario." *Canada, An Historical Magazine* 3, no. 4 (1975): 2–21.
Barman, Jean. *Sojourning Sisters: The Lives and Letters of Jessie and Annie McQueen.* Toronto: University of Toronto Press, 2003.

Baskerville, Peter. *A Silent Revolution? Gender and Wealth in English Canada, 1860–1930*. Montreal: McGill-Queen's University Press, 2008.

Baskerville, Peter. "Women and Investment in Late-Nineteenth-Century Urban Canada: Victoria and Hamilton, 1880–1901." *The Canadian Historical Review* 80, no. 2 (June 1999): 191–218.

Baxter, Judith. *Clifton Royal: The Wetmores and Village Life in Nineteenth Century New Brunswick*. Gatineau, QC: Canadian Museum of Civilization, 2004.

Beattie, Betsy. "'Going Up to Lynn': Single Maritime-Born Women in Lynn, Massachusetts, 1879–1930." *Acadiensis* 22, no. 1 (Autumn 1992): 65–86.

Beattie, Betsy. *Obligation and Opportunity: Single Maritime Women in Boston, 1870–1930*. Montreal: McGill-Queen's University Press, 2000.

Bernard, Richard M., and Maris A. Vinovskis. "The Female School Teacher in Ante-Bellum Massachusetts." *Journal of Social History* 10, no. 3 (Spring 1977): 332–45.

Blodgett, Harriet, "Preserving the Moment in the Diary of Margaret Fountaine." In Bunkers and Huff, eds., *Inscribing the Daily*, 156–68.

Bloom, Lynn Z. "Adolescence and Life Writing." In *Encyclopedia of Life Writing: Autobiographical and Biographical Forms*, Vol. 1, edited by Margaretta Jolly, 6–7. London: Fitzroy Dearborn, 2001.

Bogaard, Paul A. "Introduction: Establishing Science in the Maritimes." In *Profiles of Science and Society in the Maritimes prior to 1914*, edited by Paul A. Bogaard, 13–23. Fredericton and Sackville: Acadiensis Press and the Centre for Canadian Studies, Mount Allison University, 1990.

Bradbury, Bettina. "Surviving as a Widow in 19th-Century Montreal." *Urban History Review/Revue d'histoire urbaine* 17, no. 3 (February 1989): 148–61.

Bradbury, Bettina. "Widowhood and Canadian Family History." In *Intimate Relations: Family and Community in Planter Nova Scotia, 1759–1800*, edited by Margaret Conrad, 19–41. Fredericton: Acadiensis Press, 1995.

Bradbury, Bettina. *Wife to Widow: Lives, Laws, and Politics in Nineteenth-Century Montreal*. Vancouver: UBC Press, 2011.

Bradbury, Bettina. *Working Families: Age, Gender, and Daily Survival in Industrializing Montreal*. Toronto: McClelland and Stewart, 1993.

Bremer, Anette. "Australia: 18th- and 19th-Century Diaries and Letters." In *Encyclopedia of Life Writing: Autobiographical and Biographical Forms*, Vol. 1, edited by Margaretta Jolly, 65–7. London: Fitzroy Dearborn, 2001.

Brookes, Alan. "Out-Migration from the Maritime Provinces, 1860–1900: Some Preliminary Considerations." *Acadiensis* 5, no. 2 (Spring 1976): 26–55.

Brookes, Alan A. "The Provincials by Albert J. Kennedy." *Acadiensis* 4, no. 2 (Spring 1975): 85–101.

Brouwer, Ruth Compton. *Modern Women, Modernizing Men: The Changing Missions of Three Professional Women in Asia and Africa, 1902–1969.* Vancouver: UBC Press, 2003.

Brouwer, Ruth Compton. *New Women for God: Canadian Presbyterian Women and India Missions, 1876–1914.* Toronto: University of Toronto Press, 1990.

Brown, Elspeth. "Gender and Identity in Rural Maine: Women and the *Maine Farmer*, 1870–1875." *Maine Historical Society Quarterly* 33, no. 2 (1993): 120–35.

Buckner, Phillip A. "The 1870s: Political Integration." In *The Atlantic Provinces in Confederation*, edited by E.R. Forbes and D.A. Muise, 48–81. Toronto and Fredericton: University of Toronto Press and Acadiensis Press, 1993.

Buckner, Phillip A. "Whatever Happened to the British Empire?" Presidential Address. *Journal of the Canadian Historical Association*, New Series 4, no. 4 (1993): 3–32.

Bunkers, Suzanne, and Cynthia Huff, eds. *Inscribing the Daily: Critical Essays on Women's Diaries.* Amherst: University of Massachusetts Press, 1996.

Burke, Sara Z. "New Women and Old Romans: Coeducation at the University of Toronto, 1884–95." *The Canadian Historical Review* 80, no. 2 (June 1999): 219–41.

Burton, Valerie. "The Making of a Nineteenth-Century Profession: Shipmasters and the British Shipping Industry." *Journal of the Canadian Historical Association* 1, no. 1 (Victoria 1990): 97–118.

Buss, Helen M. "Feminist Revision of New Historicism to Give Fuller Readings of Women's Private Writing." In Bunkers and Huff, eds., *Inscribing the Daily*, 86–103.

Calder, Doris. *All Our Born Days: A Lively History of New Brunswick's Kingston Peninsula.* Sackville: Percheron Press, 1984.

Campbell, Gail G. "Disfranchised but not Quiescent: Women Petitioners in New Brunswick in the Mid-19th Century." *Acadiensis* 18, no. 2 (Spring 1989): 22–54.

Campbell, Gail G. "Nineteenth Century New Brunswick Women Travellers and the British Connection, 1845–1905." In *Canada and the British World: Culture, Migration, and Identity*, edited by Phillip Buckner and R. Douglas Francis, 76–91. Vancouver: UBC Press, 2006.

Campbell, Gail G. "Using Diaries to Explore the Shared Worlds of Family and Community in 19th Century New Brunswick." In *Writing Feminist History: Productive Pasts and New Directions*, edited by Catherine Carstairs and Nancy Janovicek, 41–57. Vancouver: UBC Press, 2013.

Carter, Kathryn. "An Economy of Words: Emma Chadwick Stretch's Account Book Diary, 1859–1860." *Acadiensis* 29, no. 1 (Autumn 1999): 43–56.

Carter, Kathryn, ed. *The Small Details of Life: Twenty Diaries by Women in Canada, 1830–1996*. Toronto: University of Toronto Press, 2002.

Chambers, Lori. *Married Women and Property Law in Victorian Ontario*. Toronto: University of Toronto Press, 1997.

Chambers-Schiller, Lee Virginia. *Liberty, a Better Husband: Single Women in America: The Generation of 1780–1840*. New Haven, CT: Yale University Press, 1984.

Clarke, Brian P. *Piety and Nationalism: Lay Voluntary Associations and the Creation of an Irish-Catholic Community in Toronto, 1850–1895*. Montreal: McGill-Queen's University Press, 1993.

Clarke, Flora. *Sisters: Canada and India*. Moncton, NB: Maritime Press, 1939.

Cohen, Marjorie Griffin. *Women's Work, Markets, and Economic Development in Nineteenth-Century Ontario*. Toronto: University of Toronto Press, 1988.

Comacchio, Cynthia R. *The Infinite Bonds of Family: Domesticity in Canada, 1850–1940*. Toronto: University of Toronto Press, 1999.

Concise Oxford Dictionary of Current English, 5th ed. Oxford: Oxford University Press, 1964.

Conrad, Margaret. "Recording Angels: The Private Chronicles of Women from the Maritime Provinces of Canada, 1750–1950." In *The Neglected Majority: Essays in Canadian Women's History*, Vol. 2, edited by Alison Prentice and Susan Mann Trofimenkoff, 41–60. Toronto: McClelland and Stewart, 1985.

Conrad, Margaret. "'Sundays always make me think of home': Time & Place in Canadian Women's History." In *Not Just Pin Money: Selected Essays on the History of Women's Work in British Columbia*, edited by Barbara K. Latham and Roberta J. Pazdro, 1–16. Victoria: Camosun College, 1984.

Conrad, Margaret, Toni Laidlaw, and Donna Smyth. *No Place Like Home: Diaries and Letters of Nova Scotia Women 1771–1938*. Halifax: Formac, 1988.

Cook, Janice. "Skinner, Emma Sophia (Fiske)." *Dictionary of Canadian Biography*, Vol. 14 (1911–1920).

Cook, Sharon Anne. *"Through Sunshine and Shadow": The Woman's Christian Temperance Union, Evangelicalism, and Reform in Ontario, 1874–1930*. Montreal: McGill-Queen's University Press, 1995.

Cottam, Rachel. "Diaries and Journals: General Survey." In *Encyclopedia of Life Writing: Autobiographical and Biographical Forms*, Vol. 1, edited by Margaretta Jolly, 267–9. London: Fitzroy Dearborn, 2001.

Couturier, Jacques Paul. "Prohibition or Regulation? The Enforcement of the Canada Temperance Act in Moncton, 1881–1896." In *Drink in Canada: Historical Essays*, edited by Cheryl Krasnick Warsh, 144–65. Montreal: McGill-Queen's University Press, 1993.

Craig, Béatrice. *Backwoods Consumers and Homespun Capitalists: The Rise of a Market Culture in Eastern Canada*. Toronto: University of Toronto Press, 2009.

Craig, Béatrice. "La transmission des patrimoines fonciers dans le Haut-Saint-Jean au XIXe siècle." *Revue d'histoire de l'Amérique française* 45, no. 2 (automne 1991): 207–28.

Craig, Béatrice, and Judith Rygiel. "Femmes, marchés et production textile au Nouveau-Brunswick au cours du XIXe siècle." *Histoire & Mesure* 15, no. 1 (2000): 83–112.

Craig, Béatrice, Judith Rygiel, and Elizabeth Turcotte. "The Homespun Paradox: Market-Oriented Production of Cloth in Eastern Canada in the Nineteenth Century." *Agricultural History* 76, no. 1 (Winter 2002): 28–57.

Cross, K. Suzanne. "The Neglected Majority: The Changing Role of Women in 19th Century Montreal." In *The Neglected Majority: Essays in Canadian Women's History*, Vol. 1, edited by Susan Mann Trofimenkoff and Alison Prentice, 66–86. Toronto: McClelland and Stewart, 1977.

Culley, Margo. *A Day at a Time: The Diary Literature of American Women from 1764 to the Present*. New York: Feminist Press of the City University of New York, 1985.

Curtis, Bruce. *Building the Educational State: Canada West, 1836–1871*. London, ON: Althouse Press/Falmer Press, 1988.

Curtis, Bruce. *The Politics of Population: State Formation, Statistics, and the Census of Canada, 1840–1876*. Toronto: University of Toronto Press, 2001.

Davey, Ian E. "The Rhythm of Work and the Rhythm of School." In *Egerton Ryerson and His Times*, edited by Neil McDonald and Alf Chaiton, 221–53. Toronto: Macmillan, 1978.

Davey, Ian E. "Trends in Female School Attendance in Mid-Nineteenth Century Ontario." *Histoire sociale/Social History* 8, no. 16 (November 1975): 238–54.

Davidoff, Leonore. "Gender and the Great Divide." *Journal of Women's History* 15, no. 1 (Spring 2003): 11–27.

Davidoff, Leonore, and Catherine Hall. *Family Fortunes: Men and Women of the English Middle Class, 1780–1850*. Chicago: University of Chicago Press, 1987.

Davies, Gwendolyn. "The Diary of Sarah Frost, 1783: The Sounds and Silences of a Woman's Exile." *Papers of the Bibliographical Society of Canada* 42, no. 2 (Fall 2004): 57–69.

Davis, Harold A. *An International Community on the St. Croix (1604–1930)*. Orono: University of Maine Studies, 1950, 1974.

Davis, Nanciellen. "'Patriarchy from the Grave': Family Relations in 19th Century New Brunswick Wills." *Acadiensis* 13, no. 2 (Spring 1984): 91–100.

Deacon, Desley. "Political Arithmetic: The Nineteenth-Century Australian Census and the Construction of the Dependent Woman." *Signs: Journal of Women in Culture and Society* 11, no. 1 (Autumn 1985): 27–47.

DeLottinville, Peter. "Trouble in the Hives of Industry: The Cotton Industry Comes to Milltown, New Brunswick, 1879–1892." *Canadian Historical Association Historical Papers/Communications historiques* 15, no. 1 (1980): 100–15.

Druett, Joan. *Hen Frigates: Wives of Merchant Captains Under Sail*. New York: Simon and Schuster, 1998.

Elliott, Bruce S. *Irish Migrants in the Canadas: A New Approach*, 2nd ed. Montreal: McGill-Queen's University Press, 2004.

Emery, George Neil. *Facts of Life: The Social Construction of Vital Statistics, Ontario, 1869–1952*. Montreal: McGill-Queen's University Press, 1993.

England, Kim, and Kate Boyer. "Women's Work: The Feminization and Shifting Meaning of Clerical Work." *Journal of Social History* 43, no. 2 (Winter 2009): 307–40.

Errington, Elizabeth Jane. "Ladies and Schoolmistresses: Educating Women in Early Nineteenth-Century Upper Canada." *Historical Studies in Education* 6, no. 1 (Spring 1994): 71–96.

Errington, Elizabeth Jane. *Wives and Mothers, School Mistresses and Scullery Maids: Working Women in Upper Canada, 1790–1840*. Montreal: McGill-Queen's University Press, 1995.

Findon, Joanne. *Seeking Our Eden: The Dreams and Migrations of Sarah Jameson Craig*. Montreal: McGill-Queen's University Press, 2015.

Fingard, Judith. "College, Career and Community: Dalhousie Coeds, 1881–1921." In *Youth, University and Canadian Society: Essays in the Social History of Higher Education*, edited by Paul Axelrod and John G. Reid, 26–50. Montreal: McGill-Queen's University Press, 1989.

Folbre, Nancy. "The Unproductive Housewife: Her Evolution in Nineteenth-Century Economic Thought." *Signs: Journal of Women in Culture and Society* 16, no. 3 (Spring 1991): 463–84.

Fournier, Constance Anne. "'Home Folks': Maritime Couples of Penobscot Bay Sustain Family and Community Ashore and at Sea." In *Of Place and Gender: Women in Maine History*, edited by Marli F. Weiner, 51–79. Orono: The University of Maine Press, 2005.

Gaffield, Chad. *Language, Schooling and Cultural Conflict: The Origins of the French-Language Controversy in Ontario*. Montreal: McGill-Queen's University Press, 1987.

Gagan, David. *Hopeful Travellers: Families, Land, and Social Change in Mid-Victorian Peel County, Canada West*. Toronto: University of Toronto Press, 1981.

Gagan, Rosemary. *A Sensitive Independence: Canadian Methodist Women Missionaries in Canada and the Orient, 1881–1925*. Montreal: McGill-Queen's University Press, 1992.

Gamber, Wendy. "A Precarious Independence: Milliners and Dressmakers in Boston, 1860–1890." *Journal of Women's History* 4, no. 1 (Spring 1992): 60–88.

Gee, Ellen. "Marriage in Nineteenth-Century Canada." *Canadian Review of Sociology and Anthropology* 19, no. 3 (August 1982): 311–25.

Ghose, Indira. *Women Travellers in Colonial India: The Power of the Female Gaze*. New Delhi: Oxford University Press, 1998.

Gidney, R.D., and W.P.J. Millar. *Inventing Secondary Education: The Rise of the High School in Nineteenth-Century Ontario*. Montreal: McGill-Queen's University Press, 1990.

Ginzberg, Lori D. *Untidy Origins: A Story of Women's Rights in Antebellum New York*. Chapel Hill: University of North Carolina Press, 2005.

Ginzberg, Lori D. *Women and the Work of Benevolence: Morality, Politics and Class in the 19th-Century United States*. New Haven, CT: Yale University Press, 1990.

Girard, Philip. "Married Women's Property, Chancery Abolition and Insolvency Law Reform in Nova Scotia, 1820–1867." In *Essays in the History of Canadian Law III, Nova Scotia*, edited by Philip Girard and Jim Phillips, 83–92. Toronto: University of Toronto Press, 1990.

Girard, Philip, and Rebecca Veinott. "Married Women's Property Law in Nova Scotia, 1850–1910." In *Separate Spheres: Women's Worlds in the 19th-Century Maritimes*, edited by Janet Guildford and Suzanne Morton, 67–91. Fredericton: Acadiensis Press, 1994.

Godfrey, W.G. "'Into the Hands of the Ladies': The Birth of the Moncton Hospital." *Acadiensis* 27, no. 1 (Autumn 1997): 27–43.

Godfrey, W.G. "Wood, Josiah." *Dictionary of Canadian Biography*, Vol. 15 (1921–1927).

Gossage, Peter. *Families in Transition: Industry and Population in Nineteenth Century Saint-Hyacinthe*. Montreal: McGill-Queen's University Press, 1999.

Gray, Charlotte. *Sisters in the Wilderness: The Lives of Susanna Moodie and Catherine Parr Traill*. Toronto: Viking, 1999.

Green, Paul, and Nancy F. Vogan. *Music Education in Canada: A Historical Account*. Toronto: University of Toronto Press, 1991.

Greenwood, Rev. Walter R. *The Early Baptists of Cambridge Parish, Queens County New Brunswick*. s.n., 1941.

Guildford, Janet. "Creating the Ideal Man: Middle-Class Women's Constructions of Masculinity in Nova Scotia, 1840–1880." *Acadiensis* 24, no. 2 (Spring 1995): 5–23.

Guildford, Janet. "'Separate Spheres': The Feminization of Public School Teaching in Nova Scotia, 1838–1880." *Acadiensis* 22, no. 1 (Autumn 1992): 44–64.

Guildford, Janet. "'Whate'er the duty of the hour demands': The Work of Middle-Class Women in Halifax, 1840–1880." *Histoire sociale/Social History* 30, no. 59 (May 1997): 1-20.

Guildford, Janet, and Suzanne Morton, eds. *Separate Spheres: Women's Worlds in the 19th-Century Maritimes*. Fredericton: Acadiensis Press, 1994.

Habermas, Jürgen. "The Public Sphere: An Encyclopedia Article (1964)." Translated by Sara Lennox and Frank Lennox. *New German Critique* 3 (Autumn 1974): 49–55.

Hacker, Carlotta. *The Indomitable Lady Doctors*. Halifax: Formac, 1984.

Hamilton, W.D. "Loggie, Alexander." *Dictionary of Miramichi Biography*. Miramichi, NB: W.D. Hamilton, 1997.

Hansen, Karen V. *A Very Social Time: Crafting Community in Antebellum New England*. Los Angeles: University of California Press, 1994.

Hansen, Linda Squires. *Those Certain Women*. Fredericton: Associated Alumnae, 1982.

Harris, R. Cole. "The Spaces of Early Canada." *Canadian Historical Review* 91, no. 4 (December 2010): 725–59.

Hartley, L. P. *The Go-Between*. London: H. Hamilton, 1953.

Hayward, George H. *Pioneer Families of Carleton County New Brunswick*. Fredericton: George Hayward, 1996.

Heaman, E.A. "Taking the World by Show: Canadian Women as Exhibitors to 1900." *The Canadian Historical Review* 78, no. 4 (December 1997): 599–631.

Heaman, Elspeth. *The Inglorious Arts of Peace: Exhibitions in Canadian Society During the Nineteenth Century*. Toronto: University of Toronto Press, 1999.

Hewitt, Martin. "Science as Spectacle: Popular Scientific Culture in Saint John, New Brunswick, 1830–1850." *Acadiensis* 18, no. 1 (Autumn 1988): 91–119.

Hewitt, Martin. "Science, Popular Culture, and the Producer Alliance in Saint John, N.B." In *Profiles of Science and Society in the Maritimes prior to 1914*, edited by Paul A. Bogaard, 243–75. Fredericton and Sackville: Acadiensis Press and the Centre for Canadian Studies, Mount Allison University, 1990.

Historical Statistics of New Brunswick. Fredericton: Statistics Canada, 1984.

Hoffman, Frances, and Ryan Taylor. *Much To Be Done: Private Life in Ontario from Victorian Diaries*. Toronto: Natural Heritage/Natural History, 1996.

Hornsby, Stephen J., Victor A. Konrad, and James J. Herlan, eds. *The Northeastern Borderlands: Four Centuries of Interaction*. Fredericton: Acadiensis Press; Orono: Canadian-American Center, University of Maine, 1989.

Houston, Susan E., and Alison Prentice. *Schooling and Scholars in Nineteenth-Century Ontario.* Toronto: University of Toronto Press, 1988.

Huff, Cynthia A. "Reading as Re-Vision: Approaches to Reading Manuscript Diaries." *Biography* 23, no. 3 (Summer 2000): 504–23.

Huff, Cynthia A. "Textual Boundaries: Space in Nineteenth-Century Women's Manuscript Diaries." In Bunkers and Huff, eds., *Inscribing the Daily*, 123–38.

Huff, Cynthia A. "'That Profoundly Female, and Feminist Genre': The Diary as Feminist Practice." *Women's Studies Quarterly* 17, no. 3 (Fall 1989): 6–14.

Huff, Cynthia A. "Writer at Large: Culture and Self in Victorian Women's Diaries." *Auto/Biography Studies* 4, no. 2 (1988): 118–29.

Hunter, Jane H. "Inscribing the Self in the Heart of the Family: Diaries and Girlhood in Late-Victorian America." *American Quarterly* 44, no. 1 (March 1992): 51–81.

Huskins, Bonnie. "The Ceremonial Space of Women: Public Processions in Victorian Saint John and Halifax." In *Separate Spheres: Women's Worlds in the 19th-Century Maritimes*, edited by Janet Guildford and Suzanne Morton, 145–59. Fredericton: Acadiensis Press, 1994.

Hutchinson, Lorna. "'God Help Me for No One Else Can': The Diary of Annie Waltham, 1869–1881." *Acadiensis* 21, no. 2 (Spring 1992): 72–89.

Inwood, Kris. "The Representation of Industry in the Canadian Census, 1871–1891." *Histoire sociale/Social History* 28, no. 56 (November 1995): 347–73.

Inwood, Kris, and Phyllis Wagg. "The Survival of Handloom Weaving in Rural Canada circa 1871." *Journal of Economic History* 53, no. 2 (June 1993): 346–58.

Jalland, Pat. *Death in the Victorian Family.* Oxford: Oxford University Press, 1996.

Jobb, Dean. *The Life and Times of Josiah Wood, 1843–1927: A Builder of Sackville.* Sackville: Tantramar Heritage Trust, 2007.

Jones, Ted. "Bebbington's Gardens Huge Attraction." *The Daily Gleaner* (Fredericton) (10 June 2000) B2.

Jones, Ted, and Anita Jones. *Fredericton and Its People, 1825–1945.* Halifax: Nimbus, 2002.

Kelly, Catherine E. *In the New England Fashion: Reshaping Women's Lives in the Nineteenth Century.* New York: Cornell University Press, 1999.

Kelley, Mary. *Learning to Stand & Speak: Women, Education, and Public Life in America's Republic.* Chapel Hill: University of North Carolina Press for the Omohundro Institute of Early American History and Culture, 2006.

Kelley, Mary. "The Sentimentalists: Promise and Betrayal in the Home." *Signs: Journal of Women in Culture and Society* 4, no. 3 (Spring 1979): 434–46.

Kerber, Linda. "Separate Spheres, Female Worlds, Woman's Place: The Rhetoric of Women's History." *Journal of American History* 75, no. 1 (June 1988): 9–39.

Klein, Kim. "A 'Petticoat Polity'? Women Voters in New Brunswick Before Confederation." *Acadiensis* 26, no. 1 (Autumn 1996): 71–5.

Lacelle, Claudette. *Urban Domestic Servants in 19th Century Canada*. Ottawa: Environment Canada (Parks), 1987.

Lane, Hannah M. "Evangelicals, Church Financing, and Wealth-Holding in Mid-Nineteenth-Century St Stephen, New Brunswick, and Calais, Maine." In *The Churches and Social Order in Nineteenth- and Twentieth-Century Canada*, edited by Michael Gauvreau and Ollivier Hubert, 109–50. Montreal: McGill-Queen's University Press, 2006.

Lane, Hannah M. "Tribalism, Proselytism, and Pluralism: Protestants, Family, and Denominational Identity in Mid-Nineteenth-Century St. Stephen, New Brunswick." In *Households of Faith: Family, Gender, and Community in Canada, 1760–1969*, edited by Nancy Christie, 103–37. Montreal: McGill-Queen's University Press, 2002.

Lane, Hannah M. "'Wife, Mother, Sister, Friend': Methodist Women in St Stephen, New Brunswick, 1861–1881." In *Separate Spheres: Women's Worlds in the 19th-Century Maritimes*, edited by Janet Guildford and Suzanne Morton, 93–117. Fredericton: Acadiensis Press, 1994.

Larocque, Peter. "'The Work Being Chiefly Performed by Women': Female Workers in the Garment Industry in Saint John, New Brunswick, in 1871." In *Fashion: A Canadian Perspective*, edited by Alexandra Palmer, 139–65. Toronto: University of Toronto Press, 2004.

Lebsock, Suzanne. *The Free Women of Petersburg: Status and Culture in a Southern Town, 1784–1860*. New York: Norton, 1984.

Lejeune, Philippe. "The 'Journal de Jeune Fille' in Nineteenth-Century France." Translated by Martine Breillac. In Bunkers and Huff, *Inscribing the Daily*, 107–22.

Lensink, Judy Nolte. "Expanding the Boundaries of Criticism: The Diary as Female Autobiography." *Women's Studies* 14, no. 1 (November 1987): 39–54.

Lewis, Kathryn Fawcett. *The Fawcetts of Sackville*. Gagetown, NB: Otnabog Editions, 2000.

Lewis, Timothy D. "Rooted in the Soil: Farm Family Persistence in Burton Parish, Sunbury County, New Brunswick, 1851–1901." *Acadiensis* 31, no. 1 (Autumn 2001): 35–54.

Little, J.I. "Death in the Lower St. John River Valley: The Diary of Alexander Machum, Jr., 1845–1849." *Acadiensis* 22, no. 1 (Autumn 1992): 122–33.

Little, J.I. "Gender and Gentility on the Lower Canadian Frontier: Lucy Peel's Journal, 1833–36." *Journal of the Canadian Historical Association* 10 (1999): 59–79.

Little, J.I. "The Fireside Kingdom: A Mid-Nineteenth-Century Anglican Perspective on Marriage and Parenthood." In *Households of Faith: Family,*

Gender, and Community in Canada, 1760–1969, edited by Nancy Christie, 77–102. Montreal: McGill-Queen's University Press, 2002.

Lystra, Karen. *Searching the Heart: Women, Men, and Romantic Love in Nineteenth-Century America*. New York: Oxford University Press, 1989.

Macdonald, Cameron Lynne, and Karen V. Hansen. "Sociability and Gendered Spheres: Visiting Patterns in Nineteenth-Century New England." *Social Science History* 25, no. 4 (Winter 2001): 535–62.

MacNaughton, Katherine F.C. *The Development of the Theory and Practice of Education in New Brunswick, 1784–1900*. Fredericton: University of New Brunswick Press, 1947.

Mallon, Thomas. *A Book of One's Own: People and Their Diaries*. New York: Ticknor and Fields, 1984.

Mancke, Elizabeth. "At the Counter of the General Store: Women and the Economy in Eighteenth-Century Horton, Nova Scotia." In *Intimate Relations: Family and Community in Planter Nova Scotia, 1759–1800*, edited by Margaret Conrad, 167–81. Fredericton: Acadiensis Press, 1995.

Mann, Susan. "Travel Lessons: Canadian Women 'Across the Pond' 1865–1905." In *Women Teaching, Women Learning: Historical Perspectives*, edited by Elizabeth M. Smyth and Paula Bourne, 177–94. Toronto: Inanna Publications and Education, 2006.

Marks, Lynne. "'A Fragment of Heaven on Earth'? Religion, Gender, and Family in Turn-of-the-Century Canadian Church Periodicals." *Journal of Family History* 26, no. 2 (April 2001): 251–71.

Marks, Lynne. *Revivals and Roller Rinks: Religion, Leisure, and Identity in Late-Nineteenth-Century Small Town Ontario*. Toronto: University of Toronto Press, 1996.

Marks, Lynne, and Chad Gaffield. "Women at Queen's University, 1895–1905: 'A Little Sphere All Their Own?'" *Ontario History* 78, no. 4 (December 1986): 331–49.

Marshall, David. "'Death Abolished': Changing Attitudes to Death and the Afterlife in Nineteenth-Century Canadian Protestantism." In *Age of Transition: Readings in Canadian Social History, 1800–1900*, edited by Norman Knowles, 370–87. Toronto: Harcourt Brace, 1998.

Martin, Jean. "Colonisation et commerce des produits forestiers : l'exemple du canton Bagot au Saguenay au milieu du XIXe siècle." *Histoire sociale/Social History* 25, no. 50 (November 1992): 359–77.

Maxwell, L.M.B. *An Outline of the History of Central New Brunswick to the Time of Confederation*. Sackville: Tribune Press, 1937.

Measner, Don, and Christine Hampson. "The Canadian Population, 1871, 1891." In *Historical Atlas of Canada, Volume II: The Land Transformed, 1800–1891*, edited by R. Louis Gentilcore, Plate 29. Toronto: University of Toronto Press, 1993.

McCall, Laura. "'Shall I Fetter Her Will?' Literary Americans Confront Feminine Submission, 1820–1860." *Journal of the Early Republic* 21, no. 1 (Spring 2001): 95–113.

McCalla, Dounglas. *Consumers in the Bush: Shopping in Rural Upper Canada*. Montreal: McGill-Queen's University Press, 2015.

McCallum, Margaret E. "Separate Spheres: the Organization of Work in a Confectionary Factory: Ganong Bros., St. Stephen, New Brunswick." *Labour/Le travail* 24 (Fall 1989): 69–90.

McCarthy, Molly. "A Pocketful of Days: Pocket Diaries and Daily Record Keeping among Nineteenth-Century New England Women." *New England Quarterly* 73, no. 2 (June 2000): 274–6.

McEwan, Cheryl. *Gender, Geography and Empire: Victorian Women Travellers in West Africa*. Aldershot, UK: Ashgate, 2000.

McGahan, Elizabeth W., ed. *Whispers from the Past: Selections from the Writings of New Brunswick Women*. Fredericton: Fiddlehead Poetry Books and Goose Lane Editions, 1986.

McInnis, Marvin. "The Fertility Transition, 1851–1891." In *Historical Atlas of Canada, Volume II: The Land Transformed, 1800–1891*, edited by R. Louis Gentilcore, Plate 30. Toronto: University of Toronto Press, 1993.

McInnis, Marvin. "The Population of Canada in the Nineteenth Century." In *A Population History of North America*, edited by Michael R. Haines and Richard H. Steckel, 388–415. Cambridge: Cambridge University Press, 2000.

McLean, Lorna R. "Single Again: Widow's Work in the Urban Family Economy." *Ontario History* 83, no. 2 (1991): 127–50.

McPherson, Kathryn. *Bedside Matters: The Transformation of Canadian Nursing, 1900–1990*. Toronto: Oxford University Press, 1996.

McTavish, Lianne. *Defining the Modern Museum: A Case Study of the Challenges of Exchange*. Toronto: University of Toronto Press, 2012.

McTavish, Lianne. "Learning to See in New Brunswick, 1862–1929." *Canadian Historical Review* 87, no. 4 (December 2006): 553–81.

McTavish, Lianne. "Strategic Donations: Women and Museums in New Brunswick, 1862–1930." *Journal of Canadian Studies* 42, no. 2 (Spring 2008): 93–116.

Medjuck, Sheva. "Women's Response to Economic and Social Change in the Nineteenth Century: Moncton Parish, 1851 to 1871." *Atlantis* 11, no. 1 (Fall 1985): 7–21.

Migneault, Gaétan. *Les Acadiens du Nouveau-Brunswick et le Confederation*. Lévis, QC: Les Éditions de la Francophonie, 2009.

Miller, Muriel. *Bliss Carman: Quest & Revolt*. St. John's, NL: Jesperson Press, 1985.

Mitchinson, Wendy. *The Nature of Their Bodies: Women and Their Doctors in Victorian Canada*. Toronto: University of Toronto Press, 1991.

Mitchinson, Wendy. "The WCTU: 'For God, Home and Native Land': A Study in Nineteenth-Century Feminism." In *A Not Unreasonable Claim: Women and Reform in Canada, 1880s–1920s*, edited by Linda Kealey, 143–56. Toronto: The Women's Press, 1979.

Moody, Barry. "Graves, Mary Elizabeth." *Dictionary of Canadian Biography*, Vol. 13 (1901-1910).

Motz, Marilyn. "Folk Expression, of Time and Place: 19th Century Midwestern Rural Diaries." *Journal of American Folklore* 100, no. 396 (April–June 1987): 131–47.

Muise, D.A. "The Industrial Context of Inequality: Female Participation in Nova Scotia's Paid Labour Force, 1871–1921." *Acadiensis* 20, no. 2 (Spring 1991): 3–31.

Murray, Stuart. "Canadian Participation and National Representation at the 1851 London Great Exhibition and the 1855 Paris Exposition Universelle." *Histoire sociale/Social History* 32, no. 63 (May 1999): 1–22.

Nerbas, Don. "Adapting to Decline: The Changing Business World of the Bourgeoisie in Saint John, NB, in the 1920s." *Canadian Historical Review* 89, no. 2 (June 2008): 151–87.

Noël, Françoise. *Family Life and Sociability in Upper and Lower Canada, 1780–1870: A View from Diaries and Family Correspondence*. Montreal: McGill-Queen's University Press, 2003.

Norling, Lisa. "Ahab's Wife: Women and the American Whaling Industry, 1820–1870." In *Iron Men, Wooden Women: Gender and Seafaring in the Atlantic World, 1700–1920*, edited by Margaret S. Creighton and Lisa Norling, 70–91. Baltimore: Johns Hopkins University Press, 1996.

Norris, Laurie Glenn with Barbara Thompson. *Haunted Girl: Esther Cox and the Great Amherst Mystery*. Halifax: Nimbus, 2012.

Nussbaum, Felicity A. *The Autobiographical Subject: Gender and Ideology in Eighteenth-Century England*. Baltimore: John Hopkins University Press, 1989.

Nussbaum, Felicity A. "Eighteenth-Century Women's Autobiographical Commonplaces." In *The Private Self: Theory and Practice of Women's Autobiographical Writings*, edited by Shari Benstock, 147–71. Chapel Hill: University of North Carolina Press, 1988.

Osterud, Nancy Grey. *Bonds of Community: The Lives of Farm Women in Nineteenth-Century New York*. Ithaca, NY: Cornell University Press, 1991.

Parr, Joy. "Notes for a More Sensuous History of Twentieth-Century Canada: The Timely, the Tacit, and the Material Body." *Canadian Historical Review* 82, no. 4 (December 2001): 719–46.

Peck, Mary Biggar, ed. *A Full House and Fine Singing: Diaries and Letters of Sadie Harper Allen*. Fredericton: Goose Lane, 1992.

Pederson, Diana. "'The Call to Service': The YWCA and the Canadian College Woman, 1886–1920." In *Youth, University and Canadian Society: Essays in the Social History of Higher Education*, edited by Paul Axelrod and John G. Reid, 187–215. Montreal: McGill-Queen's University Press, 1989.

Phillips, Mark Salber. "History, Memory, and Historical Distance." In *Theorizing Historical Consciousness*, edited by Peter Seixas, 86–102. Toronto: University of Toronto Press, 2004.

Pickles, Katie. "Locating Widows in Mid-Nineteenth Century Pictou County, Nova Scotia." *Journal of Historical Geography* 30, no. 1 (January 2004): 70–86.

Picot, J.E. *A Brief History of Teacher Training in New Brunswick, 1848–1973*. Fredericton: The Department of Education, Province of New Brunswick, 1974.

Pond, Douglas Daemon. *The History of Marysville, New Brunswick*. Fredericton: Private Printing, 1983.

Pratt, Mary Louise. *Imperial Eyes: Travel Writing and Transculturation*. London: Routledge, 1992.

Prentice, Alison. "The Feminization of Teaching." In *The Neglected Majority: Essays in Canadian Women's History*, edited by Susan Mann Trofimenkoff and Alison Prentice, 49–65. Toronto: McClelland and Stewart, 1977.

Prentice, Alison. "'Friendly Atoms in Chemistry': Women and men at Normal School in Mid-Nineteenth-Century Toronto." In *Old Ontario: Essays in Honour of J.M.S Careless*, edited by David Keane and Colin Read, 285–317. Toronto: Dundurn, 1990.

Prentice, Alison. *The School Promoters: Education and Social Class in Mid-Nineteenth Century Upper Canada*. Toronto: McClelland and Stewart, 1977.

Rayner-Canham, Marlene F., and Geoffrey W. Rayner-Canham. *Harriet Brooks: Pioneer Nuclear Scientist*. Montreal: McGill-Queen's University Press, 1992.

Reicker, Marion Gilchrist. *Those Days Are Gone Away: Queens County, N.B., 1643–1901*. Gagetown, NB: Queens County Historical Society, 1981.

Reid, John G. "The Education of Women at Mount Allison, 1854–1914." *Acadiensis* 12, no. 2 (Spring 1983): 3–33.

Reid, John G. *Mount Allison University: A History, to 1963, Volume I: 1843–1914*. Toronto: University of Toronto Press for Mount Allison University, 1984.

Rendall, Jane. "Women and the Public Sphere." *Gender and History* 11, no. 3 (November 1999): 475–88.

Ritchie, Joanne. "Amelia Holder (1855–1936)." In *The Small Details of Life: 20 Diaries by Women in Canada, 1830–1906*, edited by Kathryn Carter, 95–115. Toronto: University of Toronto Press, 2002.

Roberts, Julia. *In Mixed Company: Taverns and Public Life in Upper Canada*. Vancouver: UBC Press, 2009.

Rose, George MacLean, ed. *A Cyclopaedia of Canadian Biography: Being Chiefly Men of the Time*. Toronto: Rose Publishing Company, 1888.

Rosenblatt, Paul C. *Bitter, Bitter Tears: Nineteenth-Century Diarists and Twentieth-Century Grief Theories*. Minneapolis: University of Minnesota Press, 1983.

Rosenzweig, Linda W. *The Anchor of My Life: Middle-Class American Mothers and Daughters, 1880–1920*. New York: New York University Press, 1993.

Ross, Miriam. "Sharing a Vision: Maritime Baptist Women Educate for Mission, 1870–1920." In *Changing Roles of Women within the Christian Church in Canada*, edited by Elizabeth Gillan Muir and Marilyn Färdig Whitely, 77–98. Toronto: University of Toronto Press, 1995.

Rothman, Ellen K. *Hands and Hearts: A History of Courtship in America*. New York: Basic Books, 1984.

Roy, Muriel K. "Settlement and Population Growth." In *The Acadians of the Maritimes: Thematic Studies*, edited by Jean Daigle, 169–89. Moncton, NB: Centre d'Études Acadiennes, 1982.

Ryan, Mary P. *Cradle of the Middle Class: The Family in Oneida County, New York, 1790–1865*. Cambridge: Cambridge University Press, 1981.

Rygiel, Judith. "'Thread in Her Hands – Cash in Her Pockets': Women and Domestic Textile Production in 19th-Century New Brunswick." *Acadiensis* 30, no. 2 (Spring 2001): 56–70.

Sager, Eric. "Women Teachers in Canada, 1881–1901: Revisiting the 'Feminization' of an Occupation." *Canadian Historical Review* 88, no. 2 (June 2007): 201–36.

Seixas, Peter. "Introduction," In *Theorizing Historical Consciousness*, edited by Peter Seixas, 3–20. Toronto: University of Toronto Press, 2004.

Selles, Johanna M. *Methodists & Women's Education in Ontario, 1836–1925*. Montreal: McGill-Queen's University Press, 1996.

Smith, Arthur M. "Missionary as Collector: The Role of the Reverend Joseph Annand." *Acadiensis* 26, no. 2 (Spring 1997): 96–111.

Smith, Elizabeth, and Veronica Jane Strong-Boag. *"A Woman With a Purpose": The Diaries of Elizabeth Smith, 1872–84*. Toronto: University of Toronto Press, 1980.

Smith-Rosenberg, Carol. *Disorderly Conduct: Visions of Gender in Victorian America*. New York: Oxford University Press, 1985.

Smyth, Donna E. "'Thinking Back Through Our Mothers': Tradition in Canadian Women's Writing." In *Re(Dis)covering Our Foremothers: Nineteenth-Century Canadian Women Writers*, edited by Lorraine McMullen, 14–21. Ottawa: University of Ottawa Press, 1990.

Stacey, C.P. *A Very Double Life: The Private World of Mackenzie King*. Toronto: Macmillan, 1976.

Stairs, Michele. "Matthews and Marillas: Bachelors and Spinsters in Prince Edward Island in 1881." In *Mapping the Margins: The Family and Social Discipline in Canada, 1700–1975*, edited by Nancy Christie and Michael Gauvreau, 247–67. Montreal: McGill-Queen's University Press, 2004.

Stanley, G.F.G. "The Caraquet Riots of 1875." *Acadiensis* 2, no. 1 (Autumn 1972): 21–38.

Steinitz, Rebecca. "Travel Diaries, Journals, Logbooks." In *Encyclopedia of Life Writing: Autobiographical and Biographical Forms*, Vol. 2, edited by Margaretta Jolly, 887–9. London: Fitzroy Dearborn, 2001.

Stewart, Stormie. "The Elderly Poor in Rural Ontario: Inmates of the Wellington County House of Industry, 1877–1907." *Journal of the Canadian Historical Association* 3, no. 1 (1992): 217–33.

Taylor, Graham, and Peter Baskerville. *A Concise History of Business in Canada*. Toronto: Oxford University Press, 1994.

Theobald, Marjorie R. "The Sin of Laura: The Meaning of Culture in the Education of Nineteenth-Century Women." *Journal of the Canadian Historical Association* 1, no. 1 (1990): 257–71.

Thornton, Patricia. "The Problem of Out-Migration from Atlantic Canada, 1871–1921." *Acadiensis* 15, no. 1 (Autumn 1985): 3–34.

Toner, Peter. "New Brunswick Schools and the Rise of Provincial Rights." In *Federalism in Canada and Australia: The Early Years*, edited by Bruce W. Hodgins, et al., 125-36. Waterloo, ON: Wilfrid Laurier University Press, 1978.

Tosh, John. *A Man's Place: Masculinity and the Middle-Class Home in Victorian England*. New Haven, CT: Yale University Press 1999.

Trites, Allison A. "The New Brunswick Baptist Seminary, 1836–1895." In *Repent and Believe: The Baptist Experience in Maritime Canada*, edited by Barry M. Moody, 103–23. Hantsport, NS: Lancelot Press for Acadia Divinity College, 1980.

Ulrich, Laura Thatcher. *A Midwife's Tale: The Life of Martha Ballard, Based on Her Diary, 1785–1812*. New York: Vintage Books, 1991.

Urquhart, M.C., and K.A. Buckley, eds. *Historical Statistics of Canada*. Toronto: Macmillan, 1965, 1971.

Vachon, Pierre. "Lajeunesse, Emma (also called Marie-Louise-Cecile-Emma) (Gye) known as Emma Albani." *Dictionary of Canadian Biography*, Vol. 15 (1921–1930).
Van Die, Marguerite. *Religion, Family and Community in Victorian Canada: The Colbys of Carrollcroft*. Montreal: McGill-Queen's University Press, 2005.
Van Die, Marguerite. "Revisiting 'Separate Spheres': Women, Religion, and the Family in Mid-Victorian Brantford, Ontario." In *Households of Faith: Family, Gender, and Community in Canada, 1760–1969*, edited by Nancy Christie, 234–63. Montreal: McGill-Queen's University Press, 2002.
Vickery, Amanda. "Golden Age to Separate Spheres? A Review of the Categories and Chronology of English Women's History." *The Historical Journal* 36, no. 2 (June 1993): 383–414.
Vinovskis, Maris A. "Angels' Heads and Weeping Willows: Death in Early America." In *The American Family in Social-Historical Perspective*, 2nd ed., edited by Michael Gordon, 546–63. New York: St Martin's Press, 1978.
Waciega, Lisa Wilson. "A 'Man of Business': The Widow of Means in Southeastern Pennsylvania, 1750–1850." *William & Mary Quarterly* 44, no. 1 (1987): 40–64.
Wallace, C.M. "Tilley, Sir Samuel Leonard." *Dictionary of Canadian Biography*, Vol. 12 (1891–1900).
Wallace-Casey, Cynthia. "'Providential Openings': The Women Weavers of Nineteenth-Century Queens County, New Brunswick." *Material History Review* 46 (Fall 1997): 29–44.
Walsh, John C.S., and Steven High. "Rethinking the Concept of Community." *Histoire sociale/Social History* 32, no. 64 (November 1999): 255–73.
Ward, W. Peter. *Courtship, Love, and Marriage in Nineteenth-Century English Canada*. Montreal: McGill-Queen's University Press, 1990.
Ward, W. Peter. *A History of Domestic Space: Privacy and the Canadian Home*. Vancouver: UBC Press, 1999.
Widdis, Randy William. *With Scarcely a Ripple: Anglo-Canadian Migration into the United States and Western Canada, 1880–1920*. Montreal: McGill-Queen's University Press, 1998.
Wilson, Catharine Anne. "Reciprocal Work Bees and the Meaning of Neighbourhood." *The Canadian Historical Review* 82, no. 3 (September 2001): 431–64.
Wynn, Graeme. *Timber Colony: A Historical Geography of Early Nineteenth Century New Brunswick*. Toronto: University of Toronto Press, 1981.
Yorke, Lois. "Mabel Penery French (1881–1955): A Life Re-Created." *University of New Brunswick Law Journal* 43, no. 3 (1993): 3–49.

Young, D. Murray. "A Calendar of Life in a Narrow Valley, 1825–1843." In *A Calendar of Life in a Narrow Valley: Jacobina Campbell's Diary, Taymouth, New Brunswick, 1825–1843*, edited by D. Murray Young and Gail G. Campbell, 15–28. Fredericton: Acadiensis Press, 2015.

Zaeske, Susan. *Signatures of Citizenship: Petitioning, Antislavery, and Women's Political Identity*. Chapel Hill: University of North Carolina Press, 2003.

Secondary Sources: Unpublished

Biggs, Katherine. "Domestic Service in Saint John, New Brunswick, 1851–1891." MA thesis, University of New Brunswick, 1992.

Caplan, Hart. "'A Law Unto Oneself': Compulsory Schooling and the Creation of the Student('s) Body in New Brunswick, 1850–1914." MA thesis, University of New Brunswick, 1998.

Clarke, Mary Eileen. "The Saint John Women's Enfranchisement Association, 1894–1919." MA thesis, University of New Brunswick, 1979.

Clayton, Jenny. "'A Long Voyage Before Us': New Brunswick's Holder Family and the Nineteenth Century Seafaring Experience." MA thesis, University of New Brunswick, 2001.

Cook, Janice. "Saint John Widows, 1880–1900." Unpublished graduate essay (Hist6385), University of New Brunswick, 1992.

Coops, Lorraine. "Living By Faith: Maritime Baptist Single Women Missionaries in India, 1880–1930." PhD diss., Queen's University, 1996.

Cormier, Audrey Marie. "The Saint John County Almshouse and Workhouse: 1855–1857." Unpublished undergraduate essay (Hist5350), University of New Brunswick, 1993.

Field, Vincenzo. "The First Generation of Women at the University of New Brunswick." Unpublished graduate essay (Hist6385), University of New Brunswick, 1999.

Grant, Amber. "Young Women Who Tell a Different Story: The Diaries of Lottie Reid, Lillie Williamson, Sadie Harper and Violet Goldsmith in Late 19th and Early 20th Century New Brunswick." MA thesis, University of New Brunswick, 2009.

Huskins, Bonnie L. "Public Celebrations in Victorian Saint John and Halifax." PhD diss. Dalhousie University, 1991.

LaVorgna, Koral. "Lessons in Mid-Nineteenth-Century New Brunswick Teacher Careerism." PhD diss. University of New Brunswick, 2016.

Lewis, Timothy D. "Agrarian Idealism and Progressive Agriculture in Maritime Canada: Agricultural Leadership in New Brunswick, 1895–1929." PhD diss., University of New Brunswick, 2003.

Liebenberg, Gillian. "Handmaiden of the Church: Church of England Women of the Diocese of Fredericton, 1880–1904." Unpublished article, prepared for the Diocese of Fredericton, 2001.

Little, Sherry. "'I think I will go': Albert County Migration as seen through the Diary of Ann Eliza Rogers, 1852–1870." MA thesis, University of New Brunswick, 2012.

Mandeville, Donna Lynne. "'What a gap that leaf may make': School Enrollment in St Andrews, 1861–1881." Unpublished undergraduate essay (Hist5350), University of New Brunswick, 1999–2000.

Mandeville, Donna Lynne. "Who Went to School? School Attendance Patterns in Three British Columbia Communities in 1901." MA thesis, University of Victoria, 2002.

Munro, Celia. "A Farm Community in Pre-Confederation New Brunswick: A Case Study Based on the Diaries of Thomas O. Miles (1789–1858)." MA thesis, University of New Brunswick, 2009.

Nelson, Shelley Frances. "Links in the Chain: Maritime Women and the Protestant Missionary Movement, 1870–1925." PhD diss., University of New Brunswick, 2008.

Preston, Spencer. "A Study of the New Brunswick Grammar Schools, 1805–1861." MA thesis, University of New Brunswick, 2009.

Quinn, Shawna Stairs. "'Sympathetic and Practical Men'? School Inspectors and New Brunswick's Educational Bureaucracy, 1879–1909." MA thesis, University of New Brunswick, 2006.

Rae, Daphne. "Nineteenth-Century Midwifery: Case Studies from Britain and New Brunswick: Tradition in Transition." MA thesis, University of New Brunswick, 2002.

Thorne, Ellen. "Higher Education for New Brunswick Women: The Provincial Normal School, 1882–83." Unpublished undergraduate essay (Hist5350), University of New Brunswick, 1996.

Veer, Joanne. "Feminist Forebears: The Woman's Christian Temperance Union in Canada's Maritime Provinces, 1875–1900." PhD diss., University of New Brunswick, 1996.

Wallace-Casey, Cynthia. "'Providential Openings': The Women Weavers of Nineteenth Century Queens County New Brunswick." MA report, University of New Brunswick, 1993.

Williamson, Lorna. "From Agricultural Improvement to Industrial Affirmation: The Evolution of the New Brunswick Provincial Exhibitions, 1852–1883." MA thesis, University of New Brunswick, 2003.

Index

Acadia Ladies Seminary. *See* academies/seminaries
academies/seminaries: Acadia Ladies Seminary, 33, 87, 182–4, 262; Baptist seminary (New Brunswick), 64, 174, 344n30; College of St Joseph girls' boarding school, 64, 174; Hawes Institute (Mrs Burrill's academy, Boston), 20, 147, 172–3; Mount Allison Ladies Academy: curriculum, 179–82; enrollment, 64; experience at, 41–3, 53–4, 87; overview, 34–6, 318, supervision at, 103–5, 165–6, 241–2, 318; Prince of Wales Ladies' College, 36,
Acadians, 4, 6, 65, 176, 228; demographic analysis, 58–62, 69–70, 325, 344n32, 345n40
adolescence, 9, 14–15, 31, 37–49 *passim*, 60–5, 90–108 *passim*, 125–6, 131–3, 158–67 *passim*, 177–8, 260
age of progress, 82–5
age of sail, 30, 81–2, 88–90, 272, 282, 309–10; coasting trade, 65, 81, 146, 271–2, 310; seafaring, 25, 29, 128, 130–1, 161–2, 271–3; shipping and shipbuilding, 7, 30–1, 52–3, 81–3, 88–90, 265, 310
alcoholism, 21, 118–19, 256, 309
Allen, Frank, 36, 110–13, 322
American Civil War, 267–9; draft, 268–9
Anglicans, 24, 52, 58, 168–70, 204–6, 208, 270; baptism, 169; Christ Church cathedral (Fredericton), 19; church attendance, 35, 139–40, 142–4, 166; clergymen, 162, 169, 316; conversion, 22, 206; Madras schools, 171; St Anne's (Fredericton), 185; Sunday school, 142–3
Antwerp, Belgium, 88, 278, 281–2

Ballard, Martha, 51, 56
Baptists, 6, 25, 58, 91, 196; church attendance, 93, 183; conversion, 14; meeting, 96, 109, 131–3, 159–60, 192–6; prayer meetings, 33, 184, 192–5, 213, 238; clergy, 33, 131–2, 159–60, 194–6, 205–7, 229; revival, 191–6, 201–2, 205–7; Sunday school, 131–2, 213, 239; and temperance, 257, 260; women's

missionary society, 262, 373n21. *See also* academies/seminaries
Barman, Jean, 8
Bebbington, John, 54–5, 83, 223, 243–5, 266
bees and frolics. *See* cooperative labour
Bliss, George Jr. *See* Carman family
Bliss, George Pidgeon. *See* Carman family
Bliss, Jean. *See* Carman family
Bliss, Sarah Wetmore. *See* Carman family
Blodgett, Harriet, 39–40
Bloom, Lynn Z., 48–9
boarding, 63, 67, 101–3, 115, 133, 227–9, 238, 345n49; for high school, 37, 90–3, 165, 174, 189, 198; male boarders, 24, 26, 32, 107–8, 131, 141–3, 308, 316, 377n45; at school, 42–4, 64, 83, 96, 165, 173–4; for university, 93, 263; women teachers 3, 14, 28, 49, 65, 120, 144, 175–7, 198, 215, 231–2, 287, 312
borderlands communities, 65, 145, 267–72
"Boston States," 53, 65, 87, 146, 231, 266, 272
Bradley, Mary Coy, 230
Buchanan, James. *See* Grant family
Buchanan, Jannet Grant. *See* Grant family
Buchanan, Mary. *See* Grant family
Buchanan, William. *See* Grant family
Buenos Aires, 25, 89–90, 130, 316; carnival, 161–2, 276–8; yellow fever in, 276, 278, 384n33
businesswomen, 74, 85, 145–6, 308; dressmakers, 69, 74, 98, 229, 230; garment factory owners, 230; managing property, 138–41; market gardener, 56, 220–6, 242–5; milliners, 69, 74, 229–30; weavers, 69, 220, 230

Calcutta, 29, 162–3, 279–81
Campbell diarist: Jacobina (b.circa 1797), 15–16, 44–6 (diary), 48–51, 56, 77–8, 153, 157–8, 190–1, 207–8, 211–12 (diary), 216–19 (diary), 248, 270, 286, 312, 379n23
Campbell diarist's family: Campbell, Alexander (Sandy), 15, 211–12, 217–18, 312; Campbell, Ann, 15, 158, 211, 217–19, 312; Campbell Caroline, 15, 153, 211–12, 217–8, 312; Campbell, Dugald, 15; Campbell, Jacobina Drummond, 15, 157, 248, 312; Campbell, Ludlow, 15, 158, 211–12, 217, 312; Campbell, Patrick, 15, 157–8, 211, 217, 312; Campbell, Sally MacDonald, 158, 211, 217–18; Campbell, Tommy, 211, 218
Carlisle, Direxy, 146–7, 229
Carman diarist: Sophia (Sophy) Bliss (b.1828), 18–19, 51–2, 107, 119–20, 122, 124–6, 167–9 (diary), 208, 270–1, 286, 293, 313
Carman diarist's family: Bliss, George Jr, 19, 119–20; Bliss, George Pidgeon, 18; Bliss, Jean, 19, 119, 124, 168–9; Bliss, Sarah Wetmore, 18–19, 107, 119–20, 124, 168–9, 313; Carman, Bliss, 19, 124–6, 168–9, 313; Carman, Muriel (Murray), 19, 124–6, 168–9, 313; Carman, William, 18–19, 52, 107, 119, 124–6, 168–9, 313; Roberts, Emma Bliss, 19, 125

Carter, Kathryn, 8, 51–2
childbirth, 36, 69–70, 293. *See also* pregnancy
childhood, 60–1, 122–4, 129–30, 165, 169
Church of England. *See* Anglicans
churches: attendance, 190; church socials, 190; competition for souls, 40, 58, 196–8, 203–6, 291; as meeting places, 164, 166; and social activities 164, 306. *See also* Anglicans, Baptists, community events, Methodists, Presbyterians
civil society, 12, 253, 263
clothing, production of: dressmaking, 33, 63, 69, 74, 87, 98–9, 114, 120, 169, 229–30; fashions, 252, 272; hats, 211; homespun, 220; vests,146
Clowes, Eliza Gilbert. *See* Waltham family
coasting trade. *See* age of sail
College of St Joseph. *See* academies/seminaries
commonplace book, 15, 207–8, 270
community activities. *See* recreation
community events, 169, 209, 308; balls, 96; bazaars, 167, 169, 190, 209, 307; box/pie socials, 164, 307; circus, 306; concerts, 21, 36, 93, 111, 164, 167, 169, 179, 184, 199; entertainments, 164, 260, 307; fairs and exhibitions, 18, 84–5, 132, 160, 164, 266, 306; Loyalist celebration, 158; picnics, 97, 164, 167–8, 190, 209, 306–7; parades, 86, 306; popular lectures, 84, 96, 159, 164, 184, 187–8, 308–9; steamboat excursions, 167, 306

Confederation, 7, 85–7, 249, 310; and Fenians, 85–6; and reciprocity, 86
conjugal relationships. *See* marital relationships
Conrad, Margaret, 8, 39
consumption. *See* sickness.
cooperative labour: among extended kin 17, 79–80, 213–14, 226; among neighbours 79–80, 141, 153, 216–20; bees and frolics, 16, 216, 219; husking party, 160
correspondence, 4, 121–2, 129, 170, 259, 282, 305, 309–10; Carman, 19, 107, 124–6, 166, 168–9, 293; Estabrooks, 182–4, 239; Fullerton, 35, 42–3, 105, 180–2; Goldsmith, 186; Harper, 105–6; Hill, 20, 96, 106–7, 122–3, 137, 147, 149–51, 174, 284, 286–7; Holder, 130; Jones, 142; Loggie/Valentine, 28–9, 234–7, 273, 279–81, 318–9; MacDonald, 301; Reid/Turner, 25, 53, 88–90, 206–7, 272, 278, 281–2, 316–7; Rogers, 117, 137, 290, 315; Trueman/Wood, 26–7, 161, 180–3, 200–4, 208, 241–2, 256–9, 301, 317; Waltham, 138–40; Williamson, 109; Wolhaupter, 120
cosmopolitanism, 10, 22, 52–3, 264–5, 282, 303, 309–10
Cottam, Rachel, 46
courtship, 32, 35–6, 95–9, 104–5, 107, 110–13, 164, 307, 320; and engagement 50, 97, 105; ending of 32, 107–8, 358n32; little supervision, 96–7, 103–4, 307; love as basis of partner selection, 29, 32, 36, 104 107–8, 117; parental involvement, 95, 97, 106–7, 113; religion as factor in, 96–7; study of, 95

dairying: butter as medium of exchange, 79, 220, 227, 308; cheese making, 71, 85, 98, 304, 308; churning butter, 34, 71, 214, 216–17, 220, 239, 304; income from, 23, 71, 78, 146, 219–20, 227, 308

death and dying: changing attitudes towards, 285, 291–2, concept of a 'good death', 291–2, 301; death of children, 286, 288–9, 295; death of infants, 18–19, 31, 286, 293–4; death of parents, 60, 286, 301; death of spouse, 72, 286, 288–91. *See also* mortality rates

depression of 1870s, 18, 87, 266

DeWolfe, Leila, 234

diaries: analysis of as interdisciplinary dialogue, 39–41; comparative analysis, 52–3, and historical consciousness, 3, 5, 40–1, 53, 56, 327n3; and the life course, 48–52; as life writing, 39–40, 53–7; as material artifacts, 44–7; physical characteristics, 3, 44, 46; purpose of: 47–8; representativeness, 4–6, 9; travel, 272–3

diarists, 3–8, 303; as adolescents, 37–8, 48–9, 90, 187, 189; by age and social status, 4; British descent, 80–1; as business women, 145; in companionate marriages, 119, 305; comparative analysis of, 52, 184, 229; as daughters, 16–17, 121, and death, 285–6, 292, 300; and household, 210, 228–9, 271; independence of, 49–50, 113, 135, 144; with influence, 7; limited career options 113; living arrangements, 115–16; of Loyalist descent, 77; as married women, 50–2, 119, 129–30, 305; as mothers, 19, 121–2, 129, 305; native-born vs immigrant, 3–6, 303; as readers, 208, 270–1, 310; and religion, 190–1, 196–7, 201, 208, 260, 262; as reporters, 47, 286; as representative of many, 5–6, 59–60, 76, 90, 129, 164, 171, 189; sense of self, 5,9, 305; as settlers, 303; and shopping, 184; as siblings, 128–9; as single women, 49, 147, 242, 266, 305; stages of life, 48–52; as students of the weather, 6, 304; as teachers, 144–5, 175, 189, 241; as travellers, 87, 144–5, 158, 282; their voice, 8–9; as widows, 305

doctors: and midwives, 76, 245, 352n99, 378n52; tending patients, 55–6, 91, 194–5, 293–4, 299–301, 314, 318; women, 68, 88, 282, 360n21

economy: family, 10, 17, 23, 33, 68–71, 77–9, 135, 145–6, 210–26 *passim*, 305; farming, 25, 70–1, 157; local 24, 52, 56, 68–9, 210, 220, 225–7, 304, 307; farming/lumbering, 16–17, 23, 70, 77–81, 135, 211–13, 218, 265; lumbering, 6–7, 18, 63, 81, 135, 212, 218–21, 225–6, 265, 353n10; maritime, 30–1, 52–3, 80–82, 88–90, 135–6, 265, 303–4; provincial, 59, 71, 80–2, 86–7, 245, 265, 286, 303; seasonal, 6, 51, 78–9, 210–16, 221, 304

education. *See* schools and schooling. *See also* teaching

Else, George. *See* Estabrooks family

Estabrooks diarists: Alvaretta (Alva) (b.1869), 32, 87, 137–8,

182–4 (diary), 212, 216–17, 240–2, 286, 299–300, 315, 321; Hannah (b.1871), 32–4, 46, 49–50, 137–8, 146–7, 182–3, 237–40 (diary), 242, 286, 300, 315, 321

Estabrooks diarists' family: Else, George, 33, 212; Estabrooks, Agnes Carter, 32–4, 137–8, 183, 216–17, 238–9, 299–300, 321; Estabrooks, Arthur Shephard, 32–4, 183–4, 216, 237–40, 299–300; Estabrooks, Ellen J. (Nellie), 32–4, 238–9, 315, 321; Estabrooks, Frances (Frank) Barnes, 33–4, 238; Estabrooks, George E., 32–3, 299–300; Estabrooks, Jean, 34, 238; Estabrooks, Kenneth, 34, 238; Estabrooks, Shephard Handy, 32–3; Hayward, Reverend Amos, 33–4, 182–4, 240, 300, 321; Hayward, Lucretia Estabrooks, 33–4, 240, 321

Everett, Mary Camber. *See* Morrison family

Everett, Thomas C. *See* Morrison family

Everett, Tom. *See* Morrison family

Everett, Will. *See* Morrison family

Ewing, Juliana Horatio, 228, 231

family correspondence. *See* correspondence

family economy. *See* economy.

family social activities: extended visits, 81, 86, 101, 106, 119, 129, 157–8, 160–1, 200–1, 229; private parties, 109, 156–7, 160, 164–5, 306; social club (Xenium), 128, 164, 360n25; seasonal holidays, 19, 104, 107–9, 124, 127, 167–9, 185; visiting/calling, 44–5, 86, 98, 119, 128–9, 131–3, 154–6, 165, 217–18. *See also* games

family to community to society continuum, 9–12, 52, 94, 303–4

farming, 68–71; barn work, 34, 194, 239; calving, 44, 211; eggs, 71, 108, 214, 219, 227, 308; gendered division of labour, 51, 210–16, 219–20, 226, 246; harvesting, 6, 32, 141, 157, 214–6, 218, 244, 304; haying, 121, 143, 158, 215–6; planting, 6, 79–80, 141, 211, 214, 304; ploughing, 79, 141, 211, 213–14, 218; poultry raising, 71, 79, 108, 214, 219, 227, 300, 304; seasonal nature of, 210–19, 226; sheep shearing, 56, 63, 80, 153, 212–13, 304. *See* also gardens

fertility patterns, 69–70, 346–7n60, 347n61, 348n70

Fiske, Emma, 259–60

franchise, 247; disenfranchisement of women, 247–8

French, Mabel Penery, 188–9

Frost, Barbara Smith. *See* Jones family

Frost, Sarah, 47

Frost, Smith. *See* Jones family

Fullerton diarist: Laura Cynthia (b.1870), 34–5, 41–4 (diary), 48–54 *passim*, 84, 87, 103–5, 165–6, 179–82 (diary), 321–2

Fullerton diarist's family: Fullerton, Burgess, 34, 181; Fullerton, George, 34; Fullerton, Rosamund Lawrence, 34, 181; Fullerton, Walter, 34

funerals, 45, 132, 193, 195, 287–8, 290, 293, 300, 302, 313, 315

Gallacher, Achsah Georgia. *See* Rogers family
Gallacher, Ann Eliza: *See* Rogers diarist: Ann Eliza Rogers
Gallacher, Ella Frances. *See* Rogers family
Gallacher, Frank John Howe. *See* Rogers family
Gallacher, Isabelle Plummer. *See* Rogers family
Gallacher, John McAuley. *See* Rogers family
games, 109, 156, 162, 229, 306; ball, 90; cards, 163; whist, 112, 162; authors, 156; checkers, 133, 163; crokinole, 111–12; croquet, 96, 165, 223, 229, 306; hockey, 111–13; logomachy, 113, 133, 156; Pedro, 252, quoits, 162; tiddlywinks, 252
gardens, 141–3, 243; kitchen, 18, 71, 80, 85, 141–3, 211–26 *passim*, 250, 304; market, 18, 56, 83, 220–6, 242–5, 265–6
garment industry, 62–3, 65, 228–30, 265
gendered division of labour. *See* farming
Gilbert, Charlotte Amelia Hewlett. *See* Waltham family
Gilbert, Fannie. *See* Waltham family
Gilbert, Hannah. *See* Waltham family
Gilbert, Lucretia. *See* Waltham family
Gilbert, Thomas. *See* Waltham family
Goldsmith diarist: Violet (b.1880), 36, 48–9, 144, 178–9, 186–8 (diary), 201, 262–3, 266–7, 286, 322–3
Goldsmith diarist's family: Goldsmith, Anna Wright, 36; Goldsmith, John, Reverend, 36, 188, 267; Goldsmith, Mabel, 36, 267; Goldsmith, Margaret (Maggie), 36, 188, 267; Goldsmith, Oliver, 36
grandparents, 10, 14, 17, 25, 129
Grant diarists: Isabella (b.1807), 16–17, 47, 77–80 (diary), 98, 154–5, 212, 218, 220, 286, 312; Marjory (b.1807), 16–17, 47, 77–80, 97–98, 154–5 (diary), 218–9, 286, 312
Grant diarists' family: 212; Buchanan, James, 16, 78, 98, 154; Buchanan, Jannet Grant, 16–17, 80, 98, 218; Buchanan, Mary, 80, 98; Buchanan, William, 16, 80, 97–8, 312; Grant, Absolam, 17, 76–80, 97–8, 154–5; Grant, Alexander, 16, 98, 154; Grant, Ann (Nancy Ann) Crockett, 17, 98, 154–5; Grant, Catherine, 16–17, 78–9, 98, 155, 219–20; Grant, Charles, 17, 78–80, 98, 154–5; Grant, Elizabeth (Betsy) Barber, 17, 218; Grant, Hesadiah, 16, 154–5; Grant, James, 16, 286; Grant Jannet Buchanan, 16–17, 98, 154–5; Grant, John, 17, 154–5; Grant, Mary, 16, 79, 98, 154; Grant, William Jr., 17, 78–80, 154–5, 218; Grant, William Sr., 16, 78–80, 98, 154–5, 219; Maxwell, Catherine (Caty) Grant, 17, 154; Maxwell, Joseph, 17
grief, 286, 288, 291, 295, 299, 301–2

Hanley, Annie H. Ross Foster, 186
Harper diarist: Sarah (Sadie) Estelle (b.1875), 35–6, 46, 48, 105–6, 110–13 (diary), 156–7, 177–8, 184–5, 228, 230, 251–2 (diary), 260–1 (diary), 322

Harper diarist's family: Harper, Beatrice (Bea), 35, 112; Harper, DeBloi (Blois) D., 35, 110–11, 156, 252; Harper, Dufferin (Duff) W., 35, 111–13; Harper, Duncan, 35–6, 177; Harper, Ethel Winnifred (Winnie), 35–6, 156, 177–8, 251–2; Harper, Helen (Nell) I., 35, 110–13, 251–2; Harper, Jessie Theal, 35–6, 110, 113, 177, 252; Harper, May, 35, 112, 157, 251; Talbot, Eddie, 36
Hatheway, Ella, 259
Hayward, Reverend Amos. See Estabrooks family
Hayward, Lucretia Estabrooks. See Estabrooks family
Head, Sir Edmund and Lady, 86
Hendry, George. See MacDonald family
Hendry, Susan Belyea. See MacDonald family
Hill diarist: Mary Whitney (b.1829), 19–20, 46, 48, 50, 96, 106–7, 113, 123–4, 147–51 (diary), 156, 169, 172–4, 253–4, 284, 286–7, 302, 314
Hill diarist's family: Hill, Aaron Upton, 19, 123, 174, 286; Hill, Arthur Marcus, 20; Hill, Edgar Cutter, 20; Hill, George Frederick, 20, 96, 123, 150–1; Hill, George Stillman, 19–20, 122–4, 172–4, 286; Hill, Henry Ernest, 20, 147; Hill, Hesediah Louisa, 20, 123, 149, 314; Hill, Joanna Upton, 20; Hill, Sarah Augusta, 20, 122–4, 137, 174, 314; Hill, Sarah Upton, 19–20, 96, 106–7, 122–4, 137, 174, 253, 284, 286–7, 302
hired help, 228; farm labourers, 24, 141, 143; market garden employees, 83, 147, 214, 243–4; occasional, 150; servant/hired girl, 35, 45, 158, 219; 228
Hodge, Fanny, 54–5
Holder diarist: Susan Amelia (b.1855), 30–1, 47, 48–9, 81, 83, 99–101, 130–1, 271, 276–8 (diary), 286, 319–20
Holder diarist's family: Holder, Abraham, 30; Holder Ada, 30–1, 131, 276–8, 320; Holder Agnes (Aggie), 30–1, 99–101, 105, 130, 320; Holder, Charles, 99; Holder Edwin (Eddie), 30, 130–1; Holder, Edwin Jacob, 30–1, 83, 99–101, 130–1, 136, 276–8, 319; Holder, Frank, 30; Holder, Hannah L. Parrett, 30, 129–30, 135–6, 151; Holder, Raymond, 30; Holder, Thomas (Tommy), 30, 83, 320; Parrett, Mary Ann, 129, 319
holidays, religious and secular: Christmas, 101, 127, 131, 169; Dominion Day, 124, 167; Easter, 104, 124, 178, 188, 223, 287; Thanksgiving, 148; New Year's, 31, 41, 46, 108, 117, 125, 196, 208
households: composition of, 14, 20–1, 45, 75, 115–16, 118–19, 126, 153

immigrant vs native–born experience, 3–5, 303, 327n4
immigration, 80; immigrants, 3–5, 58, 62, 80, 118, 266, 278, 303; policy, 265–6
Inches, Janie Everett. See Morrison family
Inches, Julius. See Morrison family
India, 43, 84, 279–81, 319
inheritance, 13, 20–1, 32, 50, 72–4, 118–19, 134, 147, 312

job markets, 62–3, 144, 212, 228, 265–7
Johnson, Sarah. *See* Wolhaupter family
Johnston, Annie Eliza. See Waltham family
Johnston, Annie Townsend Gilbert. *See* Waltham diarist: Annie Townsend Gilbert Johnston
Johnston, Thomas Millidge. *See* Waltham family
Jones diarist: Emma Bertha Frost (b.1843), 23–4, 50–1, 141–4 (diary), 169–70, 286, 316
Jones diarist's family: Frost, Barbara Smith, 23; Frost, Smith, 23; Jones, Ada, 23–4, 141–4, 169–70, 316; Jones, Alma, 23–4, 141–4, 316; Jones, Hildrick, 23, 142, 144, 316; Jones, Leander, 23; Jones, Norman, 23–4, 142–3; Jones, Zebulon, 23, 50; Marley, Henrietta Jones, 23; McKeil, Julia Jones, 23

Kitchen, Fred: 232–3
Kitchen Phoebe: 126, 232

Lamont, Ellen Loggie. *See* Loggie family
Laidlaw, Toni, 8
leaving home, 61–72, 93, 103, 197
letters. *See* correspondence
Lewis, Martha Hamm, 173
Liverpool: expatriate community, 4, 29, 162–3, 272
Lockhart, Grace Annie, 87
Loggie diarists: Catherine (Kate), (b.1857), 3, 27–9, 40, 46, 48–9, 144, 176, 197–8, 234–7 (diary), 286, 318–19; Jessie (b.1859), 27–9, 48, 162–4, 236, 273, 279–81 (diary), 286, 318–9; Valentine, Margaret (Maggie) Loggie (b.1853), 27–9, 48, 82, 162–4, 234–6, 273–6 (diary), 279–81, 286, 318–19
Loggie diarists' family: Lamont, Ellen Loggie, 28, 319; Loggie, Alexander Jr., 27; Loggie, Alexander Sr., 27–9, 162, 236–7, 319; Loggie, Catherine Morrison, 27–9, 162, 234, 236–7, 273, 281, 318–19; Loggie, Donald, 28, 236–7, 319; Loggie, Herbert, 28; Loggie, John (b.1849), 28, 286; Loggie, John (b.1875), 28; Loggie, Mary, 28, 236, 280–1, 319; Loggie, Mary Jane, 28; Loggie, Rachel, 28; Loggie, Willber, 28; Valentine, William, 29, 82, 162–4, 272–3, 279, 281, 319
love as basis for marriage, 29, 36, 100–1, 104, 107–8, 117, 236
Loyalists, 13, 18, 22, 47, 77, 80, 158, 248, 278

MacDonald diarists: Ida (b.1865), 13–15, 131–3 (diary), 137–8, 158–60 (diary), 164–5, 167 (diary), 177, 215–16, 260–1, 270–1, 286, 301, 311; Janet Hendry (b.1795), 13–15, 48, 51, 80, 127, 131–3, 138, 153, 159–60, 167, 191–6 (diary), 212–14 (diary), 216, 226, 284, 286, 288–9, 301, 311–12
MacDonald diarists' family: Hendry, George, 13; Hendry, Susan Belyea, 13; MacDonald, Alexander Black Jr., 14, 132, 159, 191; MacDonald, Alexander Black Sr., 13–14, 51, 127, 138, 191–5, 212, 213–4, 284, 311; MacDonald, Beckah McDonald, 51, 193, 195, 212, 214, 288; MacDonald, Donald,

14, 51, 127, 192–5, 212–14, 284; MacDonald, Ella, 14, 127, 131–3, 159–60, 177, 301; MacDonald, Fred, 14, 127, 131–3, 159–60, 167, 192, 215–16, 301, 311; MacDonald, George Hendry, 13–14, 51, 192–6, 212–13, 286, 288–9; MacDonald, James Hendry, 14, 51, 127, 138, 192–5, 212–14, 284, 286, 301, 311; MacDonald, Jemima (Mima) MacDonald, 51, 159; MacDonald, Malcolm Campbell, 14, 51, 131–2, 159, 192, 194–5; MacDonald, Mary Mott, 127; MacDonald, Mary Jane (Sis), 14, 127, 131–3, 159, 214, 284, 311; MacDonald, Robert, 14, 127, 131–3, 159–60, 167, 215, 301, 311; MacDonald, Sarah (Sally) Smith, 14, 127, 137–8, 159–60, 192–5, 212, 214, 311; MacDonald Susannah (Susie), 14, 127, 214, 301; MacDonald, William Lewis, 14, 192–6, 301; McDonald, Susan Ann MacDonald, 14, 194–5, 286; McDonald, Thomas Earl, 195; Smith, Mary, 14, 159, 193–4, 213–14
Macdonald, Sir John A., 87
maple sugar/sugar bush, 17, 155, 167, 211, 226
marital relationships, 12, 21, 114; abusive, 21, 118–9; companionate, 116–18, 122–4
Marley, Henrietta Jones. *See* Jones family
married women's property law: dower rights 72–4; Married Women's Property Acts, 134–5, 361n4, 361–2n5
market economy, 70–1, 77–8, 210–28 *passim*, 265–7, 308, 374n1

markets, international, 7, 18, 77, 220, 265–7, 310
marriage patterns, 65–72 *passim*, 305, 345n44
Maxwell, Catherine (Caty) Grant. *See* Grant family
Maxwell, Joseph. *See* Grant family
McClelan, Senator Abner. *See* Reid family
McClelan, Anna Reid. *See* Reid family
McDonald, Susan Ann MacDonald. *See* MacDonald family
McDonald, Thomas Earl. *See* MacDonald family
McKiel,, Julia Jones. *See* Jones family
McLauchlan, Lavinia, 228, 230
McNabb, Agnes, 55, 228, 313
Mechanics Institutes, 84, 308
Medley, Bishop John, 208, 231, 270
Medley, Margaret, 208, 231, 270
Methodists, 6, 15–16, 20–3, 26–7, 32, 35–6, 49–50, 58, 147, 196–208, 253; church attendance, 42–5, 130, 136–7, 148–9; class meetings, 157, 191, 198, 207–8, 211; clergy, 30, 36, 42, 44–5, 137, 148–9, 197–8, 200–6, 218, 320–1; conversion, 22, 196–8, 203–6, 287–8; ladies' society, 20; meeting, 44, 158, 181, 190–1, 202, 205–6, 212, 213, 217–18; prayer meetings, 42–3, 110, 112, 148, 158, 180–1, 187, 206; revival, 190–1; Sunday/Sabbath school, 20, 112–13, 148–9, 211, 317; and temperance, 199–200; women's missionary society, 200, 262, 317
midwives, 51, 75–6, 230–1, 245, 375n15; and doctors, 378n52; Elizabeth Innes, 231

migration, 19, 25, 65, 73, 265–6, 271; economic causes of, 22, 116–7; international, 65, 80–1, 87–8, 265–6, 271; chain, 19, 266; westward, 266–7. *See also* out-migration

Miles diarist: Katherine (Kate) (b.1885), 37–8, 46, 48–9, 90–3 (diary), 164–5, 184–6, 323

Miles diarist's family: Miles Arnaud, 37, 91–2, 165, 323; Miles, Bruce, 37, 92, 180, 186, 323; Miles, Edgar, 37, 90–3, 165, 186, 323; Miles, George (Baby), 37, 92; Miles, Georgianna Harrison, 37, 91–2, 165, 186, 323

military officers, 52, 100, 228

missionaries, 93, 262, 269–70, 282, 307

missionary movements, 93, 96, 146, 184, 219, 307–8; and western imperialism, 262; and YWCA, 262–3

missionary societies. *See* women's missionary societies

Moore, Ann Eliza. *See* Rogers diarist: Ann Eliza Rogers

Moore, Archibald (Art). *See* Rogers family

Moore, Dodge. *See* Rogers family

Moore, Donald (Don). *See* Rogers family

Moore, Ella Kate (Ellie). *See* Rogers family

Moore, Florence. *See* Rogers family

Moore, Jennie. *See* Rogers family

Moore, Lemuel. *See* Rogers family

Morrison diarist: Lucy Everett (b.1823), 17–8, 46–52 *passim*, 54 (diary), 83, 85, 96, 156, 191, 214–16, 220–6 (diary), 227–8, 242–5, 265–6, 285–6, 313, 360n22

Morrison diarist's family: Everett, Mary Camber, 17, 222, 224; Everett, Thomas C., 17; Everett, Tom, 17–18; Everett, Will, 17–18; Inches, Janie Everett, 17, 228; Inches, Julius, 228; Morrison, Frank, 18, 54–5, 221–2, 224, 228; Morrison, Jack, 18, 54–5, 223, 228; Morrison, John A., 18, 54–5, 220–1, 223, 225–6, 242, 265–6, 313; Morrison, Julius, 18, 228; Morrison, Kate Hodge, 54–5; Morrison, Roy, 54–6; Morrison, Stewart, 18, 228; Morrison, Tom, 18, 227, 244; Morrison, William (Willie), 18, 228; Stewart, Belle Everett, 17, 227; Stewart, Luke, 227

mortality rates, 285, 384n2; infant, 70, 293, 346–7n60, 348n68; maternal 70, 347–8n64

Mount Allison Ladies College. *See* academies/seminaries

music, 91, 156, 161–2, 168, 199, 209, 237, 240–1; banjo, 161; church music, 124, 163–4, 169, 203; organ, 161, 167, 205; piano playing, 100, 156, 162, 184, 199, 216, 258, 304; practising piano, 33, 184, 216–7; violin, 133, 161, 184. *See also* singing and singing schools

music lessons, 19, 33–5, 147, 172, 180–2, 184, 240, 314. *See also* teaching music

mutual aid. *See* cooperative labour

Nation, Carrie, 188

National Policy, 62, 249; impact of, 62–3, 87–8, 249–50

navigation, 83, 320

neighbourhood, 10–11, 15, 25, 45, 94–5, 129, 151–8, 193–4, 211–13, 240, 308; development of networks, 305 networks/circles of friends: abroad, 21; generalizations about, 170, 303, 305; of individuals, 17, 19–20, 24, 147, 151, 156–7, 169; non–intersecting, 19, 52; of politicians' wives, 137; at school, 35–7; of single parents, 136; of women teachers, 67

networks/circles of kin, 16–17, 19, 35–6, 74, 94–5, 151–5, 166; broken circle, 299, 302; and children, 60; of widows, 24, 137–8

Noël, Françoise, 8

normal schools: establishment of, 7, 173–4, 231, 344n33, 375n20; exclusion of French, 345n40; life at, 36, 93, 176; preparing students for, 90, 308; value of qualification, 176, 178–9, 234, 237, 337n82; and voluntary organizations, 262, 366n28; women missionaries and, 270, 282; young women at, 7, 11, 64–5, 144, 189, 344n36

Norris, Hannah Mariah, 262

Norway, 29, 273–6

novels, 96, 116, 131, 270–1, 310, 316

nurses, 228, 230–1, 235; training, 88, 231, 245

Nye, George. *See* Wolhaupter family

Nye, Haddie Wolhaupter. *See* Wolhaupter family

out-migration, 25, 65, 81, 87–8, 144, 265–9; to Canadian West, 266–7

parents: and children, 122–7, 130–1; fathers, 12, 72, 123; mother-daughter relationships, 119–22, 125–7; *See also* childbirth, childhood

Parkin, George: 125

Parrett, Mary Ann. *See* Holder family

pensions, 15, 248

Pitt diarist: Emma Alice (b.1857), 31, 46, 81–2, 100–1, 166–7, 286, 293–5 (diary), 320

Pitt diarist's family: Pitt, Abraham Wilmot (Abe), 31, 286, 293–5; Pitt, Catherine Susannah Holder, 31, 293–4, 320; Pitt, Charlotte (Lott), 293–5; Pitt, David Leonard Jr., 31, 320; Pitt, David Leonard Sr., 31, 293–5, 320; Pitt, Edwin Jacob (Ed), 31, 46, 286, 293–5; Pitt, Katie, 293–4;

place and belonging, 5, 109, 303, 306, 328n9

politics: elections, 86, 137, 176, 214, 218, 247–53, 259, 261; petitions and petitioning, 248–9, 259, 309; political activism, 259–60; political engagement, 308–9; political parties, 241–2, 248–53; population: age of, 59; demographic characteristics of, 58–9; ethnicity of, 58–9; family size, 60; growth of, 1824–1911, 58; life course analysis of, 9, 76, 304–6; rural–urban ratios, 59, 341n7, 347n61

portraits: picture, 92, 108, 185, 187, 235–6, 239, 294; photograph, 110, 158, 186–7, 221, 235; sketch, 280

pregnancy, 69–71, 118, 120, 126–7, 137, 288, 302

Presbyterians, 34–5, 52, 58, 197–202; church attendance, 222–3, 290; clergy, 191, 197, 202, 222, 322; conversion, 14, 197; Sunday school, 234–5; St Paul's Presbyterian Church, 18, 191,

428   Index

197–8, 313; women's missionary society, 262
preserving fruits and vegetables, 56, 215–16
Protestants, 4–5, 58, 61, 64, 176, 285, 303

quilting, 16, 33, 51, 113, 153, 156, 216, 217–19, 226–7, 304

railways, 34, 86–8, 105, 124, 175, 243–7, 265–7, 310; Intercolonial Railway, 34, 86–7, 310
reading, 270–1, 310; as activity, 14–15, 29, 91, 131, 133, 169, 183, 199; devotional, 124, 181, 208, 235, 382n18; parental advice on, 29, 123; literature, 131, 162, 176, 185, 198, 208, 232, 235, 303–05; periodicals, 176, 216, 247, 269, 282, 382n16; for pleasure, 40, 124, 238–9; reading aloud, 124, 133, 216
recreation, 306–7; bicycling, 37, 93, 185–6, 274–5, 306; boating, 124, 306; dancing, 96, 156–7, 164–5, 169, 252, 306; fishing, 102, 124; skating, 42, 93, 109, 129, 166, 192, 306; snowballing, 185; snowshoeing, 111, 166, 185; swimming, 124, 306; tobogganing and coasting, 42, 166, 288, 306. *See also* games
Reid diarists: Charlotte (Lottie) (b.1859), 24–5, 48, 52–3, 85, 88, 98–9, 128–9 (diary), 164–5, 201–2, 206–7, 229, 249, 266, 272, 278, 281, 295–9 (diary), 301–2, 317; Turner, Josephine (Jo) Reid (b.1849), 24–5, 53, 82, 88–90 (diary), 98–9, 128, 161–2, 201–2, 206–7, 272, 278, 281–2, 296, 316

Reid diarists' family: McClelan, Senator Abner, 24, 99, 249; McClelan, Anna Reid, 24, 99, 128, 229, 296–7; Reid, James, 24–5, 266, 299, 302, 317; Reid, Lucinda Robinson, 24–5, 85, 128, 202, 206–7, 297–8, 317; Reid, Merritt, 24–5, 202, 266, 302, 317; Reid, Watson (Wat), 24–5, 98–9, 128–9, 201–2, 207, 266, 296, 317; Reid, William, 24–5, 98, 128, 202, 207, 249, 317; Turner, James Brewster, 24–5, 53, 88–90, 98–9, 161–2, 272, 316–17; West, Alden, 24–5, 128–9, 295–6; West, Josephine (Josie), 24–5, 128, 207, 295, 299; West, Mary Eliza Reid, 24, 99, 128, 207, 296; West, Orpah Reid, 24–5, 82, 128–9, 295–9; West, Willie, 24, 99, 128, 296
religious conversion, 14, 197–8, 203, 206, 285, 288, 291, 328n10; baptism of converts, 191–2, 194, 196–7, 205
religious revivals. *See* Baptists, Methodists
Roberts, Emma Bliss. *See* Carman family
Robb, James, 52
Rogers diarist: Ann Eliza (b.1837), 21, 48, 50, 53, 81–6 *passim*, 97, 107, 116–18, 130–7, 146, 151, 155, 160, 175–6, 229, 254–55, 266–9, 284, 286–91 (diary), 303, 314–15, 375n15
Rogers diarist's family: Gallacher, Achsah Georgia, 22, 106, 136, 175; Gallacher, Ella Frances, 22, 117–8, 136, 286; Gallacher, Frank John Howe, 22, 118, 136, 175, 266, 315; Gallacher, Isabelle Plummer, 22, 116–18, 136, 160, 175, 254–5, 266, 269, 290–1; Gallacher, John

McAuley, 22, 97, 116–18, 130, 136–7, 151, 160, 229, 266–9, 286, 289–91; Moore, Archibald (Art), 22, 315; Moore, Dodge, 22, 315; Moore, Donald (Don), 22, 315; Moore, Ella Kate (Ellie), 22, 314–15; Moore, Florence, 255; Moore, Jennie, 22, 315; Moore, Lemuel, 22, 175, 254, 269, 315; Rogers, Eleanor Dodge, 21–2, 117, 160, 267, 288; Rogers, James Horace, 21, 286; Rogers, John, 21, 117, 267, 288, 290; Rogers, John Howe, 21, 286, 288; Rogers, Margaret (Maggie), 21, 117, 155, 254–33, 290; Rogers, Mary Susan, 21, 86, 117–8, 155, 266

Roman Catholics, 4, 35, 58, 61–2, 169, 176, 203–4, 261

Ross, Annie. *See* Hanley, Annie H. Ross Foster

Santander, Spain, 89, 278

Sarton, May, 40

sawmills, 14, 18, 80, 213, 242, 311

schools and schooling: attendance, 60–1, 175–8, 233–4, 236–7; common/parish schools, 60–1, 171, 173, 175–8, 217, 234–7, 306, 308; convent schools, 64, 174, 344n32; discipline: 236–7; education, 14, 19, 20; enrollments, 60–1, 343n15, 367n7; Fredericton High School, 37, 184–6; grammar schools, 64, 83, 171–4, 251; high schools, 37–8, 90–3, 165, 174, 178, 184–6, 189; inspection of, 28, 65, 67, 173, 234–5, 237, 306; private venture, 171–2; superior, 174; textbooks, 171, 175; *See also* academies/ seminaries

schools legislation, 366n6; Schools Act of 1802, 171; Grammar Schools Act of 1805, 171–3; Schools Act of 1847, 173–4; Schools Act of 1858, 174–5; 'Free' Schools Act of 1871, 175–6, 233–4; 'Compulsory' Schools Act of 1906, 60, 178

schoolteachers. *See* teachers and teaching

science/nature, 82–4; Natural History Society of New Brunswick, 82; study of, 83–4; popular, 84

Schweickart, Patrocinio, 53

Secord, Elizabeth Smith, 88

separate spheres dichotomy, 11–12, 171–3, 210–11, 245–6, 304, 308; ideology, 82; private sphere, 210, 218, 304–5; public sphere, 303, 316; at public celebrations and entertainments; 306; in public space, 305–8

sermons: comments on, 124, 163, 185, 197–8, 200–7 *passim*, 261; farewell sermons, 93, 132; funeral sermons, 193, 195, 284–302 *passim*; texts for, 42–4, 181, 192, 194–7, 235, 287, 299

settler society, 303–4

sewing circles: denominational, 156, 190, 219, 253, 255, 307; individuals involved in, 18, 33, 238

shoemaking, 131–3, 193–4, 213, 226; in factories, 36, 88, 144, 177, 230, 265

shopping, 43, 78, 89, 100, 147–8, 157–67 *passim*, 181, 184, 308

sickness, 19, 29, 55, 69, 123, 284, 287, 315, 319; brain fever, 195; cold, 149, 183; diphtheria, 133; eczema as debilitating illness, 19, 125;

measles, 136; rheumatic fever, 318, 322; rheumatism, 188; scarlet rash, 237; seasickness, 130, 162–4; teething, 122–3; typhoid fever, 311, 316; tuberculosis/ consumption, 30, 169, 195, 284, 286–8; yellow fever, 148, 276, 278, 320, 364,n32

singing, 109, 132, 149–50, 156, 161–2, 169, 186, 237, 284, 305; choirs 110–13, 307; lessons, 43, 181

singing schools, 98, 154, 164, 190–2, 307

single women, 13, 20, 49–50, 62–68, 70, 95, 106, 113, 144–51, 166, 229–30, 262, 266–7, 282, 305, 386n1

sleighs, 6, 98, 109, 154–5, 194–5, 284

Smith, Mary. *See* MacDonald family

Smyth, Donna E., 8, 47

steamers, 6, 29, 81, 87–8, 162, 271, 274; on the St John River, 6, 100–1, 133, 159, 167, 271, 306

Stewart, Belle Everett. *See* Morrison family

Stewart, Luke. *See* Morrison family

Stiles, Lizzie, 229

Stretch, Emma Chadwick, 51–2, 56

Sunday school. *See* Anglicans, Baptists, Methodists, Presbyterians

Talbot, Eddie. *See* Harper family

Teachers Institutes, 67, 176, 237

teaching and teachers, 20, 23, 28–9, 65, 67–8, 144, 147, 171–9 *passim*, 231–7, 242–48 *passim*, 266–7, 308; feminization of, 176–8, 245–6, 376n32; teaching art, 36, 189, 241; teaching music, 33–4, 50, 147, 172, 189, 240–2, 308, 321

temperance, 199–200, 248–8, 254–62, 309, 379n23; Canada Temperance Act, 261; lodges, 110, 112, 131–3, 159, 164, 209, 252, 254–5, 260–1, 309; Prohibitory Liquor Act of 1854, 248–9. *See also* WCTU

textiles: cloth production, 63, 71, 212–13, 217–20, 227, 308; homespun, 23, 71, 212, 217–20; textile mills, 62–3, 66–7, 230, 345n48–9

theatre, 12, 165, 168

Tibbits, Mary Kingsley, 186

Tilley, Sir Leonard, 249–51

timber trade, 77–8, 81, 211, 353n10

tourism, 29, 163, 273–82

trade, 80–2; preferences: 81

transatlantic outlook, 7, 196, 270–283

travel, 52–3, 81, 87, 203–4, 271–283, 309–10; cultural comparisons, 276–283

Trent Affair, 268

Trueman diarists: Annie Rebecca (b.1851), 26–7, 48–50, 87, 102–3, 121–2, 128–9, 160–1, 198–201 (diary) 208, 241–2, 256, 262, 292, 300–1, 317–8; Wood, Laura Sophia Trueman (b.1856), 26–7, 49, 102–3 (diary), 121–2, 128, 137, 160–1, 199–204, 208, 241–2, 249–51 (diary), 256–8, 261, 291, 301, 318

Trueman diarists' family: Trueman, Albert, 26, 102, 122, 161, 199; Trueman, Rebecca Wood, 26–7, 102–3, 121–2, 161, 198–201, 241, 256–8, 301, 318; Trueman, Thompson, 26, 102–3, 122, 199–201, 250, 301, 318; Wood, Annie, 27; Wood, Dora, 27, 250–251; Wood, Eleanor (Daisy), 27, 251; Wood, Herbert, 27, 251, 301; Wood, Hester, 27; Wood, Josiah (Josie), 26–7, 102–3, 137, 161, 203,

249–51, 256, 318; Wood, William (Willie), 27, 301
Turner, James Brewster. *See* Reid family
Turner, Josephine (Jo) Reid. *See* Reid diarists: Turner, Josephine (Jo) Reid
tuberculosis. *See* sickness

Ulrich, Laurel Thatcher, 51–2
university education: 68, 87, 262–3, 270, 282, 308; Mount Allison University, 7, 26, 87, 90, 93, 261, 318, 322, 368–9n35; University of New Brunswick, 36–7, 125, 186–9, 262–3, 368–9n35
Upton, Sarah. *See* Hill, Sarah Upton

Valentine, Maggie Loggie. *See* Loggie diarists: Valentine, Maggie Loggie
Valentine, William. *See* Loggie family
Van Die, Marguerite, 8
visiting institutions, 253–4

Waltham diarist: Annie Townsend Gilbert Johnston (b.1833), 20–21, 47, 50, 118–19, 138–41 (diary), 286, 314
Waltham diarist's family: Clowes, Eliza Gilbert, 139–40; Gilbert, Charlotte Amelia Hewlett, 20–1; Gilbert, Fannie, 21, 138–9, 141; Gilbert, Hannah, 20; Gilbert, Lucretia, 21, 138–41
Gilbert, Thomas, 20; Johnston, Annie Eliza, 20–1, 50, 118, 138–9, 314; Johnston, Thomas Millidge, 20, 138; Waltham, Adeline (Lena) Miller, 21, 118, 314; Waltham, Richard Claude, 21, 50, 118–19, 314
washing: clothes, 6, 33, 51, 143, 193, 195, 212–14; dishes/pots, 221, 224; floor, 149

Waycott, Sade, 37, 90–3, 165, 185–6
WCTU (Woman's Christian Temperance Union), 93, 200, 255–62, 309, 317; membership (Sackville branch), 257; and suffrage, 258–9
weather, 6, 47, 61, 79, 177, 214, 316, 338n17, 364n4
West, Alden. *See* Reid family
West, Josephine (Josie). *See* Reid family
West, Mary Eliza Reid. *See* Reid family
West, Orpah Reid. *See* Reid family
West, Willie. *See* Reid family
widowhood: and community networks, 24, 148, 169–70; demographic analysis of, 5, 71–5; diarists' experience of, 4, 20–4, 50–1, 116, 312; diarists' marriage to widowers, 18–19, 23, 107, 286, 315, 321; and household composition, 115–16, 131; and inheritance, 134; and kin networks, 74–5, 137–8; protective legislation, 7, 135, 248; and single parent families, 45, 49, 115, 119, 130–1, 305; and social activism, 259, 318; and strategies for maintaining independence, 21, 24, 33, 50–1, 74–5, 88, 138–42, 305
Wightman, Carrie, 32, 107–9
Wightman, Fred, 32, 107–10, 158, 320–1
Williamson diarist: Lillian (Lillie) (b.1861), 31–2, 50, 107–10 (diary), 128, 158, 204–6, 320–1
Williamson diarist's family: Williamson, Benjamin, 31–2, 109, 204–6; Williamson, Frederick (Fred), 31–2, 107–9, 128, 205;

Williamson, Joseph (Joe), 31–2, 108–10; Williamson, Kate, 31–2, 108–9, 128; Williamson, Mary Haviland, 31–2, 108; Williamson, Samuel (Sam), 31–2, 108–9

Wilmot, Mrs R. (Susan), 85

Wolhaupter diarist: Mary Isoline (b.1838), 22–3, 48–50, 82, 87, 120–1, 126–7, 144–6, 197–8, 219, 229–30, 232–3 (diary), 292, 315–16

Wolhaupter diarist's family: Johnson, Sarah, 229; Nye, George, 23, 121, 126, 145, 233; Nye, Haddie Wolhaupter, 22–3, 120–1, 126, 233; Wolhaupter Benjamin, 22–3, 126–7, 145; Wolhaupter, Caroline (Carrie), 22–3, 120–1, 145, 219, 232–3; Wolhaupter, Charles, 22–3, 120, 127; Wolhaupter, Emily, 22–3, 120–1, 126–7, 145, 197, 220, 232; Wolhaupter, Gertrude, 23, 120, 127; Wolhaupter, Hanford, 22, 127, 145, 232; Wolhaupter, Margaret (Maggie), 23, 120, 127, 145, 219; Wolhaupter Samuel, 22–3, 126–7

women: urban vs rural, 6, 19, 62, 69–70, 84, 156, 229

women and science, 68, 82–4, 87, 172, 178–9

women's missionary societies, 11, 93, 190, 255, 262, 282, 307. *See also* Baptists, Methodists, Presbyterians

women's suffrage, 94, 247, 255, 258–60, 309; Saint John Women's Enfranchisement Association, 259. *See also* franchise

women's work for wages, 28, 63, 66, 68, 74, 135, 227–8, 266; clerical work, 238; clerk in store, 33–4, 49, 147, 237–40; domestic service, 49, 61–2, 65–6, 74, 87, 146, 177, 228, 230, 237; factory work, 62–3, 66–7, 87–8, 229–30; seamstresses, 24, 69, 74, 98–9, 228–30, 308, 313

Wood, Annie. *See* Trueman family

Wood, Dora. *See* Trueman family

Wood, Eleanor (Daisy). *See* Trueman family

Wood, Herbert. *See* Trueman family

Wood, Hester. *See* Trueman family

Wood, Laura Sophia Trueman. *See* Trueman diarists: Wood, Laura Sophia Trueman

Wood, Josiah (Josie). *See* Trueman family

Wood, William (Willie). *See* Trueman family

wool processing, 63, 84, 153, 212–18 *passim*, 227; carding, 45, 63, 216 226, 227; colouring wool, 63, 143, 213, 217; knitting, 217–9, 239, 304; "picking wool," 213–14, 216, 218; spinning, 24, 33, 63, 121, 143–4, 213, 216–18; washing wool, 80, 143, 212–14; weavers and weaving, 63, 69, 71, 217, 220, 226–7, 230, 245, 304

Young, D. Murray, 15, 45
Young, Eve: 230
Young, Sarah Grace: 230
YWCA (Young Women's Christian Association), 36, 93–4, 187–8, 255, 262–3